DISTRIBUTION OF RESPON
IN INTERNATIONAL

This is the second book in the series Shared Responsibility in International Law, which examines the problem of distribution of responsibilities among multiple states and other actors. In its work on the responsibility of states and international organisations, the International Law Commission recognised that attribution of acts to one actor does not exclude possible attribution of the same act to another state or organisation. However, it provided limited guidance for the often complex question of how responsibility is to be distributed among wrongdoing actors. This study fills that gap by shedding light on principles of distribution from extra-legal perspectives. Drawing on disciplines such as political theory, moral philosophy, and economics, this volume enquires into the bases and justifications for apportionment of responsibilities that can support a critique of current international law, offers insight into the justification of alternative interpretations, and provides inspiration for reform and further development of international law.

ANDRÉ NOLLKAEMPER is Professor of Public International Law at the Faculty of Law of the University of Amsterdam, Amsterdam Center for International Law (ACIL), and director of the SHARES research project.

DOV JACOBS is Assistant Professor of International Law at the Grotius Centre for International Legal Studies of Leiden University.

STUDIES ON SHARED RESPONSIBILITY IN INTERNATIONAL LAW

This series produces high-quality scholarship exploring questions of shared responsibility in international law. It provides new perspectives on the responsibility problems that arise from the increasing number of situations in which states, international institutions, and other actors engage in concerted action in the pursuit of common objectives. While such concerted action generally aims to provide beneficial outcomes, all too often it results in harmful ones. If that is the case, the multiplicity of actors involved in the concerted action may complicate the determination and implementation of international responsibility. Books in this series examine the grounds on which international law does and should allow for shared responsibility between all actors involved, and how it can be developed in a way that better enables the determination and implementation of shared responsibility.

The series includes both works on positive international law and works of a theoretical and interdisciplinary character.

The book series is part of the research project on Shared Responsibility in International Law (SHARES), which has been carried out at the Amsterdam Center for International Law (ACIL) of the University of Amsterdam from 2010 onwards.

General Editor
André Nollkaemper, Professor of Public International Law, University of Amsterdam

DISTRIBUTION OF RESPONSIBILITIES IN INTERNATIONAL LAW

Edited by
ANDRÉ NOLLKAEMPER
and
DOV JACOBS

Assistant editor
JESSICA N.M. SCHECHINGER

CAMBRIDGE
UNIVERSITY PRESS

CAMBRIDGE
UNIVERSITY PRESS

University Printing House, Cambridge CB2 8BS, United Kingdom

One Liberty Plaza, 20th Floor, New York, NY 10006, USA

477 Williamstown Road, Port Melbourne, VIC 3207, Australia

314-321, 3rd Floor, Plot 3, Splendor Forum, Jasola District Centre, New Delhi - 110025, India

79 Anson Road, #06-04/06, Singapore 079906

Cambridge University Press is part of the University of Cambridge.

It furthers the University's mission by disseminating knowledge in the pursuit of education, learning and research at the highest international levels of excellence.

www.cambridge.org
Information on this title: www.cambridge.org/9781107514621

First published 2015
First paperback edition 2018

A catalogue record for this publication is available from the British Library

Library of Congress Cataloging in Publication data
Distribution of responsibilities in international law / Edited by André Nollkaemper and Dov Jacobs ; Assistant editor: Jessica N.M. Schechinger.
pages cm
Includes bibliographical references and index.
ISBN 978-1-107-10708-3 (Hardback)
1. International law. 2. Responsibility to protect (International law) 3. Government liability (International law) I. Nollkaemper, André, editor. II. Jacobs, Dov, editor.
KZ3410.D577 2015
341.26–dc23 2015011590

ISBN 978-1-107-10708-3 Hardback
ISBN 978-1-107-51462-1 Paperback

CONTENTS

CONTRIBUTORS

ANNE VAN AAKEN is Professor for Law and Economics, Legal Theory, Public International Law and European Law at University of St. Gallen.

DANIEL H. COLE is Professor of Law and of Public and Environmental Affairs at Indiana University Bloomington, Maurer School of Law and School of Public and Environmental Affairs; Member of the Affiliated Faculty of the Vincent and Elinor Ostrom Workshop in Political Theory and Policy Analysis.

TOM DANNENBAUM is Lecturer in Human Rights at University College London.

TONI ERSKINE is Professor of International and Political Studies, School of Humanities and Social Sciences at the University of New South Wales, Canberra, Australia.

MONICA HAKIMI is a Professor of Law and the Associate Dean for Academic Programming at the University of Michigan Law School.

DOV JACOBS is Assistant Professor of International Law at the Grotius Centre for International Legal Studies of Leiden University.

EUGENE KONTOROVICH is Professor of Law at Northwestern University School of Law.

LEWIS A. KORNHAUSER is Frank Henry Sommer Professor of Law at New York University.

CHRISTOPHER L. KUTZ is C. William Maxeiner Professor of Law at the University of California at Berkeley.

ANTHONY F. LANG, JR., is Director of the Centre for Global Constitutionalism in the School of International Relations at the University of St Andrews.

SEUMAS MILLER is a professorial research fellow at the Centre for Applied Philosophy and Public Ethics (an Australian Research Council Special Research Centre) at Charles Sturt University (Canberra) and the 3TU Centre for Ethics and Technology at Delft University of Technology (The Hague).

ANDRÉ NOLLKAEMPER is Professor of Public International Law at the Amsterdam Center for International Law, Faculty of Law, University of Amsterdam, and director of the SHARES research project.

ROLAND PIERIK is Associate Professor of Legal Philosophy at the Paul Scholten Centre for Jurisprudence, Faculty of Law, University of Amsterdam.

MARGOT E. SALOMON is Acting Director of the Centre for the Study of Human Rights, London School of Economics and Political Science, where she also directs the Laboratory for Advanced Research on the Global Economy, and is Associate Professor in the Law Department.

HENRY SHUE is Senior Research Fellow at the Centre for International Studies (Department of Politics and International Relations, University of Oxford); and Senior Research Fellow (Emeritus) at Merton College, University of Oxford.

JOEL P. TRACHTMAN is Professor of International Law at The Fletcher School of Law and Diplomacy.

EDITORS' PREFACE

This is the second volume to appear in the book series Shared Responsibility in International Law. It was produced as part of the research project on Shared Responsibility in International Law (SHARES), which has been carried out at the Amsterdam Center for International Law (ACIL) of the University of Amsterdam from 2010 onwards.

This book series provides new perspectives on responsibility problems that arise from the increasing number of situations in which states, international institutions, and other actors engage in concerted action in the pursuit of common objectives. While such concerted action generally aims to provide beneficial outcomes, all too often it has resulted in harmful ones. If that is the case, the multiplicity of actors involved in the concerted action may complicate the determination and implementation of international responsibility. The book series examines the grounds on which international law does and should allow for shared responsibility between all actors involved, and how it can be developed in a way that better enables the determination and implementation of shared responsibility.

This first volume of the book series, *Principles of Shared Responsibility in International Law: An Appraisal of the State of the Art* (2014) laid the groundwork for the series as a whole, by critically reviewing the established principles of international responsibility as developed by the International Law Commission (ILC) – that are widely considered to be the state of the art in the law of international responsibility – from the perspective of shared responsibility. That volume concluded that while these principles are highly flexible, and often will allow for the determination and/or implementation of shared responsibility, they do not provide much guidance for the often complex questions of distribution of international responsibility.

Against this background, the present (second) volume of the book series considers, from extra-legal perspectives, how responsibility can and perhaps should be distributed among multiple wrongdoing actors.

Given that international law often provides no clear direction for such distribution, it engages in a fundamental enquiry into the normative bases and justifications for apportionment of responsibilities that could support an articulation of critique of current international law, and provide a basis for reform.

The third volume of the series (*The Practice of Shared Responsibility in International Law*) will explore the practice of shared responsibility in international law. Based on the recognition that the applicable rules and procedures for shared responsibility differ between particular issue-areas, it will map relevant practices of shared responsibility in more than forty issue-areas. This will enable an assessment of the fit of the prevailing principles of international responsibility, and provide further building blocks for a critique of the existing law, further development of the law, and eventually a broader theory of shared responsibility.

On the basis of the material in these first three volumes, a separate volume will consolidate the insights on the state of the law, and the possibilities for further development, into a new theory for shared responsibility in international law.

The present volume comprises fifteen substantive chapters, including a comprehensive introductory chapter. Drafts of the chapters for this volume were discussed at a seminar on 30 and 31 May 2013 in Amsterdam.

The research leading to this book has received funding from the European Research Council under the European Union's Seventh Framework Programme (FP7/2007–2013)/ERC grant agreement n° 249499, as part of the SHARES research project carried out at the ACIL.

We thank the members of the SHARES research team as a whole for their input during various stages of the project leading up to this volume, and in particular Jean d'Aspremont, Nienke van der Have, Ilias Plakokefalos, and Isabelle Swerissen for their comments on the introductory chapter. We also thank Giuseppe Dari-Mattiacci for his constructive comments on the organisation and contents of this volume. Our particular thanks go to Jessica N.M. Schechinger for her coordinating work in support of this volume and to Laura Chafey and Belinda Macmahon for editorial assistance. Finally, our thanks go to everyone at Cambridge University Press for their assistance during the production process of the volume.

André Nollkaemper and Dov Jacobs
Amsterdam
20 December 2014

TREATIES AND OTHER INTERNATIONAL LEGAL INSTRUMENTS

CASES

International courts and tribunals

Other international bodies

National courts

ABBREVIATIONS

ACIL	Amsterdam Center for International Law
AER	American Economic Review
AJARE	Australian Journal of Agricultural and Resource Economics
AJIL	American Journal of International Law
AJP	Australasian Journal of Philosophy
ANYAS	Annals of the New York Academy of Sciences
APSR	American Political Science Review
APQ	American Philosophical Quarterly
AREE	Annual Review of Energy and the Environment
ARIO	Articles on the Responsibility of International Organizations
ARSIWA	Articles on Responsibility of States for Internationally Wrongful Acts
ASIL	American Society of International Law
ASILP	American Society of International Law Proceedings
Atmos Chem Phys	Atmospheric Chemistry and Physics
Berk JIL	Berkeley Journal of International Law
BGS	British Geological Survey
BJPS	British Journal of Political Science
BoP	burdens of proof
BRICs	major developing economies of Brazil, Russia, India, and China
Brook JIL	Brooklyn Journal of International Law
BYIL	British Yearbook of International Law
Cal LR	California Law Review
CBDR	common but differentiated responsibility
CDM	Clean Development Mechanism
CERCLA	Comprehensive Environmental Response, Compensation and Liability Act
CESCR	Committee on Economic, Social and Cultural Rights
Chic JIL	Chicago Journal of International Law
CJICL	Cambridge Journal of International and Comparative Law
CJP	Canadian Journal of Philosophy

CLF	Criminal Law Forum
CLP	Current Legal Problems
CmtEDAW	Committee on the Elimination of Discrimination Against Women
CO_2	carbon dioxide
Col JEL	Columbia Journal of Environmental Law
COP	Conference of the Parties
CP	Climate Policy
CRISPP	Critical Review of International Social and Political Philosophy
CS	Current Science
DD	Development Dialogue
DES	diethylstilbestrol
DF	Disarmament Forum
DLJ	Duke Law Journal
DRC	Democratic Republic of the Congo
EC	European Communities
ECtHR	European Court of Human Rights
EIA	Ethics & International Affairs
EJBEOS	Electronic Journal of Business Ethics and Organization Studies
EJIL	European Journal of International Law
EJIR	European Journal of International Relations
EJLE	European Journal of Law and Economics
EP	Energy Policy
ET	Economic Theory
EU	European Union
EU ETS	EU's Emissions Trading System
FA	Foreign Affairs
Frontex	Frontières extérieures – European Agency for the Management of Operational Cooperation at the External Borders of the Member States of the European Union
FRY	Federal Republic of Yugoslavia
GATT	General Agreement on Tariffs and Trade
Geo JIL	Georgetown Journal of International Law
GFC	Global Financial Crisis
GHG	greenhouse gas
GLJ	German Law Journal
Glob Gov	Global Governance: A Review of Multilateralism and International Organizations
GNI	gross national income
GoJIL	Goettingen Journal of International Law

GP	Global Policy
GR2P	Global Responsibility to Protect
Grif LR	Griffith Law Review
GS	Global Society
GWP	global warming potentials
Harv ELR	Harvard Environmental Law Review
Harv ILJ	Harvard International Law Journal
Harv ILJO	Harvard International Law Journal Online
Harv LR	Harvard Law Review
HHR	Health and Human Rights
HRC	Human Rights Committee
HRQ	Human Rights Quarterly
Hydrogeo J	Hydrogeology Journal
IA	International Affairs
IACtHR	Inter-American Court of Human Rights
ICC	International Criminal Court
ICCPR	International Covenant on Civil and Political Rights
ICESCR	International Covenant on Economic, Social and Cultural Rights
ICISS	International Commission on Intervention and State Sovereignty
ICJ	International Court of Justice
ICLQ	International & Comparative Law Quarterly
ICLR	International Criminal Law Review
ICRC	International Committee of the Red Cross
ICSID	International Centre for Settlement of Investment Disputes
ICTY	International Criminal Tribunal for the former Yugoslavia
IEA	International Environmental Agreements: Politics, Law and Economics
ILC	International Law Commission
ILDC	International Law in Domestic Courts
ILM	International Legal Materials
Ill LR	University of Illinois Law Review
IMF	International Monetary Fund
Ind J Dermat	Indian Journal of Dermatology
Indiana JGLS	Indiana Journal of Global Legal Studies
IO	International Organization
IOLR	International Organizations Law Review
Iowa LR	Iowa Law Review
IPCC	Intergovernmental Panel on Climate Change
IR	International Relations
IRRC	International Review of the Red Cross

IS	International Security
ISJ	International Studies Journal
Isr LR	Israel Law Review
IT	International Theory
ITLOS	International Tribunal for the Law of the Sea
IUPJGPP	The IUP Journal of Governance and Public Policy
JE	The Journal of Ethics: An International Philosophical Review
JEEA	Journal of the European Economic Association
JEEM	Journal of Environmental Economics and Management
JICJ	Journal of International Criminal Justice
JIE	Journal of International Economics
JIS	Journal of Intervention and Statebuilding
JLE	Journal of Law and Economics
JLEO	Journal of Law, Economics, & Organization
JLS	Journal of Legal Studies
JP	The Journal of Philosophy
JPE	joint public enterprise
JPP	Journal of Political Philosophy
JRR	Journal of Risk Research
JSL	joint and several liability
JSP	Journal of Social Philosophy
JTLP	Journal of Transnational Law & Policy
LIBOR	London Interbank Offered Rate
LJIL	Leiden Journal of International Law
LOSC	United Nations Convention on the Law of the Sea
LP	Law & Policy
LT	Legal Theory
MATCH	ad hoc group for the modelling and assessment of contributions to climate change
MIJIL	Michigan Journal of International Law
Minn JIL	Minnesota Journal of International Law
MINUSTAH	United Nations Stabilization Mission in Haiti
MIT	Massachusetts Institute of Technology
MJIS	Millennium: Journal of International Studies
MNCs	multinational corporations
MoUs	Memoranda of Understanding
MSP	Midwest Studies in Philosophy
NAFTA	North American Free Trade Agreement
NATO	North Atlantic Treaty Organization
NCC	Nature Climate Change
NGOs	Non-governmental organisations
Nord JIL	Nordic Journal of International Law

NRCC	Nature Reports Climate Change
NSAs	non-state actors
NWCR	Naval War College Review
NYUJILP	New York University Journal of International Law and Politics
ODSs	ozone-depleting substances
OJEU	Official Journal of the European Union
OJLS	Oxford Journal of Legal Studies
OREP	Oxford Review of Economic Policy
PAQ	Public Affairs Quarterly
PB	Political Behavior
PBA	Proceedings of the British Academy
PD	prisoners' dilemma
Penn LR	University of Pennsylvania Law Review
Pepp LR	Pepperdine Law Review
PNAS	Proceedings of the National Academy of Sciences of the United States of America
PP	Philosophical Papers
PPA	Philosophy & Public Affairs
ppm	parts per million
PPR	Philosophy and Phenomenological Research
PS	Political Studies
PT	Political Theory
PTA	Philosophical Transactions of the Royal Society A
QJE	The Quarterly Journal of Economics
R2P	responsibility to protect
RAND JE	RAND Journal of Economics
RCADI	Recueil des cours de l'Académie de droit international de La Haye
RECIEL	Review of European Community and International Environmental Law
REE	Resource and Energy Economics
REDD	Reducing Emissions from Deforestation and Forest Degradation
RIAA	United Nations Reports of International Arbitral Awards
RIS	Review of International Studies
RtoP	responsibility to protect
SDC	Sovereign Debt Crisis
SEP	Stanford Encyclopedia of Philosophy
SHARES	Shared Responsibility in International Law
SR	Social Research
SSC	social cost of carbon

Stan ELJ	Stanford Environmental Law Journal
Stan JIL	Stanford Journal of International Law
Stan LR	Stanford Law Review
SUV	sport utility vehicle
TD	Theory and Decision
TWQ	The Washington Quarterly
UK	United Kingdom
UN	United Nations
UNDP	United Nations Development Programme
UNESCO	United Nations Educational, Scientific and Cultural Organization
UNFCCC	United Nations Framework Convention on Climate Change
UNGA	United Nations General Assembly
UNGAOR	United Nations General Assembly Official Records
UNICEF	United Nations Children's Fund
UNODC	United Nations Office of Drugs and Crime
UNTS	United Nations Treaty Series
US	United States
USD	United States dollar
Utr LR	Utrecht Law Review
VRS	Vojska Republike Srpske [Bosnian Serb Army]
Wash LR	Washington University Law Review
WILJ	Wisconsin International Law Journal
WMLR	William & Mary Law Review
WTO	World Trade Organization
WTR	World Trade Review
YJIL	Yale Journal of International Law
YLJ	Yale Law Journal

1

Introduction: Mapping the Normative Framework for the Distribution of Shared Responsibility

ANDRÉ NOLLKAEMPER* AND DOV JACOBS**

1. Introduction: identifying the starting point

Questions of distribution of shared responsibility continue to challenge international courts and other decision-makers. Examples of such questions that are discussed in the present volume are distribution of responsibility in relation to harm caused to civilians in armed conflicts;[1] climate change;[2] prosecution of pirates;[3] failure to protect social and economic rights;[4] and the global financial crisis.[5] In all these situations, the question arises who is responsible and how responsibility is to be distributed between multiple actors.

* André Nollkaemper is Professor of Public International Law at the Faculty of Law of the University of Amsterdam, and director of the SHARES Research Project. The research leading to this chapter has received funding from the European Research Council under the European Union's Seventh Framework Programme (FP7/2007–2013)/ERC grant agreement n° 249499, as part of the research project on Shared Responsibility in International Law (SHARES), carried out at the Amsterdam Center for International Law (ACIL) of the University of Amsterdam.

** Dov Jacobs is Assistant Professor of International Law at the Grotius Centre for International Legal Studies of Leiden University.

1 T. Dannenbaum, 'Public Power and Preventative Responsibility: Attributing the Wrongs of International Joint Ventures', Chapter 7 in this volume, 192; M. Hakimi, 'Distributing the Responsibility to Protect', Chapter 9 in this volume, 265.

2 C.L. Kutz, 'Shared Responsibility for Climate Change: From Guilt to Taxes', Chapter 12 in this volume, 341; D.H. Cole, 'The Problem of Shared Irresponsibility in International Climate Law', Chapter 10 in this volume, 290; H. Shue, 'Transboundary Damage in Climate Change: Criteria for Allocating Responsibility', Chapter 11 in this volume, 321.

3 E. Kontorovich, 'Pirate "Globalisation": Dividing Responsibility Among States, Companies, and Criminals', Chapter 14 in this volume, 386.

4 M.E. Salomon, 'How to Keep Promises: Making Sense of the Duty Among Multiple States to Fulfil Socio-Economic Rights in the World', Chapter 13 in this volume, 366.

5 S. Miller, 'The Global Financial Crisis and Collective Moral Responsibility', Chapter 15 in this volume, 404.

The question of distribution of responsibility is key to the understanding and application of shared responsibility in international law. In this volume, we speak of 'shared responsibility' as a matter of international law when a multiplicity of actors contributes to a single harmful outcome, and legal responsibility for this harmful outcome is distributed separately among more than one of the contributing actors.[6] If shared responsibility indeed implies a distribution of responsibility between multiple actors, it inevitably raises the question of the grounds on which such responsibility is to be distributed.

The term 'distribution', on a basic level, refers to the 'allocation' or 'division' of something between multiple persons or entities. In this volume, 'distribution' is meant to cover more than merely the implementation of the responsibility regime. It addresses the normative foundations for the actual choices that are made in terms of thinking of the allocation of responsibility among several wrongdoing entities.

While the term 'distribution' thus is relatively straightforward, the notion 'distribution of responsibility' has two separate, though interrelated, meanings deriving from the dual meaning of the term 'responsibility'.[7]

In the first meaning of 'responsibility', 'distribution of responsibilities' is concerned with how multiple actors determine *ex ante* who should do what in relation to a common purpose or a common interest. For instance, the question can be posed as to which states and international institutions must act in situations of mass atrocities[8] or in relation to the protection of social and economic rights.[9] In both examples, it is clear that while some obligations under international law (e.g., the obligation to cooperate) can rest similarly on all states and international institutions, when it comes to specific obligations (e.g., which states are obliged to take forceful measures to protect civilians), a division of tasks is necessary. In this use of the term, 'responsibility' is essentially shorthand for 'duty' or 'obligation' – terms that might

[6] P.A. Nollkaemper, 'Introduction', in P.A. Nollkaemper and I. Plakokefalos (eds.), *Principles of Shared Responsibility in International Law: An Appraisal of the State of the Art* (Cambridge University Press, 2014), 1.
[7] P.A. Nollkaemper and D. Jacobs, 'Shared Responsibility in International Law: A Conceptual Framework' (2013) 34 MIJIL 359, 365.
[8] Hakimi, 'Distributing the Responsibility to Protect', n. 1.
[9] Salomon, 'How to Keep Promises: Making Sense of the Duty Among Multiple States to Fulfil Socio-Economic Rights in the World', n. 4.

or might not be used in a strictly legal meaning.[10] Such duties or obligations then need to be distributed.

In the second meaning of 'responsibility', the expression 'distribution of responsibilities' seeks to answer the question of how responsibility is divided *ex post* between multiple actors who have contributed to a particular harm. This question is, for instance, raised in relation to harmful conduct in peacekeeping operations[11] and climate change.[12] In this meaning, the term 'distribution of responsibility' thus relates to responsibility for wrongful conduct and harmful outcomes.

In this volume, we are primarily concerned with the second meaning. The difficulty of allocating responsibility between multiple parties for wrongdoing has been puzzling courts and scholars alike, and it is this difficulty that has informed the research project from which this volume emanates.[13] However, we recognise that there is an intimate connection between the two meanings – an issue to which we will return in section 5 of this chapter.

In cases where multiple states contribute to a harmful outcome, and the test of causation does not provide an answer to the question of who is responsible for what, several possibilities arise. One option is that no state is held responsible. Another suggestion is that one state is responsible for the whole damage, no matter how large its individual contribution. A third possibility is that all states involved are responsible, but only for the part that is attributed to them. A fourth option is that all states are jointly and severally responsible, and they all are responsible for the full damage, irrespective of their own specific contributions. A fifth and final option is that states rely on some other criterion (e.g., fairness) to distribute responsibility.[14]

[10] P. Cane, *Responsibility in Law and Morality* (Oxford: Hart Publishing, 2003), 1; J.R. Lucas, *Responsibility* (Oxford University Press, 1995), 75.

[11] Dannenbaum, 'Public Power and Preventative Responsibility: Attributing the Wrongs of International Joint Ventures', n. 1.

[12] Cole, 'The Problem of Shared Irresponsibility in International Climate Law', n. 2. See also J. Brunnée, S. Goldberg, R. Lord, and L. Rajamani, 'Overview of legal issues relevant to climate change', in R. Lord, S. Goldberg, L. Rajamani, and J. Brunnée (eds.), *Climate Change Liability: Transnational Law and Practice* (Cambridge University Press, 2012) 23; M.G. Faure and P.A. Nollkaemper, 'International Liability as an Instrument to Prevent and Compensate for Climate Change' (2007) 26(A) Stan ELJ 123.

[13] Nollkaemper and Jacobs, 'Shared Responsibility in International Law: A Conceptual Framework', n. 7, at 412.

[14] For a similar distinction see A. van Aaken, 'Shared Responsibility in International Law: A Political Economy Analysis', Chapter 6 in this volume, 153, at 156.

The choice between these options is of critical importance for all actors involved, and often for the larger international community. It determines who is to act to ensure that reparation is provided and that community values are protected.

However, international law has had very little to say on the question of when and on what grounds decisions are to be made, one way or the other. The first edited volume in this series, *Principles of Shared Responsibility in International Law: An Appraisal of the State of the Art*,[15] reviewed the extent to which the current law of responsibility, as laid down by the International Law Commission (ILC), is or could be relevant in solving questions of shared responsibility, including the question of distribution. The book noted that although the Articles on Responsibility of States for Internationally Wrongful Acts (ARSIWA)[16] and the Articles on the Responsibility of International Organizations (ARIO)[17] were not designed and drafted with situations of shared responsibility in mind, the Articles did not necessarily preclude determinations of shared responsibility. The Articles are quite flexible and to some extent can be adapted to new situations. In fact, one can identify examples in the case law of various international courts and tribunals that applied such principles in a shared responsibility context.[18] However, the Articles provide only limited guidance for the *distribution* of responsibility. As a whole, the chapters in that first volume led to the conclusion that if international law is to be helpful in addressing questions of shared responsibility, it will often be necessary to look beyond the ILC legacy.[19]

This lack of guidance that international law currently provides for questions of distribution presents both practical and theoretical problems. On a practical level, this means that it is difficult for courts and tribunals to make satisfactory assessments of the forms and amounts of

[15] P.A. Nollkaemper and I. Plakokefalos (eds.), *Principles of Shared Responsibility in International Law: An Appraisal of the State of the Art* (Cambridge University Press, 2014).

[16] Articles on Responsibility of States for Internationally Wrongful Acts, ILC *Yearbook* 2001/II(2) (ARSIWA).

[17] Articles on the Responsibility of International Organizations, ILC Report on the work of its sixty-third session, UNGAOR 66th Sess., Supp. No. 10, UN Doc. A/66/10 (2011) (ARIO).

[18] *Corfu Channel (United Kingdom of Great Britain and Northern Ireland* v. *Albania)*, Merits, ICJ Reports 1949, 4; *Certain Phosphate Lands in Nauru (Nauru* v. *Australia)*, Preliminary Objections, ICJ Reports 1992, 240.

[19] P.A. Nollkaemper and I. Plakokefalos, 'Conclusions: Beyond the ILC Legacy', in P.A. Nollkaemper and I. Plakokefalos (eds.), *Principles of Shared Responsibility in International Law: An Appraisal of the State of the Art* (Cambridge University Press, 2014), 341.

reparation to be provided by one actor, in a situation where multiple actors contributed to the harm. A good illustration is the *Bosnian Genocide* case.[20] The International Court of Justice (ICJ or Court) first found that the fact that the obligation to prevent genocide rests upon a multitude of states does not reduce the obligations of each individual state. When considering whether the obligations of Serbia to prevent genocide would be affected by the action or inaction of other states, the Court held that

> it is irrelevant whether the State whose responsibility is in issue claims, or even proves, that even if it had employed all means reasonably at its disposal, they would not have sufficed to prevent the commission of genocide. As well as being generally difficult to prove, this is irrelevant to the breach of the obligation of conduct in question, the more so since the possibility remains that the combined efforts of several States, each complying with its obligation to prevent, might have achieved the result — averting the commission of genocide — which the efforts of only one State were insufficient to produce.[21]

Yet, in considering compensation, the Court found that it had not been shown that in the specific circumstances of the case, the use of the means of influence by Serbia and Montenegro 'would have sufficed to achieve the result which the Respondent should have sought'.[22] The Court declined to order Serbia and Montenegro to pay compensation.[23] This contrast between the acceptance of Serbia's obligations irrespective of the role of other states, on the one hand, and the inability to allocate the obligation to reparation to Serbia precisely because other actors were involved, on the other, is unsatisfactory.[24] At a practical level, that holds first and foremost for victims (in this case Bosnia), which then may be unable to obtain reparation.

On a theoretical level, the question of distribution requires some normative basis that needs to ground the legal framework. This normative

[20] *Application of the Convention on the Prevention and Punishment of the Crime of Genocide (Bosnia and Herzegovina* v. *Serbia and Montenegro),* Judgment, ICJ Reports 2007, 43 (*Bosnian Genocide*).

[21] Ibid., 182, para. 430. [22] Ibid., 234, para. 462. [23] Ibid.

[24] See also A. Gattini, 'Breach of the Obligation to Prevent and Reparation Thereof in the ICJ's Genocide Judgment' (2007) 18 EJIL 695, at 707–712; P. Gaeta, 'On What Conditions Can a State Be Held Responsible for Genocide?' (2007) 18 EJIL 631; M. Milanović, 'State Responsibility for Genocide: A Follow-Up' (2007) 18 EJIL 669; W.A. Schabas, 'Genocide and the International Court of Justice: Finally, a Duty to Prevent the Crime of Crimes' (2007) 4 ISJ 17.

basis has so far not been the object of a systematic study. Often, in the literature, the normative underpinnings are implied in the legal framework that is advocated, rather than being expressly articulated and justified, in particular in advocating particular primary obligations in relation to, for instance, genocide or climate change. The absence of express and fundamental articulations of a specific normative justification may in part be caused by the fact that such articulations would entail paradigms, concepts, and methodologies that are far removed from legal doctrine.

However, the normative basis for the attribution and distribution of responsibility generally, and shared responsibility in particular, has direct consequences on the mechanisms that are put in place and how they operate. A choice for one ground of distribution over the other, based on one's own moral and conceptual approach to responsibility and distribution, has immediate wider implications. For instance, a focus on the public order dimension of the legal framework might lead to ascribing obligations to provide reparation to different entities than in case one would emphasise the private interests at stake. In the former case, there may be an interest to assign obligations of cessation or reparation to all actors whose acts undermine particular public goods or values. In the latter case, it may be sufficient if one actor provides reparation, as long as the injured parties are thereby satisfied.

Another example of how competing normative or conceptual perspectives may lead to different appraisals in terms of distribution is a situation of genocide. The nature of genocide might call for rules of distribution of responsibility that strictly focus on the particular role of a particular state, and exclude joint and several liability, given the moral stigma of a finding in that direction. However, one might to the contrary argue for looser rules of distribution, with less focus on causation and more on ensuring adequate reparation of the harm, given the need to avoid impunity for such an act.[25]

So far, models of international and shared responsibility rarely provide a theoretical foundation for understanding the differences between these approaches, let alone explain the choices made between them. This in turn will impact the way judges or other decision-makers will approach the question of distribution.

The present volume responds to the practical and conceptual problems identified here. We explore articulations of the grounds on which actors,

[25] Nollkaemper and Jacobs, 'Shared Responsibility in International Law: A Conceptual Framework', n. 7, at 417–418.

participating in a collective endeavour, can be blamed for their respective contribution to a harmful outcome. Given the fact that international law often gives no clear direction for distribution in such cases, the volume inquires into the bases and justifications for apportionment of responsibilities that could support a critique of current international law, support choices in the application of the law, and could provide a basis for reform.

The volume offers a diversity of approaches. Indeed, the underlying idea is not to trace a path to a particular normative framework, but rather to map the landscape of possible normative frameworks that might apply to the distribution of responsibilities under international law.

There is not one approach that has been adopted in the various chapters. Rather, the volume brings together possible approaches that might in certain circumstances, but not necessarily, complement each other. All chapters agree on the basic intellectual premise that underlies the whole project: there is a need for the development of a comprehensive legal framework on shared responsibility, solidly argued on a normative basis, and grounded in the changing realities of the international legal order.[26] However, there are fundamental differences in the normative choices and methodologies of the chapters. Ultimately, policy choices have to be made, in light of the social, political, moral, and legal preferences of decision-makers. Against this background, the importance of this volume is that by shedding light on these policy considerations, it helps to make an informed choice.

In this sense, this book has both a modest and an ambitious objective. Modest, because it does not purport to intellectually and normatively defend a single approach to the distribution of shared responsibility.[27] Ambitious, because it aims at providing comprehensive tools for a better understanding of the concept of shared responsibility and the ensuing theoretical underpinnings in relation to the distribution of such responsibility among wrongdoers.

The various approaches to distribution in this volume are far from abstract and conceptual musings. Normative choices for distribution can have a concrete impact on the legal frameworks that are set up to address current challenges of international law. This is illustrated in

[26] Nollkaemper and Jacobs, 'Shared Responsibility in International Law: A Conceptual Framework', n. 7.

[27] Some might even argue that as legal scholars this kind of normative positioning would be beyond the scope of our function. See J. d'Aspremont, 'The Politics of Deformalization in International Law' (2011) 3(2) GoJIL 503.

many chapters in this volume, which are contextualised in relation to particular topical areas of international law, such as piracy, climate change, or the duties of the international community to protect and safeguard human rights.

All in all, this book aims to contribute to the discussion on responsibility in three dimensions: a conceptual/theoretical dimension of explaining the possible normative foundations for the distribution of responsibility; a practical dimension of setting the conceptual discussion in the context of particular areas of international law; and, ultimately, a policy dimension in providing an informed starting point for possible development of the law.

Taking account of the need for differentiation and context specificity, we will explain in this introductory chapter our methodology in mapping different approaches (section 2); identify the components of the map: that is, fundamental concepts, choices, and approaches that have an impact on questions of distribution of responsibility (section 3); identify possible grounds for distribution as these are discussed in the contributions to the volume (section 4); and discuss what all of this may mean for the construction and development of international law on responsibility (section 5). The chapter closes with a brief roadmap of the volume (section 6).

2. Mapping conceptual approaches

As noted earlier, this volume does not aim at providing the grounding for a single normative or conceptual approach to the distribution of shared responsibilities in international law, but rather to map a range of possible bases for the distribution of responsibility.

In order to map possible conceptual understandings of the distribution of responsibility, the choice was made to cover a number of approaches that provide some insight into how to address such distribution. These can be divided into four categories: an economic analysis of law; a moral philosophy approach to responsibility; a political approach; and what can be called a pragmatic normative approach. It should be noted that there are differences and disagreements *within* these approaches. An illustration in this volume is whether collective entities can be moral agents, an issue that divides moral philosophers.[28] Equally, one can note differences

[28] See discussion of this in Erskine's chapter, T. Erskine, '"Coalitions of the Willing" and the Shared Responsibility to Protect', Chapter 8 in this volume, 227, at 229–234.

between the various chapters relying on an economic analysis of law. However, it was not possible to account for all the subtleties in the various disciplinary fields considered. This volume provides the first reasonably comprehensive normative map of the ways to approach the distribution of responsibility. Future scholarly work can build on it and seek further refinement of the various approaches.

The economic analysis of law provides tools for understanding the efficient distribution of responsibility in light of economic models such as the 'tragedy of the commons' and the 'prisoners' dilemma'. It allows a better assessment of the different ways in which responsibility can be distributed, depending on both the type of responsibility that is envisioned (individual, joint, and several) and the type of reparation that is sought (individualised, collective). This approach allows Van Aaken, for example, to explain that particular types of responsibility are more likely to be conducive to international cooperation,[29] or Kontorovich to explain why privatisation of the fight against piracy might be more efficient.[30] In another application of the economic analysis of law, Trachtman argues that a choice for either rules for the allocation of responsibility *ex ante* or for general principles for the allocation of responsibility *ex post*, affect 'net benefits of internalisation of policy externalities' in different manners.[31]

The moral philosophy approach focuses more on a moral evaluation of the conduct and the blameworthiness of the entities that engage in that conduct. The distribution of responsibility then flows from this evaluation. The decision to allocate responsibility comes as a consequence of the determination of such blameworthiness (or 'moral guilt'). This approach can therefore be called deontological in nature, and moves away from the more consequentialist focus of the economic analysis of law approach, which tends to concentrate more on the allocation of liability and reparations, and less on the actual blame of the wrongdoer. In other words, the deontological approach is more likely to provide answers for the distribution of blame, while the economic analysis of law approach is more likely to provide answers for the efficient allocation of financial obligations. This moral approach allows Kutz, in the context

[29] Van Aaken, 'Shared Responsibility in International Law: A Political Economy Analysis', n. 14, at 190–191.

[30] Kontorovich, 'Pirate "Globalisation": Dividing Responsibility Among States, Companies, and Criminals', n. 3, at 387.

[31] J.P. Trachtman, '*Ex Ante* and *Ex Post* Allocation of International Legal Responsibility', Chapter 4 in this volume, 87, at 89.

of climate change, to discuss the ways in which to distribute the burden of the reduction of carbon emissions, based on the past conduct of states.[32]

The political approach sets the legal analysis of distribution in the broader discussion of political incentives for action. This approach is important in two respects. First, it recognises that most areas of international law do not exist in a political void. Issues such as climate change or the 'Responsibility to Protect' (R2P) are debated in the context of strong political oppositions and narratives, which cannot be ignored when discussing the possible evolution of the legal regimes to implement them. Second, and more conceptually, it stems from the acknowledgement that law operates within the confines of a certain political community, and legal responsibility ultimately constitutes the basis for a broader political responsibility.[33] Lang observes that 'instead of solely tying individual agents to specific actions, this initial act of locating responsibility in specific agents can be used to compel agents to engage in forms of political action that construct new political arrangements, rather than ending in punitive or even restorative consequences'.[34]

The fourth approach is that of normative pragmatism. What underlies this approach is the acceptance of the fragmented reality of the international legal order, and the suggestion that broad normative agendas can be attained in that context. The idea is that there is not necessarily a need to comprehensively rethink the legal framework in a unitary way to achieve a certain goal, but that this goal can be achieved, at least in large part, through a collection of existing legal tools. Hakimi illustrates this approach in relation to R2P, showing that a number of mechanisms already exist to ensure that some aspects of it can become a reality.[35] In the same way, Salomon explores legal tools available in order to guarantee the protection and development of socio-economic rights.[36] This approach is, to some extent, complementary to the previous three approaches in the sense that the goal to be achieved can be identified through the economic, moral, and political evaluations already discussed. The difference of this approach is that it focuses on the connections between the normative agenda and the existing legal framework. For

[32] Kutz, 'Shared Responsibility for Climate Change: From Guilt to Taxes', n. 2, at 341–342.

[33] A.F. Lang, Jr., 'Shared Political Responsibility', Chapter 3 in this volume, 62.

[34] Ibid., at 65. [35] Hakimi, 'Distributing the Responsibility to Protect', n. 1.

[36] Salomon, 'How to Keep Promises: Making Sense of the Duty Among Multiple States to Fulfil Socio-Economic Rights in the World', n. 4.

instance, Dannenbaum explains that he does not 'articulate and defend a moral account from the ground up, untethered to extant law', but instead aims to build on 'the existing normative substructure of some of the better-elaborated areas of state responsibility under international law'.[37] This has the advantage of grounding the legal discussions in pre-established rules, but also has the possible disadvantage of being affected by any limitations of these rules.[38]

These four approaches, while possibly leading to different results, are not necessarily incompatible and could even be complementary. Indeed, it is for example perfectly possible to conceive of a normative framework that focuses on victims from a deontological/moral perspective, but then resorts to an economic analysis of law in order to determine the most efficient model for claiming reparations. In the same way, a focus on the moral blame of the perpetrators does not necessarily exclude a resort to economic models or political strategies to identify the distribution of responsibility in order to ensure compliance. It all depends at what stage of the reasoning the different normative frameworks are introduced. In other words, it is not an 'either/or' situation, where policymakers would need to adopt a moral philosophy approach, for example, rather than one based on an economic analysis of the law.

This diversity and possible combination of normative preferences is made possible by two interlinked considerations. First, each model, taken in isolation, might not provide concrete solutions for every scenario. For example, the political context of responsibility will not directly help to determine the concrete moral preferences of the political community in question, and nor will a consequentialist/economic analysis of responsibility remove the need to discuss the prioritisation of acceptable consequences within a given social context. Second, this diversity is an unavoidable consequence of the complex and fragmented reality of possible societal objectives of responsibility. Indeed, reflections on responsibility cannot be made in isolation from social realities and existing preferences, which must be accommodated in the discussions. This is of course true in many areas of law. For example, criminal law is generally a combination of deontological considerations (with a focus on intention and blame) and consequentialist aspects (merely thinking

[37] Dannenbaum, 'Public Power and Preventative Responsibility: Attributing the Wrongs of International Joint Ventures', n. 1, at 193.

[38] Salomon, 'How to Keep Promises: Making Sense of the Duty Among Multiple States to Fulfil Socio-Economic Rights in the World', n. 4.

of committing a crime will not carry any criminal responsibility in the absence of any preparatory acts). In international law, comparable combinations often will apply.

With these methodological clarifications in mind, it rapidly emerges that there are a number of cross-cutting themes that inform questions of distribution, and that in varying degrees will be relevant to each of the four methodological approaches.

3. Gathering the tools for exploring the map

The chapters, taken as a whole, point to a number of fundamental preliminary questions and choices that influence the distribution of responsibility. Based on existing literature and the contributions to this volume, we identify three such questions, which concern: the structure of collective action (3.1); the objectives of international responsibility (3.2); and the nature of international responsibility (3.3).

3.1 The structure of collective action

How responsibility is distributed between multiple actors depends in large part on how one conceives the nature and structure of collective action. The notion of 'collective action' is key to shared responsibility; after all, we have defined shared responsibility as a responsibility that is not incurred by the collective, but is distributed among individual 'members' of the collective.[39] If the responsibility were to rest on a collectivity, it would no longer be shared, but instead be a responsibility of the collectivity as such.[40] Within the category of shared responsibility, therefore, questions will arise concerning the nature of the relationship between the actors within the collective, and how that affects distribution of responsibility between them.

In situations of collective action, a key question is what type of individual contribution to the eventual harm can serve as a basis for allocation of responsibility. It can be argued that the mere membership of

[39] Nollkaemper and Jacobs, 'Shared Responsibility in International Law: A Conceptual Framework', n. 7, at 368. See also L. May, *Sharing Responsibility* (University of Chicago Press, 1996).

[40] May, ibid., 116. A major reason why in the present state of international relations exclusive collective responsibility in cases of cooperative action is not an attractive option is that the organisational structures remain too weak and the power of states too strong.

a collective may be sufficient to trigger distribution of responsibility to all. Lang recalls how Hannah Arendt argued 'that simply by living in the current world, one in which we are automatically bound up in a community, we can never avoid responsibility for the actions of our states'.[41] However, all contributors to this volume seem to reject this extreme approach, and seek to identify particular structures and relations in collective action that may serve to identify some, but not all, actors as subjects of responsibility.

The relationship between members of a collective can be construed in different ways. One approach is to disaggregate the collectivity in individual 'members', and to see shared responsibility simply as the aggregation of two or more individual responsibilities. Several authors in this volume adopt this perspective. For instance, Hakimi argues that 'R2P should not posit an all-encompassing duty that falls, at once, on the entire international community. It should instead posit a bundle of more discrete duties, and responsibility for each of these duties should attach to specific outside states at a time'.[42] Pierik notes that the obvious starting point for questions of distribution is an analysis of personal responsibility: 'the conditions under which an individual human being is held responsible for the outcome of a specific choice, behaviour, or act'.[43] Given that collectivities, short of firmly established institutions, are not moral agents,[44] it follows that responsibility is to be distributed to individual components of collectivities.

Placing the emphasis on individual agents is justified by two considerations. One is that it counters the problem of unattributed obligations, which are likely to remain ineffective precisely because it is not clear who needs to perform an obligation.[45] For Hakimi, the important point is that duties for the benefit of foreign populations 'are legally operative . . . only when responsibility can be pinned on particular states at a time'.[46] Erskine observes that 'mistakenly assuming that moral responsibilities can be borne by . . . bodies that do not qualify [as moral agents in world

[41] Lang, 'Shared Political Responsibility', n. 33, at 72.
[42] Hakimi, 'Distributing the Responsibility to Protect', n. 1, at 266.
[43] Pierik, 'Shared Responsibility in International Law: A Normative-Philosophical Analysis', Chapter 2 in this volume, 36, at 39. See also Erskine, '"Coalitions of the Willing" and the Shared Responsibility to Protect', n. 28.
[44] Erskine, ibid., at 228, 229–234.
[45] V. Held, 'Can a Random Collection of Individuals be Morally Responsible' (1970) 67(14) JP 471.
[46] Hakimi, 'Distributing the Responsibility to Protect', n. 1, at 267.

politics] ... has detrimental consequences. Such missteps hamper attempts to consider, coordinate, and execute remedial action effectively and robustly'.[47] The second justification for focusing on individual actors is based on a moral perspective. It follows the idea that responsibility can only be attributed to agents that can be capable of moral agency and be blamed for their action. Moreover, this is premised on the idea that moral agents can only be responsible for their own specific acts and omissions, not those of someone else.[48]

This disaggregation of responsibility to individual actors is particularly important in situations where there is no concerted action, but rather what we call *cumulative responsibility*.[49] In such cases, we recognise the need for the injured party to be able to claim against several entities. More particularly, in those instances, in the absence of any link between the actions of these entities, there is no need to delve deeper into the nature of the collective action that led to the damage. Examples are cumulative pollution caused by two or more riparian states of an international watercourse, or climate change caused by emissions from several states.

However, shared responsibility cannot always simply be seen as the aggregation of two or more individual responsibilities. Indeed, a defining feature of many situations where issues of shared responsibility arise is that two or more actors stand in some relationship to each other, and the conduct or omission of one influences the conduct or omission of the other(s).[50] This will especially be the case in situations of concerted action. We refer to such instances as *cooperative responsibility*.[51] This covers examples such as coalition warfare, joint patrols to protect borders against immigration, or responsibility that may result from one state aiding another state in committing a wrongful act.

Whereas in the first situation responsibility can more easily be traced to individually operating states, with their conduct being able to be assessed in isolation, in the second situation the structure of the collective action can, and arguably should, influence the distribution of responsibility.

47 Erskine, '"Coalitions of the Willing" and the Shared Responsibility to Protect', n. 28, at 230.

48 Ibid., at 229–234; Pierik, 'Shared Responsibility in International Law: A Normative-Philosophical Analysis', n. 43, at 39–42.

49 Nollkaemper and Jacobs, 'Shared Responsibility in International Law: A Conceptual Framework', n. 7, at 368–369.

50 May, *Sharing Responsibility*, n. 39, at 36–38.

51 Nollkaemper and Jacobs, 'Shared Responsibility in International Law: A Conceptual Framework', n. 7, at 368–369.

As Pettit argues, the agency of a collective is actually more than the sum of its members' agency.[52] The collective and the mutual relations within it affect the position of its members. In such cases, disaggregating collective action into individual responsibility is not satisfactory if it ignores the relationship between the various agents.

This volume takes this discussion one step further. A number of chapters provide valuable insights into the structure of collective action and decision-making that is fundamental for assessing the distribution of responsibility of various entities. For instance, Miller presents a relational account of collective moral responsibility as joint responsibility.[53] In his terms, two or more individuals perform a joint action 'if each of them intentionally performs an individual action (or omission), but does so with the (true) belief that in so doing they will jointly realise an end which each of them has'.[54] While collective responsibility is ascribed to individual human beings for their contributory action, 'each is individually responsible for that outcome, *jointly with the others*'.[55]

A comparable point is made by Erskine, who, when analysing 'coalitions of the willing', considers that while the coalition cannot be a moral agent as such, it is important to take into account the relationship between its members in order to determine the scope of individual responsibilities.[56] As a result, she considers that when agents come together to form an ad hoc group, 'the enhanced capacities with which individual agents can be imbued as part of an informal association (existing or potential) lead to *magnified individual responsibilities*'.[57] Thus the structure of the collective directly influences the possibilities and types of distribution between the members of the collective.

However, it may be helpful to differentiate between various forms that the relationship between members of a collective can take. As the international legal order becomes increasingly structured by international

[52] P. Pettit, 'Responsibility Incorporated' (2007) 1 *Ethics* 117.

[53] Miller, 'The Global Financial Crisis and Collective Moral Responsibility', n. 5, at 407–408. See also S. Miller, 'Collective Moral Responsibility: An Individualist Account' (2006) 30 MSP 176; S. Miller, 'Joint Action' (1992) 21(3) PP 275; and S. Miller, 'Intentions, Ends and Joint Action' (1995) 24(1) PP 51.

[54] Miller, 'The Global Financial Crisis and Collective Moral Responsibility', ibid., at 408.

[55] Ibid., at 408 (emphasis in original). See further M.J. Zimmerman, 'Sharing Responsibility' (1985) 22(2) APQ 115; S. Miller, 'Collective Responsibility' (2001) 15(1) PAQ 65; S. Collins, 'Collectives' Duties and Collectivization Duties' (2013) 91(2) AJP 231.

[56] Erskine, '"Coalitions of the Willing" and the Shared Responsibility to Protect', n. 28, at 250–253.

[57] Ibid., at 256 (emphasis in original).

organisations and collective decisions, it is important that conceptual tools be devised to appreciate the corresponding increasingly complex nature of collective endeavours at that level. As explored in this volume, these can vary on a scale from ad hoc ventures to more institutionalised situations. In relation to the first type, Dannenbaum focuses on structures ('joint public enterprises') that are larger than individual states, yet fall short of a collectivity that can be the subject of collective responsibility.[58] For more institutionalised action, Miller emphasises the importance of predetermined rules and mechanisms.[59]

While each of these perspectives differs in terms of the weight they attach to the structure of the collective, and the assessment of the implications for distribution of responsibility, they have in common that the unit of analysis in determinations of responsibility in such cases is not just the individual members of the group, but the relations between members. This provides a critical background that points out the significance and complexity of distribution in situations of concerted action.

3.2 *The objectives of international responsibility*

The objectives of responsibility constitute a second tool to explore the map. The basic idea here is that the objectives that one assigns to, or expects from, a system of responsibility will have implications for the choice, and evaluation, of a particular model of distribution. The question of distribution when seen from the perspective of a victim looks different than when seen from the perspective of a perpetrator, or from the interest of cooperation.

A first major division can be drawn between a deontological approach (responsibility based on a duty and the moral blame of the perpetrator) and a consequentialist approach (responsibility based on the assessment of possible outcomes of the violation of the duty).

The deontological approach focuses on the moral agency of the individual agents. As noted by Pierik, this approach 'situates individual responsibility in personal agency and argues that responsibility can only be attributed to agents. Agency refers to the capacity to act deliberately and intentionally'.[60]

[58] Dannenbaum, 'Public Power and Preventative Responsibility: Attributing the Wrongs of International Joint Ventures', n. 1.

[59] Miller, 'The Global Financial Crisis and Collective Moral Responsibility', n. 5.

[60] Pierik, 'Shared Responsibility in International Law: A Normative-Philosophical Analysis', n. 43, at 41.

This approach entails several methodological steps that are relevant to distribution of responsibility. First, as discussed previously, it is necessary to identify relevant agents that might be the bearers of duties. Second, once moral agents have been identified, it is still necessary to identify criteria for the distribution of responsibility between several entities that might be responsible for the harm.[61]

The deontological approach impacts on the question of distribution of responsibility in a number of ways. In particular, it is an invitation to consider the retributive dimension of responsibility in relation to particular wrongdoers. However, one can wonder whether international law is well equipped for this, given the traditional absence of fault in discussions on the secondary rules of international law.[62] While it would seem that the 'objective responsibility' approach in international law today, which focuses on the existence of a breach of an international legal obligation per se, is compatible with the deontological approach, the irrelevance of fault (in the absence of specific rules to that effect in particular treaties) in the determination of international responsibility could be seen to be at odds with this approach.

Another impact is that a deontological approach leaves open the possibility that no one entity or state is to be blamed for a particular harm. This is seen by some as a major drawback[63] and justifies taking a consequentialist approach, whereby the existence of a harm to be repaired is the starting point, rather than the identification of a morally culpable agent.

Adoption of a consequentialist approach leads to an altogether different set of consequences in terms of distribution. The contributions to this volume identify three main goals that can be construed in consequentialist terms.[64] Each of these, and also the choice between them, has distinct consequences for distribution.

A first objective is to compensate the injured parties. This aim is backward looking, in the sense that it focuses on harm that has already

[61] These possible criteria are discussed in more detail in section 4.

[62] Nollkaemper and Jacobs, 'Shared Responsibility in International Law: A Conceptual Framework', n. 7, at 409, 411. See also E. David, 'Primary and Secondary Rules', in J. Crawford, et al. (eds.), *The Law of International Responsibility* (Oxford University Press, 2010), 27.

[63] Erskine, '"Coalitions of the Willing" and the Shared Responsibility to Protect', n. 28, at 243–244.

[64] Kornhauser, 'Incentives, Compensation, and Irreparable Harm', Chapter 5 in this volume, 120, at 121. See for similar distinctions Van Aaken, 'Shared Responsibility in International Law: A Political Economy Analysis', n. 14, at 158–161.

occurred. In terms of distribution, two points can be noted. On the one hand, a responsibility regime that aims to secure this function in effects shifts, as Kornhauser notes, the harm 'from the "victim" to one or more legally responsible agents'.[65] On the other hand, for instance, from a victim's perspective, joint and several responsibility may be most favourable, since a victim 'just needs to identify one violator and can pick the one which, first, can be brought before a court, and second, has deep pockets'.[66]

A second aim is to deter states from engaging in harmful actions in the future.[67] This aim is forward looking. If international law is to contribute to this aim, it has to create proper incentives for states.[68] This aim, too, has distinct implications for distribution. For instance, it could be argued that, from this angle, responsibility should be allocated to those actors that matter in terms of power, control, and capacity.[69] Distribution schemes that leave some actors that contribute to harm unaddressed may not be efficient, as these actors may otherwise not have an incentive to take proper care.[70]

A third aim is to secure international cooperation. This is not commonly seen as an independent objective of responsibility, and never seems to have been an aim for the ILC. However, as Van Aaken notes, different forms of responsibility are 'a crucial variable for understanding why cooperation arises (or not), since it impacts upon the propensity to cooperate in the first place'.[71] For instance, a distribution of responsibility based on independent responsibility 'would inhibit the propensity of cooperation in the first place, since the pay-off of cooperation would be potentially diminished to a great extent'.[72]

The relationship between objectives of responsibility, on the one hand, and distribution of responsibility, on the other, is made more complex since actors may pursue multiple aims that may conflict with each other. For instance, Kornhauser observes the tension between the social aims of deterrence and compensation: 'The deterrence objective requires that

[65] Kornhauser, ibid., at 121.
[66] Van Aaken, 'Shared Responsibility in International Law: A Political Economy Analysis', n. 14, at 186.
[67] Kornhauser, 'Incentives, Compensation, and Irreparable Harm', n. 64, at 121–122.
[68] Ibid. [69] See section 4.4 entitled 'The role of power'.
[70] Kornhauser, 'Incentives, Compensation, and Irreparable Harm', n. 64, at 130–132.
[71] Van Aaken, 'Shared Responsibility in International Law: A Political Economy Analysis', n. 14, at 154.
[72] Ibid., at 186.

the agent be able to avoid financial responsibility by taking socially desirable actions but, when the agent escapes financial liability, that liability must fall on the victim or be socialised through an insurance scheme.'[73] The way such potential tensions are mitigated or resolved has direct implications for distribution of responsibility.

3.3 *The nature of international responsibility*

A third exploration tool of the map is the nature of international responsibility. This is obviously closely linked to the question of the objectives of responsibility, as previously discussed. However, the question of the nature of international responsibility is situated on a meta-level and requires us to reflect on the role of responsibility in relation to the nature of the international legal order.

On this point, the distinction that we drew in previous work between its public order dimension and private dimension is of key relevance to questions of distribution.[74] The private dimension of international responsibility is exemplified in the bilateral structure of many obligations, as well as the bilateral structure of international dispute settlement, which focuses primarily on the interaction between the alleged wrongdoing state and the injured state.[75] However, certain dimensions of international law, such as the development of peremptory norms or the preference for objective responsibility in the ARSIWA, point to a more public dimension. Emphasising one dimension of responsibility over another may have direct implications for questions of distribution.

However, we also argued that it would be too simple to frame international responsibility in either a public or a private, or even in one single *sui generis* paradigm. The unitary approach to international responsibility cannot capture the various aspects of what it means to invoke the responsibility of multiple agents for particular harms, and we proposed a more differentiated approach to shared responsibility.[76]

In this volume, most chapters bring to the fore the public dimension of international responsibility. For example, Dannenbaum focuses on public enterprises; Erskine focuses on coalitions of the willing; and Shue and Kutz on climate change. They highlight, in relation to areas that are

[73] Kornhauser, 'Incentives, Compensation, and Irreparable Harm', n. 64, at 127.
[74] Nollkaemper and Jacobs, 'Shared Responsibility in International Law: A Conceptual Framework', n. 7, at 398–407.
[75] Ibid., at 432. [76] Ibid., at 415.

generally deemed to be public goods (e.g., prevention of mass atrocities, human rights, and climate change), the need to better accommodate the legal framework with the nature of international obligations. For example, climate change responsibility requires more than a traditional tort-like evaluation of causation, but brings in global historical and moral evaluations.[77] This also shows the limits of traditional models of responsibility, such as the idea of transboundary harm.[78]

This emphasis on the public order dimension of international obligations has implications for distribution of responsibility, should harm occur. It calls attention to the relevant agents who would be responsible for ensuring respect for community values at the international level. This public dimension of certain duties in relation to, for example, the prevention of mass atrocities or the protection of common goods has an uneasy relationship to the absence of a centralised international authority tasked with ensuring their respect. In that regard, the current framework of both particular sets of primary obligations (e.g., the obligation to prevent genocide or the obligation to protect social, economic, and cultural rights) and of international responsibility provides inadequate answers to the question of the exact bearers of collective duties.[79] This significantly complicates the question of distribution of responsibility.[80]

In addition to the suggestion that the United Nations might play this role,[81] various chapters propose solutions. In that respect, the varying nature of obligations, and of related responsibility, is reflected in different proposals: efficient cooperation (Kontorovich);[82] pragmatism (Hakimi

[77] Kutz, 'Shared Responsibility for Climate Change: From Guilt to Taxes', n. 2, at 342.

[78] Shue, 'Transboundary Damage in Climate Change: Criteria for Allocating Responsibility', n. 2.

[79] Nollkaemper and Jacobs, 'Shared Responsibility in International Law: A Conceptual Framework', n. 7, at 426–427.

[80] A similar unsatisfactory situation exists in relation to the question of who may invoke the responsibility of others in that respect, as the distinction between injured states and non-injured states as embodied in the ARSIWA (Articles 42 and 48 ARSIWA, n. 16). For a critical discussion see also B. Stern, 'A Plea for "Reconstruction" of International Responsibility Based on the Notion of Legal Injury', in M. Ragazzi (ed.), *International Responsibility Today: Essays in Memory of Oscar Schachter* (Leiden: Nijhoff, 2005); Nollkaemper and Jacobs, ibid. at 418–420.

[81] Nollkaemper and Jacobs, ibid. at 427.

[82] Kontorovich, 'Pirate "Globalisation": Dividing Responsibility Among States, Companies, and Criminals', n. 3.

and Salomon);[83] political cooperation (Cole);[84] or heightened rules of conduct and responsibility (Erskine, Dannenbaum, and to a certain extent, Kutz).[85] All these solutions accept the current structure of the international legal order and suggest ways to address collective aims within it.

The authors can be placed on a sliding scale of adaptation to the public order dimension of international responsibility. At one end of the scale is the breaking down of the common value into somewhat more manageable obligations that can rest on easily identifiable agents. This is the approach adopted by Hakimi and Salomon in relation to R2P and social and economic rights.[86] At the other end of the scale is the idea that certain obligations should rest on a broader category of agents. For example, Miller suggests various levels, both domestic and international, on which regulatory obligations could reside in relation to the financial crisis.[87] Along the same lines, Erskine argues that ultimately all states might have some duty to coalesce to achieve certain outcomes, even if they do not succeed.[88]

4. Criteria for distribution

In a study on distribution of responsibility, the key question is on the basis of what criteria is distribution eventually to be grounded. We have already indicated several grounds, in as much as these were related to the objectives attributed to responsibility or the construction of the nature of responsibility. It is nonetheless useful to expressly identify, briefly, the most important grounds because these, from various methodological angles, will be discussed in this volume.

[83] Hakimi, 'Distributing the Responsibility to Protect', n. 1; Salomon, 'How to Keep Promises: Making Sense of the Duty Among Multiple States to Fulfil Socio-Economic Rights in the World', n. 4.

[84] Cole, 'The Problem of Shared Irresponsibility in International Climate Law', n. 2.

[85] Erskine, '"Coalitions of the Willing" and the Shared Responsibility to Protect', n. 28; Dannenbaum, 'Public Power and Preventative Responsibility: Attributing the Wrongs of International Joint Ventures', n. 1; Kutz, 'Shared Responsibility for Climate Change: From Guilt to Taxes', n. 2.

[86] Hakimi, 'Distributing the Responsibility to Protect', n. 1; Salomon, 'How to Keep Promises: Making Sense of the Duty among Multiple States to Fulfil Socio-Economic Rights in the World', n. 4.

[87] Miller, 'The Global Financial Crisis and Collective Moral Responsibility', n. 5.

[88] Erskine, '"Coalitions of the Willing" and the Shared Responsibility to Protect', n. 28.

We emphasise that the contents and nature of such grounds for distribution will be highly context-specific. Grounds that may be relevant in one context may be much less helpful in a different setting. For example, it may be useful to distinguish between causal responsibility, legal responsibility, and financial responsibility for harm.[89] Which of those forms of responsibility matters, and is actually to be distributed, will depend on the context. It also may be useful to distinguish between types of harm that arise in particular issue-areas. Questions of distribution present themselves in quite different forms in situations of divisible harm compared to situations of indivisible harm. In cases of indivisible harm, the question is whether responsibility can really be divided among several tortfeasors. A further distinction can be made between reparable and irreparable harm. For instance, in cases of irreparable harm, the cost for victims cannot be transferred to other actors.[90]

In the subsections that follow, we will move on from such issue-specific factors and identify a number of general grounds that may be relevant for distribution of responsibility and that will be explored in this volume: obligations (4.1); causation (4.2); contributions (4.3); power (4.4); and fairness (4.5).

4.1 *Obligations*

The distribution of responsibility largely depends on the contents of primary obligations. Not all contributions made by members of a collective are legally equally relevant; it all depends on what contributions are proscribed by international law. For example, the question of distribution of responsibility in relation to climate change relies strongly on the question of what international law actually does, or does not, proscribe.

An important example of such obligations and their relevance to questions of distribution, identified in several chapters, are obligations to prevent a particular harm. Obligations to prevent, for instance, exist in relation to mass atrocities. In such cases, the contents and nature of such an obligation may be relevant for identifying which states are obliged to prevent, and possibly also for the distribution of responsibility between

[89] Kornhauser, 'Incentives, Compensation, and Irreparable Harm', n. 64, at 121.
[90] Ibid., at 122.

territorial states and third states.[91] In this respect there is an important relation between questions of jurisdiction and responsibility.[92] In this volume, this connection is particularly explored by Salomon and Hakimi.[93]

In addition to the contents of international obligations, a further relevant factor may be the nature of the relationship (or roles) between actors in a more factual sense, which may inform the application of obligations in a particular case. For instance, in the *Bosnian Genocide* case the ICJ found in the particular relationship between Serbia and Bosnia a ground to attribute responsibility to Serbia[94] which, in all likelihood, it would have not attributed to other states.

However, this volume does not limit itself to exploring obligations under existing international law. For instance, Erskine argues that in assessing the shared responsibility of members of the international community to safeguard a particular population, special responsibilities arguably come into play in arriving at an efficient and just distribution of moral burdens.[95] Such a construction of 'special responsibilities' may not immediately inform a distribution as a matter of law, but may inform the negotiation of particular solutions and possibly the development of international law.

4.2 *Causation*

An obvious factor that is relevant to the distribution of responsibility is the concept of causation. If multiple actors contribute to a harmful outcome, the first question is whether it can be determined who contributed what to the harm. This would allow for a form of proportional (or several) responsibility.[96] Relying on causation is not only instrumental

[91] Hakimi, 'Distributing the Responsibility to Protect', n. 1; Dannenbaum, 'Public Power and Preventative Responsibility: Attributing the Wrongs of International Joint Ventures', n. 1.

[92] M. Milanović, *Extraterritorial Application of Human Rights Treaties: Law, Principles and Policy* (Oxford University Press, 2011), 51.

[93] Hakimi, 'Distributing the Responsibility to Protect', n. 1; Salomon, 'How to Keep Promises: Making Sense of the Duty Among Multiple States to Fulfil Socio-Economic Rights in the World', n. 4.

[94] *Bosnian Genocide*, n. 20.

[95] Erskine, '"Coalitions of the Willing" and the Shared Responsibility to Protect', n. 28, at 258.

[96] Van Aaken, 'Shared Responsibility in International Law: A Political Economy Analysis', n. 14, at 156; Kornhauser, 'Incentives, Compensation, and Irreparable Harm', n. 64, at 124–139.

in order to achieve a distribution of responsibility, but also rests on moral grounds. As noted by Pierik, 'we can only reasonably be held responsible for the outcome(s) of our actions and decisions'.[97]

However, causation is not the tool that will fix all questions of distribution. For one thing, the contents of the standard of causation remain unsettled.[98] Courts that opt for one particular approach to causation are invariably subject to critique for choosing that over another method. The approach of the ICJ to causation in the *Bosnian Genocide* case is an example.[99]

Moreover, standards of causation are hardly neutral. Establishing causation is not a purely factual operation. There is a clear normative choice involved in selecting those causes which might entail legal responsibility. This is precisely why, as explained by Kornhauser, the distinction between causal responsibility and legal responsibility is critical.[100] Causal responsibility does not necessarily entail legal responsibility.[101]

There is a more practical limitation to relying on causation as an easy fix to questions of distribution. In many cases, there will be a problem of over-determination.[102] Specifically in the context of collective action, causation may be of limited use, since collective action might create problems in determining the causal link between conduct and consequences of the conduct. This in turn may lead to dilution of responsibility.

This is especially true if structural causes are taken into account. Salomon observes that '[i]f we take the case of biofuels: global food prices would not have skyrocketed but for the European Union and United States (US) policies on production.'[103] Likewise, Lang notes that while at one level one can think of corporations as subjects of liability for global

[97] Pierik, 'Shared Responsibility in International Law: A Normative-Philosophical Analysis', n. 43, at 39.

[98] Gattini, 'Breach of the Obligation to Prevent and Reparation Thereof in the ICJ's Genocide Judgment', n. 24, at 708.

[99] Ibid.

[100] Kornhauser, 'Incentives, Compensation, and Irreparable Harm', n. 64, at 121.

[101] Pierik, 'Shared Responsibility in International Law: A Normative-Philosophical Analysis', n. 43, at 39–40.

[102] J. Schaffer, 'Overdetermining Causes' (2003) 114 PS 23; J.G. Stewart, 'Overdetermined Atrocities' (2012) NYU Public Law & Legal Theory Research Paper Series, Working Paper No. 12–53, available at http://papers.ssrn.com/sol3/papers.cfm?abstract_id=2152670 (accessed on 1 December 2014).

[103] M.E. Salomon, 'Deprivation, Causation and the Law of International Cooperation', in M. Langford, et al. (eds.), *Global Justice, State Duties: The Extraterritorial Scope of Economic, Social and Cultural Rights in International Law* (Cambridge University Press, 2012), 259, 263–272.

harms, such as climate change, states that create corporations without proper regulation should also be considered as being responsible.[104] Several conditions can thus be identified that are relevant, yet are in themselves insufficient to generate an outcome. Choices thus have to be made on the basis of other criteria. Pierik observes in this context that it will be necessary to 'limit our analysis to those links in the causal chain of events that can be linked to actions and/or decisions that are relevant in any moral or legal sense'.[105]

There are two possible solutions to the difficulty of solving questions of distribution through causation. The first one is to remove any discussion of individual causation altogether, for instance through the application of a version of joint responsibility.[106] If the collective action has led to the damage, then each individual entity becomes individually responsible for the full outcome, irrespective of his or her actual contribution to the harm. The second one is a middle ground whereby the *principle* of responsibility would be determined by participation in the collective endeavour, while the *quantum* of responsibility would be conditional on the actual conduct of the entity. For example, in a North Atlantic Treaty Organization operation decided by the organisation, every state is in principle responsible for the conduct of the organisation, but a state that merely voted for the military action might face less responsibility than a state that actually conducted the operations on the ground. This latter solution, while in theory providing a more subtle approach to the distribution of responsibilities within organisational structures, will raise some practical difficulties.

4.3 Contributions

A third category of factors relevant to distribution of responsibility concerns the nature of contributions to a harmful outcome. This is obviously directly related to causation, but the focus here is more on the nature of contributions to harm. Various chapters point to this criterion as a key element in allocating responsibility. For instance, Shue

[104] Lang, 'Shared Political Responsibility', n. 33, at 75.

[105] Pierik, 'Shared Responsibility in International Law: A Normative-Philosophical Analysis', n. 43, at 40.

[106] Kornhauser, 'Incentives, Compensation, and Irreparable Harm', n. 64, at 132–138; Van Aaken, 'Shared Responsibility in International Law: A Political Economy Analysis', n. 14, at 168–170; Pierik, ibid., at 50–52.

points to current emissions per capita of the residents of states as a criterion for distributing responsibility in relation to climate change.[107]

A few dimensions are given special consideration in the chapters in this volume. One consists of so-called structural contributions. For example, Lang observes that while at one level one can think of corporations as subjects of liability for global harms, such as climate change, 'at a deeper level, it is the legal and political order that creates corporations that should also be responsible for the harms they commit. In other words, if states create corporations without regulatory frameworks or limits on their profit making, then the state should be considered somehow responsible'.[108]

In a number of chapters, a separate role is played by historical contributions. Salomon suggests that contemporary obligations could 'be assigned on the basis of historical responsibility for past exploitation'.[109] Likewise, Shue notes that an important factor is a state's percentage of the cumulative carbon emissions to this point.[110] Kutz makes a similar claim, grounding discussions on responsibility on past conduct and history.[111] For him, it is irrelevant whether this past conduct was, at the time, blameworthy or faultless. He considers that '[i]nsofar as this history [whether in relation to slavery or GHG emissions] is ours, so are the traces of responsibility. To be a citizen of a state is to come in a family lineage ... to be bearer of responsibility for that lineage. We must face the future in the shadow of the collective past.'[112] In other words, he rejects the idea of 'bygones are bygones' as a natural conclusion for past conduct that might have contributed to harm.

This approach has a strong socio-historical grounding in the sense that, as in other examples given previously, it allows for a better understanding of the structural conditions for the occurrence of harm. However, a number of difficulties remain. From a philosophical perspective, it

[107] Shue, 'Transboundary Damage in Climate Change: Criteria for Allocating Responsibility', n. 2, at 330.

[108] Lang, 'Shared Political Responsibility', n. 33, at 75. See also the example, quoted in section 4.2, that Salomon gives of the US and EU policies on production and their effect on global food prices; Salomon, 'Deprivation, Causation and the Law of International Cooperation', n. 103, at 259, 263–272.

[109] Salomon, 'How to Keep Promises: Making Sense of the Duty Among Multiple States to Fulfil Socio-Economic Rights in the World', n. 4, at 375.

[110] Shue, 'Transboundary Damage in Climate Change: Criteria for Allocating Responsibility', n. 2, at 333.

[111] Kutz, 'Shared Responsibility for Climate Change: From Guilt to Taxes', n. 2, at 341–342.

[112] Ibid., at 355.

does not really account for the retroactive attribution of moral culpability. Moreover, the relationship between this claim to a historical moral lineage and its implementation in a legal framework could possibly be problematic, in light of the current principles of international responsibility (such as the existence of an international obligation). More generally, it raises the question of the functions of law, and its possible limits as an adequate social tool in addressing past wrongs.[113]

4.4 *The role of power*

A fourth consideration is the role of power. Eagleton famously claimed that 'power breeds responsibility'.[114] The phrase is frequently quoted with apparent approval in international legal scholarship.[115] The notion is also framed in other terms but with the same underlying idea, for instance in the argument that responsibility originates in control.[116] There is also a strand of literature that transforms the idea into a normative proposition, for instance to the effect that responsibility should reflect power (or capacity, which is a distinct, but related, concept).[117]

Assigning responsibility to states or other actors on the basis of power makes sense. Power refers to the ability of a state to influence or control other actors, and thereby get another actor to do what it wants, if necessary even against its will.[118] In this sense power is essentially a

[113] For a discussion of this question in the context of the Armenian Genocide, see D. Jacobs 'Jumping Hurdles Backwards: The Armenian Genocide and the International Criminal Court' (2014) 14 ICLR 274.

[114] C. Eagleton, *The Responsibility of States in International Law* (New York University Press, 1928), 206. This section is partly based on P.A. Nollkaemper, 'Power and Responsibility', SHARES Research Paper 42(2014), ACIL 2014–22, available at www.sharesproject.nl.

[115] E.g. E. Paasivirta, 'Responsibility of a Member State of an International Organization: Where Will It End?' (2010) 7 IOLR 49, 51; C. Ahlborn, 'The Use of Analogies in Drafting the Articles on the Responsibility of International Organizations – An Appraisal of the "Copy-Paste Approach" –' (2012) 9 IOLR 53, 63; L. Clarke, 'Responsibility of International Organizations under International Law for the Acts of Global Health Public-Private Partnerships' (2012) 12 Chic JIL 55, 65.

[116] C. Eagleton, 'International Organization and the Law of Responsibility' (1950) 76 RCADI 319, at 385–386; W. Friedman, 'The Growth of State Control over the Individual and Its Effect upon the Rules of International State Responsibility' (1938) 19 BYIL 118, 149.

[117] J. Pattison, '*Jus Post Bellum* and the Responsibility to Rebuild' (2013) 1 BJPS 20, 22–23; D. Miller, 'Distributing Responsibilities' (2001) 9(4) JPP 453.

[118] M. Weber, *Economy and Society* (University of California Press, 1978), 53. See also M.S. McDougal, 'Law and Power' (1952) 46 AJIL 102, 107–108; C. Taylor, 'Foucault on freedom and truth' (1984) 12 PT 152, 158 (the notion of power or domination 'requires

relational phenomenon.[119] In the context of responsibility, a state can exercise power in relation to another entity by making it engage in a particular wrongful act. If so, it can be said that it then should be this state that should bear responsibility for the harm, rather than (only) the author of an act. Tracing responsibility to the actor that wields power is also justified on the basis of remedial considerations. If harm is to be prevented, those wielding the power in relation to harmful conduct should be addressed, rather than those that execute commands. Only the former actors can terminate the wrong or ensure that it is not repeated.[120]

The proposition that power breeds responsibility is particularly relevant in situations of shared responsibility. It suggests that power should be a relevant, perhaps even decisive, consideration in allocating responsibility in situations where multiple actors contribute to harm. Conversely, it could be said that if an actor is dominated by another actor, to the extent that its individual space for decision-making or its capacity to act is limited, the basis for assigning responsibility to that actor falls away.[121]

The role of power seems particularly relevant for questions of distribution in two respects. On the one hand, power underlies the very structure of the rules on responsibility that are used to distribute responsibility. Lang argues that 'power relations … exist between individuals that allow some to blame others and, in so doing, reinforce or create anew those roles. Individual persons become blameworthy or praiseworthy because of the roles we create for them'.[122]

some notion of constraint imposed on someone'). Of course, power can be conceptualised in different ways. See e.g., A. Ballesteros, S. Nakhooda, J. Werksman, and K. Hurlburt, 'Power, responsibility, and accountability: Rethinking the legitimacy of institutions for climate finance' (2010) 1 *Climate Law* 261, 265 (referring to power as the capacity to determine outcomes).

119 D.A. Lake, 'Authority, Coercion and Power in International Relations', in M. Finnemore and J. Goldstein (eds.), *Back to Basics: State Power in a Contemporary World* (Oxford University Press, 2013); D.A. Baldwin, 'Power and International Relations', in W. Carlsnaes, T. Risse, and B.A. Simmons (eds.), *Handbook of International Relations*, 2nd edn (London: Sage, 2013), 273, at 285–286; S. Strange, 'International Economics and International Relations: A Case of Mutual Neglect' (1970) 46(2) IA 304.

120 Miller, 'Distributing Responsibilities', n. 117; P.J. Kuijper and E. Paasivirta, 'EU International Responsibility and its Attribution: From the Inside Looking Out', in M. Evans and P. Koutrakos (eds.), *The International Responsibility of the European Union: European and International Perspectives* (Oxford: Hart Publishing, 2013), 35.

121 Pierik, 'Shared Responsibility in International Law: A Normative-Philosophical Analysis', n. 43, at 39–42.

122 Lang, 'Shared Political Responsibility', n. 33, at 68.

Several authors in the present volume explore the role of power, or capacity, as a specific ground for distribution of responsibilities. For instance, Salomon observes that '[o]bligations of international cooperation could be determined on the basis of the relative power it wields in international affairs manifested as influence over the direction of international trade, investment, taxation, finance, environmental policy, and development cooperation.'[123]

The concept of power has a number of more specific connotations and manifestations that can serve as grounds for distribution of responsibility. One of these is power as control. Dannenbaum observes that '[e]nterprise wrongs ought to be attributed to the participant states or organisations that hold the levers of control most relevant to preventing the type of wrongdoing in question.'[124]

Another manifestation is capacity. This is particularly relevant from a consequentialist perspective, when the question becomes who is best placed to remedy a particular harmful situation. In this context, Miller calls this 'assigning remedial responsibility according to capacity': 'if we want bad situations put right, we should give the responsibility to those who are best placed to do the remedying'.[125]

'Capacity offers both a specific and a general requirement: specific in that it is one of the bases that points to the requisite international duty-bearers, and general in that it is a prerequisite to discharging any obligation.'[126] As to the former, the Committee on Economic, Social and Cultural Rights (CESCR) has emphasised that particular obligations of international assistance and cooperation are incumbent on those states in 'a position to assist', and thus would indicate that capacity is a basis for assigning obligations.[127]

To what extent capacity serves as a ground in positive international law is controversial. In the *Bosnian Genocide* case, the ICJ referred to

[123] Salomon, 'How to Keep Promises: Making Sense of the Duty Among Multiple States to Fulfil Socio-Economic Rights in the World', n. 4, at 373.

[124] Dannenbaum, 'Public Power and Preventative Responsibility: Attributing the Wrongs of International Joint Ventures', n. 1, at 192–193.

[125] Miller, 'Distributing Responsibilities', n. 117, at 460–461, also cited in Pierik, 'Shared Responsibility in International Law: A Normative-Philosophical Analysis', n. 43, at 49.

[126] Salomon, 'How to Keep Promises: Making Sense of the Duty Among Multiple States to Fulfil Socio-Economic Rights in the World', n. 4, at 376.

[127] CESCR, General Comment No. 3, 'The Nature of States Parties' Obligations' (Article 2 (1) of the International Covenant on Economic, Social and Cultural Rights, New York, 16 December 1966, in force 3 January 1976, 999 UNTS 3), (5th Sess., 1990), UN Doc. E/1991/23 (1991), Annex III, para. 14.

the criterion as a basis for Serbia's responsibility vis-à-vis Bosnia.[128] However, as pointed out by Hakimi, the judgment is not very clear and, moreover, 'grounding responsibility primarily in each state's positive capacity would be misguided. States that are especially capable would repeatedly carry a disproportionate R2P burden, even if their involvement in the situation would lack legitimacy, even if other states are also highly capable (but less so), and even if those other states actually contributed to the problem'.[129]

This last point highlights the biggest limitation to the power-breeds-responsibility-approach: it does not necessarily square well with the idea of moral blame that underlies the deontological approach to responsibility, by sidestepping a discussion of a particular agent's moral autonomy in favour of a factual determination of who could have prevented the harm. In a sense, this approach operates as a subtle translation from a private law dimension of responsibility (who has contributed to the harm) to a more public law dimension of responsibility (who has the power/authority to ensure respect for international legal obligations, i.e., for the maintenance of public order).

4.5 *Fairness*

It is often remarked that questions of distribution are ultimately based on some sense of fairness.[130] This appears in a number of chapters of the volume. For example, in relation to climate change, Shue notes that 'since the cumulative carbon budget is a measure of a good held in common, namely the diminishing capacity to emit carbon without contributing to an intolerably great rise in temperature, the distribution of that increasingly scarce good among states and individuals is inherently a question of fairness, or as lawyers like to say, equity'.[131]

[128] *Bosnian Genocide*, n. 20, at 221, para. 430.

[129] Hakimi, 'Distributing the Responsibility to Protect', n. 1, at 281.

[130] L. Ringuis, A. Torvanger, and A. Underdal, 'Burden Sharing and Fairness Principles in International Climate Policy' (2002) 2 IEA 1; F.L. Tóth (ed.), *Fair Weather: Equity Concerns in Climate Change* (London: Earthscan, 2012); M. Prost and A. Torres Camprubi, 'Against Fairness? International Environmental Law, Disciplinary Bias, and Pareto Justice' (2012) 25(2) LJIL 379.

[131] Shue, 'Transboundary Damage in Climate Change: Criteria for Allocating Responsibility', n. 2, at 332. Other authors who refer to fairness as a basis for distribution include Dannenbaum, 'Public Power and Preventative Responsibility: Attributing the Wrongs of International Joint Ventures', n. 1, at 217, 222; and Kutz, 'Shared Responsibility for Climate Change: From Guilt to Taxes', n. 2, at 357, 362, 364.

This introduction of fairness can play a role on several levels, both *ex ante* in relation to primary rules and *ex post* in relation to secondary rules. Indeed, fairness can underlie the creation of particular obligations, as well as justify the particular distribution of responsibility should harm occur.

However, it would seem that claims to 'fairness' as a criterion for distribution have two different types of limitations. On one level, it can be considered that fairness as a concept is an empty shell that will be filled according to the normative preferences of the policy-makers. In this sense, it might not be a criterion for distribution *strictu sensu* and the conclusion of a normative discussion on responsibility, but rather the starting point of the discussion and the underlying reasons why a particular approach is adopted. Put simply, while they might not always use the term explicitly, it is likely that the authors who rely on any of the previously discussed criteria for distribution think it is fair to do so.

On another level, if there is an ambition to identify a substantial notion of fairness as an actual ground for distribution in a particular case, another problem arises: the possible absence of a shared sense of fairness that might be universally applied. As noted by Kutz in this volume, 'the logic of responsibility presupposes a context of exchange, both social and economic. Doubtless we can have duties of beneficence towards those about whom all we know is that they suffer, but responsibility is a subset of justice, and justice requires relationships. A truly global conception of responsibility requires a global conception of justice'.[132]

5. Transition to positive law

Even though this volume discusses the various normative bases mostly from an extra-legal perspective, they are fundamental in understanding and legitimising the future content, development, and application of the international law of responsibility. It can be recalled that while the law of international responsibility as construed by the ILC is generally highly flexible, in many respects it provides little guidance for solving problems of shared responsibility.[133] In that respect, the grounds of distribution articulated in this volume are relevant for providing further guidance for normative development.

[132] Kutz, ibid., at 350–351.

[133] Nollkaemper and Jacobs, 'Shared Responsibility in International Law: A Conceptual Framework', n. 7, at 363.

In connecting the extra-legal perspectives to the construction and development of international law pertaining to distribution, two questions can be distinguished: when such connections should be made, and by whom.

5.1 *The moment of distribution*

A key question for connecting the contributions to the volume to international law concerns the moment at which legal decisions on distribution of responsibility are made. A threefold distinction is helpful in this context.[134]

First, choices for a particular distribution can be made *ex ante*, by incorporating a particular distribution in the contents of rights and obligations or, as they are commonly called in international law, 'primary rules'. While discussions on responsibility often focus on *ex post facto* rules, as Kornhauser observes, such arrangements are only one means of achieving the aims of compensation and deterrence: '*Ex ante* regulation through licensing, taxing of inputs, command and control regulations, product standards, and markets in tradable permits, to name a few, are *ex ante* tools that regulate or deter actions that impose risks'.[135] This holds for international law no less than for domestic law.

Indeed, it would seem that particular approaches to distribution can often more easily connect to primary rules, rather than to principles of responsibility. For instance, while the models developed by Kontorovich operate largely within existing law relating to piracy, they also allow him to critique existing law and offer suggestions for reform.[136]

Second, choices can be included in rules on responsibility which are laid down before harm occurs. These are still *ex ante* rules, since they are laid down beforehand, even though they deal with allocation of responsibility once it has occurred. In essence, this is what the ARSIWA and the ARIO accomplish.

In this sense, the articulation of principles of distribution can underlie and induce development of the law of responsibility as developed by the

[134] Comparable distinctions are made in Trachtman, '*Ex Ante* and *Ex Post* Allocation of International Legal Responsibility', n. 31; Kornhauser, 'Incentives, Compensation, and Irreparable Harm', n. 64; and Cole, 'The Problem of Shared Irresponsibility in International Climate Law', n. 2.

[135] Kornhauser, ibid., at 121.

[136] Kontorovich, 'Pirate "Globalisation": Dividing Responsibility Among States, Companies, and Criminals', n. 3.

ILC, or within specific regimes. Although the prospects for an overhaul of the general law of international responsibility are limited, it cannot be excluded that particular principles, for instance pertaining to reparation in cases of shared responsibility, will be further developed in (judicial) practice, and that for that purpose extra-legal considerations will be of influence. More relevant is the possibility that in particular regimes, for instance relating to environmental protection or military operations, responsibility rules are designed that supplement the ILC Articles.

Third, a distributional arrangement can be determined after harm is caused. This also may be required when the grounds for determination of responsibility (as laid down *ex ante*) are flexible and/or provide limited guidance. The parties themselves, or third-party decision-makers, then need to make decisions on distribution after the harm has occurred.

The choice between the models depends on a variety of considerations. One set of considerations is the objectives and nature of responsibility. For instance, the first model may provide more guarantees that states will actually perform their obligations, a point made by Hakimi in relation to the Responsibility to Protect, and Salomon in relation to socio-economic rights.[137] Likewise, several contributions from a law and economics perspective emphasise that there will be differences between the three 'moments of distribution' in terms of the incentives they provide.[138]

Another consideration is whether particular legal relations are embedded in a strong institutional setting. As observed by Kornhauser, primary rules 'typically require a strong institutional basis for their successful creation and implementation'.[139] Likewise, *ex post* arrangement will depend even more strongly on institutional arrangements for adjudication or dispute settlement.

It should be observed, however, that there can be a close interaction between the three stages. The models are not exclusive and can fulfil comparable purposes. For instance, similar results may be achieved by *ex*

[137] Hakimi, 'Distributing the Responsibility to Protect', n. 1; Salomon, 'How to Keep Promises: Making Sense of the Duty Among Multiple States to Fulfil Socio-Economic Rights in the World', n. 4.

[138] Trachtman, '*Ex Ante* and *Ex Post* Allocation of International Legal Responsibility', n. 31.

[139] Kornhauser, ibid., at 122.

ante due diligence standards and by *ex post facto* responsibility rules.[140] Moreover, we can think of the models as a cycle in which one influences the other. Following Arendt, Lang points out that responsibility 'is not simply a legalistic move toward punishment, but is a political move toward alternative forms of action that might generate new structures and institutions'.[141] Thus, through primary rules, new forms of distribution can be established.

5.2 The distributing actors

Thought must also be given to the actors that would carry out any possible reform or evolution of the legal framework on the distribution of shared responsibility in international law.

On a general level, as noted previously, the principles of distribution can inform decision-makers in concrete cases. They underlie policy choices that have to be made in light of the social, political, moral, and legal preferences of the policy-makers and decision-makers.

How relevant such considerations are may obviously differ between different situations, depending on one's assessment of the proper roles of actors. For instance, while there is not much doubt that as the primary legislators of the international legal order, states are free to consider a wide range of policy interests, the question is whether it is for courts and tribunals to make decisions on distributions based on criteria such as power or fairness, when these are not articulated in the law itself. The response to that question will depend on one's position on the scope of the judicial function, and cannot be addressed here.[142]

The evolution of the law of international responsibility therefore depends on a combination of factors and a meeting of minds between

[140] Ibid., at 120–122; Nollkaemper and Jacobs, 'Shared Responsibility in International Law: A Conceptual Framework', n. 7, at 408.

[141] Lang, 'Shared Political Responsibility', n. 33, at 75; H. Arendt, 'Collective Responsibility', in H. Arendt, *Responsibility and Judgment* (edited and with an introduction by J. Kohn) (New York: Schocken Books, 2003), 147.

[142] In relation to the role of judges, it should also be noted that principles of distribution can be relevant as a means of interpretation. For instance, Shue observes that: 'The interpretation of international law should rest on a policy adopted toward acceptable risks of damage, especially severe damage to the defenceless'. Shue, 'Transboundary Damage in Climate Change: Criteria for Allocating Responsibility', n. 2, at 322–323.

those who reflect on the law in an academic and theoretical setting and those who are called upon to amend and implement it.

6. Structure of the volume

As indicated in section 2, this volume contains a wide variety of different approaches on the question of distribution of responsibilities. However, the volume is not organised on the basis of these different methodological approaches. This is due to the fact that some chapters reflect a mix of approaches. Moreover, various chapters relate to specific substantive issues (such as climate change) and the contrast of particular approaches on similar substantive issues can enhance our understanding of their respective merit.

As a result, the volume is roughly set out in two parts. The first part (Chapters 1–7) consists of more general discussions of questions of distribution, from a variety of angles. The second part (Chapters 8–15) consists of chapters that are more in the nature of applications of methodological approaches to particular subject areas. However, as noted, the division is not strict, and some of the latter set of chapters contain articulations of principles of distribution that are of more general relevance, just as some of the former set of chapters can inform the discussion on particular areas.

In combination, these chapters provide a broad spectrum of discussions that, together with this introduction, enhances our knowledge of the different approaches to distribution of responsibilities in situations of shared responsibility. In this sense, this volume continues to drive forward the intellectual ambition of the whole project as laid down in the initial conceptual framework: to bring together seemingly fragmented discourses from various disciplines through which an intellectual cross-fertilisation could lead to a better understanding of the dynamics of shared responsibility in international law.[143]

[143] Nollkaemper and Jacobs, 'Shared Responsibility in International Law: A Conceptual Framework', n. 7, at 438.

2

Shared Responsibility in International Law

A Normative-Philosophical Analysis

ROLAND PIERIK*

1. Introduction

This chapter analyses normative issues concerning shared responsibility among multiple actors, that is, states and/or international organisations, which have contributed to harmful outcomes that international law seeks to prevent. More precisely, the term 'responsibility' is used to refer to *ex post* responsibility for contributions to injury. The concept of independent state responsibility is well established in international law, especially in the Articles on Responsibility of States for Intentionally Wrongful Acts (ARSIWA)[1] of the International Law Commission (ILC). The question is whether international law can also make sense of the concept of *shared responsibility* of multiple actors for their contribution to a single harmful outcome.

In their seminal overview article, Nollkaemper and Jacobs conclude that current international law has a hard time keeping up with the prevailing reality of increased collaboration between states, since

* Associate Professor of Legal Philosophy at the Paul Scholten Centre for Jurisprudence, Faculty of Law, University of Amsterdam. Previous versions of this chapter were presented at the *Paul Scholten Colloquium*, University of Amsterdam, April 2013, *The SHARES Seminar on Distribution of Responsibilities in International Law*, University of Amsterdam, May 2013, the *Centre for the Study of Social Justice*, Oxford University, June 2013, and the *International Law Group Seminar*, University of Manchester, October 2013. The author wants to thank the participants at these meetings for their useful comments, especially Jean d'Aspremont, Simon Caney, Dov Jacobs, Josse Klijnsma, André Nollkaemper, Hadassa Noorda, and Ilias Plakokefalos.

1 Articles on Responsibility of States for Internationally Wrongful Acts, ILC *Yearbook* 2001/II(2), Article 1 (ARSIWA) provides that '[e]very internationally wrongful act of a State entails the international responsibility of that State', while Article 2 states that '[t]here is an internationally wrongful act of a State when conduct consisting of an action or omission' is attributable to the state and constitutes a breach of an obligation of the state. These basic principles underlie all of the ARSIWA's subsequent principles.

international law is 'the historical fruit of a primitive and horizontal conception of the international legal order'[2] that holds on to the fiction of exclusive attribution of responsibility to one single state. At the same time, however, they discern several trends in the development of the international legal order in recent decades that have led to an emerging complexity of legal relationships among various actors and a growing complexity of the interests promoted and protected by the law.[3] These trends can be recognised in the emergence of pressing issues in international law.[4] Imagine the case of two or more states contributing under the aegis of *Frontex* to joint missions to control the external borders of the European Union (EU).[5] If they are violating the rights of an asylum seeker, how should the responsibility for the outcome be distributed among the several partners? Or, consider two or more states acting collaboratively in the framework of United Nations (UN) peacekeeping. How should responsibility be attributed among the several actors when they are involved in an unintended wrongful act, for example when innocent citizens are killed by an air strike?

Two decades ago, Noyes and Smith argued that a mature system of international law should be able to comprehend the responsibility of multiple state actors for a single event.[6] However, since shared responsibility remains a relatively unknown and novel concept in international law, its discussion explores uncharted territories and novel normative questions. Nollkaemper and Jacobs have entered these uncharted territories and have provided a conceptual framework from *within* the parameters as set by positive law, using building blocks from other fields of law for their reconstruction – including concepts like 'joint and several responsibility' from private law and 'joint criminal enterprise' from international criminal law.

This chapter steps outside the legal (tool) box and provides a philosophical analysis of 'responsibility' – the normative concept that has the central stage in these discussions. Under what conditions can an actor reasonably be held responsible for a specific harmful outcome? And what

[2] P.A. Nollkaemper and D. Jacobs, 'Shared Responsibility in International Law: A Conceptual Framework' (2013) 34 MIJIL 359, at 436.

[3] Ibid., at 436. [4] Ibid., at 372.

[5] *Frontex* is the European Agency for the Management of Operational Cooperation at the External Borders of the Member States of the European Union. For more information see www.frontex.europa.eu (last accessed on 5 June 2014).

[6] J.E. Noyes and B.D. Smith, 'State Responsibility and the Principle of Joint and Several Liability' (1988) 13 YJIL 225.

consequences should this responsibility have in terms of reparations or repercussions? As such, the chapter taps into the more deontological literature in legal and political philosophy on the relation between agency and responsibility.[7] I will, in the first instance, focus on philosophical discussions, and whether or not these arguments are (or can be) adopted in domestic or international law. I do not presuppose (or pretend) that a full-blown legal defence of shared responsibility in international law can be logically deduced from such a normative-philosophical argument. I do assume, however, that such a philosophical treatise could help to put our normative intuitions into line and get our priorities right and, as such, might provide some essential normative nuts and bolts for a more conceptually grounded legal analysis of collective responsibility in international law.

This chapter is organised as follows: Section 2 contains a normative-philosophical discussion of the concept of personal responsibility, in terms of causality and agency. Section 3 translates the concept of personal responsibility into collective responsibility, and argues that a collective can be held responsible when its members, through their cooperation, can mimic the performance of a single unified agent. In addition, the general concept of 'collective responsibility' will be subdivided into two more specific conceptions: 'corporate responsibility', in which the responsibility befalls the collective as a whole, and 'shared responsibility', in which the responsibility descends to the members separately. Section 4 translates the insights of the normative-theoretical discussion to analyse the issue of distributing shared responsibility in the legal context. Section 5 employs the arguments developed in the earlier sections to analyse some issues that are central to the current discussion of shared responsibility in international law. Section 6 concludes.

2. Personal responsibility: causality and agency

What is the most fruitful way to conceptualise responsibility? Under what conditions can an actor reasonably be held responsible for a

[7] For recent philosophical work on collective responsibility see: T. Isaacs, *Moral Responsibility in Collective Contexts* (Oxford University Press, 2011); C. List and P. Pettit, *Group Agency. The Possibility, Design, and Status of Corporate Agents* (Oxford University Press, 2011); P. Pettit, 'Responsibility Incorporated' (2007) 117 *Ethics* 171; D. Miller, *National Responsibility and Global Justice* (Oxford University Press, 2007), chapter 3; T. Erskine, 'Making Sense of "Responsibility" in International Relations: Key Questions and Concepts', in T. Erskine (ed.), *Can Institutions Have Responsibilities? Collective Moral Agency and International Relations* (New York and Basingstoke: Palgrave Macmillan, 2003), 1.

harmful outcome? The most obvious starting point is an analysis of *personal responsibility*: the conditions under which an individual human being is held responsible for the outcome of a specific choice, behaviour, or act. This concept is one of the cornerstones in law and legal philosophy.[8] Within domestic law the attribution of individual responsibility for an act is essential in ascribing guilt (criminal law) or liability (the law of tort). Within liberal political philosophy, individual responsibility guides the central distinction between outcomes resulting from choices and outcomes generated by unchosen endowments.[9]

The fact *that* persons can be held responsible is widely acknowledged in legal and political philosophy, as much as it is acknowledged that not *every* person can be held responsible for *every* outcome. This generates three questions, which will be answered in sections 2.1 to 2.3. Firstly, what is so special about persons that they can be held responsible for a certain outcome, unlike for example non-human animals? Secondly, what are the conditions under which persons should be relieved of this responsibility? Finally, for what outcomes can persons be held responsible?

2.1 Responsibility and causality

A first intuition links responsibility to causality: we can only reasonably be held responsible for the outcome(s) of our actions and decisions, and not for outcomes outside our control. And indeed, causality plays a central role in discussions on responsibility, but we should not presuppose a one-to-one relationship between the two.[10] The reason is that the notion of causality is not well geared to the problem at hand. Causal responsibility is being invoked when we want to provide a factual description of *why* something occurred: for example, a forest fire. There

[8] Sections 2 and 3 of this chapter build upon on R. Pierik, 'Collective Responsibility and National Responsibility' (2008) 11(4) CRISPP 465.

[9] The question of where to draw the line between choice and circumstance has dominated the luck-egalitarian debate over the last decade. See for some key publications R. Dworkin, *Sovereign Virtue: The Theory and Practice of Equality* (Cambridge, MA: Harvard University Press, 2000), at 285–303; and G.A. Cohen, *If You're an Egalitarian, How Come You're So Rich?* (Cambridge, MA: Harvard University Press, 2000). For an overview of the debate, see M. Matravers, 'Responsibility, Luck, and the "Equality of What" Debate' (2002) 50(3) PS 558.

[10] D. Miller, 'Distributing Responsibilities' (2001) 9(4) JPP 453; L.A. Kornhauser, 'Incentives, Compensation, and Irreparable Harm', Chapter 5 of this volume, 120.

will be many conditions that have causally contributed to the fire: me clumsily lighting a match; the poor quality of the match which caused it to break during the action of striking it; the extreme dryness of the forest due to a drought; the recent cutback in government expenditures on emergency services that prevented the fire brigade from arriving in time; and so on and so forth. Given this large set of necessary but insufficient conditions for the outcome, it is impossible to single out one of them as the decisive cause of the fire. After all, each of these conditions alone would be insufficient to generate the outcome – for example, my clumsiness would have been harmless if the forest was sodden after a downpour. Moreover, our analysis in terms of causal factors does not distinguish between those causes that are within and those outside human control.

For our discussion of responsibility we should limit our analysis to those links in the causal chain of events that can be linked to actions and/or decisions that are relevant in any moral or legal sense. Thus, my clumsy behaviour should be taken into consideration; however, the extreme dryness of the forest is to be neglected, since a forest cannot reasonably be held responsible or liable in any meaningful sense.

So outcome responsibility assumes a causal component – the actor must be connected to the outcome in one way or another. On the other hand, causal responsibility does not automatically lead to outcome responsibility. Consider a market setting in which my restaurant has lost its clientele because you opened a restaurant across the street and your food is superior to mine. Although there is a causal relation between your action and my bankruptcy, your behaviour is not unjustified – competition on the basis of quality of products is perfectly legitimate in a market economy. Therefore there is no reasonable argument as to why you should be criminally prosecuted or should pay reparations.[11] This implies that our analysis of outcome responsibility should distinguish between behaviour that is appropriate, inappropriate, or forbidden in a specific situation. Thus, the case in which your skill as a cook pushed me out of the market is different from the case in which your connections to the mafia caused my bankruptcy.

2.2 *Responsibility and agency*

What are the conditions under which actors should be held responsible for a certain outcome, and under what conditions should they be relieved

[11] Ibid., Miller, at 458.

of this responsibility? In this section I tap into the deontological tradition that situates individual responsibility in personal agency and argues that responsibility can only be attributed to agents.[12] Agency refers to the capacity to act deliberately and intentionally and is usually contrasted with natural forces, which are causes that involve merely deterministic processes. The question, then, is: to what does the term 'acting intentionally' refer?

The discussion of agency is a philosophical minefield, in which one has to navigate a narrow path between free will and determinism. It is not necessary for this discussion to provide a comprehensive philosophic account of what agency consists of. I will confine myself to a description of personal agency in terms of three central conditions.[13] Firstly, when a person is faced with a choice, he or she should have an understanding of the situation in which he or she finds him or herself, the courses of action available, and their possible consequences. Secondly, he or she should be able to deliberate over these issues and choose the most preferred course of action. Third and finally, agency implies the ability *to act* upon deliberation; he or she should be able to act in such a way that the most preferred course of action is performed. These conditions can help us in our conceptualisation of agency that can be employed in our discussion of shared responsibility in the next sections.

Responsibility stems from agency because responsibility presupposes the capacity of an actor to act intentionally. In terms of Toni Erskine: 'Since moral agents possess the sophisticated deliberative capacities necessary to allow them to respond to specific types of reasoning, and to understand their actions and the probable outcomes of their actions, we ... render them vulnerable to the ascription of duties and the apportioning of moral praise and blame in the context of specific actions in a way that non-moral agents are not similarly vulnerable.'[14]

[12] In section 3.3 I relate this deontological way of arguing to the more consequential argument about outcome responsibility.

[13] This description builds upon M. Dan-Cohen, 'Conceptions of Choice and Conceptions of Autonomy' (1992) 102 *Ethics* 221, at 222; Erskine, 'Making Sense of "Responsibility" in International Relations: Key Questions and Concepts', n. 7, at 6–7, 21; V. Held, 'Can a Random Collection of Individuals Be Morally Responsible?', in L. May and S. Hoffman (eds.), *Collective Responsibility: Five Decades of Debate in Theoretical and Applied Ethics* (Savage: Rowman & Littlefield, 1991), 89, at 90; Pettit, 'Responsibility Incorporated', n. 7, at 174–175).

[14] Ibid., Erskine, at 6.

Agents cannot escape responsibility when they failed to anticipate the results of their actions through negligence or ignorance. Temporary drunkenness or inborn clumsiness do not relieve an agent from responsibility, since a responsible agent should be able to foresee the possible outcomes of his or her temporary or permanent incapacity. Moreover, agency does not presuppose extensive deliberation over each and every decision; many choices can be made without much thought and consideration. Agency implies only the *ability* to deliberate if the situation so demands. Finally, agency does not presuppose full knowledge of all possible courses of action and all their possible (side) effects. We hold people responsible for the consequences of their actions that a reasonable person would have foreseen, whether or not these consequences were intended, and whether or not they were actually foreseen by the person in question.[15] Imagine someone throwing a hand grenade into an open window, causing the death of a child.[16] Although he or she might not have been able to foresee this particular outcome, he or she still can be held responsible for it. After all, he or she could have been aware of the possible risks involved in this action. On the other hand, if he or she flips on a light switch that turns out to be booby-trapped – of which he or she could have no knowledge – thereby causing the death of a child, then he or she cannot reasonably be held responsible.

2.3 Individual agency and personal responsibility: a conclusion

Personal responsibility presupposes two things: first, a certain causal connection between the person and the outcome; and second, the capacity for intentional action on the side of the person. At the end of the day, attributing personal responsibility is not a mechanical process but a normative activity, taking 'normal powers of agents' as the norm in judging whether a particular agent should have been able to foresee the outcomes of his or her action. This is why we generally ascribe responsibility to persons above the age of reason, but not to young children and non-human animals, because they are not able to foresee and understand the consequences of their actions.

[15] Miller, *National Responsibility and Global Justice*, n. 7, at 116.

[16] This example is taken from Held, 'Can a Random Collection of Individuals Be Morally Responsible?', n. 13, at 90–91.

3. Collective responsibility

3.1 From personal to collective responsibility

The preceding section presented a description of the way in which personal responsibility is typically defended as stemming from individual agency. If we have a widely accepted idea of individual responsibility, why do we also need to conceptualise the responsibility of collectives of people? At the end of the day, collective outcomes are the aggregated result of individual actions of the members of the collective. Joining a collective does not change agents acting intentionally into mechanically operating zombies. So one could ask how collectives can have responsibilities that do not boil down, without residue, into responsibilities of individuals that constitute that collective.

One important reason to include collective responsibility in our normative repertoire is to analyse cases where the application of individual responsibility does not suffice. Consider the following examples.

Example I: On 6 March 1987, a ferry, the *Herald of Free Enterprise*, capsized when it left the Zeebrugge harbour with its bow doors still open, killing nearly two hundred people. Not a single staff member of Townsend Thoresen, the company that operated the ferry, was penalised in court because it was impossible to identify individual persons who were seriously enough at fault. At the same time an official inquiry concluded that 'all concerned in management, from the members of the Board of Directors down to the junior superintendents, were guilty of fault in that all must be regarded as sharing responsibility for the failure of management. From top to bottom the body corporate was infected with the disease of sloppiness.'[17] Eric Colvin concluded that 'ultimately . . . it was the primary requirement of finding an individual who was liable that stood in the way of attaching any significance to the organizational sloppiness that had been found by the official inquiry.'[18] Given the fact that the cause of the disaster was primarily located within the organisational structure of the company, rather than individual acts of employees, it seems more plausible to hold the company, as a collective, responsible for the negative outcome.

[17] The *Sheen Report* as discussed in E. Colvin, 'Corporate Personality and Criminal Liability' (1995) 6(1) CLF 1, at 16. See also Pettit, 'Responsibility Incorporated', n. 7, at 171.

[18] Ibid., Colvin, at 18.

Example II: Imagine seven non-acquainted passengers sitting in a subway car.[19] The second smallest person stands up, pushes the smallest to the floor, and starts beating and strangling him. If the remaining five passengers do nothing, the attacker will certainly seriously wound the victim. Although none of the passengers acting alone can stop the attacker, it is extremely plausible that jointly they can save the victim with no serious injury to themselves. Moreover, the group is small enough so that collective action will not result in confusion. Do the remaining five passengers have a joint responsibility for the outcome if they do not interfere?

The difference between these two examples indicates two things. Firstly, we should distinguish between two forms of collective responsibility: 'corporate responsibility' and 'shared responsibility'. The first example illustrates *corporate responsibility* that befalls the collective *as a* collective, without descending directly to the actors that make up the collective. The collective is considered to be a self-standing actor, organised through a clear set of internal regulations, functioning as a separate legal entity, and holding private funds separated from the funds of its members. The more these processes of deliberation, decision making, and action taking have become institutionalised routines within the collective, the easier it is to mimic the performance of a single unified agent. This makes the concept of corporate responsibility comprehensible: institutionalised routines and procedures within a collective mimic decision-making processes in the case of individual agents.

The subway car example illustrates *shared responsibility* of two or more actors for their contribution to a particular outcome that descends to the members separately, rather than resting on them as a collective. It applies in cases where the actors collaborate in one specific domain, but remain distinct and distinguishable actors in most other domains. In such ad hoc situations, with no time for explicit deliberation, shared responsibility for negative outcomes descends to individual members under two conditions: first, where it is obvious to 'normal persons' *that* collective action is required in this situation; and second, where it is obvious *what* collective action is required.

The second distinction between the examples is that they refer to two different kinds of responsibilities: the responsibility for the negative

[19] Example taken from Held, 'Can a Random Collection of Individuals Be Morally Responsible?', n. 13, at 94–96.

outcome of one's own actions, and the responsibility for failing to prevent others from doing harm. Ascribing responsibility proceeds in two steps: first, under what conditions can an actor be held responsible for certain outcomes; and second, what are the consequences that follow from this responsibility? Although both Townsend Thoresen and the five non-aggressive subway passengers can be held responsible for the specific outcome, the consequences of that responsibility will be quite different in both cases. After all, operating the vessel was the primary business for Townsend Thoresen, and the dire outcome was the direct result of the poor and faulty way this task was organised. As such, the corporation's behaviour was clearly inappropriate, given its responsibility towards the passengers on board. The corporation should therefore bear the full consequences of the outcome, both in terms of reparations and criminal repercussions.

In the subway example, the five passengers did not choose to get involved in the fight; they were forced by the situation in which they found themselves, initiated by the action of the aggressive seventh passenger. They are only indirectly responsible for the outcome: they did not act wrongly, but merely failed to intervene in another's wrong actions. They can only be prosecuted criminally for their failure to intervene, not for the outcome as a whole. In a criminal case, this implies that the consequences in terms of punishment should be less severe.

This distinction can be understood in terms of agency, as discussed earlier. Only the attacker deliberately intended the specific negative outcome and should have the primary responsibility for it. The other passengers neither initiated nor intended the fight. Helping the victim was the appropriate thing to do, but given the fact that they did not choose to get involved, and therefore were forced into the situation, their responsibility for the outcome is limited.[20] In other words, the specific context in which a particular responsibility originates determines the consequences stemming from this responsibility: the criminal consequences for the five subway car passengers – had they not intervened – should be far less severe than the consequences for the attacker.

Assigning collective responsibility implies that a collective of persons is held jointly responsible for a certain outcome. The advantage of such an approach is that the victims are relieved of the duty to investigate how the responsibility is distributed within the collective. At the same time,

[20] The most sophisticated defense of this distinction can be found in S. Scheffler, 'Doing and Allowing' (2004) 114(2) *Ethics* 215.

the concept of shared responsibility may set liberal alarm bells ringing because it 'goes against an intuition that it is only what a person does herself that can make her responsible for harmful outcomes'.[21] Under what conditions should individual responsibility for an outcome be replaced by collective responsibility? Determining whether responsibility should be ascribed to individuals or collectives implies steering a delicate middle course whereby two types of mistakes need to be avoided. I conceptualise them as follows.

Type-1 mistakes are made by persistently sticking to individual responsibility and denying the normative relevance of collective responsibility. This prevents us from ascribing remedial responsibility to a collective of perpetrators when it is impossible to determine how each participant contributed to the final outcome, leaving the victims uncompensated. Type-1 mistakes undermine a fair distribution of burdens and benefits between the perpetrators and the victims of acts. The inability of the British courts to hold Townsend Thoresen legally responsible for the negative outcome in the ferry disaster is an example of a type-1 mistake.

Type-2 mistakes occur by too readily embracing the notion of collective responsibility by too loosely including innocent bypassers as members of the responsible collective, or by too easily making group membership sufficient for responsibility for acts performed by some, even if the other members clearly demonstrated their opposition to these acts. Non-perpetrators are wrongfully included in the shared responsibility *and* the duty to pay an equal share of the expenses. In short, type-2 mistakes undermine a fair distribution of burdens and benefits between different members of the collective.

3.2 Ascribing collective responsibility through the agency model

Previously, I argued that personal agency is generally considered to be a prerequisite for personal responsibility. In a similar way, many authors assume that a collective can only be held responsible when it can be considered to be an agent, when participants in their cooperation 'mimic the performance of a single unified agent'.[22] Personal agency presupposes an understanding of one's situation, the ability to deliberate over possible courses of action and their consequences, and the ability to act in such a

[21] Miller, *National Responsibility and Global Justice*, n. 7, at 120.
[22] Pettit, 'Responsibility Incorporated', n. 7, at 179.

way that the most preferred course of action is carried out. How can the conditions for personal agency be translated into conditions for collective agency? Firstly, collectives must have the ability to make decisions as if they were a single agent *and* the ability to take action in a concerted fashion. Secondly, the responsibility should properly be attributed to the relevant agent, either to the collective as a whole – corporate responsibility – or to a set of actors that constitute the collective – shared responsibility.

Let me employ these rules to discuss whether the collectives as described in the two examples earlier could be held collectively responsible. Concerning the example of the *Herald of Free Enterprise*, Townsend Thoresen should have been ascribed corporate responsibility to compensate for the negative outcomes of the ferry disaster, because the corporation can be considered to be an agent. After all, corporations can be organised so that they 'operate through their members in such a way that they simulate the performance of individual agents'.[23] Corporations usually have institutionalised decision-making procedures that enable collective deliberation and concerted action. It is very possible to achieve a well-defined and agreed-upon division of labour within the collective, in which employees do their part and can assume that others will do theirs.[24] Moreover, firms usually have procedures for deciding which goals are desirable, how these goals should be achieved, what means should be used, and how these goals and means must be revised in light of new circumstances. A well-run corporation complies with the conditions of collective agency and responsibility: it functions as a unified actor, and holds private funds, separated from the funds of its members. Since the responsibility does not descend to the separate actors that make up the collective, the demand that it should be clear as to who is included and who is excluded is not as relevant as in the case of shared responsibility.

Concerning the second example, it is justifiable to ascribe responsibility to the five subway car passengers for the negative outcome if they failed to help the victim under two conditions: first, where it is obvious to 'normal persons' *that* collective action is required in this situation; and second, where it is obvious to 'normal persons' *what* collective action is required in order to prevent the negative outcome. We expect them to cooperate to prevent an outcome – that is, to act as a

[23] Ibid., at 172. [24] Ibid., at 179.

collective agent – when collective action is necessary and possible, and we hold them responsible if they fail to do so.[25] Although they entered the subway car as strangers, the situation in which they found themselves forced them to become an ad hoc collective and to cooperate in such a way as to prevent the unwanted outcome. Held's example is set up in such a way that collectives can be held responsible if they refuse to cooperate to prevent certain outcomes. This shared responsibility of the random collection of subway passengers is established in terms of shared agency. We can only ascribe shared responsibility when the collective is able to function as a unified actor, and when the participants can participate in some way in collective processes of deliberation and decision making. In the case of corporate responsibility, such processes are comprehensive, extensive, and institutionalised. In other situations these processes are swift, ad hoc, and implicit, for example when a group of subway passengers collectively subdues an attacker. This implies that even in the case of loose or temporary collectives, or in one-time-only events, shared responsibility can be ascribed if we can reasonably assume that the collective was able to collaborate in such a way that its members acted as a unified agent, even if only for a short period of time. On the other hand, if the circumstances were such that it was impossible for the members to coordinate their activities in such a way as to act as an agent – because the task was too complex; because there was too little time; or because the conditions were too hectic – ascribing shared responsibility is unwarranted because it would imply making a type-2 mistake. They cannot be held collectively responsible if it was impossible for 'normal persons' to act collectively in such a way that the outcome could have been prevented. They can only be held jointly responsible if they had the possibility to act as a collective agent to help the victim, but refused to do so.

In cases of sustainable and long-term cooperation between actors, shared responsibility can and should descend to individual actors when first, it is clear who is included in, and excluded from, the collective; second, when those included can participate in the collective decision making in one way or another; and third, when those who disagree with the shared goals have an exit option. The members of the collective do not have to discuss or agree on everything, but they should at least agree upon the procedures of deliberation, and each member should be able

[25] Held, 'Can a Random Collection of Individuals Be Morally Responsible?', n. 13, at 95.

to voice their disagreement.[26] This guarantees that all members of the collective can influence the collective outcome if they feel the need to do so, and thus can share responsibility for it.

3.3 Deontological and consequentialist defences of collective responsibility

My analysis of collective responsibility in terms of outcome responsibility, embedded in ideas of causal connection and agency, fits neatly into a deontological ethics that primarily focuses on the question of under what conditions a perpetrator can be considered an agent and, as such, be held responsible for the consequences of his or her actions and decisions. However, we can also encounter a second, more consequentialist justification for collective responsibility. It focuses less on the perpetrators – that is, who was responsible for bringing about this bad situation. Instead, this approach primarily focuses on the victims.

The argument is something like this: we need to help these victims, even though we cannot pinpoint precisely who exactly is causally responsible for their predicament, or because those who are responsible are unable or unwilling to pick up the tab. Miller calls this 'assigning remedial responsibility according to capacity': 'if we want bad situations put right, we should give the responsibility to those who are best placed to do the remedying.'[27] In (international) law the deontological and consequentialist justifications for collective responsibility are often used interchangeably. However, given that the normative arguments in these approaches are quite distinct, these defences should be separated conceptually. In section 5.2 I will return to this distinction between deontological and consequentialist defences of outcome responsibility in international law.

3.4 Collective responsibility and agency: a conclusion

In the preceding sections, I have developed a philosophical argument for determining outcome responsibility, and determining under what conditions an actor – an individual person or a collective of persons – can be

[26] This situation seems to be analogous to a case of personal agency in which someone is responsible for the outcome of a decision, although he or she was not fully convinced that it was the right decision.

[27] Miller, 'Distributing Responsibilities', n. 10, at 460–461.

held responsible for certain outcomes. I concluded that outcome responsibility presupposes a certain causal relation between the person and the outcome that is couched in agency: collective responsibility can be ascribed when the members of a collective are in a situation in which they can deliberate, decide, and act as a unified agent. Collective responsibility can befall the collective as a whole – corporate responsibility – or it can descend to the members separately – shared responsibility.

4. From philosophical to legal arguments

The normative-philosophical arguments discussed primarily address issues of *moral* responsibility, which do not necessarily coincide with legal responsibility, the latter being the subject of discussions of joint responsibility in domestic or international law. The currency of moral responsibility is blame or praise; the currency of legal responsibility is liability or guilt.

Legal responsibility flows from a legal system, and legal systems 'recognize, create, vary and enforce obligations'.[28] Within liberal-democratic states, one would expect a substantial overlap between prevailing moral convictions on outcome responsibility and the way these convictions are enshrined in law. Indeed, such normative-philosophical arguments are usually employed to inform, defend, or criticise actual legislation. As such, within domestic law, the philosophical debate defending moral responsibility can be considered to be a stepping-stone for legal arguments defending legal responsibility. How can the arguments of moral responsibility be translated into the context of a well-organised legal order – for example within a liberal-democratic state? The legal ascription of (shared) responsibility proceeds in two steps: first, under what conditions can an actor be held legally responsible for certain outcomes? Second, what are the legal consequences that follow from this responsibility?

In domestic law, responses by the competent authority typically fall into two categories, a distinction that coincides neatly with the separation between private and public law. The outcome may be material or non-material damage to third parties, which generates tort law cases in private law courts. Alternatively, the outcome might be the result of acts that undermine the legal order itself: cases that are handled through public

[28] L. Green, 'Legal Obligation and Authority', in E.N. Zalta (ed.), SEP (Winter 2012 edition), at 1 (available at http://plato.stanford.edu/, last accessed on 5 June 2014).

(criminal) law.[29] We can reconstruct the process of ascribing shared responsibility in domestic legal orders in a number of steps.

First, the competent authority should determine whether it is possible to unpack the cooperative action by the actors into independent actions, which would enable the authority to analyse the case in terms of independent responsibility.[30] After all, individual responsibility seems to be the more straightforward option conceptually, and collective responsibility is merely a second-best option, only to be employed when it is impossible to ascribe independent responsibility.

Second, if the cooperative action cannot be unpacked into independent actions, the competent authority should determine whether the collective could be considered to be a collective *agent*, which is a necessary prerequisite for holding the collective as such responsible for the outcome. In situations in which such collective agency can be established, the competent authority should determine whether it is a case of corporate responsibility or shared responsibility.

Third, an important consequence of ascribing collective – either corporate or shared – responsibility is that the claimant is relieved of the duty to investigate how the responsibility is distributed within the collective; the collective *as such* will be confronted with the legal consequences. Furthermore, by making it a collective responsibility, within a private law case, the burden of proof concerning this distribution of liability within the collective has moved from the victim to the perpetrators. Within a criminal law case, it enables the prosecutor to prosecute a collective, and even to ascribe shared responsibility in cases where the collective is not a legal entity.

Fourth, in the case of corporate responsibility, the legal consequences rest on the collective as such. In the example of the *Herald of Free Enterprise*, Townsend Thoresen was a legal entity with its own funds from which damages after a tort action could be paid. Concerning criminal prosecution, it is highly conceivable that persons in certain offices within the collective – those who were directly involved in this departure from Zeebrugge, those responsible for the security procedures

[29] Although the distinction between public and private law is not undisputed in law and legal theory, the attribution of responsibility in domestic law more or less follows this dichotomy.

[30] As was the case in the *Herald of Free Enterprise* example. Nollkaemper and Jacobs describe two examples of this phenomenon in international law: The *Saddam Hussein* case and *Behrami* case before the European Court of Human Rights; Nollkaemper and Jacobs, 'Shared Responsibility', n. 2, at 391.

within the company, or the highest ranking officials – could also be prosecuted personally.

Fifth, in the case of shared responsibility, the legal consequences descend to the individual members, and this can happen in several ways. Dominant in domestic tort law is the model of *joint and several* liability: the victim can recover the full amount of reparations from one of the responsible actors, who can in turn demand compensation from the other responsible actor(s) that may have contributed to the damage.[31] Another model requires that the perpetrators have a shared responsibility to pay damages. Given the shared nature of the responsibility, the default position is that all bear an equal share of that responsibility, thus disregarding the possible differences between each individual's contribution to the net outcome. Judges (or perpetrators amongst themselves) might make more finely-tuned allocations of responsibility, depending on what is known about the responsibilities, capacities, or activities of each member. Consider the example of a raging mob rampaging through a neighbourhood. If the members are held jointly responsibility for the outcome, some could be identified as ringleaders, and therefore be considered to be more liable than others.[32] In the case of the subway car incident, a healthy young person could be held more responsible for the outcome than an elderly person with a walker. Distributing responsibility over the various participants cannot be done mechanically; it is a normative choice, based on the (inherently inconclusive) information available. Indeed, such an allocation of the burden over the various perpetrators can never be a perfect reflection of their individual contribution to the collective outcome. After all, the reason why shared responsibility was invoked was precisely because the plurality of contributions and their interrelationships implies that it is very difficult, if not impossible, to disentangle the individual contributions to the outcome.

These arguments not only support ascribing collective responsibility to actors for the negative outcomes of their own decisions and actions, but also for their failure to intervene in another's wrong actions, when the situation so demands and when they are able to do so. However, such a duty to assist persons in danger is more generally acknowledged in civil law countries – see, for example, Article 450 of the Dutch Penal Code – than in common law countries. This also illustrates that even

[31] Ibid., at 422. [32] Miller, *National Responsibility and Global Justice*, n. 7, at 116–117.

though this chapter has demonstrated that there are good arguments for assigning shared responsibility, this does not always translate into legal obligations.

5. Collective responsibility in international law

Let me sum up the argument so far. I have provided a reconstruction of discussions of agency and personal responsibility, explained under which circumstances these arguments can also apply to collective actors, and described how collective responsibility can be employed in domestic law. The question, now, is how the argument can be translated into yet another context: collaborating actors in international law. States and international organisations increasingly engage in cooperative action, while the prevailing system of international responsibility suffers from a lack of clarity as to whether and when responsibility can in fact be shared, or what consequences would arise from sharing responsibility.[33] There is an increasing need for more detailed and nuanced rules governing the allocation of responsibility among states. Such a regime to regulate shared responsibility of states and/or international organisations could serve the interests of injured parties, who otherwise may have difficulty identifying the responsible entities and the scope of their responsibility – as discussed in section 3.1 in terms of type-1 mistakes. On the other hand, such a regulatory scheme might serve the interests of states by providing some predictability as to how their responsibility may be distributed among various states and attributed to them – as discussed in terms of type-2 mistakes.[34]

International law, therefore, is in need of a conception of collective responsibility.[35] One of the aims is to avoid the practice of blame shifting – or buck-passing – between the various actors involved. Widely discussed is the question of whether the Dutch government or the UN should be held responsible for the eviction of Muslims from the UN compound in Srebrenica in June 1995.[36] What can philosophical discussions, immersed in counter-factuals and thought experiments,

[33] Nollkaemper and Jacobs, 'Shared Responsibility', n. 2, at 363. For a recent treatise on collective responsibility in international criminal law see T. Isaacs and R. Vernon (eds.), *Accountability for Collective Wrongdoing* (Cambridge University Press, 2011).

[34] Nollkaemper and Jacobs, 'Shared Responsibility', n. 2, at 428. [35] Ibid., at 425.

[36] P.A. Nollkaemper, 'Dual Attribution: Liability of the Netherlands for Conduct of Dutchbat in Srebrenica' (2011) 9(5) JICJ 1143.

teach us about such cases of collective responsibility in international law? In this chapter I will not even attempt to come up with a full discussion of the issue. I will restrict myself to an approach in which I analyse specific elements in the current discussion of shared responsibility in international law from the normative perspective presented previously.

Characteristic of philosophical discussions of collective responsibility is that they focus on collectives of natural persons, and argue that a plausible story can be told whereby these collectives can, under specific conditions, be responsibility-bearing agents, over and above their individual members. The discussion of collective responsibility in international law moves one step further away from the individual person: its asks under what conditions collectives of collectives – cooperating states – can be held jointly responsible for certain outcomes.[37] However, adding another 'degree of separation' between the natural persons and the collective does not seem to preclude the possibility of ascribing shared responsibility to cooperating states in the international legal order. After all, the agency of the collective is not derived directly from the agency of their constitutive persons. Instead, an analogy argument is employed: collectives are supposed to be responsibility-bearing agents in as much as they operate in such a way that they simulate the performance of individual agents.[38]

The discussion focuses on harmful outcomes as a result of collective actions that violate international law. How should such *ex post* responsibility for contributions to injury be attributed to the various parties?

5.1 The variety of actors involved in shared international responsibility

It is clear that the actors primarily involved – states and international organisations – are formal organisations that can be considered agents in the sense of the discussion in sections 2 and 3. The questions are whether the collective of actors involved in the specific action can be held responsible for an unwanted outcome, and how that responsibility should

[37] This term refers to the term 'collectivity of collectivities' as coined by Amitai Etzioni in A. Etzioni, *The Active Society: A Theory of Societal and Political Processes* (New York: Free Press, 1968), 107; Toni Erskine describes the UN in similar terms of a collectivity of collectivities in T. Erskine, 'Assigning Responsibilities to Institutional Moral Agents: The Case of States and "Quasi-States"', in T. Erskine (ed.), *Can Institutions Have Responsibilities? Collective Moral Agency and International Relations* (New York and Basingstoke: Palgrave Macmillan, 2003), 19, at 39, note 20.

[38] Pettit, 'Responsibility Incorporated', n. 7, at 172.

be distributed among them. Firstly, we need to determine whether it is possible to unpack the cooperative action by the actors into independent actions, in which case the actors can be held responsible as separate actors. If this is not possible, it should be determined whether the collective could be considered to be a collective agent, which is a necessary prerequisite for holding the collective *as such* responsible for the outcome. In the event of collective agency, we should determine whether it is a case of corporate responsibility or shared responsibility. In some situations, collective responsibility in international law is shared responsibility, when states cooperate but remain distinct actors. In other cases they form independent international organisations with their own corporate responsibility.

The question of the distribution of responsibility among these actors is slightly more difficult to answer than in the interpersonal examples discussed earlier. The possible variety of parties involved in such collective action is much wider, and their possible interconnections can be far more complicated. One complicating issue is that in some cases the individual natural persons – officials who were directly involved in the wrongful act – should primarily be held responsible for a specific outcome. Imagine a humanitarian intervention in which several states cooperated under the aegis of the UN. During the operation one soldier, for no legitimate reason, broke specific rules of conduct that were *ipso facto* clear and straightforward. In that case, responsibility primarily rests on this specific person, regardless of how the rules of cooperation between the cooperating actors have been arranged formally. In the event that responsibility does not rest on the individual, two kinds of actors can be considered as candidates for being held responsible for the legal consequences: the state for which the official works, or the UN – the common organ under whose supervision the official was working.

Moreover, in the international arena, states can cooperate in various ways. They can cooperate bilaterally or through international or supranational organisations. Moreover, the form of cooperation through international or supranational organisations can take various sub-forms. Take, for example, *Frontex*. Most Schengen countries are also members of the EU; however, some EU countries are not party to the Schengen Treaty, while other non-EU countries participate in the Schengen cooperation.[39] If various countries with different statuses

[39] The Schengen *acquis* – Agreement between the Governments of the States of the Benelux Economic Union, the Federal Republic of Germany and the French Republic on the gradual abolition of checks at their common borders (Schengen Agreement), Schengen,

collaborate within *Frontex*, it might be quite difficult to unpack the myriad of interrelations and to distribute responsibility correctly. In other cases it might not be clear whether the 'collective of collectives' should be held responsible. First, should only the EU be held corporately responsible; second, should the various states participating in the EU be held jointly responsible; or third, should the various states participating in the EU *and* the EU *as such* be held jointly responsible?

When two or more states, through cooperative action, whether or not in a common organ, are involved in a wrongful act, it will be impossible to correctly disentangle their responsibilities because their collective agency is different from their combined individual responsibility. Pettit shows that the agency of a collective is actually more than the sum of its members' agency. As a result of negotiations and deliberative processes between the representatives of the parties establishing the common organ, the attitudes of collective agents cannot be a majoritarian or non-majoritarian function of the corresponding attitudes of the participating states. The collective attitudes and decisions are thus unique by being the attitudes and decisions of the collective. This collective agency 'may be surprising, but it is not mysterious'.[40] While group attitudes are not functions of the corresponding attitudes of individual members, they are produced by those members, and they derive all their matter and energy from what they supply.

5.2 *Consequentialist defences and outcome responsibility*

In section 3, I distinguished deontological defences of shared responsibility, which focus primarily on the perpetrators, from consequentialist ones, which focus mainly on the victims. Interestingly enough, towards the end of their article, Nollkaemper and Jacobs spell out possible foundations for shared responsibility – consent and control and the intrinsic nature of the obligation.[41] These seem to dovetail very neatly with the deontological, agency-oriented model of collective responsibility as presented in this chapter.

In addition, it might be illuminating to analyse consequentialist defences of shared responsibility in terms of the arguments as developed

14 June 1985, in force 15 June 1985, *Official Journal of the European Communities* L 239, Vol. 43, 22 September 2000, at 0013–0018.

[40] Pettit, 'Responsibility Incorporated', n. 7, at 184.

[41] Nollkaemper and Jacobs, 'Shared Responsibility', n. 2, at 428.

in this chapter, especially since deontological and consequentialist arguments are often used interchangeably in discussions in (international) law. Consequentialist defences argue for remedial responsibility according to capacity. In specific dire situations, those actors who are best placed to do the remedying are supposed to take action. A good example is provided by humanitarian interventions: the use of military force against a state with the aim of ending human rights violations being perpetrated by the state against which it is directed.

What if arguments of capacity lead certain states to participate in a well-organised humanitarian intervention abroad, and during this intervention something goes awry; for example, one of their planes mistakenly hits civilians? To what extent do such outcome-responsibility arguments have weight when participating states take up a supererogatory duty? And are these arguments similar to those employed in the example of *Frontex*, where the participating states merely organise a central domestic task jointly?

Here we need to return to the two distinct steps of ascribing responsibility: first, under what conditions can an actor or set of actors be held legally responsible for certain outcomes? And second, what are the legal consequences that follow from this responsibility?

It seems to me that the answer to the latter should be different in a *Frontex* case than in one of humanitarian intervention. After all, the activities of *Frontex* are 'business as usual' for European states: protecting their borders collectively (for reasons of efficiency and effectiveness) rather than as individual states. However, states participating in a humanitarian intervention take up the moral responsibility to help in a specific dire situation to which they are not causally connected. They undertake the task of protecting human rights although they were not involved in the actions that violated the human rights. Such actors find themselves in a situation that is similar to that of the five subway car passengers discussed earlier.

There is a clear normative distinction between a dire outcome as a consequence of conducting one's core business in a careless way and, on the other hand, a dire outcome resulting from failing to interfere appropriately in a situation in which one finds oneself, without being involved in generating the situation.

Thus, harmful outcomes resulting from incidents that arise during humanitarian interventions should have less severe legal consequences than harmful outcomes resulting from incidents that arise during *Frontex* operations. The more supererogatory a duty is, the fewer legal consequences should follow from this responsibility in case something goes awry.

This does not imply, however, that, the supererogatory character of an action implies that the actors are fully relieved from outcome responsibility. Even in the case of a humanitarian intervention, actors can be held responsible for certain outcomes of their actions, for example when the intervening parties in the humanitarian intervention mistakenly hit civilians and kill them. The fact that an actor takes up a supererogatory duty should not imply that it should not be held up to certain standards of professional behaviour, befitting the assignment. In the same way that we ascribed shared responsibility to the five subway car passengers for not intervening properly, even though they found themselves involuntarily involved in the fight, parties taking up a supererogatory duty in international law should never be able to escape evaluation of their actions through immunity claims.

In conclusion: yes, even while performing supererogatory duties, an actor or set of actors can be held legally responsible for certain outcomes; however, the legal consequences that follow from this responsibility should be less severe the more supererogatory is the duty.

5.3 *The distinction between private law and public law approaches*

Characteristic of philosophical discussions on shared responsibility is that they ignore the distinction between private law and public law responses, which is central – maybe even typical – for domestic legal analysis: an actor is either held responsible for damages in a tort action, or is criminally prosecuted. Interestingly enough, within international law this distinction is, again, less prevalent. Many scholars of international law (want to) see international law as a unitary system, to which domestic notions of private or public law cannot easily be transposed. Pellet argues that international responsibility is neither public nor private, but 'simply international'.[42] Seen from one perspective, there is much truth in this claim. The domestic distinction between private and public law is more a contingent outcome of a historical development in domestic law than an inherent legal necessity.[43] Thus, there is no evident

[42] A. Pellet, 'Can a State Commit a Crime? Definitely, Yes!' (1999) 10 EJIL 425, at 433–434.

[43] D. Kennedy, 'The Stages of the Decline of the Public/Private Distinction' (1982) 130 Penn LR 1349; C.M. Chinkin, 'A Critique of the Public/Private Dimension' (1999) 10 EJIL 387.

reason why, while developing instruments of joint responsibility in international law, theorists should follow this distinction. However, given the equally contingent patchwork of courts in international law – a constellation in which the private-public distinction can still be recognised – it might be prudent to develop a pluralist approach of joint responsibility in international law.[44] Indeed, international law did not emerge *ex nihilo*, separated from the domestic legal traditions of the states that compose the international legal order. It might be true that the distinction within domestic law between private-law and public-law ways of dealing with individual and shared responsibility may be the contingent outcome of a certain historical development. Still, there is some logic in the separation between, on the one hand, compensation for material or non-material damage to third parties, and on the other hand, punishment for acts that undermine the legal order itself.

5.4 *A conceptual problem or a problem of implementation?*

Within well-ordered nation states, law and enforcement systems ensure that there are legal consequences for those who are caught violating the law, both private and public. In this context there is a clear distinction and hierarchical relation between lawmakers and law enforcers (the state) and subjects of law (citizens and non-state actors). Regulating shared responsibility domestically boils down to regulating the interactions between citizens and non-state actors within a state. Regulating joint responsibility in international law would, however, involve states regulating and limiting their own sovereignty, their independence from one another. States resist principles of responsibility that allow them to be responsible for acts of other states on the basis of a loose involvement with those other states. Enforcing the public law function, and ensuring the integrity of the international legal order, seems to be very difficult in the current situation. The decentralised 'patchwork' nature of the international legal order, the lack of courts with compulsory jurisdiction, and the inherently consensual nature of most international dispute settlement mechanisms undermine an effective enforcement mechanism for joint responsibility in international law. States could be considered *morally* responsible, but there might not be an agent – whether supranational or not – to hold them *legally* responsible with the additional legal consequences.

[44] Nollkaemper and Jacobs, 'Shared Responsibility', n. 2, at 415.

This might lead to the conclusion that the reluctance of states to transfer power to supranational institutions and courts, and the lack of truly cosmopolitan legal institutions, might be a more significant obstacle to a firm legal establishment of shared responsibility in international law than difficulties in understanding the concept of shared responsibility in the international legal order.[45] This conclusion is supported by the fact that the European Court of Human Rights, indeed one of the few courts that does have jurisdiction over the participating states, has ruled in several multi-defendant cases.[46]

6. Conclusions

Current international law, being the historical fruit of a horizontal conception of the international legal order, is as yet incapable of correctly grasping and ascribing the responsibility of multiple state actors for a single event. This chapter has aimed to contribute to our understanding of shared responsibility in international law. It has explicitly stepped away from the way shared responsibility is conceptualised in conventional international law, and has analysed the issue from a normative-philosophical perspective. I developed the basic idea of responsibility through a discussion of personal agency and personal responsibility, and argued that shared responsibility can be ascribed when a collective can operate through its members in such a way that they simulate the performance of individual agents. I concluded that, from this perspective, it is very possible to understand the general concept of shared responsibility in international law through an analogy argument: collectives are supposed to be responsibility-bearing agents to the extent that they operate in such a way as to simulate the performance of individual agents. In that sense, the concept of shared responsibility in international law seems to be more readily acceptable in normative-philosophical debates than in conventional international law.

At the same time, I argued that it is usually very difficult to correctly allocate the shared responsibility to the involved actors. The reason why joint responsibility is usually invoked is precisely that the plurality of contributions of the involved actors and their interrelationships make

[45] On cosmopolitan legal institutions see R. Pierik and W. Werner (eds.), *Cosmopolitanism in Context: Perspectives from International Law and Political Theory* (Cambridge University Press, 2010).

[46] Nollkaemper and Jacobs, 'Shared Responsibility', n. 2, at 387.

it very difficult, if not impossible, to disentangle the individual contributions to the outcome. In international law these questions become even more complicated. Sometimes individual natural persons – officials who were directly involved in the wrongful act – should be held responsible for a specific outcome. In other cases it is a shared responsibility. However, in the international arena, states can cooperate in various ways: bilaterally, or through international or supranational organisations.

But the fact that such an allocation of responsibility can never be determined exactly should not deter philosophers and legal scholars from trying to determine this allocation as far as possible. A philosophical conceptualisation of responsibility and shared responsibility as presented here can be helpful in developing the much-needed regulations to govern the allocation of shared responsibility in international law. It may serve both the interests of injured parties, who otherwise may have difficulty identifying the responsible entities and the scope of their responsibility, *and* the interests of states, by providing some predictability as to how their responsibility might be distributed among various states and attributed to them.

3

Shared Political Responsibility

ANTHONY F. LANG JR.*

1. Introduction

In 2007, the Intergovernmental Panel on Climate Change (IPCC) issued its Fourth Assessment Report on the state of the world's climate. The report stated that '[w]arming of the climate system is unequivocal, as is now evident from observations of increases in global average air and ocean temperatures, widespread melting of snow and ice and rising global average sea level'.[1] The report presents detailed evidence for this claim and further evidence to establish what it calls the 'anthropogenic drivers' of climate change, that is, the actions brought about by human beings as opposed to those resulting from natural processes such as atmospheric changes. The report is clear that the causes attributable to human action, particularly fossil fuel use, have greatly increased climate change over the last 200 years.[2] The consequences of climate change are dire, as the report warns, including potential harm to vast numbers of inhabitants of the planet. The next report of the IPCC appeared in late 2014 and its conclusions reinforce those of previous reports.

While some have questioned the conclusions of the IPCC reports over the years, there is broad scientific consensus concerning the fact of climate change. What is missing is a global consensus about whom or what is responsible for this change. One can argue that human beings are central to this change, but when it comes to determining responsibility more precisely, this point is not helpful. It is unhelpful because the scope of climate change is global and because, in some way, all humans seem responsible for it. But the idea of responsibility is problematic here. Not

* Director, Centre for Global Constitutionalism, School of International Relations, University of St Andrews.

[1] Intergovernmental Panel on Climate Change, Fourth Assessment Report, 'Climate Change 2007: Synthesis Report' (Geneva, 2007), at 30, see www.ipcc.ch (last accessed on 5 June 2014).

[2] Ibid., at 36–41.

every person consumes the same amount of fossil fuels or food. Moreover, individual persons are located in political communities which organise their political and economic activities in ways that those individuals may or may not be able to control. A similar problem exists for states. Not all states have contributed to global climate change in the same way. And, the inherent transboundary nature of climate change has meant that even when states try in their own domestic policies to address climate change, they cannot necessarily control it.

There has been, of course, an international legal response to climate change, one built on a revision to our standard understanding of responsibility, which has come to be known as 'common but differentiated responsibility'. In 1992, at a summit in Rio de Janeiro, a treaty was drafted that entered into force in 1994. This treaty, the United Nations Framework Convention on Climate Change[3] was originally more aspirational than actionable; that is, it had little in the way of obligations and commitments that bound states to act. This changed in 1997 with the passage of the Kyoto Protocol[4] which demanded that states begin a progressive reduction in carbon emissions through a series of mechanisms such as carbon trading, or the ability to 'buy and sell' credits for carbon emissions. The Protocol gave greater specificity to the idea of 'common but differentiated responsibilities', a term in the original treaty, which placed a heavier burden on developed states to lower their carbon emissions more quickly than the developing countries. The Protocol came into effect in 2005.

The proposal for common but differentiated responsibilities has not gone down well with powerful states whose responsibilities under the terms of the Protocol are much greater than other states. The United States, which has not ratified the Kyoto Protocol because of its objections to the idea of common but differentiated responsibilities, has argued, in the words of Secretary of State John Kerry, '[p]lain and simple, all nations have a responsibility to make near-term emissions reductions'.[5] Admittedly, the United States, under the administration of President Barack Obama, has sought to respond to climate change in more active ways

[3] United Nations Framework Convention on Climate Change, New York, 9 May 1992, in force 21 March 1994, 1771 UNTS 107.

[4] Kyoto Protocol to the United Nations Framework Convention on Climate Change, Kyoto, 10 December 1997, in force 16 February 2005, 2303 UNTS 148 (Kyoto Protocol or Protocol).

[5] J. Kerry, 'Getting the US-China Climate Partnership Right', US Department of State, 19 July 2013, see www.state.gov/secretary/remarks (last accessed on 5 June 2014).

than the preceding US administration. Yet, it is undoubtedly true that the United States does not see its responsibility to respond to climate change through a differentiated lens, but through a simple lens of all states making roughly equivalent contributions.

Climate change, in other words, challenges our ideas about responsibility. Its global scope and complexity make identifying responsible agents very difficult. More importantly, simple causal notions of responsibility do not seem to capture the complexity of the issue. One idea would be to abandon the discourse of responsibility in relation to climate change because it is simply too imprecise to provide any helpful moral, legal, or political frameworks by which to respond to this issue.[6] But perhaps there exists in alternative discourses of responsibility some means by which to rethink this issue at the global level. Holding agents responsible can generate a number of possible outcomes: forcing agents to provide reparations, punishing agents who have violated rights, ensuring the continued viability of a legal order to govern environmental problems, and encouraging new modes of political action.

The proposal of the editors of this volume to explore the idea of shared responsibility in international law[7] provides one alternative that provides some new insights into climate change. This chapter will build on their idea, along with a review of moral philosophers and political theorists, to propose an understanding of responsibility that points toward political action by multiple agents across the international system as the bearers of responsibility in the international order rather than simply powerful states. This idea of political responsibility builds upon more traditional notions of responsibility, but, coupled with the idea of shared responsibility, suggests how this alternative, which I call 'shared political responsibility', provides a means by which the discourse of responsibility surrounding climate change can avoid being bogged down in discussions of causation and blame, and move toward means of action across multiple political realms.

The chapter proceeds as follows: section 2 reviews two important moral philosophers on the question of responsibility, Peter Strawson

[6] See D.H. Cole, 'The Problem of Shared Irresponsibility in International Climate Law', Chapter 10 of this volume, 290, where he argues that liability approaches to climate change are problematic in that they fail to provide incentives. I would disagree slightly with his interpretation in that the rational choice underlying his claims are not ones that I think capture the full dimensions of international politics.

[7] See P.A. Nollkaemper and D. Jacobs, 'Shared Responsibility in International Law: A Conceptual Framework' (2013) 34 MIJIL 359.

and Marion Smiley. It then moves to two political theorists, William Connolly and Hannah Arendt, as theorists of political responsibility. Building on these four theorists, the chapter then moves to a discussion of the legal theories of responsibility, concluding with Nollkaemper and Jacobs' idea of shared responsibility, which I connect to the idea of political responsibility (section 3). The fourth section of the chapter reviews various proposals for resolving climate change and evaluates them in terms of the idea of shared political responsibility that I develop in this chapter.

2. Responsibility

Through an engagement with a series of moral and political philosophers, I argue here that legal responsibility can be supplemented by what I call 'political responsibility'.[8] This means that instead of solely tying individual agents to specific actions, this initial act of locating responsibility in specific agents can be used to compel agents to engage in forms of political action that construct new political arrangements, rather than ending in punitive or even restorative consequences. This does not mean that the results of moral and legal responsibility are discarded; rather, they are enfolded into a set of practices that can lead to new actions by not only those held responsible, but by the wider community of agents. In order to develop this point, though, let me begin by exploring the idea of responsibility in moral philosophy.

Responsibility has two interrelated meanings: first, one is responsible for performing or not performing certain actions as a result of an identity or role in which one has been placed or has placed oneself; second, one can be held responsible for acting or failing to act in certain ways. The two senses are obviously interrelated in that one is held responsible after

[8] This section draws upon various pieces I have written on responsibility and punishment. These include: A.F. Lang, Jr., 'Responsibility in the International System: Reading U.S. Foreign Policy in the Middle East' (1999) 5(1) EJIR 67; A.F. Lang, Jr., 'The United Nations and the Fall of Srebrenica: Meaningful Responsibility and International Society', in T. Erskine (ed.), *Can Institutions Have Responsibilities? Collective Moral Agency and International Relations* (Basingstoke: Palgrave Macmillan, 2003), 183; A.F. Lang, Jr., 'Evil, Agency and Punishment', in R. Jeffery (ed.), *Confronting Evil in International Relations: Ethical Responses to Problems of Moral Agency* (New York: Palgrave Macmillan, 2008), 89; and A.F. Lang, Jr., 'Punishing Genocide: A Critical Reading of the International Court of Justice', in T. Isaacs and R. Vernon (eds.), *Accountability for Collective Wrongdoing* (Cambridge University Press, 2011), 92.

the fact for actions that result from the adoption of a role that creates those responsibilities. Responsibility, in turn, requires that an individual has the agency required to intend, plan, and execute the actions. Generally, we assume that only natural persons have the agency and hence responsibility for the type of action that would constitute such a violation.[9]

More often than not, we use the term responsibility in the second way, that is, we hold agents responsible for actions without specifying in advance a particular role or identity that has created this responsibility. This is because responsibility is first and foremost a moral term. That is, we tend to hold individuals responsible for their actions simply because we assume they are capable, intentional moral agents who should understand broadly conceived moral rules. This assumption about responsibility underlies a famous philosophical paper written by Peter Strawson in 1963, eventually published as 'Freedom and Resentment'.[10] He begins with a debate about the consequences for human behaviour of the thesis of determinism. The thesis of determinism – the belief that all actions are determined prior to their taking place and that human beings have no control over those actions in ways that are morally relevant – impacts our understanding of moral responsibility at its core, because if determinism is true the concept of responsibility makes no sense. Strawson seeks to prove that, even if determinism is true, responsibility still has a role to play in our interpersonal relations. In making this argument, Strawson states that responsibility must be seen in light of

> [t]he very great importance we attach to the attitudes and intentions toward us of other human beings, and the great extent to which our personal feelings and reactions depend upon, or involve, our beliefs about those attitudes and intentions.[11]

Strawson proceeds to argue that these attitudes and intentions toward others depend on the assumption that other human beings can be held responsible for their actions.

To assume that determinism is true is to adopt what Strawson calls an 'objective' rather than a 'participant' attitude toward another human person. And, to do so is

9 See R. Pierik, 'Shared Responsibility in International Law: A Normative-Philosophical Analysis', Chapter 2 of this volume, 36.

10 P. Strawson, 'Freedom and Resentment', reprinted in J.M. Fischer and M. Ravizza (eds.), *Perspectives on Moral Responsibility* (Ithaca, NY: Cornell University Press, 1993), 45.

11 Ibid., at 48.

> to see him, perhaps, as an object of social policy, as a subject for what, in a wide range of senses, might be called treatment; as something certainly to be taken account, perhaps precautionary account, of; to be managed or handled or cured or trained; perhaps simply to be avoided ... But it cannot include the range of reactive feelings and attitudes which belong to involvement and participation with others in inter-personal human relationships.[12]

Strawson's thesis challenges us to consider how interpersonal relations need to be taken into account when thinking about moral concepts. One could analyse the concept of responsibility without even considering these relationships, but to do so would undermine the role of responsibility in many of our relationships – the ability to see others as fellow human beings with whom we have concrete relationships that shape our collective lives, rather than as violators of rules who must be punished or corrected in order to be welcomed back into society. That is, Strawson's notion of responsibility reveals a role of responsibility that is not always obvious; it solidifies our relationships with each other and, in so doing, makes community life more meaningful.

Even more importantly, Strawson is making the interesting claim that without responsibility, communities make no sense. In other words, if the concept of responsibility did not exist, we could not have meaningful interpersonal relationships and, *ipso facto*, we could not have meaningful societies and political communities. In a sense, Strawson is telling us that without some notion of responsibility, social and political interactions could not exist. Strawson, of course, is writing about domestic social and political life. Yet, there is a potential for his ideas to contribute to our understanding of international or global political relations. For instance, Strawson's idea about the centrality of reactive attitudes in the deployment of responsibility could reinforce ideas of international society as theorised by figures such as Hedley Bull.[13] This tradition of thought poses itself against more structural realist arguments that do not see states as having anything other than relations of conflict; the international society idea argues that their relations arise from shared understandings of themselves as part of a community. Responsibility as theorised by Strawson might supplement this account.

More interestingly, if I turn to the idea of shared responsibility as developed by Nollkaemper and Jacobs, Strawson's argument reveals the

[12] Ibid., at 51.
[13] H. Bull, *The Anarchical Society* (New York: Columbia University Press, 1977).

potential for how these reactive attitudes toward a multiplicity of agents in the international order might enfold even a larger number of agents into some conception of global community. For instance, if I, as a citizen of the United States, see that a multinational company is polluting the Amazon rainforest, my reactive attitude to this 'finding of responsibility' can strengthen the idea that there is a larger international global or political community of which I am part and which may prompt me to act upon this realisation. Strawson's framework allows us to see how responsibility in this framework of shared responsibility might generate new political responses to global harms.

One element of Strawson's account that is under-theorised, however, is the role of power in the construction of both responsibility and even in our reactive attitudes to those claims of responsibility. One theorist who does highlight the role of power is Marion Smiley, who argues in her book *Moral Responsibility and the Boundaries of Community* that moral responsibility cannot be a function simply of our assumptions about will and intentions.[14] Rather, responsibility arises from two factors: one, the social roles that communities establish for individuals, determining whether or not they should be blamed for particular actions; and, two, the power relations that exist between individuals that allow some to blame others and, in so doing, reinforce or create anew those roles. Individual persons become blameworthy or praiseworthy because of the roles we create for them.

For example, mothers are expected to conform to certain roles in terms of raising children, roles that can mean that they are deemed to be responsible for the faults of their children in ways that fathers are not (at least according to these socially defined roles). Moreover, these roles become part of the public discourse we use to think about and act upon public problems. For instance, when reports appear arguing that children raised by stay-at-home parents tend to have fewer social problems than those who attend day care, various pundits will claim that this 'proves' that working mothers can be blamed for their children's defects. Such an assumption ignores the ways in which the role of 'mother', while certainly physical in part, is also a socially constructed role. Moreover, the ways in which we blame and praise will not simply affect the individuals at that moment, but will also have a long-term influence on how we construct the role of mother. We can meaningfully blame and praise

[14] M. Smiley, *Moral Responsibility and the Boundaries of Community: Power and Accountability from a Pragmatic Point of View* (University of Chicago Press, 1992).

individual mothers for actions in raising children, but we need to be aware of how such statements of blame and praise rely upon and recreate certain roles that partly determine the ways in which we hold mothers responsible.

Smiley's analysis demonstrates how power structures create roles for individuals that lead to attributions of responsibility. Her argument relates to Strawson's point that there is a relationship between discourses of responsibility and the social and political norms that structure community life. But, Smiley provides more precision to Strawson's account by highlighting that responsibility is not just necessary for our interpersonal relationships to work; it is more than that because it structures and is structured by the power relations that exist within that society. Her critical insight on this point is crucial to understanding the ways in which responsibility can and cannot function in international law and politics. Certainly, Smiley makes her argument in the context of domestic law and politics, and it has, I think, some important implications for international politics and law. Power is often invoked in international law and politics as the only currency. Invocations of responsibility need to be supplemented by this claim to power as well, though not just in the simplistic way that realist theory so often does. So, for instance, we might highlight not only the way in which one powerful state dominates another, but how categories of international criminal law reflect underlying power relations. One obvious example would be the ways in which the International Criminal Court has only examined cases from Africa rather than from other regions, reflecting the longstanding view of Africa as an uncivilised arena that needs to be governed by the West.

Smiley's account, while written from the perspective of moral philosophy, points us toward the political dimension of responsibility (as does Strawson's, though in a more roundabout way). Two political theorists give a different reading of the politics of responsibility, each highlighting a different dimension of the idea. The first is William Connolly. In *Identity/Difference*, Connolly explores the ways in which formulations of responsibility structure the late modern response to political life. He argues that while responsibility has had different resonances across different cultural contexts, a version of it seems to structure much of our reactions to wrongdoing and evil. For Connolly, unlike Strawson, this need for responsibility is not something to be celebrated, but something that may contain within it the 'problem of evil':

> Perhaps standards of responsibility are both indispensable to social practice and productive of injustices within it. Perhaps because every society demands some such standards, a problem of evil resides within any social practice that fulfils this demand relentlessly.[15]

Connolly argues that the demand for responsibility represents a kind of moral calculus that prevents any act of evil from slipping away unaccounted for. In our attempts to locate all wrongdoing in structures of responsibility, Connolly suggests that we force individuals into particular identities that do not accurately capture them. Put differently, the multiple levels of causality that exist in the world, and our need as humans to find clear moral and sometimes legal judgments, results in situations where the task of 'finding someone responsible' can perhaps result in outcomes that do more harm than might have been intended. The 'evil' that results, in other words, is intimately tied to our efforts to find responsible agents.

I find Connolly's critique of responsibility quite persuasive, for it reveals how responsibility is a constructed concept and how its construction does not always lead to justice. At the same time, I do not want to abandon responsibility because I agree with Strawson that it is too fundamental to our shared lives, whether at the local, national, or global levels. Rather than abandon responsibility, perhaps we need to be attentive to the kinds of identities and communities it constructs. Moreover, it may be that responsibility can generate some unexpected outcomes, ones that are not the normal moves toward punishment or sanction.[16]

The final theorist to be explored is Hannah Arendt. She develops the concept of political agency, which is the status of individuals in a community as being able to participate in the life of that community. That status sometimes results from an official body conferring it, such as in determinations of citizenship. At the same time, political agency does not stop with that official conferment. Rather, it must be continually re-inscribed by the engagement in the political, by working with and

[15] W.E. Connolly, *Identity/Difference: Democratic Negotiations of Political Paradox* (Ithaca: Cornell University Press, 1991), at 96.

[16] I have argued, however, that one of the most important functions of holding an agent responsible is to punish that agent, a move that Connolly wants to avoid. My view is that punishment is central to political life and should be one of the results of finding an individual responsible. But, in this chapter, I am trying to elucidate an alternative to punishment and sanction that may arise from discourses of responsibility. For my defence of punishment as a legitimate response to holding agents responsible, see A.F. Lang Jr., 'Crime and Punishment: Holding States Accountable' (2007) 21(2) EIA 239.

sometimes against others in the political community. Agency then results not just from the actions of others giving one an official status but from one's own political activity.

This idea of political agency is developed in Arendt's *The Human Condition*.[17] Political agency in Arendt's understanding relies on a particular understanding of action, which is how human persons reveal themselves in moments of interactions with others. It is the way in which we assert who we are, in which we create ourselves by presenting ourselves in public. Politics, which provides the constructed stage of a parliament or town meeting, provides the paradigmatic instance of moments in which the human person can be revealed. Arendt develops this concept of action in an engagement with Greek and Roman philosophers who sought to define the realm of the political. That realm, combining a Homeric agonal spirit with an Aristotelian notion of speech as the quintessentially human characteristic, results in a public space that allows for competition and conflict.

According to Arendt, the public realm is the place where 'everybody had to constantly distinguish himself from all others, to show through unique deeds or achievements that he was best of all'.[18] Indeed, it is this ability to act publicly that defines the human person:

> A life without speech and without action, on the other hand – and this is the only way of life that in earnest has renounced all appearance and all vanity in the biblical sense of the word – is literally dead to the world; it has ceased to be a human life because it is no longer lived among men. With word and deed we insert ourselves into the human world, and this insertion is like a second birth, in which we confirm and take upon ourselves the naked fact of our original physical appearance.[19]

Public political action puts us into the world and reveals the 'who' of our existence in a way that no other practice can.

Furthermore, since Arendt believes that political action is a public presentation of the self, there must be a community to whom this presentation is made. She notes that action occurs within a 'web of human relationships', a place composed both of other people acting and speaking and of the 'common world' that surrounds and anchors human interaction: 'most words and deeds are *about* some worldly objective reality in addition to being a disclosure of the acting and

[17] H. Arendt, *The Human Condition* (University of Chicago Press, 1958).
[18] Ibid., at 41. [19] Ibid., at 176–177.

speaking agent.'[20] Politics thus requires a public realm, one composed of fellow humans with an agreed upon equality, not one of merit but one of agency.

This connects to Arendt's idea of political responsibility. In her essay, 'Collective Responsibility', she distinguishes between guilt and responsibility: 'Guilt, unlike responsibility, always singles out; it is strictly personal.'[21] But while guilt is individual, responsibility can be corporate. She notes that for collective responsibility to make sense two conditions must apply:

> I must be held responsible for something I have not done, and the reason for my responsibility must be my membership in a group (a collective), which no voluntary act of mine can dissolve, that is, a membership which is utterly unlike a business partnership which I can dissolve at will.[22]

Collective responsibility applies most clearly, according to this conception, in cases where individuals are held responsible for what their governments do. The context of her argument seems to be an attempt to locate the responsibility of individuals who do not support the actions of their government but who are being held responsible for that government's actions.

Arendt takes this point even further, however. Rather than simply stating that collective responsibility is possible in these situations, she argues that simply by living in the current world, one in which we are automatically bound up in a community, we can never avoid responsibility for the actions of our states. To clarify this, she notes that only refugees are innocent of this collective responsibility, precisely because they are outside the boundaries of any community. Arendt claims that political nonparticipation, as a sign of political protest, does not alleviate this responsibility. Simply by the fact that we live in a community, we are responsible for its collective actions:

> This vicarious responsibility for things we have not done, this taking upon ourselves the consequences for things we are entirely innocent of, is the price we pay for the fact that we live our lives not by ourselves but among our fellow men, and that the faculty of action which, after all, is the political faculty par excellence, can be actualized only in one of the many and manifold forms of human community.[23]

[20] Ibid., at 182 (emphasis in the original).

[21] H. Arendt, 'Collective Responsibility', in H. Arendt, *Responsibility and Judgment* (edited and with an introduction by J. Kohn) (New York: Schocken Books, 2003), at 147.

[22] Ibid., at 149. [23] Ibid., at 157–158.

Political responsibility here connects with political agency. Rather than moral agency that seeks to connect the agent with the will, political agency and responsibility connect the individual to a wider realm, one in which the human person is celebrated in all her individuality. While it may seem strange to create a collective notion of responsibility when Arendt is so concerned with individuality, her concept of responsibility is about agency not about an internal will producing morally or legally correct outcomes. Instead, it is a responsibility that arises from an understanding that each action produces the political sphere anew. Because of the emphasis she places on the ways in which agency constructs the public sphere, Arendt's conception of responsibility arises from that participation. If the public sphere is that place where no person is made superfluous, but every person has the opportunity to enact themselves and contribute to the creation of that sphere through their deeds, acts that destroy that space will redound on all of us who have acted and continue to act in that space.[24] Constructing and sustaining the public sphere is a joint exercise, and when that sphere is closed down or parts of it are destroyed permanently, we all become responsible.

There are, of course, other versions of collective responsibility, ones that go by a variety of terms, including shared responsibility and corporate responsibility. There is an important body of literature on collective responsibility in international relations (IR) theory. One of the leading theorists here is Toni Erskine, who provides the following definition of collective moral agency:

> A collectivity is a candidate for moral agency if it has the following: an identity that is more than the sum of the identities of its constitutive parts and, therefore, does not rely on a determinate membership; a decision-making structure; an identity over time; and a conception of itself as a unit.[25]

This definition, like others that address responsibility, focuses primarily on the internal characteristics of the agent. In this account, Erskine

[24] For an argument about Arendt and her concern with the dangers of individuals becoming superfluous, see P. Hayden, 'Superfluous Humanity: An Arendtian Perspective on the Political Evil of Global Poverty' (2007) 35(2) MJIS 279.

[25] T. Erskine, 'Assigning Responsibilities to Institutional Moral Agents: The Case of States and "Quasi-States"' (2001) 15(2) EIA 67, at 72; and T. Erskine (ed.), *Can Institutions Have Responsibilities? Collective Moral Agency and International Relations* (Basingstoke: Palgrave Macmillan, 2003). See also her chapter in this volume, T. Erskine '"Coalitions of the Willing" and the Shared Responsibility to Protect', Chapter 8, 227.

focuses on the individual's will and/or knowledge in ascribing responsibility to her for past actions. Translating that approach to collective moral agents, however, requires more careful consideration, which Erskine and others provide.[26] For individuals, internal characteristics include the mind, the will, and the emotions. For collective agents, however, internal characteristics must include things like bureaucracy, constitutional structure, and/or social arrangements.

Before turning to the idea of responsibility in international law, one final distinction needs to be made. As a result of this last point, I would suggest that corporate agents are more relevant in understanding responsibility than collective ones. By this, I do not mean corporations in the purely economic sense of the term. Rather, I understand a corporation as a more formalised group structure than a collective. A collective is a group of persons, who may or may not be organised and capable of acting with intention. A corporation, on the other hand, is a group that is recognised through a formal process and has a particular structure that allows it to intend, plan, and execute actions. Holding collectives responsible is not justified, but holding corporations responsible is justified and, as Sarah Seck demonstrates, an important part of most legal systems.[27] Richard Vernon's argument that states and not nations can be held responsible and punished, an argument he poses in contrast to the famous attempt by Karl Jaspers to hold Germany responsible as a nation, could be fit into this distinction, if he called a nation a 'collective' and a state a 'corporation'.[28]

Businesses that are incorporated are designed to locate agency and responsibility in a particular structure and the wider legal order in order to avoid having any individuals within them held responsible for wrongs the corporation might commit. So, the suffering that individuals experience when a corporation is punished can be justified because the

[26] The work of Larry May is exemplary here; see L. May, *The Morality of Groups* (University of Notre Dame Press, 1987) and L. May, *Sharing Responsibility* (University of Chicago Press, 1992). For a range of debates about collective responsibility, see L. May and S. Hoffman (eds.), *Collective Responsibility: Five Decades of Debate in Theoretical and Applied Ethics* (Lanham, MD: Rowman and Littlefield, 1991).

[27] S.L. Seck, 'Collective Responsibility and Transnational Corporate Conduct', in T. Isaacs and R. Vernon (eds.), *Accountability for Collective Wrongdoing* (Cambridge University Press, 2011), at 140. While Seck provides evidence of how the law deals with corporate crime, the title of her chapter elides this important distinction between collectives and corporations.

[28] R. Vernon, 'Punishing Collectives: States or Nations?', in T. Isaacs and R. Vernon (eds.), *Accountability for Collective Wrongdoing* (Cambridge University Press, 2011), 287.

individuals involved understand that they are acting as a corporate entity recognised as such. In Seck's review of corporations as subjects of liability for global harms, such as climate change, they are on one level certainly responsible. But, at a deeper level, it is the legal and political order that creates corporations that should also be responsible for the harms they commit. In other words, if states create corporations without regulatory frameworks or limits on their profit making, then the state should be considered somehow responsible. The idea that corporate agents exist within political, legal, and even social orders points us back to the ideas developed earlier; that is, our notions of responsibility are constitutive of, and constituted by, the communities within which we live (Strawson); that these communities function through the exercise of power (Smiley); that our desire to find responsible agents results in practices that generate more harm than good (Connolly); and that one solution to these tensions is to develop ways of reconstructing the communities within which agents – corporate and personal – function by engaging in forms of new political actions (Arendt). Through these steps, we can see, then, how we might use responsibility in new ways, primarily as a political practice that might generate new political and even legal institutions and orders.

These arguments point to how wider political and legal orders create responsible agents, which I would call a 'constitutional system'. At the end of this chapter, I will demonstrate that while the global constitutional order has created states that seemingly escape liability, that order can be restructured in such a way that it places more regulatory limits on what states can do. One way to do that is to create a legal order in which states are not only held responsible but perhaps punished, something I have argued for elsewhere.[29] But in this chapter I point to some alternatives to punishment and sanction. For perhaps a better response when we hold agents responsible is to look toward alternative political forms by which the problems agents have created can be resolved. That is, following Arendt, I would like to point more toward responsibility that is not simply a legalistic move toward punishment, but is a political move toward alternative forms of action that might generate new structures and institutions. In pursuit of this objective, though, let me review one more body of literature concerning responsibility, the discourse of international legal responsibility.

[29] Lang, 'Crime and Punishment: Holding States Accountable', n. 16. See also, A.F. Lang, Jr. *Punishment, Justice and International Relations: Ethics and Order after the Cold War* (London: Routledge, 2008).

3. Responsibility in international law

In one sense, a legal discourse on responsibility is surprising, for responsibility is more of a moral or political term than a legal one. The more accurate term in the law would be 'obligation' or 'duty'. For instance, in a contractual relationship, the two parties do not have responsibilities toward each other but have obligations. Alternatively, when one has violated a law, one is considered liable rather than responsible for the harms committed. Responsibility has, one might say, a 'softer' meaning than the more precise legal terms such as 'obligation' or 'liability'.

Yet in international law there is, in fact, a robust literature on responsibility. In 2001, the International Law Commission drafted the Articles on Responsibility of States for Internationally Wrongful Acts (Articles on State Responsibility)[30] and in 2011 they passed the Articles on the Responsibility of International Organizations.[31] While these are relatively recent pieces of international law, the notion of responsibility has long been part of the international legal discourse. As Alain Pellet reminds us, responsibility is intimately tied to the central idea of the international legal order that all sovereign states are equal.[32] Pellet also points out that the fact that the French word *responsibilité* conflates the two distinct meanings of responsibility and liability;[33] perhaps a reason international law draws on the term responsibility rather than liability is because of the use of French as the diplomatic and legal language of nineteenth-century international law.

Although the term is common in international legal discourse, it includes a diversity of different meanings. Its use in traditional international law reflects something closer to 'private' or 'civil' law meanings; that is, a violation of the rights of one state by another gives rise to a need for reparations. This meaning can be found in nineteenth-century legal

[30] Articles on Responsibility of States for Internationally Wrongful Acts, ILC *Yearbook* 2001/II(2) (Articles on State Responsibility); see J. Crawford (ed.), *The International Law Commission's Articles on State Responsibility: Introduction, Text and Commentaries* (Cambridge University Press, 2003).

[31] Articles on the Responsibility of International Organizations, ILC Report on the work of its sixty-third session, UNGAOR 66th Sess., Supp. No. 10, UN Doc. A/66/10 (2011); see M. Ragazzi (ed.), *Responsibility of International Organizations* (Leiden: Brill Publishing, 2013).

[32] A. Pellet, 'The Definition of Responsibility in International Law', in J. Crawford, A. Pellet, and S. Olleson (eds.), *The Law of International Responsibility* (Oxford University Press, 2011), 3.

[33] Ibid., at 11.

discourse when the legal equality of states was emerging.[34] States were in something like a contractual relationship with each other, so a violation was a breach of that contract. But the meaning of responsibility also includes a 'public law' dimension, in which states are understood to be 'responsible' to the international community as a whole. One can see this change in the debates and discussions that surrounded the drafting of the Articles on State Responsibility. The Articles establish that a state can invoke damages by one state against it, and hence make a claim of responsibility. Yet, as James Crawford notes, this is not the only way responsibility can be invoked:

> The Articles also make provision for the invocation of responsibility in the absence of any direct form of injury, where the obligation breached is one protecting the collective interests of a group of states or the interests of the international community as a whole.[35]

In other words, built into the concept of international legal responsibility is a bifurcated understanding of the term, one that is 'private' and one that is 'public'.[36]

The other complicating element of international responsibility is that it is used in reference to both people and states. This is a recent change, one that arose as a result of the creation of international tribunals and culminating in the creation of the International Criminal Court. The ability of the international community to hold individuals responsible for war crimes, crimes against humanity, and genocide has generated two sorts of responsibility. As I have argued elsewhere, this has resulted in something like two competing constitutional orders, one where individual persons are agents and the other in which states are agents.[37]

[34] Martti Koskenniemi argues that this 'private' nature of international legal responsibility can be traced to the natural law theories of Grotius and Pufendorf. I think he is incorrect on this point, as Grotius argued from a natural law foundation in which a violation of the laws of nature was a violation of the order as a whole rather than a violation of the rights of individuals. Of course, Grotius did help create the idea of natural rights, but I am not convinced that his understanding of responsibility derives from rights rather than law. See M. Koskenniemi, 'Doctrines of State Responsibility', in J. Crawford, A. Pellet, and S. Olleson (eds.), *The Law of International Responsibility* (Oxford University Press, 2011), 45, at 47.

[35] J. Crawford, 'The System of International Responsibility', in J. Crawford, A. Pellet and S. Olleson (eds.), *The Law of International Responsibility* (Oxford University Press, 2011), 17, at 24.

[36] Nollkaemper and Jacobs, 'Shared Responsibility in International Law: A Conceptual Framework', n. 7, at 400–403.

[37] A.F. Lang, Jr., 'Conflicting Rules: Global Constitutionalism and the Kosovo Intervention' (2009) 3(2) JIS 185.

So, within the idea of international legal responsibility, there are a range of conflicting notions. André Nollkaemper and Dov Jacobs try to negotiate some of these tensions with their idea of 'shared responsibility'.[38] They propose a slightly altered understanding of the corporate/collective distinction, one that focuses less on the collective nature of the state itself and more on the range of agents in the international order who may or may not contribute to various harms. In one passage, they highlight what they see as the two possible purposes of responsibility, purposes which correspond to the distinction between the 'private' and 'public' nature of this concept: first, to protect the rights of individual agents in the international order; or second, to reinforce the centrality of law in the international political order. Further, they propose that a modified version of the idea of 'joint and several responsibility' might provide some means by which alternative uses of international responsibility can be deployed. They note that there are difficulties with applying this idea, one drawn from civil law contexts, to the public international legal order. As such, they propose some substantive and procedural variations on the international legal order that might address these tensions.

Nollkaemper and Jacobs open up the concept of responsibility through their thorough development of the idea of a 'shared responsibility'. In so doing, they widen our scope to include a range of agents in the international legal and political order whose consent and control need to be better understood as playing a crucial role in the creation of harms at the global level. Their concept is ideally placed to build upon the idea of political responsibility proposed in the previous section. Certainly, the idea of political responsibility I have developed here does not correspond with most international legal notions. But, what makes Nollkaemper and Jacobs' account helpful is that it reveals one of the obvious tensions within the international order, that is, that there are multiplicity of agents not only who can be held responsible, but who can act in order to achieve outcomes. This includes individual people, local governments, non-governmental organisations (NGOs), states, and supranational and international organisations. As suggested in the next section, there may well be agents that currently do not exist but which might need to be created in order to tackle climate change, a type of political action that Arendt would call 'natality' or the practice of creating anew. A political project

[38] See Nollkaemper and Jacobs, 'Shared Responsibility in International Law: A Conceptual Framework', n. 7 for a similar point.

arising from attributions of responsibility, such as explained by Arendt in the previous section, would certainly protect rights and reinforce the importance of the rule of law; but, I want to argue, it should also give the opportunity to a range of agents to create new ideas and visions for tackling problems such as climate change. So, prompted by the idea of shared responsibility, I want to conclude this chapter with some suggestions for how a notion of 'shared responsibility' can lead to forms of 'shared political action' in order to move forward on the problems of climate change.

4. Climate change, responsibility, and politics

There is obviously a wealth of scholarship on climate change, including the international and domestic legal dimensions. The focus of this chapter is less on the detailed analyses of the law surrounding climate change policy but instead the ways in which the idea of political responsibility might be deployed in responding to the dilemmas raised by it.

It is worth highlighting that responsibility plays a central part in discussions of climate change. As noted in the introduction, most scientific analyses point to the role that human action has played in bringing about climate change. Rather than legal, moral, or political responsibility, this point is really something closer to causal responsibility. That is, no one individual or group of individuals 'intended' to bring about climate change. Rather, it is the result of the cumulative actions of the entire human race.[39] One might argue, then, that there is no moral or legal responsibility for climate change since no agent intended it, and no agent was in any particular role that generates the responsibility to resolve the problem. Here, though, the idea of shared responsibility becomes helpful. One might go so far as to say that there is a universally shared responsibility for climate change, one that has moral and political implications. International politics and law have tried to turn this into a single multilateral treaty regime, the Kyoto Protocol, as a way to share that responsibility. But, as the political debate highlights, this responsibility is differentiated, which means that those states or companies generating more carbon dioxide (CO^2) than others will be responsible for different forms of action. This has led to debates about developing world

[39] Nollkaemper and Jacobs identity cumulative responsibility as a subgroup of shared responsibility, see 'Shared Responsibility in International Law: A Conceptual Framework', n. 7, at 368.

responsibilities in relation to developed world states, debates which have been highly contentious and which feed into the colonial legacy of the global system.

Rather than engage directly in this legal debate or try to parse out exactly which responsibilities are to be attributed to which agents, I want to highlight some alternative responses that build on the idea of responsibility for climate change but turn toward political action. Each of these actions will be located in terms of the idea of responsibility on which they rely and will be evaluated in terms of the concept of shared political responsibility that I have developed in the previous section.

4.1 *Liberal individuals and climate change*

Political philosophers have approached the problem of climate change in terms of the liberal individual, especially in terms of the individual's moral responsibilities. There is a large body of literature that seeks to address these themes, but a recent work provides one possible political response worth considering. Elizabeth Cripps argues that climate change generates a set of moral responsibilities, but the ability to fulfil these responsibilities is severely hampered by the practical problems of collective action. But Cripps does not abandon her notion of responsibility, but explores the nature of the choices that individuals have when it comes to this issue. Her argument makes an interesting move in that she suggests our failure to act will 'mar' us as individuals, resulting in a stunted conception of ourselves and our place in the world if we fail to act. In addition, because climate change requires collective action Cripps suggests that for us to reconcile the potential tensions that arise from our inability to reconcile our responsibilities we must engage in some form of collective action to address climate change.[40]

Cripps' account provides us with a morally grounded reason to act, one that moves away from the liberal account of rights toward something like a republican account of active citizenship. Yet, she does not provide any details about how that responsibility might be fulfilled, instead providing moral reasons for why we should feel responsible and how individuals should be able to translate their internal feelings of responsibility into some form of political action.

[40] E. Cripps, *Climate Change and the Moral Agent: Individual Duties in an Interdependent World* (Oxford University Press, 2013).

Some who write from within the tradition of liberal political philosophy suggest ways that we might turn this internal responsibility into concrete political actions. One political response comes from those who argue that there are a set of environmental rights that generate obligations or responsibilities in association with those rights. There are two versions of this argument. The first argues that states need to make concrete the right to a clean environment through changes to their constitutions. The clearest position along these lines comes from Tim Hayward who argues that there is a universal right to a clean environment which ought to be made part of each state's constitution.[41] Hayward adopts a Hohfeldian set of assumptions about rights and obligations, which means that any right generates a set of corresponding duties or obligations. This is the stronger notion of responsibility identified earlier, one that is not moral but strongly legal. In fact, Hayward does not use the idea of responsibility in his analysis. Moreover, his account proposes that such rights must be justiciable in order for them to be meaningful. This state-based conception of constitutional responsibility is an important move from Cripps' account of the need to act into a practical and political outcome. Yet, precisely because it is focused on national constitutions, Hayward's account does not quite correspond to the idea of shared political responsibility developed in this chapter. The idea of shared responsibility proposed by Nollkaemper and Jacobs highlights the essentially international character of certain issues, and proposes a way in which different agents, not just states, can contribute to how we might respond to this. At the same time, Hayward's idea about how states can act by changing their constitutions is an important part of the construction of this shared response.

A different but related political account comes from Andrew Dobson who proposes a form of 'environmental citizenship'.[42] Dobson's account of citizenship moves beyond the state and even beyond a liberal focus on rights. Instead, he argues for a more republican inspired notion of citizenship, one that prompts new forms of political action that transcend obligations to a single community and instead seek to formulate response to the global problems of the environment. He argues for a form of 'ecological' citizenship rather than merely environmental, the distinction being one that draws on an understanding of the human relation to the environment that goes beyond merely protecting the human race and

[41] T. Hayward, *Constitutional Environmental Rights* (Oxford University Press, 2005).
[42] A. Dobson, *Citizenship and the Environment* (Oxford University Press, 2003).

moves toward a deeper engagement with the natural world. Dobson focuses his practical responses on education, arguing that even in traditional liberal societies there is a responsibility to teach future generations about the environment in ways that go beyond their own communities.

These three accounts build on the idea of the individual agent, but take that agency in different directions. Cripps, by turning inward, suggests how the individual's moral responsibility can generate collective actions. Hayward makes concrete how that action can be turned into constitution making. And Dobson points us to how we can move beyond the liberal individual state. The modes of action proposed here do point us toward different ways we might engage in the global order, which can contribute to the idea of shared political responsibility developed in the preceding section. The ideas developed here should be read as how we might construct some actionable responses to climate change.

4.2 *Responding to international legal responsibility*

The preceding accounts focused on themes arising from the state, rights, and citizenship, although they seek to transcend them. Other efforts to deal with climate change and environmental issues begin with international elements but turn those into local action. The first comes from an innovative book by Walter Baber and Robert Bartlett, *Global Democracy and Sustainable Jurisprudence*, who address head on one of the problems of environmental politics – the debate surrounding the scientific evidence about various issues, which leaves many individuals around the world unwilling or unable to act politically to change it.[43] They argue that there is a responsibility not only to act, but to understand more clearly what is happening in the environment, something that they do not believe can be left only to the scientific community. As such, they propose the use of deliberative democracy as a means to generate political change. Importantly, writing from the perspective of international law, they suggest that there needs to be communities created around the world that can play a role in translating environmental science and political action into various forms of law making. These communities of deliberation can be structured around specific problems in communities but then translate those problems to a global scope and begin linking them together. Such groups would include scientists, political

[43] W.F. Baber and R.V. Bartlett, *Global Democracy and Sustainable Jurisprudence: Deliberative Environmental Law* (Boston, MA: MIT Press, 2009).

activists, and lawyers in an effort to create materials that could be turned into national, regional, or even international law.

This proposal maps on well with the idea of shared political responsibility developed in this chapter. Multiple sites of agency with different forms of representation might contribute to a new political movement. With both political and educative dimensions, these small councils can be part of a wider discursive structure that shares the responsibilities of climate change, but turns those shared needs into actions. It builds on the ideas of Cripps, Hayward, and Dobson in that it allows individuals to act, can contribute to national and even global constitutions, and provides a means to better educate the wider global public.

Matthew Hoffman provides evidence for how activism around climate change has emerged at a range of levels, often in response to the failure of international legal efforts to create multilateral treaties. His argument is less a normative one and more of a descriptive or explanatory one, in which he explores various 'experiments' at dealing with climate change that have arisen since the passage of the Kyoto Protocol.[44] Hoffman's account points to the ways in which schemes such as regional cap and trade agreements in North America, ones which cross the US-Canadian border, or municipal efforts to limit carbon emissions have been emerged in the fact of national failures to act. The US Congress, for instance, has failed to act on its commitments to the Kyoto Protocol which has resulted in US governors and mayors acting in their place. Additionally, Hoffman points to how multinational companies like Cisco Corporation have worked with NGOs such as the Clinton Foundation to encourage greater internet connectivity in cities to lessen the carbon impact of commuting. These efforts are prompted by the idea of responsibility, and an acknowledgement that the international legal responsibilities of states has not been translated into action. As such, actors at a number of different levels have moved responsibility from the state, to state treaty making processes, to forms of political action.

This account suggests some ways in which existing government structures, as opposed to Baber and Bartlett's proposed structures, are acting in the face of failed efforts of states. Hoffman's suggestions are useful in allowing us to see how shared political responsibility can emerge from diverse levels of government. Here we find actual descriptions of political action that can generate new insights and policies on climate change. As

[44] M.J. Hoffman, *Climate Governance at the Crossroads: Experimenting with a Global Response after Kyoto* (Oxford University Press, 2011).

Hoffman notes, these are experiments, so there is no guarantee of their success. But, as Arendt and others have argued, at times we need to engage in efforts to create new structures without full knowledge of what the outcome will be.

4.3 *Radical responsibility*

The previous examples point to ways in which political action can arise from discourses of responsibility. The last example I wish to highlight is a more radical one, drawing on a deeper ecological sentiment than the previous analyses which, as a result, challenges our accepted meanings of agency and responsibility. Jane Bennet argues in *Vibrant Matter* that an anthropocentric approach to political life fails to appreciate the complexities of agency. She argues that distinguishing between matter and life, as much of philosophical and political discourse does without thinking, ignores various ways in which political life is shaped by non-human materiality. For instance, she looks to an essay by Charles Darwin whose study of worms ended with the pithy observation that they 'make history'.[45] She acknowledges that this is a form of anthropomorphism but she embraces this accusation rather than defend against it. Using Jacques Ranciere's notion of democracy as a form of irruption, she argues that such irruptions in political life need not come from intentional human persons but can come from various forces in the wider world. Darwin's point was that worms keep in place certain artefacts and destroy others, making them authors of a kind of history. This agency is vital to how history evolves and how humans understand themselves.

How does this relate to the questions of responsibility for climate change in this chapter? Bennett only briefly refers to climate change, but her argument is directly relevant to the claims I am making. Early in her text, she highlights how responsibility assumes an intentional agent who we can identify and reward or punish if necessary. Drawing here on Connolly's critique of the politics of responsibility,[46] Bennett suggests that if we relax our assumptions about human agency and allow other forms of agency to develop, our ideas about responsibility will also evolve. Using the idea of an assemblage (from Deleuze and Guatarri), Bennett argues that responsibility is better located in 'human-nonhuman

[45] J. Bennett, *Vibrant Matter: A Political Ecology of Things* (Durham: Duke University Press, 2010), at 94–109.

[46] W. Connolly, *Identity/Difference*, n. 15, at 16–35.

assemblages'.[47] Rather than a resignation that no one is to blame, however, Bennett encourages us to consider how to respond as persons to this situation of political responsibility. She argues that we must resist a politics of blame and instead consider how we should relate to the human-nonhuman assemblages in which we are enmeshed.

This is, admittedly, a more radical response to environmental problems and is less concrete than some of the suggestions listed earlier. What it does, however, is highlight the ways in which the very concepts of agency and responsibility might be limiting our ability to respond to the environment. Bennet is a political theorist, so she argues for a politics of change. But it is a politics of change and action that force us to confront some of our ingrained assumptions about what responsibility means. And, interestingly, with her focus on the idea of assemblages, Bennet suggests a slightly different idea of 'shared politics', though perhaps without the element of responsibility. That is, her argument is one that brings together not just individual people, but a wider range of 'agents' in our understanding of the problems of climate change and our possible responses to it.

5. Conclusion

In conclusion, this chapter has built on the idea of shared responsibility in the international legal framework of Nollkaemper and Jacobs to develop an idea of shared political responsibility. In so doing, I am not trying to argue that we need to put aside legal responsibility or the international legal context. Indeed, some of what I consider to be the most innovate ideas reviewed here can take up the theme of shared responsibility and develop it in new ways. For instance, the notion of shared legal responsibility might be one way to interpret the modes of mixed political action that Hoffman describes, or the locations of deliberative action that Baber and Bartlett propose. More radically, Bennett's ideas about assemblages suggest a sharing of responsibility not only with persons but with a wider ambit of the natural world.

The primary point I wish to make is that our discourse of responsibility, while viewed through moral and legal frames, can also be seen through a political one. Arendt's idea that collective responsibility means we must accept that being part of a community generates responsibilities

[47] Bennett, *Vibrant Matter*, n. 45, at 36.

to act is one that permeates this chapter. If we expand Arendt's frame to see that we are part of the 'human' community or, in accordance with Bennett, a 'natural' community, then perhaps our modes of action will turn to new and different frames. The nature of shared political responsibility provides a possible way to act in the current global order. The problems of climate change demand nothing less.

4

Ex Ante and *Ex Post* Allocation of International Legal Responsibility

JOEL P. TRACHTMAN*

1. Introduction: shared responsibility and national measures

In the end, or '*ex post*', all international legal responsibility is individual state responsibility. Shared responsibility must be allocated somehow, even if the rule is one of joint and several liability.[1] Also joint liability can result in certainty regarding allocation, so long as the rights of contribution are clear and the factual bases for contribution are known in advance.

However, the allocation of responsibility might not be known *ex ante*. First, the principle of allocation may be uncertain. Second, even if the principle of allocation is well known, its operation may be dependent on facts that are not known, probably because they will occur in the future. To the extent that these two reasons for uncertainty *ex ante* regarding allocation are resolved, and allocation to individual countries can be determined *ex ante* on the basis of the principles, then it might be better to speak of the individual responsibility of multiple countries. Under other circumstances, where the principles of allocation are unknown, or the facts that form the basis for allocation are unknown, or both, we may speak of shared responsibility *ex ante*.

With the rise of globalisation increasing the extent to which people from different parts of the globe interact with one another, there are increasing ways in which people from different parts of the globe confer

* Professor of International Law, The Fletcher School of Law and Diplomacy. I am grateful to participants in the SHARES project, as well as to Jeffrey Dunoff, Simon Lester, Gabrielle Marceau, Petros Mavroidis, Greg Shaffer, and participants in the Georgetown Law Centre faculty workshop, for comments on an earlier draft, and to Juan David Velasco for excellent research assistance. Errors are mine.

[1] See for the concept of shared responsibility P.A. Nollkaemper and D. Jacobs, 'Introduction: Mapping the Normative Framework for the Distribution of Shared Responsibility', Chapter 1 of this volume, 1.

benefits or detriments on one another. They may do so by the way that they husband a shared resource, or regulate a dangerous activity, or respond to a shared danger.

There is no logical difference between the iconic shared responsibility situation described by the editors in their framing article,[2] in which countries are seen factually to all have a contributory causal role in causing a single problem, and any other circumstance in which the actions of one country is seen to cause harm to another country. Indeed, as the authors point out:

> The criteria that may be used in apportioning responsibilities ex ante may not be dissimilar from those used to apportion responsibilities after harm is caused. Criteria such as of capacity, contribution, control and causation will be relevant both when states ex ante agree who is to carry what burden, and when courts make ex post facto determinations of responsibility.[3]

Consider the Coasean example of a laundry that is located near a coal-fired utility that produces smoke. Coase's insight is that the harm is a result of the *joint* action of the laundry and the utility.[4] Even though we tend to place these facts in a framework of one-way causation and unilateral responsibility, Coase showed that it is equally possible to understand these facts in terms of bilateral causation and responsibility.

Causation in this sense is reciprocal, and the core question from an efficiency standpoint is how to determine whether either the utility or the laundry should change its behaviour to increase efficiency. Coase argued that under zero transaction costs, the utility and the laundry would negotiate to the efficient solution. In this analytical sense, all responsibility should be analysed as shared responsibility. The question, under positive transaction costs and with concerns regarding distributive outcomes, is how it should be allocated among the parties.

This gives rise to the Coasean question: to what extent should principles of law be established to require acting states to internalise the beneficial or detrimental effects that they impose on one another? In an important sense, this could be determined on an ad hoc basis – before each action, states could negotiate over whether the action will be taken

[2] P.A. Nollkaemper and D. Jacobs, 'Shared Responsibility in International Law: A Conceptual Framework' (2013) 34 MIJIL 359, at 366.

[3] Ibid., at 394 (citation omitted).

[4] R.H. Coase, 'The Problem of Social Cost' (1960) 3 JLE 1.

or not, and whether and to what extent compensation will be paid to the state that bears the detriment, or by the state that receives the benefit.

There are two problems with this ad hoc approach. First, it is dependent on any initial assignment of property rights that has been established in advance. If no assignment has been established, then the negotiation begins with a clean slate, and perhaps bilateral monopoly: a standoff in which neither party is willing to yield. But in the modern world, there are already legal rules that might provide a default allocation of property rights. One example is the right of territorial sovereignty. Another might be the *sic utere tuo* principle of international environmental law.

Second, the appeal of the ad hoc approach is dependent on transaction costs. As Coase showed, long-term contracting, law, or even an international organisation might be justified if it allows for more efficient action without excessive transaction costs. In other words, even assuming that a better choice would be made if the choosing state internalised the costs of its action, the costs of identifying the problem, negotiating about it, contracting over it, and enforcing the contract must be included in the calculus of whether a mechanism of internalisation is worthwhile, and which instrument of internalisation is best.

As they decide how to address these problems of policy externalities, states may use very specific legal rules that allocate responsibility for action *ex ante*, or they may use more general principles that require analysis in order to determine the allocation of responsibility *ex post*. In designing these rules, states would wish to maximise the net benefits of internalisation of policy externalities, net of transaction costs. The net benefits of internalisation include the negative effect of reduced policy autonomy ('autonomy costs'). If the costs of reduced policy autonomy exceed the benefits of internalisation, no internalisation should take place.

The purpose of this chapter is to describe and provide a normative framework for analysis of several alternative means of international legal restriction of national measures. As international law has increasingly reached into domestic regulatory processes, it has become necessary to explicitly balance different types of concerns. At the same time, the variety of restrictions on national regulatory measures has increased, and it is worthwhile to begin to compare these different types of restrictions in order to inform and critique international law making.

The traditional way in which international law restrains national action is through direct substantive prohibitions. For example, with exaggerated simplicity, you may not abridge the human rights of your citizens, you may not discriminate between goods coming from different states, and you may not engage in aggressive war. These norms can be articulated with more or less specificity. To the extent that they are articulated with less specificity, it might be said that the final allocation of responsibility must take place *ex post*, upon an evaluation of the particular circumstances of the state action or inaction. Whether curtailment of a human right is justified, whether distinct treatment is indeed illegally discriminatory or instead has a legitimate basis, and whether a war is aggressive depends on a number of factors that may only be determined in context.

But there is another emergent way in which international law restrains state action: by requiring the state to engage in a specified procedure as a condition for certain actions. This chapter provides some examples of this type of procedural predicate for national action in international law, and provides a normative framework for determining when a procedural predicate would be desirable compared to a simple prohibition on action.

1.1 Requirements regarding substance: state contingency

Law is always expressed as an 'if-then' statement: if A, B, and C, then D. The most common form of this type of if-then statement is that, if factual conditions A, B, and C are met, then the requisite elements of a particular offense are satisfied, and legal consequences D will ensue. International law is often structured this way, but alternatively, and increasingly, international legal rules specify that countries may take certain actions if, and only if, specified conditions are met. Instead of the legal consequence being a finding of violation in this logical formulation, the legal consequence is a permission for action. If the conditions were not met, the action was not permitted and is illegal. Of course, this distinction is largely one of style, or of emphasis, but the distinction is nevertheless important. States are given explicit prescriptions as to how to take specific actions.

Furthermore, in a number of observable contexts, the factual conditions are becoming more complex, requiring greater information and expertise for their determination. These complex conditions may be understood in terms of state-contingent incomplete contracting ('state contingency'), in which legal rules do not specifically determine the legality of behaviour in advance. The idea of 'state contingency' is that the application of the rule is dependent on the future state – on the facts as they arise. For example, if, and only if, there is observed (A) a surge in imports, (B) serious injury to a domestic industry, and (C) causation of B by A, then a state may be permitted (D) to impose a safeguard action restricting imports from other states. In this formulation, which is a simplification of relevant World Trade Organization (WTO) law, the legality of D (the safeguard action) is dependent on the objective existence of A, B, and C. Thus, countries are prohibited from taking the actions if the specified conditions are not met. So, in the application and enforcement of international law, it is incumbent upon countries, and upon enforcers, to determine whether the specified conditions are met.

Because the concerns of international law increasingly have to do with the external effects of the regulatory activities of countries, international legal rules are increasingly set up as complex if-then statements about the existence of specified conditions for national regulatory action. The international legal rules are state-contingent incomplete contracts. In order to take the regulatory action, these conditions must exist. The country itself, as the regulated person, is implicitly required to ensure that the conditions exist. Conversely, the action is forbidden if the conditions are not met.

In addition, those responsible for enforcement, whether they are other countries in this generally horizontal system, or international tribunals or political bodies, must determine for themselves whether these conditions exist in order to be able to determine whether the state's action is lawful. However, there are several problems with this determination by other countries and international tribunals or political bodies. First, they may not have access to the information required to make this determination ('information problems'). Second, they may not have the requisite economic, scientific, or other analytical capacity to make this determination ('expertise problems'). Third, concerns about preservation of national autonomy under globalisation may make it difficult for countries to relinquish this decision-making authority ('autonomy problems'). Under these circumstances, countries formulating international law rules may structure them in terms of conditions that relate not to the substantive existence of specified facts, but to the decision-making procedures carried out by the national authority ('procedure contingency') to determine the existence of those facts, without examining whether the country acting was actually correct in its determination.

Furthermore, although countries will negotiate different forms of state contingency and procedure contingency with their own strategic position in mind, from a purely welfare standpoint, we would expect them to seek to maximise the sum of the benefits from cooperation and the costs of information problems, expertise problems, and autonomy problems. Procedure contingency may generally implicate a lower level of information, expertise, and autonomy problems, although there may be concerns regarding whether it can adequately address cooperation problems.

State contingency is an important way in which countries allocate responsibility for the costs of action. For example, state contingency in international trade law determines whether the importing country can take trade restrictive action without compensating the exporting country.

State contingency is a special type of allocation of responsibility that sets its parameters *ex ante*, but whose application in practice is only determinable *ex post*, once the state of affairs is known: allocation of responsibility is dependent upon the state of the world pursuant to which action is taken. But state contingency often involves complex *ex post* judgments as to the state of the world when action was taken. Furthermore, state contingency can involve delegation of the task of determining whether the preconditions are satisfied to third-party decision-makers.

1.2 Specific rules and general standards regarding substance

Contracts may be structured to be more or less incomplete: to be more or less specific. Likewise, state contingent contracting, and procedure contingent contracting, can be more or less specific. If it is more specific, then the 'if' portions of the if-then statements contain specific, formally realisable components. For example, if each of the conditions for safeguards action listed previously were clear and relatively easily determinable, there would be little work for a judge or other evaluator but to make those factual determinations. On the other hand, to the extent that the if-then statement contains less specific standards, less well-defined and perhaps more difficult to determine, such as a requirement of 'due process' or a requirement that in order for discrimination to be found there must be differential treatment of 'like products', the judge or other evaluator would have more latitude, and more responsibility, in determining a violation. Under what circumstances are more specific rules superior tools compared to more general standards, and vice-versa?

1.3 Requirements regarding process: procedure contingency

Moreover, the preconditions for national action, as often found in administrative law, are increasingly procedural (procedure contingency) rather than substantive (state contingency): they require states to make certain findings in certain ways. Of course, procedure contingency is based on, and is related to, state contingency, but it is by no means the same thing. The preconditions are not substantive or factual regarding the objective state of the world, but relate to the procedure followed by the acting country to determine the state of the world.

Procedure contingency may replace state contingency, or may supplement state contingency. Where procedure contingency replaces state contingency, these procedural conditions precedent might be said to delegate to countries the job of determining the existence of the predicate facts necessary as a condition for their action. Where procedure contingency supplements state contingency, in order for a country's action to be permissible, the country must have followed the specified procedures and its resultant determination of the state of the world must in addition be determined to be objectively correct. In this case, presumably there is some intrinsic value ascribed to proper procedure. These choices necessarily involve different burdens of proof, standards of review, and allocation of workload compared to state contingency.

1.4 Interaction between state contingency, rules and standards, and procedure contingency

International law constrains national action. As countries formulate more international law, with greater constraints, they may do so through flat prohibitions, but of course 'flat' prohibitions contain requirements for judgment in determining whether the conduct at issue fits into the prohibited category, and increasingly legal rules are framed explicitly in state contingent terms. Countries may express state contingency using more specific rules or more general standards. Indeed, they may express procedure contingency also using more specific rules or more general standards. Laws may be expressed purely in terms of state contingency or purely in terms of procedure contingency, or countries may determine to establish rules that set both a state and a procedure contingency for the same action.

1.5 Structure of the chapter

In section 2, I review selected instances in international law doctrine of the use of state contingency, rules, standards, and procedure contingency. This review is intended to be exemplary, rather than comprehensive. This chapter makes explicit the choices that authors of international legal rules may make in formulating international legal rules in terms of state contingency, more specific rules or more general standards, and procedure contingency. Doctrinally, it observes a drift in international trade law towards procedure contingency, even in some cases where the relevant text seems to call for state contingency.

In section 3, I develop a normative framework for assessing these different approaches to discipline of national action. As noted, international legal rules are formulated to cause internalisation of policy externalities. But they are also formulated to preserve maximum policy flexibility for the bound countries, consistent with appropriate internalisation. Indeed, in theory they are designed to maximise the sum of the welfare benefits and detriments of (a) internalisation of externalities, (b) transaction costs, and (c) autonomy costs.

In section 4, I conclude and suggest some avenues for further research.

2. The use in international law of state contingency, rules, standards, and procedure contingency

In this section, I provide selected examples of the uses of state contingency, rules, standards, and procedure contingency. The examples addressed include exceptions for national regulatory measures that are 'necessary' for protection of human health under WTO law (section 2.1), requirements that certain types of national regulation be supported by a scientific basis under WTO law (section 2.2), fair and equitable treatment standards in bilateral investment treaties (section 2.3), the use of complementarity under the Rome Statute for the International Criminal Court (section 2.4), and proportionality relating to protection of civilians in the laws of armed conflict (section 2.5). In section 3, I develop a normative framework for evaluating these structures.

2.1 'Necessity' analysis: Brazil-Tyres

Environmental protection presents many instances in which the actions of one state have an effect on the interests of another. It may be beneficial to a particular state to block imports of goods that create adverse consumption externalities. But it may be costly to the exporting state to find alternative markets for those goods. How are states to share responsibility for these types of goods? Under WTO law, members have agreed that under certain circumstances, the exporting country would bear the costs of any barriers, but that under other circumstances, the importing country would be required to compensate the exporting country.

A recent example of this type of problem was the dispute between Brazil and the European Union (EU) over Brazil's decision to block imports of retreaded automotive tires. On its face, the dispute was about whether the importing state would be required to compensate the exporting state, but at the core of this dispute was the question of which state would bear the costs of disposal of used tires. The EU benefited from the export of retreaded tires, while Brazil was concerned about the environmental damage that would come from the disposal of these retreaded tires after they reached the end of their useful life. Retreaded tires have a shorter useful life than new tires, and therefore have greater adverse consumption externalities.

The *Brazil-Tyres* case arises in this contentious terrain of overlap between trade policy and environmental policy. Free trade and national environmental protection measures are not always consistent. Yet the parties to the WTO decided, and committed in WTO law, that even where a national environmental protection measure would otherwise violate a free trade rule of the General Agreement on Tariffs and Trade (GATT),[5] the national environmental measure would generally be permitted, subject to certain conditions. It is important to recognise that members of the WTO were serious both about allowing great flexibility for national environmental measures, and about establishing some conditions so that this flexibility is neither unlimited nor abused. It is also important to recognise that by establishing the WTO dispute settlement system, members decided that WTO panels, and the Appellate Body on appeal, would generally decide disputes about the scope of this flexibility.

The *Brazil-Tyres* case,[6] decided by the WTO Appellate Body in 2007, presents a challenge to the analytical resources available in WTO dispute settlement. In *Brazil-Tyres*, the WTO dispute settlement tribunals seem to have shirked their responsibility to make substantive determinations of objective conditions of action in accordance with the WTO treaty.[7]

[5] General Agreement on Tariffs and Trade, Geneva, 30 October 1947, in force 1 January 1948, 55 UNTS 187 (GATT).

[6] *Brazil – Measures Affecting Imports of Retreaded Tyres*, Appellate Body Report, 17 December 2007, WT/DS332/AB/R (*Brazil-Tyres*).

[7] For a more detailed treatment, see C.P. Bown and J.P. Trachtman, 'Brazil – Measures Affecting Imports of Retreaded Tyres: A Balancing Act' (2009) 8 (Special Issue 1) WTR 85.

The Panel and the Appellate Body were called upon to decide the scope of Brazil's retained flexibility under WTO law to maintain an import ban on certain retreaded tires. In these decisions, the Panel and Appellate Body explored the scope of their own responsibility to evaluate and weigh several factors in connection with these types of cases under the exceptional provision of GATT relating to human health: Article XX(b).

Indeed, Article XX(b) is a good example of the type of state contingency pursuant to which WTO member countries divided responsibility for the trade detriments that may arise from health and certain types of environmental protection: to the extent that the trade detriments are necessary to protect human, animal, or plant life or health, the exporting country must bear the burden of reduced market access.[8]

As discussed in more detail in section 3, an optimal test in this type of case, unconstrained by treaty text, from the standpoint of global welfare maximisation, would simply use cost-benefit analysis to determine whether the national measure produces net benefits, or net cost-reductions, compared to alternative measures that might be considered (including inaction). Thus, a full cost-benefit analysis in this context would evaluate the following parameters on a global basis, considering the profiles of proposed alternatives: first, alue of the regulatory goal; second, contribution of the measure to achieving the regulatory goal; third, cost of the regulatory measure; and fourth, cost to trading partners via the mechanism of a restriction on trade.

Indeed, rational countries would write this test into their agreements, assuming that the transaction costs of carrying out this analysis do not exceed the benefits of carrying out the analysis.[9] In this type of case, interpreting the 'necessity' test of Article XX(b) (and Article XX(d)) GATT, the WTO Appellate Body has consistently spoken of a test that weighs and balances to some degree each of the four factors mentioned previously,[10] but it has never documented in an opinion its application of

[8] Interestingly, in the Appellate Body Report in the *Asbestos* case, the Appellate Body suggested that the state maintaining a trade barrier justified under Article XX(b) might be required to provide trade compensation to the exporting state under the doctrine of non-violation nullification or impairment. *European Communities – Measures Affecting Asbestos and Asbestos-Containing Products*, Appellate Body Report, 21 March 2001, WT/DS135/AB/R.

[9] J.P. Trachtman, 'Trade and ... Problems, Cost-Benefit Analysis and Subsidiarity' (1998) 9 EJIL 32.

[10] See e.g., *Korea – Measures Affecting Imports of Fresh, Chilled and Frozen Beef*, Appellate Body Report, 10 January 2001, WT/DS161/AB/R, WT/DS169/AB/R.

this type of test, or insisted that panels actually apply this type of balancing test.

Most importantly, in *Brazil-Tyres*, the Appellate Body has shown itself unwilling to evaluate for itself, or to require a panel to evaluate, in any but the most gross categories, any of these four factors. Yet, one might ask, if you consider these factors, but you do not evaluate them, in the sense of assessing their magnitude, and you do not compare them with one another – the costs with the benefits – how do you determine which domestic measures are acceptable and which are not? It seems that the only responsible answer is that without careful evaluation of these factors by the decision-maker, its only strategy other than ignorance is deference. This is the situation in which the Appellate Body found itself, and the result has been extreme deference to the importing country, but it is difficult to reconcile this degree of deference with the Appellate Body's treaty mandate.

It appears that the Panel, and the Appellate Body, sought to be deferential to Brazil's regulatory autonomy, especially in the environmental context. It is easy to see why this is an attractive course. But in order to rationalise deference, and a move in effect from state contingency to procedure contingency, the decisions have done much violence to text, to precedent, and to legal logic. The Appellate Body seemed to move to procedure contingency by virtue of the fact that it deferred to Brazil's balancing of the relevant factors.

Should the Appellate Body require panels to seek greater analytical capacity, perhaps in the form of expert assistance, in order to perform a more extensive analysis of these factors in particular cases? Until the Appellate Body does so, we can say that the rule has effectively been transformed from one of state contingency to one of procedure contingency, pursuant to which the international legal discipline applies to check whether the member seems, on the member's own analysis, to have selected the less trade restrictive alternative.

2.2 SPS requirements of scientific basis: EU-Hormones

When the WTO was established in 1995, additional requirements were imposed on the process of national product regulation, beyond those that applied under the GATT. These requirements give exporting countries greater opportunities to require importing countries to compensate them for barriers to trade. Responsibility is shared between importing and exporting countries based on a determination of whether the importing country complied with these requirements. Interestingly, in this area as well, WTO law seems to focus not on the substance of national regulation, but on the procedure for formulating national regulation.

Both the WTO Agreement on Technical Barriers to Trade[11] (TBT Agreement) and the WTO Agreement on the Application of Sanitary and Phytosanitary Measures[12] (SPS Agreement) contain requirements regarding the process for establishing product regulations. For example, key provisions of the SPS Agreement provide that countries must ensure that SPS measures are based on scientific principles (Article 2.2), and that a reflection of this requirement is that governments must base any SPS measure on an assessment of the risks to human, animal, or plant life or health, taking into account risk assessment techniques developed by relevant international organisations (Article 5.1). The risk assessment must identify the diseases, pests, etc. a country wants to prevent in its territory, identify the potential biological and economic consequences associated with such diseases, and evaluate the likelihood of entry, establishment, or spread of these diseases (Article 5.3). In the assessment of risks, available scientific evidence must be considered, as well as relevant processes and production methods; inspection, sampling and testing methods, and the prevalence of specific diseases or pests and environmental conditions (Article 5.2).

At the core of the European Union's appeal in the 2008 *Canada/ United States-Continued Suspension* case was the argument that the panel had substituted its own judgment for that of the relevant WTO member: the European Union.[13] The Appellate Body clarified that 'the review power of a panel is not to determine whether the risk assessment undertaken by a WTO Member is correct, but rather to determine whether that risk assessment is supported by coherent reasoning and respectable scientific evidence and is, in this sense, objectively justifiable'.[14] That is, the test is not state contingency but procedure contingency.

[11] Agreement on Technical Barriers to Trade, 15 April 1994, in force 1 January 1995, 1868 UNTS 120 (TBT Agreement).

[12] Agreement on the Application of Sanitary and Phytosanitary Measures, 15 April 1994, in force 1 January 1995, 1867 UNTS 493 (SPS Agreement).

[13] *United States – Continued Suspension of Obligations in the EC – Hormones Dispute*, WT/DS320/AB/R, European Communities' Appellant's Submission, para. 248 (*Continued Suspension*).

[14] *United States – Continued Suspension of Obligations in the EC – Hormones Dispute*, Appellate Body Report, 14 November 2008, WT/DS320/AB/R, para. 590.

A panel must also determine whether the results of the risk assessment 'sufficiently warrant' the SPS measure.[15] In first looking at expert opinion, and then examining whether the European Union's risk assessment agreed with this opinion, the Panel gave too little deference to the member's retained autonomy to engage in its own risk assessments.[16] Therefore, the Appellate Body determined that 'the Panel failed to conduct an objective assessment of the facts of the case, as required by Article 11 of the Dispute Settlement Understanding, in determining whether the European Communities' risk assessment satisfied the requirements of Article 5.1 and Annex A of the SPS Agreement'.[17]

Accordingly, the Appellate Body reversed the Panel's finding that the European Union failed to satisfy the requirements of Article 5.1 and Annex A, paragraph 4, of the SPS Agreement. In the earlier discussion of *Brazil-Tyres*, it was seen that a balancing test may be very demanding to apply in technical terms, and that panels may avoid carrying out these tests as described.[18] In fact, these tests may require the panel to second-guess some of the public policy evaluations that governments often carry out in order to determine their measures. This type of second-guessing is precisely the type of judicial exercise that has been rejected under the scientific basis provisions of the SPS Agreement. Indeed, the Appellate Body decision in the *Continued Suspension* case may be understood along parallel lines, as an interpretation of the SPS Agreement that limits the scope of international judicial scrutiny of national use of science as a basis for public policy.

2.3 Fair and equitable treatment under international investment law: Metalclad v. Mexico

In another area of international economic law – international investment law – home countries and host countries share responsibility for harm to investments in the host country in a similar way: restrictions on national action giving rise to host country responsibility contain elements of state contingency and procedure contingency. As to procedure contingency, the International Centre for the Settlement of Investment Disputes'

[15] Ibid., para. 591. [16] Ibid., paras. 598–602. [17] Ibid., para. 616.

[18] Bown and Trachtman, 'Brazil – Measures Affecting Imports of Retreaded Tyres: A Balancing Act', n. 7.

(ICSID) arbitral decision in the case of *Metalclad* v. *Mexico*[19] provides an important example.

North American Free Trade Agreement (NAFTA)[20] Article 1105(1) provides as follows:

> Each Party shall accord to investments of investors of another Party treatment in accordance with international law, including fair and equitable treatment and full protection and security.

In the *Metalclad* case, applying Article 1105(1) of NAFTA, the Tribunal found that:

> Mexico failed to ensure a transparent and predictable framework for Metalclad's business planning and investment. The totality of these circumstances demonstrates a lack of orderly process and timely disposition in relation to an investor of a Party acting in the expectation that it would be treated fairly and justly in accordance with the NAFTA.[21]

This is a clear example of international investment law constituting a kind of global administrative law,[22] in this case providing for procedural review of environmental permitting in Mexico.

2.4 Complementarity in the ICC

Complementarity is an emerging approach to the role of international law and institutions. It makes the use of international law and institutions contingent on failure by countries to take sufficient *procedural* steps. In this way, it can be understood as a type of procedure contingency: it does not require that national prosecutions convict guilty defendants – it merely requires that appropriate prosecutions take place. A leading example of complementarity can be seen in the Rome Statute of the International Criminal Court (ICC).[23]

[19] *Metalclad Corporation* v. *The United Mexican States*, ICSID Case No. ARB(AF)/97/1, Award, 30 August 2000 (*Metalclad*).

[20] North American Free Trade Agreement (NAFTA), Washington, 17 December 1992, in force 1 January 1994, (1993) 32 ILM 289.

[21] *Metalclad Corporation* v. *The United Mexican States*, n. 19, para. 99.

[22] See G. Van Harten and M. Loughlin, 'Investment Treaty Arbitration as a Species of Global Administrative Law' (2006) 17 EJIL 121 (emphasising other aspects of international investment law as global administrative law).

[23] Rome Statute of the International Criminal Court, Rome, 17 July 1998, in force 1 July 2002, 2187 UNTS 90.

The jurisdiction of the ICC is intended to be complementary to national criminal jurisdiction. Therefore, under Article 17 of the Rome Statute, a case otherwise within the ICC's jurisdiction will be inadmissible when it 'is being investigated or prosecuted by a State which has jurisdiction over it, unless the State is unwilling or unable genuinely to carry out the investigation or prosecution' and under other related circumstances.[24] Conversely, the powers of the ICC to act in relation to a case become effective only where the relevant states are unwilling or unable to carry out the investigation or prosecution. Note that this arrangement can be characterised in either of two ways: first, as a limited delegation by states to the ICC, or second, as a limited delegation by the ICC to states. As a limited delegation to states, it ensures that states have a certain measure of incentives to investigate or prosecute relevant crimes, or simply supplements their capabilities where they are unable to do so.

2.5 *Proportionality in the law of armed conflict*

Jus in bello proportionality requires that the damage to civilians caused by an act of war not be excessive in relation to the anticipated military advantage.[25] Specifically, Article 51(4) of the Additional Protocol to the Geneva Convention of 1977[26] provides that 'indiscriminate attacks are prohibited'. Article 51(5) provides that '[a]mong others, the following types of attacks are to be considered as indiscriminate (a) . . . and (b) An attack which may be expected to cause incidental loss of civilian life, injury to civilians, damage to civilian objects, or a combination thereof, which would be excessive in relation to the concrete and direct military advantage anticipated.'

Similarly, Article 8(2)(b)(iv) of the Rome Statute of the International Criminal Court provides that the following is a war crime, subject to the jurisdiction of the ICC: 'Intentionally launching an attack in the knowledge that such attack will cause incidental loss of life or injury to civilians or damage to civilian objects or widespread, long-term and

[24] See *The Prosecutor* v. *Francis Kirimi Muthaura, Uhuru Muigai Kenyatta and Mohammed Hussein Ali*, Case No. ICC-01/09-02/11 OA, 30 August 2011, at 13, para. 35 (finding that Kenya had not adequately shown that it satisfied the requirement to investigate or prosecute).

[25] Protocol Additional to the Geneva Conventions of 12 August 1949, and relating to the Protection of Victims of International Armed Conflicts (Protocol I), Geneva, 8 June 1977, in force 7 December 1979, 1125 UNTS 3, Article 51(5)(b).

[26] Ibid., Article 51(4).

severe damage to the natural environment which would be clearly excessive in relation to the concrete and direct overall military advantage anticipated.' This formulation provides some clarification that the intent and knowledge of the attacker, as well as the military advantage anticipated by the attacker, are critical to the analysis. Under this formulation, if the incidental loss is far greater than the achieved advantage, it is still possible for the attacker to be innocent, so long as his anticipation of loss is not excessive in relation to his anticipation of advantage. Of course, these elements are quite incommensurable.

The attacker is required to engage in a procedure designed to determine whether its attack is proportionate.[27] The law of armed conflict principle of precaution similarly requires attackers to engage in a procedure designed to protect civilians.[28] These rules seem to constitute a type of procedure contingency. They require that a procedure be followed as a predicate for action, not that a specific set of substantive facts be true as a predicate.

3. Normative evaluation

In section 2, I described instances of state contingency in international law, noting that state contingency may be framed in more specific 'rules' and in less specific 'standards'. Rules involve greater *ex ante* specification, and standards provide for more *ex post* specification of responsibility. I also described instances of procedure contingency in international law. What is the utility of international legal rules that incorporate state contingency? When are more specific rules superior to less specific standards? Finally, why would countries use procedure contingency instead of state contingency? This section develops some frameworks for analysis of the utility of these different types of legal rules.

[27] J.-M. Henckaerts and L. Oswald-Beck, 'Customary International Humanitarian Law Volume I: Rules', International Committee of the Red Cross (Cambridge University Press, 2005) (ICRC Rules), Rule 14; M. Cohen-Eliya, 'The Formal and Substantive Meanings of Proportionality in the Supreme Court's Decision Regarding the Security Fence' (2005) 38 Isr LR 262, at 288–289.

[28] 'Precaution requires that, before every attack, armed forces must do everything feasible to: (i) verify the target is legitimate, (ii) determine what the collateral damage would be and assess necessity and proportionality, and (iii) minimize the collateral loss of lives and/or property.' Report of the Special Rapporteur on Extrajudicial, Summary or Arbitrary Executions, Philip Alston, 28 May 2010, para. 58, citing Additional Protocol I, n. 25, Article 57; Ibid., ICRC Rules, Rules 15–21.

These issues do not seem relevant to the iconic areas of shared responsibility, such as the classic case of degradation of an environmental commons. However, they are relevant to the construction of new rules by which to address these iconic areas of shared responsibility: the designers of these rules will need to choose between *ex ante* specification by virtue of rules, and *ex post* specification through application of standards, and between state contingency and procedure contingency.

3.1 International law and policy externalities: the value of taking into account the concerns of other states

According to the subsidiarity principle, states should have no concern with the activities of other states, unless those activities cause external effects. Broadly speaking, there should be no international law without international external effects, including the effects entailed by public goods, economies of scale, and regulatory competition. These external effects may be physical, market-transmitted ('pecuniary'), moral, or aesthetic. They may be beneficial or harmful.

Thus, for example, the financial regulation, environmental regulation, or other regulation (or deficiencies therein) in one state may be associated with adverse or beneficial effects (negative or positive externalities) in other states. Externalities may be addressed through rules of jurisdiction that accord the affected state control over the injurious behaviour.

Thus, there will be circumstances in which international cooperation is useful in order to cause states to internalise externalities: to establish congruence between decision-making authority and the effects of the exercise of authority. In an increasingly interdependent world, we would expect increasing instances in which the national exercise of authority has consequences for people outside the national political community. Thus, the Pigovian function of international law is to bring the international effects of national decisions to bear on national authorities, where, as Coase pointed out, it is worthwhile in transaction cost terms to do so. This is the only way to address issues of shared responsibility.

3.2 Incomplete contracts and state contingency

Henrik Horn notes that a complete contract that specifies permissible policies in all possible states of the world is simply infeasible: the costs of writing and enforcing any such agreement are prohibitive even assuming heroically that governments are able to specify *ex ante* all the regulatory needs, and needs for exceptions, that may arise in the future.[29] So, no international legal regime is ever completely specified in terms of rules.

The GATT provisions described in *Brazil-Tyres*, the SPS provisions addressed in *Continued Suspension*, and the rule of proportionality in the law of armed conflict, can be regarded as components of state contingent contracts, delegating to the dispute settlement process, where available, the task of determining the state. But these provisions refer to a state that is described by virtue of conditions such as less trade restrictive alternative, lack of scientific basis, proportionality, etc. The implication is that in these contexts, the degree to which state contingencies result in beneficial internalisation of externalities (i.e., in contract completeness) needs to be examined *ex post*.

Analysing the GATT national treatment rules in these terms, Horn develops a model in which for given tariff commitments, a marginally binding national treatment provision will increase government welfare, but moving beyond this and further tightening national treatment may reduce welfare. A state-contingent rule is efficient.

The problem caused by tariff bindings combined with a hypothesised strict national treatment rule (one that is unable to use regulatory categories to distinguish between products) is that insofar as imported products cause externalities, governments no longer can use the tariff to offset these externalities. Instead they must use domestic instruments, which, because of national treatment, must apply equally to local and imported goods. As a result, an importing country that is being forced to abide by an equal or non-discriminatory taxation requirement will set a uniform domestic tax that is, from an international efficiency point of view, too high with regard to the domestic product (which is assumed not to produce a negative externality), and too low with regard to the imported product (which is assumed to produce a negative externality).

As a consequence, provided the externality problem is sufficiently severe, the imposition of national treatment may be internationally inefficient.[30]

[29] H. Horn, 'National Treatment in the GATT' (2006) 96 AER 394.

[30] Costinot develops a model showing that national treatment results in standards that are excessively restrictive, due to failure to take account of the interests of foreign producers exporting to the regulating market. On the other hand, under a regime of mutual recognition in which each state undertakes to accept as satisfactory the regulation of the home state of the exported good, standards will be too low due to a race to the bottom effect in which the regulating government fails to account for foreign externalities. See A. Costinot, 'A Comparative Institutional Analysis of Agreements on Product Standards' (2008) 75 JIE 197.

But the GATT national treatment rule is much more nuanced than the hypothesised strict rule. Horn explains that information about government preferences is at the core of the problem that a more nuanced national treatment is intended to solve:

> If we were to assume that such information [regarding government preferences in order to determine the first best solution] is verifiable, in the context of the present model there would exist an even simpler solution than the market access rule: a provision simply requesting the parties to "set internal taxes to their first-best levels." This would implement the first-best outcome even if tariff negotiators were myopic, as long as the tariffs were set sufficiently low, since this would leave room to set total taxes at the first-best level, once the state of nature is realized. Presumably, the reason why we do not see such a provision lies in the difficulty to prove whether a set of taxes that benefits domestic interests, and harms foreign interests, is chosen to exploit neighbors, or because the importing government's preferences are such as to make the chosen taxes efficient from a global point of view. That is, it requires the adjudicator to effectively determine the intent behind the de facto discriminatory taxes, something the Appellate Body in the WTO has repeatedly (but not always very convincingly) claimed to be irrelevant to its decisions.[31]

The question raised by Horn is whether domestic regulators are engaging in first-best regulation, or instead are motivated by protectionism. The necessity requirement of Article XX(b) of GATT and the scientific basis requirement imposed by the SPS Agreement may be said to respond to precisely this question: how do we determine the intent behind *de facto* discrimination – how do we get closer to a requirement to set internal regulation at its first-best level? While there is no WTO law requirement that domestic regulators set internal regulations to their first-best levels, the necessity requirement and the scientific basis requirement achieve a closer approximation of this test than mere national treatment. Under this type of regime, a country will only be assigned responsibility if it fails to set these taxes or regulations at first-best levels.

The scientific basis requirement at issue in *Continued Suspension* is a means for determining the intent of an SPS measure, just as the less trade restrictive alternative analysis of the Article XX(b) necessity standard, applied in *Brazil-Tyres* is a means for determining the intent of health measures under the GATT. But all of these standards seem motivated by

[31] Horn, 'National Treatment in the GATT', n. 29, at 402.

a concern to prevent states from adopting measures intended adversely to affect the competitive position of imported products.

Although the scientific basis test and necessity test can therefore be regarded as proxies by which to measure intent, the Appellate Body reports in *Continued Suspension* and *Brazil-Tyres* make clear they are weak tests. In the case of SPS measures, governments are free to apply whatever level of protection they deem appropriate, a minority scientific view is enough to justify a measure, and panels have no business assessing what is 'good science', evaluating whether the risk assessment undertaken by a government is 'correct', or giving more weight to the majority view in the scientific community. In the case of measures covered by Article XX(b) GATT, panels do not evaluate except superficially whether the importing state has chosen the less trade restrictive alternative, or whether alternative measures actually could achieve the selected level of protection.

Insofar as specific SPS measures that are adopted by governments are targeted at market failures that have effects on national objectives, any international negative spillovers associated with the SPS measures that are adopted will reflect national preferences and attitudes towards risk, and the fact that such preferences and attitudes will differ across countries. The SPS Agreement makes a marginal additional contribution in further completing the WTO 'contract' compared to the potential outcome of litigation of such cases under GATT alone.

3.3 State contingency: rules and standards

States negotiate treaties *ex ante* to govern actions *ex post*. In order to do so, they must describe which actions will have which consequences. They can do so with lesser or greater specificity. All international agreements, like all contracts, are incomplete. States may specify how they are to be completed either by stating with specificity the conditions of application of the rule, or by delegating to future decision-making the determination of whether those conditions are satisfied.

In the rules versus standards literature, a law is a 'rule' *to the extent that* it is specified in advance of the conduct to which it is applied.[32] Thus, a law against littering is a rule to the extent that 'littering' is

[32] For an introduction to the rules versus standards discussion in law and economics, see L. Kaplow, 'General Characteristics of Rules', in B. Bouckaert and G. De Geest (eds.), *Encyclopedia of Law and Economics* (Cheltenham: Edward Elgar, 1998); L. Kaplow, 'Rules

well-defined. Must there be an intent not to pick up the discarded item; are organic or readily bio-degradable substances covered; is littering on private property covered; is the distribution of leaflets by air covered? Any lawyer knows that there are always questions to ask, so that every law is incompletely specified in advance, and therefore incompletely a rule.

A standard, on the other hand, is a law that is farther toward the more general end of the spectrum, in relative terms. It establishes general guidance to both the person governed and the person charged with applying the law, but does not specify in detail in advance the conduct required or proscribed. Incompleteness of specification may not simply be a result of conservation of resources. It may be a more explicitly political decision to either agree to disagree for the moment, to avoid the political price that may arise from immediate hard decisions, or to cloak the hard decisions in the false inevitability of judicial interpretation. It is important also to recognise that the incompleteness of specification may represent a failure to decide how the policy expressed relates to other policies. This is critical in the trade area, where often the incompleteness of a trade rule relates to its failure to address, or incorporate, non-trade policies.

Rules are more expensive to develop than standards, *ex ante*, because rules entail specification costs, including drafting costs and negotiation costs, as well as the strategic costs involved in *ex ante* specification. In order to reach agreement on specification – in order to legislate specifically – there may be greater costs in public choice terms.[33] On the other hand, standards often involve greater *ex post* costs. These *ex post* costs include the costs of *ex post* decision-making after the circumstances calling for a decision arise, but also include the agency costs associated with delegation to a judicial, administrative, or other *ex post* decision-maker. The *ex post* decision-maker may shirk its duties or may be subject to conflicts of interest. The principal may be hampered by asymmetrical availability of information. The principal may control its agent with greater specification – with more rules, but may also utilise required

Versus Standards: An Economic Analysis' (1992) 42 DLJ 557. See also, C.R. Sunstein, 'Problems with Rules' (1995) 83 Cal LR 955.

33 See G.K. Hadfield, 'Weighing the Value of Vagueness: An Economic Perspective on Precision in the Law' (1994) 82 Cal LR 541, at 550, citing L.R. Cohen and R.G. Noll, 'How to Vote, Whether to Vote: Strategies for Voting and Abstaining on Congressional Role Calls' (1991) 13 PB 97.

procedures, transparency, and requirements for logical reasoning in order to control its agent. In this sense, procedure contingency may supplement state contingency utilising standards.

Rules are generally thought to provide greater predictability. There are two moments at which to consider predictability. First, is the ability of persons subject to the law to be able to plan and conform their conduct *ex ante*, sometimes known as 'primary predictability'.[34] The second moment in which predictability is important is *ex post*, after the relevant conduct has taken place. Where the parties can predict the outcome of dispute resolution – where they can predict the tribunal's determination of their respective rights and duties – they will spend less money on litigation. This type of predictability is 'secondary predictability'. Both types of predictability can reduce costs. As we consider the relative allocative efficiency of potential outcomes, we must recognise that there is a temporal distinction between rules and standards. Standards may be used earlier in the development of a field of law, before sufficient experience to form a basis for more complete specification is acquired. In many areas of law, courts develop a jurisprudence that forms the basis for codification – or even rejection – by legislatures. With this in mind, legislatures may set standards at an early point in time, and determine to establish rules at a later point in time.[35]

Kaplow points out that where instances of the relevant behaviour are more frequent, economies of scale will indicate that rules become relatively more efficient. For circumstances that arise only infrequently, it is more difficult to justify promulgation of specific rules. In addition, rules provide compliance benefits: they are cheaper to obey, because the cost of determining the required behaviour is lower. Rules are also cheaper to apply by a court: the court must only determine the facts and compare them to the rule.

It is not possible to consider the costs and benefits of rules and standards separately from the strategic considerations that would cause states to select a rule as opposed to a standard. Where adjudication of an international legal rule is unlikely, which is the case for most international legal rules, specific rules may result in greater compliance, which might be understood as a benefit. This is the role of the concept of 'precision' advanced in the 'legalisation' literature on international law.[36]

[34] For this use of the terms 'primary predictability' and 'secondary predictability', see W.F. Baxter, 'Choice of Law and the Federal System' (1963) 16 Stan LR 1, at 3.

[35] Kaplow, 'General Characteristics of Rules', n. 32, at 10.

[36] K.W. Abbott, R.O. Keohane, A. Moravcsik, A.-M. Slaughter, and D. Snidal, 'The Concept of Legalization' (2000) 54 IO 401.

Johnston analyses rules and standards from a strategic perspective, finding that, under a standard, bargaining may yield immediate efficient agreement, whereas under a rule, this condition may not obtain.[37] He considers a rule a 'definite, ex ante entitlement' and a standard a 'contingent, ex post entitlement'.[38] Johnston notes the 'standard supposition in the law and economics literature . . . that private bargaining between [two parties] over the allocation of [a] legal entitlement is most likely to be efficient if the entitlement is clearly defined and assigned ex ante according to a rule, rather than made contingent upon a judge's ex post balancing of relative value and harm'.[39] He suggests this supposition may be incorrect:[40] 'When the parties bargain over the entitlement when there is private information about value and harm, bargaining may be more efficient under a blurry balancing test than under a certain rule.'[41] This is because under a certain rule, the holder of the entitlement will have incentives to 'hold out' and decline to provide information about the value to him of the entitlement. Under a standard, where presumably it cannot be known with certainty *ex ante* who owns the entitlement, the person not possessing the entitlement may credibly threaten to take it, providing incentives for the other person to bargain. Johnston points out that this result obtains only when the *ex post* balancing test is imperfect, because if the balancing were perfect, the threat would not be credible. This provides a counter-intuitive argument for inaccuracy of application of standards.[42]

It is easy to see a standard, combined with mandatory dispute settlement, as a way to complete incomplete contracts, *ex ante*, in a way that can under particular circumstances minimise costs of contracting. Horn, Maggi, and Staiger examine the GATT, finding that it includes an interesting combination of '*rigidity*, in the sense that contractual obligations are largely insensitive to changes in economic (and political) conditions, and *discretion*, in the sense that governments have substantial leeway in the setting of many policies'.[43]

[37] J.S. Johnston, 'Bargaining under Rules versus Standards' (1995) 11 JLEO 256.

[38] Ibid., at 256. [39] Ibid. (citations omitted).

[40] See also C.M. Rose, 'Crystals and Mud in Property Law' (1988) 40 Stan LR 577 J.P. Trachtman, 'Externalities and Extraterritoriality', in J.S. Bhandari and A.O. Sykes (eds.), *Economic Dimensions in International Law: Comparative and Empirical Perspectives* (Cambridge University Press, 1998), 642.

[41] Johnston, 'Bargaining under Rules versus Standards', n. 37, at 257. [42] Ibid., at 272.

[43] H. Horn, G. Maggi, and R.W. Staiger, 'Trade Agreements as Endogenously Incomplete Contracts' (2010) 100 AER 394, at 406.

Under significant uncertainty as to the future state of affairs, states would wish to establish complex state-contingent contracts. For example, the magnitudes of first, the benefits of environmental protection, and second, the benefits of unimpeded free trade in particular products that may violate environmental rules, are uncertain. However, contracting is costly, limiting the ability to specify state-contingencies. On the other hand, by specifying general 'standards', and delegating to dispute settlement bodies the responsibility to apply these standards, states are able to include complex state-contingency in their contracts, with significantly less variable contracting costs.

3.4 *Procedure contingency: judicial review*

Whenever externalities are internalised, the decision-maker is induced to take account of the external effects. Procedure contingency can serve to require the decision-maker directly to take account of the external effects, within the prescribed procedure, without necessarily bearing responsibility for the adverse effect.

In a sense, the relationship among (a) states party to a multilateral agreement, (b) individual states that may be accused of violation, and (c) dispute settlement under the multilateral agreement, is analogous to the relationship among (aa) a legislature, (bb) administrative agencies, and (cc) courts charged with judicial review. Just as a legislature may provide for judicial review in order to control the discretion of administrative agencies under their statutory authorisation, states party to a multilateral agreement may provide for dispute settlement in order to control the discretion of individual states under the agreement. There is no doubt that procedural rules can have substantive effects.

As noted, there are a number of different types of review that may be applied to national decisions. I will focus here on review by an international court of, first, national interpretation of treaty requirements, second, national regulation, and third, national agency determinations or adjudications.

Review of national interpretation of treaty requirements is not a traditional international law function, but is a core international law function. That is, the traditional approach to treaty obligations is implicitly to allow each state to interpret its obligation for itself, subject to informal diplomatic discourse. In the WTO, in investment treaties, in the European Union, and in other specialised areas, dispute settlement tribunals are accorded mandatory jurisdiction to determine whether states' interpretations of their obligations are accurate. One of the main functions of the WTO Appellate Body has been to interpret the WTO treaty, in accordance with customary international law rules of interpretation. This type of review is best understood as a technique for ensuring that states comply with their treaty obligations as objectively determined: it is a departure from the international law default rule of auto-interpretation.

The treaty context here is quite different from the administrative law context. In the United States, the *Chevron* rule calls for substantial deference to agencies in interpreting their authorising statutes. While this has important rationales in the domestic context, given the more contractual relationship between parties to international treaties, it would be strange to provide substantial deference to national treaty interpretations.[44] To which state would we defer – the complainant or the respondent? More specifically, in the horizontal federalism context the relationship between agencies and a legislature is nuanced and has elements of verticality in which the agency is subordinate to the legislature. On the other hand, in the international setting, the core of the international legal relationship is still largely between states in a more purely horizontal relationship.

Review of national regulation becomes more interesting. Here, we can see in *Brazil-Tyres* and in *Continued Suspension* that WTO law can be understood as imposing procedure contingency *as to national regulatory measures* in particular fields. To some extent, as noted at the outset of this chapter, these procedure contingency requirements can be understood in terms of policy externalities as a kind of 'virtual representation' of foreign persons in the policy process: the procedure contingency induces states to make appropriate findings showing that they considered less protectionist alternatives, or that they had a scientific basis for their action.

> Most scholars argue that the transparency of an agency, its duty to consult the stakeholders, weight their arguments and give the reasons for its decision, amount to a form of 'soft accountability' which is an acceptable substitute for classic electoral mechanisms where these do not fit the institution.[45]

[44] See S.P. Croley and J.H. Jackson, 'WTO Dispute Procedures, Standard of Review, and Deference to National Governments' (1996) 90 AJIL 193.

[45] P. Magrette, 'The Politics of Regulation in the European Union', in D. Geradin, R. Muñoz, and N. Petit (eds.), *Regulation Through Agencies in the EU: A New Paradigm*

In the administrative law context, process review examines the regularity of the process by which the regulation is produced. The United States Supreme Court has applied a 'hard look' review to the agency process of establishing rules.[46] In the administrative law context, a group that is currently in power in a legislature may anticipate that it will be out of power in the future, and seek to insulate its legislation from interference by a future government through administrative action.[47]

In an analogous sense, a treaty partner able to negotiate a treaty today may seek to insulate the counterparty's performance from interference by a future government of the counterparty. Treaty partners are increasingly aware of the need to analyse the extent to which their counterparties are likely over time to comply with their commitments.[48] They can do so by requiring the counterparty to establish structural mechanisms through procedure contingency rules. While the counterparty may indeed violate both the procedure contingency and a related state contingency, violation of the procedure contingency will require it to maintain a constant violation, or to demean its own rule of law. That is, it will need to either decline to establish the required procedure, or refuse to follow the required procedure in a particular circumstance.

Foreign country counterparties might use procedure contingency to reduce the likelihood that the domestic government will renege on its commitments. As Terry Moe suggests, there are various structural means by which to constrain a future government to carry out a particular policy: first, write a detailed law that imposes rigid constraints on the administrative mandate and decision procedures; second, establish requirements for professional decision-making, since professionals resist political interference; third, oppose formal provisions that enhance political oversight and involvement; or fourth, favour judicial review of agency decision-making.[49]

of European Governance (Cheltenham: Edward Elgar, 2005), at 12 (discussing regulatory agency accountability).

46 *Citizens to Preserve Overton Park* v. *Volpe*, 401 US 402 (1971); *Motor Vehicle Manufacturers Association* v. *State Farm Mutual Automobile Insurance Company*, 463 US 29 (1983). Under these precedents, the reviewing court does not engage in *de novo* review, but instead determines whether the agency action is reasonable.

47 T.M. Moe, 'The Politics of Bureaucratic Structure', in J.E. Chubb and P.E. Peterson (eds.), *Can the Government Govern?* (Washington: Brookings, 1989), 267, at 274.

48 J.P. Trachtman, 'International Law and Domestic Political Coalitions: The Grand Theory of Compliance with International Law' (2010) 11 Chic JIL 127.

49 Moe, 'The Politics of Bureaucratic Structure', n. 47, at 274–275.

On the other hand, there are converse structural means to impede a future government in carrying out a particular policy: first, detailed provisions for political control of agency action, including legislative veto and monitoring; second, participatory agency decision-making procedures, including judicial review; or third, requirements for agency decision-making to be accompanied by detailed evidence and objective analytical statements, also facilitating judicial review.[50]

Review under international law of national agency determinations or adjudications may be understood in a similar way: states are permitted to act, as in to impose an SPS measure, only upon the establishment of certain facts. For example, the WTO Appellate Body in important contexts relating to contingent protectionism such as safeguards actions, has found that the standard of review of national agency determinations is not *de novo* review – WTO panels are not required to check the facts that form the basis for the action, but are only required to check the procedure by which the national agency checked the facts that form the basis for the action.

Once countries understand the level of review required, they can set their procedures in such a way as to comply with the requirement. It is entirely possible that their procedure would superficially comply, while the substance of their determination is false. In order to set up its system this way, the country doing so would in effect have to sacrifice its own rule of law and the integrity of its legal system. If the national authorities apply the correct standard, and follow the correct procedure, they are unlikely to stray too far from the intent of the international legal rule.

3.5 *Procedure contingency: burdens of proof*

Eric Talley makes the following statement about the welfare stakes involved in determining burdens of proof (BoP):

> This criticality of process in general – and the BoP in particular – may be especially salient in cases where the economic stakes are high, and where the informational environment is complex, opaque, and difficult to navigate. In such situations, it is plausible that no single entity – not the jury, not the judge, not attorneys, not the parties themselves – has full and complete command of all the "facts" pertinent to a legal dispute. It is here where the burden allocation may be the most influential in catalyzing

[50] Ibid., at 275–276.

> information discovery, reducing verification costs, and ultimately contributing to overall welfare policy goals.[51]

Of course the type of procedure contingency discussed in this chapter is not the same thing as a BoP. Rather, procedure contingency, when it appears alone, can best be analogised to a conditional presumption to the effect that *if* the procedure followed by the respondent country conforms to legal requirements, then we will presume that the substantive act taken by the respondent country conforms to the relevant legal requirements. The core problem to which BoPs respond, and to which procedure contingency seems to respond as well, is the inability of the decision-maker – in our case the international tribunal – directly to observe the conditions of liability.

For example, in the *Brazil-Tyres* and *Continued Suspension* cases, the international tribunal is unable directly to observe the intent of the regulating state. In the WTO context, procedure contingency may be understood as establishing a presumption that, if requisite procedures are followed, then it is appropriate to presume that the intent is non-protectionist.

What is the rationale for making these presumptions? Under a decision-theoretic approach, as described by Talley, 'the fact-finder's role is tantamount to a welfare-minded social planner, using adduced evidence to learn and make decisions within an information-constrained environment. The evidence produced in a case enables an uncertain fact-finder to "update" her assessment of the case (possibly in a Bayesian manner) in light of that evidence'.[52] This is consistent with the approach to national treatment taken by Horn in the WTO context.

Where the critical facts are not directly observable by the fact-finder, the fact-finder must determine whether to rely on other facts that are statistically correlated with the critical facts. The decision-maker must assess their correlation, and weigh the costs of false negatives and false positives, as well as the costs of inquiry, in order to determine how to proceed. In international law, it is difficult to assess how a decision-maker would weigh the costs of false negatives and false positives. It might be that false positives (erroneous findings of violation) are more costly, because of a weighting in favour of untrammeled sovereignty (*in*

[51] E.L. Talley, 'Law, Economics, and the Burden(s) of Proof', in J.H. Arlen (ed.), *Research Handbook on the Economics of Torts* (Cheltenham: Edward Elgar, 2013), 305, at 306.

[52] Ibid., citing E. Feess, G. Muehlheusser, and A. Wohlschlegel, 'Environmental liability under uncertain causation' (2009) 28 EJLE 133.

dubio mitius). Alternatively, if the adjudicator has a view that the permitted action is normatively unattractive, it might determine that false negatives are not very costly, at least insofar as the adjudicator is concerned about the public welfare. However, in the special case in which the false negatives and false positives are weighted equally, reliance on the presumption can be justified where it is more likely than not that the other facts are indicative of the critical facts. More generally, a welfare-minded social planner would optimise given the relative probabilities, and the relative costs of false negatives and false positives.

International legal rules, like domestic rules of criminal and civil responsibility, generally allocate the initial burden to the complainant to show a violation. And so, in the trade law areas described earlier, it is up to the complainant to show a violation of the relevant rule. Here, it might be said that, especially in the trade remedies area, the procedures that form the basis for procedure contingency will often be easier for the complainant to observe than the actual facts that are the basis for state contingency.

As we consider these ideas regarding BoP, we might ask what inferences we can draw regarding the likely effects of the move from state contingency toward procedure contingency documented in section 2? For one, provided that the procedures required by procedure contingency are not unreasonable for states to follow, we would expect procedure contingency to represent greater latitude for national action than state contingency. But this does not necessarily suggest greater efficiency, reduced litigation, or increased success for respondents in litigation. Litigation might not be reduced, because the greater flexibility for state action could induce states to hew less closely to legal requirements, giving other states more reason to complain, and greater chances for success.[53]

In addition, the actual regulatory purpose may be quite difficult to observe. So, if the optimal bargain – the optimal shared responsibility – among states in the trade and environment or trade and health context would involve prohibition of measures that are motivated by protectionism, it seems plausible that other facts might be selected for evaluation because they are good proxies for protectionist intent.[54] The proxies that have been chosen in this area have included (a) discrimination in the

[53] See A.E. Bernardo, E.L. Talley, and I. Welch, 'A Theory of Legal Presumptions' (2000) 16 JLEO 1.

[54] See Trachtman, 'Trade and ... Problems, Cost-Benefit Analysis and Subsidiarity', n. 9, at 40.

national treatment sense, (b) failure to choose the less trade restrictive alternative (necessity), and (c) failure to base the measure on a scientific risk assessment.

3.6 Procedure contingency: information and expertise asymmetry

Countries that take regulatory action often have engaged in serious public policy studies in order to determine their action. The examples of procedure contingency provided in this chapter involve circumstances where the regulating country can be expected to have superior access to information, and to have deployed superior expert analysis, compared to anything likely to be deployed by other countries that may complain about the regulating country's action, and compared to anything likely to be readily available to international tribunals. It may be highly impractical, and can be very costly, to double-check these analyses. Even within the domestic legal system, we sometimes defer to the knowledge and expertise of those subject to the law, as in the legal doctrines of the business judgment rule in corporate law, or the due diligence defense in securities law. These domestic doctrines can be understood in terms of procedure contingency.

The international law of cooperation frequently couches its obligations using concepts that make sense to experts, but that are not readily applied by laypersons. Obligations under the SPS Agreement utilise and refer to biological knowledge, many obligations under other WTO law utilise and refer to economic knowledge, and the law of armed conflict concept of proportionality refers to military knowledge. In applying these types of provisions, a tribunal has little choice but to defer to experts – the question is whether to defer to national experts of the respondent country, or to hire independent experts.

In the WTO, panels are permitted to establish 'expert review groups' under Article 13.2 of the WTO Dispute Settlement Understanding. This facility has not been used yet, but it seems well-designed for use in cases where the panel must make complex scientific or economic determinations. Panels have called upon individual experts in eight cases: *US/Canada-Hormones Continued Suspension*, *EC-Biotech*,[55]

[55] *European Communities – Measures Affecting the Approval and Marketing of Biotech Products*, Panel Report, 29 September 2006, WT/DS291/R, WT/DS292/R, WT/DS293/R Add.1 to Add.9 and Corr.1 (*EC-Biotech*).

Japan-Apples,[56] *Australia-Salmon*,[57] *EC-Asbestos*[58] (initial panel and Article 21.5 panel), *Japan-Agricultural Products*,[59] *US-Shrimp*,[60] and *EC-Hormones*.[61] However, in none of these cases have panels consulted experts on economic issues. In a number of cases, panels have sought expert or other information from international organisations, such as the International Monetary Fund, the World Intellectual Property Organization, Codex Alimentarius, and the World Customs Organization.

Engaging expert review groups to work through the difficult issues would relieve panels of a burden that they generally cannot bear. Article 13 of the WTO Dispute Settlement Understanding has been found to provide panels with broad flexibility to utilise experts. So it is curious that economic experts have not been used.

It might be argued that it is better to have the litigants bring their own experts, and have the panel determine which experts present the better argument. However, panels generally lack the expertise to critique complex scientific or economic analyses. 'A non-expert cannot independently and directly check complex theoretical propositions that do not have simple observational consequences ... Whatever checking the non-expert can manage must rely on indirect devices like demeanor, credentials, and reputation.'[62]

In any particular circumstance, it will require a complex calculus to determine whether to defer to national knowledge and expertise through exclusive procedure contingency, or to add state contingency and provide an independent expert review of complex facts. Part of the benefit of deference is to avoid chilling good faith national determinations – this is a kind of subsidiarity. Part of the detriment of deference is the risk of

[56] *Japan – Measures Affecting the Importation of Apples*, Report of the Appellate Body, 26 November 2003, WT/DS245/AB/R (*Japan-Apples*).

[57] *Australia – Measures Affecting Importation of Salmon*, Report of the Appellate Body, 20 October 1998, WT/DS18/AB/R (*Australia-Salmon*).

[58] *European Communities – Measures Affecting Asbestos and Asbestos-Containing Products*, Panel Report, 18 September 2000, WT/DS135/R and WT/DS135/R/Add.1, as modified by the Report of the Appellate Body, 21 March 2001, WT/DS135/AB/R (*EC-Asbestos*).

[59] *Japan – Measures Affecting Agricultural Products*, Report of the Appellate Body, 22 February 1999, WT/DS76/AB/R (*Japan-Agricultural Products*).

[60] *United States – Import Prohibition of Certain Shrimp and Shrimp Products*, Report of the Appellate Body, 12 October 1998, WT/DS58/AB/R (*US-Shrimp*).

[61] *EC Measures Concerning Meat and Meat Products (Hormones)*, Report of the Appellate Body, 16 January 1998, WT/DS26/AB/R, WT/DS48/AB/R (*EC-Hormones*).

[62] S. Brewer, 'Scientific Expert Testimony and Intellectual Due Process' (1998) 107 YLJ 1535, at 1538.

bias. But there are a number of other costs and benefits to be weighed in determining how to proceed.

4. Conclusion

This chapter provides a normative framework for analysis of state contingency and procedure contingency in international law. It would be useful to develop greater theoretical and empirical understanding of the ways in which international legal structures are designed to use state contingency and procedure contingency, and rules and standards, to regulate national action, and to provide for shared responsibility. What are the advantages and disadvantages of each structure? With what parameters of specific international contexts does each structure match well? This chapter only begins to suggest the responses to these questions.

State contingency and procedure contingency are ways of providing for the completion of incomplete contracts in international law. They are ways of providing that regulating countries must take into account the concerns of other affected states, either by refraining from action where the concerns articulated in state contingency are not met, or by following a procedure designed to take into account the concerns of other affected states. As national regulation and globalisation grow, we can expect to see increasing state contingency and procedure contingency.

Countries engaged in cooperation may articulate their state contingency or procedure contingency with greater or lesser precision – with rules or standards. Where adjudication takes place, standards implicitly allocate authority to the tribunal responsible for adjudication. Rules involve greater *ex ante* costs, but can provide economies of scale where the relevant issue will arise frequently. In the absence of adjudication, rules, being more precise and thereby making it easier for third countries to observe compliance or violation, may induce greater compliance than standards.

How can countries choose between state contingency and procedure contingency? Where the relevant conditions are easier for the regulated country to observe, and difficult for other countries or tribunals to observe, procedure contingency may be superior to state contingency. Procedure contingency may be an appropriate substitute for state contingency where following the appropriate procedures is a close proxy for the existence of the desired conditions. Where the procedural requirements are not perfectly statistically correlated with the desired conditions, it is necessary to assess their correlation, and weigh the costs of false negatives and false positives, as well as the costs of inquiry, in order to determine whether to use them as proxies. Procedure contingency can operate as a kind of virtual representation of outsiders to regulatory processes. Furthermore, procedure contingency can be used by other countries to embed a set of considerations within the administrative and legal processes of the obligee country, making compliance less susceptible to subsequent political shifts. In effect, domestic rule of law in the obligee country is made hostage to compliance.

The aforementioned considerations may suggest why countries would choose specific international legal mechanisms in order to cause other countries to internalise certain externalities in their regulatory decision-making. These considerations do not seem relevant to the iconic areas of shared responsibility, such as the classic case of degradation of an environmental commons. However they seem relevant to the construction of new rules by which to address these iconic areas of shared responsibility: the designers of these rules will need to choose between *ex ante* specification by virtue of rules, and *ex post* specification through application of standards, and between state contingency and procedure contingency. They may thus serve as a guide to countries seeking to formulate international legal mechanisms in order to establish shared responsibility.

This chapter contributes to an increased focus of global administrative law studies on the way in which international legal structures regulate national administrative action. Most global administrative law studies have focused on the administrative law analysis of *international* legal structures. This chapter shows the rich potential for scholarship in the reverse area: administrative law analysis of international legal rules that restrict national action.

5

Incentives, Compensation, and Irreparable Harm

LEWIS A. KORNHAUSER*

1. Introduction

Many individual, organisational, and corporate activities impose a risk of harm on individuals, their property, or the environment generally. Society regulates these risks in a variety of ways. This chapter focuses on the use of *ex post* liability rules that impose liability on one or more actors deemed 'responsible' for the harm. In domestic legal systems, *ex post* liability rules typically regulate the basic relations between private individuals; intentional torts, accidents between strangers, and most contractual relations are governed by *ex post* liability rules. *Ex post* regulation of harm might play an equally significant role in international legal contexts as, in many international law contexts, institutions for the creation and implementation of *ex ante* regulatory instruments are scarce and underdeveloped.[1]

* Frank Henry Sommer Professor of Law, New York University. I thank Vanessa Casado-Perez for her excellent research assistance. The Filomen d'Agostino and Max E. Greenberg Research Fund of the New York University School of Law provided financial assistance. I thank participants at the SHARES Conference in Amsterdam in May 2013 for helpful comments. All websites were last accessed in June 2014.

[1] I make the distinction between *ex ante* and *ex post* as it is used by economic analysts of law. Nollkaemper and Jacobs (P.A. Nollkaemper and D. Jacobs, 'Shared Responsibility in International Law: A Conceptual Framework' (2013) 34 MIJIL 359, at 365) elide three different senses to this distinction, only one of which corresponds to the distinction as used in the text. Each sense identifies a different decision that might come before (*ex ante*) or after (*ex post*) a relevant event. In each case, the relevant event is the realisation of the harm that gives rise to the dispute. Economic analysts consider the relevant decision to be the regulatory action of the government. When regulation is *ex post*, harm is a necessary condition for government application of a rule; this idea is central to Nollkaemper and Jacobs. They use the same terms, however, to mark two different distinctions. On occasion, the *ex ante/ex post* distinction refers to the timing of the creation (or recognition) of the defendant's legal obligations. Common law rule-making is often regarded (and criticised) for creating obligations after the agent has acted and caused a harm whereas, when legislators enact a statute, it imposes obligations going forward. The distinction

I shall distinguish three aspects of the assignment of responsibility.[2] First, the law determines what I shall call *causal responsibility*; it identifies which actor or actors created the risk. Second, the law assigns what I shall call *legal responsibility* for the harm; it identifies those actors who must 'remedy' the harm. Finally, the law determines *financial responsibility* for whatever remedy the law provides.

These three forms of responsibility are related in complex ways. First, the complexity arises in part from the tension between two distinct motivations for a liability regime. On the one hand, the law, through the liability regime, may seek to mitigate the risks that led to the harm. This aim is forward looking; society wants agents to take actions that reduce the risks and hence, on average, the realised harms from these risks. I shall sometimes call this aim, *deterrence*[3] and sometimes the *incentive* aim.

On the other hand, a liability regime seeks to compensate the 'victim' of the harm. This aim is backward looking. A liability regime accomplishes this compensation by 'shifting' the realised harm from the 'victim' to one or more legally responsible agents. I shall call this aim *compensation*.

Society has other means, both legal and non-legal, for achieving the twin aims of compensation and deterrence. *Ex ante* regulation through licensing, taxing of inputs, command and control regulations, product standards, and markets in tradable permits, to name a few, are *ex ante* tools that regulate or deter actions that impose risks. In most instances, these regulatory techniques complement rather than replace

relied on the text is independent of this distinction; the timing of the regulatory action of the government is independent of the manner in which an obligation is created. Finally, the terms occasionally mark a distinction between rules that create incentives for agents looking forward and rules that resolve disputes. As defined in the text, however, *ex ante* and *ex post* regulation both create incentives for agents looking forward. The legal rule places a contingent price on risk-creating actions. When a risk is realised and harm occurs, the agent pays; *ex ante*, when making her decision, the agent weighs the *expected* costs she will face – the costs of an injury weighted by the probability that her action will lead to injury.

2 Again, Nollkaemper and Jacobs use the term 'responsibility' slightly differently. They distinguish responsibility from reparation. Responsibility for them encompasses more than causal responsibility, the first aspect of assignment of liability discussed in the text, but falls short of a duty to repair or compensate. By contrast, their idea of reparation apparently includes the other two aspects of responsibility discussed above: the obligation to remedy and financial responsibility for that remedy. Ibid., at 412.

3 In many ways, this term is misleading as it may suggest that society seeks to *eliminate* the risk when, in fact, society definitely does not aim at risk elimination. A more precise statement of the social attitude towards a risk requires that we articulate the social objective function which will generally involve multiple goods, some of which are promoted by activities that carry the risk and some of which are lost when the risk is realised.

regulation through *ex post* liability rules, though, as noted, they typically require a strong institutional basis for their successful creation and implementation.

The law also may *shift* the burdens created by the realised harm. More precisely, society may *spread* the risk through insurance or other mechanisms. Insurance requires the bearer of financial responsibility to have made a prior premium payment in exchange for the right to indemnification from the insurer for the loss. Other mechanisms typically spread losses among taxpayers by providing 'social insurance' to the individual financially responsible.

A second source of complexity in the relation among the three types of responsibility arises from the nature of the harms that risky activities cause. Much of the legal literature treats harms in an undifferentiated way and understands the aim of compensation as one of 'making the victim whole'. This approach only makes sense for certain types of harms, specifically monetary losses (or losses of property) and certain types of what I shall call 'transient personal injury'. In these instances, the victim can in fact be made whole, at least in the economist's sense of delivering a bundle of goods that makes the victim, from her own perspective, as well off after suffering the harm as she would have been had the harm not occurred. Harms for which an agent can be made whole I shall call 'monetary harms' or 'financial harms'.[4]

Not all harms however are financial harms. Some harm is *irreparable.* Irreparable harms cannot be shifted or spread. The victim alone bears them; as a consequence, I shall argue, deterrence should play the dominant role in the assignment of legal responsibility and the determination of the extent of financial responsibility.

The harm to an agent who loses her eyesight in an industrial accident cannot be shifted to the employer or the supplier of the equipment that caused or contributed to the accident. Though the agent receives 'compensation', she remains blind.[5] Similarly, when a nuclear power plant

[4] When harm is purely financial, there is a sense in which there is no victim. The action of one or more agents causes a loss; the liability rule then identifies who must bear that loss. The legal rule thus, in some sense, identifies the 'victim' by assigning responsibility for the financial loss. As the next paragraph indicates, not all injuries are, like financial losses, transferable.

[5] Of course, the law might shift the pecuniary losses of income to the employer or supplier, or spread that pecuniary loss through disability insurance. After this monetary transfer, however, the agent remains blind and she cannot be compensated *ex post* for that loss. She cannot be 'made whole' under any reasonable understanding of that term. Notice that an

discharges significant radioactive materials into the environment and contaminates water and soil so that it is not fit for human habitation, no monetary transfers may repair the damage. It will thus be useful in what follows to distinguish two aspects of a damage award: compensatory damages and risk-reducing damages.[6]

When a single tortfeasor causes a financial harm, a standard liability rule can fully satisfy both the compensation and the deterrence aims.[7] When a single tortfeasor causes an irreparable harm or when multiple tortfeasors cause any harm, irreparable or not, the compensatory aim may conflict with the deterrence aim. So, for example, in the case of monetary harm only caused by multiple tortfeasors, a rule of strict liability satisfies the compensation aim but it will distort the incentives of at least one of the tortfeasors.[8]

This chapter uses the economic analysis of law to illuminate the relations among the three allocations of responsibility: causal responsibility, legal responsibility, and financial responsibility. Section 1 offers a brief introduction to the economic analysis of liability rules. It emphasises the role of irreparable injury in structuring the effects of these

agent might purchase insurance against loss of eyesight, if such a market existed, but the face value of that purchase does not reflect the value to her of her eyesight. Insurance merely transfers income from the state of the world in which the agent has sight to the state of the world in which she is blind. She will transfer income from one state to the other until the marginal value of money in the two states is equal.

6 Damages for torts in the United States fall into three legal categories: pecuniary damages, pain and suffering, and punitive damages. Pecuniary damages encompass all pecuniary harm: damage to property, medical expenses, and lost wages. When personal injury is transient, 'pain and suffering' might be interpreted as 'compensatory' in the sense of compensating the agent for welfare losses suffered from personal injury. On this account, a plaintiff who has suffered a broken arm, incurs welfare losses for the periods during which her arm has not reached its healthy state; we can imagine that a transfer of some finite sum in each period she is 'not whole' would provide the plaintiff with an equivalent amount of well-being she would have had in the healthy state. A permanent personal injury such as blindness or death, however, presents a different situation. It is not clear that any finite sum could compensate the victim for her lost welfare; we require a different approach to calculating pain and suffering. From an economic perspective, that approach would set damages so as to create optimal incentives on the defendant to reduce risk to the socially optimal level. We might understand punitive damages similarly. Notice that these risk-reducing damages operate like a fine or a tax; the economic account requires some justification for transferring these amounts to the victim. See A.M. Polinsky and Y.-K. Che, 'Decoupling liability: optimal incentives for care and litigation' (1991) 22(4) RAND JE 562.

7 This claim rests on a characterisation of the victim as the party on whom the loss 'initially' fell. The requisite rule is then one of strict liability.

8 Again, this claim rests on some non-legal basis for the identification of the victim.

liability rules on deterrence and compensation. Sections 2 and 3 use the insights of this economic analysis to reflect on the assignment of responsibility to international governmental organisations ('international organisations' or 'organisations'). The activities of international organisations present a particularly interesting setting in which to examine these liability issues, as many such activities impose irreparable injury. Section 2 discusses abstract features of international organisations. Section 3 considers two stylised examples, patterned on two actual incidents. First, the actions of the United Nations Children's Fund (UNICEF) in funding the construction of wells in Bangladesh that were tainted with arsenic; and second, the introduction of cholera into Haiti by the United Nations Stabilization Mission in Haiti (MINUSTAH). In this chapter, I largely ignore the actual *ex post* liability legal regime governing international organisations.[9] Rather, I sketch the underlying economics of various doctrines that apply to private actors and in many contexts to sovereign governments, and that might be applied to international organisations.

2. Economic analysis of joint and several liability

This section outlines the economic analysis of accident law. The first subsection sets out the basic elements in the context of an accident caused by the actions of a single agent. The second subsection considers the more complex case in which the accident arises from the actions of two agents, on one of whom the loss initially falls. The third subsection uses these concepts to analyse the case in which the accident arises from the actions of two or more agents, none of whom initially bears the loss. The final subsection briefly discusses vicarious liability which may be understood as a form of joint and several liability.

2.1 The (second) simplest tort

Economic analysis of accident law emphasises the deterrent function of liability rules. It begins from an assumption that the legal rules are

[9] As laid down in the Articles on the Responsibility of International Organizations, ILC Report on the work of its sixty-third session, UNGAOR 66th Sess., Supp. No. 10, UN Doc. A/66/10 (2011) (ARIO). See for a comprehensive assessment of these rules P.A. Nollkaemper and I. Plakokefalos (eds.), *Principles of Shared Responsibility in International Law: An Appraisal of the State of the Art* (Cambridge University Press, 2014).

instruments designed to further social objectives. Typically, analysts assume that society seeks to maximise social welfare but little in the argument turns on the content of the social objective.[10]

Within this framework, analysts investigate how individuals respond to legal rules in general and liability rules in particular. Liability rules create incentives; rationally self-interested individuals make socially desirable decisions only if they see the full costs and benefits of their actions. Imposing liability for harm caused thus may improve decision making from a social perspective as, otherwise, the decision-maker may fail to see the full costs of her decisions.

Accidents arise in myriad ways. The simplest accident is an act of god in which the harm an individual suffers results from purely non-human causes. Such accidents are rare, if they exist at all, as human agency can mitigate almost any risk. Typical natural disasters such as earthquakes, hurricanes, and floods cause harm to individuals who have chosen to build on or near seismic faults, in flood plains, or in regions historically subject to such threats. Moreover, they could have constructed structures more resistant to earthquake shocks or wind and water damage. In any case, in these instances, where human agency plays no role in the causation of the harm, deterrence is not possible. Compensation, of course, is possible but an insurance scheme rather than a liability scheme is the appropriate institutional response.

Consider, then, the next simplest accident situation in which the actions of a single agent determine the likelihood that the accident occurs. Suppose that the harm caused by the accident falls on a passive third party. In this context, the society wants to assign causal, legal, and financial responsibility to the same agent, the one whose actions determine the likelihood that the harm will occur. A rule of strict liability accomplishes this end.[11]

A simple example may clarify the argument. Suppose a single defendant, when he undertakes an action, may do so with more or less care. For simplicity, suppose that the defendant may take an action that yields her a benefit of 125; when acting she may take either no care (at a cost of

[10] The analysis, that is, assumes that the law is an instrument for achieving certain aims and that agents respond to the incentives created by the legal rules. A liability rule thus puts a 'price' on specific conduct; that price reflects the value of the harm incident to the conduct undertaken.

[11] A rule of negligence that set the standard of care appropriately would also achieve the social objective. The rule of negligence, however, assigns legal and financial responsibility not to a non-negligent agent who caused the harm but to the victim.

zero) or 'full care' at a cost of 5; if the defendant takes no care the probability of an injury is .7 while if she takes full care the probability of an accident falls to .1. When an accident occurs it causes pecuniary losses of 100 to a third party (whom we shall call plaintiff). Under a rule of no liability, a self-interested agent takes no care as she then receives a net return of 125 though she causes expected losses of 70. She takes no care because, under a no liability rule, she does not bear the loss. Under a rule of strict liability by contrast she takes full care, garnering a net benefit of 110: 125 in gross benefits from the activity less the cost 5 of taking care and less the expected losses of 10.[12]

Two complications arise in this context; both concern the appropriate extent of financial responsibility. Common law liability regimes typically equate the extent of financial responsibility with the amount of harm caused. This measure of financial responsibility may be inadequate if the policymaker pursues an objective function different from the maximisation of social welfare or if the injurer causes irreparable harm.

Consider the first complication. Assume that the harm is purely financial. When society seeks to minimise the social costs of accidents – the costs of preventions plus the expected harm – (or to maximise the social benefits of engaging in the activities that (jointly) cause the harm), a rule of strict liability with the amount of financial responsibility set equal to this amount induces agents to adopt the socially appropriate level of care.

When society pursues a different objective, however, the law cannot align all three assignments of responsibility. Suppose, in an extension of the prior example, that society seeks to minimise not the social cost of accidents but the probability that the accident will occur (conditional on the activity taking place at a fixed level). In the extension the agent can make care expenditures of 5 as before and reduce the probability of an accident to .1 or she can make care expenditures of 10 and reduce the probability of an accident to .08. Under a rule of strict liability the agent

[12] Of course the agent does not realise benefits of 110. When, with probability .9, the harm is not realised, the agent realises benefits of 120; but, with probability .1, the harm is realised and the agent receives benefits of 20, her benefit of 125 less the cost 5 of care and less the harm 100. This example illustrates the 'problem of social cost'. R. Coase, 'The Problem of Social Cost' (1960) 3 JLE 1 famously argued that the assignment of the liability rule did not affect the efficient allocation of resources (though it might affect the distribution of wealth) when frictionless bargaining among parties was possible. Such bargaining might seem plausible in the stylised example in the text but, in real world situations, such bargaining is often infeasible.

will choose to expend 5 on care as this maximises her private expected return, which is, as before, 110. But if society seeks to minimise the probability of an accident, conditional on allowing the activity, then it should use a negligence rule with a standard of care set at 10. If the agent meets the standard of 10, her expected, indeed certain, return is 115 and the passive victim suffers an expected loss of 8; the agent's return exceeds the maximum return she can receive for being negligent, which is 110. If we fix financial responsibility equal to the harm caused, then the optimal rule is a negligence rule with the standard of care set appropriately.[13]

A negligence rule potentially separates causal responsibility from legal and financial responsibility. When the agent meets the standard of care and an accident happens, the agent is causally responsible for the harm, but she is neither legally nor financially responsible for the harm.[14] Negligence rules highlight the tension between the social aims of deterrence and compensation; in this context, society cannot simultaneously deter and compensate through the tort system alone. The deterrence objective requires that the agent be able to avoid financial responsibility by taking socially desirable actions but, when the agent escapes financial liability, that liability must fall on the victim or be socialised through an insurance scheme.

The second complication arises when the harm is irreparable. Even if the causal agent is legally and financially responsible, the victim cannot be made whole. This conclusion is apparent when the irreparable harm is death. Clearly, no amount of compensation to the decedent's heirs can compensate the decedent for her loss of life. This conclusion holds even though the decedent herself purchased life insurance as the amount of life insurance purchased bears no relation to the decedent's valuation of her life. Indeed, the amount of insurance that an agent purchases against the risk that causes the irreparable harm does not reflect her valuation of the harm. Insurance transfers money from the agent in one state of the world to the same agent in another state of the world; that is from the agent in the unharmed state to the agent in the harmed state. An agent makes such transfers only if additional money would be (marginally)

[13] In this stylised model, we index the standards of care by the cost of taking care. Then the standard should be set at a cost equal to the minimum of expected total social cost. This standard minimises the probability of an accident as, for any higher standard, it is cheaper for the agent to be negligent. She thus acts as she would under a strict liability rule and adopts the social cost minimising level of care.

[14] A rational agent, faced with these incentives, would choose to meet her standard of care when the standard is set 'optimally'.

more valuable to her in the harmed state than in the unharmed state. Putting to one side the bequest motive, money has no value to a deceased agent; her marginal utility of money is zero and she has no reason to buy insurance. Indeed, an agent without a bequest motive would like to transfer money from the deceased state to the living state as money has no value to her when dead; she would like to sell today any prospective wrongful death claims that she might acquire tomorrow.

To understand this claim requires a model of personal injury.[15] Consider an individual who cares about both her wealth and her 'health'. Irreparable injuries such as blindness, paraplegia, or death reduce her level of 'health'. Given a state of health, the individual always prefers more wealth to less. Similarly, given a level of wealth, the individual always prefers to be healthier than less healthy.

Insurance permits the individual to transfer wealth from a healthy state to a less healthy one. She pays a premium in the healthy state. In the event she becomes unhealthy, the insurance company pays the policy amount. Health insurance, for example, pays the individual's medical costs in the event she becomes unhealthy and disability insurance delivers a stream of payments in the event of disability. Life insurance pays the face value of the policy to beneficiaries in the event of the individual's death.

The insurance payments, however, do not 'make the individual whole'. The insurance company cannot restore the individual's health; or, put differently, the individual cannot 'transfer health' from her healthy to her less healthy state. Insurance against blindness transfers money from the state in which the individual is sighted – she pays a premium – to the state in which she is blind. After the insurance payment, the individual still cannot see.[16]

[15] More formally, assume that the agent has preferences over her wealth w and her health h. Under suitable assumptions, these preferences may be represented by a utility function $u(w, h)$. Suppose that (w, h) represents the agent's initial endowment of wealth and health. Suppose the agent suffers a personal injury so that her health status falls to a level $h' < h$. Presumably, her preferences reflect a positive valuation of health; that is, for any level of wealth v, the agent prefers (v, h) to (v, h'), or in utility terms, for all v, $u(v, h) > u(v, h')$. Moreover, when $h = d$, where d is death, her level of wealth does not affect her well-being; she is indifferent between (v, d) and (v', d) for any v and v'. Obviously, then, for $h = d$, there is no amount of wealth w' such that $u(w', d) = u(w, h)$. Clearly, this same inability to compensate may occur for other types of personal injury.

[16] It is not clear what 'making whole' means when the harm is irreparable. It might mean that the agent should receive sufficient compensation to make her welfare in the harmed state equal to her welfare in the unharmed state: that is, choose damages d so that

Thus, in this model, an individual purchases insurance against the risk of a specific personal injury when her marginal utility of money in the injured state is higher than her marginal utility of money in the healthy state. An individual insures to some extent against blindness because the marginal value of money in the blind state is higher than in the sighted state; with that money the individual can purchase 'substitutes' for her sight: seeing eye dogs, individuals to read to her, braille lessons, a chauffeur to drive her, etc.[17]

If the marginal value of money is identical in the two states, she will not purchase any insurance. A common object may, for example, have sentimental value to the agent. The object is easily and cheaply replaced but the value attaches to the particular token of the object the agent has. If the object is lost, however, she has no reason to change the extent or pattern of her expenditures. Though she might insure for the replacement value of the object she would not insure for its sentimental value.

The fact that an agent might not purchase any insurance or very little insurance does not indicate that the agent places a low value on the adverse event. As noted, an agent may not purchase any insurance that pays out only on her death. We should not conclude from this fact that she places a low value on her life. Paying a premium now to have money when she is dead is simply undesirable; she would rather spend money to reduce her risk of death.

All irreparable injuries share this feature; insurance can only transfer wealth from the agent in the healthy state to the agent in the 'injured state'; but if money is less valuable to the agent after suffering the irreparable injury than before, she will have no reason to transfer income to the injured state. Thus, when activities create risks of irreparable injury, the deterrence and compensation motives separate. Should the

$u(v + d, h') = u(v, h)$. Two comments about this formula are important. First, d may not exist; there may be no amount of money that, in the state h' restores the agent to her pre-injury level of well-being. When h' is death, this observation is straightforward. Second, the amount d of compensation does not quite place the agent in identical positions as neither her marginal utility of money nor her marginal utility of health will be identical in the harmed and unharmed states. That is, a monetary windfall would be less valuable to her in the harmed state than in the unharmed state; conversely, additional irreparable harms may have different effects on her in the two states.

17 Of course, her expenditures in some areas may be less than they were when she was sighted. She will spend less money on entrance fees to art exhibits and perhaps movies. But she may attend more concerts or buy more songs from iTunes. Whether the marginal utility of money is higher in the less healthy state will depend on how these increases and decreases net out.

third party be held liable, the agent would receive a damage award but this award would not compensate her for her loss.[18] Nevertheless, society has a reason to hold third parties responsible for the personal injuries to which their actions contribute, as reducing the risk of personal injury generally (and hence the amount of personal injury that occurs in society) is important.[19]

2.2 *Two-actor accidents*

Most accidents occur in more complex environments in which more than one agent makes decisions that causally affect the outcome. In these contexts the conflict between deterrent and compensatory aims of the law are stronger. In this section, I briefly consider the next simplest situation in which the actions of two agents causally contribute to the creation of a risk that, if realised, will impose harm on one of the two agents.

Consider an accident between strangers. A and B each engages in an activity that each might pursue with more or less care. An accident may result from their activities; the probability that an accident occurs depends on A's choice a of care and B's choice b of care. The accident causes harm to one of the parties, say B. To begin, assume that the harm is only financial.

The analysis has begun with an assignment of causal responsibility; each agent's action contributes to the risk of harm and each is thus causally responsible. How should legal and financial responsibility be allocated? If the assignment of responsibility is not contingent on the level of care of at least one of the parties, the deterrence aim of a liability rule cannot be fully met.[20] Consider three different, 'absolutist' rules: legal and financial responsibility on A (strict liability), legal and financial responsibility on B (no liability), and A and B equally responsible (the sharing rule). Under rules of strict liability or no liability, only one agent bears the full costs of her decision making: A under strict liability and

[18] As we saw, in the case of death, there is no amount of money that will restore the dead agent to the level of well-being she had when alive. In less extreme cases, compensation increases the injured agent's well-being but it does not make her 'whole' in the sense of putting her in a position identical to her pre-injury state.

[19] Society, of course, might mitigate these risks through mechanisms other than liability rules. The account thus far does not explain why victims of personal injury should receive compensation beyond the (possibly substantial) pecuniary losses that they incur.

[20] Again, I ignore other legal routes to inducing appropriate care choices.

B under no liability. The non-responsible agent is thus irresponsible and takes too little care.[21] Under a sharing rule, each bears only part of the loss and consequently each takes too little care; accidents happen too frequently.[22]

A negligence rule that conditions the legal and financial responsibility of A on her choice of care level can, when standards of care are set appropriately, induce both parties to take the socially optimal levels of care.[23] Similarly, a rule that conditions the legal and financial responsibility of B on his choice of care can also induce both parties to take optimal care. Negligence rules like these 'show' the full cost of an agent's decision to *each* agent. Suppose, for instance, that A faces a negligence rule. The agent whose responsibility is conditioned on her choice sees the cost of being negligent, while the other agent directly bears those costs when the first is non-negligent.[24]

Thus, under negligence rules, causal responsibility will always diverge from legal and financial responsibility. The deterrent and compensatory aims are also in tension. Under a negligence rule, financial responsibility falls on only one party.

When potential harm includes irreparable injury, the agent has an incentive to take care to reduce the risk of personal injury to herself even if a liability rule assigns liability to another party. In some, symmetric instances, the drivers on a freeway for example, both parties face a risk of

[21] This conclusion depends on the technology of accident prevention. If the choices of each party are alternatives: only one of them need to take care to prevent it, then, to maximise social welfare, only one of them should take care. But this technological structure is unusual. In most instances, the socially optimal decisions require each to take care. Under a rule of strict liability A takes too much care and B too little, while under no liability A takes too little care and B too much.

[22] S. Shavell, *The Economic Theory of Accident Law* (Cambridge, MA: Harvard University Press, 1987) provides an introduction to the economic analysis of accident law. The models he develops focus on pecuniary loss not personal injury. He identifies the set of rules that minimise social costs when agents choose only care levels. When agents choose both care and activity levels – not only how carefully they drive but also how many miles per unit time, no liability rule achieves the first-best; Shavell identifies the structure of analysis for determining which liability rules are second-best.

[23] B's legal and financial responsibility is thus similarly conditioned on A's choice of care level. If A is non-negligent, then B bears financial responsibility for the harm; if A is negligent, A bears financial liability for the accident.

[24] These conclusions should be hedged by suitable caveats. The negligence rules minimise social costs relative only to certain decisions. If both agents choose activity levels as well as care levels, for example, no rule can induce both parties to adopt the care levels and activity levels that maximise social welfare.

irreparable harm; this symmetry may induce each agent to take adequate care when faced with only paying pecuniary damages equal to the financial harm.[25] When the risk of irreparable injury is asymmetric, however, the agent who faces no risk of irreparable must bear, or at least face, financial responsibility that exceeds the financial harm if her care decisions are to appropriately reflect the risk of injury her decisions impose on the victim, the agent who suffers irreparable harm.

Even in simple environments, then, devising liability rules that simultaneously create appropriate incentives for multiple actors requires that responsibility be allocated so that each agent 'sees' all the costs and benefits that her actions impose on all other parties. Typically, allocations that create appropriate incentives will allocate legal and financial responsibility differently.

This complex coordination problem is made more difficult when one accounts for the possibility of settlement. Plaintiffs and defendants bargain in the shadow of the law and it is the shadow, not the law itself, that determines each agent's incentives. Defendants in determining how much care to take, that is, do so in light of the amounts they expect actually to pay, rather than the amount the law requires in the event they lose the litigation.

2.3 *Joint and several liability*

In many circumstances, a harm results to a third party because of the actions of multiple agents.[26]

Complex risks of this sort may be governed either by a regime of several-only liability or a regime of joint and several liability. Under several-only liability, each responsible agent is legally and financially responsible only for 'her share' of the harm. Under joint and several liability, each potentially responsible agent is legally and financially responsible for the entire harm.

Regimes of joint and several liability are complex and different regimes allocate legal and financial responsibility among causally responsible agents in radically different ways. To begin, however, it is useful to

[25] J.H. Arlen, 'Reconsidering Efficient Tort Rules for Personal Injury: The Case of Single Activity Accidents' (1990) 32 WMLR 41.

[26] For a survey see L.A. Kornhauser, 'Economic analysis of joint and several liability', in J.H. Arlen (ed.), *Research Handbook on the Economics of Torts* (Northampton: Edward Elgar, 2013), 199.

contrast regimes of joint and several liability with a regime of several-only liability. Under several-only liability, each tortfeasor is responsible for the wrong that she caused; the regime thus presupposes that the court can distinguish the wrongs caused by each tortfeasor from the wrongs caused by other tortfeasors.[27] When the wrong is indivisible, however, the wrongs are not easily assignable to tortfeasors; in these cases a regime of joint and several liability applies.[28] In these cases, joint and several liability reallocates the risk of the insolvency of one or more defendants as well as the costs of collection of damages. More importantly, as will be explained later, the value of a claim under joint and several liability is at least as great as, and often exceeds, the value of parallel claims under several-only liability.

Regimes of joint and several liability are complex along several dimensions. I discuss three dimensions: contribution, claim reduction, and allocation of orphan shares. In a regime of no contribution, a plaintiff who prevails at trial against multiple tortfeasors chooses from which tortfeasors to collect her award. Should she collect the entire award from a single defendant, that defendant bears the entire cost. By contrast, under a regime of joint and several liability with contribution, the defendant from whom the plaintiff has collected her award has a right of action for the allocated shares of the other defendants against whom the plaintiff has prevailed.[29] A regime of joint and several liability with

[27] The next sentence specifies the claim in this sentence to a particular way in which the wrongs for which different tortfeasors are responsible are indistinguishable. It focuses on indivisibility of the harm. But sometimes the 'harms' are indistinguishable in the sense that plaintiff cannot identify which defendant harmed her. Each defendant created an identical risk but we cannot tell which risk was realised. Some US courts have applied joint and several liability to these cases under the rubric enterprise liability. See *Sindell* v. *Abbott Laboratories*, 26 Cal. 3d 588 (1980), cert. denied 449 US 912 (1980) in which the California Supreme Court held liable all firms that marketed diethylstilbestrol (DES) even though plaintiffs (in a class action) were unable to determine whose DES pills they had consumed. These cases present a different set of issues than those discussed in the text. Vicarious liability, discussed later, presents a third set of issues.

[28] L.A. Kornhauser, 'An Economic Analysis of the Choice between Enterprise and Personal Liability for Accidents' (1982) 70 Cal LR 1345 provides an example. Suppose A fires a shotgun at P and injures P's arm, while B fires a pistol at P and injures P's leg. These harms are 'divisible'; several-only liability allocates the arm injury to A and the leg injury to B. Suppose, on the other hand, that A and B fire identical weapons at P, with both bullets killing him. P's death is an indivisible harm and the courts impose a regime of joint and several liability on both A and B.

[29] Under some regimes with contribution, the paying defendant may have a claim against settling defendants as well.

contribution thus assigns responsibility among multiple tortfeasors based on its determination of an allocable share.

How is the allocable share determined? Are not 'indivisible harms' unallocable?[30] The division of financial responsibility apparently contradicts the underlying condition that joint and several liability applies only when harm is indivisible. But this contradiction is apparent rather than real. There are two cases. First, suppose both A and B are legally responsible for P's death. The harm, death, is unitary; each was causally responsible for exactly the same harm (on the assumption that the action of each was sufficient to cause P's death). In these instances, shares are typically allocated *pro rata*, that is, responsibility for the award is divided equally among the responsible defendants.

Second, suppose, by contrast, that each agent's action is necessary to cause the harm but neither is sufficient. In these instances, shares may be allocated in proportion to some measure of the defendants' causal responsibility for the harm or, under a negligence regime, proportional to each's fault. CERCLA,[31] the United States (US) statute governing responsibility for resolving contamination of soil and groundwater caused by the release of hazardous waste into the environment, illustrates a complex variant of this class of harms. It allocates responsibility in proportion to the amount of wastes released. For simplicity, assume that each responsible party deposited the same toxic chemical at a waste site; any amount released into the environment would have caused harm but the amount of harm increases with the total amount of waste deposited. If the marginal cost of remediation is increasing in the total amount of contaminant deposited, then we cannot allocate this marginal increase to one or the other agent; proportional sharing seems appropriate.[32]

Claim reduction determines the effect of the plaintiff's settlement with one defendant on her remaining claims against litigating tortfeasors. Claim reduction rules vary across jurisdictions. Some jurisdictions have adopted a *pro tanto* set-off rule that reduces the plaintiff's claim against

[30] We might also ask whether indivisible harms are irreparable. Indivisibility and irreparability characterise harms along two different dimensions. Indivisibility concerns the relation of the harm to those causally responsible for it while irreparability concerns the nature of the harm itself. Defendant 1 who cuts off V's arm and defendant 2 who severs V's leg have each inflicted an irreparable harm on V, but the harms are divisible.

[31] Comprehensive Environmental Response, Compensation and Liability Act of 1980, 42 USC sections 9601–9675 (CERCLA).

[32] In this example, generators are the only defendants. The site owner (and transporters) are, under the statute, also responsible.

litigating defendants by the amount of the settlement reached with another defendant. Other jurisdictions have adopted an *apportioned* set-off rule that reduces the plaintiff's claim against litigating defendants by the settling defendant's allocable share of the claim.

Rules governing claim reduction and contribution play a significant role in structuring the choice between settlement and litigation; that choice, in turn, determines the final allocation of financial responsibility for damages created by the liability regime. Interestingly, when all (solvent) parties settle, each defendant pays the same amount in settlement regardless of the size of her allocable share.

The final element of a regime of joint and several liability that I shall discuss allocates the burden created by the insolvency of some, but not all, defendants. Under a rule of legal contribution, the party from whom the plaintiff chooses to collect her judgement bears responsibility for all orphan shares. Under an equitable rule, solvent parties divide the burden of orphan shares in proportion to their own allocable shares. Under a legal rule, the solvent party from whom the plaintiff has chosen to collect the judgement bears the entire burden of the orphan shares.

It is (relatively) straightforward to see the extent to which joint and several liability serves the social aim of compensation. It distributes financial responsibility among the legal responsible defendants. As a consequence, other defendants bear the risks of insolvency of some of the defendants.[33]

Understanding the incentive effects of joint and several liability, however, is much more complex. This complexity arises from several sources. First, the value of litigation depends on the degree of correlation among the plaintiff's prospects for success in the litigation against the various defendants. Second, the price that the liability rule places on an agent's behaviour depends on the settlement process. Finally, the impact of insolvency is difficult to untangle.

To begin simply, however, observe that the incentive and compensation aims of the rules will again be in tension. Even when the plaintiff is passive, the presence of multiple defendants reproduces the difficulties

[33] This statement is not strictly true. As discussed below, the value of a claim under joint and several liability exceeds the value of parallel claims under a regime of several-only liability. As the number of solvent, responsible defendants declines, however, the value of the claim under joint and several liability decreases and approaches the value of the claim against a single defendant. In one sense, then, plaintiff bears part of the risk of insolvency of a defendant because that insolvency decreases the value of her claim.

that arose in the two-agent accident case previously discussed. The legal rule has to 'show' the full cost of the harm to each agent. Yet the compensation criterion restricts recovery to the amount of the financial harm. A negligence rule can accomplish this feat, but, again, in equilibrium, no rational defendant will be negligent and financial responsibility will fall on the victim. By contrast, under strict liability, the victim will be compensated but each defendant will take too little care as she does not see the full cost of her actions.[34]

Of course, as noted earlier, when there is irreparable harm, limiting financial responsibility to financial harm implies that the defendants will take too little care even under a negligence regime. Financial responsibility has to be increased beyond the level of financial harm to induce parties to take appropriate care.

Let us return now to the more interesting aspects of the incentive effects of joint and several liability. Suppose that there are exactly two defendants, R and C, who have caused the plaintiff harm. The plaintiff's prospects of success against R may be more or less correlated with her prospects of success against C. Contrast, for example, an antitrust action grounded in conspiracy with an unusual tort to be described shortly. In the antitrust case, the plaintiff only prevails against R if she prevails against C; her prospect of success against R is perfectly correlated with her prospect of success against C. If the plaintiff prevails against R she prevails against C and if the plaintiff loses to R she loses to C. This perfect correlation results from the elements of proof against each and relies on identical evidence.

In *Boca Grande Club* v. *Florida Power and Light*[35] by contrast, the plaintiff's prospects of success against R and C were independent. The plaintiff's husband and son, both inexperienced sailors, had rented a yacht from the Boca Grande Club. The yacht's high mast struck a cable slung by Florida Power and Light from a bridge. Husband and son were both electrocuted. The plaintiff alleged that the yacht club negligently rented inexperienced sailors an inappropriate boat and that Florida Power and Light negligently let its power cable hang too low. To prevail

[34] See L.A. Kornhauser and R.L. Revesz, 'Sharing Damages Among Multiple Tortfeasors' (1989) 98 YLJ 831. They note that one can reproduce the negligence result under a more complex strict liability regime that mirrors the negligence regime but simply shifts the default bearer of liability.

[35] *Boca Grande Club Inc.* v. *Florida Power & Light Company Inc.*, 511 US 222 (1994); the facts appear in the opinion of the lower court, 990 F. 2d 606 (11th Cir. 1993).

against the yacht club, the plaintiff must rely on completely different evidence than she must rely on to prevail against Florida Power and Light. Knowledge of the outcome of the plaintiff's suit against the yacht club tells us nothing about her prospects of success against the power company.

When the plaintiff's prospects of success against the two defendants are perfectly correlated, the expected value of litigation against both is identical to the expected value of litigation under a regime of several-only liability. If, for example, the plaintiff's prospect of success against the pair is .5 and the claim is for USD 1,000,000, then the expected value of her claim is USD 500,000. When plaintiff's prospects of success are independent, however, the expected value of the plaintiff's claim under joint and several liability exceeds the expected value of the parallel claims under a regime of several-only liability. Suppose that the plaintiff's prospects of success against each defendant is again .5. Under several-only liability, the value of her claim is again USD 500,000. Under a regime of joint and several liability, by contrast, the expected value of her litigation is USD 750,000 because, to receive the full amount of USD 1,000,000, she need prevail against only one of the two defendants and this event happens with a probability of .75.[36] This heightened probability of success has important consequences for settlement negotiations. In general, for two defendants, we know that the value of the claim to a plaintiff is at least as great as the value of the corresponding claims under several-only liability.[37]

It is important to note that settlement, under a rule that allocates legal responsibility proportionally to fault or cause, allocates financial

[36] She loses both law suits with probability .5x.5 = .25 so her probability of prevailing against at least one defendant is .75.

[37] The claim was first proven in L.A. Kornhauser and R.L. Revesz, 'Multi-Defendant Settlements: The Impact of Joint and Several Liability' (1994) 23 JLS 41, at 73–75. For a survey of the relevant literature see Kornhauser, 'Economic analysis of joint and several liability', n. 26. The claim is true for all degrees of correlation in plaintiff's prospects of success except when the prospects of success are perfectly correlated and the regime includes the apportioned rather than the *pro tanto* set-off rule. Note that the value of a claim is always at least as great as the expected value of litigation, but it may be higher because the plaintiff may be able to extract additional funds through settlement. We know much less about settlement behaviour when there are more than two defendants though it remains true that the expected value of litigation under joint and several liability exceeds the expected value of litigation under several-only liability and hence that the value of a claim under joint and several liability is at least as great under joint and several liability.

responsibility differently than it would be allocated if the case were litigated to a conclusion. Thus, if both defendants settle, they settle for equal amounts regardless of the size of their relative shares. If, in equilibrium, the plaintiff settles with one defendant and litigates with the other, she settles with the defendant responsible for the larger share.

These settlement behaviours bear on the assessment of the fairness of a liability regime as well. Often, analysts assess the fairness of a regime in terms of the formal allocation of legal and financial responsibility by the legal rule. The actual allocation, however, is mediated by settlement and settlement amounts are not, under joint and several liability, necessarily proportional to the shares that would be allocated were a dispute litigated to a conclusion.

Further, the assessment of fairness depends on one's reference point. Under joint and several liability, an agent with a very small allocated share of financial responsibility bears a large share of financial responsibility if agents with more significant allocable shares are insolvent.[38] From the perspective of the defendant, its disproportionate financial liability is unfair; but the injured plaintiff is the other alternative bearer of financial responsibility.

2.4 *Vicarious liability*

Vicarious liability imposes liability on a principal for those wrongs of her agent that were done in the course of the agent's employment. The law thus allocates responsibility among at least three parties: the injured plaintiff, the defendant-agent, and the defendant-principal. Specifically, vicarious liability allows the plaintiff, when the defendant-agent is legally and causally responsible, to collect her award from the principal rather than the agent. The principal may then seek indemnity from the agent if the agent is solvent and if the employer so chooses. In the event of the full or partial insolvency of the agent, then, vicarious liability shifts pecuniary losses and risk-reducing damages to the principal rather than the plaintiff.

Vicarious liability thus apparently separates legal responsibility from causal responsibility. In principle, the principal may have taken no action

[38] The text assumes a regime that has a rule of contribution. If the regime does not permit contribution then an actor with a small allocable share may bear the entire financial responsibility if the plaintiff chooses to enforce the entire judgement against that defendant. Any unfairness here results from the bar on contribution.

beyond hiring the agent. The assignment of legal and financial responsibility in the absence of causal responsibility thus rests on the fact that the principal has benefitted from the agent's actions and not that the principal has otherwise acted wrongly. On the other hand, the assignment of legal and financial responsibility may rest also on a recognition of the difficulties that a plaintiff would face in establishing the causal responsibility of the principal.

Nevertheless, the shadow of causal responsibility lurks behind vicarious liability. The principal, after all, may take greater or less care when hiring individuals and it has supervisory authority over the agent and determines the incentive structure within which the agent acts. More concretely, the principal assigned the agent the task in the accomplishment of which she caused the plaintiff's injury. The principal typically structures that task and supervises the agent her duties. The principal may have failed to exercise due care in any of these tasks.

Vicarious liability thus has incentive effects that may induce principals to reduce risks appropriately. We may approach this argument in two ways. First, the principal may have available *ex ante* or even *ex post* incentive mechanisms not available to state law. The employer might screen its agents more carefully, supervise them more intensively, or adopt back-up systems that eliminate or mitigate risks caused by a single agent. An employer might be held responsible under a negligence standard for failure to take some of these actions; but proof of the agent's negligence might be more direct and less costly than establishing negligence on the part of the principal.

Vicarious liability is a form of joint and several liability. Its justification rests on one of the two standard justifications for joint and several liability: it shifts the risk of insolvency of the defendant-agent from the plaintiff to the defendant-principal. This justification treats the principal as an insurer of the agent on the grounds presumably that the agent's wrong occurred in the course of her employment and hence worked to the benefit of the principal.

3. Responsibility of international organisations

A large number of international and supra-national organisations undertake daily myriad tasks. These tasks often seek to accomplish much good, but in the pursuit of that good they can cause significant harm; we thus all have an interest that these organisations pursue these tasks carefully. In this, international organisations do not differ from multinational corporations, not-for-profit organisations, or governments, the former of which, at least, are subject to liability for wrongs they commit.

In this section, I pursue three tasks. First, I sketch the law governing international organisations. Second, I identify some differences between international organisations and private actors that might bear on the desirability of imposing liability on them for wrongs. Finally, I briefly characterise different classes of actions that an international organisation might undertake and that might merit different treatment.

3.1 *The law governing liability of international organisations*

This chapter addresses the liability regime governing international organisations as defendants. The situation of an international organisation that is a defendant differs from that of an individual defendant in two important respects. The international organisation is a corporate, sovereign entity.

The legal regime governing the responsibility of international organisations for wrongs to others is, in one sense complex, and in another sense quite simple. Complexity arises from the multiple, potential sources of law under which an international organisation might be responsible. International organisations do not operate on 'international' territory; they operate, as multinational corporations do, on the territory of many different nations in each of which they might, in principle, be governed by domestic law. By treaty and by statute, however, international organisations are generally immune from suit. In the United States, the scope of that immunity is quite broad, though controversial. The International Organization Immunities Act of 1945 granted many international organisations the same status as foreign states.[39] The Foreign Sovereign Immunities Act of 1976 more clearly defined and restricted the extent of immunity of sovereign states;[40] but the extent to which it modified the immunity enjoyed by international organisations is controversial.[41]

[39] International Organization Immunities Act of 1945, 22 USC section 288a(b): '[i]nternational organizations, their property and their assets, wherever located, and by whomsoever held, shall enjoy the same immunity from suit and every form of judicial process as is enjoyed by foreign governments, except to the extent that such organizations may expressly waive their immunity for the purpose of any proceedings or by the terms of any contract.'

[40] Foreign Sovereign Immunities Act of 1976, 28 USC 1602 et seq.

[41] Contrast *Brzak* v. *United Nations*, 597 F. 3d 107 (2d Cir. 2010), cert. denied 131 S. Ct. 151 (2010) which held that the Foreign Sovereign Immunities Act did not affect the absolute

In addition, international organisations are subject to international law and may not violate its norms. The nature and extent of these obligations are controversial; the United Nations (UN) General Assembly's taking note of the International Law Commission's Articles on the Responsibility of International Organizations (ARIO)[42] has not lessened the controversy.[43] The ARIO envision a legal regime that has the basic elements of vicarious liability,[44] joint and several (or, at least, shared) responsibility,[45] and piercing the corporate veil to hold member states responsible.[46]

From a practical perspective, however, the legal regime governing the liability of international organisations is relatively simple: international organisations are immune from suit under domestic law and, typically, under international law no court may have jurisdiction. Given the lack of a forum in which to hold them accountable, international organisations are legally and financially responsible only for those wrongs for which they choose to be responsible; and in many contexts the extent of liability is on their own terms. Typically, international organisations establish internal procedures to process grievances from employees and third parties, but these fora are not obviously impartial and may deny claims that, to outsiders, appear valid.[47]

3.2 *Incentives and accountability in international organisations*

International organisations are not typical collective entities that function within a complex liability regime. They are neither natural persons nor for-profit corporations. They typically have beneficent missions. They sit outside domestic governments. Further, neutral fora for adjudication

immunity of the UN granted by the Convention on the Privileges and Immunities of the United Nations (1 UNTS 15), to which the United States is a signatory, with *OSS Nokalva, Inc.* v. *European Space Agency*, 617 F. 3d 756 (3d Cir. 2010) holding that the restrictions on sovereign immunity of states applied to international organisations as well. For an account of the state of US law, see A.I. Young, 'Deconstructing International Organization Immunity' (2012) 44 Geo JIL 311.

42 ARIO, n. 9.

43 For a taste of the controversy see issue 1 of volume (2012) 9 of the IOLR.

44 Article 6 ARIO, n. 9.

45 Article 48 ARIO, n. 9.

46 Articles 58–62 ARIO, n. 9.

47 The claim of Haitian cholera victims, discussed in section 4 below provides an example.

and resolution of claims against them are at best rare and at worst non-existent. How do these features bear on the assignment of responsibility to them?

Under the common law, charitable institutions and governments long benefitted from immunity from suit for their wrongful acts. Two related arguments for a time sustained this legal regime; both focus on the not-for-profit nature of these entities. First, both charitable enterprises and governments act, at least in principle, for the public benefit. Imposition of liability would obviously increase the cost of providing these public benefits and, presumably, decrease their supply. If charitable organisations were liable for wrongs that they negligently caused, the argument goes, individuals would be less likely to engage in charitable endeavours. Similarly, if governments were liable for wrongs that they negligently caused, the government would either limit the extent of its activity or abandon it.

A conclusion that the cost should not be imposed, however, does not follow from the claim or even the fact that tort liability would reduce the supply of charitable endeavours. The provision of public benefits, just as the provision of private benefits, might impose external costs – costs not seen by the decision maker; if those external costs exceed the public benefits then it is socially better that the provision of benefits not occur. Similarly, if those external costs can be reduced or eliminated by the delivery of the benefits in a more careful way, then society would be better off if more care were taken; the net social benefits delivered by charitable organisations would increase. A liability regime that internalised those external costs and induced better, more careful policies from charitable organisations and governments would thus be socially beneficial.

The second justification for immunity rests on the assumption that charitable organisations, governments, and their agents will not respond to economic incentives created by liability rules. This assumption seems unwarranted, or, at least, no more warranted than a similar assumption about for-profit enterprises and their agents. Not-for-profits and governments operate within budgets that require the organisation to make trade-offs about different uses of its funds and limit the scale of its activities. These resource allocation decisions parallel those made in for-profit organisations; well-run not-for-profit organisations make these decisions in a manner consonant with economic theory. Better government and better provision of public benefits by charitable organisations should thus result when a liability rule forces the organisation to include the external costs in its decision.

These immunities have eroded,[48] at least in the United States, for charitable institutions and for local governments though not for 'sovereigns' so that these entities now face substantially the same liability regime as private principals and agents.[49]

One other issue arises. Liability often arises substantially after an agent has acted wrongfully. Soil contamination from releases of hazardous waste into the environment may occur decades after the waste was deposited. The agents who undertook the wrongful acts may have left the principal's employ; indeed the long time horizon implicated in these decisions may render it difficult to transmit appropriate incentives to the agent. Vicarious (or direct) liability of the government may seem unfair because the state population may have changed radically over that time; the citizens who benefitted from the action will not be the set of citizens who must pay the damages. In the private context, this problem is mitigated by the existence of securities markets; the shareholders who incur the liability purchased the shares in a competitive market that should have priced the expected liability. No such pricing mechanism exists for individuals immigrating to a jurisdiction. International organisations, however, are more similar to governments than to publicly traded corporations.

International organisations differ from sovereign governments in one other important respect. Sovereigns, at least those in democratic states, are accountable to the electorate. If the government persistently ignores the external costs and benefits of its actions and acts inappropriately, the electorate will punish these actors at the polls. International organisations, by contrast, are not politically accountable.

Not-for-profits are not politically accountable either. Many not-for-profits are essentially self-perpetuating managers of assets. Each may face a market test in the sense that each has to raise money to underwrite its operations. But this market is very thinly tied to performance as a glance at the ratio of administrative expenses to total budget would suggest. It is even more thinly tied to performance on specific projects. Imposing legal and financial responsibility imposes a very minimal form of accountability on these organisations.

[48] This erosion has occurred both through judicial decision and statutory innovation.

[49] Sovereign immunity, however, has not eroded for the United States and its states. Typically, however, these governments enact statutes that partially waive immunity from suit. In some instances, not-for-profits are liable only for gross negligence.

3.3 *A taxonomy of tasks*

Individuals, corporations, not-for-profits, governments, and international organisations undertake a wide range of activities. Some activities occur in the ordinary course of living or business. An agent of the entity, in the course of her employment, drives from point A to point B. Her vehicle might strike a pedestrian. Both the agent and the entity should take care in these contexts.

But bureaucracies also plan, adopt, and execute policies. The Federal Tort Claims Act, the statute that waives the sovereign immunity of the United States, does not waive immunity for policy decisions, a category that, as the examples that follow suggest, is difficult to describe. One might ask whether policy decisions should benefit from protection from immunity. Many policy decisions are made in an environment rife with uncertainty both about the underlying nature of the crisis to be resolved or activities to be regulated and about the best solution to these problems. In these contexts, many policies will fail but we might nonetheless not want to stifle policy responses. On the other hand, we want policy makers to take reasonable care in the formation of policy. The arguments for liability for wrongs incident to day-to-day tasks apply equally to policy decisions. The policy maker should take into account the potential adverse consequences that her decisions may have. For-profit entities face liability for similar policy decisions. If a corporation creates an innovation and introduces it to the market, it will be responsible for any harms the product causes.

4. Two examples

Two examples may help make concrete the nature of the inquiry that might arise were international organisations subject to legal responsibility for their actions. As such agencies often act together and through agents issues of joint and several liability as well as vicarious liability will arise.

4.1 *Poisoned wells*

Until the early 1970s, surface water from lakes, ponds, and rivers constituted the primary source of drinking water in (what is now) Bangladesh. These sources were often contaminated with water-borne diseases that were killing roughly 250,000 children a year.[50] To solve this problem UNICEF spearheaded a project to provide groundwater from tube wells in Bangladeshi villages. In fact, UNICEF funded the first 900,000 tube wells dug in Bangladesh.[51] The World Bank also contributed funding. Many of these wells, however, are contaminated with arsenic and have led to the largest mass chemical poisoning in history.[52]

Controversy exists both as to when authorities knew or should have known of the contamination. UNICEF claims that, at the time of their initial funding, no one suspected that ground water in Bangladesh might be tainted. Geochemists, however, dispute that claim, contending that testing for arsenic would have been reasonable and inexpensive.[53]

International agencies claimed to have learned of the problem in 1998. Workers at the Dhaka hospital in Bangladesh, however, treated cases of arsenic poisoning among Bangladeshis in the early 1980s and claim to have notified authorities in 1985.[54] Saha reported a case of arsenic poisoning in West Bengal in 1983.[55] One activist sampled well water in 1988 and had it analysed by a Belgian firm; that analysis found arsenic.[56] Similarly, the World Bank claims that no groundwater was tested for arsenic until 1993; yet one engineer based in Dhaka contends he found arsenic in the wells in the late 1980s.[57] More broadly, authorities in neighbouring West Bengal in India, in the same watershed as Bangladesh, knew of arsenic contamination by 1991.[58]

50 F. Pearce, 'Who is to blame for Bangladesh's arsenic poisoning?', The Courier UNESCO, January 2001, 10, at 10.

51 Ibid.

52 Ibid. UNICEF's representative in Dhaka estimates that they will have *identified* all the contaminated wells by 2030, ibid., at 11. The standard for arsenic in drinking water in the United States is 10 micrograms per liter; in India and Bangladesh, the standard is 50 micrograms per liter. Actual concentrations in groundwater in Bangladesh appears to be roughly 180 micrograms per liter. P. Ravenscroft, W.G. Burgess, K.M. Ahmed, M. Burren, and J. Perrin, 'Arsenic in groundwater of the Bengal Basin, Bangladesh: Distribution, field relations, and hydrogeological setting' (2005) 13 Hydrogeo J 727, at 728, 733–734. The standard in the United States was 50 micrograms per liter until 2001. United States Environmental Protection Agency, 'Arsenic Rule', see water.epa.gov/lawsregs/rulesregs/sdwa/arsenic/regulations.cfm.

53 Pearce, 'Who is to blame for Bangladesh's arsenic poisoning?', n. 50, at 11.

54 Ibid.; also M. Mushtaque and R. Chowdhury, 'Arsenic Crisis in Bangladesh,' Scientific American (August 2004), at 87.

55 K.C. Saha, 'Melanokeratosis from arsenical contaminated tubewell water' (1984) 29 Ind J Dermat 37.

56 Pearce, 'Who is to blame for Bangladesh's arsenic poisoning?', n. 50, at 11.

57 Ibid.

58 Ravenscroft et al., 'Arsenic in groundwater of the Bengal Basin, Bangladesh', n. 52, at 728.

Contaminated water is generally drawn from wells that have a depth of 30 to 70 metres. Water above 20 metres and below 200 metres has concentration levels that meet health standards. Knowledge of the extent and nature of arsenic levels in ground water might thus have led either to no use of contaminated aquifers (and a concomitant drive to purify surface waters) or to exploitation of even contaminated aquifers in a safer manner.

A complex social process led to the poisoning of a vast population. To allocate responsibility requires that we unravel this complex process. UNICEF and the World Bank funded the digging of tube wells in Bangladesh. But other individuals and agencies participated in this endeavour as well. Most obviously, the government of Bangladesh knew of the project and has primary responsibility for the assurance of water quality in its territory. In addition, various other foreign aid institutions participated in funding the preliminary (and subsequent) engineering studies. These of course were conducted by consultants. The wells themselves were dug by contractors. All of these agents causally contributed to the harm.

Millions of Bangladeshis suffered an irreparable harm to their health and welfare. In addition, these individuals require new sources of untainted water. How should responsibility be allocated among the parties who causally contributed to this public health disaster? The issues raised are complicated in part because the government of Bangladesh was in part causally responsible for the mass disaster as it neither had provided clean water nor tested groundwater for high concentrations of arsenic. Bangladesh should thus be a co-defendant partially responsible.[59]

If this were a domestic tort, we would ask what duties were owed to the affected population and when. Clearly, someone should have tested the water for arsenic at some point. The question is: when? Testing should have occurred once relevant officials knew or should have known two facts: first, that arsenic levels in drinking water were a public health hazard; and second, there was some chance that groundwater in Bangladesh was contaminated. All relevant actors should have known at the time UNICEF initiated funding that arsenic in drinking water was dangerous. After all, arsenic was a known poison. Moreover, in 1975,

[59] One might argue, however, that the World Bank and other development agencies were digging the wells precisely because of the inadequacies of the government of Bangladesh.

the US Environmental Protection Agency had issued a rule permitting concentrations of no more than 50 micrograms per litre.[60]

Whether the testing should have occurred at the time the project was initially conceived thus depends on when the relevant parties had or should have had knowledge of a possibility of arsenic in the ground water. Such knowledge might have arisen either from direct knowledge of the presence of arsenic in the water or from indirect knowledge inferred from observed instances of arsenic poisoning (which should then have prompted water testing).[61] The first cases of arsenic poisoning were observed in hospitals in the area in the early- to mid-1980s. The number of cases proliferated. By 1998, the international organisations had acknowledged the existence of a public health crisis and turned to remediation.

The date at which we determine the wrongdoing occurred determines the set of wrongdoers that should be held legally responsible. Suppose that agents should have known that tests of water quality were appropriate by 1980. Then the set of legally responsible wrongdoers would consist of the financing agents that included UNICEF and the World Bank,[62] various governmental organisations and consultants who performed or failed to perform tests, and arguably various agencies of the Bangladeshi government.

Financial harm here consists of the costs of remediation which, in this instance, would require the provision of safe drinking water for the affected areas. Irreparable harm includes both the death and disability of a large percentage of the Bangladeshi population and damage to local ecosystems. These harms are preventable, but not compensable and

60 See United States Environmental Protection Agency, 'Arsenic Rule', n. 52.

61 In the early 1990s, an engineer employed by the British Geological Survey (BGS), under a grant from the UK Overseas Development Agency, surveyed the water quality in the aquifers in Bangladesh to determine whether it was toxic to fish or humans. The engineer took water samples from roughly 150 tubewell sites. The water was analysed but not tested for the presence of arsenic. The BGS published a report in 1992; that report outlined the results of the study that concluded that, on the basis of the tests done, the sampled water was safe to drink. The report was distributed to, among others, officials in the Bangladeshi government. Roughly 700 individual Bangladeshis, all suffering from arsenic poisoning brought suit against the BGS and the governmental body of which it was a part. The suit was dismissed for failure to state a cause of action on the grounds that the defendants had no duty to the plaintiffs. See *Sutradhar* v. *Natural Environment Research Council* [2004] EWCA Civ. 175; [2004] PNLR 30 (and judgement of the House of Lords upholding the lower court decision, see [2006] UKHL 33).

62 Other wells may have been financed by national development aid agencies. The British agency, for example, appears to have financed tube wells for irrigation purposes.

financial responsibility has to be set so as to give appropriate incentives to agents to reduce the risk of their occurrence.

If financial responsibility is apportioned, apportionment might correspond to the relative degree of causal responsibility. One might measure this causal responsibility by reference to the number of wells financed by each agency and/or by the number of wells in the untested or faultily tested (arsenic tainted) aquifer. The financing agents should be held jointly and severally, causally, and legally responsible because their financing decisions were directed at digging these wells in the region; the legal responsibility of the testing agencies, however, rests on their faulty testing of the relevant aquifers.

4.2 Cholera

In January 2010, a massive earthquake struck Haiti, killing thousands, leaving hundreds of thousands homeless, and destroying a large portion of the limited infrastructure of the country. Sometime after 10 October and before 20 October 2010, cholera claimed its first victim in Haiti.[63] Within a year, roughly 4,000 people had died. As of 5 May 2013, there had been approximately 650,000 cases of cholera and over 8,000 deaths.[64] The epidemic has contaminated the largest river in Haiti, the valley of which is the primary location of agricultural production.

Cholera arrived in Haiti with the deployment of a contingent of Nepalese soldiers at the Mirebalais camp of the MINUSTAH. These soldiers arrived in Haiti between 8 and 24 October 2010. Each soldier

[63] Reports often describe the victim as the first in 100 years, but it is not clear that there was in fact a prior cholera victim in Haiti. Indigenous strains of cholera in Haiti are not pathogenic and records do not include reports of prior epidemics that might have been cholera.

[64] See the report of the Ministry of Health and Population of Haiti, Rapports journaliers du MSPP sur l'évolution du choléra en Haiti, Rapport du 05 mai 2013 at www.mspp.gouv.ht/site/index.php?option=com_content&view=article&id=120&Itemid=1. There is some question about the reliability of the official statistics. From the reported figures, the death rate is slightly more than 1.2 per cent, down from a rate of 1.7 per cent early in the epidemic. See A. Cravioto, C.F. Lanata, D.S. Lantagne, and G. Balakrish, 'Final Report of the Independent Panel of Experts on the Cholera Outbreak in Haiti (UN Independent Panel)', Institute for Justice & Democracy in Haiti, at www.ijdh.org/2011/05/topics/health/final-report-of-the-independent-panel-of-experts-on-the-cholera-outbreak-in-haiti-u-n-independent-panel/ (Final Report). According to the expert panel, a 'well-managed' cholera outbreak should have a mortality rate of less than 1 per cent, Final Report, 8.

had had a medical exam prior to deployment to Haiti, but only those with relevant symptoms would have been tested for cholera even though cholera is endemic to South Asia and many infected people are asymptomatic. In addition, after their medical examinations and prior to deployment, the Nepalese contingent was given ten days leave.[65]

The Mirebalais camp had inadequate sanitary facilities. It had black water containers but the water was not purified on site; it was collected by a Haitian contractor. There is evidence both that the base was discharging fecal matter directly into the Artibonite watershed[66] and that the Haitian contractor was disposing of the black water improperly in open pits near the base and the river.[67] The epidemiological evidence and evidence at the site thus strongly suggest the newly deployed Nepalese MINUSTAH contingent as the source of the epidemic. Microbiological analysis confirms that the strain of cholera in Haiti derives from the distinctive strain present in South Asia.[68]

There are thus a multitude of actors causally responsible for the release of a deadly infectious agent into the population: first, the Nepalese military deployed troops after an inadequate medical screening that failed to detect or use prophylactic measures to prevent cholera in the deployed troops; second, MINUSTAH that had inadequate facilities for treatment of biological waste at its Mirebalais camp, had inadequate standards for waste treatment and inadequate monitoring of its bases and contractors; third, the Haitian Ministry of Health that had no early warning procedures for cholera in place as well as other Haitian governmental bureaus that had failed to provide a more secure and sanitary system of provision of potable water; fourth, the private Haitian contractor who disposed of the waste illegally; and fifth, the UN itself either vicariously or more directly in its failure to provide adequate guidelines for waste removal.

We have an indivisible, irreparable injury or set of injuries that were jointly caused by multiple agents. How should legal and financial liability

65 Ibid., Final Report, at 8, 12–13; J.M. Katz, *The Big Truck That Went By: How the World Came to Save Haiti and Left Behind a Disaster*, 4th edn (New York: Palgrave Macmillan, 2013), at 232.

66 See a video from the news agency Al Jazeera 'UN investigates cholera spread in Haiti', 27 October 2010, at www.youtube.com/watch?v=gk-2HyQHUZ0.

67 See Final Report, n. 64, at 21–22; and Katz, *The Big Truck That Went By*, n. 65, at 228–231.

68 Final Report, n. 64, at 28.

be allocated?[69] We have identified two issues: the amount of financial responsibility and how it should be distributed. Establishing the amount is beyond the scope of this chapter. I note, however, that limiting financial responsibility to the funds necessary to remove the hazard of cholera is inadequate in deterrence terms as it does not reflect the full social costs created by the actions of the responsible parties.[70] A territory free of the cholera pathogen is of significant value to a country with inadequate health and sanitation facilities, and a government unable to provide them.

In principle, Nepal, the UN, the Haitian government, and the private contractor should bear financial responsibility. Three of these entities,

[69] The following paragraphs are purely normative as the United Nations has denied responsibility for the cholera epidemic, invoking its sovereign immunity. See the press release, 'Haiti cholera victims' compensation claims 'not receivable' under immunities and privileges convention, United Nations tells their representatives', 21 February 2013, SG/SM/14828 at www.un.org/News/Press/docs/2013/sgsm14828.doc.htm. It is not clear on what grounds the UN rejected the claim. Perhaps they relied on the conclusion of the Final Report of the Panel of Independent Experts on the Cholera Outbreak in Haiti which concluded: 'The introduction of this cholera strain as a result of environmental contamination with feces could not have been the source of such an outbreak without simultaneous water and sanitation and health care system deficiencies. These deficiencies, coupled with conducive environmental and epidemiological conditions, allowed the spread of the *Vibrio cholerae* organism in the environment, from which a large number of people became infected. *The Independent Panel concludes that the Haiti cholera outbreak was caused by the confluence of circumstances as described above, and was not the fault of, or deliberate action of, a group or individual.*' Final Report, n. 64, at 29 (emphasis in original). The panel consisted of experts on epidemiology, microbiology, and infectious diseases competent to reach conclusions about causal responsibility. It indeed concluded that the Nepalese troops introduced cholera into Haiti. Its conclusion concerning legal and financial responsibility, however, is unwarranted. The quoted paragraph virtually blames the victim. MINUSTAH, as most UN peacekeeping forces, arrived in Haiti precisely because the state was unable to provide basic security services. It could not have come as a surprise that the water, sanitation, and health care systems of Haiti were deficient; according to UN data, 'Haiti', UN data, http://data.un.org/CountryProfile.aspx?crName=Haiti, gross national income per capita (in 2010) in Haiti is USD 609.0 (The CIA world factbook estimates purchasing power parity per capita income in Haiti in 2012 as USD 1300 making it the 20th poorest country in the world, see www.cia.gov/library/publications/the-world-factbook/geos/ha.html). According to the Haitian Ministry of Health, it has annual per capita health care expenditures of USD 27. 'Haiti at a glance', at www.haitihealthministries.org/haiti/. These facts would give reason for the UN to take extra care, given its knowledge of the fragility of the infrastructure, rather than rely on it as a form of 'contributory negligence' of the state (though obviously not of the individual cholera victims).

[70] One might argue that it is not possible to restore the pathogenic environment in Haiti to its pre-cholera state in September 2010.

however, are virtually judgement proof as they have few if any funds available to satisfy a judgement.[71] Under a regime of joint and several liability the UN would thus be financially responsible for the full amount.

5. Concluding remarks

The rules governing legal and financial responsibility for wrongs promote two distinct and sometimes conflicting goals: the provision of appropriate *ex ante* incentives on agents to take appropriate care and the compensation of victims. To resolve this conflict, liability regimes must often allocate causal, financial, and legal responsibility for the harm caused differently. We see this separation most starkly, perhaps, in regimes of vicarious liability that assign legal and financial responsibility to an employer that is not causally responsible for the harm. The separation, however, recurs in negligence regimes.

This conflict between the two goals arises whenever the actions of multiple agents causally contribute to the harm. The conflict is exacerbated, however, when the actions cause irreparable harm because, in this case, full compensation is not possible. Society thus has additional reason to promote the prevention of the risk. The inability to compensate for irreparable harms thus shifts attention from the compensatory structure of a legal regime to its incentive structure. The importance of the incentive structure increases as the severity and extent of the irreparable harm increases.

International organisations undertake many activities that impose risks of irreparable harm to the lives and health of large, vulnerable populations. We thus have strong reason to subject these organisations to liability regimes that provide incentives for these organisations to act responsibly and carefully. When multiple agents causally contribute to these harms, a regime of joint and several liability may be appropriate. Regimes of joint and several liability, however, are complex and the

[71] Nepal had gross national per capita income of USD 549.0 in 2010. UN data, 'Nepal', see http://data.un.org/CountryProfile.aspx?crname=Nepal, less than that of Haiti though the CIA estimates 2010 purchasing power parity per capita income in 2012 as identical to that of Haiti at USD 1300. Both these governments thus have limited resources available to compensate victims without significant reductions in essential services to other, needy citizens. The two governments are thus functionally judgement proof. The private contractor is, presumably a small operator with little capital beyond the trucks used to transport waste. These assets are likely to be far below its share of financial responsibility.

optimal structure of such regimes may vary with the underlying causal structure that generates those harms. In domestic law, for instance, joint and several liability functions differently in the context of antitrust law than in the context of the regulation of hazardous waste. The development of regimes of joint and several liability in international contexts should thus attend to the varying structures of harm and harm prevention to which the regimes are applied.

6

Shared Responsibility in International Law: A Political Economy Analysis

ANNE VAN AAKEN*

1. Introduction

Problems that can only be resolved through international cooperation are increasing. As a consequence, states are cooperating with each other and with international organisations more than ever, but often not sufficiently to solve the problems. Consequently, the question arises as to how the problems of public goods (or bads)[1] can be solved cooperatively[2] given that there is no central world government. State sovereignty essentially requires us to rely on voluntary provision and contributions. When social scientists analyse the potential for cooperation on global public goods, they focus on the benefits derived from cooperation and on the game theoretic structures under which cooperation may arise; they have until now, however, neglected to study state responsibility and, especially,

* Professor for Law and Economics, Legal Theory, Public International Law and European Law, University of St. Gallen; Guisanstr. 36, CH-9010 St. Gallen; Tel: ++41-71-2243370; Email: anne.vanaaken@unisg.ch. I would like to thank the participants of the SHARES Workshop in May 2013 for very helpful comments as well as André Nollkaemper and Giuseppe Dari-Mattiacci for very helpful critique. Special thanks go to Tobias Lehmann for extraordinary help in the game theoretic part (section 4) and to Luis Montilla with editing the footnotes. All remaining errors are of course mine.

[1] Public goods are non-excludable and non-rivalrous. Once provided, no country can be prevented from enjoying a public good, nor can any country's enjoyment of the good impact upon the consumption opportunities of other countries. Classic examples are prevention of climate change, preventing the outbreak of a new contagious disease, or keeping weapons of mass destruction out of the hands of terrorists. Nevertheless, they differ in important respects and they cannot just be treated altogether; they have to be classified sensitive to the manner that they are supplied. S. Barrett, *Why Cooperate? The Incentive to Supply Public Goods* (Oxford University Press, 2007), 1 et seq.

[2] See from a game-theoretic perspective, T. Sandler, *Global Challenges. An Approach to Environmental, Political, and Economic Problems* (Cambridge University Press, 1997); and Barrett, *Why Cooperate?*, ibid.

its different forms of apportionment when responsibility is shared.[3] I submit that this is a crucial variable for understanding why cooperation arises (or not), since it impacts upon the propensity to cooperate in the first place.

In most cases, cooperative structures may entail responsibility vis-à-vis other states or vis-à-vis third parties. Responsibilities in international law[4] can be shared between different states when they are responsible together for providing a public good or for preventing a public bad (such as climate change), between states and international organisations (such as in situations of peacekeeping), and between states and/or international organisations and non-state actors (NSAs) (such as in case of provision of vaccination in developing countries). In all those constellations, violations of rights of subjects of international law or human rights can occur. In an increasing number of situations, multiple actors are responsible for harmful outcomes.

Legal scholars have analysed state responsibility from a doctrinal perspective, but the law remains opaque in situations of multiple states. As was stated 25 years ago, '[t]he law of multiple state responsibility is undeveloped. The scholarly literature is surprisingly devoid of reference to the circumstances or consequences of multiple state responsibility.'[5] This has not changed since then: 'The law, or at least its application, is currently in many respects uncertain, unsatisfactory,

[3] State responsibility is analysed from an economic contract theory perspective, but only questions of attribution and vicarious liability are treated as if states were firms: see, E.A. Posner and A.O. Sykes, *Economic Foundations of International Law* (Cambridge, MA: Harvard University Press, 2013), 113 et seq. They do not mention the problem of shared responsibility.

[4] I define 'responsibility' as in P.A. Nollkaemper and D. Jacobs, 'Shared Responsibility in International Law: A Conceptual Framework' (2013) 34 MIJIL 359, at 365: 'We use the term "responsibility" to refer to *ex post facto* responsibility for contributions to injury.' I will use the term 'shared responsibility' more broadly then they do. They define shared responsibility by four main features (at 366 et seq.): 1) responsibility of multiple actors; 2) contribution to a single harmful outcome (whereby harm is understood as broadly encompassing all situations in which actors violate their obligations toward others); 3) shared responsibility *strictu sensu* refers to situations where the contributions of each individual cannot be attributed to them based on causation (I will not follow that, but understand it more broadly, since both situations – identification or no identification – are crucial for the analysis); and 4) 'the responsibility of two or more actors for their contribution to a particular outcome is distributed to them separately, rather than resting on them collectively'.

[5] J.E. Noyes and B.D. Smith, 'State Responsibility and the Principle of Joint and Several Liability' (1988) 13 YJIL 225.

and even chaotic.'[6] Analysing the legal consequences of multiple state responsibility (state responsibility as *explanans*) is slowly gaining ground,[7] but what has not been analysed is how the norms on multiple state responsibility impact upon the willingness of states to cooperate,[8] and how this can be designed optimally to secure cooperation.[9] This chapter attempts to fill that gap by using a political economy approach.[10] Norms on state responsibility are thus viewed as *explanans* for the cooperation of states (the *explanandum*).[11] I will analyse the rules and their effects, thus identifying the pay-offs for parties under different rules, and will then look at the incentives of the parties with respect to the initial stage of the game, and see which rules influence the propensity to cooperate.[12] I will also take into account the consequences for the other goals of state responsibility and the arising trade-offs. This kind of functional analysis addresses the issue of how we get to the optimal state responsibility mechanism (normative, depending on the identified goals of state responsibility), with a special consideration of the problem of the participation constraint of states[13] (i.e., whether they would enter into cooperation in the first place).

[6] A. Orakhelashvili, 'Division of Reparation between Responsible Entities', in J. Crawford, et al. (eds.), *The Law of International Responsibility* (Oxford University Press, 2010), 647, at 664.

[7] See the SHARES Project and the articles cited in this chapter, as well as the other chapters in this volume.

[8] Although social scientists have studied how different sanctioning mechanisms impact upon cooperation, since they affect *ex ante* expectations, they have not yet studied the impact of the sanctioning mechanism, known as state responsibility, on the willingness of states to cooperate.

[9] Nollkaemper and Jacobs, 'Shared Responsibility', n. 4, at 398.

[10] By political economy, I mean to study the 'why' questions (why we have institutions, independent courts, or the laws of responsibility) using as explanatory variables the 'who' questions (who are the actors – legislators, executives, judges, interest groups – that participate in shaping the law) and 'what' motivates them (their preferences) on the one hand and on their constraints (power, resources, given institutions and law, etc.) on the other hand. A change of the behaviour is attributed to changes in the constraints. In this given case, the question is how different norms of state responsibility impact upon the willingness of states to cooperate. For details, see A. van Aaken and J. Trachtman, 'Political Economic of International Law: Towards a Holistic Model of State Behavior', in A. Fabricotti (ed.), *Political Economy of International Law: A European Perspective* (Cheltenham: Edward Elgar, 2016 *forthcoming*)

[11] Similar to economic contract theory, which asks what contracts rational parties would write in order to generate efficient outcomes. For an international law application, see R.E. Scott and P.B. Stephan, *The Limits of Leviathan. Contract Theory and the Enforcement of International Law* (Cambridge University Press, 2006).

[12] In an equation, this would look like the following: propensity to cooperate = f (norms on state responsibility, game played, factual problem to be solved, etc.).

[13] This is a term from economic contract theory denoting the cost-benefit calculus of an actor as to whether or not to cooperate.

This chapter focuses on questions of shared responsibility, which are captured in Article 47 of the Articles on Responsibility of States for Intentionally Wrongful Acts (ARSIWA).[14] Article 47 is unclear about how responsibility is apportioned. The legal possibility of having one state responsible for the whole harm is embedded in the ARSIWA, under which responsibility can arise solely due to an attributed international wrongful act (responsibility of conduct). The allocation of responsibility poses the biggest problem, since causality and/or behaviour may not be easily observable or verifiable by other states or a third party. In principle, there are five possibilities: first, no state is held responsible; second, a state is responsible for the whole damage, no matter how large its part in the contribution (independent responsibility); third, a state is responsible only for the part that is attributed to it (proportional or several-only responsibility);[15] fourth, each state is jointly and severally liable;[16] and fifth, each state assumes vicarious responsibility if acting through an international organisation – this is partially captured by the International Law Commission (ILC) Articles on the Responsibility of International Organizations (ARIO).[17] An in-depth analysis of the ARIO is still missing.[18]

These solutions can be viewed from two perspectives. On the one hand, they can be viewed from the perspective of states that do not want to be held responsible for acts (or omissions) they did not commit (participation constraint of states), as has been held unerringly by the

[14] Articles on Responsibility of States for Intentionally Wrongful Acts, ILC *Yearbook* 2001/II(2) (ARSIWA).

[15] Proportional liability means that each defendant is only held responsible for their proportionate share of the loss, however the criterion of attribution is defined. If, for example, causality is the criterion and you have caused 10 per cent of the loss, you will only be responsible for that 10 per cent. The difference from the other rules is simple: under proportional liability each liable defendant is responsible only for the proportion of the loss or damage that a court determines is just, taking into account each defendant's relative level of comparative responsibility; under joint and several liability (JSL), the defendant is responsible for the whole harm but can ask other contributors to reimburse; under independent responsibility, the latter possibility does not necessarily exist.

[16] JSL is most often compared or contrasted with an alternative rule usually called 'proportional liability' (or several only), on the one hand, or independent responsibility, on the other.

[17] Articles on the Responsibility of International Organizations, ILC Report on the work of its sixty-third session, UNGAOR 66th Sess., Supp. No. 10, UN Doc. A/66/10 (2011) (ARIO).

[18] But see now the contributions in M. Ragazzi (ed.), *Responsibility of International Organisations* (Leiden: Brill, 2013). There is no political economy analysis though.

European Court of Human Rights (ECtHR) (which stated that responsibility may lead to non-cooperation in peacekeeping missions).[19] On the other hand, they can be viewed from the perspective of the injured party. From the victims' point of view, it is always better to have joint and several liability (JSL) of the different actors. Not only does one not need to figure out exactly who is responsible (which is sometimes quite a tedious task, even for lawyers), but chances are that there is jurisdiction of some court on the issue and no immunities[20] (holding international actors responsible is difficult enough, and holding several actors responsible together rarely happens). In short, the risk of verification of who is responsible, the risk of insolvency, and so on, is shifted to the injurers. Nevertheless, JSL is not what is necessarily observed in international law. Also, it impacts upon the propensity of states to cooperate. How do the other possibilities fare? The best solution in most cases, and which may even lead to cooperation of states as a dominant strategy under certain circumstances, is proportional (or several only) responsibility, as compared with no, or independent, responsibility. JSL, from this perspective, lies in between independent and proportional responsibility.

Section 2 asks what goals a responsibility regime is intended to achieve. State responsibility, for example, determines if and how a victim (a third party) can get compensation. Only clarity on those goals will allow us to conduct a comparative institutional analysis on the question of which responsibility regimes are adequate for certain problems and

[19] *Agim Behrami and Bekir Behrami* v. *France* and *Ruzhdi Saramati* v. *France, Germany and Norway*, App. No. 71412/01 and App. No. 78166/01 (ECtHR, 2 May 2007) (joint admissibility decision), para. 111 (Polish Government): 'A finding that States were severally liable for participating in peacekeeping and democracy-building missions would have a devastating effect on such missions notably as regards the States' willingness to participate in such missions.' See also paras. 90, 94, and 101 (noting the submissions and oral statements of Norway, France, and Denmark). For a critical discussion see T. Dannenbaum, 'Translating the Standard of Effective Control into a System of Effective Accountability: How Liability Should be Apportioned for Violations of Human Rights by Member State Troop Contingents Serving as United Nations Peacekeepers' (2010) 51 Harv ILJ 113, at 184, 185: 'it is unclear that the expected cost of potential rights violation liability would be enough to offset the benefits they currently reap from participating in peacekeeping missions'.

[20] See for the problems of process and jurisdiction Noyes and Smith, 'State Responsibility and the Principle of Joint and Several Liability', n. 5, 231 et seq., as well as Nollkaemper and Jacobs, 'Shared Responsibility', n. 4, 430 et seq.

what trade-offs between different responsibility goals arise. Section 3 analyses how the norms on state responsibility currently accommodate multiple actors. The ARSIWA will be at the forefront of the discussion, since they are the default rules if no special treaty regime exists. Nevertheless, the current institutional framework cannot ignore the primary rules that are applicable: both primary and secondary norms are deeply intertwined when setting incentives for states. I will then describe the possible games being played by states when cooperating to provide public goods or to prevent public bads. The question is whether two or more states will cooperate under different apportionment systems under the law of state responsibility. Four such systems are compared: no responsibility, proportionality (or several) responsibility, independent responsibility, and JSL. Game theory shows under which game a particular attribution role fares best to foster cooperation. This gives theoretical guidance to Article 47 of the ARSIWA, also for law-application (section 4). Section 5 will, first, elaborate on hypotheses on the circumstances under which states may assume JSL, which is the best solution from a victim's point of view; second, make suggestions on how to overcome trust and commitment problems that might be responsible for the currently unsatisfactory state of state responsibility; and third, suggest other solutions where this might not be possible. Section 6 concludes.

2. Goals of the responsibility regime

Theories on responsibility (including state responsibility) can be analytical or normative, but this distinction is not clear-cut: whenever we try to understand why we have a certain regime in the first place (analytical; explanation of existing rules), those theories can be criticised or confirmed from a normative perspective.[21] Although normatively certain goals might be desirable (e.g., full compensation of harm), they might not be achievable because of the participation constraint of states. Thus, from a functional perspective, the question is under what circumstances states will agree to what kind of responsibility, taking the incentives of states to participate in cooperative ventures into account (this is different from municipal systems, where liability or responsibility norms can be imposed and enforced).

[21] J.L. Coleman and G. Mendlow, 'Theories of Tort Law', in E.N. Zalta (ed.), SEP (Fall 2010 edition), available at http://plato.stanford.edu/ (last accessed on 5 June 2014).

An important distinction cuts across, namely whether goals of responsibility are instrumental or non-instrumental.[22] Instrumental theories would look at the underlying problems to be solved by responsibility rules, especially how cost allocation (in a broad sense) should be done. This, in turn, depends on the goals that should be achieved by the cost-allocation regime: costs can be allocated efficiently (such as to the cheapest cost avoider[23] or the cheapest 'insurer'),[24] or fairly (to those who contributed most to the violation of international law or to the harm).[25] In international law, one important additional factor is the probability that states may consent to the rules – otherwise no cooperation would take place.

In contrast, non-instrumental theories posit that responsibility is better understood as a way of giving expression to certain moral or political principles (such as rights, duties, redress).[26] Two duties are commonly formulated. Duties of the first order are *duties not to injure*. These duties establish norms of conduct (primary rules in international law). Duties of the second order are *duties of repair* (secondary rules; that is, state responsibility norms). Instrumental and non-instrumental goals are not disconnected: the imposition of duties creates incentives if the duty is somehow entrenched with consequences.[27]

We can then determine several goals of state responsibility. The first is reparation of the harm done (non-instrumental). Next are the preservation of peace via regulating the consequences of violations of international law; deterrence through the setting of incentives to adhere to

[22] Ibid., at section 1.3.2. Whereas normative or philosophical approaches look for grounds for duties or rights, an instrumental perspective asks which duties we should have in order to have good consequences. For an excellent treatment of moral duties in shared responsibility constellations, see L. May, *Sharing Responsibility* (Chicago University Press, 1992).

[23] R.H. Coase, 'The Problem of Social Cost' (1960) 3 JLE 1.

[24] G. Calabresi, *The Costs of Accidents, A Legal and Economic Analysis* (New Haven, CT: Yale University Press, 1970), at 303 et seq.

[25] D. Rosenberg, 'Casual Connection in Mass Exposure Cases: A "Public Law" Vision of the Tort System' (1984) 97 Harv LR 849, at 858: 'Individualized determination of the causal connection also comports with deeply rooted notions of moral responsibility and just compensation.'

[26] This ties in with what Nollkaemper and Jacobs, 'Shared Responsibility', n. 4, at 372 et seq. call the 'moralization' of international law.

[27] Those can be legal or non-legal (e.g., reputational); see extensively R. Brewster, 'Reputation in International Relations and International Law', in J.L. Dunhoff and M.A. Pollack (eds.), *Interdisciplinary Perspectives on International Law and International Relations. The State of the Art* (Cambridge University Press, 2013), 524.

international law and thereby reducing norm violations; loss allocation (that is, rational distribution of losses either between victims and responsible states or between different responsible subjects of international law); and administrative efficiency (that is, responsibility rules that are efficient and workable, and accessible for the victims). Last but not least, if the regime is a common enterprise for the common good (such as peacekeeping missions), the goal is to secure the cooperation of the states involved.[28] Note that if cooperation is not desired because it involves an unlawful activity in the first place, such as undertaking a war or an act of aggression, all arguments concerning the responsibility rules are reversed: the rule should be such that it hinders cooperation (i.e., independent responsibility fares best).[29]

In short, there are three main goals: first, to compensate the injured parties; second, to deter states from engaging in harmful actions in the future; and third, to secure international cooperation. Only the first two are usually mentioned in the legal literature;[30] the third is neglected – wrongly, in my opinion. Those goals cannot easily be achieved simultaneously. As with reservations to treaties, the trade-off between two principles needs to be kept in mind: on the one hand, the need of the international community to have states participating in treaties or joint actions (universality), and on the other hand, the integrity of the legal system by holding states responsible, and upholding the international rule of law by guaranteeing compensation of victims. In section 4, the chapter will show under which institutional and factual conditions the trade-off occurs and how it could be mitigated. This trade-off helps, in my view, to understand the norms and the (limited)[31] international case law currently existing for state responsibility. It is also connected to the understanding of the mixed

[28] Dannenbaum, 'Translating the Standard of Effective Control', n. 19, at 114 proposes a 'liability framework (which) better realizes the fundamental goal of attributing liability to the entity most responsible for the wrongdoing, thus structuring incentives so as to minimize violations, while simultaneously expanding the access of victims to juridical recourse and proper remedy'.

[29] Cf. C. Chinkin, 'The Continuing Occupation? Issues of Joint and Several Liability and Effective Control', in P. Shiner and A. Williams (eds.), *The Iraq War and International Law* (Oxford: Hart Publishing, 2008), 160.

[30] See, e.g., Orakhelashvili, 'Division of Reparation between Responsible Entities', n. 6, at 647.

[31] J. Crawford, *State Responsibility* (Cambridge University Press, 2013), at 326: 'noticeable lack of judicial and arbitral authorities'.

public/private nature of state responsibility.[32] The traditional private understanding that any injury caused gives rise to an obligation of reparation is well entrenched in international law. The famous dictum of the Permanent Court of International Justice echoes this: 'it is a principle of international law, and even a general conception of law, that any breach of an engagement involves an obligation to make reparation'.[33] This amounts to a private law approach,[34] which is related to the traditional concept of sovereignty and inter-state relationships, serving the interests of the respective nation-state, and securing the first goal: compensation for the injured parties.

But how does this connect to the problems we are facing with global public goods and bads? Is the private law approach still adequate? The private law 'repair shop' for those problems is JSL – holding on to the principle of reparation that harm done must be compensated, since JSL is always better from a victim's perspective.[35] But can the other two goals (deterrence and cooperation) be captured by other incentives for norm conformity of states? The ARSIWA have moved in this direction. Pellet talks about a 'revolution' in international law.[36] Damage is not a prerequisite for responsibility; rather it is necessary and sufficient under Articles 1 and 2 of the ARSIWA that only two elements are present: breach and attribution. This imposes a responsibility of conduct, not result (as in administrative law, where a fine can be imposed for crossing a red light without injuring anyone). This move towards an 'objectivization'[37] of international responsibility (or the public law dimension)[38] stresses the second goal: the deterrence or incentive function. Although this goal is surely desirable, it produces potential trade-offs with securing the third goal – the cooperation of states, especially in public good constellations. Depending on the responsibility rule chosen, states will be more or less willing to cooperate.

[32] Nollkaemper and Jacobs, 'Shared Responsibility', n. 4, at 398 et seq.

[33] *Factory at Chorzów (Germany* v. *Poland)*, Merits, Claim for Indemnity, Judgement No. 13, 1928 PCIJ Series A-No. 17, at 29.

[34] A. Pellet, 'The Definition of Responsibility in International Law', in J. Crawford, et al. (eds.), *The Law of International Responsibility* (Oxford University Press, 2010), 3, at 5, 11 et seq.

[35] Nollkaemper and Jacobs, 'Shared Responsibility', n. 4, at 397.

[36] Pellet, 'The Definition of Responsibility in International Law', n. 34, at 9.

[37] Ibid., at 8, 15, and 9: 'international law must be respected independently of the consequences of a violation and any breach entails the responsibility of its author'.

[38] Nollkaemper and Jacobs, 'Shared Responsibility', n. 4, at 401 et seq.

3. State responsibility *de lege lata*

Every action (or omission) carries the danger of responsibility, governed by the ARSIWA as default rules. They are applicable to the extent that there is no special treaty regime governing the (harmful) activities in question.[39] In the ARSIWA, the term 'responsibility' is used for wrongful action,[40] whereas 'liability' is usually used for lawful action resulting in harm.[41] The current law of state responsibility is rather opaque, especially in instances of joint cooperation of states. The general principle of state responsibility is independent responsibility of states, although the ARSIWA contain several exceptions to it.[42] Article 47 of the ARSIWA[43] deals with the situation of a plurality of responsible states in respect of the *same wrongful act*[44] and starts from the general principle that 'each State is separately responsible for the conduct attributable to it, and that responsibility is not diminished or reduced by the fact that one or more other States are also responsible for the same act'.[45] Thus, a situation can arise where only one state is held responsible for the violation (conduct), although many states contributed to it: one state could be held responsible for the whole harm (result), independently of its contribution.

The Commentaries specify that the responsibility of a state should not be reduced even if another state is also involved in the perpetration of the same wrongful act.[46] It is thus conceptually based on 'individual' or

[39] They also do not distinguish between the source of obligation breached, be it crime, contract, or tort. Cf. Crawford, *State Responsibility*, n. 31, at 51 and J. Crawford, 'The System of International Responsibility', in J. Crawford, et al. (eds.), *The Law of International Responsibility* (Oxford University Press, 2010), 17, at 21 et seq. Cf. *Case concerning the difference between New Zealand and France concerning the interpretation or application of two agreements concluded on 9 July 1986 between the two States and which related to the problems arising from the Rainbow Warrior Affair*, Decision, (1990) 20 RIAA 217, at 251, para. 75, and the ICJ in *Gabčíkovo-Nagymaros Project (Hungary / Slovakia)*, Judgement, ICJ Reports 1997, 7, at 38–39, paras. 46–48.

[40] Cf. Article 2 ARSIWA, n. 14.

[41] For a juxtaposition, see Pellet, 'The Definition of Responsibility in International Law', n. 34, at 10 et seq.

[42] Articles 16–18 ARSIWA, n. 14. Orakhelashvili, 'Division of Reparation between Responsible Entities', n. 6, at 650 et seq.

[43] Cf. Article 47 ARSIWA, n. 14 and Article 48(1) ARIO, n. 17, contains a similar provision.

[44] Commentary to the Articles on Responsibility of States for Internationally Wrongful Acts, ILC *Yearbook* 2001/II(2) (ARSIWA Commentary), Commentary to Article 41, para. 1.

[45] Ibid., Commentary to Article 47, para. 1; Crawford, *State Responsibility*, n. 31, at 327.

[46] Ibid., Commentary to Article 47, para. 1; and Orakhelashvili, 'Division of Reparation between Responsible Entities', n. 6, at 657.

'independent' state responsibility,[47] where each state's responsibility is determined separately, being based on a concept of an international order where states act alongside, rather than together, in intermingled ways. Therefore, 'principles of international law that correspond to the needs of an era characterized by joint and coordinated, rather than independent, action'[48] are still largely missing. One of the main problems is that 'there are fundamental problems with defining joint responsibility in terms of the "same wrongful act" [conduct, AvA] rather than (as is done in some domestic systems) in terms of the "same injury" [result, AvA]'.[49] This is especially painful in situations of global public goods, be they created jointly or independently, since their non-provision leads to the 'same injury', but every state may have contributed in part. Nevertheless, Article 47 of the ARSIWA is in principle open to any attribution: it neither explicitly recognises a rule of joint and several responsibility, nor 'does it exclude the possibility that two or more States will be responsible for the same internationally wrongful act',[50] and thus responsibility could also be partitioned proportionally. Following Nollkaemper and Jacobs, shared responsibility *strictu sensu* is defined as situations in which individual causal contributions cannot be determined, and the allocation of responsibility thus cannot be fully based on principles of individual responsibility as previewed in the ARSIWA (and, potentially, independent responsibility).[51]

Can international law borrow from municipal law for the solution to the problem? Here, opinions in the doctrine are divided, but from a functional perspective, which is used here, it makes a lot of sense to consider solutions found in municipal law to solve similar problem structures.[52] This is, as a first step, just a theoretical consideration. In

[47] I follow Nollkaemper and Jacobs, 'Shared Responsibility', n. 4, at 381: 'Under the principle of independent responsibility, the state or international organization (as the case may be) is responsible for its own conduct and its own wrongs. That is, it is responsible for the conduct that is attributable to it and that is deemed in breach of its obligations.'

[48] Ibid., at 361. [49] Ibid., at 396.

[50] ARSIWA Commentary to Article 47, para. 6, n. 44; Crawford, *State Responsibility*, n. 31, at 331.

[51] Ibid.; and Crawford, ibid., at 367.

[52] See e.g., *Oil Platforms (Islamic Republic of Iran* v. *United States of America)*, Judgement, ICJ Reports 2003, 161, at 324 (Judge Simma, Separate Opinion); R. Alford, 'Apportioning Responsibility Among Joint Tortfeasors for International Law Violations' (2011) 38 Pepp LR 233; and Nollkaemper and Jacobs, 'Shared Responsibility', n. 4. Against the use of municipal terms such as 'joint and several', 'joint', 'solidary' (solidaire), cf. I. Brownlie,

deciding whether those solutions can be considered common legal doctrine, drawing on municipal tort law, we need to differentiate between concerted action and cumulative action.[53] *Concerted action* describes circumstances in which states engage in common or joint conduct which breaches an international obligation. For example, two states may participate in a commercial joint venture that causes environmental damage, or joint troops may commit a breach of humanitarian law. Independent action, by contrast, describes situations where states breach obligations with respect to a single event independently. Those cases may arise, for example, in environmental law where states do not adhere to fishing quotas or emission standards set by an international treaty. Those instances are called *cumulative action*.[54] Here, the injured party is in principle able to make claims against each entity, since these entities acted independently from each another. Nevertheless, if the cause of the damage cannot be divided amongst them (for instance because causality is not observable), any of the tortfeasors can be held fully responsible – just like in the case of tortfeasors acting in concert. It would thus not matter whether A *and* B were acting together or whether A *or* B acted when causality cannot be clearly assigned, although that might make a difference from the perspective of a state considering whether to cooperate in the first place. The ARSIWA do not distinguish between cumulative and concerted action.[55]

Principles of Public International Law, 6th edn (Oxford University Press, 2003), at 440, who finds municipal analogies 'unhelpful'. Also, the ILC cautions against the uncritical use of municipal concepts in international law: see ARSIWA Commentary, Article 47, para. 3, n. 44: 'analogies must be applied with care'. However, insofar as the traditions of some countries may reflect general principles of law, they are of relevance in the interpretative process as a source of law under Article 38 of the ICJ Statute.

[53] Noyes and Smith, 'State Responsibility and the Principle of Joint and Several Liability', n. 5, at 228 et seq.

[54] Here, the harm results from a multiplicity of actions. Although each of the actions has contributed cumulatively (like overfishing or CO_2 emissions), none alone would have caused the harm to the same extent.

[55] Cf. ARSIWA Commentary, Article 47, para. 2, n. 44: 'For example two or more States might combine in carrying out together an internationally wrongful act in circumstances where they may be regarded as acting jointly in respect of the entire operation. In that case the injured State can hold *each responsible State to account for the wrongful conduct as a whole.* Or two States may act through a common organ which carries out the conduct in question, e.g., a joint authority responsible for the management of a boundary river. Or one State may direct and control another State in the commission of the same internationally wrongful act by the latter, such that both are responsible for the act.' (emphasis added by the author).

In the constellation of public goods, states rarely act in isolation, but they can act cumulatively or in concert.[56] Theoretically, there are three possibilities of designing responsibility of cooperating states for an unsatisfactory outcome (i.e., if the public good is not provided or if third parties are hurt), leaving out the possibility of acting through an international organisation. First, states are assigned independent responsibility, and one state might need to pay for the whole damage, even if a plurality of states was engaged in the damaging action/omission.[57] This is the predominant situation of state responsibility as codified in the ARSIWA. Second, if there are multiple tortfeasors, responsibility could be attributed to all via JSL. Third, the responsibility may be attributed proportionally (several only). All of them have different consequences for the propensity to cooperate. I will shortly describe how those are used *de lege lata*.

3.1 *Independent responsibility*

The general principle of allocation of responsibility for joint action is that each state is separately responsible, and this responsibility is not reduced or diminished due to the fact that the state was acting jointly with other states.[58] The ARSIWA Commentaries justify this with the general principle of responsibility in international law as stated in Article 2 of the ARSIWA, where each state is separately responsible for wrongful conduct attributable to it, not the damage done. In the view of the ILC, the principle of independent responsibility reflects the position under general international law that, in the absence of an agreement to the

[56] Crawford, *State Responsibility*, n. 31, at 325, footnote 1, lists several possibilities in which the combined action of more than one state might result in wrongful conduct: joint conduct, conduct of several states separately causing aspects of the same harm or injury, action via a common organ, agency, independently wrongful conduct involving another state, incitement of a wrongful act, voluntary assistance in the commission of a wrongful act (complicity, Article 16 ARSIWA, n. 14). Cf. for the latter, e.g., the complicity in the intervention in Iraq (presuming it was wrongful), see H.P. Aust, *Complicity and the Law of State Responsibility* (Cambridge University Press, 2011); G. Nolte and H.P. Aust, 'Equivocal Helpers – Complicit States, Mixed Messages and International Law' (2009) 58 ICLQ 1.

[57] Omissions are included in the definition of an 'internationally wrongful act' in Article 1 ARSIWA: see ARSIWA Commentary, Article 1, para. 14, n. 44, and Crawford, *State Responsibility*, n. 31, at 49.

[58] Brownlie, *Principles of Public International Law*, n. 52, at 441.

contrary,[59] the general principle must be such that each state can be sued for the whole damage. The ILC draws on the International Court of Justice (ICJ or Court) case *Certain Phosphate Lands in Nauru*,[60] where Australia, the sole respondent, had administered Nauru as a trust territory under the Trusteeship Agreement also on behalf of other states (New Zealand and the United Kingdom). Australia argued that it could not be sued alone by Nauru, but only jointly with the other two states concerned. The Court dismissed this argument[61] but left open the question of 'whether reparation would be due from Australia, if found responsible, for the whole or only for part of the damage Nauru alleges it has suffered, regard being had to the characteristics of the Mandate and Trusteeship Systems and, in particular, the special role played by Australia in the administration of the Territory'.[62] The case was later settled, so there is no decision on apportionment.[63]

3.2 Proportional responsibility

Proportional (or several only) responsibility is not excluded by Article 47 of the ARSIWA, even though it is not explicitly mentioned anywhere. As Nollkaemper and Jacobs state, '[t]he issue has not been explored and to our knowledge has not been raised in practice.'[64] Proportional responsibility depends crucially on the criteria of attribution, since proportion always needs a relator (in proportion to what?). The criteria for

[59] ARSIWA Commentary, Article 47, para. 3, n. 44.

[60] *Certain Phosphate Lands in Nauru (Nauru* v. *Australia)*, Preliminary Objections, ICJ Reports 1992, 240.

[61] Ibid., at 258–259, para. 48. 'Australia has raised the question whether the liability of the three states would be "joint and several" (solidaire), so that any one of the three would be liable to make full reparation for damage flowing from any breach of the obligations ... and not merely one third or some other proportionate share. This ... is independent of the questions whether Australia can be sued alone. ... It cannot be denied that Australia had obligations under the Trusteeship Agreement, in its capacity as one of the three States forming the Administering Authority, and there is nothing in the character of that Agreement which debars the Court from considering a claim of a breach of those obligations by Australia.'

[62] Ibid., at 262, para. 56.

[63] Australia agreed to pay the full amount of Nauru's claim and the other governments contributed. See Agreement between Australia and the Republic of Nauru for the Settlement of the Case in the International Court of Justice concerning *Certain Phosphate Lands in Nauru*, Nauru, 10 August 1993, in force 20 August 1993, 1770 UNTS 379. This amounts then to a kind of JSL.

[64] Nollkaemper and Jacobs, 'Shared Responsibility', n. 4, at 429.

attribution are themselves an unclear notion in international law.[65] Those rules serve the purpose of legal certainty in terms of the allocation of the responsibility in two ways: the acting state knows what it will be held responsible for, and the injured party should then know from whom to claim reparations.[66] Those criteria can be capacity,[67] contribution, control,[68] and causation (amongst others). The allocation of a proportion can be done in the phase of finding responsibility in the first place under Article 2 of the ARSIWA, or at a later stage of reparation, if responsibility is confirmed for a plurality of states and reparations (e.g., damages) have to be allocated.

Let us turn to the first phase. Causality foremost can restrict responsibility under the ARSIWA.[69] Causation arises in the work of the ILC as a conceptual limit to be employed in ascertaining the quantum of compensation owed to the injured state. Article 31(1) of the ARSIWA deals with the question of a causal link between the internationally wrongful act and the injury. It is only '[i]njury ... caused by the internationally wrongful act of a State' for which full reparation must be made. This phrase clarifies that 'the subject matter of reparation is the injury resulting from and ascribable to the wrongful act, rather than any and all consequences flowing from an internationally wrongful act'.[70] Causality is a necessary and thus confining, but not a sufficient, condition for responsibility. The allocation of injury or loss to a wrongful act is a normative and not only a historical or causal process.[71] Thus, whilst causality can set out limits to responsibility and also function as a criterion of attribution to allocate responsibility proportionally, it is not always possible to determine

[65] D. Caron, 'The Basis of Responsibility: Attribution and Other Transsubstantive Rules', in R.B. Lillich and D.B. Magraw (eds.), *The Iran-United States Claims Tribunal: Its Contribution to the Law of State Responsibility* (Ardsley: Transnational Publishers, 1998), 109. See also F. Messineo, 'Attribution of Conduct', in P.A. Nollkaemper and I. Plakokefalos (eds.), *Principles of Shared Responsibility in International Law: An Appraisal of the State of the Art* (Cambridge University Press, 2014), 60; and J.D. Fry, 'Attribution of Responsibility', in P.A. Nollkaemper and I. Plakokefalos (eds.), *Principles of Shared Responsibility in International Law: An Appraisal of the State of the Art* (Cambridge University Press, 2014), 98.

[66] As here, Orakhelashvili, 'Division of Reparation between Responsible Entities', n. 6, at 649.

[67] As, for example, in climate change discussions.

[68] Mainly relevant in peacekeeping missions.

[69] See Caron, 'The Basis of Responsibility', n. 65, at 153: 'The relationship between causation and attribution is clear in the sense that causation serves as a limit on the scope of State Responsibility for attributable acts.'

[70] ARSIWA Commentary, Article 31, para. 9, n. 44.

[71] Ibid. Article 31, para. 10.

causality, and other criteria need to be used.[72] Which one that is depends on the issue area, and should ideally be dealt with in primary law.[73]

The proportionality rule is nevertheless in principle ideally suited to the task of resolving the problem of causal indeterminacy. Under this rule, the expected responsibility confronting the state equals the losses attributable to its illegal conduct. By giving states precisely the incentive needed to induce them to take optimal care, such a rule enables the system to achieve its optimal deterrence objective.[74] As will be shown, it is also the rule that best fosters cooperation between states.

Proportional responsibility can also be constructed in such a way that it comes into play only at the second stage, the allocation of losses. Here, in the first stage, independent responsibility would be found, but in the second stage, a state would only be responsible for the part attributed to it (via causality or otherwise).

3.3 *Joint and several liability*

Overall, explicit JSL is scarce in international law.[75] Article 47 of the ARSIWA allows JSL however, and thus independent responsibility can turn into JSL if there is a way to recover from other responsible states. The large absence of explicit JSL in international law (contrary to municipal law) is often deplored in legal scholarship.[76] This is certainly correct from a compensation perspective, since for any victim (state or non-state) it is much easier to recoup reparations from one single state, not only for reasons of procedure and jurisdiction, but also because it might be factually difficult for a victim to identify the tortfeasor due to unclear causality or an asymmetric information account of the victim.

Instances for constructing a general principle of JSL have not been followed up until now, although Judge Bruno Simma elaborated on JSL

[72] As has been noted by Caron, 'The Basis of Responsibility', n. 65, at 153, 'causation as an aspect of State responsibility is, relative to municipal law developments, an undeveloped area of international law'.

[73] In peacekeeping missions, it could be any form of command and control criterion; in climate change, it could be CO_2 emissions.

[74] For details see Rosenberg, 'Casual Connection in Mass Exposure Cases', n. 25, for tort litigation in the United States. His analysis is equally valid for public international law.

[75] The ECtHR's jurisprudence, however, has some cases with JSL, e.g., *Ilaşcu and others* v. *Moldova and Russia*, App. No. 48787/99 (ECtHR, 8 July 2004).

[76] Brownlie, *Principles of Public International Law*, n. 52, at 440: 'A rule of joint and several liability in delict should certainly exist as a matter of principle, but practice is scarce.'

in his minority opinion in the *Oil Platforms* case.[77] In this case, the United States alleged that Iran had violated its treaty obligations by laying mines in the Persian Gulf during the decade-long Iran-Iraq war.[78] It was unclear who laid the mines. Judge Simma concluded, after a comparative municipal tort law analysis, that the 'principle of joint- and several responsibility . . . can properly be regarded as a "general principle of law" within the meaning of Article 38, paragraph 1 (c), of the Court's Statute'.[79] The majority opinion did not elaborate on that point.[80]

In the *Eurotunnel* Arbitration,[81] the question was whether the United Kingdom and France could be jointly and severally liable for not having taken measures against the incursion of illegal immigrants using the Channel Tunnel and causing damage to its operators (the Channel Tunnel Group Ltd. and France Manche S.A.).[82] Whereas France held that 'if there is to be a responsibility that responsibility ... has to be accepted jointly and severally',[83] the United Kingdom argued that 'there is no basis in international law for claims of joint liability or joint and several liability'.[84] Furthermore, it argued that an obligation of joint policing and coordinating the activities of the two states would 'invent(s) an obligation of result'.[85] Although the *Eurotunnel* tribunal found entitlement to damages in arbitration against the governments of France and the United Kingdom, the tribunal held, after looking at the contracts that were concluded (and thus not relying on the ARSIWA), that to 'the extent that the Claimants' case depends on the thesis of joint and several responsibility, i.e., the per se responsibility of one State for the acts of the other, it must fail'.[86]

[77] *Oil Platforms*, n. 52, at 324 (Judge Simma, Separate Opinion).
[78] Ibid., at 172, 174 (majority opinion).
[79] Ibid., at 358, para. 74 (Judge Simma, Separate Opinion).
[80] Ibid., at 218, para. 124 (majority opinion).
[81] *Eurotunnel Arbitration (The Channel Tunnel Group Ltd & France-Manche S.A.* v. *the Secretary of State for Transport of the Government of the United Kingdom of Great Britain and Northern Ireland and le ministre de l'équipement, des transports, de l'aménagement du territoire, du tourisme et de la mer du Gouvernement de la République française)*, Partial Award, (2007) 132 ILR 1 (*Eurotunnel*).
[82] Ibid., para. 163: the claimants alleged that '[a]ny violation caused by the Governments' respective acts and omissions in the context of policing, security and frontier controls should, in addition to engaging the specific responsibilities of the relevant Government, also be attributable to both Governments jointly since these actions are manifestations of the Governments' joint failure to co-operate and co-ordinate their actions in making appropriate provision in relation to policing, security and frontier controls.'
[83] Ibid., para. 170. [84] Ibid., para. 171. [85] Ibid., para. 172. [86] Ibid., para. 187.

Some instances are known, however, especially in treaty law, and they might serve as examples as to how to model JSL, even if it is absent in most treaties. A caveat should be mentioned though: the treaties usually deal with issues where strict liability is foreseen; that is, the action as such is lawful, whereas the ARSIWA deal with wrongful acts. The Convention on International Liability for Damage Caused by Space Objects (Liability Convention)[87] mentions JSL. In Article II, a launching state is strictly liable to pay compensation for damage caused on the surface of the earth or to aircraft in flight by its space object. When more states jointly launch a space object, they are jointly and severally responsible for any damage caused.[88] Exoneration from strict liability (and therefore JSL) is only granted to the extent that a launching state establishes that the damage resulted from another state's gross negligence or from an intentional act or omission. Thus, in instances of JSL in lawful activities, damage is necessary: it thus imposes responsibility of result, not conduct. Clearly, those treaties are *lex specialis* to the ARSIWA; more so, since they deal with risky lawful activities.[89]

4. What games do states play?

We turn now to one important goal of state responsibility: its impact on the propensity of states to cooperate in the first place. One explanation given in the literature for the current state of state responsibility, where independent responsibility is dominant in practice, is the principle of sovereignty, defined in terms of independence and liberty from other states since 'states resist principles of responsibility that require them to be responsible for conduct other than their own'.[90] This argument can be reformulated from a game-theoretical perspective: in which responsibility constellations will states cooperate to provide public goods? Game theory can help to explore and refine those explanations further, since it

87 Convention on the International Liability for Damage Caused by Space Objects, London, Moscow, and Washington D.C., 29 March 1972, in force 1 September 1972, 961 UNTS 187 (Liability Convention).

88 Similarly, UN General Assembly Resolution UN Doc. A/RES/47/68 (1992), which proclaims 'Principles Relevant to the Use of Nuclear Power Sources in Outer Space', similarly provides for strict liability as well as joint and several liability (at Principle 9).

89 ARSIWA Commentary, Article 47, para. 5, n. 44.

90 Nollkaemper and Jacobs, 'Shared Responsibility', n. 4, at 386.

analyses strategic interaction[91] of different players – in our case, states.[92] When states cooperate in solving common problems, they face trade-offs in their interests. Rephrasing this diagnosis in more abstract terms permits us to show where the problems in cooperation lie, and why and how institutional structures, including apportionment under Article 47 of the ARSIWA, can be designed to overcome those problems, since it highlights the underlying problem structure and motivations of the players. In game-theoretic terms, state responsibility changes the pay-off structure of states and therefore their willingness to cooperate. In different games, which result from different underlying problem structures, the pay-off structure changes in various ways and thus generates different incentives to cooperate.

The most important issue is to define the content of the pay-offs: this can be either only the loss of the parties themselves from non-cooperation, or it can also be the externalities caused by non-provision of the public good (such as the loss of a small island if China and the United States do not cooperate on climate change). It can also be an externality arising from the provision of a public good (i.e., from cooperation). The classical case would be a peace-keeping mission that involves human rights violations of third parties.

The question is whether two or more states[93] will cooperate under different state responsibility systems. I will again compare four such systems: no responsibility, proportional responsibility, independent responsibility, and JSL.[94] Two major constellations have to be distinguished. The

[91] Interactive choices that cause agents' (peoples', firms', or nations') pay-offs to be interdependent are nominated as 'strategic'; that is, what one player will do depends on what he or she believes the other players will do. See Sandler, *Global Challenges. An Approach to Environmental, Political, and Economic Problems*, n. 2, at 25. More generally, for the application of game theory to law and international relations, see D.G. Baird, R. Gertner, and R.C. Picker, *Game Theory and the Law* (Cambridge, MA: Harvard University Press, 1994); J.D. Morrow, *Game Theory for Political Scientists* (Princeton University Press, 1994).

[92] Game theory is not an end in itself, but merely a useful tool, and other theories might also contribute to explain states' behaviour. In particular, the trust game is not only used in economics and international relations scholarship, but also in sociology: see V. Buskens, *Between Hobbes' Leviathan and Smith's Invisible Hand* (The Hague: Eleven International Publishing, 2011), at 27. Furthermore, I use the rational choice assumption here as a first step; another interesting endeavour would be to use behavioural economics. See extensively (but not analysing state responsibility issues) A. van Aaken, 'Behavioral International Law and Economics' (2014) 55 Harv ILJ 421.

[93] The game-theoretical model will show only two states, but the rationale remains the same even if more players are involved.

[94] One could also compare responsibility rules with fault (negligence or intent), but since fault does not play a role under the rules of ARSIWA, this will be left out here.

first are constellations where actions are performed in isolation, but each action depends on what the others do. Treaties concerned with controlling pollution, climate change, or overfishing are examples, such as exceeding fishing quotas leading to overfishing, or not reducing emissions as requested by the Kyoto Protocol.[95] This is a case of *cumulative action*. Here, states face a prisoners' dilemma (PD) game where their cumulative actions lead either to a good result, in the case of adherence to the law or, in the case of violation, to a negative outcome (section 4.1).

The second are constellations where states can voluntarily come together in a *concerted action* to provide a public good as described above, but may face responsibility for violations that occur during the mission. Cooperation is understood as a joint undertaking. The harm occurs while both states work on this joint undertaking. Here, states pursue joint positive goals and need to cooperate in order to achieve a cooperative surplus; a violation is but an (usually) unintended side-effect of the cooperative provision of the public good. States play a trust game in this case.[96] They can also use an international organisation for the task, whereby the international organisation is either solely responsible, or may reclaim either *pro rata* from all members (if contributions vary according to ability to pay: the deep pocket approach), or proportionally (such as from those states that contributed most to the harm), or by JSL (section 4.2). Section 4.3 summarises the findings.

4.1 *Prisoners' dilemma constellations*

A PD has an incentive structure that – without additional mechanisms – makes cooperation of states unlikely in the first place (without considering state responsibility).[97] If every player acts rationally individually, the collective outcome is sub-optimal. The game applies to any number of participants that seek a collective response to a problem in which the gain from reneging on one's commitment can give a defector a short-term

[95] Kyoto Protocol to the United Nations Framework Convention on Climate Change, Kyoto, 11 December 1997, in force 16 February 2005, 2303 UNTS 148 (Kyoto Protocol).

[96] Treaties can manage trust relationships, but how exactly they do so varies with the type of transaction: see Buskens, *Between Hobbes' Leviathan and Smith's Invisible Hand*, n. 92, at 27 et seq. Possibilities are e.g., guarantees and 'hostages'.

[97] See e.g., J.L. Goldsmith and E.A. Posner, *The Limits of International Law* (Oxford University Press, 2005).

advantage over cooperation and is applicable in cumulative action constellations.[98] In the following, the situations of a PD without responsibility (section 4.1.1); with independent responsibility (section 4.1.2); with proportional responsibility (section 4.1.3); and with JSL (section 4.1.4) will be discussed.

4.1.1 No responsibility

The pay-offs here depict only the gains from (non-)cooperation – the harm to third parties does not enter the pay-offs. This game is known from the so-called arms race and is prevalent in many other constellations of cumulative action. How does the game look in a world where no state responsibility exists (or there is no injured party claiming)?[99]

Table 6.1 *Simple Prisoners' Dilemma*

	State II		
		Defection	Cooperation
State I	Defection	2,2*	4,1
	Cooperation	1,4	3,3

* The underlining denotes an equilibrium.

Although cooperation has a higher pay-off for both states, both of them will defect, no matter what the other state does (the pay-off of 4 for defection is higher than the pay-off of 3 for cooperation). The dominant strategy for each state is defection; there is a unique equilibrium – defection, defection – and therefore, states will not cooperate (in a one-shot game). They end up in the cell with a pay-off of 2 for both (Nash equilibrium),[100] although they could have achieved a pay-off of 3 for both, if cooperating. In the PD the equilibrium is thus non-cooperative, with pay-offs (2,2). There are many mechanisms that can solve this social dilemma: once a game is repeated (open-ended), the pay-off matrix may change, since the pay-off of defection declines and the pay-off of

98 For a game with many participants, see Sandler, *Global Challenges. An Approach to Environmental, Political, and Economic Problems*, n. 2, at 31.

99 The first number is the pay-off of State I, the second number the pay-off of State II. The underlined numbers represent a Nash equilibrium. For reasons of simplicity, probabilities are not explicitly modelled: the pay-off is the expected pay-off.

100 A Nash equilibrium is a concept of a non-cooperative game involving two or more players, in which each player is assumed to know the equilibrium strategies of the other players, and no player has anything to gain by changing only their own strategy.

cooperation rises due to reputational effects. All this has been widely researched in international law and international relations.[101] What is the problem with failing to ensure that there is cooperation? From the perspective of the parties, the problem is that each of them loses 1 (3-2=1), and thus the total loss of the parties is 2 (i.e., only the loss of non-cooperation) – harm to third parties is not even included.

4.1.2 Independent responsibility

How do the incentives change once responsibility exists and externalities to third parties are taken into account? The role of state responsibility (and the different rules of apportionment) has not been investigated, although sanctioning has been proposed as a mechanism to overcome the social dilemma.[102] There is an additional social loss that the parties do not take into account if there is no responsibility (for instance, a loss for other victims of pollution). But this is relevant if state responsibility exists. Typically, the amount to be paid is somewhat related to the loss. We are interested in the amount of compensation (denoted X).[103] Note that the higher is X, or the expected compensation E(X),[104] the smaller is the pay-off from cooperation for the states. Every payment of compensation thus diminishes the expected pay-off of states. Let us now turn to independent responsibility, where a state can be held responsible for the whole harm to third parties independent of its contribution.

[101] Goldsmith and Posner, *The Limits of International Law*, n. 97; A. Guzman, *How International Law Works: A Rational Choice Theory* (Oxford University Press, 2008); Posner and Sykes, *Economic Foundations of International Law*, n. 3.

[102] See Sandler, *Global Challenges. An Approach to Environmental, Political, and Economic Problems*, n. 2, at 32.

[103] $X > 2$ if the punishment is larger than the actual damages. But we could also have $X < 2$, if for some reason there is under-compensation. This is, in turn, crucial because the equilibrium under the various rules depends on X, but for reasons of simplicity we assume that X is the exact amount of damage done to third parties.

[104] $E(X)$ = expected compensation (i.e., the probability of having to pay the whole claim * X). E denotes that we deal with expected compensation, which is subjective (whereas X only is objective). For simplicity, all states have the same subjective probability of being held responsible in case of independent responsibility: they do not know whether they or another state will be held responsible. Note that this is different for proportional responsibility where a half/half split is assumed for simplicity, and thus E is not needed (X is objective). This might not hold in practice since, for example, states with deep pockets are more likely to be sued. In this case, expected damages might surpass the contribution to the damage, and from the perspective of that state, the game turns into a trust game.

Table 6.2 *Prisoners' Dilemma with Independent Responsibility*

		State II	
		Defection	Cooperation
State I	Defection	2-E(X),2-E(X)	4-E(X),1-E(X)
	Cooperation	1-E(X),4-E(X)	3,3

The dominant strategy is defection if E(X)<1 (small expected damages); the game then shows a unique equilibrium – defection, defection. Therefore, states will never cooperate if they face the risk of being held responsible for the whole harm, even if they did not cause it.

But if E(X)>1, where there is a high expected compensation,[105] then the game becomes a trust game (it has two equilibria). This is counter-intuitive and may be explained by the fact that the stakes are so high (i.e., state responsibility as a sanctioning device) that it is better to cooperate. There are thus two equilibria, depending on the expected responsibility with regard to third parties. This can easily be seen because responsibility reduces the pay-off uniformly in all cases except the case of cooperate/cooperate. Therefore, it does not change the decision of, say, state I under the assumption that state II defects: state I's pay-off when it cooperates, and state I's pay-off when it defects, go down by the same amount. So defection remains a best response to defection by the other party. But if state II cooperates, than the rule makes the pay-off of state I with cooperation higher than its pay-off with defection. Therefore, cooperation is now state I's best response to state II's decision to cooperate. So cooperate, cooperate is also an equilibrium.

To summarise: if the expected damages are small, defection remains the dominant strategy as in a PD with no responsibility. If the expected damages are large, the game turns into a trust game with two equilibria: that is, the behaviour of states is indeterminate. Higher expected sanctions thus augment the propensity to cooperate.

[105] For example, because the damage caused is very great or there are more third parties suing. Note that also here, over- and under-compensation is possible, for cooperation depends on the *ex ante* belief of states.

4.1.3 Proportional responsibility

The game changes in the case of proportional apportionment:[106]

Table 6.3 *Prisoners' Dilemma with Proportional Responsibility*

	State II		
		Defection	Cooperation
State I	Defection	2-X/2,2-X/2	4-X,1
	Cooperation	1,4-X	3,3

With proportional apportionment, the dominant strategy is cooperation if, and only if, $X>2$.[107] There is thus a unique equilibrium – cooperation, cooperation (3,3). Therefore states will always cooperate. Note, though, that this holds only if the expected reparation is higher than the gains from defection. In this case, proportional responsibility is always better than independent responsibility, since states will always cooperate (because there is only one equilibrium). We can expect X to be very high (larger than 2) in, for example, climate change constellations. But if $1<X<2$, then the game becomes a trust game with two equilibria – defection, defection, and cooperation, cooperation – and equals, from the cooperation viewpoint, independent responsibility with large damages.

To summarise: if the expected damages are high, states will always cooperate under proportional responsibility, whereas this is not assured under independent responsibility. If the expected damages are very small ($X<1$), they will defect, since then we are close to the pay-offs of the game without responsibility. If expected damages are in the middle range ($1<X<2$), the game is indeterminate, since there are two equilibria and it turns into a trust game. All then depends on the expected behaviour of other states.

[106] Note that for reasons of simplicity, responsibility is shared in a perfect way in this matrix: that is, half/half, assuming that states can be attributed exactly half of the damage (this, in turn, of course depends on the attribution criterion). If states are asymmetric with respect to their pay-offs, this may complicate matters.

[107] This follows from: $1 > 2\text{-}X/2$, which implies $X>2$; and $3 > 4\text{-}X$, which implies $X>1$. X/2 denotes that the assumption is a half/half split. This assumption is taken for reasons of simplicity and denotes thus an objective probability (this is why there is no E (X), which denotes subjective probabilities). This assumption of a half/half split is without loss of generality. If the share is not half/half, then the threshold (in our case 2) shifts accordingly.

4.1.4 Joint and several responsibility

What happens with JSL? JSL lies in the middle of the two extremes.[108] Whether it is closer to independent responsibility or to proportional apportionment depends on the probability of recovering the 'overpaid' share from the other states. Depending on the indemnity rule between the states, JSL is closer to independent or proportional responsibility. If that rule is zero (or is *de facto* zero), it is similar to independent responsibility; if the rule is 100 per cent, it equals proportional apportionment. The latter case is unlikely, however, since we can expect recovery to involve costs, whether diplomatic costs or costs of dispute settlement and enforcement. Thus JSL is never as good as proportional responsibility from a cooperation perspective (although not under the compensation perspective).

4.2 Trust game constellations

Let us turn to cooperative ventures of states where they come together for concerted action. At the forefront of international cooperation is trust: 'the nature of many risks requires cooperation, coordination, and trust between a range of stakeholders who have diverging interests and different perceptions of the (potential) risks involved'.[109] We define 'risk' here as the risk, first, of being held responsible that the cooperative outcome is not achieved; and second, of being attributed the wrong caused by other players in the game. I submit that international cooperation in common ventures is best illustrated by a trust game.[110] While in a PD there is a conflict between individual rationality and mutual benefit, in a trust game what is rational for one player to do depends on his or her beliefs about what the other will choose.[111] The game describes a conflict between the risk of responsibility for actions the state did not cause (or omissions it did not commit), on the one hand, and the desire for social gains by cooperation, on the other. The stag hunt game

[108] Again, for reasons of simplicity, it is assumed that that E(X) is the same for all parties: that is, the damages are split half/half. Surely, if one country is more solvent, that country will be targeted first. Other considerations might make the probabilities different: media damage, internal politics, ability to fight back, fear of retaliation, etc. If the chances to recover from other countries is zero, this will shift JSL close to independent responsibility: that is, if a party bears the full X and the other bears nothing, then that party will always choose to defect.

[109] M.B.A. v. Asselt and O. Renn, 'Risk Governance' (2011) 14 JRR 431, at 435.

[110] Other names for it, or its variants, include 'assurance game', 'coordination game', and 'trust dilemma', and its applicability immediately becomes clear for international cooperation.

[111] B. Skyrms, *The Stag Hunt and the Evolution of Social Structure* (Cambridge University Press, 2004), 3.

models the underlying problem structure of the strategic interests of the players: rational agents are pulled in one direction by considerations of risk of responsibility, and in another by considerations of mutual benefit expected from cooperation.[112] The game was first described by Jean-Jacques Rousseau. Two individuals go out hunting and each hunter can choose to hunt either a stag (deer) or a hare, the hare being worth less than the stag (also pro rata). Neither knows what the other hunter will do. If they both concentrate on hunting the stag, they will gain a bigger price, but they need the cooperation of the other. If each hunter assumes that the other hunter may not cooperate, they will choose to shoot the hare in order to ensure having meat on the dinner table.[113] It all depends what one player thinks the other player will do. Trust is often not present, which hinders cooperation in the first place: this is the so-called social dilemma. In this case, states will prefer to play a lone hand, although they would gain from cooperation.

Rational players can coordinate on the stag hunt (not choosing the hare hunt), which gives them a better pay-off, but they need a measure of trust to do so. Several dynamics can lead to a Nash equilibrium in which the players hunt the stag (and are thus better off). Most of the trust dynamics tested in experiments are independent of institutions.[114] But trust problems can be solved by many means, such as by having a central government (reliable enforcement); by creating network structures (as in eBay sellers' ratings); long-term relationships;[115] and a reputation for being trustworthy.[116] As Lenin stated long ago, 'trust is good but control is better'. In game-theoretic terms, the term 'control mechanisms' refers to the possibility of punishing or rewarding a partner in subsequent transactions in repeated trust problems.[117] Thus we also find institutional

[112] For details of the stag hunt game see ibid., at 5–9. He holds that a stag hunt describes much more aptly most of those situations where political scientists used to assume a PD. Indeed, in certain situations with repeated interactions, the PD turns into a stag hunt game. While Hobbes, reframed in game-theoretical terms, would assume a PD, the stag hunt would be the appropriate game to describe a social contract (ibid., at xii). If international law creates a minimal social contract in international relations, assuming a stag hunt in situations of cooperative efforts of states should be the correct game.

[113] The game was first described by Jean-Jacques Rousseau and is deemed to be almost as important a game as the more renowned PD game in international relations.

[114] On trust as a social mechanism, see E. Fehr, 'On the Economics and Biology of Trust' (2009) 7 JEEA 235. Individual beliefs can be changed by communication and social norms. This is more likely in small communities which know each other well.

[115] Buskens, *Between Hobbes' Leviathan and Smith's Invisible Hand*, n. 92, at 17 et seq.

[116] On reputational mechanisms in international law, see for an overview Brewster, 'Reputation in International Relations and International Law', n. 27.

[117] Buskens, *Between Hobbes' Leviathan and Smith's Invisible Hand*, n. 92, at 23.

structures that punish defection:[118] state responsibility as a sanctioning device is one of them.

In the following, the situations of a trust game without responsibility (section 4.2.1); with independent responsibility (4.2.2); with proportional responsibility (4.2.3); and with JSL (4.2.4) will be discussed.

4.2.1 No responsibility

Let us look at the structure of the game situation without any responsibility.

Table 6.4 *Trust Game without Responsibility*

		State II	
		Defection (hare)	Cooperation (stag)
State I	Defection (hare)	1,1	1,0
	Cooperation (stag)	0,1	3,3

If one player thinks that the other one will not cooperate, he or she is better off when playing alone (hunting the hare: pay-off of 1, because he or she would end up with nothing (0) if they did not do so). They would end up hunting the hare (pay-off of 1,1). Only if they believe that the other player will also concentrate on hunting the stag will they do so and catch the stag (3,3). Two equilibria exist in this game, and which one is chosen depends on trust; it therefore depends on what one player thinks the other player will do.

4.2.2 Independent responsibility

Let us look first at independent responsibility, which carries the risk of being held responsible for harm to third parties caused by one or more other states.

[118] Skyrms, *The Stag Hunt and the Evolution of Social Structure*, n. 111, at 9, et seq. and Buskens, ibid., at 24. Another mechanism to overcome trust problems is the 'learning mechanism'. Institutional learning mechanisms are able to generate trust by monitoring or peer-review. The difference between the control mechanism and the learning mechanism is that control is based on the anticipation of behaviour of the players in the future, while learning is based on information obtained from the players in the past.

Table 6.5 *Trust Game with Independent Responsibility*

		State II	
		Defection (hare)	Cooperation (stag)
State I	Defection (hare)	1-E(X),1-E(X)	1-E(X),0-E(X)
	Cooperation (stag)	0-E(X),1-E(X)	3,3

Under this condition there is no dominant strategy. There are two equilibria in pure strategies – defection, defection; and cooperation, cooperation.[119] Which one is chosen depends on trust, as in the situation without state responsibility. Therefore, it depends on what a state thinks the other state will do – here, trust-creating mechanisms, apart from state responsibility, come into play. With independent responsibility, the trust game always remains a trust game (two equilibria), irrespective of the expected damages. Note the difference with the PD situation, where under independent responsibility the game turns into a trust game only if E(X)>1; otherwise defection is the dominant strategy.

4.2.3 Proportional responsibility

Let us look at proportional apportionment, where I again assume a half/half splitting of responsibility without loss of generality.

Table 6.6 *Trust Game with Proportional Responsibility*

		State II	
		Defection (hare)	Cooperation (stag)
State I	Defection (hare)	1-X/2,1-X/2	1-X,0
	Cooperation (stag)	0,1-X	3,3

The dominant strategy is cooperation if, and only if, X>2.[120] We then have a unique equilibrium – cooperation, cooperation (3,3). With proportional apportionment, states will thus always cooperate, even in the absence of trust. If X<2, the game remains a trust game with two equilibria; again, trust is crucial for cooperation. Note that if damages are high,

[119] This is because 1-E(X) is always > than 0-E (X), and 1-E(X) is always < 3. Thus it does not matter how high the expected damages are; the structure of the pay-offs remain unchanged.

[120] X again denotes compensation to third parties. This follows from: 0 > 1-X/2, which implies X>2; and 3 > 1-X, which implies X>-2.

there is no difference between a PD and a trust game under proportional responsibility: both lead to cooperation as a unique equilibrium.

4.2.4 Joint and several responsibility

For JSL, the same reasoning applies as in the PD: it depends on the probability of recovery as to whether the JSL situation resembles the proportional or the independent apportionment.

4.3 Summary of the findings on cooperation of states

Assuming that cooperation is desirable, there is thus a clear ranking of outcomes. The first best is cooperation/cooperation; the second best is indeterminate with two equilibria depending on trust; and the third best is defection/defection. In a world without responsibility, in cases of cumulative action, states will not cooperate; whereas, in cases of concerted action it depends on their mutual trust. We can now distinguish between two situations: one with high damages and one with low damages.

In PD situations – that is, situations of cumulative action – we can show a clear ranking: independent responsibility will lead to non-cooperation if the harm is not too serious. In contrast, if the harm is very serious and the state risks being held responsible for the whole damage, it is unclear whether states will cooperate. This is counterintuitive and can be explained by the effect of punitive damages. Then the costs of non-cooperation can become higher than the costs of potential responsibility, and the game changes into a trust game. In the case of proportional liability, states will always cooperate if damages are high, and thus it is better for cooperation than independent responsibility. Where damages are intermediate, the game changes into a trust game with two equilibria. Only if damages are very small will states defect, and the situation will be the same as if there were no responsibility. JSL may thus work either way: if damages are high and/or recovery from other states is likely, then cooperation is more likely, since the structure is similar to proportional responsibility with high E(X). If damages are low and/or the probability of recovery is low, cooperation is not secured, since the structure is more similar to independent responsibility. All thus depends on recovery from the other states, and it can cut both ways: in the direction of either independent responsibility (no recovery) or proportional responsibility (perfect recovery).

Let us turn to instances of concerted action; that is, a trust game. Having 'no state responsibility' or having 'independent responsibility' changes nothing in terms of cooperation (it all depends on trust), but

Table 6.7 *Summary of Consequences of Responsibility Regimes for Cooperation*

Cumulative Action (PD) **Concerted Action (TG)**	**High damages**	**Intermediate damages**	**Low damages**
No responsibility	PD: Non-cooperation	PD: Non-cooperation	PD: Non-cooperation
	TG: Indeterminate	TG: Indeterminate	TG: Indeterminate
Independent responsibility	PD: indeterminate	—	PD: Non-cooperation
	TG: Indeterminate	TG: Indeterminate	TG: Indeterminate
Proportional responsibility	PD: cooperation	PD: Indeterminate	PD: Non-cooperation
	TG: cooperation	—	TG: Indeterminate

'proportional responsibility' surely leads to cooperation. Assuming that the third-party victim is always compensated, then 'proportional' responsibility strictly dominates 'independent' responsibility – that is also intuitively convincing in the case of high damages. If the likelihood of the third-party victim being compensated changes to zero (e.g., because there is immunity), this amounts to a system without state responsibility, and cooperation depends on trust. In concerted action constellations, contrary to a PD, other trust-generating mechanisms can be used to solve the cooperation problem, independently from state responsibility.

The game-theoretical analysis could show that it may impact the propensity of states to play the game in the first place if responsibilities are assigned in a way that a player is subject to responsibility above and beyond the harm caused by the violator's unlawful conduct. That is, independent responsibility, especially in low damages situations, is worse than proportional responsibility. A perfect JSL situation with full recovery sets the same incentives for cooperation as proportional responsibility. Apart from sovereignty concerns, incentive problems may thus militate against norms of state responsibility, which would hold all states either independently responsible for the whole, or jointly and severally liable (with less than full recovery) for the risk that third parties are hurt (as in peacekeeping missions). In trust games, if trust in the other actors is not secured, states may prefer to play a lone hand, although they would gain from cooperation. This reverses with proportional apportionment in combination with high amounts of damages: interpreting Article 47 of the ARSIWA in that way would better secure cooperation of states, even in a PD situation. This implies that in spite of considerations of fairness and compensation of victims, one needs to be cautious as to how state responsibility should be designed.

5. The trade-off problem from a political economy perspective

We can now judge the current state of state responsibility. The first criticism is that not one size fits all – as we have seen, it is necessary to distinguish different constellations in the primary law (which deals with different problem structures).[121] Clearly, the first best option is to be able to draw on *ex ante* arrangements that states would need to agree before

[121] In the same vein, Nollkaemper and Jacobs, 'Shared Responsibility', n. 4, at 398 et seq., section: 'Moving Away from the Unity of the Law of International Responsibilty'.

acting together as to how to distribute responsibility *ex post*.[122] Surely the ARSIWA and the ARIO give some guidance, but they also leave space for filling those gaps in cases of shared responsibility; thus a tribunal should have some guidance as to how to apply Article 47 of the ARSIWA.[123] The following analysis is intended to provide such guidance, showing the trade-offs between the different goals when determining responsibility. First, the trade-off problems will be described (section 5.1); second, potential solutions will be shown (section 5.2).

5.1 *Trade-off between the different goals of state responsibility*

As set out in section 2, three main goals of the law of international responsibility can be formulated: first, to compensate the injured parties; second, to deter states from engaging in harmful actions in the future (and therefore preserve peace); and third, to secure international cooperation. Those goals cannot easily be achieved simultaneously. Let us look at the apportionment principles in detail, this time from a compensation perspective, taking into account the participation constraint of states.

From a compensatory perspective, there are good grounds for finding JSL; it is the first best option from the perspective of the injured party.[124] Under JSL, a litigant can claim against one defendant only and recover the whole reparation from that one defendant, regardless of how many other defendants are also responsible for the damage. It is sufficient for the claimant to identify one or more parties that are responsible for the same loss. That defendant might then – with a limited probability –

[122] Cf. ibid., at 393: 'After all, whether or not two states are jointly responsible for a particular act is first and foremost governed by what states have actually agreed to, whether in drafting their primary obligations or in providing for specific secondary rules of responsibility. If states and other actors wish to prevent the above-noted problems of too much or too little responsibility, they simply should agree on the modalities of sharing ex ante.'

[123] Ibid., at 407. For discussion of the danger that the ARSIWA might restrict judges unduly and are unable to cope with the development of international law, see D. Caron, 'The ILC Articles on State Responsibility: The Paradoxical Relationship Between Form and Authority' (2002) 96 AJIL 857.

[124] 'The real reason for the rule that each joint tortfeasor is responsible for the whole damage is the practical unfairness of denying the injured person redress simply because he cannot prove how much damage each did, when it is certain that between them they did all.' *Summers* v. *Tice*, 33 Cal. 2d 80 (1948), at 85, quoted from *Oil Platforms*, n. 52, at 354 et seq., para. 67 (Judge Simma, Separate Opinion). See also extensively Dannenbaum, 'Translating the Standard of Effective Control', n. 19, at 170, who proposes JSL since it is the best solution from a victim's perspective.

recover from other defendants *ex post* but it has to bear *ex ante* a disproportionally large share of the burden. JSL can (but need not) provide an indirect path to proportional liability, provided all defendants are available and able to pay.[125] The risk of recovery is shifted to the defendant states, away from the injured parties.[126] One joint tortfeasor then serves as an 'insurer' of another.[127]

States can be hold jointly and severally liable only if their concurrent acts brought about the harm to the injured party. The acts of the defendants do not have to be simultaneous: they must simply contribute to the same event. For example, assume that one state diverts a river and another one later pollutes it. Together this leads to a disruption of water supply for a third state. JSL is applicable in both instances of cumulative and concerted action. The classic reason the law imposes joint liability is when the harm is 'indivisible', in order to deter wrongdoing by those acting together.[128] JSL thus shifts the risks of recovery and the burden of proof of attribution to the defending states (away from victims). Although that fosters the first goal (reparation), it impacts upon the third (cooperation). This was clearly stated in the submissions of governments in the *Behrami* and *Saramati* cases.[129] On the one hand, it gives states an incentive to monitor each other, since they might be held responsible for each other; on the other hand, it might promote shirking by states in case they expect not to be responsible for the full costs of their behaviour. Depending on the recovery probability and the ability to monitor, it may thus inhibit cooperation. In cases of concerted action (a trust game), control mechanisms are much easier to institutionalise than in instances of cumulative action (a PD situation) and, thus, cooperation is more likely in the former constellations, even under JSL. Also in cases where trust is present, JSL might mitigate the participation constraint problem depending on the recovery possibilities. JSL is therefore a second best option (in comparison with proportional responsibility)

[125] New Zealand Law Commission, 'Review of joint and several liability', Issue Paper 32 (2012), available at http://ip32.publications.lawcom.govt.nz/uploads/NZLC-IP32-Review-of-Joint-and-Several-Liability.pdf, at 4 (last accessed on 5 June 2014).

[126] L.A. Kornhauser, 'Economic Analysis of Joint and Several Liability', in J. Arlen (ed.), *Research Handbook on the Economics of Torts* (Cheltenham: Edward Elgar, 2013), 199.

[127] Ibid., as well as *Eurotunnel*, n. 81, para. 177: 'In other words someone who is jointly and severally liable takes the risk of a partner's insolvency, disappearance or non-amenability to suit.'

[128] Kornhauser, 'Economic Analysis of Joint and Several Liability', n. 126.

[129] See *Behrami and Saramati*, n. 19.

from an incentive point of view of states, but a first best option from the victims' perspective.

Independent responsibility is clearly, from a state's perspective, the worst outcome, and would inhibit the propensity of cooperation in the first place, since the pay-off of cooperation would be potentially diminished to a great extent (although more so in PD than in trust games). From a victim's perspective, independent responsibility is a second best outcome after JSL, since it just needs to identify one violator and can pick the one which, first, can be brought before a court, and second, has deep pockets.

Under proportional responsibility, the plaintiff has to identify all the defendants and claim a proportionate share from each of them. It requires the plaintiff to claim and prove a percentage or share of his or her loss from each defendant, who may of course contest both the attribution to them and the appropriate share. This is difficult and sometimes impossible for a plaintiff. Under proportional liability the share allocated to an insolvent or absent defendant cannot be recovered by the plaintiff unless there is a further rule to re-allocate uncollectable shares. What is important here is that under proportional responsibility, the risk of who should bear the cost of the loss, and also who bears the risk of a defendant not paying, is shifted to the claimant, thus impacting upon the first goal of compensation, but it secures cooperation of states much better, as was shown earlier.

To summarise: whenever possible, from a compensatory perspective, JSL is best; independent responsibility is second best; and proportional responsibility is the worst. In contrast, from a cooperation point of view, responsibility should be attributed to the state directly and proportionally. Furthermore, only when actors take responsibility for their actions will incentives in the institutional setting be such that harm will be avoided (the second goal of deterrence). Acting without consequences does not usually get the incentives right: neither for the level of activities, nor for the scope of negligence or wilful acts (although the latter considerations are immaterial in the ARSIWA).[130] Furthermore, only if the other actors trust their cooperative partners to abide by the law will they cooperate. Moreover, states will not easily assume independent responsibility for their joint actions, since they

[130] L.A. Kornhauser and R.L. Revesz, 'Joint Tortfeasors', in M. Faure (ed.), *Encyclopedia of Law and Economics*, 2nd edn (Cheltenham: Edward Elgar, 2009), 625.

would otherwise run the risk of being held responsible (solely for the whole violation, or jointly and severally) for something they did not do or could not control.

5.2 *Institutional suggestions*

If criteria of attribution are not clarified *ex ante*, states might be reluctant to delegate the decision concerning them to international tribunals. Only if they are clarified can individual responsibility be attributed. Even if the criterion is clear, observability and verifiability of the behaviour is often difficult. The best option here would be to extend monitoring and compliance mechanisms. Clear assignment of responsibilities is not only a prerequisite of the rule of law for those harmed by the activities, but also a prerequisite of trust, which in turn is crucial for cooperation. If players do not have clear responsibilities, shirking is a lot easier, and its detection and verification is much harder. This is not to say that trust-generating mechanisms are non-existent in the current treaties. They are there, but they should be emphasised even more. Only by those means can murky responsibilities, where causality is not easily observable or verifiable, be clarified, thus enabling individual responsibility to be proportional to the contribution of the harm (whatever the criterion for attribution is), fostering cooperation (even in PD games), and helping claimants to identify tortfeasors.

What happens in cases where apportionment is simply impossible? As was asked by Judge Simma in the *Oil Platforms* case, 'can neither of the ... States be held responsible because it is impossible to determine precisely who did what?'[131] On the one hand, he recognised the difficulty with making a finding of responsibility where apportionment is impossible. On the other hand, he excluded as unfair a solution in which no one would be held responsible (impacting upon the first goal of compensation). This is especially important in situations of cumulative actions, since each contribution is often non-observable (e.g., in climate change). This calls for using proxies in order to be able to determine proportional responsibility, for example the share of CO_2 emissions. Another solution is to shift the burden of proof[132] of attribution from the victim to the joint tortfeasors. But states will not easily

[131] *Oil Platforms*, n. 52, at 354, para. 65 (Judge Simma, Separate Opinion).
[132] Ibid., at 355, para. 68.

consent to treaties or joint actions if they risk bearing responsibility for actions of other states. I will outline instances where states are more likely to agree to JSL, since it is best from a compensatory perspective, and some institutional suggestions for dealing with shared responsibilities in international law.

Let us turn to the case of cumulative but independent action of states (the PD situation). Although states might have agreed through a treaty to achieve a common goal (like sustaining fisheries),[133] each state acts independently and has less control over the others' actions. Each state has to rely on compliance mechanisms to trust that other states will contribute to the public good. When the injured party is able to claim against one state only for the whole damage, that might have consequences for the consent to collective action in situations of 'cumulative action' in the first place.[134] It is in those situations where non-compliance mechanisms are not necessarily considered to be a matter of state responsibility (thus de-connecting potential reparations from a violation of an international norm; the public law dimension). Although this might be deplored,[135] it is explicable by states avoiding taking on responsibility where attribution might be unclear, and thus individual action is burdened with the risk of being attributed responsibility without action of the respective defendant state.[136] One needs to note, however, that deterrence is most likely in instances where reparations loom – in all other cases, only reputational sanctions are present. State responsibility is thus a crucial solution to the cooperation problem, as could be shown by game theory. If reputational sanctions are considered an equivalent to 'small damages', this might lead to a breakdown of cooperation in those instances.

Let us turn to instances of concerted action (the trust game situation). Here, consent to a joint undertaking for providing a public good is common (e.g., peacekeeping). This makes mechanisms for creating trust easier than in situations of cumulative actions. It is therefore more likely that states will agree to JSL. Nevertheless, it has some downsides from the

133 There are, of course, instances where states act completely independently from each other, as in the *Oil Platforms* case, n. 52.

134 See in the same vein Nollkaemper and Jacobs, 'Shared Responsibility', n. 4, at 369.

135 Ibid., at 407, attribute it to a more public law approach to those issues, in that compliance procedures are primarily concerned with securing public power, to limit abuses of power, and to further the rule of law.

136 Ibid.

perspective of the cooperating states. The incentives for victims to go for the 'easiest' state are huge: criteria for choosing the state might be its 'deep pockets', consent to mandatory jurisdiction of the ICJ, or the reputational sensibility of that state. There is thus a risk that the state will find itself in a *de facto* situation of independent responsibility, especially if recourse is unlikely.

The question is, under what circumstances would states agree to JSL, given that this rule best serves the victims' desire for compensation? I submit that they would do so if several circumstances are met; the range is to be found on a continuum. First, it is explicable that JSL is consented to in lawful activities (as in the Liability Convention). States thereby know beforehand that they are consenting to very risky but desirable activities in which each country involved has an interest in participating in the common enterprise; the expected benefit from the joint activity is often greater than the risk of being held liable for the actions of another state. Second, in instances of strict liability for states (usually liability for lawful behaviour), it is more likely that they will also consent to JSL, since the potential negligent behaviour of other states, which is usually very difficult to detect and verify, does not play a role.[137] Third, the smaller the project (in scope, time, and potential damages), the more likely it is that states will consent to JSL, since the behaviour of other cooperating states can be better monitored and controlled. Also, trusting on the basis of a small sum is easier than trusting on the basis of a potentially undefined large sum for reparations. Fourth, the cooperation needs to be well-defined in scope. The clearer the definition of the common task, and the more controllable it is, the higher the likelihood that there will be consent to JSL. This is what we see, for example, in the Liability Convention, since launching a space object is an activity that is well-defined in scope. Fifth, the closer the cooperative relationship is between the states, the higher the degree of trust and the greater the likelihood they will agree to JSL. It is also possible to introduce caps on responsibility if states cooperate through a treaty (or a soft-law agreement, as in peacekeeping). This could be combined with an 'insurance mechanism' and would change pay-offs accordingly. Another possibility is to create funds *ex ante* to compensate victims or to create insurance solutions, as is already done in the International

[137] Kornhauser and Revesz, 'Joint Tortfeasors', n. 130.

Convention on Civil Liability for Oil Pollution Damage, which provides for mandatory insurance for tanker owners.[138]

Trust can be generated through international organisations since those may not only solve the trust problem but also the responsibility problem, because then the international organisation could be held responsible for insufficiently fulfilling its tasks (leaving aside the immunity problem). The question is what mechanisms can be created, first, to enhance trust even more, and second, to create clear responsibilities among the actors, but this must be left to further research.

6. Outlook

Global problems, and therefore the provision of global public goods as well as the prevention of global public bads, are becoming ever more prominent – and with those problems, so does the need for global cooperation. Whereas social scientists ask under what circumstances states cooperate, lawyers ask inter alia who is responsible when something goes wrong and the public good is either not provided (such as climate change mitigation), or it is provided, but simultaneously third parties are injured (such as in peacekeeping missions). This chapter was a first attempt to bring those two strands of thought together by asking how shared responsibility impacts upon the propensity of states to cooperate in the first place. Depending on how state responsibility is designed, the participation constraint of states in cooperative ventures comes into play. If international cooperation is desirable, one needs to take this constraint into account. It therefore seems reasonable to look at the game that states (and other actors) are playing when collaborating. While the compensation perspective has been rightfully considered, the other side of the equation needs to be taken into account as well, by using state responsibility as *explanans* for the propensity of states to cooperate in the first place. *Grosso modo*, if cooperation is desired, independent responsibility is not the best solution. Article 47 of the ARSIWA should be interpreted in a way that allows, if it is possible in any way, for proportional responsibility or JSL, with the possibility of recourse in order to accommodate the victim's perspective.

Note that all the arguments can be reversed in those cases where cooperation is not desired. If the common undertaking itself (hunting

[138] International Convention on Civil Liability for Oil Pollution Damage, New York, 29 November 1969, in force 19 June 1975, 973 UNTS 3.

the stag as such, not the individual action) is unlawful (such as a common invasion of a third country), JSL or even independent responsibility for the whole harm (as in the ARSIWA) should be found for deterrence reasons, since it destabilises the unlawful relationship. This reasoning is well-known from competition law or fighting corruption, but it also applies to the desired hindrance of cooperation of states.

While this chapter is a first attempt to explore the impact of state responsibility norms on the cooperative behaviour of states, further elaboration on the exact circumstances and institutional features is surely needed.

7

Public Power and Preventive Responsibility

Attributing the Wrongs of International Joint Ventures

TOM DANNENBAUM*

1. Introduction

What ought to happen legally when multiple states and international organisations participate in an institutionally thick cooperative venture that subsequently engages in wrongdoing? To whom should such wrongdoing be attributed?

The question is a pressing one. States and organisations are engaging with increasing frequency in cooperative enterprises of growing sophistication. The pursuit of international law's core objectives of peace, security, justice, human rights, and development depends on that trend continuing and perhaps accelerating.[1] Yet the legal regime of responsibility for wrongs that occur in the course of international cooperation remains disturbingly immature.[2] Responding to that lacuna, this chapter proposes a way of thinking about responsibility for a particular form of cooperative action – what I term here the joint public enterprise (JPE). My claim is that the normative principle underpinning the *ex post*

* Lecturer in Human Rights, University College London. I owe great thanks to the conveners of and participants in the conference at which the papers were discussed, and especially to Kristen Boon for her excellent comments as the discussant of an earlier draft of this chapter in that forum.

[1] Consider some of the greatest threats to those objectives (adapted from the UN Charter's preamble): terrorism, depleting fishing stocks, climate change, wrongdoing by multinational corporations, refugee flows, peacekeeping, transnational wars, piracy, water resources, and global health.

[2] Independent responsibility remains dominant. Commentary to the Articles on Responsibility of States for Internationally Wrongful Acts, ILC *Yearbook* 2001/II(2) (ARSIWA Commentary) at 64; Articles on Responsibility of States for Internationally Wrongful Acts, ILC *Yearbook* 2001/II(2) (ARSIWA); P.A. Nollkaemper and D. Jacobs, 'Shared Responsibility in International Law' (2013) 34 MIJIL 359; I. Brownlie, *Principles of Public International Law*, 8th edn (Oxford University Press, 2008), 457.

attribution of JPE wrongdoing should be that of reciprocity between public power and preventive responsibility. Enterprise wrongs ought to be attributed to the participant states or organisations that hold the levers of control most relevant to preventing the type of wrongdoing in question.[3] The proposal has two primary virtues. First, it aligns *ex post* attribution in JPEs with a deep moral principle that already undergirds state responsibility in unilateral contexts. Second, it strikes the right balance between preventing wrongdoing and encouraging cooperation.

Sections 2 and 3 define the question and identify the alternative answers advanced thus far. Sections 4 and 5 then seek a guiding normative principle to select among those alternatives. Here, I look not to articulate and defend a moral account from the ground up, untethered to extant law, but instead to understand and build on the existing normative substructure of some of the better-elaborated areas of state responsibility under international law. Running through the doctrines of preventive due diligence, the responsibility to protect, and the attribution of state organs' conduct is a common normative thread: asserting legitimate public power entails a reciprocal duty to prevent wrongdoing of global concern. The immanence of this principle in more developed adjacent domains of the law gives it two advantages as a foundational tenet of JPE attribution: legitimacy in a world of plural values and a preliminary promise of viability. The final two sections elaborate and hone a JPE attribution regime built on this principle.

2. Why JPEs? Why attribution? Why wrongdoing?

Before proceeding to the core argument, it is necessary to define and justify its scope, starting with its focus on JPEs. JPEs arise when multiple states or international organisations cooperate to form a public organ or venture with partially merged processes of decision making and action. Unlike international organisations, however, JPEs lack full legal personality, and are ordinarily temporary.[4] Classic examples include, first,

[3] This expands on earlier arguments regarding UN peacekeeping. T. Dannenbaum, 'Translating the Standard of Effective Control into a System of Effective Accountability' (2010) 51 Harv ILJ 113, at 156–183 (Dannenbaum, 'Translating'); T. Dannenbaum, 'Finding Balance in the Attribution of Liability for the Human Rights Violations of U.N. Peacekeepers' (2010) 51 Harv ILJO 69 (Dannenbaum, 'Finding Balance'); T. Dannenbaum, 'Killings at Srebrenica, Effective Control, and the Power to Prevent Unlawful Conduct' (2012) 61 ICLQ 713, at 719–727 (Dannenbaum, 'Killings at Srebrenica').

[4] Cf. Articles on the Responsibility of International Organizations, ILC Report on the work of its sixty-third session, UNGAOR 66th Sess., Supp. No. 10, UN Doc. A/66/10 (2011) (ARIO); Commentary to the Articles on the Responsibility of International Organizations,

'common organs' – public entities created collectively by a number of states or organisations to act on their behalf, like the trusteeship administration of Nauru;[5] and, second, multilateral operations in which states place their organs at the disposal of another state, international organisation, or group thereof, such as peacekeeping operations and multinational military forces.[6] Today, JPEs also include ventures that fit into neither of those classic paradigms. Frontex operations, for example, involve cooperation between a European Union (EU) agency, a host state, and personnel contributors in which all three exercise some autonomy, despite the host's formal supremacy.[7] Other examples include ventures like the Joint Investigation Team in which German, Dutch, and Europol participants engage in merged police and investigative operations,[8] and the Tilburg prison (rented from the Netherlands by Belgium, staffed by Dutch guards, and run by a Belgian Prison Director).[9] JPEs may operate extraterritorially for all participants,[10] extraterritorially for active participants at the invitation of a passive host,[11] or on an active participant's territory.[12]

Key features distinguish JPE wrongdoing from other shared wrongdoing. First, unlike non-collaborative aggregations of independent wrongdoing,[13]

ILC Report on the work of its sixty-third session, UNGAOR 66th Sess., Supp. No. 10, UN Doc. A/66/10 (2011) (ARIO Commentary), at 52–172, paras. 87–88, Article 2(a) ARIO; *Reparation for Injuries Suffered in the Service of the United Nations*, Advisory Opinion, ICJ Reports 1949, 174.

5 ARSIWA Commentary, n. 2, at 44, 64, 124; *Certain Phosphate Lands in Nauru (Nauru* v. *Australia)*, Preliminary Objections, ICJ Reports 1992, 240.

6 Article 6 ARSIWA, n. 2. In addition to the UN, regional actors like the EU, UN Doc. S/RES/1671 (25 April 2006), and ECOWAS, UN Doc. S/RES/2085 (20 December 2012) also lead peacekeeping missions. Similarly, both the UN, UN Doc. S/RES/2098 (28 March 2013), and regional actors like NATO, UN Doc. S/RES/1386 (20 December 2001), command multi-national military operations. Sometimes leadership is shared, as in NATO's and the UN's dual-key system in Bosnia, UN Doc. S/RES/836 (4 June 1993), para. 10.

7 I. Mann, *The EU's Dirty Hands* (Human Rights Watch, 2011), at 10–18, 38–45.

8 Netherlands Ministry of Defense, Press Release, 'German-Dutch Team Join Forces Against Pirates', 23 November 2011.

9 Government of the Netherlands, Press Release, 'Lower House Agrees to Placement of Belgian Detainees in Tilburg', 19 January 2010.

10 UN Doc. S/RES/678 (29 November 1990); UN Doc. S/RES/1973 (17 March 2011).

11 The classic peacekeeping scenario.

12 Frontex missions take this form, but also involve high seas operations. E. Papastavidris, '"Fortress Europe and FRONTEX": Within or Without International Law?' (2010) 79 Nord JIL 75.

13 See *Ilaşcu and others* v. *Moldova and Russia*, App. No. 48787/99 (ECtHR, 8 July 2004), paras. 352, 385, 393; *Corfu Channel (United Kingdom of Great Britain and Northern Ireland* v. *Albania)*, Merits, ICJ Report 1949, 4, at 15–23, 36; Council of Europe,

collective failures to engage in required cooperation,[14] or contributory fault,[15] JPEs are cooperative. Second, unlike collaborations between a state or international organisation and entities lacking international legal personality, JPEs involve multiple participants with full international legal personality.[16] Third, JPEs' merged structure of action distinguishes them both from collaborative but independent action,[17] and from scenarios in which the decisions of a merged entity are implemented independently.[18]

These distinctions emphasise why JPEs pose a unique problem for *ex post* attribution. In most shared international wrongs, it is relatively straightforward to isolate the conduct of each state or organisation and thus solve the first-order problem of attribution. The key challenges in those other contexts are instead: first, apportioning liability when the aggregation of the distinguishable state and international organisation acts leads to a single harm, and second, determining the scope of

Parliamentary Assembly, 'Lives lost in the Mediterranean Sea: who is responsible?' Doc. 12895 (5 April 2012).

14 States must cooperate to combat *jus cogens* violations, protect the environment, and further development. See Article 41 ARSIWA, n. 2; *Gabčíkovo-Nagymaros Project (Hungary/Slovakia)*, Judgment, ICJ Reports 1997, 7, paras. 112–113, 141–143; Rio Declaration on Environment and Development, UN Doc. A/CONF.151/5/Rev.1 (1992), reprinted in (1992) 31 ILM 874 (Rio Declaration), Principles 5, 7, 9, 11–14, 19; United Nations Convention on the Law of the Sea, Montego Bay, 10 December 1982, in force 16 November 1994, 1833 UNTS 3 (LOSC), Articles 194, 197, 199–200, 207–208, 210–212; UN Millennium Declaration, UN Doc. A/RES/55/2 (18 September 2000); International Covenant on Economic, Social and Cultural Rights, New York, 16 December 1966, in force 3 January 1976, 993 UNTS 3, Articles 2(1), 11(1), 23.

15 Article 39 ARSIWA, n. 2; Article 39 ARIO, n. 4.

16 On state collaborations with entities lacking international legal personality, see discussion at n. 59–61; *Application of the Convention on the Prevention and Punishment of the Crime of* Genocide *(Bosnia and Herzegovina* v. *Serbia and Montenegro)*, Judgment, ICJ Reports 2007, 43, paras. 235–241 (*Bosnian Genocide*).

17 Such as *refoulement* (see discussion at n. 71), or one state allowing another to use its territory to do wrong. Definition of Aggression, UN Doc. A/RES/3314 (XXIX) (14 December 1974) Article 3(f); *El-Masri* v. *The Former Yugoslav Republic of Macedonia*, App. No. 39630/09 (ECtHR, 13 December 2012), para. 206. More generally, see Article 16 ARSIWA, n. 2; *Bosnian Genocide*, ibid., paras. 416–424.

18 This distinction is not always appreciated. See, e.g., N. Gal-Or and C. Ryngaert, 'From Theory to Practice' (2012) 13 GLJ 511, at 513. On independent implementation of collective decisions, see *Bosphorus Hava Yollari Turizm Ve Ticaret Anonim Şirketi* v. *Ireland*, App. No. 45036/98 (ECtHR, 30 June 2005), paras. 137, 152–156; *Kadi and Al Barakaat International Foundation* v. *Council of the European Union and Commission of the European Communities* [2008] ECR I-6351, joined cases C-402/05 P and C-415/05 P; *Commission* v. *Kadi* [2013] ECR Case C-584/10 P, C 593/10 P, C 595/10 P (2013); *Nada* v. *Switzerland*, App. No. 10593/08 (ECtHR, 12 September 2012). See also ARIO, n. 4, at 105–110.

vicarious responsibility among states and organisations.[19] JPEs are different. The issue is not just 'who pays for the damage?', but 'who do we understand to have committed the wrong?' The uniquely thorny nature of that latter question warrants focusing on JPE attribution in isolation.

Finally among matters of scope, I use the term *wrongs* (rather than legal breaches) purposely to single out illegal action of public concern to the global community.[20] The legal category of duties *erga omnes* provides doctrinal substance to this concept.[21] However, in addition to the narrow list elaborated by the International Court of Justice (ICJ) thus far,[22] I include aspects of environmental law, the full corpus of human rights, and the humanitarian aspects of the laws of war.[23]

I focus on global wrongs for three reasons.[24] First, because they cause 'irreparable harm', the consequentialist imperative is prevention more than compensation.[25] Second, because attributing wrongdoing entails public condemnation (rather than merely bilateral responsibility),

[19] Distinguishing *ex post* attribution and *ex post* liability, see Nollkaemper and Jacobs, 'Shared Responsibility in International Law', n. 2, at 414; R. Pisillo-Mazzeschi, 'Forms of International Responsibility for Environmental Harm', in F. Francioni and T Scovazzi (eds.), *International Responsibility for Environmental Harm* (London: Graham and Trotman, 1991), 15.

[20] Cf. P.A. Nollkaemper, 'Constitutionalization and the Unity of the Law of International Responsibility' (2009) 6 Indiana JGLS 535; N.H.B. Jorgensen, *The Responsibility of States for International Crimes* (Oxford University Press, 2000). The ILC's refusal to draw such a distinction (ARSIWA Commentary, n. 2, at 55, 111) sits uneasily with the status it accords *erga omnes* and *jus cogens*. ARSIWA Commentary, n. 2, at 33, 56, 110–116, 126–128.

[21] *Barcelona Traction, Light and Power Company, Limited (Belgium* v. *Spain)*, Second Phase, ICJ Reports 1970, 3, para. 33 (*Barcelona Traction*).

[22] Ibid., para. 34 (including prohibitions on aggression, genocide, slavery, and racial discrimination); *East Timor (Portugal* v. *Australia)*, Judgment, ICJ Reports 1995, 90, para. 29 (adding self-determination).

[23] See United Nations Framework Convention on Climate Change, New York, 9 May 1992, in force 21 March 1994, 1771 UNTS 107 (UNFCCC), preamble and Article 3(1); Rapporteur F. Orrego Vicuña, *Responsibility and Liability Under International Law for Environmental Damage*, Institut de Droit International (1997), Articles 23, 28; Human Rights Committee (HRC), General Comment 31, UN Doc. CCPR/C/21/Rev.1/Add.13 (2004), para. 2. The exclusion of humanitarian and human rights protections from the system of countermeasures emphasises their global, rather than bilateral, value. Article 50 ARSIWA, n. 2.

[24] Despite the lack of a formal doctrinal distinction, the normative differences between public from private wrongs warrant separate analysis. Nollkaemper and Jacobs, 'Shared Responsibility in International Law', n. 2, at 372–373, 405, 408.

[25] See Chapter 5 of this volume L.A. Kornhauser, 'Incentives, Compensation, and Irreparable Harm', 120.

it should be rooted in a robust underlying institutional moral responsibility. Third, whereas liability apportionment is central to the private dimension of *ex post* responsibility, attribution is its public dimension.[26]

3. Doctrinal dissension

Currently on the table in one form or another are five approaches to attributing JPE wrongdoing: authorial control, operational control, blanket multiple attribution, the *Nicaragua* interpretation of 'effective control', and the broader interpretation of 'effective control' that I have advocated elsewhere and elaborate here – call it 'preventive control'.[27] Sections 4–6 identify the normative principle that ought to guide attribution and explain why the first four approaches fall short in that respect. To frame that discussion, this section sketches the alternative attribution regimes and the rationales offered for each. For the most part, the rebuttal of these rationales is left for section 6.

The authorial control test holds that if a JPE exists pursuant to the authorisation and delegation of one or more of the participants, enterprise conduct is to be considered the conduct of those authorial participants and none of the others. Thus, in *Behrami*, the European Court of Human Rights (ECtHR) attributed the conduct of United Nations (UN)-authorised, North Atlantic Treaty Organization (NATO)-led troops in Kosovo exclusively to the UN (and *not* to NATO or any state participant).[28] The International Law Commission (ILC) also advocates an authorial control standard, although only for the narrower category of 'common organs', like the Nauru trusteeship managed by Australia but authorised by Australia, New Zealand, and the United Kingdom (UK).[29]

26 Nollkaemper and Jacobs, 'Shared Responsibility in International Law', n. 2, at 414.

27 See sources cited at n. 3.

28 *Agim Behrami and Bekir Behrami* v. *France* and *Ruzhdi Saramati* v. *France, Germany and Norway*, App. No. 71412/01 and App. No. 78166/01 (ECtHR, 2 May 2007), paras. 132–141. Initially, the Court persisted with this 'ultimate authority and control' test. *Kasumaj* v. *Greece*, App. No. 6974/05 (ECtHR, 7 July 2007); *Gajić* v. *Germany*, App. No. 31446/02 (ECtHR, 28 August 2007). More recently, however, the Grand Chamber equivocated between 'ultimate authority and control' and 'effective control' (discussed later in the chapter). *Al-Jedda* v. *the United Kingdom*, App. No. 27021/08 (ECtHR, 7 July 2011), para. 84.

29 ARSIWA Commentary, n. 2, at 64, 124; R. Ago, 'Seventh Report on State Responsibility', ILC *Yearbook* 1978/II(2), at 99. On Nauru, see *Certain Phosphate Lands in Nauru*, n. 5, paras. 45–47; Ibid, Separate Opinion of Judge Shahabuddeen, para. 4; Trusteeship Agreement for the Territory of Nauru (Australia-UK-New Zealand), approved by the UNGA on

A few other courts and states have adopted or asserted this test.[30] The rationale is that it reflects the authorial entity's 'obligation to ensure that it can exercise effective authority and control over the way in which its delegated powers are being exercised'.[31]

Although also emphasising formal hierarchy, the second approach attributes enterprise conduct to the entity with operational command and control, whether or not it is the authorial entity. In 2008, the District Court in The Hague applied this test to impute the acts of the Dutch peacekeeping battalion at Srebrenica to the UN.[32] The rulings have since been reversed,[33] but the standard remains popular and is asserted by the UN and troop-contributing states in most peacekeeping operations.[34]

Some advocates of this standard claim that holding contributing states responsible for wrongs occurring in a mission under another entity's operational control would deter contributions, undermining valuable international cooperation.[35] This position is misleading. By the same logic, effective attribution to the entity with operational control would

1 November 1947, 10 UNTS 3. Australia (with contributions from the UK and New Zealand) settled with Nauru, obviating final judgment. Agreement between Australia and the Republic of Nauru for the Settlement of the Case in the International Court of Justice concerning *Certain Phosphate Lands in Nauru*, Nauru, 10 August 1993, in force 20 August 1993, 1770 UNTS 379. Except for common organs, the ILC rejects authorial control, as does the UN Secretariat. ARIO, n. 4, at 87–88, 110.

30 *Anglo-Chinese Shipping* v. *United States*, 127 F. Supp. 553 (Fed. Cl. 1955); *Eurotunnel Arbitration (The Channel Tunnel Group Ltd & France-Manche S.A.* v. *the Secretary of State for Transport of the Government of the United Kingdom of Great Britain and Northern Ireland and le ministre de l'équipement, des transports, de l'aménagement du territoire, du tourisme et de la mer du Gouvernement de la République française)*, Partial Award, (2007) 132 ILR 1, para. 179; *Legality of Use of Force (Serbia and Montenegro* v. *United Kingdom)*, Transcript, CR 1999/25 (12 May 1999), at 16 (Federal Republic of Yugoslavia advocating authorial control).

31 D. Sarooshi, *The United Nations and the Development of Collective Security* (Oxford University Press, 1999), 164.

32 *Hasan Nuhanović* v. *the Netherlands*, ECLI:NL:RBSGR:2008:BF0181 (Rechtbank's-Gravenhage, 10 September 2008) (*Nuhanović* District Court) para 4.9 (identifying the 'operational command and control' test); ibid. para 4.14.1 (the Netherlands would have been attributed with the act only if it had 'cut across' UN command, directing Dutchbat 'to ignore' or 'to go against' UN orders.).

33 See sources cited at n. 44.

34 ARIO, n. 4, at 88; UN Secretary-General, 'Administrative and Budgetary Aspects of the Financing of the United Nations Peacekeeping Operations', UN Doc. A/51/389 (1996), paras. 7–8; Dannenbaum, 'Translating', n. 3, at 153.

35 *Al-Jedda*, n. 28, para. 68; M. Simons, 'Dutch Peacekeepers Are Found Responsible for Deaths', *The New York Times*, 7 September 2013, at A3. The UN has indicated that its acceptance of exclusive responsibility is partly 'political'. ARIO, n. 4, at 88.

undermine the very same ventures by deterring states and international organisations from adopting an operational leadership role. In peacekeeping, the latter danger is obviated by UN immunity.[36] But that 'solution' entails eviscerating the proscription of such wrongs in the context of international cooperation. Rather than articulating a defensible attribution framework, its supporters are really advocating attribution to no one.[37] A genuine rationale for the operational control test would instead need to identify operational control as the relevant superior feature in a *respondeat superior* narrative.[38]

A third category of frameworks, yet to find judicial affirmation, would expand attribution to a broader subset. The more conservative version would attribute JPE conduct to both those with operational or authorial control *and* any entity that supplied the individual perpetrators of the wrong.[39] A more expansive version would attribute wrongful JPE conduct to *all* enterprise participants, irrespective of venture control or connection to the individual perpetrators.[40] The rationale for such automatic joint attribution is that it maximally protects victim compensation and ensures robust deterrence.

Ultimately, the authorial control, operational control, and blanket joint attribution tests all focus on general enterprise structure, rather than the specifics of the wrongful conduct.[41] This is a mistake. What makes JPEs unique among public ventures is that they disaggregate the concentrated power that a state ordinarily holds over its organs and agents, distributing the levers of command, authority, and control in various ways depending on the negotiated compromise underpinning the particular enterprise. The result is that the influence of any given state or international organisation over conduct varies significantly depending

[36] See, for example, *Mothers of Srebrenica* v. *the Netherlands and the United Nations*, ECLI: NL:HR:2012:BW1999 (Supreme Court of the Netherlands, 13 April 2012), upheld in *Stichting Mothers of Srebrenica and others* v. *the Netherlands*, App. No. 65542/12 (ECtHR, 11 June 2013), paras. 135–170.

[37] The UN 'accepts' attribution while asserting universal immunity and diverting claims to an inadequate internal system. Ibid.; Dannenbaum, 'Translating', n. 3, at 121–129.

[38] Section 6 rebuts such a rationale.

[39] J.J. Paust, 'The U.N. Is Bound By Human Rights' (2010) 51 Harv ILJO 1, at 8.

[40] A standard asserted unsuccessfully on behalf of Saddam Hussein in a suit against twenty-one members of the coalition that invaded Iraq in 2003. *Saddam Hussein* v. *Albania and others*, App. No. 23276/04 (ECtHR, 14 March 2006). See also Human Rights Watch's work on Frontex operations in Greece, which demands the withdrawal of all contributing states. Mann, *The EU's Dirty Hands*, n. 7, at 46–52, 55.

[41] There are marginal exceptions. See n. 32 on 'cutting across' the chain of command.

not just on that participant's position in the enterprise, but also on the nature of the impugned conduct. For JPEs, a contextual, conduct-specific standard of attribution is more likely to pair legal attribution with moral responsibility and optimal incentives.

This is the appeal of the 'effective control' standard adopted by the ILC and several courts in the context of one particular form of JPE: the placement of multiple states' and international organisations' organs at the disposal of an international organisation.[42] There are at least two relevant interpretations of 'effective control', so this divides into two alternative standards.

This chapter deepens the normative foundations of the 'preventive control' interpretation that I have advocated elsewhere and extends it to all JPEs.[43] The Hague Court of Appeal adopted a version of this standard in 2011 which was affirmed two years later by the Dutch Supreme Court.[44] The preventive control framework is detailed in section 6, but four features warrant foregrounding. First, for any given wrong, it inquires of each enterprise participant whether that participant held the levers of control most relevant to preventing the type of wrongful conduct in question.[45] Second, those levers include not just the authority to direct, but also authority over training, discipline, hiring, promotion, criminal jurisdiction, and more. Third, which of these levers underpins responsibility depends on the type of wrongful conduct. Finally, preventive control can be shared.

[42] Article 7 ARIO, n. 4; ARIO Commentary, n. 4, at 87. See *Hasan Nuhanović* v. *the Netherlands*, ECLI:NL:GHSGR:2011:BR0133 (Gerechtshof's-Gravenhage, 5 July 2011); also ILDC 1742 (NL 2011) (*Nuhanović* Court of Appeal). Upheld in: *The Netherlands* v. *Hasan Nuhanović*, ECLI:NL:HR:2013:BZ9225 (Supreme Court of the Netherlands, 6 September 2013) (*Nuhanović* Supreme Court). See also *R (on the Application of Al-Jedda) (FC)* v. *Sec'y of State for Def.* [2007] UKHL 58. Upheld in: *Al-Jedda*, n. 28, paras. 80, 84.

[43] Dannenbaum, 'Translating', n. 3, at 157. The ILC terms mine a 'wide meaning' of effective control. ARIO, n. 4, at 93, fn. 129. I argue that it is the optimal interpretation of Article 7 ARIO, n. 4. Dannenbaum, 'Killings at Srebrenica', n. 3, at 721. However, that conversation is tangential here, since many JPEs are not covered by Article 7.

[44] *Nuhanović* Court of Appeal, n. 42. In affirming the Court of Appeal's interpretation of effective control without caveat, the Supreme Court eschewed its Procurator General's advice to use a narrower interpretation. *Nuhanović* Supreme Court, n. 42, paras. 3.11.2–3.11.3, 3.12.2–3.12.3; P.A. Nollkaemper, 'Procurator General of the Dutch Supreme Court Concludes to Reject Appeal against Srebrenica Judgment', SHARES Blog, 3 May 2013. Drawing the connection to my proposal, see ARIO, n. 4, at 93, fn. 129.

[45] *Nuhanović* Court of Appeal, n. 42, paras. 5.8–5.9; Dannenbaum, 'Translating', n. 3, at 157; Dannenbaum, 'Killings at Srebrenica', n. 3, at 721.

The dominant alternative interpretation of 'effective control' is that used by the ICJ in *Nicaragua* and later judgments to evaluate state responsibility for the wrongs of non-state armed groups.[46] Adapted to JPEs, this would attribute enterprise conduct to the state or organisation that 'directed or enforced the perpetration of [the wrongful] acts'.[47] When the conduct is directed by one of the state or international organisation enterprise participants, this test is attractive. But it breaks down in the common case that the wrong occurs in the absence of such directions, or even in contravention thereof.[48]

It would be implausible to attribute such wrongful conduct straightforwardly to a state or international organisation when performed by one of its organs acting alone (as is uncontroversial legal orthodoxy), and yet to leave precisely the same wrongful conduct of an otherwise identical JPE organ completely unattributed to *any* legal person merely because the organ is the collaborative product of a number of states and organisations.[49] Filling that implausible attribution gap would mean supplementing the *Nicaragua* test with a presumptive rule of attribution to a particular participant for enterprise conduct not occurring pursuant to state or international organisation direction. Such a presumption has mixed doctrinal credentials, but the more important point here is that it sacrifices the value of a conduct-specific test.[50] Any confluence between

[46] *Military and Paramilitary Activities in and against Nicaragua (Nicaragua* v. *United States of America)*, Merits, ICJ Reports 1986, 14, para. 115 (*Nicaragua*); *Bosnian Genocide*, n. 16, paras. 397–401; *Armed Activities on the Territory of the Congo (Democratic Republic of the Congo* v. *Uganda)*, Judgment, ICJ Report 2005, 168, paras. 146–147 (*Armed Activities*).

[47] *Nicaragua*, ibid., para. 115. See also *Armed Activities*, ibid., para. 146; *Bosnian Genocide*, n. 16, paras. 397, 400. Some advocate attributing JPE conduct to the state or organisation 'giving the orders'. M. Milanović and T. Papić, 'As Bad as it Gets' (2009) 58 ICLQ 267, at 282.

[48] P. Rowe, 'United Nations Peacekeepers and Human Rights Violations' (2010) 51 Harv ILJ 69, at 76 (most peacekeeper wrongs contravene superior orders).

[49] Non-attribution is the typical result of applying the *Nicaragua* test to non-state actor conduct. *Nicaragua*, n. 46, para. 116; *Bosnian Genocide*, n. 16, paras. 413–415; *Armed Activities*, n. 46, para. 160. Applied to JPEs, this would contradict the ILC framework. ARIO, n. 4, at 88, 95.

[50] Under Article 7 ARIO, n. 4, the seconded organ's conduct is attributed to the receiving international organisation 'if the organization exercises effective control over that conduct'. Since Article 6 ARIO, n. 4 and Article 4 ARSIWA, n. 2 hold that a state's or organisation's organs' conduct is attributable to that state or organisation, one might argue that whenever the receiving entity lacks effective control, organ conduct is attributable to the lender. The Dutch Procurator General and the ECtHR hint at this, but both equivocate by also emphasising the lender's control. Nollkaemper, 'Procurator General of

the presumption and actual institutional influence over the conduct in any given case would be serendipitous.

The preventive control approach is alone among JPE attribution frameworks in tracking institutional influence in all contexts. In doing this, it instantiates legally the deeper normative reciprocity between public power and preventive responsibility that underpins various more mature rules of international responsibility – most obviously, those on preventive due diligence.

4. Vigilant prevention of wrongdoing in international law

The principle that states have a duty to act vigilantly to prevent wrongdoing within their spheres of power is central to international law's approach to ensuring global values. In its early guise, this doctrine of preventive due diligence developed in a context of bilateral state relations, and it remains significant in certain bilateral realms.[51] But even in that form it has always been premised on the notion that claiming sovereign authority entails a fundamental duty to use that power in a way that protects those most vulnerable to wrongdoing within its sphere. That idea provided the foundation for legal frameworks governing: first, neutrality, in which the state must prevent private actors within its jurisdiction from using force transnationally;[52] second, states' obligations vis-à-vis one another's citizens, in which the state has a duty to prevent harm to foreign nationals,[53] foreign investors,[54] and diplomatic and

the Dutch Supreme Court Concludes to Reject Appeal against Srebrenica Judgment', n. 44; *Al-Jedda*, n. 28, paras. 80–86. It is difficult to reconcile such a framework with the ECtHR's endorsement of dual attribution (ibid., para. 80) or the ILC's Commentaries. Dannenbaum, 'Killings at Srebrenica', n. 3, at 720–721. Further confusing matters, and seemingly rendering Article 7 ARIO, n. 4 redundant, other authorities have suggested the opposite presumption (that conduct *ultra vires* is attributable to the receiving entity, not the lender). ARIO, n. 4, at 96; *Nuhanović* District Court, n. 32, paras. 4.8–4.15; *Behrami*, n. 28, paras. 133–135.

51 *Barcelona Traction*, n. 21, paras. 33–35, 88.

52 *Caroline Incident: Daniel Webster's letter to Henry Fox* (24 April 1841); *Alabama claims of the United States of America against Great Britain*, Award, (1872) 29 RIAA 125.

53 *British Claims in the Spanish Zone of Morocco (Great Britain/Spain)*, Award, (1924) 2 RIAA 615; *Janes et al. (United States of America* v. *United Mexican States)*, Award, (1926) 4 RIAA 82.

54 This remains a bilateral frame. *Noble Ventures, Inc.* v. *Romania*, Award, ICSID Case No. ARB/01/11 (2005), para. 164; *Elettronica Sicula S.p.A. (ELSI) (United States of America* v. *Italy)*, Judgment, ICJ Report 1989, 15.

consular premises and officials[55] in its territory; and third, non-violent transboundary harm, in which states must prevent private entities from polluting neighbouring states.[56]

In line with international law's (partial) transition from a regime focused on bilateral inter-state relations to a regime of global public normativity, preventive vigilance is now central to the legal frameworks for quelling global terrorism, upholding human rights, protecting the global environment, and combating mass atrocity. At the normative crux of these regimes is the reciprocity between the state's claim to legitimate power and its duty to prevent wrongs of global concern.

The contours of the state's preventive responsibility regarding transnational armed groups are the subject of heated debate, but few would deny the central legal importance of such a duty.[57] The ICJ offered the most modest (and heavily criticised) articulation of the standard when it held that the Democratic Republic of the Congo (DRC) – a profoundly weak state lacking control over the relevant territory – was for those reasons excused from engaging in significant preventive action.[58] More expansively, others point to Security Council support for, near-universal acceptance of, and extensive participation in the American response to Al-Qaeda's 2001 attacks, which involved waging war on Afghanistan on the grounds that it had 'harboured' Al-Qaeda.[59] This stimulated an ongoing debate as to whether the state's duty to act vigilantly to prevent actors on its territory from launching transnational attacks might be transforming into a rule whereby preventive failure could underpin attribution with the attack (and thus trigger the attributed state's vulnerability to lawful defensive force).[60] This remains a minority view, but regardless of ongoing disagreements as to the appropriate trigger for

[55] *United States Diplomatic and Consular Staff in Tehran (United States of America* v. *Iran)*, Judgment, ICJ Reports 1980, 3 (*Consular Staff in Tehran*), paras. 63–68.

[56] *Trail Smelter (United States of America* v. *Canada)*, Award, (1938) 3 RIAA 1905.

[57] Declaration on Friendly Relations, UN Doc. A/RES/2625, UN Doc. A/8028 (24 October 1970), at 123; Definition of Aggression, n. 17, Article 3(f); *Armed Activities*, n. 46, paras. 162, 300.

[58] Ibid., paras. 301–304. But see ibid., Separate Opinions of Judges Kooijmans, para. 82, and Tomka, paras. 1–6.

[59] D. Jinks, 'State Responsibility for the Acts of Private Armed Groups' (2003) 4 Chic JIL 83, at 89.; V.-J. Proulx, 'Babysitting Terrorists' (2005) 23 Berk JIL 615, at 637–638.

[60] Y. Dinstein, *War, Aggression, and Self-Defence*, 5th edn (Cambridge University Press, 2012), 261; T. Franck, *Recourse to Force* (Cambridge University Press, 2002), 54; G. Travalio and J. Altenburg, 'Terrorism, State Responsibility and the Use of Military Force' (2003) 4 Chic JIL 97, at 100–111; Proulx, ibid., at 637; Jinks, ibid., at 89–90.

lawful defensive force, the basic preventive duty is clear.[61] It has been strengthened and operationalised over the past 15 years in a series of Security Council resolutions.[62]

Duties of preventive vigilance have also taken on a public dimension in environmental law.[63] Moving beyond bilateral harm, the ICJ has recognised the state's obligation to ensure that private actors under its jurisdiction respect the *global* environment,[64] emphasising the stakes for 'the whole of mankind'.[65] Upholding this preventive legal obligation is considered a core governmental duty.[66]

Perhaps most notable, however, has been the rise of preventive duties in human rights law. Many human rights treaties lack explicit provisions obligating the state to use its sovereign power affirmatively to prevent human rights violations by private actors.[67] It was not until the 1980s that the preventive dimension of human rights obligations under these treaties came to the fore.[68] In an early and influential statement of this responsibility, the Inter-American Court of Human Rights held that states must organise 'all the structures through which public power is

[61] Questioning the expansion of lawful defensive force, see, C. Gray, *International Law and the Use of Force*, 3rd edn (Cambridge University Press, 2008), 135.

[62] Prior to 11 September 2001, see, for example, UN Doc. S/RES/1267 (15 October 1999). Since the attacks, the Council has issued a slew of resolutions on this issue, starting with UN Doc. S/RES/1373 (28 September 2001).

[63] Articles 3–6 UNFCCC, n. 23; Principles 2, 11, 16 Rio Declaration, n. 14; Articles on Prevention of Transboundary Harm from Hazardous Activities, ILC Report on the work of its fifty-third session, UN Doc. A/56/10 Supp. No. 10 (2001), at 370, 372 (Article 3), 393, 395, 411; *Pulp Mills on the River Uruguay (Argentina* v. *Uruguay)*, Judgment, ICJ Reports 2010, 14, paras. 101, 187, 197, 204, 223, 265; Articles 192–194, 196, 199, 207–212 LOSC, n. 14; *Responsibilities and Obligations of States Sponsoring Persons and Entities with Respect to Activities in the Area*, Advisory Opinion, Seabed Disputes Chamber of the International Tribunal for the Law of the Sea, Case No. 17, (2011) 50 ILM 458 (*ITLOS Advisory Opinion 2011*), paras. 99–120.

[64] *Legality of the Threat or Use of Nuclear Weapons*, Advisory Opinion, ICJ Report 1996, 226, para. 29 (*Nuclear Weapons*); *Gabčíkovo-Nagymaros*, n. 14, para. 53. See also Rio Declaration, n. 14, Principle 2.

[65] *Gabčíkovo-Nagymaros*, ibid., paras. 53, 140. See also *Nuclear Weapons*, ibid., at 505–507 (Judge Weeramantry, dissenting).

[66] Vicuña, *Responsibility and Liability Under International Law for Environmental Damage*, n. 23, Article 3; P. Birnie and A. Boyle, *International Law and The Environment*, 2nd edn (Oxford University Press, 2002), 112. See also *ITLOS Advisory Opinion 2011*, n. 63, para. 112.

[67] V.P. Tzevelekos, 'In Search of Alternative Solutions' (2010) 35 Brook JIL 155, at 182.

[68] See H. Shue, *Basic Rights*, 2nd edn (Princeton University Press, 1996), 52; A. Eide, Report on the Right to Adequate Food as a Human Right, UN Doc. E/CN.4/Sub.2/1987/23 (7 July 1987), at 34–36, 112–115, 167–181.

exercised, so that they are capable of juridically ensuring the free and full enjoyment of human rights. [They] must prevent, investigate and punish any violation of the rights recognized by the Convention'.[69] This basic preventive responsibility has now been endorsed and affirmed repeatedly across human rights regimes.[70]

The strength of the reciprocal link between the state's claim to legitimate power and the duty to exercise that power preventively is spotlighted in its extraterritorial application. *Non-refoulement* prohibits the state from transferring individuals under its control to a state where they would be at risk of severe abuse (even when the former state's agents are holding the persons on the territory of the latter).[71] States have been found to have a duty to prevent rights violations by private persons acting in foreign territories over which they exercise effective control,[72] and by private persons over whom they have preventive influence.[73] This latter doctrine may prove especially important in regulating

[69] *Velásquez Rodriguez* v. *Honduras*, IACtHR, (Ser. C) No. 4 (1988), para. 166.

[70] A. Mowbray, *The Development of Positive Obligations under the European Convention on Human Rights by the European Court of Human Rights* (Oxford: Hart Publishing, 2004); *Delgado Páez* v. *Colombia*, Communication No. 195/1985, Human Rights Committee, UN Doc. CCPR/C/39/D/195/1985 (1990); HRC, General Comment 20, UN Doc. HRI/GEN/1/Rev.1 (1992), paras. 2, 10, 13; HRC, General Comment 31, n. 23, paras. 6, 8; Committee Against Torture, General Comment 2, UN Doc. CAT/C/GC/2 (2007), paras. 18–24; Committee on Economic, Social and Cultural Rights (CESCR), General Comment 12, UN Doc. E/C.12/1999/5 (1999), para. 15; *MFHR* v. *Greece*, European Committee of Social Rights, Complaint No. 30/2005 (2006), para. 192; *SERAC and CESR* v. *Nigeria*, Communication No. 155/96 (2001), African Commission on Human and Peoples' Rights, paras. 46, 58, 61, 63, 65–66; Basic Principles and Guidelines on the Right to a Remedy and Reparation for Victims of Gross Violations of International Human Rights Law and Serious Violations of International Humanitarian Law, UN Doc. A/RES/60/147 (16 December 2005) (Basic Principles on the Right to a Remedy), para. 3; O. De Schutter et al., 'Commentary to the Maastricht Principles on Extraterritorial Obligations of States in the Area of Economic, Social and Cultural Rights' (2012) 34 HRQ 1084, at 1134 (De Schutter, 'Commentary to the Maastricht Principles'). But see M. Hakimi, 'State Bystander Responsibility' (2010) 21 EJIL 341, at 367–371 (limiting the duty to a narrow category of abuses).

[71] *Al-Saadoon and Mufdhi* v. *the United Kingdom*, App. No. 61498/08 (ECtHR, 2 March 2010).

[72] HRC, General Comment 31, n. 23, para. 10; *Loizidou* v. *Turkey*, App. No. 15318/89 (ECtHR, 23 March 1995), paras. 62–64. Conversely, even when a state lacks control over part of its territory, it retains 'a duty to take all the appropriate [preventive] measures which it is still within its power to take'. *Ilaşcu*, n. 13, para. 313.

[73] The ECtHR required Russia to use its 'dissuasive influence' (later termed 'decisive') to restrain the breakaway Transdniestrian regime in Moldova. *Ilaşcu*, n. 13, para. 387. See also De Schutter et al., 'Commentary to the Maastricht Principles', n. 70, at 1136–1137.

multinational corporations.[74] Overall, the extraterritoriality of human rights illustrates the tight link between the scope of the state's preventive responsibilities and the scope of its asserted power, a point sharpened by the ECtHR's holding that human rights obligations abroad can be 'divided and tailored' to reflect the nature of the state's control.[75]

These developments in human rights have become intertwined with the preventive dimension of the laws of war.[76] Building on belligerent occupiers' duty to restore public order, the ICJ found Uganda responsible for failing to act vigilantly to prevent 'rebel groups acting on their own account' from violating human rights and humanitarian law in the Eastern DRC.[77] The Inter-American Court has interpreted Additional Protocol II and Common Article 3 to impose a similar duty on states with respect to the violations of non-state actors in internal armed conflicts.[78]

Perhaps the most explicit articulation of the deep normative reciprocity discussed throughout this section is the 'responsibility to protect' (R2P).[79] Still searching for a clear legal status, R2P is currently a complex cluster of *lex lata* and *lex ferenda*.[80] It is, in my view, best understood as an expression of the normative foundation of an evolving legal regime – the blueprint for the legitimation of sovereign power under a humanised international law. It transforms sovereignty from a shield into a bundle of powers justified because they enable the prevention of wrongs of global concern.[81] Seen in this light, R2P captures the moral reciprocity between

[74] J. Ruggie, *Guiding Principles on Business and Human Rights*, UN Doc. A/HRC/17/31 (2011) Annex, Part I; De Schutter et al., 'Commentary to the Maastricht Principles', n. 70, Article 25(c), at 1135–1136, 1139–1145; CESCR, Statement on the Obligations of States Parties Regarding the Corporate Sector and Economic, Social and Cultural Rights, UN Doc. E/C.12/2011/1 (2011), para. 5.

[75] *Al-Skeini and others* v. *the United Kingdom*, App. No. 55721/07 (ECtHR, 7 July 2011), para. 137.

[76] Basic Principles on the Right to a Remedy, n. 70, para. 3.

[77] *Armed Activities*, n. 46, paras. 178–180, 219–229, 248–250.

[78] *The Mapiripán Massacre* v. *Colombia*, IACtHR, (Ser. C) No. 134 (2005), para. 114.

[79] International Commission on Intervention and State Sovereignty, *The Responsibility to Protect* (2001) ch. 7 (ICISS Report); UN Doc. S/RES/1674 (2006), para. 4; 2005 World Summit Outcome, UN Doc. A/RES/60/1 (24 October 2005), para. 138; UN Secretary-General, Implementing the Responsibility to Protect, UN Doc. A/63/677 (2009), at 8–9.

[80] See C. Stahn, 'Responsibility to Protect' (2007) 101 AJIL 99; Chapter 9 of this volume, M. Hakimi, 'Distributing the Responsibility to Protect', 265.

[81] ICISS Report, n. 79, paras. 1.35, 2.14–2.15, 2.30–2.32; High-level Panel on Threats, Challenges and Change, 'A more secure world: our shared responsibility', UN Doc. A/59/565 (2004), paras. 29–30; Stahn, ibid., at 118.

public power and responsibility – a foundational principle that makes normative sense of the rise of the range of preventive duties described above.

Indeed, one can read R2P as holding the legitimacy of state power *contingent* on its preventive use. A state that fails to protect its people from atrocity loses temporarily the basic sovereign right not to be subject to forceful external intervention, with preventive responsibility extending to the international community.[82] Precisely what this means is hotly disputed, but the latter duty is widely thought to apply at least to the UN Security Council – notably, the body with the most expansive claims to legitimate global public power – and it has been suggested that the permanent members bear a special obligation not to obstruct such action.[83] Here, too, the basic moral reciprocity is apparent.

In a final case illustrating the doctrinal reach of that underlying principle, the ICJ held the Federal Republic of Yugoslavia (FRY) responsible under the Genocide Convention[84] for failing to make 'the best efforts within [its] power to try and prevent' Vojska Republike Srpske (VRS) [Bosnian Serb Army] atrocities in Bosnia.[85] Responsibility hinged on the FRY's 'capacity to influence effectively' the génocidaires' actions (whether or not it could have stopped the genocide).[86] Notwithstanding caveats emphasising the FRY's special links to the VRS and the former's failure to abide by a provisional measures ruling, the judgment adds to the broad trend towards recognising in law the normative reciprocity between public power and the responsibility to use it to prevent wrongdoing of global concern.[87]

Four features of this trend warrant emphasis. First, the *ex ante* duty to prevent such wrongdoing is not reflected in a strict responsibility *ex post* – if the state acts with vigilance, it is not responsible for wrongs it was unable to prevent.[88] Second, even if the state fails to act with

[82] ICISS Report, n. 79, para. 2.25; L. Feinstein and A.-M. Slaughter, 'A Duty to Prevent' (2004) FA (R2P is 'nothing less than the redefinition of sovereignty itself').

[83] ICISS Report, n. 79, ch. 6, especially para. 6.21. A. Peters, 'The Responsibility to Protect and the Permanent Five – The Obligation to Give Reasons for a Veto', in J. Hoffmann and P.A. Nollkaemper (eds.), *Responsibility to Protect: From Principle to Practice* (Amsterdam University Press, 2012), 199.

[84] Convention on the Prevention and Punishment of the Crime of Genocide, Paris, 9 December 1948, in force 12 January 1951, 78 UNTS 277 (Genocide Convention).

[85] *Bosnian Genocide*, n. 16, para. 438.

[86] Ibid., paras. 430, 434, 462.

[87] For the caveats, see ibid., paras. 429, 430, 435.

[88] P.-M. Dupuy, 'Reviewing the Difficulties of Codification' (1999) 10 EJIL 371, at 379. See *Corfu Channel*, n. 13, at 18–22; *Armed Activities*, n. 46, para. 300; *Velásquez-Rodriguez*, n. 69, paras. 172–175; *Bosnian Genocide*, n. 16, para. 430.

vigilance, it is not attributed with the ensuing wrongs; its violation is the separate delict of failing to prevent.

Third, however, in the areas of greatest global public concern, the line between attribution and preventive failure is blurring. Some now argue that states that fail to prevent private human rights abuses or transnational uses of force should be held responsible *ex post* for the underlying wrong (not just preventive failure) and judicial decisions are occasionally ambiguous on this issue.[89] Moreover, any technical distinction is anyway of reduced significance if the consequences are the same (such as if failing to prevent transnational terrorism makes a state liable to defensive force).

Fourth, and most significantly, the doctrine of preventive vigilance is a trans-substantive principle (arguably, a general principle) by which lines of responsibility are drawn between states and fundamental wrongs.[90] Although what counts as the diligence due is highly contextual, there is a consistent normative core: states have a duty to act vigilantly and reasonably within their sphere of lawful influence to prevent wrongdoing of global concern. The separation of delicts is misleading in this respect. There is no due diligence violation unless the wrong itself occurs; the *ex ante* vigilance obligation is only a ground for *ex post* responsibility vis-à-vis *the core global wrong*. A state that fails to act with vigilance will not be responsible *ex post* if the core wrong does not occur. Preventive due diligence is thus functionally far closer to attribution than the delictual distinction allows. The global wrong is the same; the difference is in the route by which the state is connected to it.[91]

This is important. On the prevailing legal account, rules of preventive vigilance and rules of attribution are classified as primary and secondary rules, respectively.[92] Critics have noted that purportedly secondary rules of international law often import or create primary obligations.[93] But the

[89] *El-Masri*, n. 17, paras. 206, 211; *Velásquez-Rodriguez*, n. 69, para. 177; *Cyprus* v. *Turkey*, App. No. 25781/94 (ECtHR, 10 May 2001), paras. 76–77. See sources and discussion at n. 59–60 and n. 109, 112–114.

[90] Tzevelekos, 'In Search of Alternative Solutions', n. 67, at 160; De Schutter et al., 'Commentary to the Maastricht Principles', n. 70, at 1135–1136; *Corfu Channel*, n. 13, at 22; *Trail Smelter*, n. 56; Hakimi, 'State Bystander Responsibility', n. 70, at 345. But see *Bosnian Genocide*, n. 16, para. 429.

[91] *Velásquez-Rodriguez*, n. 69, para. 172 (a private 'act *which violates human rights* . . . can lead to international responsibility of the State . . . because of the lack of due diligence to prevent the violation') (emphasis added).

[92] ARSIWA Commentary, n. 2, at 31, 38–39.

[93] Nollkaemper and Jacobs, 'Shared Responsibility in International Law', n. 2, at 408–412.

reverse point is no less powerful: as a trans-substantive method of drawing a line of responsibility between the state and an underlying primary wrong, preventive due diligence shares key features with secondary rules on attribution.[94] Both define a legally significant connective link between state and wrongdoing.

This functional commonality, explored in the next section, is crucial, because underpinning the connective analysis in *both* contexts (due diligence and attribution) is a deeper normative commonality. Namely, the moral reciprocity between the state's claim to (and exercise of) public power, and its duty to use that power to prevent wrongdoing of global concern.[95] The normative resonance of that principle in both of these contexts, and across substantive domains sets the stage for starting with that reciprocity in assessing responsibility for JPE wrongdoing.

5. Due diligence, attribution, and drawing lines of responsibility

At the crux of the functional similarity between preventive vigilance and attribution is the fact that state responsibility is always at least minimally vicarious.[96] This is not to deny the moral reality of state responsibility – states and international organisations have morally significant agential features that warrant holding them (and not only their members or agents) responsible for official conduct.[97] However, because state action just is some combination of human acts (albeit acts defined and enabled by their institutional context), state responsibility necessarily involves drawing a normative link between the state and the conduct of natural persons.[98] And on prevailing moral and legal understandings, this connection is not merely one of direct causation, whereby human agents carry out institutionally defined obligations. State organs and their constituent individuals take initiative; they act beyond, and sometimes

[94] Defending what look like primary rules in its complicity framework, the ILC explains that they are 'derivative' of the underlying wrong. ARSIWA Commentary, n. 2, at 65. The same could be said of a preventive vigilance failure.

[95] *Armed Activities*, n. 46, Separate Opinion of Judge Tomka, para. 2.

[96] The ILC's work on state responsibility began with the *protection* of aliens. United Nations, *The Work of the International Law Commission*, 4th edn (1988), at 91. Compare sources cited at n. 53. See also C. Chinkin, 'A Critique of the Public/Private Dimension' (1999) 10 EJIL 387, at 395.

[97] Cf. P. Pettit, 'Responsibility Incorporated' (2007) 117 *Ethics* 171.

[98] ARSIWA Commentary, n. 2, at 35.

contrary to, what is institutionally required. But as long as they engage in 'official' conduct, the dominant view attributes their acts to the state.[99]

The line of responsibility connecting the state to such conduct is not obvious. Indeed, emphasising the distinction between the perpetrators and the state, and thus the need for a normative account of the latter's responsibility, one way in which a legally responsible state may be required to repair victims is by punishing the perpetrators.[100]

Making sense of the state's *ex post* responsibility for the conduct of agents acting on initiative or even contrary to instructions requires a moral narrative that connects the behaviour of the agent to the failures of the state institution. Much like the contexts described in section 4, that narrative is a story of preventive responsibility reciprocally entailed by claiming or holding public power.

The functional congruity of vigilance and attribution analyses in this context is plain from the structure of judicial examinations of wrongdoing of global public concern. When such a wrong is not directed or authorised by the relevant state authorities, the judicial evaluation of *ex post* responsibility involves considering potential normative connections between the state and the wrongful conduct, including both direct attribution and a failure of preventive vigilance, often considered in turn.[101]

The normative congruity of the two forms of linking is most obvious in the case of an organ acting *ultra vires*.[102] The state holds – or has the capacity to hold – significant levers of control over its organs. It is the combination of that heightened preventive capacity with the importance of restraining those who wield public power that drives the moral narrative underpinning a strict institutional duty to prevent *ultra vires* wrongdoing by state officials.[103] Giving voice to this narrative, the ECtHR held in *Ilaşcu* that state authorities 'are under a duty to impose

[99] Article 7, ARSIWA, n. 2; Article 8 ARIO, n. 4.

[100] ARSIWA Commentary, n. 2, at 106.

[101] See, for example, *Bosnian Genocide*, n. 16, para. 379; *Consular Staff in Tehran*, n. 55, paras. 58, 61; *Ilaşcu*, n. 13, para. 313; *Velásquez-Rodriguez*, n. 69, paras. 165–167.

[102] Although not without criticism, state responsibility arising from private wrongs and from public organs acting *ultra vires* have both been termed 'indirect' or 'vicarious'. Special Rapporteur R. Ago, 'Eighth Report on State Responsibility', ILC *Yearbook* 1979/II(1), at 4.

[103] Hakimi, 'State Bystander Responsibility', n. 70, at 356; D.D. Caron, 'The Basis of Responsibility', in R.B. Lillich and D.B. Magraw (eds.), *The Iran-US Claims Tribunal* (Ardsley: Transnational, 1998), at 109, 138; M.N. Shaw, *International Law*, 5th edn (Cambridge University Press, 2003), 700; B.A. Frey, 'Small Arms and Light Weapons: The Tools Used to Violate Human Rights' (2004) 3 DF 37, at 40.

their will [on their subordinates] and cannot shelter behind their inability to ensure that it is respected'.[104]

In this scenario and that of a failure of preventive vigilance, the underlying wrong is motivated by the will and initiative of a natural person. In both cases, the moral basis of the state's responsibility with respect to that wrong is in its failure to prevent the wrongful conduct.[105] Emphasising precisely this parallel, a former UN Special Rapporteur observes, '[i]n addition to *preventing* violations committed by *state agents*, human rights law obligates states to use *due diligence to prevent* harm … caused by armed *individuals and groups*.'[106] The common moral narrative is one of the reciprocity between public power and prevention. As discussed below, the different legal applications of that concept are explained not by a deviation from the reciprocity principle, but by different regulatory dangers in the two contexts.

An alternative to the reciprocity narrative might emphasise that state organs act on *behalf* of the state in a way that the private natural persons under its jurisdiction do not.[107] They represent it, and act in furtherance of its projects, and this representative function might be thought to underpin the attribution of their conduct. The problem with this is that, in acting *ultra vires*, state organs diverge from the state's projects and often fail to advance its interests. Moreover, *de facto* organs – which are subject to the same attribution rules – do not 'represent' the state at all; their connection to the state is defined solely by their subjection to its control.[108] These contours of *ultra vires* attribution are explained better by a moral account rooted in the state's obligation to prevent global wrongful conduct as a reciprocal entailment of its claimed or asserted public power than they are by one focused on the idea of organs acting on behalf of states.

[104] *Ilaşcu*, n. 13, para. 319. See also *Youmans (United States of America* v. *United Mexican States)*, Award, (1926) 4 RIAA 110, para. 14; *Velásquez-Rodriguez*, n. 69, para. 171.

[105] Compare *Ilaşcu*, n. 13, to *Armed Activities*, n. 46, para. 246 ('Uganda violated its duty of vigilance by not taking adequate measures to ensure that *its* military forces did not' loot and plunder.) (emphasis added). See also Chinkin, 'A Critique of the Public/Private Dimension', n. 96, at 395.

[106] Frey, 'Small Arms and Light Weapons', n. 103, at 41 (emphasis added).

[107] There are contexts in which principles other than control and reciprocity underpin attribution. Article 9 ARSIWA, n. 2; ARSIWA Commentary, n. 2, at 43; Caron, 'The Basis of Responsibility', n. 103, at 128.

[108] *Bosnian Genocide*, n. 16, paras. 391–392.

Of course, if this is true, one might ask why the legal operationalisation of that basic normative principle differs meaningfully in the preventive vigilance and attribution contexts. The state is strictly responsible for the *ultra vires* wrongs of its organs, but only responsible under a due diligence standard for the wrongs of private persons acting within the scope of its claimed or exercised public power. If the prevention of such wrongs is part of what it means to exercise public power legitimately, why should the same test of responsibility not apply in both cases?

This question is at the heart of long-running criticisms of the public/private divide in international law.[109] And that is telling. The divergent operationalisation of preventive reciprocity reflects the ideas that some functions are quintessentially public in character,[110] and that the state must ensure *without fail* that these functions (but not private actions) are exercised lawfully.[111] It is, in other words, rooted in the public/private distinction.

Critics of that distinction variously emphasise four things. First, dissensus as to which functions are *quintessentially* public, and significant variance in the functions actually allocated to public entities.[112] Second, the fact that a disproportionate number of the human rights violations suffered by women occur in the 'private' sphere, whereas men suffer a disproportionate share of 'public' violations.[113] Third, the relative invisibility of multinational corporations in a regime focused on public actors.[114] And, finally, the lack of a meaningful normative distinction between terrorists and the states that 'harbour' them.[115] Overall, the worry is that the public/private divide allows for wrongs that ought to be concerns of the international community to be sheltered from international law.[116]

[109] H. Charlesworth and C. Chinkin, *The Boundaries of International Law* (Huntington: Juris, 2000), at 59–61.

[110] ARSIWA Commentary, n. 2, at 39–49.

[111] States contracting such functions to private actors do so at their own legal risk. *B. d. B. et al.* v. *the Netherlands*, Communication No. 273/1989, Human Rights Committee, UN Doc. A/44/40 (1989); CESCR, General Comment 19, UN Doc. E/C.12/GC/19 (2008), para. 46. See also ARSIWA Commentary, n. 2, at 38.

[112] H. Charlesworth et al., 'Feminist Approaches to International Law' (1991) 85 AJIL 613, at 626; Chinkin, 'A Critique of the Public/Private Dimension', n. 96, at 388.

[113] Charlesworth, 'Feminist Approaches to International Law', ibid.; UN Commission on Human Rights, Report of the Special Rapporteur on Violence Against Women UN Doc. E/CN.4/1996/53 (1996), paras. 26–31.

[114] See discussion and sources at n. 120.

[115] See discussion and sources at n. 59–61.

[116] Chinkin, 'A Critique of the Public/Private Dimension', n. 96.

The preventive vigilance obligations described in section 4 offer a way to accommodate that concern without eliminating the public/private distinction. They allow international law to respond to violence against women, the wrongdoing of multinational corporations, and transnational terrorism.[117] They narrow the public/private divide so as to mitigate its pathologies. However, although this narrowing is a virtue, the public/private distinction remains normatively significant, particularly in operationalising the principle of preventive reciprocity.

First, the state's preventive control over the *ultra vires* acts of its organs vastly exceeds its preventive control over the acts of private individuals within its jurisdiction. It is through state processes that individuals are selected to be entrusted with public power, through state systems that they are trained and prepared for it, and under state supervision, in the context of a state organisation, subject to state discipline, and under state organisational rules that they exercise it. This warrants different expectations regarding the state's capacity to control conduct.[118]

Second, when state organs and agents engage in wrongs of global public concern, they wield great power over human victims. Endowed with the coercive force of a public authority, the public actor has a significantly greater opportunity than does her private analogue to inflict such wrongs on those who lack the equivalent means to defend themselves. Indeed, in many cases, the public perpetrator would be the very actor to whom such potential victims would most plausibly turn for protection when faced with an analogous private threat.[119] This undermining of self- and other-help in response makes it especially important that abuses of public power be prevented by the state.[120]

[117] See discussion and sources at n. 120 (multinationals) and n. 57–62 (counter-terrorism). On violence against women, see, for example, Committee on the Elimination of Discrimination Against Women (CmtEDAW), General Recommendation 19, in UN Doc. A/47/38 (1992), para. 9; *AT* v. *Hungary*, Communication No. 2/2003, CmtEDAW, in UN Doc. A/60/38 (Part I) Annex III (2005), paras. 9.2–9.6; *Opuz* v. *Turkey*, App. No. 33401/02 (ECtHR, 9 June 2009), paras. 146–149, 191.

[118] See generally *Restatement (Third) Of Agency* section 2.04 (2006); P.S. Atiyah, *Vicarious Liability in the Law of Torts* (Oxford: Butterworths, 1967), at 15–18. Preventive duties intensify with control. Hakimi 'State Bystander Responsibility', n. 70, at 357–368; *Juan Humberto Sánchez* v. *Honduras*, IACtHR, (Ser. C) No. 99 (2003), para. 111.

[119] The typical public perpetrators of wrongs of global concern are in the security sector.

[120] Some multinational corporations exercise similar power, which helps to explain why their status under international law is a point of such tension. Ruggie, *Guiding Principles on Business and Human Rights*, n. 74; C. Albin-Lackey, 'Without Rules' (Human Rights Watch, 2013); S. Ratner, 'Corporations and Human Rights' (2001) 111 YLJ 443.

Third, and perhaps most important, is the different *nature* of the state's preventive control over public and private actors. The most potent mechanisms through which states can prevent private actors from inflicting wrongs of global concern involve using the tools of law enforcement and national security.[121] Holding the state strictly responsible for the wrongs of private actors within its jurisdictional sphere would demand implicitly the zealous use of these tools.[122] Given the tendency for the zealous use of these tools to violate human rights, a strict responsibility to eliminate threats from private actors would itself threaten the very global human values motivating the preventive duty, and unfairly condemn states that seek to strike an optimal balance on precisely that dimension.[123] By holding states responsible only when they fail to enact reasonable preventive measures, the vigilance standard avoids upsetting that balance.[124]

Preventing global wrongs by state organs or agents raises very different institutional concerns. The levers of preventive control held by the state over its organs are manifold. They do not depend on law enforcement, and they do not carry the danger of overzealous prevention inflicting new global harms. Moreover, given the heightened importance of protecting against the infliction of such harms by public authorities (due to potential victims' vulnerability to those authorities and public authorities' status as victims' primary protective recourse), the imperative to exercise those preventive levers is especially acute. As a result, when the state fails to rein in violations by organs or agents, there is a sense of condemnation of the state itself, even if there is no specific evidence of institutional failure.[125]

This reflects a presumption (typically vindicated) that when state organs engage in wrongs of global public concern, there *must* have been

[121] Other tools, like education, are also important.

[122] Caron, 'The Basis of Responsibility', n. 103, at 127.

[123] *Bámaca Velásquez* v. *Guatemala*, IACtHR, (Ser. C) No. 70 (2000), para. 174; *Osman* v. *the United Kingdom*, App. No. 23452/94 (ECtHR, 28 October 1998), para. 116; J.A. Hessbruegge, 'The Historical Development of the Doctrines of Attribution and Due Diligence in International Law' (2004) 36 NYUJILP 265, at 276–277.

[124] Vigilance is deeply connected to balancing in human rights adjudication. *Ilaşcu*, n. 13, para. 332.

[125] *Ilaşcu*, n. 13, para. 319 (the state 'cannot shelter behind' the *ultra vires* nature of the act); *Al-Skeini*, n. 75, Separate Opinion of Judge Bonello, para. 16. Attribution merges with blame. L. Comiteau, 'Court Says the Dutch are to Blame for Srebrenica Deaths', Time Magazine, 6 July 2011.

some institutional preventive failure at some level.[126] Of course, institutional imperfections and failures that *could* lead to wrongful conduct of global concern are common to all states. However, this does not lessen the sense that those states for which these failures *do* lead to such wrongdoing are properly condemned for it – a judgment rooted in an organisational analogue to moral luck.[127]

In sum, the vulnerability of the potential victim; the degree of preventive power available to the state; the importance of prevention in the context of irreparable harm; and the lack of overwhelming global human values militating in the opposite direction – underpin the state's strict *ex post* responsibility for the *ultra vires* wrongs of its organs. At the heart of that judgment is the assessment that preventing such wrongs is central to the sovereign legitimacy of the state and that this responsibility is especially pointed for those most tightly under its control.

6. Attribution and lawful joint public enterprises

The reciprocity between claimed or asserted public power and preventive responsibility is no less important a foundational normative principle in the context of JPE wrongdoing than it is with respect to the unilateral contexts described previously. And the considerations that affect how that principle is operationalised in unilateral contexts should also inform its legal operationalisation in the context of merged multilateral ventures. This leads to analysing JPE wrongdoing on two levels. The primary line of responsibility for such wrongs – elaborated in this section – should be one of strict attribution to at least one of the enterprise participants. Secondarily, as discussed in section 7, additional participants should be responsible for maintaining preventive vigilance.

The case for attributing JPE wrongs to at least one participant state or organisation rests on the same factors underpinning strict attribution in the unilateral context: the strength of potential preventive control, the robust imperative that it be maintained and exercised, the fact that JPEs wield public authority, and the reduced danger (relative to private

126 Vindication may come via retrospective inquiry. See Public Works and Government Services of Canada, *Dishonoured Legacy* (1997); Netherlands Institute for War Documentation, *Srebrenica: A 'Safe Area'* (2002).

127 T. Nagel, 'Moral Luck', in *Mortal Questions* (Cambridge University Press, 1979), at 24–38; B. Williams, 'Moral Luck', in *Moral Luck* (Cambridge University Press, 1981), at 20–39.

wrongdoing) of overzealous enforcement. In determining the object of that attribution, the guiding principle, as identified in sections 4–5, must be the reciprocity between claimed or asserted public power and the responsibility to use it to prevent wrongdoing. In the context of a JPE, that means focusing on the distribution of levers of control relevant to prevention – a distribution that varies with enterprise structure and with the nature of the wrongful conduct.

The exercise of public authority over human persons and the imperative that this power is not to be exercised abusively is no less significant for JPEs than it is for states acting unilaterally. Such enterprises, by definition, exercise public authority, and their constituent members wield public power with respect to those with whom they interact. When they engage in wrongdoing of global concern, they often do so as the putative protectors of the very principles that they violate.[128] As such, like state actors, JPEs undermine their own existential foundation when they violate core global human values.[129] And, as in the unilateral context, the zealous exercise of the levers of control by which JPE wrongdoing might be prevented – levers like training, discipline, personnel selection, leadership, and so on – do not carry the inherent threat to global human values that is posed by the zealous exercise of state power to prevent private actors from engaging in similar wrongs.

Ultimately, then, just as it is important that the public acts or omissions of a state organ be attributed to that state even when the individual perpetrators act *ultra vires*, so it is for the same reasons important that official JPE conduct be attributed to one or more of the participating states and international organisations. In a sense, this conclusion is uncontroversial; as canvassed in section 3, the need to attribute enterprise acts to at least one participant is widely accepted. The debate is over what this entails.

Recognising the foundational importance of the reciprocity between public power and preventive responsibility illuminates that choice. Attributing JPE wrongdoing based on the reciprocity principle would align JPE legal responsibility with the deeper normative sense of institutional responsibility manifest in adjacent legal contexts. It would affirm and entrench the contemporary reframing of public power as a trigger for international responsibility, rather than a shield against international interference.

This matters because legal responsibility for inflicting *wrongs* of global public concern carries with it condemnation. Fairness to the legally

[128] For example, Dannenbaum, 'Translating', n. 3, at 119–120. [129] Ibid.

responsible state demands that attribution with such wrongdoing reflect some basic principle of organisational moral responsibility. Fairness to those wronged demands the same, particularly in light of the fact that a core aspect of reparation for such wrongs is the 'satisfaction' of an official judgment holding the responsible party to account.[130] From both perspectives, *ex post* legal responsibility ought to reflect a plausible account of deeper moral responsibility. Founding attribution on the reciprocity principle does that in a way that preserves normative consistency across adjacent domains.

An additional perspective from which any attribution regime should be evaluated is consequentialist. As a matter of global public order, and to the extent that legal responsibility creates incentives for state and international organisation action, those incentives ought to be balanced so as to deter JPE wrongs without undermining international cooperation.

In each of these respects, the preventive control standard introduced in section 3 is superior to its four alternatives. Stated most succinctly, this rule attributes JPE wrongs to any participant state(s) or international organisation(s) holding a sufficient concentration of the lawful levers of control relevant to preventing the type of wrongful conduct in question. The recent use of something like this test in the Dutch courts is an important step forward, but it lacks specificity, and leaves the contours of the standard largely undefined.[131] The framework that follows elaborates a more comprehensive vision.

The analysis starts with a typology of enterprise conduct. Although necessarily enterprise-specific, a typical classification includes: (i) conduct pursuant to commands or directions that generate a duty to obey; (ii) conduct pursuant to commands or directions that generate a duty to disobey (such as manifestly criminal orders); (iii) conduct pursuant to authorisations creating a sphere of discretion that includes the wrongful conduct; (iv) conduct *ultra vires*; and (v) conduct caused by resource constraints or intra-enterprise excuse.[132] The attribution analysis builds on this in four steps.

130 For example, *Bosnian Genocide*, n. 16, paras. 460–462; T. Dannenbaum, 'The International Criminal Court, Article 79, and Transitional Justice' (2010) 28 WILJ 234, at 281–286.

131 Dannenbaum, 'Killings at Srebrenica', n. 3, at 719–727; *Nuhanović* Supreme Court, n. 42, paras. 3.11.3, 3.12.2, 3.12.3. Since the final edit of this chapter, the District Court in The Hague has improved significantly on the Nuhanović reasoning in this respect, accommodating my core critique in 'Killings at Srebrenica'. See *Stichting Mothers of Srebrenica v. the Netherlands and the United Nations*, ECLI:NL:RBDHA:2014:8748 (16 July 2014), paras. 4.41, 4.57–4.60, 4.89, 4.94–4.95, 4.98, 4.114–4.115.

132 Applying this to peacekeeping, see Dannenbaum, 'Translating', n. 3, at 158–183.

Step 1: In the case of conduct undertaken pursuant to a command, direction, or authorisation [conduct (i–iii)], the analysis would identify whether the initial mandate to perform the wrong originated outside of the enterprise [step 1] or within the enterprise [step 2]. If the former, the wrongful conduct would be attributed to the state or international organisation whose organ proclaimed the initial requirement or permission.

Additional lines of attribution could then be layered on top of this baseline. First, if the command or direction were such as to trigger a duty to disobey [conduct (ii)], then the state(s) or international organisation(s) holding preventive control over the obedient executors of the order or directive would also be attributed with the conduct [see step 3]. Similarly, if the conduct were within the scope of the natural perpetrators' organisational discretion [conduct (iii)], the state(s) or international organisation(s) with preventive control over those natural persons would also be attributed with the conduct [see step 3]. However, conduct occurring pursuant to a command or direction *not* generating a duty to disobey [conduct (i)], would not be attributed to any actors other than the state(s) or international organisation(s) from which the mandate originated.

Step 2: Suppose, however, that the order requiring or authorising the wrongful conduct originated *within* the enterprise. This would raise two alternative possibilities: either the intra-enterprise actor who originated the wrongful order acted within her mandate, or she acted *ultra vires*. If she acted within her mandate in issuing the wrongful command, direction, or authorisation, then the analysis would proceed precisely as in step 1 to identify the originator of that permissive mandate, with the same consequences for attribution. If, on the other hand, she acted *ultra vires*, then the analysis would proceed as stipulated in step 3.

Step 3: A preventive control analysis would be applied to all official conduct *ultra vires* and to the scenarios identified in the paragraphs immediately preceding. As in unilateral action, this would involve a strict responsibility analysis, not a vigilance test. Rather than examining the reasonableness of the efforts taken to prevent the wrongful conduct, it would require an assessment of the *de jure* and *de facto* distributions of the levers of control relevant to preventing that type of wrong. Those state(s) or international organisation(s) with a concentration of such levers would be attributed with responsibility, regardless of how they actually exercised their control. The levers of control relevant to this analysis would vary depending on the enterprise and the impugned conduct.[133] In many scenarios they would include: disciplinary authority, authority over personnel selection, authority to structure enterprise subunits; authority over training, authority to dismiss individuals from the enterprise, authority to select enterprise leaders, responsibility for enterprise legal advice, and criminal jurisdiction.[134]

The rule of step 3 is that all states or international organisations holding a concentration of these levers of preventive control over one or more enterprise members involved in the wrongful conduct (except those acting pursuant to orders that did not trigger a duty to disobey [conduct (i)]) would be attributed with the conduct. The rare scenario in which none of the participant states or international organisations holds a sufficient concentration of preventive levers is discussed in section 7.

Step 4: The final step applies a special rule to wrongdoing caused by 'intra-enterprise excuse'. In this scenario, a subunit or individual member of the JPE is forced to engage in the wrongful conduct by necessity, duress, or an equivalent excuse, the conditions of which were caused by another JPE participant. Responsibility in this scenario would take one of two forms, depending on the legal status of the excuse-creating act. When that act is unlawful, responsibility for the excused act would be determined by applying steps 1–3 to the excuse-creating actor. However, when the excuse-creating act is lawful, responsibility reverts instead to the state or international organisation with overall operational control of the enterprise, because such wrongs are best prevented through operational coordination.

This four-step framework provides for shared attribution in a range of scenarios.[135] On the private dimension of responsibility, this raises the question of liability apportionment – a vexed issue given the obstacles to enforcing international contribution and indemnity. However, public responsibility need not be apportioned at all; attribution to one entity does not dilute simultaneous attribution to another. Thus, although the method for sharing liability is important (and likely requires a scheme of

[133] Wrongs in Tilburg Prison, Mediterranean Frontex patrols, UN peacekeeping in the DRC, and ISAF operations in Afghanistan demand different preventive mechanisms, as do criminal and non-criminal wrongs.

[134] Dannenbaum, 'Translating', n. 3, at 160–164. See also Basic Principles on the Right to a Remedy, n. 70, para. 23; *Nuhanović* Court of Appeal, n. 42, para. 5.10; ARIO, n. 4, at 87–88; *Nuhanović* Supreme Court, n. 42, paras. 3.10.2, 3.11.3.

[135] On shared 'effective control', see *Al-Jedda*, n. 28, para. 80; *Nuhanović* Court of Appeal, n. 42, para. 5.9; *Nuhanović* Supreme Court, n. 42, para. 3.11.2; ARIO, n. 4, at 83.

joint and several liability), the specifics of such a scheme are beyond the scope of this chapter.

Ultimately, the virtues of the proposed framework are twofold. First, it reflects the normative reciprocity described earlier; when a state or international organisation holds a sufficient concentration of levers of preventive control over those involved in a JPE, its strict responsibility is to ensure that they do not participate in wrongdoing of global concern. Second, by holding responsible only the entities best placed to prevent the wrongdoing, the proposed framework calibrates incentives so as to recognise not just the importance of deterrence, but also the global value of international collaboration.[136]

It is worth pausing to reflect on the importance of international cooperation because it in fact informs both of these virtues. An advocate of broader attribution might respond to the preceding discussion by observing that the distribution of levers of preventive control in a JPE is itself the result of a collective choice by all participants. States contributing peacekeepers cede operational control to the UN; New Zealand and Britain ceded administrative control over Nauru to Australia; border guard contributors cede control to Frontex and the host state; and the UN and contributing states often cede operational control of a Chapter VII authorised military force to a lead state or international organisation.

The objection has force. After all, when states cede control over public functions to private actors, they do not escape responsibility for wrongdoing by those actors.[137] Relinquishing their preventive authority in that way is just another way of failing to take adequate preventive measures. The fact that the failure occurs earlier in the process is immaterial. Analogous reasoning in the JPE context has underpinned arguments in favour of attributing the UN with all acts of UN-authorised military forces, even when the UN cedes operational control to one of the participant entities.[138] Framed in this way, authorial control is depicted as an element of preventive control. Indeed, one might take the point further and argue that even non-authorial, contributing states have a preventive power in that they voluntarily cede control over their organs or agents when they second them to an enterprise over which they do not have complete control. Here, too, the contributing state could have

[136] Deterrence may occur through condemnation, reparations, or outcasting. On the latter: O.A. Hathaway and S. Shapiro, 'Outcasting' (2011) 121 YLJ 252.

[137] ARSIWA Commentary, n. 2, at 42–43.

[138] Sarooshi, *The United Nations and the Development of Collective Security*, n. 31, at 164.

made its contribution conditional on retaining total control over its personnel.

Insightful though this objection is, four reasons militate in favour of an attribution framework that reflects only the *actual* distribution of the levers of control in the JPE as negotiated, not authorial or contributory status (and the implicit power to have designed a different structure).

First, a state's delegation of public functions to a private actor is not analogous to a state or international organisation ceding control to a JPE. Delegation to a private actor without preventive checks involves freeing the function from the preventive control of *any* international legal person. If such abdication were to relieve the state of responsibility, it would eliminate international responsibility for the function entirely. Relinquishing preventive control to another state or international organisation does not extinguish international responsibility; it merely changes the international legal person responsible. Second, as long as the participant(s) with preventive control are attributed with the wrong, the framework fulfils the reciprocity principle and creates incentives for wrong prevention. Third, and crucially, ceding control is essential to rich and effective international collaboration, which is, in turn, vital to realising the promise of international law. Conversely, encouraging each venture participant to retain all levers of control and to interfere preventively in JPE functioning would undermine the advancement of global values. Fourth, the application of preventive due diligence can address the core danger of responsibility evasion *without* thereby undermining international cooperation.

The final two points warrant greater elaboration – the third here, the fourth in section 7. The vital role of thick international cooperation in realising international law's core objectives is manifest in a broad range of cooperative ventures, including many JPEs. Indeed, the enforcement of international law is itself *dependent* on effective international collaboration.[139] And yet, the very reason that cooperation is so vital – the absence of a global sovereign – is also one of the key reasons it is so difficult to achieve and sustain. International collaboration requires states ordinarily subject to little superior coercion to cede control to other states and international organisations in contexts in which they often have significant interests. This can be achieved only through careful

[139] Hathaway and Shapiro, 'Outcasting', n. 136.

negotiation and compromise – a process over which no participant has unilateral control.

It is a mistake to assume that because the United Nations, for example, holds authorial control over a multilateral military force, that it therefore has the power to determine the distribution of levers of control. Its options are determined through negotiation, and they are likely to be limited to an operation in which it cedes control or no operation at all. For the same reason, many states will rarely have the realistic option of retaining greater control over their contributions to a JPE. The options facing a state considering sending a contingent of border guards on a Frontex mission may be to withhold the contingent altogether, or to accept that it must cede some levers of control to Frontex and the host state.

It would be unfair and counterproductive to human values to attribute conduct to a state or international organisation whose only modes of preventive action would have been to refuse to participate in a lawful collaboration under the agreed terms, to violate those terms, or to withdraw from the venture altogether.[140] Moreover, even when a given state or organisation *could* negotiate the retention of total control over its contributions to a lawful JPE, it would rarely be desirable that it do so. Quite the contrary, the unification of decision-making and control in collaborative ventures augments their efficacy and coherence.[141] Some of the gravest cases of JPE wrongdoing have occurred in ventures in which control was insufficiently unified and integrated.[142]

Given the value of international cooperation and the challenge of achieving it, as long as control is held by at least one participant with international legal personality, as long as legal obligations are not circumvented, and as long as the right to reparation is not nullified, a preventive control analysis ought to reflect the *actual* distribution of control agreed by participants, not a hypothesis about what authorial or other entities *might or might not* have relinquished in an alternative enterprise structure. Deference to the compromise that was reached is an important virtue.

Preventive control has important advantages over the alternative attribution frameworks for JPE wrongdoing. By incorporating the reciprocity principle, it aligns legal JPE responsibility with the deeper moral

[140] Dannenbaum, 'Finding Balance', n. 3, at 107–111.
[141] ICISS Report, n. 79, para. 7.20.
[142] Ibid.; Dannenbaum, 'Finding Balance', n. 3, at 115–116.

underpinnings of legal responsibility in adjacent domains. By tying responsibility to prevention, it provides the best framework for deterrence. And by sharing attribution only when the nature of the conduct and the distribution of powers are such that multiple actors directed the action or held significant levers of preventive control, it honours the imperative of international collaboration.

7. Addressing the limits of the preventive control framework

Despite these virtues, three potential objections to the proposed attribution framework warrant attention. First, it may be vulnerable to manipulation by powerful states. Second, its conduct-sensitivity places a significant epistemic and evidentiary burden on claimants and adjudicators. Third, rare JPE wrongdoing may occur over which no entity holds a concentration of the levers of preventive control.

The first worry is that powerful states would design enterprise structures so as to ensure sufficient influence to achieve their objectives, while avoiding the costs of responsibility for collateral wrongdoing. This threat is particularly pernicious in contexts in which the participant to which key levers of control are ceded is immune from legal action, is likely to be unmoved by international responsibility, is too weak to exercise that control effectively, is insolvent, or is unbound by the relevant legal regime.

This danger is genuine, but it does not weigh against the preventive control model. On the contrary, with the sole exception of blanket multiple attribution (which itself poses a severe threat to international cooperation), the alternative attribution regimes discussed in section 3 are all significantly *more* vulnerable to manipulation of this kind. A preventive control test involves conduct-specific factual analysis, and ignores the formal ceding of authority unless it reflects a genuine transfer of factual control. In contrast, the operational and especially authorial control tests enable powerful states to cede *de jure* authority and thereby wash their hands of responsibility, despite retaining robust factual influence over enterprise conduct. States are traditionally more reluctant to relinquish many of the levers of preventive control described above than they are willing to cede formal authority. And when they *do* relinquish those factual elements of control, they lose considerable influence over enterprise activity. In short, although manipulation cannot be eliminated, the proposed regime is structured to guard against it while continuing to encourage international cooperation.

Moreover, the attribution regime would not operate in isolation. As in the case of unilateral action, it would work alongside preventive vigilance requirements. Under that two-level analysis, JPE participants not attributed with the conduct would be assessed for whether they exercised vigilance in ensuring the lawful conduct of the enterprise, or whether they should have engaged in reasonable preventive measures, such as applying diplomatic pressure on their co-participants or assisting under-resourced states with training or other support.[143] In addition to combating manipulation, this would recognise the escalating responsibility of all participant states and international organisations to act preventively as wrongdoing becomes increasingly endemic to an enterprise. Unlike blanket joint attribution, however, it would avoid undermining desirable collaboration.

Supplementary vigilance analysis of this sort could be particularly useful in the context of UN peacekeeping. Although more likely to attribute wrongful peacekeeper conduct to troop-contributing states than most other attribution regimes, the preventive control framework does attribute wrongful conduct exclusively to the UN in some contexts.[144] Given UN immunity, and the woeful inadequacy of the internal claims system, an accountability gap remains in those scenarios.[145] However, under a supplementary vigilance standard, states might be held responsible for failing to pressure the organisation to institute a robust and transparent claims review system.[146]

Preventive vigilance could also provide the basis for the responsibility of states and organisations that contribute to JPEs through means other than personnel. Depending on the likelihood of misuse, the provision of resources, objects, or even territory may generate obligations on contributing states to seek assurances and impose conditions on the use of their contributions, or to withhold those contributions if it becomes apparent they are being misused.[147]

[143] Cf. *Ilaşcu*, n. 13, paras. 333, 336–352.

[144] See Dannenbaum, 'Translating', n. 3, at 165–183.

[145] Ibid., at 121–129.

[146] Cf. Secretary-General, Draft Model Status of Forces Agreement for Peace-Keeping Operations, UN Doc. A/45/594 (1990), Article 51 (providing for a never-instituted claims commission for UN peacekeeping).

[147] Analogously, consider the principle of *non-refoulement*. See n. 71. Peacekeeping is often funded and equipped by non-troop-contributors. 'Troop and Police Contributors' at www.un.org/en/peacekeeping/resources/statistics/contributors.shtml; 'Financing Peacekeeping' at www.un.org/en/peacekeeping/operations/financing.shtml (last accessed on 5 June 2014). On territory, consider the Tilburg prison, n. 9.

A second danger of the preventive control framework is epistemic. Authorial control, operational control, and blanket multiple attribution all provide victims with clarity as to the party liable for JPE wrongdoing. Simply knowing that the JPE perpetrated the violation is enough to know which entity to sue. Conduct-specific tests lack that clarity. The preventive control test, in particular, requires a case-by-case assessment of the *de facto* and *de jure* distributions of the levers of control with respect to each wrong (not to mention the complication of intra-enterprise excuse).

This is a genuine procedural disadvantage of the system. However, precisely because that disadvantage is procedural, it is best remedied with a procedural, rather than a substantive, response – namely, adopting a victim friendly evidentiary presumption on attribution. Given that state and international organisation participants in a JPE have greater knowledge of the distribution and use of the relevant levers of preventive control in specific operations than does any claimant or court, once a JPE wrong is proven, it would be just to shift to the defendant state or organisation the burden of establishing that it did not hold the relevant levers of control over the impugned conduct.[148]

The final danger of the framework is that of non-attribution in the case that no state or international organisation holds a concentration of the relevant levers of preventive control over certain enterprise wrongs – whether due to private contracting or an unusually fragmented enterprise structure. Despite the general advantages of basing attribution on the actual power distribution that is negotiated and applied, it would be a mistake to leave such conduct unattributed.[149]

The fact that the preventive control 'relinquished' by participants in JPEs is ordinarily taken up by others with international personality is one of the key reasons it makes sense to focus on the actual negotiated structure of preventive control. When that context does not obtain, the case for reverting to an authorial control test strengthens. Simultaneously, the reasons against authorial control weaken. First, attribution to authorial entities would be the only way of deterring wrongful conduct in that context, and may stimulate the repossession of preventive control by one or more participants. Second, a joint enterprise with a widespread lack of preventive control is less likely the result of a carefully brokered compromise among entities reluctant to cede control, and more likely the

148 Cf. *Corfu Channel*, n. 13, at 18; *Velásquez-Rodriguez*, n. 69, paras. 135–136; ARSIWA Commentary, n. 2, at 72.

149 Ibid., at 42–43; ARIO, n. 4, at 88, 95.

result of states or international organisations deliberately insulating themselves from responsibility. Third, the value of lawful international cooperation loses its overriding normative weight when it is attainable only through the creation of entities that exercise public power in a way that is invisible to international law, out of control, and shielded from accountability. Ultimately, then, when a JPE is structured to eliminate the levers of preventive control, authorial states and international organisations must be attributed with its wrongs.

8. Conclusion

The reciprocity between claimed or asserted public power and preventive responsibility has become an increasingly important moral foundation of legal responsibility in contemporary international law. Its standing in a world of plural values emphasises its merit and viability as the normative basis from which to develop a regime of responsibility for the wrongs of joint public enterprises. With a few caveats outlined in section 7, enterprise wrongs ought to be attributed to the participant states or organisations that hold the levers of control most relevant to preventing the type of wrongdoing in question. This regime builds on the reciprocity between public power and preventive responsibility while affirming the importance of thick international collaboration in advancing international law.

8

'Coalitions of the Willing' and the Shared Responsibility to Protect

TONI ERSKINE*

1. Introduction

There has been widespread support for the idea that the so-called international community has a remedial moral responsibility to protect vulnerable populations from mass atrocities when their own governments fail to do so. Moreover, military intervention may, when necessary, be one means of discharging this proposed 'responsibility to protect' or, more colloquially, 'RtoP'.[1] But, where exactly is this responsibility located? In other words, which body or bodies can be expected to discharge a duty to safeguard those who lack the protection of – or,

* Professor of International and Political Studies, School of Humanities and Social Sciences, University of New South Wales, Canberra, ACT, AUSTRALIA, t.erskine@unsw.edu.au. The argument presented here was first published as T. Erskine, '"Coalitions of the Willing" and Responsibilities to Protect: Informal Associations, Enhanced Capacities and Shared Moral Burdens' (2014) 28(1) EIA 115. I am very grateful to the editors of *Ethics & International Affairs* for granting me permission to include a revised version in this volume. I am also indebted to Richard Beardsworth, Alex Bellamy, Chris Brown, Peter French, Harry Gould, Anthony Lang, Jr, Larry May, James Pattison, Don E. Scheid, two anonymous EIA referees, and the editors of both EIA and this volume for incisive written comments on earlier versions of this chapter, and to Stephanie Collins, Ned Dobos, David Estlund, Jeroen Gunning, Kimberley Layton, Seth Lazar, Richard Ned Lebow, Nishank Motwani, Nic Southwood, Daniel Warner, Jeni Whalan, and Alireza Yunespur for their valuable engagement with particular points.

1 As RtoP is often, inaccurately, treated synonymously with military intervention on humanitarian grounds, two points of clarification should be offered. First, RtoP is articulated as a comprehensive 'three-pillar' strategy. Military intervention contributes to the third pillar, which sets out the international community's 'Timely and Decisive Response' when states manifestly fail to protect their own populations (and can also, conceivably, contribute to the second pillar in the form of preventative peacekeeping). Second, while military intervention as a means of responding to this failure is the focus of this chapter, sanctions and diplomatic strategies are examples of alternative, or preliminary, means. See the Outcome Document of the 2005 United Nations World Summit, UN Doc. A/RES/60/1 (24 October 2005), paras. 138, 139; and the Secretary-General's 2009 Report on Implementing the responsibility to protect, UN Doc. A/63/677 (12 January 2009).

indeed, come under threat from – their own government? A particularly pressing context for this question arises when the United Nations (UN) is unwilling or unable to act, and there is no one state to fill the breach, no 'agent-of-last-resort' to invoke Michael Walzer's phrase (along with all of the controversy and potential risks that he acknowledges reliance on such a protector entails).[2]

This chapter will examine 'coalitions of the willing', or temporary, purpose-driven, self-selected collections of states, and sometimes non-state and inter-governmental actors, as one (likely provocative) answer to this question. It will also explore how the informal nature of such associations complicates, and should inform, the judgements of moral responsibility that we make in relation to them. In undertaking both tasks, it will offer a practical and demanding account of *shared responsibility* in world politics. Moreover, it will illustrate the importance of two crucial, preliminary steps towards this volume's stated goal of determining how responsibility is to be distributed between agents in cases of concerted action: i) analysing how our expectations of discrete agents – and our evaluations of their acts and omissions – should be recalibrated when they participate in (or are in a position to participate in) a cooperative endeavour with other agents; and (as a second step made possible in part by the first) ii) clearly identifying the relevant agents amongst whom duties might be allocated or blame apportioned.

I will begin by briefly recounting what I call a 'model of institutional moral agency' in order to explain why it is conceptually coherent and necessary in practice to assume that moral responsibilities can be borne by formal organisations (such as states, multinational corporations (MNCs) and intergovernmental organisations), but why it seems theoretically and practically problematic to talk about the moral responsibilities of *informal* associations.[3] I will then focus on coalitions of the willing as prominent, and challenging, examples of the latter category, before raising misgivings about my own rather stark distinction if it

[2] M. Walzer, 'The Politics of Rescue', (1995) 62(1) SR 53, at 64.

[3] This chapter follows on from qualified arguments for understanding states and intergovernmental organisations (such as the UN) as bearers of moral responsibilities in world politics. See T. Erskine, 'Assigning Responsibilities to Institutional Moral Agents: The Case of States and Quasi-States' (2001) 15(2) EIA 67; and T. Erskine, '"Blood on the UN's Hands"? Assigning Duties and Apportioning Blame to an Intergovernmental Organizations' (2004) 18(1) GS 21. The arguments in each article have been revised and updated as chapters 3 and 4, respectively, of T. Erskine, *Locating Responsibility: Institutional Moral Agency and International Relations* (in preparation).

means that accounts of moral responsibility must be reduced to the members – or potential members – of such coalitions in a way that neglects the moral significance of their acting together. Prompted by these concerns, I will explore important arguments by Virginia Held and Larry May about moral responsibility in relation to informal associations and identify insights that can be taken from these positions to refine our expectations and evaluations of the actions associated with such collectivities in world politics. Finally, I will consider the particular implications of these insights for addressing how the widely espoused duty to intervene to rescue vulnerable populations can be understood in relation to coalitions of the willing. Perhaps most controversially, this analysis will lead to a proposal that, under certain circumstances, states and other entities have a duty to form such ad hoc associations – and may be held to account when they fail to do so.

2. A model of institutional moral agency[4]

Claims to moral responsibility are ubiquitous in world politics. Such statements make use of two different, but closely related, understandings of responsibility. Prospective moral responsibility involves *ex ante* judgements regarding acts that ought to be performed, or forbearances that must be observed. Retrospective moral responsibility entails *ex post facto* assessments of a particular event or set of circumstances for which an agent's acts or omissions were such that the agent is the object of praise or blame. The forward-looking variation is heard in assertions of duty and obligation;[5] the backward-looking variation emerges most often in charges of blame and accountability. Statements by two UN secretaries-general, both contemplating the consequences of inaction in the face of widespread human rights violations, provide respective examples of each

[4] This section draws on discussions of this model in the following: Erskine, 'States and Quasi-States', n. 3, reprinted in T. Erskine (ed.), *Can Institutions Have Responsibilities? Collective Moral Agency and International Relations* (New York: Palgrave Macmillan, 2003), 19; T. Erskine, 'Making Sense of "Responsibility" in International Relations – Key Questions and Concepts', in Erskine (ed.), *Can Institutions Have Responsibilities?*, ibid., 1; Erskine, 'Blood on the UN's Hands', n. 3; Erskine, 'Locating Responsibility: The Problem of Moral Agency in International Relations', in C. Reus-Smit and D. Snidal (eds.), *The Oxford Handbook of International Relations* (Oxford University Press, 2008), 699; and T. Erskine, 'Kicking Bodies and Damning Souls: The Danger of Harming "Innocent" Individuals While Punishing "Delinquent" States' (2010) 24(3) EIA 261.

[5] I am using 'moral responsibilities', 'duties', and 'obligations' interchangeably to indicate actions or forbearances that one is deemed bound to perform or observe.

understanding. '[T]he international community has a moral responsibility', Ban Ki-moon declared in 2012, 'to stop the bloodbath and find peace for the people of Syria'.[6] Apportioning moral responsibility for approximately 800,000 deaths in 1994, Kofi Annan lamented that 'the international community' is 'guilty of sins of omission' in the context of the Rwanda genocide.[7] These statements exemplify the judgements of moral responsibility so commonly voiced in world politics. However, they also highlight the worrying ambiguity that often accompanies them, and is apparent in key articulations of RtoP, by suggesting that duties might somehow be assigned, and blame apportioned, to the international community – an entity that would seem incapable of unified, purposive action in the first place.

Importantly, to be intelligible, judgements of moral responsibility must be directed towards entities capable of responding to ethical imperatives. In other words, they must be directed towards *moral agents*, or those bodies that possess capacities to contemplate, recognise the significance of, and ultimately execute different courses of action. Overlooking those bodies that qualify as moral agents in world politics when considering how best to respond to crises, or mistakenly assuming that moral responsibilities can be borne by those bodies that do not qualify, each has detrimental consequences. Such missteps hamper attempts to consider, coordinate, and execute remedial action effectively and robustly. They also result in missed opportunities to determine what went wrong when crises are neither prevented nor mitigated. Avoiding such shortcomings is particularly pressing in just those cases that prompt calls to protect vulnerable populations – when inaction can have far-reaching and tragic consequences, and failing to learn from past mistakes deprives us of the knowledge needed to make meaningful pledges of 'never again'.

Yet, identifying moral agents in world politics is far from straightforward. Most philosophers understand moral agency exclusively in terms of individual human beings. Such an assumption seems unnecessarily limiting. In theory, it flies in the face of the observation that the norms, rules, procedures, practices, and cultures of formal organisations frame

[6] UN Secretary General Ban Ki-moon, speaking at Drake University in Des Moines, Iowa, attributed by his spokesperson, M. Nesirky. See 'Int'l community has moral responsibility to end violence in Syria: UN chief', English.news.cn, 20 October 2012, at http://news.xinhuanet.com/english/world/2012-10/20/c_131918013.htm (accessed on 30 April 2013).

[7] 'Rwanda genocide "must leave us always with a sense of bitter regret and abiding sorrow", says Secretary-General to the New York Memorial Conference', 26 March 2004, United Nations Press Release, SG/SM/9223 AFR/870 HQ/631.

and channel the decisions and actions of those individual human beings within them – with the result that these organisations can reach decisions and act in ways not adequately described in terms of the sum of decisions and actions of their constituents. In practice, such an assumption severely restricts often consequential assessments of moral responsibility in relation to some of the most pressing problems in world politics: when prescriptions for action and accounts of wrongdoing risk being incomplete if directed only at individual human beings. Duty and blame, in the context of certain acts and omissions, seem more accurately attached to the organisations themselves.

Given these objections to the idea that individual human beings exhaust the class of moral agent – along with the point that bodies like financial institutions, states, MNCs, and the UN, for example, are often described as bearers of duties and appropriate objects of blame in practical discourses in world politics (in a way that might be unexamined, but that I do not think is always meant as shorthand for referring to individual human actors) – it makes eminent sense to consider the possibility that such collectivities also qualify. This potential is usefully gestured towards within the disciplines of International Relations (IR) and international law. A number of prominent movements within IR imbue certain collectivities (most notably states) with agency;[8] contributions to international law defend the legal personality of an even broader range of collectivities (such as states, MNCs, and intergovernmental organisations).[9] Yet, work within both fields either sidesteps or precludes a question that would address the ethical implications of the sophisticated capacities that they thereby already attribute to formal organisations in the international realm: namely, can certain collectivities be *moral* agents?[10] Raising such a question links unexamined assumptions

[8] The same approaches, however, refuse to characterise as agents those bodies with arguably comparable capacities, such as intergovernmental organisations. For both points, see Erskine, 'Locating Responsibility: The Problem of Moral Agency in International Relations', n. 4, at 702–704.

[9] See, for example, J. Crawford, *State Responsibility: The General Part* (Cambridge University Press, 2013); and J. Crawford, A. Pellet, and S. Oleson (eds.), *The Law of International Responsibility* (Oxford University Press, 2010). For an account of the relationship between assumptions of legal personality and the understanding of moral agency being addressed here, see Erskine, *Locating Responsibility: Institutional Moral Agency and International Relations*, n. 3, chapter 2.

[10] IR's general neglect of this question prompted the project within which the present work is situated. This project has also included a collaborative dimension, which has produced inter alia Erskine (ed.), *Can Institutions Have Responsibilities?*, n. 4. For the argument that

within IR and international law to important philosophical enquires in a way that could inform and refine our understanding of responsibility in international law and politics.

Fortunately, this question has received sustained attention elsewhere. Focusing primarily on business firms, Peter French challenges what he identifies as an 'anthropocentric bias' in our moral reasoning and aims to illustrate that corporations can be 'moral persons'.[11] Borrowing terminology from geology, he distinguishes between what he calls an 'aggregate collectivity' ('merely a collection of people') and a 'conglomerate collectivity' ('an organization of individuals such that its identity is not exhausted by the conjunction of the identities of the persons in the organization').[12] He concludes that the latter are 'full-fledged members of the moral community, of equal standing with the traditionally-acknowledged residents: human beings'.[13] Moreover, in an article on duties to respond to nuclear dangers, Onora O'Neill highlights parallels between the capacities of individual human agents and those of institutions, and argues that institutions can also be agents for whom ethical reasoning is both accessible and action-guiding.[14]

Adding to and elaborating upon French's account of 'conglomerate collectivities', and inspired by O'Neill's 'thin theory of institutional agency',[15] I have proposed that a collectivity qualifies as a moral agent if it possesses five characteristics: first, an identity that is more than the sum of the identities of its constitutive parts, or what might be called a 'corporate' identity; second, a decision-making structure that can commit the group to a policy or course of action that is different from the

many movements in IR *preclude* questions of specifically moral agency by being methodologically predisposed to avoiding ethical analyses, see Erskine, 'Locating Responsibility: The Problem of Moral Agency in International Relations', n. 4, 703.

11 P. French, *Collective and Corporate Responsibility* (New York: Columbia University Press, 1984), at 46–47.

12 Ibid., at 5, 13.

13 Ibid., at 32. Note that my account of institutional moral agency, summarised here, does not go quite as far as French in maintaining that formal organisations are 'members of the moral community . . . of equal standing with . . . human beings'. While both individual human beings and formal organisations can qualify as moral agents, or bearers of duties, I argue that only the former are 'moral patients', or entities to which duties are owed. See Erskine, *Locating Responsibility: Institutional Moral Agency and International Relations*, n. 3, chapter 2.

14 O. O'Neill, 'Who Can Endeavour Peace?' (1986) 16 CJP 41 (special issue, supplementary vol. 12).

15 Ibid., at 61–67.

individual positions of some (or all) of its members;[16] third, mechanisms by which group decisions can be translated into actions (thereby establishing, with the previous criterion, a capacity for purposive action); fourth, an identity over time; and, fifth, a conception of itself as a unit (meaning simply that it cannot be merely externally defined).[17] I refer to collectivities that have these qualifying features as 'institutional moral agents'. They can be subject to the assignment of duties and the apportioning of blame in the context of particular acts and omissions in a way that is not reducible to their individual constituents – as long as they enjoy the (limited) independence from other agents and structural constraints necessary to perform the requisite actions.[18] (Neither individual human nor institutional moral agents can coherently be expected to discharge a duty in the absence of enabling conditions.) To avoid misunderstanding, this proposed model in no way precludes or undermines the moral agency of those individual human actors, or subgroups, that constitute the institutional moral agent. Rather, moral agency exists simultaneously at different levels, and moral agents at all levels can be responsible for concurrent, complementary, or even coordinated acts and omissions.

In light of this model, one might ask which collectivities in world politics would be able to respond to the proposed moral imperative to protect vulnerable populations. Although each case warrants detailed examination beyond the scope of this chapter, one might argue that most states and many intergovernmental organisations (including the UN and, perhaps, some regional alliances of states such as the North Atlantic Treaty Organization (NATO) and the Arab League) possess the sophisticated, integrated capacities for deliberation and action that allow them to qualify as institutional moral agents.[19] As moral agents, they could

[16] Although I was inspired by French's account of 'corporate moral personhood' in offering this criterion, Philip Pettit's work on why certain decision-making structures make possible group agency has also been influential. My description of this criterion moves some way towards Pettit's conception, but is less stringent. See French, *Collective and Corporate Responsibility*, n. 11, chapters 3–4; and P. Pettit, *A Theory of Freedom: From the Psychology to the Politics of Agency* (Oxford University Press, 2001), chapter 5.

[17] Each of these criteria is set out in detail in Erskine, *Locating Responsibility: Institutional Moral Agency and International Relations*, n. 3, chapter 2.

[18] This final qualification highlights the crucial point that even those bodies that qualify as moral agents cannot exercise this agency in all circumstances. See Erskine, 'States and Quasi-States', n. 3, at 79–83; and O'Neill, 'Who Can Endeavour Peace?', n. 14, at 51.

[19] It is possible that if the Arab League and NATO were to qualify as institutional moral agents, they would only do so precariously. This is a tentative conclusion comparable to that reached about the UN, another body that similarly balances supra-national

reasonably be expected to discharge such a duty in accordance with established moral guidelines and in the context of enabling conditions.[20] They could also, then, be blamed for the acts or omissions that derogate from this duty.

3. Coalitions of the willing as a 'hard case'

Coalitions of the willing, however, belong to a broad category of unlikely candidates for institutional moral agency: informal associations, or those collectivities that lack formal organisational structures and decision-making procedures. Informal associations are prominent in both the scholarly domain of IR and the practical world of international politics. 'International society', 'epistemic communities', 'transnational advocacy networks', and 'communities of practice' are all informal associations that are notable, and fruitful, objects of analysis in IR.[21] Terrorist networks, protest movements, and coalitions of the willing – as well as the more amorphous collectivities known respectively as 'the international community', 'the (global) market', 'the media', and 'the Internet' – are examples of informal associations regularly invoked in practical discourses and debates.[22] Each would *prima facie* struggle to be considered

structures and processes with a commitment to its member states' sovereignty. For the conclusion that the UN might possess moral agency only 'transiently', see Erskine, 'Blood on the UN's Hands', n. 3, at 41. For a discussion of the Arab League and NATO, which focuses specifically on their respective decision-making structures, see Erskine, *Locating Responsibility: Institutional Moral Agency and International Relations*, n. 3, chapter 4.

20 Regarding the first qualification, that an institutional moral agent might reasonably be expected to discharge a duty 'in accordance with established moral guidelines', it should be noted that the model proposed here says nothing about the source or substance of the moral demands to which formal organisations are expected to conform. These are important, but separate, considerations. The focus is, instead, on the question of who – or what – can respond to *what we understand to be ethical imperatives.*

21 See, for example, the following: scholarship from IR's 'English School' on international society, such as I. Clark, *The Vulnerable in International Society* (Oxford University Press, 2013); the special issue of IO (1992) 46(1) and M.K.D. Cross, 'Rethinking Epistemic Communities Twenty Years On' (2013) 39 RIS 137 on epistemic communities; M. Keck and K. Sikkink, *Activists Beyond Borders: Advocacy Networks in International Politics* (Ithaca, NY: Cornell University Press, 1998) on transnational advocacy networks; and, E. Adler and V. Pouliot, 'International Practices' (2011) 3 IT 1 on communities of practice.

22 The examples of nations, the Internet, and the international community are highlighted and briefly discussed in Erskine, 'States and Quasi-States', n. 3, at 72–73. Al-Qaeda, coalitions of the willing, international advocacy networks, and international society are raised as 'hard cases' of 'less formal organizations' in 'Locating Responsibility: The

a duty-bearer in its own right – and this matters to how we interpret, judge, and respond to the assertions of moral responsibility made in relation to them. Of this diverse range of examples, coalitions of the willing are a particularly interesting case because they have been regularly ushered into (and occasionally conspicuously excluded from) recent, prominent discussions of moral responsibility in world politics, including discussions of RtoP. They also provide an exceptionally challenging case because they do not straightforwardly fail to meet every criterion for institutional moral agency, but, rather, demand careful consideration of the degree to which they might satisfy at least some.

3.1 Defining 'coalitions of the willing'

Coalitions of the willing are common phenomena in world politics. The label is most often used for associations that are summoned and established in cases of military intervention – with or without UN authorisation, and frequently on proposed humanitarian grounds – but is also applied in the context of single-issue campaigns involving norm promotion.[23] The term has achieved relatively recent currency. It was reportedly used for the first time in 1990–1991, when a United States (US)-led, UN-authorised coalition of the willing responded to Iraq's invasion of Kuwait,[24] and was employed again in the late 1990s in the context of

Problem of Moral Agency in International Relations', n. 4, at 705. Each of these examples is also addressed in Erskine, *Locating Responsibility: Institutional Moral Agency and International Relations*, n. 3, chapters 2 and 6.

[23] In 'Stretching the Model of "Coalitions of the Willing"', Centre for International Governance and Innovation, Working Paper No. 1, October 2005, at http://papers.ssrn.com/sol3/papers.cfm?abstract_id=857444 (accessed on 31 March 2013), A.F. Cooper proposes two 'models' of coalitions of the willing along these respective lines, with the former represented by the 2003 Gulf War coalition. I do not accept the stark dichotomy proposed by Cooper (perhaps because I do not see the 2003 coalition as paradigmatic), and, rather, understand both as falling under one general category. Nevertheless, Cooper's paper is valuable for highlighting the significance of the label beyond the 2003 iteration.

[24] The claim that this is when the label was coined is made by L.P. Bloomfield in '"Coalition of the willing" is world's best weapon', The Baltimore Sun, 21 April 2002. Note that Bloomfield asserts that the phrase is used as 'shorthand for military action blessed by the U.N. Security Council but carried out by a pick-up team of member countries'. I do not take the label to connote action necessarily authorised by the UN Security Council – nor is this the current prevalent connotation of coalition of the willing, particularly given its usage in the year following Bloomsfield's op-ed.

the campaign to prohibit anti-personnel landmines.[25] A coalition of the willing established around NATO, which included some non-NATO states, intervened in Kosovo in 1999 on humanitarian grounds without UN Security Council backing. In the same year, an Australia-led, UN-endorsed coalition of the willing intervened in East Timor. The 2003 US-led group of states that launched a 'preventive' war against Iraq – one that was also subsequently, and rather improbably, justified on humanitarian grounds – has arguably been the most prominent, and infamous, example of such a coalition. In 2011, a multinational coalition of the willing led by the United States took military action to protect civilians in Libya (followed shortly after by NATO control of the military effort) under the authority of UN Security Council Resolution 1973. Most recently, respective calls have been made to establish a coalition of the willing to advance the climate change agenda,[26] and, in the absence of UN Security Council authorisation, to put a halt to the violence in Syria.[27]

Despite the differences between the various examples just listed, an important set of shared features tie them together. Coalitions of the willing are self-selected (and often self-authorised) constellations of states and sometimes intergovernmental and non-state actors (including, for example, regional alliances of states and private military and security

[25] L. Axworthy, 'Address by the Hon. Lloyd Axworthy', Minister of Foreign Affairs [Canada], to the United Nations Commission on Human Rights, Geneva, Switzerland, 30 March 1998. Cited by Cooper in 'Stretching the Model', n. 23, at 1.

[26] The former executive secretary of the UN Framework Convention on Climate Change, Yvo de Boer, has called for a 'coalition of the willing' to confront global warming in the absence of a formal international agreement. This is reported in J. Leake and B. Webster, 'No Hope for Climate Change', The Australian, 29 November 2010. See also T. Hale, 'A Climate Change Coalition of the Willing' (2011) 34(1) TWQ 89.

[27] US Senator John McCain, among others, proposed that the United States form a 'coalition of the willing' to intervene in Syria in 2012. See 'Transcript of Piers Morgan Tonight: Interview with John McCain, Aired July 19, 2012 – 21:00 ET', at http://transcripts.cnn.com/TRANSCRIPTS/1207/19/pmt.01.html (accessed on 16 March 2013). There was also a flurry of calls for such a coalition a year later, particularly following the Syrian government's alleged chemical weapons attack on its own people. See, for example, P. Lewis, 'Syria: Chemical Weapons and the Spectre of War', 27 August 2013, at www.chathamhouse.org/media/comment/view/194007 (accessed on 28 August 2013). As this volume goes to press, a US-led coalition has begun airstrikes against the so-called 'Islamic State' (ISIS) in Syria with neither UN Security Council authorisation nor the *formal* consent of the Syrian government (but justified by US officials as collective self-defence of Iraq). Although the Obama administration has used the label 'core coalition' for this newly established, informal association of states, it is widely referred to as a 'coalition of the willing' in media coverage.

corporations, respectively)[28] that come together to respond to a specific crisis and, in responding, act outside the control of any formal, overarching organisation to which they might already belong. The members of a coalition of the willing are thereby temporarily united in pursuit of a common purpose, but the coalition itself lacks an established organisational and decision-making structure. For those coalitions of the willing that either convene or are implored to materialise in order to engage in military intervention on humanitarian grounds, the issue of their authority to act invariably arises. As such, two clarifications are in order. First, the circumstances under which a coalition of the willing might intervene militarily on humanitarian grounds include both those in which the UN has effectively 'subcontracted' such an ad hoc association to act (to use Thomas Weiss' term),[29] and those in which the members of a coalition of the willing put themselves forward as agents of intervention when the UN is unwilling or unable to act at all.[30] I will refer to the associations in each case as 'subcontracted' and 'vigilante' coalitions, respectively.[31] The second point of clarification follows from this and concerns when I understand the UN as failing to act. As a body that has both explicitly assumed a moral responsibility to intervene in cases of mass atrocity, and has claimed a monopoly on authorising interventions conducted by other agents, the UN derogates from this responsibility when it fails to act *either* by deploying troops itself *or* by providing approval for another body to act in its place. Either failure can conceivably have one of two

[28] I am grateful to James Pattison for highlighting the contribution of private military and security companies to several recent humanitarian interventions (predominantly in the sense of performing logistical services – with Sierra Leone, where they adopted a role in the combat, as a notable exception).

[29] T.G. Weiss, 'The Humanitarian Impulse', in D.M. Malone (ed.), *The UN Security Council: From the Cold War to the 21st Century* (Boulder CO: Lynne Rienner, 2004), 37, at 46.

[30] Each sub-category includes coalitions of the willing established for what are often referred to as 'robust peacekeeping' or 'peace enforcement' operations. Note, however, that I exclude UN-led (as distinct from UN-authorised) operations from the general category of coalition of the willing, whether traditional peacekeeping forces, enforcement operations, or something in the increasingly blurred area between the two. Not only does this exclusion accord with how the label 'coalition of the willing' is generally employed, but I understand UN-led operations to demonstrate the UN's (albeit frequently inadequate) mechanism for acting on the basis of its decisions, and thereby as exemplifying the UN's own capacity for purposive action. See Erskine, 'Blood on the UN's Hands', n. 3, at 30–31.

[31] The latter label is inspired by C. Brown, 'Moral Agency and International Society: Reflections on Norms, the UN, the Gulf War, and the Kosovo Campaign', in Erskine (ed.), *Can Institutions Have Responsibilities?*, n. 4, 51, at 60–61, where he draws an analogy between coalitions of the willing and vigilante bands.

sources: a *decision* not to deploy troops or not to provide authorisation to other bodies to intervene; or the *inability* to act due to a decision-making stalemate (brought on by the exercise of the veto in the Security Council), or lack of resources (often in the form of insufficient material support from its member states). Questions of authority – including whether the UN should have a monopoly on authorising intervention in cases of humanitarian crises – are, of course, important.[32] Yet, whether or not vigilante coalitions of the willing should have the legal authority to intervene in cases of mass atrocity and large-scale loss of life is distinct from a possibility that will be explored in this chapter: that both subcontracted and vigilante coalitions (or at least their constituents) have a *moral obligation* to intervene in certain urgent circumstances.

Coalitions of the willing receive little attention as subjects for academic study in IR, and have been ignored within philosophical discussions of collective responsibility (perhaps unsurprisingly given the hitherto largely domestic focus of such analyses).[33] Moreover, despite their concrete presence in military interventions on humanitarian grounds, they are conspicuously absent from recent RtoP reports and policy documents. Significantly, the seminal 2001 report, *The Responsibility to Protect*, drafted by the International Commission on Intervention and State Sovereignty (ICISS), acknowledges the potential necessity of vigilante coalitions, 'ad hoc coalitions … acting without the approval of the Security Council', engaging in military intervention for human protection purposes if the Security Council 'fails to discharge … its responsibility in conscience-shocking situations crying out for action'.[34] However, when the UN member states unanimously endorsed RtoP at

[32] For a sophisticated analysis of whether the UN Security Council possesses unconditional exclusive legitimacy to authorise military interventions on humanitarian grounds – along with a proposal for an original alterative – see A. Buchanan and R.O. Keohane, 'Precommitment Regimes for Intervention: Supplementing the Security Council' (2011) 25(1) EIA 41.

[33] An exception that spans both can be found in Brown's brief engagement with coalitions of the willing in 'Moral Agency and International Society', n. 31, at 60–63. See also the even briefer engagement in Erskine, 'Blood on the UN's Hands', n. 3, at 39, footnote 53. Rare instances of attention to the category of coalition of the willing within IR are also found in Cooper, 'Stretching the Model', n. 23; and, in the context of assessments of multilateral military cooperation, in P. Weitsman, *Waging War: Alliances, Coalitions, and Institutions of Interstate Violence* (Stanford University Press, 2013); and S.E. Kreps, *Coalitions of Convenience: United States Military Interventions after the Cold War* (Oxford University Press, 2011).

[34] International Commission on Intervention and State Sovereignty (ICISS), *The Responsibility to Protect* (Ottawa: International Development Research Centre, 2001), at 54–55.

the 2005 World Summit, it was made explicit that the responsibility to protect deemed to be borne by the international community must be discharged exclusively through the Security Council (with, perhaps predictably, no mention of coalitions of the willing).[35]

If we accept that there is a responsibility to protect vulnerable populations from serious human rights abuses (a claim that has not only become increasingly widely accepted, but is also a prime example of what is broadly understood to be a moral imperative – and has been couched in such terms since its inception), then considering who should, and indeed can, discharge this responsibility when the UN fails to act is fundamental. The coalition of the willing is an obvious candidate for consideration. The question of how we understand such coalitions – whether as entities that we can reasonably expect to bear moral burdens, or as ad hoc associations of individual duty-bearers – necessarily follows. In order to respond, it might prove useful to return to the proposed criteria and interrogate the preliminary judgement that coalitions of the willing fail to qualify as institutional moral agents.

3.2 *Are coalitions of the willing institutional moral agents?*

A coalition of the willing struggles to meet the first criterion for institutional moral agency: that it possess an identity that is more than the sum of identities of its constitutive parts. Indeed, the importance that is often placed on the precise membership of such a coalition is indicative of this difficulty.[36] Moreover, a considerable obstacle to a consistent and

[35] This endorsement leaves a legitimate role for subcontracted coalitions of the willing, particularly as the UN Charter places on all member states a duty to implement Security Council decisions; yet precludes vigilante coalitions when the UN fails to act. See 2005 World Summit Outcome Document, n. 1, paras. 138 and 139; and, for member states' obligations to implement the decisions of the Security Council, see Charter of the United Nations, San Francisco, 26 June 1954, in force 24 October 1945, 1 UNTS 16 (UN Charter), Article 25.

[36] One example is the significance attached to the identities of the particular members of the 2003 Gulf War coalition. A White House press release, dated 27 March 2003, lists the forty-nine states that ostensibly made up the coalition, see 'Coalition Members', The White House archives, available at http://georgewbush-whitehouse.archives.gov/news/releases/2003/03/20030327-10.html (accessed on 25 March 2013). Notably, this archived document underwent a number of retrospective changes between 2003 and 2005, posted under the guise of the original – including, in one version, the removal of Costa Rica, which had vehemently objected to being included in the original list. (For an overview of the unacknowledged revisions made to this historical record, see S. Althens and K. Leetaru, 'Airbrushing History, American Style', available at www.clinecenter.illinois.

convincing corporate identity is the coalition's failure to satisfy the second criterion. The absence of an established decision-making mechanism at the level of the coalition prevents the diverse perspectives, preferences, and policies of its members (along with their potentially very different motivations for association) from being channeled into a position that is more than an agglomeration of discrete individual stances. Any independent identity that the coalition as a whole might achieve therefore remains partial and precarious at best.

Deliberation does, of course, take place between the members of the coalition – and is necessary for the coordinated action that its constituents come together to achieve. Yet, rather than the formal decision making of so-called structured institutions such as the UN, NATO, and (all but failed) states, which entails codified rules and established practices for arriving at policies, the coalition of the willing relies on what might be called *informal* decision making.[37] This involves negotiation, bargaining, and consensus-building among various constituents in the absence of existing organisational structures and decision-making procedures.[38] In the case of both subcontracted and vigilante coalitions assembled for military interventions, one member often takes the lead (whether a state such as the United States or a regional alliance such as NATO).[39] Other coalitions of the willing, most notably those committed

edu/research/airbrushing_history/ (accessed on 25 March 2013).) See also Cooper's assessment (Cooper, 'Stretching the Model', n. 23, at 5) that even in the case of norm-generating coalitions (such as the anti-landmine coalition, which he contrasts with the 2003 Gulf War coalition on the grounds that the focus of the former 'has tended toward the collective rather than the individual members'), identifying individual members mattered greatly.

[37] For the term 'structured institution', see, inter alia, K.A. Shepsle 'Rational Choice Institutionalism', in R. A.W. Rhodes, S.A. Binder, and B.A. Rockman (eds.), *The Oxford Handbook of Political Institutions* (Oxford University Press, 2006), 23, at 27. On decision making and 'failed states', see Erskine, 'States and Quasi-States', n. 3, at 78–79.

[38] My use of 'informal' in this context is informed by work on 'informal governance' and relates specifically to the *process* through which decisions are reached and policies are made. See, for example, the contributions to T. Christiansen and C. Neuhold (eds.), *International Handbook on Informal Governance* (Cheltenham: Edward Elgar, 2012), and, for this particular nuance, Christiansen and Neuhold, 'Introduction', in ibid., 1, at 4. For a different view, that even informal deliberative mechanisms would allow a group to qualify as what I call an 'institutional moral agent', see S. Collins, 'Collectives' Duties and Collectivization Duties' (2013) 91(2) AJP 231. I am grateful to Jon Herington for drawing my attention to common themes in this argument and Collins' piece.

[39] See G.F. Oliver, 'The Other Side of Peacekeeping: Peace Enforcement and Who Should Do It?', in H. Langholtz, B. Kondoch, and A. Wells (eds.), *International Peacekeeping: The Yearbook of International Peace Operations*, vol. 8, (Leiden: Martinus Nijhoff, 2002), 99.

to norm promotion, tend to be less hierarchical in negotiating courses of action.[40] Yet, both cases display a further feature frequently associated with informal decision making: the inability to translate calls for collective action into decisions that are binding upon the group as a whole if such proposals depart from the positions of some of its members.[41]

In sum, informal decision making establishes and holds together the loose association of agents (or, indeed, fails to do so); achieves some consensus on a general course of action; and coordinates individual contributions (often imperfectly), with the specifically military command-and-control function of those coalitions assembled for interventions commonly provided through a single chain within the lead organisation.[42] Crucially, there is no overarching decision-making apparatus that can be said to both direct the actions and represent the intentions of the collectivity as a whole. With respect to the third criterion – that the collectivity have mechanisms by which decisions can be translated into actions and policies can be implemented – although the individual members of the coalition can carry out their respective decisions in order to coordinate their actions, and can even choose to follow the instructions of a lead agent, the lack of a decision-making structure at the level of the coalition impedes *corporate* purposive action.

As an association that is by definition temporary, a coalition of the willing also stumbles at the fourth, identity-over-time criterion. A degree of continuity is necessary for it to make sense to talk about the moral expectations that we have of a collectivity performing certain actions at some point in the future. Logically, a coalition of the willing cannot be assigned duties prospectively when it does not exist prior to what is often taken to be the duty-generating event or set of circumstances that its constituents band together to confront. Moreover, it follows that, as a

According to Oliver, this is both a common scenario when it comes to military action by coalitions of the willing and an ideal one – but ideal only, he qualifies, in relation to *subcontracted* coalitions.

40 Cooper, 'Stretching the Model', n. 23, at 5.

41 On the non-binding forms of cooperation that often define informal governance in international politics, see T. Conzelmann, 'Informal governance in international relations', in T. Christiansen and C. Neuhold (eds.), *International Handbook on Informal Governance* (Cheltenham: Edward Elgar, 2012), 219.

42 Oliver, 'The Other Side of Peacekeeping', n. 39, at 113. Note that Oliver describes the specific decision process relating to the conduct of force as usually resting on 'a single national chain'. It is notable that the lead actor often does not enjoy complete compliance by the military personnel of the other members of the coalition, who do not totally relinquish their own chains of command and (potentially conflicting) rules of engagement.

group, it cannot incur blame retrospectively for failing to discharge duties that it could not have been assigned in the first place.[43] This judgement is crucial for many of the cases being addressed: that is, when an ad hoc coalition is called to action to respond to the gross violation of human rights, but no such entity yet exists. It also highlights one of the vital questions that this chapter seeks to address. *To whom* – or *to what* – can duties be assigned in such a case?

However, it might be wise to pause on this criterion and consider another set of circumstances. Coalitions of the willing enjoy some continuity once they have been established, even if this is unlikely to represent the persistence of a corporate identity. Some are surprisingly eclectic (the 1990-1991 Gulf War coalition, for example, comprised liberal democracies, traditional Arab states, and more radical Arab states, including Syria) and render an enduring association highly unlikely. Yet, others are relatively homogeneous, with many of their members bound together by overlapping regional and international associations that both predate and outlive the particular coalition in question (such as the 1999 Kosovo coalition).[44] In each case, once a coalition of the willing has been established, questions of prospective and retrospective moral responsibility arise in relation to the specific timeframe in which it exists. The proposed responsibility to respond, which the members come together to uphold, does not exhaust the range of possible duties to be discharged when the response takes the form of military action to protect vulnerable populations. Rather, other duties are also recognised in the context of that action: that military intervention be conducted discriminately and proportionately, for example. Questions remain of where these duties rest and where blame for their breach is to be apportioned. Convincing answers depend on the moral status of the coalition of the willing. Insight into this status is, in turn, revealed in the difficulty that such coalitions have in meeting the previous criteria – even if, once established, they can have a (limited) identity over time. Finally, the criterion that the collectivity be self-asserting is easily met by a coalition of the willing, given that its

[43] Erskine, 'Blood on the UN's Hands?', n. 3, at 31.

[44] This point is inspired by Brown, who usefully distinguishes between the Gulf War and Kosovo coalitions in terms of what their members do and do not have in common (aside from a temporary, shared purpose). See Brown, 'Moral Agency and International Society', n. 31, at 61–62.

constituents are self-selected and explicitly committed to both a common goal and collective action.[45]

Even acknowledging the diversity within the category of coalition of the willing, and understanding each criterion for institutional moral agency as being able to be satisfied by degree (rather than constituting an all-or-nothing test), coalitions of the willing do not possess the sophisticated, integrated capacities for deliberation and action that would allow them to qualify.[46] According to this analysis, coalitions of the willing are not moral agents; the moral responsibility to protect vulnerable populations must be borne elsewhere. Individual states and other institutional agents might have duties to intervene, and can be blamed for inaction (or acting disproportionately or indiscriminately). However, such prescriptions and evaluations must remain exclusively at the level of those agents that make up the temporary association. We cannot coherently talk about assigning duties or apportioning blame to the coalition itself.

4. A gap in the analysis? Moral responsibilities and informal associations

This might seem a logical end-point to this analysis. Yet, three related concerns remain, each of which cautions against treating coalitions of the willing as mere aggregates of individual agents acting independently for the purposes of addressing questions of moral responsibility. First, if moral responsibly must be attributed to individual states (and possibly non-state and intergovernmental actors), rather than the ad hoc associations that they might come together to form, there will be some cases in which no state (or other actor) can be expected to discharge a duty to protect a population from egregious human right violations simply because each, as a discrete agent, lacks either the capacities or enabling conditions to do so.[47] If the UN is also unable to respond, then we seem

[45] I am assuming here that they have not been merely co-opted into the coalition without their knowledge or consent and would not consider the coalition to extend to such actors. I am thinking of the case of Costa Rica and the 2003 coalition when making this qualification. See n. 36.

[46] See Erskine, 'States and Quasi-States', n. 3, at 79, for a discussion of the criteria for institutional moral agency often being met by degree.

[47] Even though unilateral military action would remain a viable option for a few great powers, possessing the power and resources to engage in military action is not the same thing as having the capacity effectively to protect a population at risk. The ability to

to have no choice but to concede that *no agent* can reasonably be burdened with a duty to protect the vulnerable population. This is eminently unsatisfactory. Second, accounts of moral responsibility with respect to some informal associations, such as coalitions of the willing, seem to resist being reduced without remainder to their component parts. If their members can accomplish things acting in concert that they cannot achieve when acting individually, this must somehow affect our judgements of moral responsibility in relation to them, even though the coalition that they come together to form cannot be a moral agent in itself. Third, coalitions of the willing are not amorphous collectivities in the way that the international community is. They are not purposive actors in themselves, but they nevertheless seem to possess something that at least resembles a capacity for purposive action.[48] Meeting *some* of the criteria addressed to a limited degree does not take the coalition of the willing far enough to qualify as an institutional moral agent. Nevertheless, its informal deliberative capacity, the continued (albeit temporary) association of its members, and its constitution by actors who have come together to participate in a common project are features that, combined, seem morally significant. Perhaps informal associations like coalitions of the willing should not be so easily dismissed in assessments of moral responsibility.

Philosophers such as Virginia Held and Larry May have focused on questions of moral responsibility in the context of just those types of collectivity that I have argued cannot bear moral responsibilities at the corporate level: associations that lack formal organisational structures and decision-making procedures. Insights from their work provide a more nuanced and demanding account of moral responsibility in relation to informal associations in world politics than has been alluded to so

understand the local culture and political situation, and to generate trust amongst those to be rescued, are also imperative for an effective humanitarian intervention, and will mean that an obvious 'agent of last resort' does not, in most cases, have the capacity to discharge the duty. Furthermore, it should be noted that the perception that unilateral action is illegitimate provides an external normative constraint that pushes even powerful states towards multilateral action.

48 On this point, it is perhaps no coincidence that a few IR scholars attribute to informal associations some degree of 'independent' and 'collective' agency, 'informal agency', or 'agent-like moral effects'. See, respectively, Cross, 'Rethinking Epistemic Communities', n. 21, at 153, 156; Brown, 'Moral Agency and International Society', n. 31, at 51, 58, 63; and Clark, *The Vulnerable*, n. 21, at 17.

far – and one that will complement the analysis of institutional moral agency already offered.

4.1 *Held's 'random collection'*

The question that Held set out to answer in an oft-cited 1970 article is reflected in its title: 'Can a Random Collection of Individuals be Morally Responsible?'.[49] The types of group that she wishes to hold up to scrutiny are those that contingently share a time and place, but lack any specific decision-making procedures.[50] We might, she suggests, think of unacquainted passengers riding together on a train or pedestrians sharing a sidewalk as thereby belonging to this category. Neither would have specific methods for deciding to act. Indeed, the groups that she addresses fail to qualify as institutional moral agents on each and every criterion offered in this chapter. They also, I will suggest, stand in a potentially instructive relationship to the types of ad hoc association overlooked in recent articulations of RtoP.

Held makes two claims. First she argues that, *in some circumstances*, a random collection – or, more accurately, those that make up such a collection – may be held responsible for not acting.[51] The specific circumstances in which they may be held responsible are those in which the following conditions are met: a) the individuals constituting the random collection were faced with a stranger in dire need of rescue and the gravity of the crisis demanded a response; b) these individuals could have rescued the stranger by acting together, even though no one in the group could have done so acting independently; c) the required action was 'obvious' and its foreseeable outcome 'clearly favourable'; and, d) carrying out this action would have been possible without prior deliberation or special coordination between the individuals and would

[49] V. Held, 'Can a Random Collection of Individuals Be Morally Responsible?' (1970) 67 (14) JP 471.

[50] From this point, I will use 'random collection' to refer to the type of collectivity that Held has in mind, regardless of challenges that this is not the most appropriate label. See, for example, S. Bates, 'The Responsibility of "Random Collections"', in L. May and S. Hoffman (eds.), *Collective Responsibility: Five Decades of Debate in Theoretical and Applied Ethics* (Lanham, Maryland: Rowman and Littlefield, 1991), 101.

[51] Despite the ambiguity of her language in places, Held's position here supports my contention that moral responsibility is *distributive* amongst the members of a group that lacks a formal decision-making structure.

not have been open to disagreement.[52] As my intention is to apply Held's argument at the international level, it is worth noting that the extent to which the fourth condition can be met when we are talking about discrete states, rather than individual human beings, is questionable. It is difficult to imagine a scenario in which collective action involving states would require neither prior deliberation nor special coordination.[53] This condition would therefore *prima facie* shield individual states from any expectation that they engage in remedial collective action outside a pre-existing organisational structure. An exemption of this sort would have potentially tragic consequences in those cases in which no formal intergovernmental organisation was willing or able to act to discharge a moral responsibility, such as the proposed imperative to protect vulnerable populations. The duty would thereby go unmet without any agent having derogated from its moral responsibility to respond. However, before lamenting that states would be let off the moral hook given Held's analysis, this application to international relations might be valuably pursued – and the apparent leniency of this condition qualified – in the context of her subsequent assertion.

According to Held's second claim, even in some cases in which a random collection cannot be held responsible for failing to perform an action, the individuals who constitute it may be held responsible for not 'forming [themselves] into an organized group capable of deciding which action to take'.[54] The specific example that she constructs to convey this argument is worth relating. Held describes three pedestrians, who are strangers to each other, walking down an isolated street when '[a] small building collapses':

> A man inside is trapped; he calls to the three for help. He is bleeding from a lower-leg injury and needs immediate assistance. All four persons know

[52] Held, 'Random Collection', n. 49, at 476. Note that I take the fourth condition to be implicit in both the second and third conditions and in Held's analysis of several hypothetical scenarios.

[53] I think that individual states each reducing carbon emissions to collectively address climate change might be an example here. However, it should be added that, even in this context, prior deliberation and special coordination *would* be required to establish effective global environmental policies.

[54] Held, 'Random Collection', n. 49, at 476. Again, Held's language is ambiguous, and she seems, momentarily, to suggest that we can apportion blame to the random collection itself. (She uses 'itself' where I have inserted 'themselves', above.) However, in the context of her argument it is clear that she means to apportion responsibility to the individuals within it.

> that a tourniquet should be applied to his thigh, but this cannot be done until various beams are removed, and removing any would require the strength of all three. The three observers do not agree on how to proceed.[55]

Each person makes a different proposal, they argue, do not act, and the man slowly bleeds to death. Held observes that *any* of their proposed actions would have saved the man, and a 'reasonable person' should have known that any action would have been better than none; '[t]he problem was deciding which to take.' She concludes that we cannot hold the members of the random collection responsible for the non-performance of the action (given the fourth condition outlined previously), but that they 'can be held responsible for failing . . . to adopt a decision method' and thereby transforming themselves into the sort of group that might have been capable of the deliberation and coordination required for an effective response.[56]

Intuitively, Held's judgement appears flawed in two respects – at least in the context of the domestic case that she illustrates. First, she seems too forgiving in concluding that the individuals are not responsible for failing to act when they are unable to reach an agreement (but are, rather, responsible for not forming themselves into the sort of group that would have been capable of acting), if, as she maintains, it is abundantly clear that *any* action would have been better than no action at all. Surely, then, each individual should have accepted the gravity of the situation, suppressed his or her own desire to orchestrate the rescue, and simply gone along with the others.[57] A more appropriate scenario for the individuals to have been spared responsibility would have been one in which it were *not*, in fact, clear that any action would have been better than none. Perhaps a false move of one beam, for example, would have conceivably resulted in the death of the trapped man – or indeed all four individuals. Such a scenario would have provided good reason for not contributing immediately to any proposed action, and would have genuinely required a group of individuals capable of some degree of deliberation over the consequences of possible actions and having the ability to coordinate

[55] Ibid., at 479. [56] Ibid.

[57] To the degree that one of the pedestrians had done this, I think that her responsibility would have been mitigated, even if the members of the group had failed to respond collectively. This qualification matters if neither of the other two pedestrians would similarly compromise to the extent necessary to cooperate in a situation in which the collaboration of only two individuals would have been insufficient to avert tragedy.

themselves to execute the considered course. Second, if transformation into a group capable of this sort of deliberation had been necessary, it does not seem plausible to suggest that the individuals could have achieved this in the time they had to move the beams without the victim bleeding to death.

Yet, when an analogy is drawn with a possible set of circumstances at the international level, and states (or even regional organisations of states) represent the pedestrians, Held's judgement becomes more compelling in both respects. First, whether the crisis is a malfunctioning nuclear power plant (such as the one involved in the Fukushima Daiichi nuclear disaster of 2011), or the mass violation of human rights in another state (such as Rwanda in 1994, or Syria from 2012), the situation is going to be infinitely more complex than simply moving three beams. Indeed, in such complex crises, it is not obvious that just *any* action would be better than none. Some actions will worsen rather than improve the situation, or cause more overall harm than good. Second, in many (although not all) cases of international crisis, there *is* time for relevant agents to transform themselves from a random collection into a group capable of accomplishing objectives that would be beyond their reach if they were each facing the crisis either in isolation or as part of a completely non-integrated aggregate. (This potential is particularly important in the absence of a formal, permanent organisation willing and able to respond, and given that either establishing or reforming such an organisation would require a prohibitively longer time frame.) Genocidal intent, for example, is often clearly articulated before it is acted upon: weapons might be stockpiled, hatred incited, human beings rhetorically reduced to 'cockroaches'.[58] In short, crises – or at least their escalation – may be anticipated, leaving time to establish some capacity for deliberation and special coordination between relevant agents. This is where Held's analysis and an exploration of moral responsibility in the context of coalitions of the willing come together in a particularly meaningful way.

Held's argument provides purchase in addressing certain, apparently intractable, cases in world politics in which the gravity and imminence of a crisis demands a response, and yet no agent seems able to act effectively on its own. Inspired by Held's position, one might propose that *even if*

[58] This is, of course, the description offered by both Radio Télévison Libre des Milles Collines in Rwanda in 1994, and Muammar Qaddafi in Libya in 2011 to refer to Tutsis and anti-Qaddafi demonstrators, respectively.

remedial action requires both a multilateral effort on the part of available agents (because of the limited capacities or constraining conditions faced by each), and prior deliberation and special coordination between them (because the requisite action is neither immediately obvious nor beyond disagreement), and *even if* these agents are not part of some pre-existing organisational structure that would facilitate such cooperation, there nevertheless remains a moral imperative for them to do something. Namely, they each have a duty to contribute to establishing the type of collectivity capable of the requisite collective action. It is important to emphasise that Held actually suggests that members of a random collection be held responsible for failing to transform themselves into an 'organized group' – comparable to those formal organisations that I argue qualify as institutional moral agents.[59] (For Held, an 'organized group' has 'a method for deciding to act: it has officials who can act in its name, or a voting procedure ... or customary procedures to guide its actions'.)[60] Yet, her argument, and the particular time-sensitive, life-and-death examples that she invokes, actually point towards an intermediary type of association that the members of her random collection have an obligation to form themselves into: an *informal association*, loosely organised and capable of some deliberation leading to coordinated action, but lacking the organisational or decision-making trappings of a structured institution.

Applying Held's argument to the international level – but with the crucial clarification that loose organisational structures may be sufficient for the deliberation and coordination needed to support some forms of collective action – leads to a compelling, and potentially controversial, suggestion. One might propose that individual states (and non-state and intergovernmental actors) each have an obligation, in the absence of a viable alternative, to contribute to the establishment, and then functioning, of an informal, temporary association for the purposes of responding to a particular crisis effectively, robustly, and in time to mitigate disaster. This seems especially persuasive in the worrying case where there is no

[59] Held's 'organized groups', like my institutional moral agents, can be held morally responsible at the corporate level for acts or omissions in a way that is not distributive amongst their members. See Held, 'Random Collection', n. 49, at 474–475. Indeed, I share Held's view that moral responsibility at the level of the formal organisations *cannot* be distributive amongst its individual members, although, as noted, these members might be individually responsible for concurrent, complementary and even co-ordinated acts and omissions.

[60] Held, 'Random Collection', n. 49, at 479.

formal organisation (whether the UN or some other potential 'agent of justice') that can be expected to discharge a duty to respond (either because of external, constraining conditions or the agent's own limited capacities for deliberation and action) – and no hope of reforming or creating one in the limited time needed for an effective response.[61]

Of course, once such an ad hoc coalition has been established, we are talking about neither a 'random collection of individuals' in Held's sense, nor what I have called an institutional moral agent. Rather, we are addressing what was formerly a random collection of individuals who have together transformed themselves into something between the two: that is, an informal association made up of actors who have come together in pursuit of a common goal. For consideration of such an intermediary category of collectivity, Larry May's work is invaluable.

4.2 May's 'middle position'

May observes that the structures of informal associations (such as amateur sports teams and mobs) 'enable their members to perform actions that they could not have performed on their own'.[62] Moreover, he argues that the 'in-between status' of the mob in particular – 'a status somewhere between a random collection of individuals and an organized group' – should prompt us to re-think the requisite features for coherently talking about a group acting.[63] In constructing his argument, May focuses on the significance of relationships and, specifically, the notion of solidarity.

He maintains that collective action and responsibility can be predicated on individuals in groups, insofar as one refers to *both* individual persons *and* the relations among them. He thereby adopts an alternative to both my position as outlined in this chapter (that some collectivities can be moral agents, and therefore the bearers of duties, in their own right) and the 'individualist' insistence that accounts of group action and responsibility are always reducible to descriptions of the actions and responsibilities of their individual human constituents.[64] May explains his 'middle position' as follows:

[61] The phrase 'agent of justice' is taken from O. O'Neill, 'Agents of Justice' (2001) 32(1–2) *Metaphilosophy* 180.

[62] L. May, *The Morality of Groups: Collective Responsibility, Group-Based Harm and Corporate Rights* (University of Notre Dame Press, 1987), 26.

[63] Ibid., at 37. [64] Ibid., at 9.

> My own view is that social groups should be analyzed as individuals *in relationships*. Groups themselves do not exist in their own right; but the individuals who compose groups also are often not understandable as acting in isolation from one another.[65]

In distinguishing his position from that of French, May argues that French is wrong both to assert that a 'conglomerate' somehow entails a group that is ontologically independent of its individual members in relationships *and* to assume that an 'aggregate' is straightforwardly reducible to its individual members.[66] While I agree with French that certain collectivities have identities that are more than the sum of their constitutive parts – and in a way that is morally significant – May's point that French's aggregates are not always reducible to descriptions of individual action is a compelling one. In other words, I adopt the more radical 'minority position' (explicitly rejected by May) that certain types of collectivity can qualify as moral agents in their own right,[67] but nevertheless maintain that there is something in May's more moderate stance that is important for certain collectivities that neither meet the criteria for institutional moral agency outlined earlier nor can be adequately described in terms of Held's random collections. In short, May's argument is important for collectivities such as coalitions of the willing.

May reminds us that French actually, albeit briefly, distinguishes between two different types of aggregate collectivity: 'the sort whose definition explicitly involves spatial/temporal contiguity' and 'the sort defined in terms of a common characteristic or feature'.[68] (Neither has formal organisational structures or decision-making procedures.) However, French does not treat the distinction as significant and maintains that descriptions of the actions of both are reducible to the actions of their individual constituents, with consequences for questions of moral responsibility. May challenges this and suggests that only the former, what he calls 'random aggregate groups', actually supports French's position that they are reducible to the actions of their individual

[65] Ibid. (emphasis in the original). [66] Ibid., at 22–23.

[67] Philip Pettit has also championed a position that is comparable to the one that I have outlined. Indeed, Pettit draws the comparison, and describes both of our arguments as representing a 'minority position'. See P. Pettit, 'Responsibility Incorporated' (2007) 117 (2) *Ethics* 171, at 172, footnote 3. See also C. List and P. Pettit, *Group Agency: The Possibility, Design and Status of Corporate Agents* (Oxford University Press, 2011).

[68] May, *The Morality of Groups*, n. 62, at 22–23; French, *Collective and Corporate Responsibility*, n. 11, at 12–13.

constituents. As for the latter, May proposes that this 'subclass of aggregates, those defined in terms of a common feature, is surely not one which can be understood as a summation of the parts of persons who compose it'.[69] Offering mobs and teams as examples of this subclass, he maintains that 'both groups are defined by reference to the solidarity which allows the members of the group to engage in *joint purposive behaviour*'.[70] This middle ground between groups that I have argued are capable of corporate purposive action and groups such as Held's 'random collections', which are reducible to the actions of their constituents, promises to tell us something important about moral responsibility in world politics in general and about the reasonable expectations that we might have of coalitions of the willing in response to humanitarian crises in particular.

Two points of clarification should, however, be offered about how I propose to use May's work in this respect. First, although I agree with May's important point that there is more than one type of 'aggregate collectivity', I disagree with his claim that individuals and relationships are all that there is. Some collectivities *can* achieve a status independent of their constituents. Second, while I am drawing on May's insight that individuals in informal associations act in a way that cannot be simply reduced to the actions and intentions of individuals acting in isolation, it is important to emphasise that by applying this insight to an analysis of coalitions of the willing I am not using May's work in a way that he would – or could, given the totality of his argument – endorse. This is because, going back to the previous point, I am assuming that the sorts of collectivities to which he denies independent ontological standing are actually the individuals in the informal associations being addressed. States, and possibly other institutional agents, are to my coalitions of the willing what individual human actors are to May's mobs and amateur sports teams. This is not a problem for me given my arguments surrounding institutional moral agency, but it would be a problem for May's very different 'middle position'.

Importantly, May effectively introduces another category of collectivity: those entities that lack formal organisational structures, but that 'can facilitate joint action or common interest' nonetheless.[71] Within this category May includes collectivities that have 'informal organizational

[69] May, ibid., at 22. [70] Ibid. (emphasis added). [71] Ibid., at 23.

structures' and those 'such as mobs' that 'can attain unity even though they are not organized at all'.[72] Both types of collectivity, May argues, are distinct from those random collections of persons 'which do not have the ability to engage in joint action'.[73] Although the latter variation (which May understands to be exemplified by mobs) is less useful to the discussion here, the former would seem logically to be the type of collectivity that the individuals within Held's random collection have an obligation to contribute to establishing under certain circumstances – at least in the short term, given the time constraints that she assumes.[74] Indeed, May's account of the often overlooked characteristics of such informally organised collectivities provide the foundation for a potentially valuable supplement to analyses of moral responsibility made possible by the model of institutional moral agency outlined previously.

5. The moral significance of acting in concert: coalitions of the willing and responsibilities to protect

The proposal that I have taken from Held's article is the following: if there is a duty to perform a particular action, and if individual agents can come together to perform this action when they could not have performed it individually, then they each have an obligation to contribute to establishing the type of group necessary for this duty to be discharged. The examples that she invokes in constructing this argument gesture towards a category of informally organised associations whose members are nevertheless capable of some degree of deliberation and special coordination. May's work is valuable in giving substance to this category. From May, I have taken the point that social relationships and their participants' shared interests and desire to work towards a common goal can make possible what he calls 'joint purposive behaviour'.

It is important to clarify here that I hesitate to take this further and accept that group action and intention are possible in the case of informal associations; I do not think that solidarity can replace a formal organisational structure and decision-making procedures, and thereby allow for purposive action in a way that is not ultimately distributive amongst the

[72] Ibid. [73] Ibid.
[74] Again, this is a conclusion that I have reached given what I take to be the logic of Held's argument, rather than a position that Held herself asserts.

members of the association.[75] The thought of somehow melding together the actions and intentions of these constituents seems unrealistic – and worrying, particularly if one then treats each constituent as somehow complicit in the ostensible actions of the informal association as a whole. Despite my defending the view that formal organisations that meet specific criteria are capable of purposive action, and can thereby coherently be understood to bear moral responsibilities at the corporate level, I do not think that the same is true for informal associations. When it comes to this category of collectivity, descriptions of actions and intentions, and corresponding ascriptions of moral agency and responsibility, are reducible to their individual constituents, *as long as one recognises that such accounts are different in important ways from accounts of individuals acting independently or in isolation.*[76]

This difference is encompassed by what I take to be the defining feature of '*joint* action', '*shared* activity' or '*collective* action':[77] an outcome or effect that could not have resulted from the mere summation of individual acts. Importantly, the necessarily unified, concerted endeavours of individual agents that characterise such action vary in both sophistication and the capacities necessary to perform them – a point that is particularly important if we are considering joint action at the international level. Some types of joint action – including that which Held suggests the members of her 'random collections' can be blamed for not performing given certain conditions – require only limited cooperation between individual agents. Others demand some degree of prior deliberation and special coordination. Following May (to the point that draws on his analysis of groups with informal organisational structures, but not as far as to embrace his analysis of those that lack them, such as mobs), I will refer to the latter, more sophisticated variation as *joint purposive action.*[78] To be able to exercise joint purposive action, the

[75] I am thereby rejecting a move that I associate with both May in *The Morality of Groups*, n. 62, and David Miller (who draws on May) in D. Miller, 'Holding Nations Responsible' (2004) 114 *Ethics* 240.

[76] I think that my reductive account of shared activity and shared intention (when it comes to informal associations such as coalitions of the willing) departs in significant ways from May's position – and that of Miller – but this requires further explanation and analysis beyond the scope of this chapter.

[77] I will treat these interchangeably.

[78] There are differences between how I understand joint purposive action and how May understands what he calls 'joint purposive behaviour'. Nevertheless, the general concept, as presented in this chapter, is inspired by May's important *The Morality of Groups*, n. 62.

members of a collectivity must have the following: compatible interests (although not common or even necessarily complementary motivations);[79] a concomitant willingness to cooperate – something that might be called 'participatory intention';[80] and the capacity to deliberate (however informally) in order to coordinate their actions (even imperfectly) in circumstances in which the required collective action is not obvious but, rather, open to disagreement.[81] Joint purposive action is thereby distinct from action that is best described at the level of the organisation as a whole and that generates coherent accounts of moral responsibility that cannot be reduced to its individual constituents. The model of institutional moral agency, presented previously, aims to explore the latter (and to define the collectivities capable of it), but overlooks the moral significance of the former. Coalitions of the willing are capable of – and, indeed, created to exercise – joint purposive action.

With the potential for joint purposive action comes *shared responsibility*. By shared responsibility I mean responsibility that is necessarily distributive amongst the individual members of a collectivity for outcomes that can only be achieved when they act in concert. I am not, however, suggesting that joint purposive action thereby entails diminished responsibility on the part of each member of the group. From such a perspective, the fact that multiple actors are required to discharge a duty would mean that the responsibility of each to act is somehow reduced – and that each could only be blamed in fraction for failing to do so. Moral responsibility, by this view, is diluted when it is shared. I do not mean this at all. Rather, the position that I am proposing involves the individual constituents of those informally organised groups capable of this more sophisticated type of collective endeavour bearing *greater* individual responsibility than they would bear if they were acting independently. It also, by extension, suggests that we should have greater expectations of the individuals within random collections that have the potential to contribute to establishing such groups than we should have of individual agents who do not have this opportunity (because they find

79 The divergent motivations of those agents participating in joint action must not undermine cooperation, of course, but they might nevertheless be radically different and 'incompatible' in the sense that they could not be held simultaneously by the same agent without a substantial degree of cognitive dissonance.

80 See C.L. Kutz, 'Acting Together' (2000) 61 PPR 1.

81 The first two criteria are for joint action broadly (but are perhaps required to a greater degree for what I am calling joint purposive action); the third criterion is specifically for joint purposive action.

themselves either isolated or part of a random collection whose other constituents lack a willingness to cooperate).

5.1 *Joint purposive action, enhanced capacities, and redefined individual responsibilities to protect*

The arguments of both Held and May allow me to build on a relatively simple, but crucial insight: that agents who come together, even in an informal association, to work towards a shared goal are able to achieve things by cooperating that they would not be able to achieve independently. This potential for *enhanced capacities* prompts me to suggest that individual agents (including states, non-state actors, and intergovernmental organisations) should come together to form such an ad hoc group, in the absence of a viable alternative and when confronted with a moral imperative that would otherwise go unmet.[82] This also leads me to propose that there is reason to have *greater* expectations of these individual agents – both when they are already members of an informal association with the capacity for joint purposive action and when they find themselves in a 'random collection' with the opportunity to form such an association. In other words, the enhanced capacities with which individual agents can be imbued as part of an informal association (existing or potential) lead to *magnified individual responsibilities.*

This argument regarding capacities for joint purposive action and attendant shared responsibility is directly relevant to considerations of who can – and should – discharge the proposed remedial responsibility to protect vulnerable populations.[83] Indeed, if we accept the proposed moral responsibility to protect vulnerable populations as a starting point, and maintain that the 'just cause' criterion was met in the case of the

[82] I acknowledge that this proposal requires another qualifying condition: that the cost of acting not be unacceptably high. For now, this qualification is assumed; exactly what it should entail will be examined in future work. I am grateful to one of EIA's anonymous reviewers for highlighting its importance.

[83] Interestingly, an early iteration of the 2005 UN endorsement of RtoP included the statement 'we recognize our *shared responsibility* to take collective action' (emphasis added). This assertion was replaced by '[w]e are prepared to take collective action in a timely and decisive manner' in para. 139 of the 2005 World Summit Outcome Document, n. 1, following an objection to the explicit acknowledgment of an obligation that the earlier version entailed. This amendment is highlighted by J. Welsh, 'Who Should Act? Collective Responsibility and the Responsibility to Protect', in W.A. Knight and F. Egerton (eds.), *The Routledge Handbook on the Responsibility to Protect* (New York: Routledge, 2012), 103, at 109.

2011 intervention in Libya, this argument has implications not only for how we judge the actions of those states that formed a coalition in order to carry out UN Resolution 1973 (these actions were *required* – and not merely due to states' UN Charter-defined responsibilities to implement Security Council decisions), but also for what would have been required in a counterfactual case of no resolution. In such a case, either a state capable of acting independently would have had a duty to intervene (Walzer's 'agent of last resort'), or, more plausibly (given both the diverse range of capacities needed for an effective humanitarian intervention and the constraining perception of illegitimacy that threatens to accompany unilateral action), individual states, and possibly non-state and intergovernmental actors, would have each had an obligation to contribute to a collectivisation process, and then, as part of a joint endeavour, to respond to the crisis. Importantly, when such institutional moral agents have enhanced capacities as members of an informal association, or the opportunity to acquire enhanced capacities by contributing to the establishment of an informal association, the greater expectations placed on each of them also translate into increased vulnerability to blame if there is a failure to respond.[84] There is a compelling case for considering the possibility of shared responsibility for *joint omissions* or *inaction in concert* in certain cases.[85]

5.2 Distributing responsibilities and apportioning blame amongst relevant agents

Although Held's collapsing-building scenario vividly illustrates the logic behind this proposed imperative, the relative simplicity of her example avoids a question that is likely to arise in the international case being examined. Namely, how should moral burdens be distributed amongst the members, and potential members, of a coalition of the willing? Held's 'random collection' is populated only by three proximate pedestrians,

[84] An individual agent's vulnerability to blame is diminished, however, if other agents required for joint action refuse to cooperate, or if the deliberation made possible once an informal association has been established results in a reasonable decision that intervention should not be pursued (because it is likely to result in greater harm than good, for example).

[85] Compare to May, *Sharing Responsibility* (The University of Chicago Press, 1992), 73–124. These points are explored in detail in T. Erskine, *Locating Responsibility: Institutional Moral Agency and International Relations*, n. 3, chapter 6, in a section entitled, '"Dithering in concert": collective failures and joint omissions'.

each of whom is needed for a successful rescue. In contrast, the understanding of joint purposive action and shared responsibility developed earlier in this chapter reveals the international community to comprise a *multitude* of (contingently) duty-bearing agents in cases of mass atrocity.[86] In the sense that distance precludes neither knowledge of a crisis nor the opportunity to respond, the international community as a whole is a comparable 'random collection' (in Held's sense) and each state is a bystander. Practical decisions need to be made about who is best placed to act. After all, these institutional agents are capable of different types and degrees of contribution to a collective rescue, and the active participation of all is not required in order to achieve it. Moreover, and separately, the shared responsibility discussed earlier might weigh especially heavily on some members of the international community – those who have assumed a particular role to safeguard the population in question, for example, or those who have played some part in the events leading up to the crisis. Given both points, it makes sense to mention the factors of *capacity*, *special responsibilities*, and *culpability* that arguably come into play in arriving at an efficient and just distribution of moral burdens (whether we are talking about assigning responsibilities or apportioning blame) in such complex cases of concerted action – even if a detailed examination of each must be left to others.[87]

Agents' particular capacities can generate expectations of who amongst those that bear a shared responsibility to protect should act in a particular case. Significantly, the capacities required to contribute to an effective collective rescue have not been understood in this chapter exclusively in terms of military might, but also, for example, as cultural and political knowledge of the crisis and (given the imperative to collectivise and the nature of informal deliberation) skills to negotiate effectively between competing interests. Moreover, different capacities are valuable at the respective points at which I have proposed there is an imperative

[86] 'Contingently' because both the necessary initial move of collectivising and the subsequent joint endeavour depend on the cooperation of other agents (and are thereby beyond the ultimate control of each).

[87] For valuable discussions of how remedial responsibilities are variously generated and assigned, see D. Miller, 'Distributing Responsibilities' (2001) 9(4) JPP 453, and, in the specific context of responding militarily to grievous human rights abuses, M. Walzer, 'The Politics of Rescue', n. 2; J. Pattison, *Humanitarian Intervention & The Responsibility to Protect: Who Should Intervene?* (Oxford University Press, 2010); and K.-C. Tan, 'The Duty to Protect', in T. Nardin and M.S. Williams (eds.), *Humanitarian Intervention, NOMOS* XLVII (New York University Press, 2006), 84, at 96–101.

for action: at the point where states (and other institutional agents) each have a duty to contribute to establishing an informal association; and at the point where the members of the resulting coalition each have a duty to consider, to coordinate, and – if viable – to participate in a response.[88] It is notable that an appeal to capacity thus understood entails neither a problematic reliance on a single, powerful, and potentially over-burdened 'agent of last resort', nor the risk of ineffectiveness and charges of illegitimacy that might accompany unilateral action. Rather, such an appeal points most convincingly to multilateral action.

Moreover, within the 'random collection' that is the international community, there will be institutional agents with assumed, role-dependent and, perhaps, community-based special responsibilities to protect particular vulnerable populations.[89] These agents might thereby be identified amongst the wider aggregate of those who each bear a shared responsibility to protect such populations as carrying a heavier burden – in terms of a greater expectation to act or to contribute to the costs of collective action. Finally, one might consider the possibility that certain agents have contributed in various ways and to various degrees to creating the crisis in question. This possibility cautions against taking the analogy with Held's scenario to imply that all states and other agents in world politics confronted with the problem of vulnerable populations at risk from their own governments are merely innocent bystanders.[90] Some members of the international community are *culpable* bystanders – not direct participants in the atrocity to be prevented or mitigated, but blameworthy to some degree for the context in which it is possible.[91] We

[88] On the former point, May makes the case that a leadership capacity should bolster our moral expectations of a particular agent when a group needs to be established in order to discharge a duty. See May, *Sharing Responsibility*, n. 85, at 114.

[89] An intriguing proposal for designated states to assume special responsibilities to intervene to protect particular populations if they should ever require it is made by Buchanan and Keohane in 'Precommitment Regimes for Intervention', n. 32. Special responsibilities that attach to 'institutionally specified roles' are usefully discussed by M.O. Hardimon in 'Role Obligations' (1994) 91(7) JP 333. For an account of community ties and relationships giving rise to special responsibilities, see Miller, 'Distributing Responsibilities', n. 87, at 462–463; and S. Scheffler, *Boundaries and Allegiances: Problems of Justice and Responsibility in Liberal Thought* (Oxford University Press, 2001), at 97–110.

[90] I am grateful to Richard Jackson for making this point when I presented this argument at the OCIS conference in Sydney in July 2012.

[91] France's alleged culpability for events leading up to the Rwandan genocide comes to mind, for example. See D. Kroslak, 'The Responsibility of Collective External Bystanders in Cases of Genocide: the French in Rwanda', in Erskine (ed.), *Can Institutions Have Responsibilities?*, n. 4, 159.

might place added weight on their existing responsibility to contribute to remedial collective action – and also apportion to them an added burden of blame if no action is taken.

Crucially, the argument defended in this chapter stipulates that these factors (however defined and negotiated), and any resulting proposal for a differential allocation of burdens amongst the existing or potential members of a coalition of the willing, can neither eclipse nor extinguish the enduring shared responsibility borne by each member of the international community to ensure, in the absence of a viable alternative, that an informal association is established and acts to protect a vulnerable population from immediate danger. After all, precisely those situations in which agents who are expected to fill certain roles, perform particular tasks, and shoulder specific burdens manifestly fail to do so prompted this discussion in the first place. Each member of the international community has a shared responsibility to support both a collectivisation process and the collective endeavour the resulting informal association makes possible when such expectations are not met.

5.3 *Accompanying (on-going and long-term) responsibilities*

None of this is to say, however, that all moral responsibilities are somehow discharged when an ad hoc group of agents comes together and acts in concert to respond to a crisis in the absence of a viable alternative. Here it might be useful to return, again, to Held's example of the victim of the collapsing building. Even if individual actors have an immediate responsibility to form a temporary, informal association, and cooperate in order to save a victim facing a profound threat, such emergency measures, and even their possible success, do not mitigate the ongoing and long-term responsibilities both to create the conditions conducive to avoiding this sort of accident in the first place (by promoting the construction of safe buildings), and to ensure that a more suitable agent is in place to respond (by establishing robust and reliable emergency services). In the international realm, alongside the immediate – and transient – imperative that institutional agents act in concert when faced with a grave crisis that would otherwise be unattended, it is necessary to recognise the ongoing prospective moral responsibilities both to create an environment in which such crises are prevented and to build and bolster formal 'agents of justice' with the will, resources, and procedures in place to act.

This final moral responsibility is crucial because the informal associations that satisfy the immediate imperative are, in many ways, imperfect alternatives. Informal associations such as coalitions of the willing may be capable of joint purposive action, and may even boast a speed and flexibility in responding to crises that some formal organisations (such as the UN) lack when their rigid, formal decision-making structures are slow to arrive at a course of action or result in stalemate. However, these associations also have limits. Unlike (effectively functioning) structured institutions, they have neither the potentially sophisticated capacity for deliberation manifest in highly developed mechanisms for accessing and processing information, nor the capacity for institutional learning whereby an organisation is able to reflect on past experiences (and the consequences of previous acts and omissions) in a way that allows calculated revisions to policies, practice, codes of conduct and organisational culture.[92] Nor is there the same potential within such informal associations to integrate coherently the roles of their constituents and thereby achieve a comparably complex level of coordinated action. Accordingly, both individual human and institutional moral agents also have an obligation to create, empower or reform those formal organisations best able to respond to crisis so that such ad hoc arrangements do not exhaust our options in the future.

6. Conclusion

Coalitions of the willing *cannot* coherently be considered bearers of duties. Our calls to action and cries of condemnation in the wake of action that is stalled, ineffective, or deemed unjust must be directed instead towards the states, non-state actors, and intergovernmental organisations that variously constitute (or could constitute) them. And, even while such statements of moral responsibility are reasonably directed towards the members (or potential members) of these ad hoc associations, our attention should also remain focused on reforming and enabling the formal organisations for which coalitions of the willing act as either necessary supplements or, more controversially, unauthorised substitutes. Yet, these are only some of the conclusions that follow from

[92] I argue that this capacity for 'institutional learning' results from the combination of an established decision-making procedure and an identity over time in formal organisations that meet the criteria for institutional moral agency. See Erskine, *Locating Responsibility: Institutional Moral Agency and International Relations*, n. 3, chapter 5.

the preceding argument. It has also yielded a more nuanced account of moral responsibility in relation to informal associations in world politics than the model of institutional moral agency could hope to offer on its own. This account, in turn, has far-reaching implications for our responses to practical problems, such as how to make sense of the widely accepted, and detrimentally vague, claim that 'the international community' has a moral responsibility to respond to mass atrocities, and how to organise ourselves to discharge this collective commitment.

Informal associations (which lack established organisational structures and decision-making procedures) do not qualify as institutional moral agents and cannot bear moral burdens at a corporate level. This judgement is important. However, the proposed model of institutional moral agency dismisses these types of collectivity too quickly with such a stark assessment and, therefore, fails to address important problems of moral responsibility in world politics. Fortunately, the same model allows us to understand certain bodies in world politics as themselves constituted by institutional moral agents. It thereby makes accessible valuable lessons from the work of philosophers such as Held and May, who focus on informal associations at the domestic level populated by their individual human counterparts.

Consideration of the work of Held and May helps us to identify two categories of collectivity that lack formal organisational structures and decision-making procedures: 'random collections' of agents that contingently share a time and place; and, associations made up of agents that share a common purpose and have developed an informal organisational structure and deliberative capacity in order to pursue it. Both are distinct from those formal organisations (such as the UN and NATO) that are themselves made up of institutional moral agents, and are at least conditionally capable of deliberation and action at the corporate level. While the members of the former are only able to achieve (very limited) joint action that does not require prior deliberation and special coordination, the constituents of the latter can realise more sophisticated forms of cooperation, or what I have labeled 'joint purposive action'.

The members of informal associations capable of joint purposive action can address injustices and respond to crises (and, indeed, produce harm) in ways that far surpass what they could each achieve if acting on their own. Our prescriptions and evaluations of their actions should thereby be different in significant ways to those that we would make if these agents were acting independently. In short, their enhanced capacities within these associations lead to magnified responsibilities on the part of each individual agent. Significantly, however, this argument does not support the simple conclusion that we should only have greater expectations of agents if and when they become members of such informal associations. (There could then be a perverse disincentive to form such associations in the face of crises.) When confronted with what is commonly held to be a duty-generating crisis, and in the absence of a viable alternative, our expectations should attach, in the short term, to those individual agents able to contribute to establishing the sort of informal association needed to discharge the duty. In the wake of duty-generating crises that were neither prevented nor mitigated, blame should be apportioned not only to those individual and institutional moral agents who caused harm (by acting maliciously, recklessly, or negligently), and to those individual and institutional agents who could have responded but did not, but also to those who failed to collectivise to create a temporary, informal, and arguably imperfect association necessary for urgent remedial action.

With respect to the hard case addressed in this chapter, this argument suggests that in order to discharge the responsibility to protect vulnerable populations in situations of gross human rights abuses, and in the absence of a single institutional agent willing and able to respond, individual states, non-state actors, and intergovernmental organisations each have a duty to contribute to establishing an informal association capable of joint purposive action and then to participate in an effective response. This conclusion will understandably raise a number of concerns, particularly when we are talking about vigilante coalitions of the willing. Primary among these concerns must be whether the imperative that agents contribute to such informal associations can be appropriated as a convenient cover for some to circumvent intergovernmental organisations (and international law) for their own advantage – in other words, to surreptitiously bypass the UN as the designated 'custodian of collective legitimacy'.[93]

I do not deny that this can be – and has been – a motivation for establishing such associations. Nevertheless, if the value of such informal, collective action is brought out of the shadows cast by denial and wishful thinking (manifest in the mythical abilities of the so-called international community, or misplaced confidence in a frequently weak and constrained UN), and if the vigilante coalition of the willing is acknowledged

[93] This phrase is taken from I.L. Claude Junior, 'Collective Legitimisation as a Political Function of the UN' (1966) 20 IO 267.

as an alternative that is sometimes *necessary* when designated 'agents of justice' are unwilling or unable to respond, then explicit guidelines can be set regarding the conditions under which such collective action is genuinely required. Important questions of what these guidelines should look like, which amongst a multitude of duty-bearing institutional agents should be identified to come together and act in concert in a particular case and according to what criteria, and how ensuing tasks and costs are to be distributed, necessarily follow. By proposing that the nature of informal associations, such as coalitions of the willing, should profoundly affect our prescriptions and evaluations of the acts and omissions of their constituents (and potential constituents), this chapter aims both to offer a more demanding account of moral responsibility in relation to such entities in world politics and to set the stage for these crucial, further questions.

9

Distributing the Responsibility to Protect

MONICA HAKIMI*

1. Introduction

Over the past several decades, the central focus of international law has shifted from protecting only sovereign states to protecting individuals.[1] Still, the worst imaginable human rights abuses – genocides, ethnic cleansings, crimes against humanity, and systemic war crimes – occur with alarming frequency. And the international response is often slow or ineffectual.

The most recent development for addressing this problem is the 'responsibility to protect', an idea that has received so much attention that it now goes simply by R2P. R2P stands for two basic propositions.[2] First, each state must protect its population from atrocities. This proposition is well established in international law, but experience demonstrates that states sometimes fail their own populations. R2P's key innovation is its second proposition: that the broader international community should step in, when necessary, to help at-risk populations. Unlike the first proposition, the second one is widely understood not to be legally operative.[3] And the extent to which it otherwise influences states is, at best, speculative and contested.[4]

* Professor of Law and the Associate Dean for Academic Programming, University of Michigan Law School. This chapter is derived from an article that was originally published as M. Hakimi, 'Toward a Legal Theory on the Responsibility to Protect' (2014) 39 YJIL 241.

[1] See, e.g., R. Teitel, *Humanity's Law* (Oxford University Press, 2011), at 9, 37.

[2] See, e.g., International Commission on Intervention and State Sovereignty (ICISS), 'Report on the Responsibility to Protect' UN Doc. A/57/303 (2001), Annex, paras. 2.30–2.31 (ICISS Report); UN Secretary-General, 'Implementing the Responsibility to Protect', UN Doc. A/63/677 (12 January 2009), para. 11.

[3] See, e.g., G. Evans and R. Thakur, 'Correspondence, Humanitarian Intervention and the Responsibility to Protect' (2013) 37 IS 199, at 205; C. Stahn, 'Responsibility to Protect: Political Rhetoric or Emerging Legal Norm?' (2007) 101 AJIL 99, at 109.

[4] Compare, e.g., A.J. Bellamy and P.D. Williams, 'The new politics of protection? Côte d'Ivoire, Libya and the responsibility to protect' (2011) 87 IA 825, at 826: arguing that R2P

Part of R2P's challenge is conceptual. The United Nations (UN) and almost all of the scholarly literature support a particular vision for R2P – of outside states banding together and doing everything possible to help at-risk populations. R2P is said to fall simultaneously on all outside states or to favour their collective action. As for what these states should do, the possibilities are almost endless. R2P emerged from the debate on humanitarian interventions and has always been associated with the use of force. A forcible intervention might be the only way to avert ongoing atrocities. But R2P has never been exclusively about forcible interventions. Recently, the conversation about R2P within the UN has shifted to the varied non-forcible and proactive measures for trying to prevent atrocities from breaking out.[5] Such measures include, for example, programmes to build domestic institutions or alleviate internal tensions. In the end, then, the vision for R2P that dominates current thinking is incredibly diffuse and open-ended.[6]

This chapter critiques that vision and offers an alternative. I argue that R2P should not posit an all-encompassing duty that falls, at once, on the entire international community. It should instead posit a bundle of more discrete duties, and responsibility for each of these duties should attach to specific outside states at a time.[7] In particular, an outside state should be

has helped shape a 'new politics of protection' that might affect the response to particular crises; with S. Mohamed, 'Shame in the Security Council' (2013) 90 Wash LR 1191, at 1251: doubting that 'shaming based on the notion of a responsibility to protect yields productive results'; and D. Rieff, 'R2P, R.I.P', Op-Ed., *New York Times*, 7 November 2011: arguing that using R2P to justify regime change in Libya delegitimised the concept and damaged its 'prospects of becoming a global norm'.

[5] UN Secretary-General, 'Responsibility to Protect: State Responsibility and Prevention', UN Doc. A/67/929 (9 July 2013), paras. 30–64; UNSG, 'Implementing the Responsibility to Protect', n. 2, para. 44.

[6] See, e.g., A.J. Bellamy, 'The Responsibility to Protect – Five Years On' (2010) 24 EIA 143, at 144: 'profound disagreements persist about the function, meaning, and proper use of R2P.'; H. Cuyckens and P. De Man, 'The Responsibility to Prevent: On the Assumed Legal Nature of Responsibility to Protect and its Relationship with Conflict Prevention', in J. Hoffman and P.A. Nollkaemper (eds.), *Responsibility to Protect: From Principle to Practice* (Amsterdam University Press, 2012), 111, at 111: describing 'a conceptual entanglement that significantly compounds the practical operationalisation of the RtoP concept'.

[7] Some philosophers have argued that a moral duty to intervene militarily can fall on specific outside states. See, e.g., J. Pattison, *Humanitarian Intervention and the Responsibility to Protect: Who Should Intervene?* (Oxford University Press, 2010), 182; L. Glanville, 'On the Meaning of "Responsibility" in the "Responsibility to Protect"' (2011) 20 Grif LR 482, at 494–496. My vision builds on that philosophical argument but differs from it in two respects. First, I focus on legal, not moral, duties. Second, I focus on duties that do not involve the use of armed force.

responsible as a result of its own conduct or relationships. This vision for R2P is preferable to the one that now dominates R2P thinking because this vision builds on existing international law. International law has already begun to assign states duties for the benefit of foreign populations, and the current trajectory is to continue expanding these duties. The duties are legally operative, however, only when responsibility can be pinned on particular states at a time.

My goal in this chapter is to offer a framework for refining the R2P idea – that is, for identifying when atrocities do or should trigger an outside state's responsibility. Rooting this framework in international law, as opposed to in mere policy proposals, might be beneficial for two reasons. First, because international law has already begun to account for the interests that animate R2P, existing legal arrangements have descriptive and predictive value for R2P. They shed light both on the extent to which global actors already support R2P and on the prospects for success going forward. Second, tethering R2P to international law might make it more effective. International law might help broaden R2P's base of support, influence the behaviour of outside states, or legitimise efforts to hold particular outside states responsible.[8]

Because I focus on states' legal duties, I do not address the right to use armed force for humanitarian purposes. Though outside states sometimes have that right,[9] any duty to use armed force would be completely out of touch with current expectations. First, the duty would be extraordinarily onerous if it were assigned to only one or a small handful of states. Second, international law never requires – and is skittish even about permitting – cross-border violence.[10] Still, states might have to use other levers of power, like economic or diplomatic measures, to benefit a foreign population. These other measures might be less effective than force at averting a particular crisis, but they also are less burdensome for the acting state and less intrusive on the territorial state. As such, an

[8] An extensive literature now examines the mechanisms by which international law might influence states' human rights practices. See, e.g., B.A. Simmons, *Mobilizing for Human Rights: International Law in Domestic Politics* (New York: Cambridge University Press, 2009), 357; and R. Goodman and D. Jinks, 'How to Influence States: Socialization and International Human Rights Law' (2004) 54 DLJ 621.

[9] Although international lawyers debate whether outside states may use military force for humanitarian ends without the UN Security Council's authorisation, states clearly have this right when they act pursuant to such authorisation. Charter of the United Nations, San Francisco, 26 June 1945, in force 24 October 1945, 1 UNTS 16 (UN Charter), ch. VII.

[10] Article 2(4) UN Charter, ibid.

outside state might realistically be expected to take these measures even if it would rather not.

Before I proceed, one note about terminology might be helpful. The R2P literature uses the word 'responsibility' to suggest some kind of moral or legal duty. However, as André Nollkaemper and Dov Jacobs explain in their concept paper, international law usually uses 'responsibility' as a term of art not for the duty itself but for the consequence of not satisfying a duty; a state that violates a duty is responsible for that violation.[11] I use 'responsibility' in this latter sense. Nevertheless, I use 'R2P' for the idea that states should protect at-risk populations.

2. The unfulfilled promise of collective duties

Almost all of the R2P literature envisions outside states implementing R2P collectively – by banding together to help at-risk populations. This vision drives even the language that is used to articulate R2P. R2P's burdens are said to fall first on the territorial state and then on the international community as a whole. Two kinds of legal claims support this vision. One is that an R2P duty falls simultaneously on all outside states, such that they all must satisfy the same basic standard in any R2P scenario. To use the concept paper's terminology, this claim is for states' *shared* responsibility: responsibility would be pinned on every state that does too little for the at-risk population. The second claim is for states' *collective* responsibility: responsibility for not satisfying a duty would fall not on states themselves but on their collective organisations, like the UN. Neither of these claims on R2P is likely to gain legal traction in the near term.

2.1 Assigning R2P to all outside states simultaneously

The claim that R2P demands action by all outside states simultaneously has some authoritative support but remains almost entirely aspirational. This claim treats all outside states as if they are in the same boat; none is uniquely obligated to help the at-risk population or responsible when that population suffers. As David Miller has explained, 'an undistributed duty ... to which everybody is subject is likely to be discharged by nobody unless it can be allocated in some

[11] P.A. Nollkaemper and D. Jacobs, 'Shared Responsibility in International Law: A Conceptual Framework' (2013) 34 MIJIL 359, at 365.

way'.[12] To appreciate the problem, consider three discrete contexts in which the claim appears, plus evidence that it is inoperative.

First, the 1949 Geneva Conventions require states to 'ensure respect' for the Conventions 'in all circumstances'.[13] This language is widely interpreted to mean that every party must try to avert ongoing war crimes, no matter where or by whom the crimes are committed.[14] State officials verbally endorse that interpretation[15] but regularly ignore it in practice.[16] Moreover, states that stand by in the face of ongoing war crimes are rarely, if ever, held responsible.[17]

Second, the Articles on State Responsibility, which the International Law Commission (ILC) adopted in 2001,[18] aim to identify when states are responsible for violating international law and what follows from these violations. The ILC spent decades developing the Articles and, from early on, sought to attach special consequences to especially egregious violations. In the end, the Articles declare that all '[s]tates shall cooperate

[12] D. Miller, *National Responsibility and Global Justice* (Oxford University Press, 2007), 98; see also A.J. Bellamy, 'Conflict Prevention and the Responsibility to Protect' (2008) 14 Glob Gov 135, at 147.

[13] Geneva Convention for the Amelioration of the Condition of the Wounded and Sick in Armed Forces in the Field, Geneva, 12 August 1949, in force 21 October 1950, 75 UNTS 31 (First Geneva Convention), Article 1; Geneva Convention for the Amelioration of the Condition of Wounded, Sick and Shipwrecked Members of Armed Forces at Sea, Geneva, 12 August 1949, in force 21 October 1950, 75 UNTS 85 (Second Geneva Convention), Article 1; Geneva Convention relative to the Treatment of Prisoners of War, Geneva, 12 August 1949, in force 21 October 1950, 75 UNTS 135 (Third Geneva Convention), Article 1; Geneva Convention relative to the Protection of Civilian Persons in Time of War, Geneva, 12 August 1949, in force 21 October 1950, 75 UNTS 287 (Fourth Geneva Convention), Article 1 (collectively 1949 Geneva Conventions).

[14] J.-M. Henckaerts and L. Doswald-Beck, International Committee of the Red Cross, *Customary International Humanitarian Law* (New York: Oxford University Press, 2005), 509; G. Gaja, 'Do States Have a Duty to Ensure Compliance with Obligations *Erga Omnes* by Other States?', in M. Ragazzi (ed.), *International Responsibility Today: Essays in Memory of Oscar Schachter* (Leiden: Brill Publishing, 2005), 31, at 33–34.

[15] See the customary international humanitarian law database of the International Committee of the Red Cross (ICRC), Rule 144 at www.icrc.org/customary-ihl/eng/docs/v2_rul_rule144 (last accessed in July 2014).

[16] See, e.g., International Committee of the Red Cross, 'Improving Compliance with International Humanitarian Law: ICRC Expert Seminars' (October 2003), at 3–8; C. Focarelli, 'Common Article 1 of the 1949 Geneva Conventions: A Soap Bubble?' (2010) 21 EJIL 125.

[17] See, e.g., T. Pfanner, 'Various Mechanisms and Approaches for Implementing International Humanitarian Law and Protecting and Assisting War Victims' (2009) 91 IRRC 279, at 305–306.

[18] Articles on Responsibility of States for Internationally Wrongful Acts, ILC *Yearbook* 2001/II(2) (ARSIWA).

to bring to an end ... serious breach[es]' of peremptory norms.[19] The category of peremptory norms is notoriously indeterminate but, by all accounts, includes mass atrocities.[20] Thus, any duty to cooperate on peremptory norms should come into play in scenarios that implicate R2P.

Yet the ILC's Articles do not even try to identify the conduct that would satisfy a duty to cooperate – or, therefore, when a state might be responsible for not cooperating. Though the ILC posits that cooperation can be 'non-institutionalized', it clearly assumes that most cooperation will occur through international organisations.[21] The ILC does not identify what states must do in these organisations, other than simply participate.[22] More significantly, the ILC acknowledges that any duty to cooperate to end violations of peremptory norms might still be aspirational and not (yet) effective law.[23]

Finally, in its 2008 judgment in the *Genocide* case, the International Court of Justice (ICJ or Court) determined that the Genocide Convention[24] obligates states to try to avert genocidal conduct in and by third states.[25] This interpretation is progressive and potentially far-reaching. It arguably requires every party to the Convention to act in the face of genocide. After all, every party has the same obligation under the Convention's text. However, the ICJ limited that expansive implication. The Court explained that the duty to prevent genocide requires different measures of each state, depending on that state's particular tools for addressing a crisis.[26] As a practical matter, an outside state that lacks

[19] Commentary to the Articles on Responsibility of States for Internationally Wrongful Acts, ILC *Yearbook* 2001/II(2) (ARSIWA Commentary), Commentary to Articles 1–2.

[20] Ibid., Commentary to Article 40 ARSIWA, paras. 2–6; A. Orakhelashvili, *Peremptory Norms in International Law* (New York: Oxford University Press, 2006), at 50–66.

[21] ARSIWA Commentary, n. 19, Article 41 ARSIWA, para. 2; see also N.H.B. Jørgensen, 'The Responsibility to Protect and the Obligations of States and Organisations under the Law of International Responsibility', in J. Hoffman and P.A. Nollkaemper (eds.), *Responsibility to Protect: From Principle to Practice* (Amsterdam University Press, 2012), 125, at 129.

[22] ARSIWA Commentary, n. 19, Article 41, para. 2.

[23] Ibid., Article 41, para. 3.

[24] Convention on the Prevention and Punishment of the Crime of Genocide, Paris, 9 December 1948, in force 12 January 1951, 78 UNTS 277 (Genocide Convention).

[25] *Application of the Convention on Prevention and Punishment of Crime of Genocide (Bosnia and Herzegovina* v. *Serbia and Montenegro)*, Judgment, ICJ Reports 2007, 43, para. 438 (*Genocide* case). Serbia inherited this case when the Federal Republic of Yugoslavia (FRY) dissolved. Although the Court assessed the conduct of the FRY, not of Serbia as such, I use 'Serbia' interchangeably with the 'FRY' for ease of reference.

[26] *Genocide* case, ibid., para. 430.

any nexus to or mechanisms for averting a crisis might not have to do anything at all.[27] The claim that every state must try to avert genocide seems more expansive than the ICJ's own interpretation and is, in any event, unsupported by state practice. Here again, the claim that a legal duty attaches to all outside states simultaneously is inoperative.

2.2 *Assigning R2P to international organisations*

An alternative claim seeks to attach the R2P duty not to individual states but rather to their collective organisations. The claim that international organisations must implement R2P is usually directed at the UN Security Council (Council) and reflects, at least in part, R2P's historic association with the use of force.[28] Some have argued for requiring the Council to act in humanitarian crises,[29] or for restricting the use of the veto in such cases.[30] Yet the R2P claim against international organisations is not directed exclusively at the Council. For instance, the UN Secretary-General has identified varied proactive measures that different kinds of organisations might coordinate or implement.[31]

The claim that an R2P duty attaches to international organisations is likely to confront serious hurdles in the near term. First, the UN Security Council and its regional analogues are run by states. If R2P duties are not functional when they demand that all outside states act simultaneously, why would the duties become functional simply by demanding that states act through collective organisations? The demand on any particular state

[27] But cf. *The Netherlands* v. *Hasan Nuhanović*, ECLI:NL:HR:2013:BZ9225 (Supreme Court of the Netherlands, 6 September 2013), finding that Dutch peacekeepers unlawfully evicted from their base Bosnian men who were later killed in Srebrenica.

[28] For the argument that regional organisations should have a residual duty that kicks in if the Security Council does not act, see ICISS Report, n. 2, paras. 6.28, 6.31–6.35; and K.M. Haugevik, 'Regionalising the Responsibility to Protect: Possibilities, Capabilities and Actualities' (2009) 1 GR2P 346, at 350–351.

[29] See, e.g., UN Secretary-General, 'We the Peoples: The Role of the United Nations in the 21st Century', UN Doc. A/54/2000 (27 March 2000), para. 219; ICISS Report, n. 2, para. 6.24; L. Arbour, 'The Responsibility to Protect as a Duty of Care in International Law and Practice' (2008) 34 RIS 445, at 454.

[30] See, e.g., UNSG 'Implementing the Responsibility to Protect', n. 2, para. 61; ICISS Report, n. 2, para. 6.21; A. Blätter and P.D. Williams, 'The Responsibility Not to Veto' (2011) 3 GR2P 301, at 313–320; A. Peters, 'Humanity as the A and Ω of Sovereignty' (2009) 20 EJIL 513, at 539.

[31] UNSG, 'Implementing the Responsibility to Protect', n. 2, paras. 28–48; see also A.J. Bellamy, 'Making RtoP a Living Reality: Reflections on the 2012 General Assembly Dialogue on Timely and Decisive Response' (2013) 5 GR2P 109, at 122–124.

would still be diluted, both because of the number of states involved and because holding particular states responsible would mean piercing the organisation's veil.

Second, the relevant bodies in these organisations are, at bottom, political bodies. They have broad discretion to decide whether and how to help at-risk populations, and they ultimately may decide to do nothing.[32] This does not mean that international organisations may do whatever they please. For example, the UN Security Council is generally expected to account for human rights interests when it makes decisions.[33] But the Council has considerable discretion to weigh those interests against the countervailing considerations that favour or disfavour a particular decision.[34] Proposals to further constrain the Council's discretion,[35] including proposals on R2P,[36] have had little success. The idea that the Council is obligated to respond to humanitarian crises is, in José Alvarez's words, 'absurdly premature and not likely to be affirmed by state practice.'[37]

Third, even if international organisations had an R2P duty, the extent to which the duty could meaningfully be enforced is unclear. International organisations are rarely held responsible for international legal violations.[38] Part of the reason for the dearth of relevant practice is that

32 N. Krisch, 'Article 39', in B. Simma et al. (eds.), *The Charter of the United Nations: A Commentary*, 3rd edn (Oxford University Press, 2012), 1272, at 1275–1276.

33 N. Krisch, 'Article 41', in *The Charter of the United Nations: A Commentary*, ibid., 1305, at 1317: 'the [Security Council] has recognized that, when taking action under Art. 41, it is bound to take into account the humanitarian consequences and human rights implications'.

34 N. Krisch, 'Introduction to Chapter VII: The General Framework', in *The Charter of the United Nations: A Commentary*, n. 32, 1237, at 1258.

35 See, e.g., B. Fassbender, *UN Security Council Reform and the Right of Veto: A Constitutional Perspective* (New York: Springer, 1998), 263–275 (describing proposals to constrain the veto); I. Johnstone, 'Legislation and Adjudication in the UN Security Council: Bringing Down the Deliberative Deficit' (2008) 102 AJIL 275, at 303–307 (arguing for a set of procedural reforms to decrease the Council's 'deliberative deficit' and increase its legitimacy).

36 See, e.g., ICISS Report, n. 2, paras. 6.13–6.27.

37 J.E. Alvarez, 'The Schizophrenias of R2P', in P. Alston and E. MacDonald (eds.), *Human Rights, Intervention, and the Use of Force* (New York: Oxford University Press, 2008), 272, at 275, 282.

38 Commentary to the Articles on the Responsibility of International Organizations, ILC Report on the work of its sixty-third session, UNGAOR 66th Sess., Supp. No. 10, UN Doc. A/66/10 (2011) (ARIO Commentary), Commentary to Article 2, para. 5: '[o]ne of the main difficulties in elaborating rules concerning the responsibility of international organizations is due to the limited availability of pertinent practice'. Note that the United

international and national courts commonly lack jurisdiction over claims against international organisations.[39] However, even the more informal enforcement tools that are used against scofflaw states – like countermeasures or verbal denunciations – might be maladapted for international organisations.[40] International organisations are likely to be less responsive to such enforcement than are individual states because international organisations are more diverse and less unified. A claimant who tries to enforce an R2P duty against an organisation presumably would have to convince many states, not just one, to take that duty seriously.

3. The potential of individual duties

The claim that outside states should together implement R2P translates poorly to international law. No matter whether the claim is directed at all outside states simultaneously or at states' collective organisations, it is unlikely to garner support from international law. Instead, R2P should offer a framework for obligating and then holding responsible *particular* outside states. Each state should have multiple, discrete duties relating to R2P. And in any given case, responsibility for one or another duty should attach to the state or small handful of states that, because of their own conduct or relationships, have unique ties to the situation. This alternative vision for R2P is appealing because it is already rooted in international law and thus has the potential to gain traction going forward.

Nations sometimes compensates states or individuals for particular kinds of harms, but when it makes such payments, it typically preserves its discretion not to make them and denies that they are legally required. See Secretary-General's Bulletin: 'Financial Regulations and Rules of the United Nations', Rule 105.12, UN Doc. ST/SGB/2003/7 (9 May 2003); J.E. Alvarez, 'Revisiting the ILC's Draft Rules on International Organization Responsibility' (2011) 105 ASILP 344, at 347; A. Telestsky, 'Binding the United Nations: Compulsory Review of Disputes Involving UN International Responsibility Before the International Court of Justice' (2012) 21 Minn JIL 75, at 87–88.

[39] See A. Reinisch, 'Securing the Accountability of International Organizations' (2001) 7 Glob Gov 131, at 139–41. The jurisdictional limitations do not provide the full answer because third-party dispute resolution bodies sometimes have jurisdiction to adjudicate claims against international organisations. See, e.g., Agreement Between the United Nations and the United States of America Regarding the Headquarters of the United Nations, U.S.-UN, 26 June 1947, approved by the UNGA on 31 October 1947, 61 Stat. 3416, Article 8, section 21(a); Convention on the Privileges and Immunities of the United Nations, New York, 13 February 1946, in force 17 September 1946, 1 UNTS 15, Article 8, section 30.

[40] See ARIO Commentary, n. 38, Article 51, paras. 4, 6.

Some readers might instinctively worry about encouraging outside states to act individualistically. Working through an international organisation or with other states can curb a state's opportunistic impulses or legitimise efforts to help the at-risk population. In contrast, acting alone gives the outside state more leeway to exploit its power for its own gains, to the potential detriment of the territorial state or population. This worry is understandable but should not be overstated. Outside states that want to act opportunistically may already do so.[41] They may take non-forcible measures, without going through an international organisation, to help at-risk populations. The question is when to convert that right into a duty – when to require outside states to take measures that they might otherwise forego. Any such duty could be crafted to lessen, rather than increase, the risk of individual states acting invidiously. For instance, certain R2P duties might kick in only after an outside state has inserted itself into a situation. Such duties might dissuade states from getting involved in the first place or might influence states that are involved to act benevolently.

Other readers might object that my vision is instead too cautious. The duties that exist or realistically might emerge in international law will sometimes be too weak to protect people from atrocities. The chances of success might be higher if states banded together, or if responsibility fell on states that were not already implicated in the situation by virtue of their own conduct or relationships. Yet the vision that I advance would establish only a floor – not necessarily a ceiling – of what outside states might do. States that want to do more always could. Further, even if R2P's legal articulation is limited in the ways that I suggest, its normative impulse and rhetoric might be available to advocate for more robust, discretionary, and collective action.

[41] International law differentiates between non-forcible measures that comply with an acting state's legal obligations and non-forcible measures that do not comply. Compliant measures are lawful. ARSIWA Commentary, n. 19, ch. II, para. 2. Non-compliant measures are usually unlawful but might be excused as countermeasures, if they are taken against a scofflaw state. In most circumstances, countermeasures are available only to states that have been specifically injured by the scofflaw's breach. But the weight of state practice suggests that, in cases involving especially egregious human rights violations, countermeasures are available to all states. See E.K. Proukaki, *The Problem of Enforcement in International Law* (London: Taylor and Francis, 2010), 204–207; C.J. Tams, *Enforcing Obligations Erga Omnes In International Law* (Cambridge University Press, 2005), 208–251.

3.1 *Theoretical foundations*

I turn, then, to demonstrating that this vision for R2P is rooted in existing international law. International law has two natural starting points for thinking about R2P duties: human rights law and the law on state responsibility. These two bodies of law provide a foundation for assigning states duties that benefit foreign populations, and then for allocating the associated responsibilities.

3.1.1 The seeds for crafting R2P duties

Human rights law and the law on state responsibility both seek to prescribe R2P-relevant conduct. Like R2P, human rights law is fundamentally concerned with protecting people from harm. This body of law recognises a broad range of rights – for instance, rights to life, liberty, health, and food.[42] It then assigns states three kinds of duties to help realise those rights.[43] *Duties to respect* are paradigmatic duties not to intrude on rights. For instance, a duty to respect the right to life prohibits states from arbitrarily killing people. A duty to respect the right to food prohibits states from intentionally starving people. *Duties to protect* require states to try to restrain third parties from violating rights. Protecting the right to life means taking reasonable steps – or as sometimes stated, exercising due diligence – to prevent murder. Depending on the circumstances, a duty-holding state might have to clamp down on gang-related violence or try to incapacitate someone who is about to detonate a bomb. Finally, *duties to fulfil* require states to help realise positive liberties. These duties are unlike the other two in that they do not assume a single, identifiable abuser. Fulfilling the right to life might mean guaranteeing emergency medical care or responding competently to a natural disaster.

That taxonomy of human rights duties is conceptually useful for R2P. It reminds us that one objective – like avoiding unnecessary losses of life – can justify multiple duties. States might have to achieve that objective in different ways. Moreover, disaggregating the objective might

[42] See, e.g., International Covenant on Civil and Political Rights, New York, 16 December 1966, in force 23 March 1976, 199 UNTS 171 (ICCPR); International Covenant on Economic, Social and Cultural Rights, New York, 16 December 1966, in force 3 January 1976, 993 UNTS 3 (ICESCR).

[43] See, e.g., O. De Schutter et al., 'Commentary to the Maastricht Principles on Extraterritorial Obligations of States in the Area of Economic, Social and Cultural Rights' (2012) 34 HRQ 1084, at 1090.

make it more manageable. Rather than establish one daunting duty to avoid unnecessary losses of life, human rights law establishes three more concrete duties. R2P would benefit from a similar approach. R2P is currently fashioned as an all-encompassing duty to protect – a duty to try to shield people from third-party atrocities. R2P might instead articulate a bundle of more discrete duties.

The question, then, is how to define those duties. Human rights law provides a potentially useful model for R2P but would have to be further developed to support R2P. As a matter of positive law, human rights law applies principally in a state's own territory, for the benefit of its own population.[44] The current trend is to expand the extraterritorial scope of application of human rights law.[45] Yet this trend is contested and deeply under-theorised.[46] Most decisions that apply human rights law extraterritorially do so by reference to state control. The more control a state exercises in an extraterritorial setting, the greater the likelihood that the state will be held to its human rights duties. But the relevant decisions lack a coherent account of when and why control matters.[47] These decisions vary on the kinds of extraterritorial control that trigger a state's human rights duties;[48]

[44] See, e.g., Article 2(1) ICCPR, n. 42; *Legal Consequences of Construction of Wall in Occupied Palestinian Territory*, Advisory Opinion, ICJ Reports 2004, 136, para. 109 (*Wall* advisory opinion); *Al-Skeini and others* v. *the United Kingdom*, App. No. 55721/07 (ECtHR, 7 July 2011), paras. 131–132.

[45] See M. Milanović, *Extraterritorial Application of Human Rights Treaties* (Oxford University Press, 2011), 1; J. Cerone, 'Jurisdiction and Power: The Intersection of Human Rights Law & the Law of Non-International Armed Conflict in an Extraterritorial Context' (2007) 40 Isr LR 396, at 431–436.

[46] See, e.g., Human Rights Committee, 'Second and Third Periodic Reports of the United States of America Submitted Under Article 40 of the Covenant on Civil and Political Rights', Annex I, UN Doc. CCPR/C/USA/3 (28 November 2005); Human Rights Committee, 'Information Received from the United Kingdom of Great Britain and Northern Ireland on the Implementation of the Concluding Observations of the Human Rights Committee', UN Doc. CCPR/C/GBR/CO/6/Add.1 (3 November 2009), para. 24.

[47] Milanović, Extraterritorial Application of Human Rights Treaties, n. 45, at 264.

[48] The question here is whether duties to respect *always* apply extraterritorially on the ground that a state is always presumed to control its own conduct. Compare, e.g., Human Rights Committee, *Delia Saldías de López* v. *Uruguay*, UN Doc. CCPR/C/13/D/52/1979 (29 July 1981), para. 12.3: 'A State party [may not] perpetrate violations ... on the territory of another State, which violations it could not perpetrate on its own territory'; and *Issa and others* v. *Turkey*, App. No. 31821/96 (ECtHR, 16 November 2004) (same); and *Alejandre and others* v. *Cuba*, Case 11.589, Inter-American Commission on Human Rights, Report No. 86/99, Case 11.589, OEA/Ser.L/V/II.106 doc. 6 rev. (1999), para. 25 (same); with, e.g., *Al-Skeini*, n. 44, para. 131: 'acts of the Contracting States performed ... outside their territories can [trigger human rights duties] only in exceptional cases'.

on whether factors other than control can trigger these duties;[49] and on whether the duties are always triggered simultaneously or can be triggered piecemeal, depending on the circumstances of a case.[50] Further, whatever the extraterritorial scope of a state's ordinary human rights duties, its R2P duties might be more expansive. Outside states might reasonably have more demanding duties in cases of atrocity. Indeed, the treaties that specifically regulate states on atrocities – the Geneva and Genocide Conventions – are widely understood *not* to be territorially limited.[51] Thus, R2P might build on human rights law but needs more conceptual work. R2P must justify assigning duties to outside states in cases of atrocity.[52]

Likewise, R2P might build on the law on state responsibility. Recall that the Articles on State Responsibility claim a unique enforcement duty – a duty to cooperate on enforcement – in cases of atrocity. Like R2P, this claim is motivated by the idea that some human rights violations are so egregious that they justify a serious response.[53] But alas, any duty to cooperate is not yet functional. The ILC could not identify the level or kind of cooperation that is required of outside states. Again, R2P must do its own conceptual work.

[49] Compare, e.g., C. Droege, 'The Interplay Between International Humanitarian Law and International Human Rights Law in Situations of Armed Conflict' (2007) 40 Isr LR 310, at 325–335: reviewing cases and concluding that 'the basic requirement for extraterritorial application ... is effective control, either over a territory or over a person'; with, e.g., *Victor Saldaño* v. *Argentina*, Petition, Inter-American Commission on Human Rights, Report No. 38/99, OEA/Ser.L/V/II.102 doc. 6 rev. (1998), para. 17: 'a state ... may be responsible under certain circumstances for the acts and omissions of its agents which produce effects ... outside that state's own territory', and De Schutter, 'Commentary to the Maastricht Principles on Extraterritorial Obligations of States in the Area of Economic, Social and Cultural Rights', n. 43, at 1149–1154: asserting that duties to fulfil apply extraterritorially on the basis of states' capacities.

[50] Compare, e.g., *Banković and others* v. *Belgium and 16 other states*, App. No. 52207/99 (ECtHR, 12 December 2001), para 65: asking about 'the scope and reach of the entire Convention system of human rights' protection', with, e.g., *Al-Skeini*, n. 44, para. 137: explaining that a state might have a duty to secure rights 'that are relevant to the situation of [a particular] individual', and that '[i]n this sense, ... the Convention rights can be "divided and tailored"'.

[51] Articles 2–3 of the 1949 Geneva Conventions, n. 13; *Genocide* case, n. 25, para. 183; and *Application of the Convention on Prevention and Punishment of Crime of Genocide (Bosnia and Herzegovina* v. *Serbia and Montenegro)*, Preliminary Objections, ICJ Reports 1996, 595, para. 31.

[52] M.E. Salomon, 'How to Keep Promises: Making Sense of the Duty Among Multiple States to Fulfil Socio-Economic Rights in the World', Chapter 13 in this volume, 366.

[53] See ARSIWA Commentary, n. 19, Article 12, para. 7.

3.1.2 The seeds for grounding R2P responsibilities

The human rights duties and the supposed duty to cooperate raise a follow-up question for my vision for R2P: if the duties go unsatisfied, when and why would particular outside states be responsible? The answer, I argue, must be extracted from the intersection between human rights law and the law on state responsibility. Under these two bodies of law, responsibility relating to human suffering stems from either the state's own misconduct, the state's unique relationship with the malfeasant, or a messy combination of both.

To start, consider a state's well established duty not to commit atrocities in its territory. A territorial state that commits atrocities violates this duty and is responsible. But of course, the state cannot itself commit atrocities; the state is just a concept. A more accurate formulation is that the state is responsible if *its agents* commit atrocities. That formulation highlights three important points relating to state responsibility. First, state responsibility results from the concurrent application of so-called primary rules and secondary rules. The primary rules in human rights law prescribe certain conduct. Secondary rules in the law on state responsibility identify whether that conduct is attributable to a state and, if so, what follows from a breach.

Second, as Nollkaemper and Jacobs demonstrate, the doctrinal distinction between the law's primary and secondary rules is not always crisp.[54] One set of rules sometimes turns on the other. For example, any duty to cooperate on enforcement under the law on state responsibility would kick in for only some primary rules – namely, the rules on peremptory norms. Likewise, the duty to respect in human rights law requires a state to prevent its agents from committing atrocities precisely because they are its agents – as defined by the secondary rules on state responsibility. Under the law on state responsibility, state agents have particular kinds of relationships with the state. State officials, of course, qualify as agents.[55] So do people who are not formally officials but nevertheless act on the state's behalf. For example, the Articles on State Responsibility posit that, when a state effectively controls someone's conduct, the person becomes an agent while committing that conduct.[56]

[54] Nollkaemper and Jacobs, 'Shared Responsibility in International Law: A Conceptual Framework', n. 11.

[55] ARSIWA Commentary to Article 4, n. 19.

[56] Ibid., Commentary to Article 8.

Third, a state is responsible for its agent's misconduct because the state is expected to oversee its agents and ensure that they behave. To be clear, the state is responsible even if it did not actually oversee or control a particular agent. Control over someone can create an agency relationship if that relationship does not otherwise exist,[57] but a lack of control over someone who already qualifies as an agent does not dissolve the agency relationship or relieve the state of responsibility.[58] The whole point of this responsibility regime is to encourage the state to establish control over its agents.

I have argued in another work that human rights duties to protect reflect a similar logic.[59] A state is not expected to oversee third parties – that is, people who are not its agents – to the same extent that it oversees its own agents. Consequently, a state is not responsible every time a third party violates rights. Duties to protect are due diligence duties, meaning that the state is responsible only if it (or more precisely, its agents) should have done more to restrain the third party. Moreover, whether a state should have made that effort depends largely on the nature of its relationship with the third party. A state must try to restrain third parties in its territory because of its governance relationship with those people. States exist, at least in part, to maintain order and enforce the law against inhabitants who might intrude on individual liberties.

I demonstrate later in this chapter that where international law already renders an *outside state* responsible for human suffering it likewise does so on the basis of the state's own conduct or relationships. These grounds for pinning responsibility on a state are in tension with two other grounds that appear in the R2P literature. First, most of the R2P literature assumes that all outside states are in the same boat – that none has a legally relevant nexus to the at-risk population that justifies holding it, but not all other outside states, responsible. In fact, outside states can be differently situated relative to the at-risk population. Some outside states might participate in or contribute to a humanitarian crisis, or might have

[57] Ibid.

[58] ARSIWA Commentary to Article 4, n. 19, para. 9: 'it is . . . irrelevant whether the internal law of the State in question gives the [State] power to compel the [agent] to abide by the State's international obligations'. Ibid., Article 5, para. 7: 'there is no need to show that the conduct was in fact carried out under the control of the State'; ibid., Article 7, para. 2: asserting that the state is responsible even where the agent 'has manifestly exceeded its competence'.

[59] M. Hakimi, 'State Bystander Responsibility' (2010) 21 EJIL 341.

a unique relationship with the perpetrators. These factors justify pinning responsibility on *those* outside states, even if not on all others.

Second, some have proposed grounding outside state responsibility in the state's positive capacity to help the at-risk population.[60] This proposal arguably finds support in the *Genocide* case. Recall that the ICJ interpreted the Genocide Convention to require outside states to try to prevent genocide. The ICJ then asserted that this duty is contingent on each state's 'capacity to influence' the perpetrators.[61] Yet the ICJ did not understand capacity to mean the state's overall military, financial, or diplomatic might. It understood capacity in relational terms:

> This capacity itself depends, among other things, on the geographical distance of the State concerned from the scene of the events, and on the strength of the political links, as well as links of all other kinds, between the authorities of that State and the main actors in the events. The State's capacity to influence must also be assessed by legal criteria, since it is clear that every State may only act within the limits permitted by international law; seen thus, a State's capacity to influence may vary depending on its particular legal position vis-à-vis the situations and persons facing the danger.[62]

The nature of the state's relationship with the perpetrators affects whether the state can and should exert its influence over them.

In the *Genocide* case, the ICJ was clearly focused on that relational question. The ICJ underscored that, even though the perpetrators were not Serb agents, they received immense guidance and support from Serbia.[63] Serbia's dubious conduct – its support for an armed group in another state – gave it a unique relationship with that group. Precisely for that reason, Serbia both could have and should have tried to restrain the group's members from committing genocide. Although the judgment used the word 'capacity', it provides at best mild support for grounding responsibility in a state's positive capacity to help. The judgment is instead consistent with my approach. Serbia's responsibility is justifiable because of a messy mix of its conduct and relationship with the Bosnian Serbs.

[60] See, e.g., Pattison, *Humanitarian Intervention and the Responsibility to Protect*, n. 7, at 182; Arbour, 'The Responsibility to Protect as a Duty of Care in International Law and Practice', n. 29, at 455.

[61] *Genocide* case, n. 25, para. 430. [62] Ibid.

[63] Ibid., paras. 422, 434–438; see also *Prosecutor* v. *Tadić*, Judgement, ICTY Case No. IT-94-1-A, 15 July 1999, para. 156.

In any event, grounding responsibility primarily in each state's positive capacity would be misguided. States that are especially capable would repeatedly carry a disproportionate R2P burden, even if their involvement in the situation would lack legitimacy, even if other states are also highly capable (but less so),[64] and even if those other states actually contributed to the problem. Moreover, grounding responsibility primarily in each state's positive capacity would absolve states that are incapable, rather than encourage these states to develop some capacity.[65] Of course, states *are* disparately capable and should not have to do more than they can reasonably bear. An outside state that cannot satisfy an R2P duty unless it abandons other, more important duties might have a more lenient R2P duty or be excused altogether from a particular duty. But if the vast majority of outside states can reasonably satisfy a duty, then their responsibility should not be allocated on the basis of their positive capacities.

3.2 Preliminary remarks on the R2P bundle

A foundation for outside state responsibility exists in international law but must be further developed to support R2P. In the subsections that follow, I outline four plausible bases for holding an outside state responsible. These four bases vary in the extent to which they are already established in international law. But each builds on the law's existing foundation and pins responsibility on particular outside states by virtue of their own conduct or relationships. To be clear, my goal here is not to review comprehensively the law on outside state responsibility. Neither is

[64] K.-C. Tan, 'The Duty to Protect', in T. Nardin and M.S. Williams (eds.), *Humanitarian Intervention: Nomos XLVII* (New York University Press, 2006), at 84, 102.

[65] Perhaps for these reasons, human rights bodies generally assume that states either have or can develop the capacity to secure basic rights, at least in their own territories. See, e.g., *Assanidze* v. *Georgia*, App. No. 71503/01 (ECtHR, 8 April 2004), para. 139: explaining that the territorial state's control over an autonomous republic created a 'presumption of competence'. Moreover, these bodies are generally unsympathetic to the idea that a state is absolved of its human rights duties by virtue of its incapacity. See, e.g., Human Rights Committee, 'Comments: United Republic of Tanzania', UN Doc. CCPR/79/Add.12 (28 December 1992), para. 5: emphasising that a reduction in available resources 'does not exempt the State party from the full and effective application of the Covenant'. Indeed, even the body that oversees the ICESCR, which expressly defines states' duties by reference their capacities, see ICESCR, n. 42, Article 2(1), assumes that all states can and must realise a minimum core of ICESCR rights. See Committee on Economic, Social and Cultural Rights, General Comment No. 3, 'The Nature of States Parties' Obligations', UN Doc. E/1991/23 (14 December 1990), para. 10 (CESCR General Comment 3).

it to endorse this particular bundle of duties, or even to suggest that every duty in this bundle is realisable. My goal is simply to show that my vision for R2P – which would establish multiple R2P duties and assign responsibility on the basis of each state's conduct or relationships – has roots in and can continue to build on international law.

3.2.1 Duty to respect

To begin, outside states might be responsible for participating in atrocities. This responsibility might seem obvious because it already has solid support in international law,[66] but it is completely absent from the R2P discourse. The R2P literature typically asserts a duty to respect only for the territorial state. The omission for other states might be an unfortunate oversight, or it might reflect a lingering discomfort with applying human rights duties extraterritorially. In either event, responsibility for participating in extraterritorial atrocities exists or could easily develop in international law. Indeed, it is difficult to imagine any state claiming a right to participate in atrocities just because it acts abroad.

3.2.2 Duty to protect

An outside state that does not itself participate in atrocities might have to try to restrain third-party participants; it might have an extraterritorial duty to protect. Such duties have already begun to emerge in international law. So far, they appear to be triggered by two kinds of relationships. First, an outside state that exercises governmental authority over an area might have to take measures to restrain the inhabitants from committing atrocities – as it would in its own territory.[67] The ICJ's *Armed Activities* decision is a case in point. The ICJ determined that Uganda had occupied portions of the Democratic Republic of the Congo (DRC) and, therefore, had 'to protect the inhabitants of the occupied territory against acts of violence, and not to tolerate such violence by any

[66] Articles 2–3 of the 1949 Geneva Conventions, n. 13: not limiting obligations geographically; *Application of the Convention on Prevention and Punishment of Crime of Genocide (Bosnia and Herzegovina* v. *Serbia and Montenegro)*, Preliminary Objections, n. 51, para. 31: finding that the obligations under the Genocide Convention are not geographically limited.

[67] Much of the legal literature articulates a slightly different proposition: that extraterritorial duties to protect are triggered by a state's physical control over foreign territory. I explain why that articulation is descriptively inaccurate and perhaps undesirable in Hakimi, 'Toward a Legal Theory on the Responsibility to Protect', n. *, at 270–271.

third party'.[68] An occupying state, by definition, exercises governmental authority over foreign inhabitants.[69] The fact that the state already exercises such authority justifies requiring it to exercise that authority *in a particular way* – to prevent the inhabitants from intruding on one another's rights.

Second, a state's extraterritorial duties to protect might be triggered if it substantially supports the third party that perpetrates atrocities. Recall that, in the *Genocide* case, the ICJ highlighted Serbia's support for the Bosnian Serbs who committed genocide. Serbia was responsible for not trying harder to prevent genocide. Similar relationships – in which a state gives a non-state group considerable support but does not actually participate in the group's conduct – are, unfortunately, common. In *Ilaşcu* v. *Moldova*, the European Court of Human Rights found that Russia had such a relationship with Moldovan groups that violated rights in Moldova; Russia was responsible.[70] In *Georgia* v. *Russia*, Georgia claimed that Russia likewise supported groups that violated rights in Georgia. The ICJ dismissed Georgia's case on jurisdictional grounds,[71] but an order on provisional measures suggested that, even if Russia did not control the groups' conduct so as to create an agency relationship and trigger a duty to respect, Russia should have satisfied a duty to protect.[72] It should have pressured the groups not to violate rights.

In short, certain kinds of relationships already seem to trigger extraterritorial duties to protect. An outside state might have these duties if it exercises governmental authority over or substantially supports the

[68] *Armed Activities on Territory of the Congo (Democratic Republic of the Congo* v. *Uganda)*, Judgment, ICJ Reports 2005, 168, para. 178.

[69] Article 42 of the Regulations concerning the Laws and Customs of War on Land, annexed to the Convention (IV) respecting the Laws and Customs of War on Land, The Hague, 18 October 1907, in force 26 January 1910, 1 Bevans 631.

[70] *Ilaşcu and others* v. *Moldova and Russia*, App. No. 48787/99 (ECtHR, 8 July 2004), paras. 392–394. The Court's justification for holding Russia responsible is unclear. The court sometimes suggested that Russia was responsible for the abuses themselves. See ibid., para. 393: 'there [was] a continuous and uninterrupted link of responsibility on the part of the Russian Federation'. But the Court also described the duty with language indicative of a duty to protect – i.e., as a duty that required the state to 'attempt to put an end to the . . . situation'. Ibid.

[71] *Application of the International Convention on the Elimination of All Forms of Racial Discrimination (Georgia* v. *Russian Federation)*, Preliminary Objections, ICJ Reports 2011, 70, paras. 156–185.

[72] *Application of the International Convention on the Elimination of All Forms of Racial Discrimination (Georgia* v. *Russian Federation)*, Provisional Measures, ICJ Reports 2008, 353, para. 149.

perpetrators. The state would be responsible in these circumstances if it failed to exercise due diligence to restrain the perpetrators. The diligence that is due would depend on the circumstances but might entail taking economic, diplomatic, or criminal measures against the perpetrators, or putting in place standards or processes that inhibit atrocities. A particular state would have to take those measures, even though other outside states would not, because the one already involved itself in the situation and entangled itself with the third party.

3.2.3 Duty not to obstruct

No matter whether a state must actively try to restrain a third-party perpetrator, it might be prohibited from obstructing the protective measures that third parties pursue. A duty not to obstruct is, at best, nascent in current practice and so lacks precise content. But in essence, such a duty would prohibit outside states from impeding measures to protect at-risk populations. Because states can reasonably disagree about which such measures are appropriate, a state that obstructs one measure might be responsible only if it does not pursue a meaningful alternative, or only if it cannot justify its obstruction by a sufficiently weighty countervailing interest.

A duty not to obstruct would build on two claims that have become quite prominent in the R2P literature: (1) the claim that states must cooperate to end violations of peremptory norms, and (2) the claim that the permanent members of the UN Security Council must not use their veto in R2P cases. First, a duty not to obstruct overlaps with the claimed duty to cooperate because, by definition, an obstructing state fails to cooperate. Still, the duty not to obstruct would be less onerous. An outside state would not have to take affirmative steps to cooperate; it simply would have to avoid getting in the way. Moreover, whereas not cooperating is often passive and pervasive, obstructing usually involves overt acts that can be identified and pinned on particular states. Second, a duty not to obstruct overlaps with the claimed duty not to veto. Using the veto might be obstructive; it might prevent the Council from acting to protect an at-risk population.[73] Yet the veto is only one of many ways in which states can act obstructively.

[73] See, e.g., Arbour, 'The Responsibility to Protect as a Duty of Care in International Law and Practice' n. 29, at 453: arguing for reassessing the use of the veto on the ground that states should 'cease inhibiting other states from discharging their duty to protect when those states are willing and able to discharge their obligations'.

The early stages of the recent crisis in Syria illustrate these points. In the UN Security Council, China and Russia repeatedly vetoed or threatened to veto resolutions that would have put pressure on the Assad regime.[74] This conduct might be evidence of obstruction but is not dispositive. States could reasonably disagree about what to do in Syria and, therefore, about the content of particular Security Council resolutions. Looking outside the Council reveals a broader pattern of obstructionism. China and Russia were consistently among a handful of states in the UN General Assembly[75] and Human Rights Council[76] that voted against resolutions condemning the Assad regime. These two states also declined to participate in multilateral meetings that sought to pressure Assad either to step down or to find a political solution to the crisis.[77] Further, although China and Russia largely synchronised their positions in multilateral arenas, Russia did more of the dirty work. For example, Russia repeatedly shipped military equipment to the regime even after its atrocities were apparent.[78] This broader pattern of behaviour suggests that China might have acted obstructively and that Russia very likely did.

The Syria case is also illustrative because it suggests that a duty not to obstruct might be developing informally. States and other actors persistently pressured Russia[79] and, to a lesser extent,

[74] See, e.g., UN SCOR, 67th Sess., 6810th meeting, UN Doc. S/PV.6810 (19 July 2012) (record of Council meeting at which Russia and China vetoed a draft resolution); UN SCOR, 67th Sess., 6711th meeting, UN Doc. S/PV.6711 (4 February 2012) (same).

[75] See, e.g., UN GAOR, 66th Sess., 124th plenary meeting, UN Doc. A/66/PV.124 (3 August 2012) (vote of 133-12-31); UN GAOR, 66th Sess., 97th plenary meeting, UN Doc. A/66/PV.97 (16 February 2012) (vote of 137-12-17).

[76] See, e.g., Human Rights Council Res. 21/26, 'Situation of Human Rights in the Syrian Arab Republic', 21st Sess., 28 September 2012, UN Doc. A/HRC/RES/21/26 (17 October 2012) (vote of 41-3-3); Human Rights Council Res. 20/22, 'Situation of Human Rights in the Syrian Arab Republic', 20th Sess., 6 July 2012, UN Doc. A/HRC/RES/20/22 (16 July 2012) (vote of 41-3-3).

[77] See, e.g., Ministry of Foreign Affairs of the Russian Federation, 'Comment of the Russian Foreign Ministry Spokesman Alexander Lukashevich in Relation to the Meeting of "Friends of Syria" in Paris' (6 July 2012), at www.mid.ru/bdomp/brp_4.nsf/e78a48070f128a7b43256999005bcbb3/462ce2c8456b8b1144257a38003006ef!OpenDocument: on Russia's and China's decisions not to attend the meeting in Paris, last accessed on 5 July 2014.

[78] See, e.g., M.R. Gordon and E. Schmitt, 'Russia Signals Syrian Support with Missiles', *New York Times*, 17 May 2013, at A1.

[79] E. Barry and R. Gladstone, 'Russia Says Syrian Plane Impounded by Turkey Had Radar Gear, Not Arms', *New York Times*, 13 October 2012, at A6: reporting on Turkey's confrontation with Russia concerning Russia's supplies to Syria; S. Erlanger, 'Merkel

China[80] to stop obstructing international action in Syria. Even if this pressure failed to yield any results, the fact that others applied the pressure suggests that they understood the two states, and especially Russia, to be acting reprehensibly. Further, the fact that these other actors pressured Russia and China, but not states that neither obstructed nor cooperated in any international action, demonstrates that a duty not to obstruct might gain traction even if a duty to cooperate cannot.

3.2.4 Duty to assist

Finally, outside states might have to help foster conditions that are inhospitable to atrocities. The nature of this assistance can vary, from transferring material resources, to training local actors, to rebuilding domestic institutions. Such assistance is similar in kind to that which satisfies human rights duties to fulfil. The R2P duty would differ from a duty to fulfil, however, because the R2P duty would focus on realising negative, not positive, liberties. The goal would be to shield people from third-party harms by reducing the risk of atrocities breaking out. Still, the hurdles that have confronted extraterritorial duties to fulfil would almost certainly confront the R2P duty, as well.

The claim that states must give foreign assistance to help people abroad has circulated for decades, usually in the context of pressuring developed states to alleviate severe poverty in developing states.[81] However, the claim is still of questionable authority and has not been

and Sarkozy Share Anger Over Syria Stalemate and Urgency Over Greece', *New York Times*, 7 February 2012, at A12: reporting that Western leaders publicly criticised Russia; R. Gladstone and A. Lowrey, 'Amid Reports of a New Massacre, Nations Seek to Step Up Pressure on Syria', *New York Times*, 7 June 2012, at A8: reporting on US pressure; N. Kulish and N. MacFarquhar, 'Putin Rejects Intervention But Fears Civil War in Syria', *New York Times*, 2 June 2012, at A8: reporting on French and German pressure; N. MacFarquhar, 'Residents Flee Damascus as Battle Enters its Fifth Day', *New York Times*, 20 July 2012: reporting on UK pressure.

80 J. Kanter, 'China Assures Europe on Debt Aid', *New York Times*, 21 September 2012, at A11: reporting on pressure from the European Union; S.L. Myers and J. Perlez, 'No Movement on Major Disputes as Clinton Meets with Chinese Leaders', *New York Times*, 6 September 2012, at A10: reporting on US pressure.

81 CESCR, 'General Comment No. 15 (2002): The Right to Water', UN Doc. E/C.12/2002/11 (20 January 2003), paras. 30, 34; Office of the UN High Commissioner for Human Rights, 'Report on the Relationship Between Climate Change and Human Rights', UN Doc. A/HRC/10/61 (15 January 2009), paras. 84–85. See also Salomon, 'How to Keep Promises: Making Sense of the Duty Among Multiple States to Fulfil Socio-Economic Rights in the World', n. 52, this volume.

especially effective in practice.[82] The ICJ recognised in its *Wall* advisory opinion that duties under the International Covenant on Economic, Social and Cultural Rights (ICESCR)[83] – which include duties to respect and protect but are paradigmatically duties to fulfil – are 'essentially territorial'.[84] Further, developed states have consistently resisted the idea that they are obligated to give foreign assistance.[85] Although these states sometimes endorse the idea that 0.7 percent of their gross domestic products ought to go to development aid, few states have actually achieved that goal.[86]

Aid for R2P looks a lot like human rights and development aid. For example, the UN Secretary-General has proposed using R2P aid to educate local actors about human rights, build domestic institutions, redress severe poverty, and enhance the positions of women and disadvantaged minorities.[87] These proposals are unlikely to gain legal traction simply by linking them to R2P. On the contrary, the experience with the UN Millennium Development Goals demonstrates that developed states resist the claim that foreign assistance is obligatory even when the underlying policy objectives have broad and high-level support. The hurdles to establishing an R2P duty to assist are, in the end, substantial.

For this duty to have any prospect of success, it must identify the grounds for holding specific tightfisted states responsible. Because an R2P duty to assist would entail redistributing wealth or expertise, it might account for states' positive capacities in ways that other R2P duties do not. Still, positive capacity is an insufficient basis for assigning responsibility. In any given case, many outside states that have the capacity to give will not. Responsibility should instead be grounded in

[82] De Schutter, 'Commentary to the Maastricht Principles on Extraterritorial Obligations of States in the Area of Economic, Social and Cultural Rights', n. 43, at 1094: 'disagreement persists as to the legally binding nature of the obligation of international cooperation as expressed in the [ICESCR]'.

[83] See n. 42. [84] *Wall* advisory opinion, n. 44, para. 112.

[85] See, e.g., Commission on Human Rights, 'Report of the Open-Ended Working Group to Consider Options Regarding the Elaboration of an Optional Protocol to the International Covenant on Economic, Social and Cultural Rights on its Second Session', UN Doc. E/CN.4/2005/52 (10 February 2005), para. 76; P. Alston, 'Ships Passing in the Night: The Current State of the Human Rights and Development Debate Seen Through the Lens of the Millennium Development Goals' (2005) 27 HRQ 755, at 777.

[86] See Millennium Development Goal (MDG) Gap Task Force Report 2012, 'MDG 8: The Global Partnership for Development: Making Rhetoric a Reality', at 10, Fig. 2, (UN, 2012).

[87] See UNSG, 'Implementing the Responsibility to Protect', n. 2, paras. 28–48: discussing proactive measures for satisfying R2P's objectives.

a state's own conduct or relationships. For example, an outside state might be responsible for not helping a population if the state contributed to the risk of atrocities breaking out or if the state has a unique relationship with the population, such as one rooted in a colonial past. The point is that grounding responsibility in the state's conduct or relationships is consistent with the law's theoretical foundations and thus a way to develop the law going forward.

4. Conclusion

This chapter has proposed a new vision for R2P and presented a rudimentary framework for implementing that vision. I have argued that R2P should not posit an all-encompassing duty that falls, at once, on the entire international community. R2P should instead posit a bundle of more discrete duties, and responsibility for each duty should attach to specific outside states at a time. This latter vision is appealing because it is anchored in existing international law and follows the law's current trajectory. As such, this vision has both descriptive and predictive value. It explains how international law already supports R2P and how international law might realistically develop to continue supporting R2P going forward.

Whether international law will actually develop along these lines is another question. States are highly unlikely to ratify a new treaty on R2P or to expand the jurisdiction of courts or other bodies that might develop and enforce new R2P duties. In the near term, any further prescription and enforcement on R2P is likely to occur informally – as states, international organisations, and civil society groups craft new norms on R2P and put pressure on states that deviate from those norms. These disparate actors might work together to articulate a set of non-binding norms on R2P. They might incorporate their preferred norms into official documents, like the UN Secretary-General's reports on R2P. And they might apply these norms to sanction particular outside states.

The informality of that process presents both an opportunity and a challenge for R2P. The opportunity is that global actors who are committed to R2P can apply and enforce their preferred duties, even absent a clear consensus on what the duties require or whether the duties qualify as law. In other words, they can use my framework to try to push the law in their preferred direction. This is also R2P's challenge. Operative R2P duties will not develop unless the commitment to them is sufficiently broad and deep that enough global actors decide either to satisfy the duties voluntarily or to enforce the duties against deviant states. That level of commitment might not exist. But if it does – and there is some reason for optimism – then R2P should offer a vision that resonates with different actors and can actually gain legal traction.

10

The Problem of Shared Irresponsibility in International Climate Law

DANIEL H. COLE*

1. Introduction

International climate governance represents a case of shared *ir*responsibility. The United Nations (UN) Framework Convention on Climate Change (UNFCCC),[1] the Kyoto Protocol,[2] and subsidiary agreements purport to establish both shared and common-but-differentiated responsibilities; yet the global community as a whole has yet to make credible and enforceable commitments that would actually accomplish the UNFCCC's stated goal of preventing 'dangerous anthropogenic interference with the climate system'.[3] At Cancun in 2010, the parties to the framework convention agreed that increases in global mean temperatures should be restricted to no more than 2° (Celsius) above pre-industrial levels,[4] which would require a reduction in annual global greenhouse gas (GHG) emissions of at least 80 per cent from 1990 levels by 2050.[5] However, the

* Professor of Law and of Public and Environmental Affairs at Indiana University Bloomington, Maurer School of Law and School of Public and Environmental Affairs; Affiliated Faculty Member, Vincent and Elinor Ostrom Workshop in Political Theory and Policy Analysis. Thanks are due to Scott Barrett, James Crawford, Giuseppe Dari Mattiacci, David Fidler, Peter Grossman, Dov Jacobs, André Nollkaemper, Ilias Plakokefalos, Josephine van Zeben, and participants in the 2013 SHARES Seminar on the Distribution of Responsibilities in International Law in Amsterdam, for their many helpful comments and suggestions on drafts of this paper. The author remains solely responsible for the contents. All websites were last accessed on 5 June 2014.

1 United Nations Framework Convention on Climate Change, New York, 9 May 1992, in force 21 March 1994, 1771 UNTS 107 (UNFCCC).

2 Kyoto Protocol to the United Nations Framework Convention on Climate Change, Kyoto, 11 December 1997, in force 16 February 2005, 2303 UNTS 148 (Kyoto Protocol).

3 Article 2 UNFCCC, n. 1.

4 'The Cancun Agreements: Outcome of the work of the Ad Hoc Working Group on Long-term Cooperative Action under the Convention', COP Decision 1/CP.16 (2010), at http://unfccc.int/meetings/cancun_nov_2010/session/6254/php/view/decisions.php.

5 Allianz Group and World Wildlife Fund, 'Climate Change & the Financial Sector: An Agenda for Action' (June 2005), at www.wwf.org.uk/filelibrary/pdf/allianz_rep_0605.pdf.

only existing multilateral mitigation agreement, the 1997 Kyoto Protocol, virtually guarantees continuing *net* increases in *global* emissions of greenhouse gases (GHGs).[6] That Protocol was scheduled to expire at the end of 2012, but was extended as member states failed to agree on a successor mitigation agreement that might be even slightly effective. Consequently, the existing international regime for climate change does virtually nothing to avoid 'dangerous anthropogenic interference with the climate system'.

This chapter describes the current state of 'shared irresponsibility' for climate change, and explores a couple of possible solutions including: first, a liability-based approach, which some international lawyers have been advocating;[7] and second, an emerging interdisciplinary literature recommending various 'polycentric' approaches that would supplement or replace the UN process, which relies on global treaties among hundreds of state actors with varying interests and incentives. The key for any solution is to alter the existing incentives and/or interests of states so that they accept *and* share responsibility to mitigate greenhouse gas emissions.

Section 2 briefly explains climate change as a collective-action problem, which largely explains the lack of progress on climate change so far. Moving from 'shared irresponsibility' to shared responsibility on climate change is primarily a matter of resolving those collective-action problems. Obviously, that is no easy task, but it is a task upon which game theory sheds some light. Section 3 asks what type of 'game' international climate negotiations represent. The answer to that question is important because, if the climate 'game' is a prisoners' dilemma (PD), as several scholars have suggested,[8] then a cooperative solution – where 'cooperation' amounts to accepting and sharing responsibility – is not just unlikely but strictly impossible. I argue, however, that the climate 'game' is more in the nature of an Assurance Game with uncertain pay-offs (expected values), which has both cooperative and non-cooperative equilibria. If I am right about that, then

[6] See, e.g., D.H. Cole, 'Climate Change and Collective Action' (2008) 61 CLP 229, at 230.

[7] See, e.g., R. Verheyen, *Climate Change Damage and International Law: Prevention Duties and State Responsibility* (Leiden: Martinus Nijhoff, 2005); D.A. Grossman, 'Warming Up to a Not-So-Radical Idea: Tort-Based Climate Change Litigation' (2003) 28 Col JEL 1; J. Kilinski, 'International Climate Change Liability: A Myth or a Reality?' (2009) 18 JTLP 377.

[8] G. Brennan, 'Climate change: a rational politics view' (2009) 53 AJARE 309; K. Pittel and D.T.G. Rübbelke, 'Transitions in the negotiations on climate change: from prisoner's dilemma to chicken and beyond' (2012) 12 IEA 23; F. Grundig, H. Ward and E. R. Zorick, 'Modeling Global Climate Negotiations', in U. Luterbacher and D.F. Sprinz (eds.), *International Relations and Global Climate Change* (Cambridge, MA: MIT Press, 2001), 153. It is not clear, however, that those scholars were referring the 'Prisoners' Dilemma' in the strict sense in which I employ it. See section 3.

cooperative (shared-responsibility) solutions to the climate change problem are neither ruled-out *ab initio* nor ensured, but are contingent on circumstances, some of which might be within the control of state actors. Sections 4 and 5 consider alternative mechanisms for inducing greater cooperation among actors in the climate 'game'. Section 4 considers and rejects the liability-based approach advocated by some international legal scholars because of legal and procedural hurdles. Moreover, using liability to promote mitigation of greenhouse gas emissions could prove counterproductive; rather than inducing cooperation, it might reduce incentives for states to participate in international regimes (i.e., to share responsibility). Section 5 explores, in a somewhat more optimistic vein, emerging 'polycentric' approaches to climate change. Such approaches are framed in various ways – as 'regime complexes', 'building blocks', 'tipping sets', etc. – but they share a supposition that sub-global (and even sub-national) processes could bring about a more effective and robust climate mitigation regime by altering the incentives and interests of (virtually) all states.

This chapter is more analytical than normative, but the analysis is informed by the following normative values: first, whatever we believe about the best (or second-best) climate policy is irrelevant if it is not feasible – normative assertions untethered to positive diagnoses of the problems we confront are likely to be unproductive or even counterproductive; second, the analyses in this chapter presume a welfare-consequentialist goal, which is, of course, fully consistent with the UNFCCC's main objective of 'avoiding dangerous anthropogenic interference with the climate system'; and third, 'shared responsibility' (as a reality rather than a mere concept) cannot simply be imposed from above but must be *accepted* or *taken* by parties. The allocation of costs and benefits of climate change or climate change prevention is a secondary, which is not to say an unimportant, consideration. Finally, the analysis, if it is sufficiently persuasive, could point us in certain normative directions and away from others.

2. Climate change as a collective-action problem

Climate change is the greatest collective-action problem the international community has confronted.[9] This is true for several reasons, which I will list before briefly discussing:

[9] This section provides a very brief treatment of issues discussed at length in Cole, 'Climate Change and Collective Action', n. 6. Cf. S. Barrett, *Why Cooperate? The Incentive to Supply Global Public Goods* (Oxford University Press, 2007), at 9: 'Global climate change may or

1. It is an 'aggregate effort' problem that is truly global in scope, in that GHG emissions from anywhere contribute to climate change everywhere.[10] In other words, for any solution(s) to the climate change problem to succeed, responsibility for mitigating greenhouse gas emissions must be widely shared.
2. Uneven distribution of costs and benefits expected from moderate climate change reduces incentives for wide sharing of responsibility.
3. Lingering scientific and social-scientific uncertainties about social-welfare effects from various emissions and atmospheric concentration levels of GHGs complicate determinations of how much mitigation is required.
4. Concerns about energy supply and the lack of sufficient quantities of affordable substitutes to fossil fuels for at least the next 20–30 years create countervailing incentives for most, if not all, states.

Climate change is a problem of truly global proportions because GHG emissions from any location in the world contribute to climate change everywhere. A stable climate, once thought of as a pure 'public good' (meeting both technical requirements of non-rivalrousness of consumption and inability to exclude),[11] has proven to be a 'common-pool resource',[12] as defined by Vincent and Elinor Ostrom.[13] A 'common-pool resource' is a congestible or subtractable public good, where upon reaching some threshold point of congestion, overuse, or subtraction, consumption becomes rivalrous, though non-excludability persists. The combination of

may not be the most important problem facing us today, but it is almost certainly the hardest one for the world to address.'

[10] Barrett, *Why Cooperate?*, ibid., at ch. 3.

[11] See, e.g., P. Cramton and S. Soft, 'International Climate Games: From Caps to Cooperation', Global Energy Policy Center Research Paper No. 10-07 (20 August 2010), at www.cramton.umd.edu/papers2010-2014/cramton-stoft-international-climate-games.pdf.

[12] It is extremely important not to confuse or conflate a 'common-pool resource' (CPR) with a 'common-property regime' (also CPR). The former is a resource system defined by subtractibility/congestibility and non-exclusivity. The latter is a potential solution to problems of overuse arising from nature of common-pool resources. A common-property regime is a system of common-property rights/regulations created by local users/actors to restrict their own access to and use of the common-pool resource. In other words, a common-property regime is one mechanism (among others, including formal governmental regulation and privatisation) for introducing some exclusivity where exclusivity previously was absent. See generally E. Ostrom, *Governing the Commons: The Evolution of Institutions for Collective Action* (Cambridge University Press, 1990).

[13] V. Ostrom and E. Ostrom, 'Public Goods and Public Choices', in M.D. McGinnis (ed.), *Polycentricity and Local Public Economies: Readings from the Workshop in Political Theory and Policy Analysis* (Ann Arbor: University of Michigan Press, 1999), 75, at 77–79.

rivalrousness in consumption and non-excludability leads 'inexorably' to Hardin's 'tragedy of the commons', *unless* exclusivity can somehow be imposed *via* institutional mechanisms. Indeed, the purpose of climate mitigation law is to introduce some amount of exclusion by fiat, pursuant to a binding contract entered into by state actors.[14]

Before the Industrial Revolution, the climate system was for all practical purposes a global public good because aggregate human emissions of the GHGs were insufficient to push the climate system out of an equilibrium that was determined exclusively by natural forces. In other words, human use of the climate system was non-rivalrous and non-exclusive. But human emissions of GHGs since the onset of the Industrial Revolution (generally dated to around 1850) have increased exponentially, and atmospheric concentration levels of carbon equivalents have reached a threshold level at which the stability of the climate system is threatened.[15] The climate system has reached a carbon-congestion point, which renders it a common-pool resource rather than a pure 'public good'.

That the climate system is now a 'common-pool resource' rather than pure 'public good' is implicit in notions such as 'carbon budgets'. A carbon budget is a scientific estimate of aggregate amounts of carbon dioxide equivalents humans (from all countries) can emit over a certain period time (usually, the middle of this century) without breaching a threshold at which the atmosphere, because of over-congestion of GHGs, might tip into a new and potentially dangerous equilibrium.[16] If the global climate were completely non-rivalrous in consumption, like pure 'public goods', the carbon budget would be infinite.

As a matter of positive political-economy and game theory, the climate change problem is not just about living within a carbon budget to sustain

[14] I take it as given that the option of privatisation of the climate is impossible (or, at least, infeasible). An international agreement could be conceived as taking the form either of Hardin's state-regulatory solution or Ostrom's common-property solution to avert the tragedy of open access.

[15] See, e.g., Intergovernmental Panel on Climate Change (IPCC), Climate Change 2007: Synthesis Report, at 36–37.

[16] I am using the phrase 'carbon budgets' as it is used in the climate policy literature, in contrast to the very different meaning that phrase has in the ecological literature. Compare, e.g., T. Kanitkar et al., 'Carbon budgets for climate change mitigation – a GAMS-based emissions model' (2013) 104 CS 1200, at 1201 (addressing issues of distribution of a global 'carbon budget' of 1000 CtCO2 for 2000–2050 to prevent dangerous interference with the climate system); and G.M. Woodall et al., 'Biota and the World Carbon Budget' (1978) 199 *Science* 141, at 141 (referring to the 'carbon budget' as a scientific determination of net sources and sinks).

a common-pool resource. It is about doing that while securing reliable and affordable energy supplies for both developed and developing countries.[17] The existence of such inconsistent goals (given current technologies) greatly complicates policy approaches to climate change. The main sources of GHG emissions, including energy production and consumption, industrial production, and transportation, are critical components of economic development and growth, which no country on earth, least of all those in the developing world, would willingly sacrifice, especially when any state's efforts to reduce emissions can so easily be offset by increasing emissions elsewhere – a problem known as 'leakage'. Any state that unilaterally reduced its GHG emissions, at substantial cost to its economy, to ameliorate the climate problem might be a 'sucker',[18] as other states have incentives to free-ride on its efforts (i.e., not to share responsibility). Those incentives are what make climate change a collective-action problem in the first place.

If, for example, the United States, the world's leading *per capita* emitter of GHGs (and second to China in nominal annual emissions), unilaterally curtailed (that is, reduced to zero) its *net* carbon-dioxide emissions (emissions minus sinks that absorb carbon dioxide), those reductions would be completely offset within a few short years by increasing emissions from developing countries.[19] The global climate would almost

[17] See Cole, 'Climate Change and Collective Action', n. 6, at 238–239.

[18] Elinor Ostrom often stated as a truism of positive political-economy that 'no one wants to be a "sucker"'. See, e.g., Ostrom, *Governing the Commons*, n. 12, at 44; S. Crawford and E. Ostrom, 'A Grammar of Institutions' (1995) 89 APSR 582, at 596.

[19] In 2011, the United States was responsible for *net* carbon-dioxide emissions of 5.612.9 gigatons of CO_2 equivalents. See US EPA, 'Inventory of U.S. Greenhouse Gas Emissions and Sinks: 1990–2011', EPA 430-R-13-001 (12 April 2013), at 2–4, Table 2-1 'Recent Trends in U.S. Greenhouse Gas Emissions and Sinks (Tg CO_2 Eq.)'. Total global emissions that same year amounted to approximately 34 gigatons of CO_2 equivalents. See Planbureau voor de Leefomgeving Netherlands Environmental Assessment Agency, 'Trends in global CO_2 Emissions', Table 28 A1.2. Subtracting 2011 US emissions from that total would leave 27.4 gigatons of CO_2 equivalents. Thus, in 2011 the United States was responsible for 16.5 of global CO_2 emissions; it is, after all, a major emitting country. But developing country emissions increased in 2011 alone by one gigaton of CO_2 equivalents. At that rate, developing countries would offset a complete decarbonisation of the US economy in less than six years. This does not mean that unilateral decarbonisation of the US economy would not be a good thing from a climate change perspective. To estimate its overall effect, we would have to run the numbers through an 'integrated assessment model', combining emissions data and climate sensitivity models in Monte Carlo analyses to derive a probability density function of damages from various levels of change in global mean temperature. On the nature of integrated assessment models and variations among them, see, e.g., E.A. Parson and K. Fisher-Vanden, 'Integrated Assessment Models of Global Climate Change' (1997) 22 AREE 589.

Table 10.1 *Effects of 2.5°C GMT increase on GDP (mean estimates)*

Country	Net cost (or benefit) as per cent of GDP
USA	0.45
China	0.22
Japan	0.50
OECD Europe	2.83
Russia	−0.65
Eastern Europe	0.71
Africa	3.91
India	4.93

certainly benefit to a limited extent from the approximately six years' of grace provided by US decarbonisation, but it would merely delay by that amount of time an overall doubling of preindustrial concentration levels of greenhouse gases (unless the US example caused other countries to follow suit, as hopefully it would).

The political problem of climate change is compounded by the unequal distribution of costs and benefits that economists expect will result from changes in global mean temperatures, rising sea-levels, and other consequences. Moderate climate change is likely to create winners (at least relatively speaking, and perhaps nominally) as well as losers among nations. Those that expect to 'win' obviously have different incentives in climate change negotiations from those that expect to 'lose'. By way of illustration (the precise estimates of which should be taken with several pinches of salt),[20] consider Table 10.1, from a 2000 study by William Nordhaus and Joseph Boyer:[21]

On Nordhaus and Boyer's estimates, big losers from moderate climate change would include India and Africa. Western Europe would also

[20] This table is merely for illustration because Nordhaus's integrated assessment models of climate change have evolved since 2000, and it is unlikely that the damage estimates predicted by this particular study are spot on. Analysts using other integrated assessment models with differing parameter values yield much higher damage estimates for all countries, including the United States and China. See, e.g., N. Stern, *The Stern Review on the Economics of Climate Change* (Cambridge University Press, 2007). However, Nordhaus and Boyer's assessment of the *relative* allocation of harm among regions reflects a general consensus. No economic assessment of *moderate* climate change suggests that all areas of the world will be (more or less) equally harmed or benefited. All economists agree that the countries likely to suffer the most harm are precisely the countries that have historically emitted the least GHGs.

[21] W.D. Nordhaus and J. Boyer, *Warming the World: Economics Models of Global Warming* (Cambridge, MA: MIT Press, 2000), at 91, Table 4.10.

suffer significant harm, while the United States, China, and Eastern Europe would suffer very little socio-economic harm. Russia would actually be a net beneficiary of moderate climate change, which goes some way toward explaining why Russia held out for 'side payments' (in the form of 'hot air' credits, which are emissions allowances unrelated to actual emissions) to sign and ratify the Kyoto Protocol.[22]

Whenever some members of the international community expect to win while others lose, negotiating treaties that would distribute gains and losses while balancing conflicting imperatives, such as climate stability and energy security, becomes problematic. The equilibrium solution is overwhelmingly likely to be the lowest common denominator of all the parties – something like the Kyoto Protocol – which would not resolve the problem.[23] In other words, to the extent parties agree to share responsibility at all, the level of aggregate responsibility will be insufficient.

Just as importantly, we lack technological substitutes for fossil fuels that would allow states to decarbonise, if not painlessly, then at least at some reasonable cost.[24] According to the International Energy Administration's *World Energy Outlook 2012*, fossil fuels (coal, gas, and oil) are expected to continue supplying the vast majority of the world's energy needs at least through 2030, a period during which global energy demand is expected to increase by more than one-third.[25] During that same period we need to be in the process of reducing *global* emissions of GHGs by approximately 80 per cent to avoid exceeding a target concentration level of 450 parts per million by 2050.[26] It is a tall order, even assuming (perhaps heroically) that states quickly become more willing than they have been so far to cooperate.

Given the facts of the climate problem, it is not surprising that more than two decades of international negotiations have so far produced

[22] D.H. Cole, 'Regulatory Cost-Benefit Analysis and Collective Action', Institute for Policy Integrity New York University School of Law, Working Paper No. 2009/1 20–22 (May 2009), at http://policyintegrity.org/files/publications/2009_1.pdf, at 21.

[23] Cole, 'Climate Change and Collective Action', n. 6, at 254; M. Inman, 'The climate change game' (2009) 3 NRCC 130, at 132.

[24] This is part of what makes the climate change problem so very different from, and so much more difficult than the ozone problem. Cole, 'Climate Change and Collective Action', n. 6, at 238–242.

[25] International Energy Agency, World Energy Outlook 2012, at www.worldenergyoutlook.org/publications/weo-2012/.

[26] IPCC, Fourth Assessment Report, Working Group III, Box 13.7, at www.ipcc.ch/index.htm.

disappointing results. Agreements have been few, and achievements modest at best. The agreements include

- a workable but weak framework convention, the United Nations Framework Convention on Climate Change;[27]
- a frail and seriously flawed (but recently extended) mitigation treaty, the Kyoto Protocol,[28] which by design is fully consistent with a net increase in global GHG emissions;[29] and
- a mixed bag of (legally non-binding) add-ons to the Kyoto Protocol, including REDD+,[30] the Marrakech Accord,[31] and the Copenhagen Accord.[32]

Because the climate agreements, and their various problems, have been comprehensively canvassed in both scholarly and popular literatures,[33] this chapter will not review them except insofar as they relate directly to recommended mechanisms for enhancing shared responsibility in the sections that follow.

3. The nature of the climate change game

Climate change often is portrayed as a Prisoners' Dilemma – perhaps the ultimate PD.[34] Were that truly the case, no purpose would be served trying to conceive cooperative solutions because PDs, properly understood, do not allow for cooperative solutions.[35] Given the pay-off

[27] See http://unfccc.int/2860.php. [28] Kyoto Protocol, n. 2.

[29] See, e.g., Cole, 'Climate Change and Collective Action', n. 6, at 230.

[30] REDD+ (Reducing Emissions from Deforestation and Forest Degradation) is an offset programme that developed separately from the UNFCCC process but has since been incorporated into it. See 'About REDD+', UN-REDD Programme, at www.un-redd.org/aboutredd/tabid/582/default.aspx.

[31] 'The Marrakesh Accords' and 'The Marrakesh Declaration', at http://unfccc.int/cop7/documents/accords_draft.pdf.

[32] Ibid.

[33] Cole, 'Climate Change and Collective Action', n. 6; D. Victor, *The Collapse of the Kyoto Protocol and the Struggle to Slow Global Warming* (Princeton University Press, 2001); Q. Scheirmeier, 'The Kyoto Protocol: Hot air' (2012) 491 *Nature* 656.

[34] P.J. Wood, 'Climate Change and Game Theory' (2011) 1219 ANYAS 153, at 168; D. Helm, 'Climate change policy: why has so little been achieved?'(2008) 24 OREP 211, at 234; T. Irwin, 'Implications for climate-change policy of research on cooperation in social dilemmas', World Bank Policy Research Working Paper No. 5006 (1 July 2009), at 3.

[35] Often, the label 'Prisoners' Dilemma' (PD) is used quite loosely to describe all manner of problems that might or might not have cooperative solutions. Indeed, it has become fashionable to talk about cooperative solutions to iterative PD games, but as I have pointed out before, any PD (single-play or iterative) that admits any cooperative solution is not strictly speaking a PD. The only way a cooperative solution to a PD can exist is to

structure of a PD (which is what makes a PD a PD), non-cooperation is a unique Nash equilibrium solution. The only way a cooperative solution can be achieved is by altering the pay-offs (which would make the PD no longer a PD, but some other kind of game).

However, the climate change game is not a PD because, like virtually all other common-pool resource problems,[36] it possesses multiple equilibria, which might be either cooperative or uncooperative. In other words, climate change is in the nature of what Amartya Sen has called an 'Assurance Game', which possesses uncertain, probabilistic pay-offs (expected values rather than certain values). Those pay-offs are determined by an array of variables, most notably levels of trust, which depend in turn on factors such as credibility of commitments and the ability to monitor performance and sanction non-compliers. Those factors affect the perceived probability that, if the first mover cooperates (e.g., accepts responsibility to mitigate GHG emissions), so then will subsequent movers.[37]

In the Assurance Game, pay-offs are not certain values but expected values with probabilistic pay-offs, where p is a probability assigned to a pay-off. In its simplest form, the pay-off matrix appears as follows: [38]

		Player 2	
		Cooperate	Defect
Player 1	Cooperate	$p_2 7$, $p_1 7$	$(1-p_2)-1$,5
	Defect	5,$(1-p_1)-1$	5,5

With expected values as specified in the matrix, cooperation (shared responsibility) is the dominant strategy for both parties so long as the probability of mutual cooperation remains above 0.75.[39] But if the probability of mutual cooperation falls to 0.74, then the expected value from cooperation falls to 4.92, which is lower than the pay-off from

change the pay-offs, in which case the problem is no longer (and may never have been) a true PD (which by definition entails a single non-cooperative solution as a Nash equilibrium). See D.H. Cole and P.Z. Grossman, 'Institutions Matter! Why the Herder Problem Is Not a Prisoners' Dilemma' (2010) 69 TD 219.

[36] Ibid.

[37] Ibid. See also A. Sen, 'Isolation, assurance, and the social rate of discount' (1960) 81 QJE 112.

[38] From Cole and Grossman, 'Institutions Matter! Why the Herder Problem Is Not a Prisoners' Dilemma', n. 35, at 228.

[39] $EV_1 = (.75)\ 7 + (.25)-1 = 5$.

defection (5). At that point (and at all probabilities lower than 0.75), non-cooperation on climate mitigation would become the dominant strategy – sometimes referred to as a 'risk dominant' strategy.[40] In reality, of course, the climate change game is iterative and long-form, involving many more than two parties; and the probabilistic pay-offs presented in the simple two-by-two matrix would only represent expected valuations of cooperation and non-cooperation at each decision node in the iterative game. In addition, the losses suffered from non-cooperation may not be symmetrical between the parties, as the pay-off matrix presupposes. However, the pay-off matrix does accurately illustrate the multiple equilibria of an Assurance Game.

In the climate change context, the probability of mutual cooperation is based largely on the credibility of commitments, which in turn reflect the relative ease of monitoring and enforcing those commitments.[41] The greater the credibility of commitments to abate GHG emissions, the more likely major emitting countries would be to attain a more efficient (in the aggregate) equilibrium. The greater the level of distrust – the less countries believe that others would follow their lead in cooperating – and the greater their level of risk aversion (not for climate change itself but for investments to resolve the problem), the more likely the global community would remain at a globally inefficient equilibrium, possibly equivalent to the outcome of a PD. So, even if the climate change game is not, strictly speaking a PD, it might turn out like one.[42] Indeed, such an outcome seems more likely than not at present, given the lack of progress on cooperative solutions. But unlike the strict PD that undesirable outcome is not preordained by the pay-offs, which in a PD are deliberately structured by the criminal justice system.[43] The current bad equilibrium in climate negotiations might be flipped to a better equilibrium, although just how this might be accomplished remains uncertain and contested.

[40] R. Gardner, *Games for Business and Economics* (New York: Wiley, 1995).

[41] S. Barrett, 'Credible Commitments, Focal Points, and Tipping: The Strategy of Climate Treaty Design', in R.W. Hahn and A. Ulph, *Climate Change and Common Sense: Essays in Honour of Tom Schelling* (Oxford University Press, 2012), 29; S. Barrett, 'Climate treaties and the imperative of enforcement' (2008) 24 OREP 239.

[42] Accord S. Barrett and A. Dannenberg, 'Climate negotiations under scientific uncertainty' (2012) 109 PNAS 17372. Barrett believes that the current pay-off structure of pay-offs to climate negotiations remain like those of a PD. See S. Barrett, 'Climate treaties and approaching catastrophes' (2013) 66(2) JEEM 235.

[43] Cole and Grossman, 'Institutions Matter! Why the Herder Problem Is Not a Prisoners' Dilemma', n. 35, at 221, 223, 224.

4. Can liability motivate shared responsibility for climate change mitigation?

If the climate change game has at least the potential for a cooperative equilibrium, as I have suggested, the next task is to identify potential mechanisms that might shift players toward such an equilibrium solution from the current uncooperative equilibrium. This section assesses two general recommendations for improving the incentives of GHG emitting countries to cooperate in reducing their emissions: first, a liability-based regime under which countries harmed as a result of climate change might sue countries alleged to have *caused* the harm (*a la* the *Trail Smelter* arbitration); second, a 'polycentric' approach to climate policy-making that might (or might not) dispense with the UNFCCC process. Any polycentric approach (or set of such approaches) would allow for (relatively speaking) 'bottom-up' development of climate policies via unilateral, bilateral, or multilateral state, regional, and local actions. Such actions would provide an opportunity for experienced-based learning about what works and does not work at various levels of climate governance. Recognising, of course, that no panacea (or one-size-fits-all) solutions exist for the climate change problem (excluding the negligible possibility of an unexpected short-term technological change that would immediately provide reliable and inexpensive substitutes for fossil fuels), experimentation with multiple potential solutions is more likely to prove fruitful (over time) than continuing down a singular, globally negotiated path that has been fruitless since its adoption more than 20 years ago.

One solution, promoted with increasing frequency, even desperation, by international legal scholars,[44] is litigation to establish state liability for extraterritorial harm resulting from the GHG emissions of major emitting countries, such as the United States. Harm from climate change already is manifest in various locales around the world, but nowhere more so than in low-lying islands and peninsulas, where climate change-induced sea-level rise is inundating land and displacing persons. For instance, the island of Kutubdia, off the coast of Bangladesh, is rapidly sinking into the Bay of Bengal. In just the last 20 years, the island's total area has been halved, six of the island's villages have been swamped, and 40,000 of its inhabitants have fled to higher

[44] See, e.g., Verheyen, *Climate Change Damage and International Law*, n. 7, at ch. 6.

ground.[45] The question is whether those poor climate refugees and the government of Bangladesh should be entitled to compensation from countries such as the United States and the European Union (EU) that are responsible for the lion's share of GHG emissions over the past 150 years? As a matter of simple justice, the answer to this question seems obvious: states should be liable for environmental harm, including climate harm, they cause to other states and their citizens. Very quickly, however, difficult legal, jurisdictional, and policy questions arise, which belie facile answers.

4.1 The notion of 'state responsibility' in international law

It has been argued, with substantial justification, that the international legal notion of state responsibility is 'not well adapted to the environmental field'[46] on several grounds, including (a) the absence of a consensus definition of 'environment' (not a trivial matter when the extent of state responsibility depends substantially on that term's definition); (b) the brute fact that 'in modern society, damage to the environment cannot be completely avoided',[47] but is 'inherent in industrial development';[48] and (c) the 'disgraceful solidarity of States in front of the degradation of the human environment to which they all contribute'.[49] Indeed, one might posit the existence of an international customary principle of environmental *abuse*. Nevertheless, state responsibility for international environmental harms is well established, if only in the minds of international lawyers.

Norms of international environmental protection have emerged since the early twentieth century primarily from two sources: first, treaties and other agreements, which are quasi-contractual arrangements establishing

45 J. Vidal, 'Sea change: the Bay of Bengal's vanishing islands', *The Guardian*, 29 January 2013. Similar stories have been told about low-lying Pacific Island nations, such as Tuvalu. See, e.g., 'Tuvalu about to disappear into the ocean', *Reuters*, 13 September 2007. But according to recent reports several of those coral atolls have actually been growing in size, rather than shrinking. See N. Bryant, 'Low-lying Pacific islands "growing not sinking"', BBC News, 3 June 2010 (claiming that Tuvalu and other low-lying islands will 'still be there in 100 years' time', but might not be habitable). Disparate factual claims about whether or not islands are sinking highlights the kind of evidentiary problems that claimants of climate harm might confront before international courts and tribunals.

46 C. Nègre, 'Responsibility and International Environmental Law', in J. Crawford, A. Pellet, and S. Olleson (eds.), *The Law of International Responsibility* (Oxford University Press, 2010), 803, at 803–804.

47 Ibid. 48 Ibid. 49 Ibid.

mutual legal responsibilities among states (which may be shared equally or 'common but differentiated');[50] and second, the customary international legal principle of 'no harm', according to which states (supposedly) have a general duty to avoid engaging in acts causing substantial extraterritorial environmental harm.[51] Breaches of treaty-based or customary law-based duties can give rise to state liability. However, even in the strongest factual circumstances imaginable, such as Bangladesh suing the United States for harm to Kutubdia and its residents, a negative outcome is predictable at a fairly high confidence level.

4.1.1 Potential liability under the UNFCCC and Kyoto Protocol

First, consider the source of potential legal liability. Bangladesh could try to sue the United States before the International Court of Justice (ICJ) under the UNFCCC or the customary no-harm rule, but not under the Kyoto Protocol. Because the United States has not ratified the Protocol, it is not legally bound by its terms. So, immediately, the most prominent source of legal climate mitigation obligations is off the table. Of course, other parties to the Kyoto Protocol might be sued (e.g., for violating emission-reduction obligations). But even assuming some parties are in violation of those very modest obligations, it is not clear that a basis for litigation exists because subsidiary agreements to the Protocol establish automatic (if ineffective) penalties for noncompliance,[52] which could be read to preempt party-*v.*-party lawsuits, under the international legal doctrine of *lex specialis*.[53]

[50] The UNFCCC imposes a shared obligation to avoid dangerous climate change, but the Kyoto Protocol creates 'common but differentiated' responsibilities with respect to mitigation: only developed countries (listed in Annex I of the UNFCCC) have specific emissions-reduction targets under the Protocol.

[51] See section 4.1.2.

[52] The primary penalty for failure to meet emission-reduction obligations under the Kyoto Protocol is a 30 per cent reduction in the emissions-reduction target for the following compliance period. Decision 27/CMP.1 (2005), Annex, 'Procedures and mechanisms relating to compliance under the Kyoto Protocol', FCCC/KP/CMP/2005/8/Add.3, at www.ciesin.columbia.edu/repository/entri/docs/cop/Kyoto_COP001_027.pdf. The penalty is much less significant than it appears because a penalised party is allowed to 'borrow' from one compliance period to the next, and so never actually has to suffer the penalty. X. Wang and G. Wiser, 'The Implementation and Compliance Regimes under the Climate Change Convention and Its Kyoto Protocol' (2002) 11 RECIEL 181, at 196.

[53] According to the doctrine of *lex specialis*, special rules of international law take precedence over more general rules governing state responsibility. Article 55 of the ILC's Articles on State Responsibility provides that its 'articles do not apply where and to the extent that the conditions for the existence of an internationally wrongful act or the content or

Moreover, suing co-parties of treaties hardly provides a solid basis for further cooperation in ongoing negotiations to develop a workable global mitigation regime. For example, a lawsuit against the EU, which arguably has taken more action to mitigate emissions than any other state actor, would do little to encourage it to take more action, and might actually discourage EU member states from cooperating.

But what about a theoretical lawsuit against the United States for violating its legal obligations under the UNFCCC, which the United States *has* ratified? A threshold question is whether the UNFCCC imposes *legally enforceable* obligations to reduce GHG emissions. Scholars have offered different answers to that question: on one view, the UNFCCC imposes only very limited legally enforceable obligations, which do not include actual emission-reductions;[54] on another view, the UNFCCC imposes actual, though not specific, emission-reduction obligations.[55] Probably the strongest case for a legally enforceable commitment to reduce emissions is found in Article 4(2)(a) of the UNFCCC, which provides that parties 'shall adopt national policies and take corresponding measures on the mitigation of climate change, by limiting its anthropogenic emissions of greenhouse gases'.[56] As Michael Faure and André Nollkaemper have observed, this provision, though 'still rather vague', nevertheless 'stipulate[s] a commitment' and 'arguably could be the basis of a liability claim'.[57]

implementation of the international responsibility of a State are governed by special rules of international law.' See Articles on Responsibility of States for Internationally Wrongful Acts, ILC *Yearbook* 2001/II(2) (ARSIWA). Scholars disagree about the applicability of *lex specialis* in the context of the climate treaties. Compare Verheyen, *Climate Change Damage and International Law*, n. 7, at 143 (arguing that *lex specialis* does not apply) and T. Thorp, 'Climate Justice: A Constitutional Approach to Unify the Lex Specialis Principles of International Climate Law' (2012) 8 Utr LR 7, at 15 (providing reasons to believe that *lex specialis* does apply to the climate treaties, preempting other remedies).

[54] D. Bodansky, 'The United Nations Framework Convention on Climate Change: A Commentary' (1993) 18 YJIL 451; S. Barrett and R. Stavins, 'Increasing Participation and Compliance in International Climate Change Agreements' (2003) 3(4) IEA 349, at 350 (referring to the UNFCCC's goal of reducing GHG emissions from developed countries as 'non-binding').

[55] See, e.g., Verheyen, *Climate Change Damage and International Law*, n. 7. Some scholars seem caught in between these two groups. See M. Faure and P.A. Nollkaemper, 'International Liability as an Instrument to Prevent and Compensate for Climate Change' (2007) 26A Stan ELJ 123.

[56] Article 4(2)(a) UNFCCC, n. 1.

[57] Faure and Nollkaemper, 'International Liability as an Instrument to Prevent and Compensate for Climate Change', n. 55, at 143.

Obviously, if the UNFCCC does not create legally binding obligations, the inquiry is complete. But let us suppose, following Faure and Nollkaemper (among others), that Article 4(2)(a) creates a binding obligation on which liability might be based. Has the United States failed to 'adopt national policies and take corresponding measures on the mitigation of climate change, by limiting its anthropogenic emissions of greenhouse gases'? The US Environmental Protection Agency has imposed substantive regulations limiting power-plant and automobile emissions of greenhouse gases, under the Clean Air Act.[58] The federal government also has established by regulation a schedule for the social cost of carbon (SSC), which all executive branch agencies must factor into their regulatory analyses.[59] By raising the estimated costs of major federal regulations that might result in emissions of GHGs, the SSC presumably (at some point) would affect actual emissions.

Are those 'policies and measures' sufficient to meet the obligations created by Article 4(2)(a) of the UNFCCC? If not, do state and regional policies to reduce GHG emissions, including California's 'Global Warming Solutions Act',[60] also count as US measures to comply with UNFCCC obligations? Unfortunately, the Convention itself fails to specify any metric for judging the sufficiency of state efforts to reduce GHG emissions. It only calls on parties to implement policies and measures that would reduce GHG emissions as against business as usual, and that the United States has done.[61] Even China, which has no obligations under Article 4 of the UNFCCC, has established policies and measures designed to reduce its GHG emissions as against business

[58] Clean Air Act of 1970, 42 USC. For descriptions of current EPA regulations relating to climate change, see www.epa.gov/climatechange/EPAactivities/regulatory-initiatives.html; www.whitehouse.gov/sites/default/files/omb/inforeg/social_cost_of_carbon_for_ria_2013_update.pdf. A rule regulating carbon emissions from new power plants currently is in the process of being finalised. The proposed rule can be read at www.regulations.gov/#!documentDetail;D=EPA-HQ-OAR-2011-0660-0001. In addition, the Obama Administration recently announced that it would promulgate a rule regulating carbon emissions from existing power plants. See Executive Office of the President, 'The President's Climate Action Plan' (June 2013), at www.whitehouse.gov/sites/default/files/image/president27sclimateactionplan.pdf.

[59] Interagency Working Group on Social Cost of Carbon, United States Government, Technical Support Document – Technical Update on the Social Cost of Carbon for Regulatory Impact Analysis – Under Executive Order 128666 (May 2013), at www.whitehouse.gov/sites/default/files/omb/inforeg/social_cost_of_carbon_for_ria_2013_update.pdf.

[60] Global Warming Solutions Act of 2006, Assembly Bill 32.

[61] See n. 50 and 51.

as usual,[62] which underscores just how easily any legal burden the UNFCCC actually creates might be satisfied.

Even accepting at face value the most optimistic interpretation of the UNFCCC for invoking liability, the practical wisdom of such a move is questionable. Given the strong disagreements that characterised the UNFCCC's negotiation, and the compromises necessary to create even a modest 'framework convention', imposing liability on member states for violating provisions of such a *framework* convention could well prove counterproductive. More than anything, sued parties might become inclined to simply withdraw from the treaty. And what recourse would that leave harmed states? Perhaps even more importantly, what would be the prospective effect on future negotiations of 'framework conventions' about sensitive, complex, and highly contentious issues? Would countries become more likely or less likely to sign on to documents they believe represent only a first step toward negotiating a fully-fledged regime, but which could later might be (re-)interpreted as a source of legal liability? The question would seem to answer itself.

The real possibility that states might withdraw from the UNFCCC to avoid liability, if an international tribunal used it as a basis for liability, reflects a more general problem with litigating violations of multilateral treaties. In most cases, states could avoid liability for violating treaties simply by exiting them.[63] Indeed, Canada withdrew from the Kyoto Protocol, which it previously had ratified, ostensibly for that reason.[64] The fact of free withdrawal underscores the fact that 'responsibility' cannot be imposed from above in the international climate regime but must be voluntarily accepted.

[62] D.I. Stern and F. Jotzo, 'How ambitious are China and India's emissions intensity targets?' (2010) 38 EP 6776 (concluding that China will have to adopt ambitious carbon mitigation policies to achieve its voluntary carbon-intensity target).

[63] In rare cases, such as the Ozone Accords (Vienna Convention, Montreal Protocol, et al.) states cannot avoid the ban on production and sale of listed ozone-depleting substances simply by withdrawing from the accords because the treaties including trade sanctions to enforce compliance, including against non-parties. See, e.g., J.D. Werksman, 'Trade Sanctions Under the Montreal Protocol' (2006) 1 RECIEL 69. Trade sanctions do not appear, however, in most environmental treaties, including the UNFCCC and the Kyoto Protocol. And while their use in the Ozone Accords has not yet led to problems, the use of trade sanctions in international agreements can give rise to disputes before the World Trade Organization. See generally S. Barrett, 'The strategy of trade sanctions in international environmental agreements' (1997) 19 REE 345.

[64] 'Canada pulls out of Kyoto protocol', *The Guardian*, 12 December 2011.

4.1.2 Potential liability under the customary 'no-harm' rule

The overall weakness of the international climate treaty regime has led to the promotion of a liability-based regime, using the 'no-harm' rule of customary international law, not so much as a substitute but as a spur to international negotiations.[65] The basic idea is that if recalcitrant states, such as the United States, can be made to pay for the harm their GHG emissions cause in other countries, they will be incentivised to share responsibility by reducing their GHG emissions and engaging more positively with the rest of the international community in multilateral negotiations resulting, hopefully, in more effective climate treaties. But it remains to be seen whether litigation under the no-harm rule is a viable option; and even if it is, it might not create the positive incentives to share responsibility that its proponents anticipate.

In order to establish liability under the no-harm principle, following the lone precedent of the *Trail Smelter* arbitration, a claimant would have to prove by clear and convincing evidence that emissions originating in the defendant state caused it injury of 'serious consequence'.[66] Proponents of the liability-based approach to GHG mitigation, including Roda Verheyen, argue forcefully that these burdens are not especially onerous. In my view, the legal obstacles are more formidable than some international lawyers suppose, as evidenced by the fact that not a single harmed country has so far even attempted to bring a claim (even for declaratory judgment, which avoids the need for voluntary acceptance of jurisdiction by the defendant country or countries) against a major emitting country.

To illustrate the problems a climate plaintiff would confront, let us take as a hypothetical case *Bangladesh* v. *US*, for harmed caused to the Island of Kutubdia and its residents. To give the complaining country the strongest possible case, assume that the facts, as stated, are true: the Island of Kutubdia's total area has been halved, six of the island's villages have been swamped, and 40,000 of its inhabitants have fled to higher ground. Further assume that the causal link between

[65] See, e.g., J. Gupta, 'Legal Steps Outside the Climate Convention: Litigation as a Tool to Address Climate Change' (2007) 16 RECIEL 76, at 85 (concluding that 'the potential threat of future litigation . . . might itself give strong incentives to governments to address climate change more seriously'); D. Hunter, 'The Implications of Climate Change Litigation for International Environmental Law-Making', in W. Burns and H. Osofsly (eds.), *Adjudicating Climate Change: State, National, and International Approaches* (Cambridge University Press, 2009), 357.

[66] *Trail Smelter (United States of America* v. *Canada)*, Award, (1938) 3 RIAA 1905, at 1965.

anthropogenic GHG emissions and rising global sea-levels is reasonably robust; and that Bangladesh and the United States both submit to the jurisdiction of the ICJ. The question presented to the ICJ is whether the United States has breached its duty towards Bangladesh to ensure that actions in its territory do not cause harm of 'serious consequence' to the territory of another state.

In order for Bangladesh to prevail on that question several elements must be established, including most prominently causation, foreseeability, and harm of 'serious consequence'. Given the facts, there can be little doubt that the injuries suffered by Bangladesh from sea-level rise are of 'serious consequence'. But to what extent did emissions from the United States *cause* those injuries? Put in a different way that more clearly highlights the problem, had the United States not emitted the GHGs that contributed to rising sea levels, would the consequences for the Island of Kutubdia be substantially less 'serious'?

The question presumes that the United States could be held liable only for the damage caused by its own emissions. Some climate liability proponents suggest that international courts might adopt a rule of joint and several liability,[67] under which the United States could be held liable for the all the harm from global emissions of GHGs, but with a right to sue those other countries for contribution. Other scholars have observed that no such rule exists in international law.[68] Article 47 of the Articles on State Responsibility allows for liability of a 'plurality of responsible States'.[69] The Commentaries to the Article make clear that each responsible state is liable only for the harm it individually causes.[70] In this case, we are concerned with the potential responsibility of the United States for damage to Bangladesh from sea-level rise; and under the ARSIWA, the United States will be held liable, if at all, only for the injuries arising from emissions emanating from its territories.

The scientific basis for resolving questions of attribution of climate damages remains soft. We possess a fair idea of historic US contributions to global GHG emissions since the middle of the nineteenth century:

[67] Verheyen, *Climate Change Damage and International Law*, n. 7, at 268–273.

[68] I. Brownlie, *System of the Law of the Nations: State Responsibility, Part I* (Oxford University Press, 1983), 189.

[69] ARSIWA, n. 53; J. Crawford, *State Responsibility: The General Part* (Cambridge University Press, 2013), 327.

[70] Commentary to the Articles on Responsibility of States for Internationally Wrongful Acts, ILC *Yearbook* 2001/II(2) (ARSIWA Commentary), Commentary to Article 47 ARSIWA.

approximately 29 per cent.[71] But quantifying the overall human effect, independent of natural drivers, for purposes of establishing legal responsibility remains problematic.[72] Scientists are 'very confident that most of the observed large-scale changes in surface temperature over the twentieth century are externally driven'.[73] But 'externally driven' does not equate to human-caused.[74] Relevant external factors include anthropogenic aerosol cooling, solar activity, and volcanic activity, as well as anthropogenic GHG emissions.[75] Disentangling those factors is a tricky business. While the Intergovernmental Panel on Climate Change (IPCC) has concluded unequivocally that the climate is warming, and that 'most of the observed increase in global average temperatures since the mid-twentieth century is *very likely* due to the observed increase in anthropogenic GHG concentrations',[76] it has not yet attempted to quantify the human contribution to climate change in a way that would be useful for litigants and jurists.

Ten years ago, the Oxford physicist Myles Allen cautioned that more scientific research was required to resolve the problem of attribution before emitters could be held legally liable for the impacts of their emissions.[77] Arguably, that remains the case today for states as well as for private emitters. Liability proponent Roda Verheyen puts great stock in a single study attributing 60–70 per cent of observed warming to anthropogenic emissions with an extremely high level of certainty.[78] Whether the ICJ would put so much stock in a single study, when the IPCC itself has yet to provide a percentage attribution at *any* confidence level, is doubtful. And in the absence of an overall attribution level of global mean temperature increase to anthropogenic emissions, no one can assert with confidence how much of the global mean temperature increase can be attributed specifically to American emissions, let alone how much sea-level rise is attributable to emissions from the United States.

[71] K.A. Baumert, T. Herzog, and J. Pershing, 'Navigating the Numbers: Greenhouse Gas Data and International Climate Policy' (World Resources Institute, 2005), at 32, Fig. 6.1.

[72] See generally M. Allen et al., 'Scientific Challenges in the Attribution of Harm to Human Influence on Climate' (2007) 155 Penn LR 1353.

[73] Ibid., at 1370. [74] Ibid., at 1371. [75] Ibid., at 1374.

[76] IPCC, 2007 Synthesis Report, n. 15, at 30, 39.

[77] M. Allen, 'Liability for climate change' (2003) 421 *Nature* 891, at 891–892.

[78] Verheyen, *Climate Change Damage and International Law*, n. 7, at 259, citing J. Grieser, T. Staeger and C.-D. Schönwiese, *Statische Analyse zur Früherkennung globaler und regionaler Klimaänderungen aufgrund des anthropogenen Treibhauseffektes. Berichte des Instituts für Meteorologie und Geophysik* (Frankfurt am Main: Eigenverlag des Instituts, 2000).

Even if we could determine state attribution with a degree of accuracy that might persuade the ICJ, the *foreseeability* of harm remains at issue. Liability proponents argue with substantial justification that at least since 1992 the potential harm from GHG emissions has been foreseeable.[79] But if state responsibility only dates from 1992,[80] then, as Roda Verheyen and co-author Richard Tol note, the ambit of the no-harm rule would envelope not just the United States and other developed countries, but also China, India, and other developing countries that have been emitting GHGs in increasing quantities since that date.[81] As a consequence, the extent of potential US culpability would shrink. Based on data from the US Energy Information Administration,[82] in 1990 the United States was responsible for approximately 23 per cent of global emissions (below its average of 29 per cent contribution from the mid-nineteenth century to 2002).[83] By 2011, the United States was responsible for just 16.5 per cent of global GHG emissions.[84] If we simply average those two figures, the United States would be responsible for 19.75 per cent of the foreseeable harm suffered by Kutubdia from *anthropogenic* GHG emissions (that is, minus natural forces driving global mean temperatures and sea-level rise). If human emissions are responsible for, say, 60 per cent of total increases in global mean temperatures *and* sea-level rise since 1992 (a significant assumption to be sure), then US responsibility for Kutubdia's harm would by 19.75 per cent of 60 per cent, or about 12 per cent. China's liability could turn out to be roughly similar.

One final, vitally important, procedural issue remains to be resolved: the standard of proof for the claimant to prevail. Roda Verheyen has called for a 'preponderance of the evidence' standard, according to which

79 Verheyen, *Climate Change Damage and International Law*, n. 7, at 181. See also R.S.J. Tol and R. Verheyen, 'State responsibility and compensation for climate change damages – a legal and economic assessment' (2004) 32(9) EP 1109, at 1118.

80 Tol and Verheyen, ibid. suggest earlier dates for establishing foreseeability, including 1827, when Fourier first posited a relationship between concentrations of carbon dioxide and radiative forcing in the atmosphere, and the 1950s, when monitoring data from Antarctica and Hawaii provided a basis for the first in-depth research on the implications for the global climate of increasing atmospheric concentration levels of GHGs. But given the extent of scientific uncertainty, 1992 seems a more reasonable date on which to base foreseeability.

81 Ibid.

82 See 'World Carbon Dioxide Emission by Region, Reference Case, 1990–2030', at http://photos.mongabay.com/09/forecast_co2.jpg.

83 See n. 71 and accompanying text.

84 D. Clark, 'Which nations are most responsible for climate change?', *The Guardian*, 21 April 2011.

the claimant only has to show that its injuries more likely than not resulted from the defendant's conduct.[85] But our only existing precedent, the 1935 *Trail Smelter* arbitration, expressly established a more burdensome 'clear and convincing evidence' standard. Scant reason exists to presume, especially in the absence of any test case, that the ICJ would abandon that precedent today. Assuming the ICJ followed the *Trail Smelter* tribunal in applying a 'clear and convincing' evidence standard, the consequences for Bangladesh's hypothetical case against the United States would be potentially fatal. Even the staunchest advocate of liability for climate harm would have a difficult time arguing that the existing scientific basis for assessing cause-and-effect relations between emissions from a specific country and specific harms somewhere else is sufficiently advanced to meet such a standard of proof.

In sum, a liability claim for harm from climate change based on the customary no-harm rule remains an uphill fight for any claimant. That could explain why we do not see climate claimants rushing to the ICJ, despite the encouragement of several international law scholars, who are like lawyers in search of clients.[86] Another reason is the virtual certainty that defendant states would not agree to be tried before the ICJ. Once again, they only have to share responsibility if they want to do so. In the absence of mandatory jurisdiction, a prospect no one considers realistic, any suggestion that a liability regime might play a significant role in ameliorating climate change seems pie-in-the-sky.

This conclusion might be tough to accept for lawyers, who are by training and temperament accustomed to look to the courtroom as a

[85] Verheyen, *Climate Change Damage and International Law*, n. 7, at 291, 331.

[86] In 2011, the governments of Palau and the Marshall Islands, small island nations in the Pacific, asked the United Nation's General Assembly (UNGA) to seek an advisory opinion from the ICJ, under Article 96 of the Charter of the United Nations, addressing the responsibility of GHG-emitting states to ensure that emissions arising within their boundaries do not harm other states. 'Palau seeks UN World Court opinion on damage caused by greenhouse gases', United Nations News Service, 22 September 2011. Individual countries cannot themselves request advisory opinions from the ICJ, but can ask the UNGA to do so. A UNGA request would be in the form of a resolution enacted by majority vote (of those states that cast votes), which is not easily obtained. So far, the UNGA has not acted on the request of Palau and the Marshall Islands. If it did so, the question would be submitted to the ICJ, but the Court would not necessarily be bound to answer the question submitted; and if it did answer the question, its advisory opinion would not be binding; nor would it provide any remedy. The only advantage of seeking an advisory opinion as Palau and the Marshall Islands have done, as opposed to filing a direct claim for harm, is that the UNGA resolution requesting an advisory opinion obviates the requirement of consent by 'defendant' states.

primary forum in which to redress grievances. We lawyers naturally react to unjust social and environmental insults by looking for some 'wrongdoer' to sue (even if it seems, as in the case of GHG emissions, that everyone is a 'wrongdoer' to some extent). And legal liability sometimes has proven a useful tool for environmental protection, at least in domestic courts (though not in the climate-change context).[87] The fact remains that we hardly ever see environmental claims brought before international tribunals. The *Trail Smelter* arbitration remains a unique exception (albeit one that seems to have spawned a vast rule). Scant reason exists for optimism about the prospects for spurring shared responsibility for climate change via litigation, let alone resolving the climate-change problem, one court case at a time.

5. Polycentric approaches to climate change: of 'regime complexes',[88] 'building blocks',[89] 'bottom-up approaches'[90] and 'tipping sets'[91]

If international courts are unable to contribute significantly to a global climate change solution, we are forced back onto a political process that so far has proven incapable of coming to grips with the problem. But the fact that global negotiations have made little progress so far does not mean progress is impossible. In the first place, and contrary to facile nostrums, such as 'global problems require global solutions',[92] *global* agreements are not a *sine qua non* for progress. Scholars from diverse disciplines have, in recent years, started calling for more 'polycentric'

[87] Even the strongest tort claims in domestic courts have failed. See *Native Village of Kivalina and city of Kivalina* v. *ExxonMobil Corp. and others*, 696 F. 3d 849 (9th Cir. 2012), (rejecting claim for relocation costs by tribal village in Alaska inundated by rising seas).

[88] R.O. Keohane and D.G. Victor, 'The Regime Complex for Climate Change', Harvard Project on International Climate Agreements, Discussion Paper 10–33 (January 2010).

[89] R.B. Stewart, M. Oppenheimer, and B. Rudyk, 'Building Blocks for Global Climate Protection', NYU Center for Law, Economics and Organization, Law and Economics Research Paper Series, Working Paper No. 12–43 (January 2013).

[90] R. Leal-Arcas, 'Top-Down and Bottom-Up Approaches for Climate Change Negotiations: An Analysis' (2011) 6 IUPJGPP 1.

[91] G. Heal and H. Kunreuther, 'Tipping Climate Negotiations', in R.W. Hahn and A. Ulph (eds.), *Climate Change and Common Sense: Essays in Honour of Tom Schelling* (Oxford University Press, 2012), 50.

[92] See, e.g., M. Grasso, 'A normative ethical framework in climate change' (2007) 81 *Climatic Change* 223, at 224.

approaches to climate governance, arguing that the UN process should not be (if it ever has been) the 'only game in town'.[93]

A diversity of polycentric approaches has been recommended, including, in brief:

- 'Building blocks', which are smaller-scale regional or sectoral policies that can be linked together.[94]
- A 'regime complex', comprised of 'highly fragmented collections of institutions, with no identifiable core and weak or nonexistent linkages between regime elements'.[95]
- A 'bottom-up approach . . . that begins with details and works up to the highest conceptual level', as found for example in the field of investment protection, which relies on more than 2,700 bilateral investment protection agreements and virtually no multilateral agreements.[96]

What do these various 'polycentric' approaches have in common, and how would they differ from the existing UNFCCC approach? All global or multilateral legal regimes are multi-scalar in the trivial sense that they inevitably rely on member states (sharing responsibility) for implementation and compliance. A 'polycentric' approach to climate change represents not only governance at multiple scales, but nodes of decision making at various levels of governance that are not necessarily hierarchical. Instead of lower-level government agencies simply carrying out orders from above, polycentrism envisions an array of government-service providers, interacting with one another and with consumers of public goods or 'common-pool resources'. Some of those government-service providers may be organised in hierarchies *a la* business firms in markets for private goods. But they may also be competitive, in the sense that they offer alternative approaches to resolving similar problems. Thus, in a polycentric system providers of public goods and services both compete and cooperate in providing public goods and services

[93] E. Ostrom, 'Nested externalities and polycentric institutions: must we wait for global solutions to climate change before taking action at other scales?' (2012) 49 ET 353; D.H. Cole, 'From Global to Polycentric Climate Governance' (2011) 2 *Climate Law* 395. See also J.E. Aldy, S. Barrett, and R.N. Stavins, 'Thirteen Plus One: A Comparison of Global Climate Policy Architectures' (2003) 3 CP 373 (observing that '[e]nvironmentalists have supported the Kyoto Protocol partly because it has been "the only game in town"').

[94] Stewart, Oppenheimer and Rudyk, 'Building Blocks for Global Climate Protection', n. 89.

[95] Keohane and Victor, 'The Regime Complex for Climate Change', n. 88, at 3–4.

[96] Leal-Arcas, 'Top-Down and Bottom-Up Approaches for Climate Change Negotiations', n. 90, at 4, footnote 19.

that private markets are likely to under-supply because of the inability to internalise sufficient private benefits.[97]

The chief implication of a polycentric approach for climate change governance is not (necessarily) the abandonment of global negotiations under the UNFCCC, but reduced reliance on the UN process as the sole or even predominant mechanism for obtaining GHG emissions reductions from major emitting countries. The focus would not shift to any particular substitute process; rather, a multiplicity of processes, in the nature of policy experiments, would be encouraged. Experiments that prove promising would be emulated, scaled up (if feasible), and perhaps linked with other promising and compatible systems. While not strictly 'bottom-up' in the conventional economic (Hayekian) sense of that term,[98] polycentric climate institutions might be referred to as *relatively* bottom-up, in the sense that they *evolve* from national or even sub-national policy experiments, rather than global-level negotiations, which often crowd out national and sub-national experiments and learning.

The impetus toward a less centralised approach to climate change did not come from a single source but emerged over the course of a few years among a diverse group of scholars, including Elinor Ostrom, Robert Keohane, David Victor, Richard Stewart, and the present author. In some respects, their recommendations have been less normative than positive – recognising that climate policy already was becoming polycentric, as governance units at various levels, including some private actors, were implementing policies and measures of their own outside the purview of the UNFCCC process. In some cases, their actions reflected dissatisfaction with the pace of global negotiations; in other cases, lower-level actions were taken in anticipation of national or international developments (not all of

[97] On the polycentric approach generally, see V. Ostrom, C. Tiebout, and R. Warren, 'The Organization of Government in Metropolitan Areas: A Theoretical Inquiry' (1961) 55 APSR 831; V. Ostrom, 'Polycentricity (Part 1)', in M.D. McGinnis (ed.), *Polycentricity and Local Public Economies: Readings from the Workshop in Political Theory and Policy Analysis* (University of Michigan Press, 1999), 52; V. Ostrom, 'Polycentricity (Part 2)', in M.D. McGinnis (ed.) *Polycentricity and Local Public Economies: Readings from the Workshop in Political Theory and Policy Analysis* (University of Michigan Press, 1999), 119.

[98] See, e.g., W. Easterly, 'Institutions: Top Down or Bottom Up?' (2008) 98 AER 95 (referring to 'bottom up' in the traditional economic sense of spontaneous emergence of institutions from social norms, customs, traditions and values of individuals, as opposed to the 'top-down' imposition of institutions by political leaders). In the climate policy context, 'bottom-up' typically refers to institutional mechanisms deployed at the sub-global level by political leaders (or entrepreneurs). See Leal-Arcas, 'Top-Down and Bottom-Up Approaches for Climate Change Negotiations', n. 90.

which have materialised). Whatever their impetus, the various policies and measures introduce at different levels of public and private governance are, in effect, experiments in climate policy, which scholars and policy analysts might assess for potential emulation, scaling up, and linkage.

Following is a select (and far from complete) list of policies and measures adopted at national and sub-national levels over the past several years, but not as Kyoto Protocol compliance mechanisms:

- US EPA regulations of greenhouse gases.
- China's unilateral promise (now codified) to reduce its carbon-intensity of production.
- California's 'Global Warming Solutions Act'.
- The Regional Greenhouse Gas Initiative (RGGI).
- Portland, Oregon's plan to reduce GHG emissions by 20 per cent below 1990 levels by 2010.
- Berkeley, California's FIRST programme (to finance residential solar-heating systems).
- The Cement Sustainability Initiative (CSI), created in 2002 by ten large cement manufacturers to reduce GHG emissions in production.
- The now-defunct Chicago Climate Exchange, a private emissions-trading market.[99]
- British Petroleum's early efforts to reduce carbon emissions from pipeline leaks.[100]

These are all examples of public and private governance units at various levels *accepting* responsibility for reducing GHG emissions, in most cases without any direct connection to UN-based structures. Jouni Paavola has provided a handy table (Table 10.2) illustrating the variety of sub-global mechanisms that are already in use (somewhere) to mitigate GHG emissions:[101]

Even the EU's Emissions Trading System (EU ETS),[102] which started as a Kyoto compliance mechanism, has attained an identity distinct

[99] For details on this programme and the others listed above, see Cole, 'From Global to Polycentric Climate Governance', n. 93, at 406–409. See also J. Paavola, 'Climate Change: The Ultimate Tragedy of the Commons?', in D.H. Cole and E. Ostrom (eds.), *Property in Land and Other Resources* (Cambridge Massachusetts: Lincoln Institute of Land Policy Press, 2012), 417, at 426 (discussing the Cement Sustainability Initiative).

[100] See J. Browne, 'Beyond Kyoto: The Carbon Challenge', FA, July/August 2004.

[101] Paavola, 'Climate Change: The Ultimate Tragedy of the Commons?', n. 99, at 428, Table 14.1.

[102] See e.g. http://ec.europa.eu/clima/policies/ets/index_en.htm.

Table 10.2 *Institutional Diversity in Polycentric Climate Change Governance*

Type and Level	Conventional	Hybrid	Voluntary
Global	Kyoto Protocol; post-Kyoto targets; adaptation funding	Carbon markets; REDD	Business sector initiatives
Regional	EU ETS	Regional carbon markets; insurance provision and underwriting	Adaptation clearinghouses
National	Climate change, energy, and other legislation	Carbon markets; public-private partnerships in carbon capture & storage; insurance provision and underwriting	Adaptation networks of local governments
Local	Climate-proofed zoning; property tax regimes; joint mitigation and adaptation	Public-private partnerships	Carbon-neutral communities

from the Kyoto Protocol, offering an alternative path to climate mitigation. Elsewhere,[103] I have written about the EU ETS's more modest, careful, and altogether superior approach to emissions trading, compared to the Kyoto Protocol. The EU Commission, which designed the ETS, learned lessons (that the Kyoto parties ignored) about conditions (and limits) for successful emissions trading from earlier US experiments, such as the Clean Air Act's acid rain programme. Although the EU ETS suffers from some well-known design flaws of its own, including the lack of an allowance price-floor to avert financial collapse of carbon markets in the wake of economic recession,[104] its dominant

[103] Cole, 'From Global to Polycentric Climate Governance', n. 93, at 409–411.

[104] See, e.g., European Commission, Report from the Commission to the European Parliament and the Council, 'The State of the European carbon market in 2012', COM(2012)

position as the world's largest and most well-developed market provides an opportunity, at least, for it to serve as a more reliable and replicable alternative to Kyoto's irredeemably flawed trading and offset programmes. In fact, when it designed the ETS, the European Commission fully intended to influence the future development of global carbon markets.[105] That is to say, it was *taking responsibility* for promoting a more effective global carbon market.

Because the EU and its member states are such large players in virtually all emissions markets (mostly as buyers), they can and have *de facto* amended the Kyoto Protocol via domestic legislation to improve the environmental integrity of trading markets. For example, when the EU amended the ETS in 2009 to prohibit member states from complying with ETS targets by using Clean Development Mechanism (CDM) credits from fraud-ridden HFC-23 projects in China, that unilateral act (which took effect in 2013) has pretty much ended China's scam, which was facilitated by inherent defects (e.g., reliance on counterfactual emissions) in the design of the CDM programme. The EU also has unilaterally adopted an ambitious emissions-reduction target of 20 per cent by 2020, offering to increase that emissions-reduction target to 30 per cent if other major emitting countries *shared responsibility* by committing to emissions reductions of 20 per cent.[106] So far, other major emitting countries have not followed suit. The EU has also tried to cajole major emitting countries into sharing responsibility for GHG emission reductions by unilaterally imposing carbon taxes on international flights to and from EU destinations.[107] That effort has not worked, either. But the main point is that the EU has demonstrated how actions taken at a regional or domestic level can have a salutary effect on GHG emissions.

To the extent other countries replicate the EU ETS or design something even better, which can be linked with the ETS and other, similar

652 final 10 (14 November 2012), at http://ec.europa.eu/clima/policies/ets/reform/docs/com_2012_652_en.pdf (discussing a price floor as one option to reduce volatility and to prevent price drops resulting from temporary economic disruptions).

105 Cole, 'From Global to Polycentric Climate Governance', n. 93, at 410.

106 European Commission, 'EU greenhouse gas emissions and targets', at http://ec.europa.eu/clima/policies/g-gas/index_en.htm. See also J. Cludius, H. Forster and V. Graichen, 'Greenhouse Gas Mitigation in the European Union: An Overview of the Current Policy Landscape', World Resources Institute Working Paper, November, 2012, at www.wri.org/publication/ghg-mitigation-eu-policy-landscape.

107 See, e.g., 'EU freezes controversial aviation carbon tax', EUbusiness, 13 November 2012.

trading markets, a global carbon market might emerge (though not spontaneously) from 'bottom-up'. Such formal linkages would amount to an actual *sharing of responsibility* for climate change mitigation. The EU's recent agreement to link its ETS with Australia's new trading scheme is one small step in that direction. The EU has also held preliminary talks with California about linking the world's two largest carbon trading markets.[108] Should that happen, those linked national- and sub-national-level schemes could completely supplant the Kyoto Protocol's fatally flawed mitigation programmes, yielding a net improvement for global climate policy.

Perhaps even more importantly, combined efforts of major emitting countries (taking and sharing responsibility) could *tip* global climate negotiations into a more cooperative equilibrium.[109] As Geoffrey Heal and Howard Kunreuther have explained, a 'tipping set' of countries taking action on climate change could create a 'net return to the choice of this strategy for other agents'.[110] In other words, they could alter the incentives of other states to favour a broader distribution and sharing of responsibility for reducing emissions. This has happened before, for example in the global switch from leaded to unleaded gasoline. That switch involved three major incremental costs: first, innovating a reliable and cost-effective anti-engine-knock alternative to lead-based gasoline; second, adapting refineries to produce the new fuel; and third, modifying auto engines to use it. The United States led in innovating and mandating alternatives, which other countries could then easily adopt. Once the United States mandated lead-free gasoline (domestically), American automakers were required to adjust car designs accordingly. Automakers in other countries could not, of course, be required to play by American rules except on American soil. But the United States is such an important export market for most Japanese and European car-makers that those companies had market incentives to modify their engines accordingly. Once the alternative gasoline formulas and engines to burn it were widely available, the costs to all other countries of moving to unleaded fuel were 'negligible'.[111] In this case, shared responsibility for reducing atmospheric lead levels was spurred

[108] F. Carus, 'EU plans to link emissions trading scheme with California', *The Guardian*, 7 April 2011.

[109] On the idea of 'tipping points' generally, see T.C. Schelling, *Micromotives and Macrobehavior* (New York: W.W. Norton & Company, 1978).

[110] Heal and Kunreuther, 'Tipping Climate Negotiations', n. 91, at 55.

[111] Ibid., at 53.

by the unilateral acceptance of responsibility by a single country, the United States.

Climate change undoubtedly represents a more difficult problem to solve than taking the lead out of gasoline – not least because of the lack of available substitutes for fossil fuels. Indeed, all of Heal and Kunreuther's examples of successful tipping sets involve technological substitutions that are not on the near-term horizon for carbon-based fuels.[112] However, Heal and Kunreuther demonstrate generally that

> the climate negotiation game has a tipping set if (a) the cost of joining a treaty drops as the number of joiners rises; (b) there is a cost to not joining that is constant or rising with the number who have joined; and (c) if once a sufficient number have joined this cost exceeds the cost of joining for those who have not yet joined.[113]

A group of cooperating countries (sharing responsibility) is far more likely to constitute a 'tipping set' if they are 'strategically important countries', defined as those having 'the largest reinforcing effects on others'.[114]

We already know that the EU cannot be a tipping set of one in climate negotiations, despite its proven ability to amend *de facto* elements of the existing global regime. Whether the eventual combination of carbon trading schemes in the EU, Australia, and California might provide a 'tipping set' is uncertain. Indeed, there is reason to doubt the existence of tipping set for climate policy that does not include either China or the United States. However, those two countries recently began bilateral negotiations on GHG reductions, which potentially could lead to a 'tipping set'.[115] Simply put, if a relatively small set of countries cannot

[112] For a non-technological example of a tipping mechanism, see Barrett, 'Credible Commitments, Focal Points, and Tipping', n. 41, at 45, noting that, if a critical mass of countries join a treaty with trade restrictions as a compliance enforcement mechanism, other countries will have an incentive to join and comply. The Ozone Accords successfully used trade restrictions as a tipping mechanism. Even in that case, however, the availability of technological substitutes to ozone-depleting substances (ODSs) were crucial to the successful negotiations, including presumably the agreement to impose trade sanctions as an enforcement device against both parties and non-parties. It is extremely unlikely that the Montreal Protocol would have been agreed to, with or without trade sanctions, but for the existence of reliable and not-too-costly ODS substitutes. See Cole, 'Climate Change and Collective Action', n. 6, at 239–241.

[113] Heal and Kunreuther, 'Tipping Climate Negotiations', n. 91, at 57.

[114] Ibid.

[115] See, e.g., H. Schneider, 'U.S., China agree on climate steps to curb emissions', *Washington Post*, 10 July 2013.

tip global climate negotiations towards a potential welfare-improving equilibrium, little hope exists for global climate negotiations to find a better equilibrium. Either way, shared responsibility cannot be *imposed* but must be *accepted.*

6. Conclusion

Global climate negotiations have made little progress since the adoption of the Kyoto Protocol in 1997, which itself marked no real progress towards resolving the climate change problem. Despite the well-meaning efforts of climate negotiators and the intellectual contributions of international lawyers, global negotiations have become so paralysed that even marginal improvements to the Kyoto Protocol's ineffectual regime have remained out of grasp. In frustration, some legal scholars have begun calling for litigation against perceived recalcitrant states, such as the United States. At best, litigation is unlikely to do much good; at worst, it could create disincentives for major emitting states to take on any treaty-based obligations. Even if liability might be imposed (which seems unlikely), responsibility must be accepted or taken voluntarily.

Another option is to broaden the focus of attention from the global roving cocktail party of climate negotiations, with their thousands of participants, to smaller-scale efforts currently arising all over the world to actually reduce carbon emissions. Rather than dismissing those efforts as meaningless for a global problem like climate change, scholars and policy makers ought to be studying the actions of those who are actually taking responsibility to see which lower-level programmes are effective and might be emulated, scaled-up, and/or linked with other programmes to create a 'regime complex' or a 'tipping set' that could lead to a broader sharing of responsibility for climate change mitigation. Such efforts are not a quick fix, let alone a panacea solution for climate change. After all, the Assurance Game of climate change does not guarantee cooperative solutions. But less formal and more consistent communication and trust-building efforts between individual, major emitting countries could hardly yield worse results than the formal, global negotiations of the UN process. Hardly a ringing endorsement or a prediction of great success for polycentric approaches, but it realistically reflects the daunting nature of the collective-action problem we confront.

11

Transboundary Damage in Climate Change Criteria for Allocating Responsibility

HENRY SHUE*

'It could therefore be argued that the lack of effective federal action in the United States to mitigate climate change constitutes a breach of its customary obligation to prevent transboundary damage ... In the absence of carbon-neutral states, all states contribute to climate change through the emission of greenhouse gases and the degradation of greenhouse gas sinks. The international community tolerates this ... An injured state can therefore only invoke the responsibility of states whose contributions to climate change exceed the standard of tolerance.'[1]

1. Introduction: damage and excess

What exactly constitutes the transboundary damage caused by the failure to take effective action to avoid making climate change worse than it otherwise would be? The quoted observations by Lefeber indicate that what will be considered damage under international law is relative to which causal contributions to climate change are judged to be excessive – damage and excess go together. Implicitly this invokes a picture of the climate situation that we do well to make explicit. The conceptual picture is constructed around two zones, respectively, of resignation and indulgence, the first planet-wide and the second country-specific. First, it is accepted that a certain amount of climate change beyond what has already happened is going to occur. Second, it has been accepted that every state may continue to contribute to a certain extent to further

* Senior Research Fellow, Centre for International Studies (Department of Politics and International Relations, University of Oxford); Senior Research Fellow (Emeritus), Merton College, University of Oxford. This chapter has benefitted from comments by Anja Karnein, Dov Jacobs, André Nollkaemper, and Luke Tomlinson.

[1] R. Lefeber, 'Climate Change and State Responsibility', in R. Rayfuse and S.V. Scott (eds.), *International Law in the Era of Climate Change* (Cheltenham: Edward Elgar, 2012), 321, at 340, 346.

climate change in a manner that does not count as excessive, and is therefore not to be considered as a source of transboundary damage.

The former planet-wide zone of resignation is not entirely a product of the latter country-specific zones of indulgence and arises partly out of necessity, not policy. One part of the explanation of additional climate changes fated to come is the 'commitment' already built into the planetary system by greenhouse gas (GHG) emissions that have already been injected into the atmosphere, but have yet to play out their full effect. Sea-level rise, for example, will continue for centuries as a result of emissions that have already occurred.[2] This means that, leaving aside dangerous hubristic experiments like the extreme varieties of climate engineering,[3] we must because of necessity allow for some degree of additional climate change – at least a minimal zone of resignation.[4] In addition, some continuing emissions are inevitable for a few years. But how extensive that planetary zone of resignation must be also depends very much in fact on the extent of the zone of indulgence we choose as a matter of policy to grant to states in the future – where we draw the line beyond which the production of emissions and the destruction of sinks count as excessive, and are judged to cause transboundary damage.

I shall argue that we must specify the planetary zone of resignation first on the basis of the seriousness of the damage at risk for everyone, and then must specify any national zones of indulgence accordingly, so that the chosen planetary zone of resignation is not exceeded through extravagant claims for national indulgence on the basis of outmoded notions of state sovereignty. The interpretation of international law

[2] J.A. Church, P.U. Clark, A. Cazenave, et al., 'Sea Level Change', in T.F. Stocker, D. Qin, G.-K. Plattner, et al. (eds.), *Climate Change 2013 – The Physical Science Basis*, Working Group I Contribution to the Fifth Assessment Report of the Intergovernmental Panel on Climate Change (Cambridge University Press, 2014), 1137; S. Solomon, G.-K. Plattner, R. Knutti, and P. Friedlingstein, 'Irreversible Climate Change Due to Carbon Dioxide Emissions', (2009) 106 PNAS 1704; and M. Schaeffer, W. Hare, S. Rahmstorf, and M. Vermeer, 'Long-term sea-level rise implied by 1.5°C and 2°C warming levels' (2012) 2 NCC 867, online at www.nature.com/nclimate/journal/vaop/ncurrent/full/nclimate1584.html (last accessed on 5 June 2014).

[3] See C. Hamilton, *Earthmasters: The Dawn of the Age of Climate Engineering* (New Haven and London: Yale University Press, 2012), at ix: 'For sheer audacity, no plan by humans exceeds the one now being hatched to take control of the Earth's climate. Yet it is audacity born of failure, a collective refusal to do what must be done to protect the Earth and ourselves from a future that promises to be nasty, brutish and hot.'

[4] This is made more palatable if one assumes that adaptation can be successful in response to this degree of change. Human lives – and entire species of plants and animals – will, however, be lost.

should rest on a policy adopted toward acceptable risks of damage, especially severe damage to the defenceless.

Hence, before we reflect on the line-drawing issues raised by the specification of 'excess', we must grasp the kinds of damage that excess in this realm produces. The twinned causes, excessive degradation of sinks and excessive emissions, produce in combination twinned sets of effects. First, of course, they directly cause the various interrelated phenomena that are referred to as climate change itself. These phenomena, singly and in multiple combinations, then yield multiple indirect effects on human societies, including crop failures, destruction of dwellings and other property, threatening changes in disease patterns (like the northern movement of 'tropical' diseases and their vectors) and in temperature patterns, and much else, including some locally positive effects. I shall not elaborate this first set of damages – physical changes and their social effects – here, since they are increasingly appreciated.

These changes in the climate threaten, if they continue far enough, to undermine the most fundamental conditions of human welfare and modern human societies, which is highly significant legally. The levels of wealth to which developed societies cling and developing societies aspire were possible because human societies had gradually adapted more and more successfully to the current conditions on this planet, which had remained as they were for about 10,000 years, but are now being changed by us. The Agricultural Revolution that occurred at the dawn of this period in the history of the earth's climate made possible surplus food and consequently expanding human settlements that have turned into the metropolises, mega-metropolises, and nation-states that have hosted the Industrial Revolution, the Information Revolution, and the other developments that have created the wealth many of us currently enjoy and the social infrastructure that has allowed the human population to explode several times over.

The agriculture at the base of this social pyramid is, however, strikingly fragile, and the weather cannot change beyond certain points without disruptions in the supply of food that would initially yield price fluctuations and subsequently produce scarcities, to neither of which the poorest humans would be able to adjust.[5] Any 'standard of tolerance'

[5] See J.R. Porter, L. Xie, A. Challinor, et al., 'Food Security and Food Production Systems', in V. Barros, C. Field, K. Mach, et al., *Climate Change 2014: Impacts, Adaptation, and Vulnerability*, Working Group II Contribution to the Fifth Assessment Report of the Intergovernmental Panel on Climate Change (Cambridge University Press, 2014), ch. 7.

in this area deserves sharp scrutiny, as does any interpretation of state sovereignty that would grant license to undermine the very preconditions of the viability of the units claiming it. Any suggestion that state sovereignty ought to include license to engage in activities that risk undermining such fundamental conditions of life would be absurdly self-defeating. It is clearly vital that the customary prohibition on transboundary damage be considered *jus cogens* in the case of damage that risks undermining the essential physical underpinnings of human agriculture and the rest of the human economy.

Indeed, one might plausibly posit 'a primitive social contract at the international level whereby the international community, as a reified entity, owes a sort of sovereign duty to protect its subjects, in the same way that a state must protect its citizens against crime. In this sense, the duty is clearly a shared obligation and owed by the international community as a whole . . . and by all states constituting that community, irrespective of their special relationship to the injured state'.[6] As we shall see, this would have powerful implications for who could bring legal actions.

2. Cumulative carbon: the science

The second kind of damage produced by sink-destruction and emissions-production is quite different from the first set, and more profoundly socially mediated. The standard way of specifying the extent of what I am calling the planetary zone of resignation is to say that we will attempt to prevent an increase in average global temperature, compared to the average temperature prior to the Industrial Revolution, of more than two degrees Celsius (2°C), which of course means accepting a temperature rise of 2°C. In effect, a line is being drawn between two degrees of 'tolerable' worsening of the climate and further intolerable worsening. It is generally understood that the first two degrees of rise is far from unproblematic, but this is widely believed to be the most ambitious goal that might be politically feasible. The goal of 2°C informally adopted in Copenhagen and formally embraced in Cancun rests on drawing this line here.[7] Leaving

6 P.A. Nollkaemper and D. Jacobs, 'Shared Responsibility in International Law: A Conceptual Framework' (2013) 34 MIJIL 359, at 427.

7 See 'The Cancun Agreements: Outcome of the Work of the Ad Hoc Working Group on Long-Term Cooperative Action under the Convention', Decision 1/CP.16, in *United Nations Framework Convention on Climate Change (UNFCCC), Report of the Conference of the Parties on Its Sixteenth Session, Addendum, Part Two: Action Taken by the Conference of the Parties*, UN Doc. FCCC/CP/2010/7/Add. 1 (2011), para. 4.

aside the question whether 2°C is the best place for the line, we must choose some number. We must specify how much climate change is too much, and thereby how much and which kinds of damage we accept (in trust for the future generations who will mostly be the ones who suffer it).

An impressive number of recent scientific analyses have converged on the suggestion that once a political decision has been reached about the amount of temperature rise that will be accepted, we can best think in terms of a cumulative carbon budget for that amount of temperature rise.[8] The single factor that predicts most accurately the most likely amount of temperature change beyond the pre-Industrial Revolution temperature is the cumulative amount of carbon emitted since the beginning of the Industrial Revolution – since, say, 1750. The total *cumulative* amount of carbon emissions since 1750 is what matters – rather than, say, the current annual global emissions – because of the extraordinarily long atmospheric residence time of carbon dioxide. Once carbon dioxide is injected into the atmosphere it remains for a lengthy period – for many molecules, the residence time in the stratosphere is millennia – so the atmospheric total continues to swell decade after decade.[9] The strong correlation between

[8] This determination is of course probabilistic: the concentration makes a given temperature the most likely one. Other factors are also at work. Two companion studies converged upon the conceptual point: M.R. Allen, D.J. Frame, C. Huntingford, et al., 'Warming Caused by Cumulative Carbon Emissions Towards the Trillionth Tonne' (2009) 458 *Nature* 1163; and M. Meinshausen, N. Meinshausen, W. Hare, et al., 'Greenhouse-Gas Emission Targets for Limiting Global Warming to 2°C' (2009) 458 *Nature* 1158 (with supplementary information online). The conceptual point was first laid out in an accessible manner in M.R. Allen, D.J. Frame, K. Frieler, et al., 'The Exit Strategy' (2009) 3 NRCC 56, at 57. A policy relevant follow-up study is N.H.A. Bowerman, D.J. Frame, C. Huntingford, et al., 'Cumulative Carbon Emissions, Emissions Floors and Short-Term Rates of Warming: Implications for Policy' (2011) 369 PTA 45. A further analysis of the policy implications of carbon dioxide's lengthy lifespan relative to other greenhouse gases is: H.D. Matthews, S. Solomon, and R. Pierrehumbert, 'Cumulative Carbon as a Policy Framework for Achieving Climate Stabilization' (2012) 370 PTA 4365. For a more sophisticated discussion of the science than mine in the text, see R.T. Pierrehumbert, 'Cumulative Carbon and Just Allocation of the Global Carbon Commons' (2013) 13 Chic JIL 2. The significance of the cumulative carbon budget has now been confirmed by the IPCC – see M. Collins, R. Knutti, J.M. Arblaster, et al., 'Long-term Climate Change: Projections, Commitments and Irreversibility', in T.F. Stocker, D. Qin, G.-K. Plattner, et al. (eds.), *Climate Change 2013 – The Physical Science Basis*, Working Group I Contribution to the Fifth Assessment Report of the Intergovernmental Panel on Climate Change (Cambridge University Press, 2014), 1029, at 1033.

[9] P. Ciais, C. Sabine, G. Bala, et al., 'Carbon and Other Biogeochemical Cycles', in T.F. Stocker, D. Qin, G.-K. Plattner, et al. (eds.), *Climate Change 2013 – The Physical Science Basis*, Working Group I Contribution to the Fifth Assessment Report of the Intergovernmental Panel on Climate Change (Cambridge University Press, 2014), 465, at 472–473.

total cumulative carbon emitted since the Industrial Revolution began and rise in average global temperature since the Industrial Revolution began means that for any amount of temperature rise chosen as the political goal of efforts to deal with climate change, the atmospheric scientists can calculate the approximate cumulative carbon budget that makes it more likely than not that the temperature goal will not be exceeded. For a rise of no more than 2°C, for instance, the cumulative carbon budget is around one trillion tonnes. This budget is already more than half used up – emissions from 1750 to date are over 580 gigatonnes – and if emissions continue on the trajectory of the last 20 years, the remainder of the budget will be exhausted in 26 years, in 2040.[10]

3. Cumulative carbon: the significance

For our purposes particular numbers are primarily illustrative. The significance lies in the basic logic: for any given total of cumulative carbon emissions – any given cumulative carbon budget – there is a most likely temperature rise. As humanity exceeds that cumulative carbon budget, the probability of lower average global temperatures than the target falls, and the probability of higher temperatures rises.

So far, as the observation initially quoted from Lefeber indicates, we have tended to believe that for each state in the international system a national zone of indulgence could be specified in terms of permissible additional GHG emissions: 'An injured state can therefore only invoke the responsibility of states whose contributions to climate change exceed the standard of tolerance.'[11] If we frame our challenge in terms of the global carbon budget, however, we begin to see that the current pattern of thinking nation-by-nation is highly problematic.

Above all, the cumulative carbon budget is global. Emissions must be summed not only over time since 1750 but over all nations. This reveals one of the dangers of thinking in terms of national zones of indulgence: it allows it to seem appropriate to do calculations from the bottom – national (or in the case of the European Union (EU), regional) – level up. But this is a mistaken procedure. It is the global total of emissions that must be restricted to the cumulative carbon budget for whichever goal of temperature rise has been chosen. There is no guarantee – indeed, no real prospect – that bottom-up allowances will sum to only the

[10] See TrillionthTonne.org, http://trillionthtonne.org (last accessed on 20 June 2014).
[11] Lefeber, 'Climate Change and State Responsibility', n. 1, at 340, 346.

maximum global total compatible with the desired temperature rise. This would require some truly miraculous 'invisible hand'. Failure in the mitigation enterprise is certain unless the allowances for nations/regions are reached with a view to a global total that is fixed first on the basis of the temperature rise to which human agriculture and other human enterprises can successfully adapt rapidly enough. Emissions targets must be viewed from the top down – from the chosen global goal to the national/regional allowances that will in fact lead to that goal.

This is by far the lesser stringency, however. The greater discipline lies in the fact that the remaining balance of 'allowable' emissions, whatever the appropriate total budget is, is rapidly diminishing through our currently undisciplined carbon emissions free-for-all. The point is not to delay the day on which the trillionth tonne of carbon is emitted, but to keep that day from coming – ever. This is not a political constraint that can be fiddled – this is a feature of planetary dynamics.

Obviously, then, in order to avoid the infliction of the transboundary damages inherent in further climate change we need to specify national/regional emissions allowances, at least some of which decline so rapidly that total global cumulative carbon emissions into the atmosphere never reach one trillion tonnes, if we are serious about the goal of a temperature rise no greater than 2°C. In short, net injections of carbon dioxide into the atmosphere must reach zero before the atmospheric total reaches one trillion tonnes. Basically, we must promptly find an exit from the fossil-fuel/carbon regime that now dominates the planet and has brought us both industrial society and climate change.

Yet contemporary societies cannot function without massive supplies of energy. Exiting the carbon regime, then, requires entering a non-carbon regime. The transition to an alternative energy regime will require courageous leadership and great exertion because it will be constantly attacked by fossil-fuel interests, the value of whose capital assets – the proven reserves of coal, oil, and gas – will turn out to be a financial bubble if humanity acts against climate change.[12] This is not the place to

[12] See Carbon Tracker Initiative, *Unburnable Carbon – Are the world's financial markets carrying a carbon bubble?* (2011) at www.carbontracker.org/wp-content/uploads/downloads/2012/08/Unburnable-Carbon-Full1.pdf; and Carbon Tracker Initiative and Grantham Research Institute on Climate Change and the Environment, *Unburnable Carbon 2013: Wasted capital and stranded assets* (2013) at http://carbontracker.live.kiln.it/Unburnable-Carbon-2-Web-Version.pdf (both last accessed on 5 June 2014). Carbon interests tend instead to support climate engineering, which would allow the fossil-fuel regime to continue business as usual – see Hamilton, *Earthmasters*, n. 3.

analyse alternative paths for the energy transition, and I have considered one strategy elsewhere.[13]

4. Profligate emissions: four allocation principles

Here the question is: what in the circumstances that the international system of states confronts constitutes the transboundary infliction of damage? And it should now be evident that the damage is of two varieties. The first set is the infliction of the phenomena constituting climate change itself and their social effects. The second is the generation of carbon emissions that exhaust an excessive share of the remaining cumulative carbon budget. Both kinds of damage result from excessive emissions, but each is revealed by viewing the excessive emissions from a different perspective. From one perspective the excessive emissions are additional causal contributors to the floods, droughts, and other disruptions that constitute climate change itself. From another perspective the excessive emissions are encroachments on the shrinking global cumulative budget, needed by others, of emissions that will most likely not produce a temperature rise of more than 2°C.

Conceptually this has the great disadvantage of making the standard of 'excessive' depend upon a question of distribution, namely, when is a nation consuming more than its share of the shrinking remaining budget? However, we cannot avoid this complication because it is a crucial element of the international situation. All states in the international system must share a single budget of carbon emissions that shrinks with every emission by every state. Excessive climate emissions are doubly damaging across borders. One kind of action – excessive carbon emissions – is both increasing the supply of supposedly tolerable climate difficulties and reducing the supply of energy that can be consumed without causing clearly intolerable climate difficulties.

What does it mean concretely for a state's emissions to exceed its share enough to inflict the second variety of damage? We can call these 'profligate emissions'. In order to specify a baseline against which to

[13] Essentially the strategy is a global version, with transnational subsidies, of the kind of feed-in tariffs pioneered by Germany – for a sketch, see H. Shue, 'Climate Hope: Implementing the Exit Strategy' (2013) 13(2) Chic JIL 381; reprinted in H. Shue, *Climate Justice: Vulnerability and Protection* (Oxford University Press, 2014), 319. And for fuller details, see T. Banuri and N. Hällström, 'A Global Programme to Tackle Energy Access and Climate Change' (2012) 61 DD 264.

measure what is profligate we must confront a central question concerning shared responsibility: on the basis of what criteria responsibility can be allocated between multiple parties.[14] What would be the basis for a judgment that a particular state's emissions are profligate? The negative answer to the question is: no single factor establishes that emissions are profligate because each individual measure is partial and contentious in its own ways, especially if advanced as the only factor that matters. But if all or several of the most relevant factors converge in the case of a particular state, that constitutes a compelling case. Here are the four most relevant factors.

First, the most important factor is how strenuous the state's efforts have been to reduce its emissions. One could not reasonably accuse a state of excessive emissions if it were engaged in ambitious, robust, and multi-pronged efforts to cut its emissions rapidly. Accordingly, a good score on this factor would count strongly against any charge of excessive emissions, perhaps even if the states' emissions remained undesirably high by an objective standard. No state could be found guilty of transboundary damage as a result of excessive emissions if it were basically doing everything it could reasonably be expected to do to reduce its emissions. And a bad score on this factor would count strongly in favour of the judgment of excess, especially because the standard of international law is due diligence: 'The obligation is a due diligence obligation . . . Compliance requires states to adopt, implement, supervise, and enforce policies and measures to achieve the objective, in this case policies and measures that prevent, limit, or reduce the emission of greenhouse gases, i.e. mitigation action.'[15] In sum, the first factor embodies the legal requirement of due diligence and is reasonable in common-sense terms as recognising good-faith effort.

Second, a further factor is what kinds of costs the state would need to impose upon its own residents in order to do more to constrain carbon emissions than it is now doing. In effect, a high score on this consideration might function as a justification for a low score on the first.[16] It would not be reasonable to expect a state to make strenuous efforts to constrain its carbon emissions if, for example, many of its residents suffer from 'energy poverty' in, for instance, being unable to afford the

[14] Nollkaemper and Jacobs, 'Shared Responsibility', n. 6, at 393.

[15] Lefeber, 'State Responsibility', n. 1, at 334, citing *Pulp Mills on the River Uruguay (Argentina* v. *Uruguay)*, Judgment, ICJ Reports 2010, 14, para. 197.

[16] I examine later some ways of measuring these factors.

electricity necessary for a decent life, and the only energy that could affordably be provided to those deprived residents is carbon-based energy.

If, by contrast, the state's residents have among the highest per capita rates of energy consumption in the world, they certainly can reasonably be asked to manage with less. Indeed, it is precisely for the sake of energy-deprived people who can potentially afford nothing other than carbon-based energy that energy-rich people must not unnecessarily exhaust the remaining carbon budget in a wasteful or frivolous manner. The cumulative carbon budget is after all strictly zero-sum: whatever the rich consume becomes unavailable for the deprived.[17] In short, the second factor embodies the legal excuse of necessity and is reasonable in common-sense terms as a form of fairness that acknowledges genuine needs.

The third factor to consider, then, is the current emissions per capita of the residents of the state in question, which are a direct measure of the extent of their ongoing appropriation of resources from the shrinking common pool. This objective measure should be qualified by the first two factors. If, in accord with the first, the state is making a maximum effort to restrict its emissions, then it is perhaps exercising due diligence even if the objective level of its members' appropriation is higher than ideal for now. Adequate effort makes up to some degree for inadequate results. Similarly, if, in accord with the second, the state could not restrict its emissions without depriving its residents of energy that they need for a decent life, it would be unreasonable to accuse it of transboundary damage even if its emissions were objectively higher than ideal. It is not fair to expect the sacrifice of the fulfilment of genuine needs.

If, by contrast, the state is neither doing its best to reduce emissions nor unable to reduce them without depriving its members of essentials, and its emissions per capita are high, this evidently indicates that its emissions are profligate, and it is inflicting both kinds of transboundary damage on the rest of the world. If emissions per capita are exceptionally high, this shows that the profligate emissions are produced in flagrant disregard of other peoples.

It may be objected to the third factor that the people of different states have different needs and so it is not reasonable to expect equal per capita emissions from everyone. The content of the objection is correct, but the

[17] I have explored this more fully in Shue, 'Climate Hope: Implementing the Exit Strategy', n. 13.

objection is irrelevant. The third factor neither supposes that emissions ought to be the same per capita nor that it is somehow automatically wrong for one state's per capita emissions to be higher than another's. It assumes only that if a state's emissions are among the highest in the world, it bears the burden of explanation why they should be so high, given the urgency of reducing emissions overall. If the state is making great efforts to reduce emissions (first factor) or its weather is especially extreme (example of second factor), the higher emissions might be either excusable or justifiable.

Most important, the objection ignores the fundamental point that the cumulative carbon budget is zero-sum. Each person's emissions are emissions that no one else may ever have, and this makes the extent of emissions a profoundly distributive question – a question of fairness.[18] Some extremely good reason would need to apply to any emissions that are at all high, much less among the highest in the world, in light of the double damage high emissions are wreaking: exacerbating climate change itself and its social effects and exhausting the remaining balance of 'tolerable' emissions within the cumulative carbon budget. High per capita carbon emissions hasten the day when no significant further carbon emissions will be compatible with an acceptable limit on average global surface temperature, and they entail that fewer persons – even persons who can afford no other kind of energy – can emit before that day is reached. Emissions that are exceptionally high and are not falling rapidly are virtually impossible to justify.

Fourth, an additional important factor is the state's percentage of the cumulative carbon emissions to this point.[19] This is based on three separate but converging reasons. The first reason is simply that cumulative emissions are, so to speak, what it is all about. Because carbon resides for so very long in the atmosphere once it arrives there, the crucial factor in how severe climate change becomes is the cumulative total of carbon emitted, as we have already seen. It would consequently be exceedingly strange in assessing the international role of various states in climate change to give little weight to their performance on the dimension that matters the most: the cumulative.

[18] I explain this more fully in connection with the fourth factor, which similarly rests on distributive considerations.

[19] It is well worth considering whether the most relevant variant of this factor is per capita cumulative emissions. I leave this aside here.

The second reason is that past emissions are hardly unrelated to the stringency now required in future emissions. On the contrary, the remaining carbon budget is as small as it is precisely because past emissions have been as great as they have. A Faulkner character (a lawyer) famously said: 'The past is never dead – it's not even past.'[20] Nowhere is this more true than here. More carbon could be emitted in the future without driving the temperature rise beyond an additional 2°C if less carbon had been emitted in the past. The entire cumulative carbon budget is zero-sum across time. So little of the budget is left for the future because so much has been used in the past. Who used up the amount that is gone is of central significance.

The third reason in support of this fourth factor is this: since the cumulative carbon budget is a measure of a good held in common, namely the diminishing capacity to emit carbon without contributing to an intolerably great rise in temperature, the distribution of that increasingly scarce good among states and individuals is inherently a question of fairness, or as lawyers like to say, equity. And to deprive people of their fair share of a vital good is to damage them. Distributive issues are unavoidable here because a shared good must be divided. To try to deny that this distribution raises normative issues is implicitly to make the preposterous claim that a procedure under which the richest grab whatever they want until it is all gone is a normatively acceptable procedure for the division of such a valuable scarce good. The state's percentage of total cumulative emissions is the most obviously direct measure of the extent of its appropriation so far of this good held in common by the people of all states. This standard can be interpreted in a number of different ways – as we shall see later, it may be fairer to deduct from each nation's absolute total the emissions that were essential for the provision of basic necessities to its population, or to deduct the emissions before the effects of emissions were understood. But the basic contention that cumulative emissions indicate the share taken out of the commons seems difficult to deny.

So the four allocation principles that I am proposing should be considered in order to judge when a state's emissions are profligate are: first, extent of effort to reduce emissions ('due diligence'); second, costs of possible additional reductions ('necessity'); third, current emissions per

[20] G. Stevens, in W. Faulkner, *Requiem for a Nun* (London: Vintage, 1996 [1950]), Act I, scene iii, at 85.

capita (actual results to date); and fourth, percentage of total cumulative emissions (national encroachment on global budget).

5. The US case: causal and moral responsibility for profligacy

By way of illustration, let us consider whether United States (US) emissions are profligate. The situation of the United States with regard to the first and second factors is quite straightforward. Concerning the first, the United States has exerted very little effort to reduce emissions. To this day it still lacks any national limit on emissions of GHGs in general or emissions of carbon in particular and any legislation (like a carbon tax or an emissions trading scheme) designed to reduce emissions; it has rejected the one relevant binding multilateral treaty (Kyoto Protocol);[21] the upper level of its federal legislature (the Senate) is openly contemptuous of measures to deal with climate change; the lower level (House of Representatives) in 2011 rejected by a vote of 240 to 184 the proposition that 'Congress accepts the scientific findings ... that climate change is occurring, is caused largely by human activities, and poses significant risks for public health and welfare';[22] and its emissions grew 4.7 per cent between 1990 and 2012, the latest year for which it gives its own statistics.[23] Concerning the second factor, it is one of the most affluent societies on earth and could easily reduce emissions significantly by reducing energy waste and curtailing entirely unnecessary uses of energy. The status of the United States with regard to the first two factors requires very little discussion: it has not remotely displayed due diligence, and it has no excuse of necessity whatsoever.[24]

The third factor in judging which emissions are excessive is current per capita emissions. If, following David Weisbach, one considers all six

[21] Kyoto Protocol to the United Nations Framework Convention on Climate Change, Kyoto, 10 December 1997, in force 16 February 2005, 2303 UNTS 148 (Kyoto Protocol).

[22] Hamilton, *Earthmasters*, n. 3, at 85–86.

[23] United States Environmental Protection Agency, 'National Greenhouse Gas Emissions Data' (April 2014) at www.epa.gov/climatechange/Downloads/ghgemissions/US-GHG-Inventory-2014-Chapter-2-Trends.pdf (last accessed on 28 June 2014).

[24] To be fair, it ought to be noted that this extreme level of failure is true only of the federal government. Some regions (combining several states), individual states, individual cities, and voluntary associations of citizens are working vigorously to try to counteract Washington's backwardness. For examples, see J. Garofoli, 'California, China to Link Climate-Change Efforts', San Francisco Chronicle, 13 September 2013; and M.L. Wald, '8 States Teaming Up to Support Electric Cars', *New York Times*, 24 October 2013.

Kyoto Protocol GHGs and leaves aside the countries with the smallest total emissions, the United States has the sixth highest per capita emissions in the world.[25] The three highest are oil producers, whose emissions presumably come mainly from oil production, not emission-generating consumption, each with less than one-half of one per cent of global emissions: Qatar, United Arab Emirates, and Kuwait. The next three are both producers of fossil fuel and extreme emission-generating consumers: Australia [coal], Canada [tar sands bitumen], and the United States [coal, oil, and gas]. Of the top twenty in per capita emissions the United States produces by far the highest percentage of the world total: 15.7 per cent. On this factor, then, the United States is not the worst, although it does extremely poorly. And it has neither the justification that it is making robust efforts to cut emissions, nor the excuse that the current emissions are necessary to lift citizens out of poverty.

The fourth and final factor is cumulative emissions, which are a more controversial matter and can be calculated in some significantly different ways, three of which merit discussion. Benito Müller, Niklas Höhne, and Christian Ellermann have provided sophisticated analyses of the main issues in two complementary articles using the data set originally assembled by the ad hoc group for the modelling and assessment of contributions to climate change (MATCH).[26] First, Müller, Höhne, and Ellermann begin by quantifying the relative causal contributions of the world's various nations to climate change, interpreting climate change specifically as 'changes in mean global temperature', and taking the relative causal contributions to be the relative sizes of the cumulative sums of emissions of all six anthropogenic Kyoto-counted greenhouse gases over each nation's sovereign territory between 1890 and 2005,

[25] D. Weisbach, 'Negligence, Strict Liability, and Responsibility for Climate Change' (2011–2012) 97 Iowa LR 521, at 548, Table 8. The main limitation of Weisbach's discussion is that he relies largely on domestic conceptions of responsibility and liability.

[26] B. Müller, N. Höhne, and C. Ellermann, 'Differentiating (Historic) Responsibilities for Climate Change' (2009) 9 CP 593; and C. Ellermann, N. Höhne, and B. Müller, 'Differentiating Historical Responsibilities for Climate Change', in P.G. Harris (ed.), *China's Responsibility for Climate Change: Ethics, Fairness and Environmental Policy* (Bristol: Policy Press, 2011), 71. As the similarity of titles and identity of authors suggests, both articles cover much of the same ground, but Ellermann, et al. devotes special attention to China, while Müller, et al. provides more analysis of alternative conceptions of responsibility. Citations for further information on MATCH are provided in Müller, et al., at 594. Because the figures in this analysis are for all six Kyoto gases, they are not strictly comparable to the carbon budget, which concerns only carbon. However, because carbon is the dominant gas among the Kyoto six, they are broadly comparable.

weighted according to their respective constant 1995 global warming potentials (GWP) as standardly employed under the Kyoto Protocol.[27] Thus 'the share of a country's . . . contribution to climate change is given by their share in global historic GWP-weighted GHG emissions'.[28] Some selected 'causal contribution shares' are: United States (19.7 per cent), EU-25 (17.8 per cent), China (10.8 per cent), Russia (6.5 per cent), Brazil (4.3 per cent), India (3.9 per cent), and Japan (2.8 per cent).[29]

One of the main conceptual points in these twin articles is that causal contribution and moral responsibility are not the same, and any given agent may have (a percentage of the total) moral responsibility that is either less or greater than (the percentage of) that agent's causal contribution. As a general proposition, this is certainly true. One may not be morally responsible for some effects one has caused, and one may be morally responsible for some states of affairs that one has not caused. Unfortunately, in specifying how moral responsibility differs from causal responsibility considerable complication comes in.[30] The next two calculations consider two of them respectively.

In both cases, Müller, Höhne, and Ellermann use what they call 'a (bottom-up) allowance-based methodology', which permits various allowances, based on various different factors relevant to responsibility, to be incorporated into the calculations in order to reflect facets of the difference between national causal responsibility and national moral responsibility:[31]

[27] Müller, Höhne, and Ellermann, 'Differentiating (Historic) Responsibilities for Climate Change', ibid., at 595, 597; Ellermann, Höhne, and Müller, 'Differentiating Historical Responsibilities for Climate Change', ibid., at 72, 76.

[28] Müller, Höhne, and Ellermann, 'Differentiating (Historic) Responsibilities for Climate Change', n. 26, at 601; Ellermann, Höhne, and Müller, 'Differentiating Historical Responsibilities for Climate Change', n. 26, at 83.

[29] Ibid. (fewer countries specified). This analysis considers all the greenhouse gases covered by the Kyoto Protocol, not carbon alone. For the suggestion that the costs of, in particular, any necessary air extraction of carbon dioxide be allocated in proportion to cumulative emissions, since climate change is so closely proportional to cumulative emissions, see J. Hansen, M. Sato, R. Ruedy, et al., 'Dangerous human-made interference with climate: a GISS modelE study' (2007) 7 Atmos Chem Phys 2287.

[30] We are of course concerned with legal responsibility under international law, which they did not attempt to consider. But I believe their discussion still turns out to be instructive for our purposes, and I come to international legal responsibility in light of their analysis later.

[31] Müller, Höhne, and Ellermann, 'Differentiating (Historic) Responsibilities for Climate Change', n. 26, at 598; Ellermann, Höhne, and Müller, 'Differentiating Historical Responsibilities for Climate Change', n. 26, at 77.

> The idea is that allowances may be allocated to emitters, which they can use against their emissions in calculating their level of responsibility. It is, in general terms, analogous to the system of tax allowances used in most countries in differentiating the tax burden. There can be different kinds of such 'climate change responsibility allowances', depending on the (moral) justification for their allocation.[32]

Some allowances are applied per capita, and some are not; each allowance might be set at any of many different levels, and the level chosen needs to be justified morally.[33] This becomes highly complex and contentious, and I will mention only one per capita and one national allowance.

Secondly, then, one might think that every nation is entitled to a certain basic level of emissions and that it would be unfair to hold a nation responsible for using its initial 'basic allowance' of emissions.[34] This is analogous to the tax-free income at the bottom of many tax tables. Müller, Höhne, and Ellermann quite reasonably assign their basic allowance per capita. Obviously, all per capita quotas serve in fact, other things equal, to reduce the responsibility of the more populous nations and increase the responsibility of the less populous ones. Consequently, the causal contribution shares given previously, adjusted by their chosen basic allowance, yield shares of what they call 'strict responsibility'[35] as follows: United States (25.6 per cent), EU-25 (19.1 per cent), Russia (7.3 per cent), China (6.4 per cent), Brazil (5.2 per cent), Japan (2.8 per cent), and India (0.3 per cent) – compared to the first calculation of their 'causal contribution shares', China falls below Russia, and India falls to the bottom of this list, because of its low emissions (3.9 per cent causal contribution share) combined with its large population size (16.9 per cent of world population).[36] The United States moves even farther into the top spot.

[32] Ibid.

[33] My own fear is that the moral complexity will make the allowance component of the methodology collapse of its own weight in a manner that is indeed precisely analogous to many national tax codes, which desperately need simplification.

[34] I initially argued for this view in H. Shue, 'Subsistence Emissions and Luxury Emissions' (1993) 15(1) LP 39; reprinted in S.M. Gardiner, S. Caney, D. Jamieson, and H. Shue (eds.), *Climate Ethics: Essential Readings* (New York: Oxford University Press, 2010), 200; and in H. Shue, *Climate Justice*, n. 13, at 47.

[35] This is entirely distinct from strict liability and is therefore a somewhat unfortunate label.

[36] Müller, Höhne, and Ellermann, 'Differentiating (Historic) Responsibilities for Climate Change', n. 26, at 603; Ellermann, Höhne, and Müller, 'Differentiating Historical Responsibilities for Climate Change', n. 26, at 85 (fewer countries specified).

Thirdly, just as one cannot be morally responsible for having engaged in basic activities everyone must engage in, it is also widely thought that one cannot be morally responsible for consequences that one neither intended nor even foresaw.[37] Thus, it might be thought that a nation whose people were excusably ignorant of the effects on the climate of their emissions cannot be held morally responsible for those effects or blamed for those emissions.[38] This assumption is the basis for what these articles call an 'epistemic allowance', which they implement, not per capita, but nationally, simply by excluding all emissions before 1990. That year is chosen 'on the grounds that after that year, which saw the beginning of the UNFCCC [United Nations Framework Convention on Climate Change] negotiations and the publication of the first IPCC [Intergovernmental Panel on Climate Change] reports, no government could reasonably plead ignorance of the problem'.[39] If one then looks only at emissions from 1990 through 2005, then compared to the second calculation of 'strict responsibility' (which adjusts causal shares for basic allowances), the share of epistemically constrained 'limited responsibility' that falls on China almost doubles to 12 per cent, and the shares of the United States and EU each fall by more than one-fifth to 20.1 per cent and 12.3 per cent, respectively.[40]

Focusing exclusively on the United States and comparing the three measures, the United States has a 'causal contribution share' of 19.7 per cent, a 'strict responsibility share' of 25.6 per cent, and a 'limited responsibility share' (1990–2005 emissions only) of 20.1 per cent. Rather than plunge into the myriad issues concerning which, if any, of these three measures might be most appropriate for which purposes – presumably, different measures for different purposes – and at which level each of the two allowances should be set, I would like to suggest that two facts stand out starkly.

[37] I have suggested that this is less obvious than it may seem in the case of climate change in 'Historical Responsibility', Technical Briefing for Ad Hoc Working Group on Long-term Cooperative Action under the Convention [AWG-LCA], SBSTA, UNFCC, Bonn, 4 June 2009, at http://unfccc.int/files/meetings/ad_hoc_working_groups/lca/application/pdf/1_shue_rev.pdf (last accessed on 5 June 2014). But I ignore my own (minority) view here.

[38] I discuss this somewhat more fully later in this chapter.

[39] Müller, Höhne, and Ellermann, 'Differentiating (Historic) Responsibilities for Climate Change', n. 26, at 604; Ellermann, Höhne, and Müller, 'Differentiating Historical Responsibilities for Climate Change', n. 26, at 86.

[40] Ibid.

First, whichever of these three measures of cumulative emissions one uses, the United States share is always the largest in the world; and second, for all the philosophical complexities attendant upon judgments about the relative merits of (these and other) alternative calculations of shares, the United States never falls significantly below 20 per cent of the total for all nations on earth. This seems to me to be basically all that one needs to know. In sum, the United States has made the largest – and absolutely a very substantial – contribution to the creation of climate change and consumed the largest portion of the cumulative carbon budget (factor four), while doing very little about it (factor one) with no plausible excuse (factor two) and continuing to this day to emit at one of the highest per capita rates in the world (factor three) – the third highest among industrial nations.[41]

6. The US case: legal responsibility

Our concern here of course is specifically with legal responsibility for transboundary damage, which is not discussed as such by Müller, Höhne, and Ellermann. But I think the implication of their work is clear. Pure causal responsibility (measure 1) would be apposite only if the relevant standard were strict liability, but strict liability is not the legal standard for transboundary damage. Nor can I see any basis in international law for using their 'limited responsibility' (measure 3), which qualifies causal responsibility by ignoring all emissions prior to 1990 on epistemic grounds.[42] Knowledge or lack of knowledge would be relevant only if fault needed to be established, but 'in international law, liability does not depend on fault and is established on the basis of attribution and breach alone'.[43] As I have noted already, the United States is in any case the worst offender by all three measures.

[41] Cumulative emissions per capita as of 2010 show the United States is emitting more than three times as much as China and more than three times the world average – see Ellermann, Höhne, and Müller, 'Differentiating Historical Responsibilities for Climate Change', n. 26, at 81, Figure 4.3.

[42] D. Weisbach analyses cumulative per capita emissions since 1990 only – see Weisbach, 'Negligence, Strict Liability, and Responsibility for Climate Change', n. 25, at 562, Table 9. The US has the 10th highest per capita emissions since 1990; China ranks 107th and India 154th. Of states that are neither oil-producers nor very small, only Canada (5th) and Australia (6th) are worse than the US

[43] M.G. Faure and P.A. Nollkaemper, 'International Liability as an Instrument to Prevent and Compensate for Climate Change' (2007) 43A Stan JIL 123, at 145.

Their somewhat misleadingly named 'strict responsibility' (measure 2), which qualifies causal responsibility by applying a per capita 'allowance' for emissions necessary (given the existing energy regime) for a decent life, is presented by them as one reading of moral responsibility. I would suggest, however, that it is also the core of one reasonable way to try to quantify 'excess' emissions in the sense prohibited by international law. In my terminology it could be construed as already being a reading of the fourth factor (cumulative emissions) qualified by the second factor (necessity). I would simply suggest also considering the first factor (extent of due diligence) and the third factor (results to date) in assessing the wrongfulness of state behaviour.

The most contentious aspect of using their conception of 'strict responsibility' as a reading of responsibility under international law would, I imagine, be the setting of the specific level of the allowances, an issue that I have not pursued. Some people would, I suspect, consider the level at which Müller, Höhne, and Ellermann have set their allowances too low, that is, as interpreting 'necessity' too strictly. However, it is worth observing that since the allowance is per capita and the US population is far smaller than some other, poorer nations with growing emissions (notably, China and India), the higher the allowance is set, the worse the United States looks. A possible challenge would be to find non-arbitrary bases for a particular level. Nevertheless, the suggestion that some per capita adjustment should be made to the absolute amount of emissions to reflect the fact that until we escape the fossil-fuel regime a certain amount of emissions are very temporarily unavoidable – and certainly were in the past – seems sound.

7. Conclusions

Fundamentally, the current situation is urgent precisely because so much of the cumulative carbon budget has already been used up. The single largest factor explaining why the global carbon allowance will be exhausted so soon is the percentage of the global sinks already filled by emissions from the United States: at least 19.7 per cent. The primary contributor to the exhaustion of the cumulative carbon budget is the United States, whose total cumulative emissions remain to this day the largest in the world. US emissions are profligate, and flagrantly so.[44]

[44] According to two recent authoritative reports in a series done for the World Bank by what is perhaps the most highly respected research centre on climate science, the

I believe, therefore, that cases for transboundary damage ought to be brought against the United States in international courts by some of the states that are, and will be, suffering the most from, for example, sea-level rise.[45]

Further, if one accepts the suggestion mentioned earlier that the thickening of the web of international norms is moving the international situation closer to a 'primitive social contract', thus heightening the aspects of shared responsibility that are analogous to domestic public law, it is natural to conceive of the obligation not to undermine the fundamental pre-conditions of human life as an *erga omnes* obligation and to see enforcement action by any state, whether directly injured itself or not, 'essentially as a public prosecutor' acting on behalf of the most vulnerable segments of humanity.[46] Humanity cannot grant an individual state a permissive zone of indulgence allowing profligate emissions and hope to have a prayer of maintaining a manageable planetary zone of acceptance. It is incoherent to think otherwise, and current extreme US interpretations of sovereignty as permitting its current reckless behaviour are insupportable in the real world of scientific laws.[47] Flagrant actors like the United States may continue to make staying within a 2°C rise in temperature impossible until the costs are raised by others.[48] Litigation under customary international law by both injured states and other states acting in the global public interest to restore legality might be one useful tool.

Potsdam Institute for Climate Impact Research and Climate Analytics, the planet is currently on track for a disastrous 4°C temperature rise – double the limit adopted in Cancun in 2010 – see World Bank, *Turn Down the Heat: Why a 4°C Warmer World Must Be Avoided* (Washington: World Bank, 2012); and World Bank, *Turn Down the Heat: Climate Extremes, Regional Impacts, and the Case for Resilience* (Washington: World Bank, 2013).

45 See R.J. Nicholls, N. Marinova, J.A. Lowe, et al., 'Sea-level rise and its possible impacts given a "beyond 4°C world" in the twenty-first century' (2011) 369 PTA 161.

46 Nollkaemper and Jacobs, 'Shared Responsibility', n. 6, at 420. Also see H. Shue, 'Historical Responsibility, Harm Prohibition, and Preservation Requirement: Core Practical Convergence on Climate Change' (2015) 2 *Moral Philosophy and Politics* 7.

47 I have developed the point about sovereignty a little more fully in H. Shue, 'Eroding Sovereignty: The Advance of Principle', in R. McKim and J. McMahan (eds.), *The Morality of Nationalism* (New York: Oxford University Press, 1997), 340; reprinted in Shue, *Climate Justice*, n. 13, at 142.

48 The United States is not alone, of course. It is quite easy to make cases as well against, for example, Canada in light of its choice to fail to comply with its minimal legal obligations under the Kyoto Protocol and the lengths to which it is going to develop the environmentally harmful tar sands bitumen, and Poland, for its refusal to reduce its consumption of coal and its veto of leadership in this area by the EU.

12

Shared Responsibility for Climate Change: From Guilt to Taxes

CHRISTOPHER L. KUTZ*

1. Introduction

The enormous actual and anticipated costs of human-caused climate change are a product of both past and future. The now-industrialised nations of Western Europe and North America have contributed over half of carbon dioxide (CO_2) emissions over the last century, even if the European nations have made aggressive efforts to reduce their future carbon impact. By contrast, the swiftly industrialising nations have made a lesser historical contribution (for example India and China have contributed roughly 11 per cent) but are projected to make proportionately much larger aggregate future contributions than North America and Europe.

Climate change will cause large future costs, whether in the form of reduced productivity (if energy restrictions are implemented); mitigation costs (to fend off rising sea waters and reduce the risks of violent weather and drought); prevention costs (through large-scale geo-engineering); or pure damages. The question of who will bear those costs, and how they might be allocated or transferred between states, has been one of, if not the, most important issues impeding meaningful international agreement on remedies and reductions. In particular, the debate has centered around the implications of a principle of 'historical responsibility', favoured by, for example, China and India. Such a principle would impose the principal burden of present and future costs on states historically responsible for the CO_2 rise, independent of future contributions. By contrast, European and North American nations have urged principles of allocation that pay greater heed to current and future causal contributions, based partly on the grounds that current generations

* C. William Maxeiner Professor of Law, University of California at Berkeley. All websites were last accessed on 5 June 2014.

cannot be taxed to pay for the contributions of excusably ignorant prior generations. By contrast, they argue, states now pursuing development goals in full awareness of the risks of climate change must accept a significant burden of responsibility for these choices.

This chapter takes up the debate about historically-versus future-based allocations of responsibility in both an ethical and an empirical dimension. The ethical dimension of the chapter concerns how one might justify either historical or prospective responsibility for citizens, in relation to the acts of others, whether compatriots or not. I will consider the problems of reasonable historical ignorance and political change, as variables affecting allocation. I will also take up the question of the priority of relative deprivation of current or future individuals, as against prospective responsibility. Lastly, I will take up the question of what forms of political and legal institutions might be best suited to the problem of global allocation, specifically whether global taxes, trading schemes, and/or direct wealth or technology transfers are best suited.

2. The problem

The current situation is extremely unfortunate: 2013 marked the passing of the 400 parts per million (ppm) CO_2 benchmark, a symbolic threshold significant both for the absolute level of CO_2 in our atmosphere, and for the pace at which we reached it. Seeking the relatively modest target of a two degrees Celsius (2°C) rise in temperatures will require reductions dwarfing the Kyoto Protocol[1] levels – levels that did not find any accord with the largest current emitters of CO_2 – and future cuts in the neighbourhood of 80 per cent from 1990 levels. China has been rapidly implementing low-carbon energy technologies – but even more quickly adding coal-fired electricity generation. India and Brazil also forecast a quickly increasing rate of greenhouse gases (GHGs) production, through the quickly increasing energy, transportation, and agricultural sectors. The future share of emissions from the major developing economies of Brazil, Russia, India, and China (the BRICs), assuming no great policy shift, is expected to account for two-thirds of total GHG emissions.

Extrapolating from these trends, and notwithstanding a genuine if variable commitment by the European Union and the United States (US) to carbon reduction, the world can expect a continuously increasing

[1] Kyoto Protocol to the United Nations Framework Convention on Climate Change, Kyoto, 10 December 1997, in force 16 February 2005, 2303 UNTS 148 (Kyoto Protocol).

CO_2 level and a temperature increase estimated to exceed 2°C. While experts differ in the details of their proposals, we can take Nicholas Stern's 2008 calculations as a reasonable starting point for discussion purposes.[2] According to Stern, in order to stabilise GHG levels at less than 500ppm in CO_2 equivalents, a level thought possibly sufficient to avert catastrophic climate change, the world as a whole must reduce its emissions by 50 per cent (relative to 1990 levels) by 2050, to an average level of 2 tons of CO_2 per person. Even with much higher per capita cuts in the developed world (of roughly 80 per cent of 1990 emissions by 2050), this carbon budget constraint puts enormous strain on both developed and developing nations to reduce current and/or expected carbon emissions. As Stern says, the 2 ton per capita target is so low that even equitable adjustment between developed and developing states will not offset the fact that all states will have to make dramatic adjustments.[3]

The implications of such a programme are daunting, since it effectively relies on a de-carbonisation of the energy and transportation sectors, through technological innovation, and a halt to deforestation. Because contemporary developed nation living standards have been built on the back of a fossil fuel economy, without a carbon budget, as are the aspirations of the developing world, reconciling global anti-poverty economic development with a newfound strict carbon budget can seem like squaring the circle.[4] I do not mean to dismiss the possibility that the

[2] N. Stern, 'Key Elements of a Global Deal on Climate Change', London School of Economics and Political Science (30 April 2008), at http://eprints.lse.ac.uk/19617/1/Key_Elements_of_a_Global_Deal-Final_version(2)_with_additional_edits_post_launch.pdf.

[3] By way of comparison, excluding the United States and Canada, developed country emissions are about 10-12T per capita; the United States and Canada are in the 18-20T range; China is at about 5T. Source: M. Wolf, 'Living with limits: growth, resources, and climate change' (2012) 12(6) CP 772.

[4] It is true that post-war France, Sweden, and Japan have come to rely on nuclear power and other low-carbon alternatives for their electricity needs, as part of their development programmes. But we are clearly in a period of transition away from nuclear power, and it is unclear whether the turn to natural gas (accelerated since the Fukushima accident) is merely a short-term bridge to renewable and carbon-neutral generation, or will be a significant long-term part of energy production. Indeed, French Prime Minister Manuel Valls has just announced that France will reduce its nuclear dependence to 50 per cent by 2025. See 'Quand Manuel Valls prônait la sortie du nucléaire,' *Le Monde*, 2 April 2014. The movement away from nuclear power, and China and India's rapid growth of coal consumption (which involves building a lot of coal infrastructure) suggests that global development and carbon-intense usage will continue hand in hand. See International Energy Agency, '2013 Key World Energy Statistics', at www.iea.org/publications/freepublications/publication/KeyWorld2013.pdf, especially at 46 et seq.

technological innovation that we seek may itself drive economic growth – and it is certainly possible that even industries unconcerned with carbon emissions may come to find alternative energies more attractive than eventually dwindling fossil fuel supplies. But the contemporary environment is essentially one in which we are asked to trade off immediate and enduring costs, in reductions in consumption and productivity, against gathering and potentially catastrophic costs of ecological calamity, for ourselves and future generations.[5] It is, as Martin Wolf has remarked, a potentially zero-sum calculation we are asked to make. And for that, we need to muster to the utmost our moral and policy courage.

Now, on the most pessimistic assessment of current responses, we may be well past the point of facing a choice between making investments in mitigation versus accepting short-term costs in adaptation and response. We may have settled for response rather than prevention. But the bill must be paid – either a preventative bill that all logic and decency says should be paid as soon as possible; over the next 50 years; or a clean-up bill that will need to be paid bit by bit. This is a scandal of human rationality, to be sure: we are effectively hiding from the problem under current policies.[6] At best, Western Europeans are congratulating themselves that a historical (but volatile) investment in nuclear power, plus a declining economy, will mark the way to the much more difficult cuts that are to come. The United States can congratulate itself that the windfall of natural gas is easing emissions considerably. But though the modest emissions decreases of the United States and Europe are promising, they are not yet at a level that can stanch the rise of temperatures. Globally speaking, we are digging ourselves quickly into a deepening hole, with no plans to stop digging.

For purposes of this chapter, I stipulate the following two points, despite current pessimistic trends: first, that an international agreement that will significantly mitigate warming is possible, at substantial cost; and second, that the costs of dealing with the consequences of the inevitable warming cannot simply be left where they fall, mostly on the poorest of the world's

[5] For a comprehensive discussion of the harms of a 2-degree rise, see A. Guzman, *Overheated* (New York: Oxford University Press, 2012). Guzman counts disease and regional conflict as the foremost risks of climate change, and those risks will rise sharply before much progress can be made, even under an optimistic political scenario.

[6] I do not regard the problem as linked to the dispute about future discount rates on investment decisions. The costs we would avoid through mitigation, or repair through adaption, are fundamentally non-monetisable costs in human suffering and death (as well as intrinsic environmental costs in mass extinction).

poor in Africa and Asia, but will be shared on a progressive basis by the wealthier nations. My aim is to discuss how we might best think about national responsibility for the costs of climate change adaptation and mitigation: what are the ethical principles for allocating responsibility between and among nations? My discussion will concern both ethical principles and the moral psychology necessary to give those principles motivational effect. Although I will mostly consider the question of responsibility from the perspective of the developed world – that is, of nations who have produced most of the cumulative emissions – I will also discuss the responsibilities of developing states. My general argument is that we do well to pay heed to the collective responsibilities of individuals *as* citizens of particular states, both historically and projectively, in thinking about climate change responsibilities. This is for four basic reasons:

First, our politics are organised collectively, around nation-states. Accounts that treat collective interests as irrelevant to underlying moral facts will fail to apply to the system of law and politics we have developed.

Second, conceptually, the collective aspect of GHG production matters – the significant outflows of GHG come from joint projects, usually enacted at a national scale: power facilities, manufacturing and heave industry, large-scale agriculture and deforestation. We need an account of the problem that is true to its origins.

Third, psychologically, collective motivations matter – they are how we focus and coordinate our most important political commitments. Given that climate change is the paradigm of a collective action problem, in which success depends on broad cooperation while the incentives to free-ride are enormous, we must be able to make use of the collective solutions we have developed as moral animals.[7]

Fourth, tapping these motivations may enable some progress towards the kind of systems necessary to tame climate change.

This chapter is organised as follows. First, I lay out a conceptual vocabulary for dealing with the moral concept of responsibility, and relate that moral concept to the legal concept at the centre of this volume's discussion. Next I apply this concept to the doubly shared issue of responsibility for climate change mitigation – doubly shared because the responsibility encompassed not merely the shared responsibility of citizens of many states, but also the shared responsibility of those states. My approach

[7] The collective action aspects of the problem are well-discussed by Seumas Miller, in his contribution to this volume, S. Miller, 'The Global Financial Crisis and Collective Moral Responsibility', Chapter 15, 404.

is to argue for a conception of shared *legal* responsibility that allows legal and political obligations to be supported by a plausible moral psychology. In my view, any significantly redistributive political and economic institutions must, to be feasible, be able to draw on the resources of actual moral psychology: the capacity of individuals and collectives to see themselves as rightful 'owners' of the responsibilities attributed to them. Attempting to impose financial liabilities on states, and the citizens whose taxes cover those liabilities, will be met with evasion and resistance unless citizens and their political leaders can come to see those liabilities as embedded in a coherent story about responsibility and the claims of justice, both distributive and corrective. In other words, an account of responsibility must meet demands for both philosophical coherence and psychological realism.[8] Last, I will offer a preliminary argument for the virtues of a system of carbon taxation rather than tradable emissions permits, as best fitting the psychological constraints I discuss.

3. What is responsibility: individual and collective?

There is no room to develop here a full theory of individual moral responsibility to account for responsibility for global climate change, nor would it evidently be useful. Our commonsense practices of attributing responsibility, and much of the philosophy theorising those practices, emerges from purely local, individual contexts that do not generalise to the broad-scale, long time horizon, marginal individual effects characteristics of the climate change problem. Nonetheless, we do need a more specific vocabulary for this discussion.[9]

First, I want to make some distinctions between three types of responsibility, recognising that different theorists use different labels.[10]

[8] This point is akin to the demand John Rawls makes, that a theory of justice needs to be sensitive to the 'strains of commitment' to the ideal it designates – that is, such a theory needs to be embedded in a moral psychology. See J. Rawls, *A Theory of Justice*, rev. edn (Cambridge: MA: Belknap Press, 1999), sec. 29, as well as ch. 8 ('The Moral Sentiments'). See also S. Krause, *Civil Passions: Moral Sentiment and Democratic Deliberation* (Princeton University Press, 2008).

[9] I develop a number of these points at greater length in C.L. Kutz, *Complicity: Ethics and Law for a Collective Age* (New York: Cambridge University Press, 2000); and C.L. Kutz, 'Responsibility', in J.L. Coleman and S. Shapiro (eds.), *The Oxford Handbook of Jurisprudence and Philosophy of Law* (New York: Oxford University Press, 2001).

[10] For a somewhat different set of terms, although with overlapping conclusions, see Chapter 2 in this volume, R. Pierik, 'Shared Responsibility in International Law: A Normative-Philosophical Analysis', 36.

When we tie a past event to the doings of an agent, we ascribe responsibility for that event to that agent: this can be called *attributability*, and it is fundamentally retrospective. The crucial point is that attributability is only weakly normative. Accounts of causal responsibility are attributive in the sense that they construct an explanatory narrative between an act and a later event, attributing the latter to the former. They are weakly normative in that an ascription of responsibility need not import a judgment of blame or a demand for response. I can ascribe responsibility for the torn living room rug to my puppy, without thinking my puppy is the kind of thing that can be subject to genuine blame. The judgment is normative in that, in any event resting on a host of conditions and contributing causes, we seek some rather than others in making our ascription – and changing our interests or values may change our ascription. I may come to see that the role of my son in leaving open the kitchen door is a better explanation of the rug's destruction by the puppy, because it was a more unusual event – or the choice of the rug maker to soak his wool in a saline solution that tastes good to a dog. Such quasi-factual judgments may lead to a judgment of blame, but are not the same.

Next, we have responsibility in the sense of *accountability*. Accountability is referred to as 'responsibility' in the primary sense in the Articles on State Responsibility.[11] Though accountability is often treated as a synonym for responsibility (and in ordinary language often is that), it is worth marking a conceptual distinction. While puppies, winds, and children all can be the subjects of ascriptive responsibility, only those kinds of agents that are proper targets of what philosopher Peter Strawson famously called the 'reactive attitudes', including gratitude and resentment, can be accountable.[12] To be accountable is to be a proper subject for these attitudes, and, more to the point, to be someone from whom a response (or account) is claimed, or to whom a sanction (or a benefit) may be administered. Accountability, then, is something like liability to praise or blame, but we should recognise that those two words mark only two points on a much broader spectrum of accountability

[11] Articles on Responsibility of States for Internationally Wrongful Acts, ILC *Yearbook* 2001/II(2) (ARSIWA). Chapter IV of the ARSIWA provides that responsibility is a state of liability to repair or indemnify, in virtue of a breach of an international obligation attributable to a state. For discussion, see P.A. Nollkaemper and D. Jacobs, 'Shared Responsibility in International Law: A Conceptual Framework' (2013) 34(2) MIJIL 359.

[12] There is, of course, a fourth sense of responsibility as a capacity to be accountable, presumed in my treatment here. See P. Strawson, 'Freedom and Resentment' (1962) 48 PBA 1.

relations. You may be accountable to give an explanation, which may show why you are neither to be praised nor blamed, for instance because you were sleepwalking (and so non-responsible in the capacity sense). Or you may be accountable in needing to repair damage you caused, for which you are ascriptively responsible, even though, again, you were not to blame. Moral, like legal, regimes of strict or vicarious liability exist: if my children break your window through their play, because of a freak bounce of a ball, I must still offer to fix your window (though perhaps you must refuse the offer, if I have not been negligent in supervising my children). Or, to take a further example, if in backing up my car I run over your cat who has run under my wheels, I surely must get out of the car, find you, and bring you your cat with my condolences.

The last relevant form of responsibility is *projective responsibility*: responsibility for future conduct. This is duty-based responsibility, where these duties arise from specific roles we inhabit, voluntarily or not, from prior ascriptions of responsibility and accountability, or from general moral (or political or legal) duties. We are responsible, going forward, to pay our debts and clean up our messes; to act as good children of our parents and parents of our children; to care as good stewards of the earth; to respect each other as moral equals; and to manifest that respect in our material treatment of each other. Such responsibility entails a liability to moral assessment – to fault and blame, praise and respect. It is the social and psychological counterpart to a morality of duty.

I also want to emphasise two aspects of this conception of responsibility: responsibility, in all three of these senses, is *socially embedded* and *relational*. By 'socially-embedded', I mean that the particulars of any ascription of responsibility, accountability, capacity, or duty are highly relativised to a particular social location. Behaviour that in some times or cultures is seen as unremarkable, or not an appropriate object of social commentary, becomes in others a mark of social shame. The history of the gradual European rejection of public bodily emissions, described by Norbert Elias, renders vividly the historical relativity of these norms.[13] A similar relativity, both historical and geographic, characterises pollution norms. In North America, no more than forty years ago, it was utterly unremarkable to throw a bag of garbage from a car onto the highway, while now the same act would bring social opprobrium and a stiff fine. Meanwhile, the absence of a littering norm is evident in many

[13] N. Elias, *The Civilizing Process* [Über den Prozeß der Zivilisation, 1939] (Oxford: Blackwell Publishers, 1994).

developing countries.[14] Responsibilities to future generations come to make ethical and epistemic sense as we come to understand processes of change and resource exhaustion. The list could be extended. I offer here an observation about our social practices of responsibility, not an argument for a deep moral relativism. It may well be true, and I think it is, that there are certain things for which we should be held responsible, independent of whether our society licenses the practice now. But the judgments we actually make about responsibilities, both retrospective and projective, necessarily rest on a constellation of values, habits, and presumptions that vary with our location in society, and our society's location in space and time.

The point about relationality is more controversial, and has deeper implications. While I have been writing as though judgments or ascriptions of responsibility are brute metaphysical facts, inscribed in a metaphorical heavenly book of accounts, they are in fact judgments we make of each other – moreover, of others with whom we claim (perhaps falsely) to share a social understanding. To be in a position to ascribe responsibility is to already be in a relation with another in which it makes sense, even vicariously, to make moral demands on that other agent. This point holds, at least, for accountability and projective responsibility: it does not make sense for me to blame someone for a harm to a third party unless I stand in a relation to that person that has content going beyond the mere ascription of blame. To take an extreme example, there is a kind of category mistake in blaming, say, a slave trader for the crimes he committed. We can fault him, regard him as ascriptively responsible, and so forth – but to hold him to account supposes that we can imagine ourselves in actual confrontation with him – a confrontation that our temporal dislocation does not permit. Less extremely, but perhaps more controversially, imagine that we discover that a remote tundra population is deliberately releasing large amounts of methane into the atmosphere, by burning peat. If there are no common social or commercial ties that bind us, talk of accountability seems beside the point – and this is true from the tundra population's perspective towards us as well.

Let us see how these points illuminate the discussion of climate change. First, the debate over historical responsibility has been, for the

[14] The emergence of cleanliness norms, both for individual bodies and for public spaces, is obviously tightly linked to issues of class and wealth, but not exclusively so. The wealthy, in any period, have never had greater compunctions about the industrial pollution from their capital assets than any other group.

most part, a debate between people who agree on the ascriptive point, but disagree about accountability. In particular, it is uncontested that the majority of cumulative GHG emissions date from the beginning of the Industrial Revolution through, say 1990, and are ascribable to the developed Western world. Disagreement centres on whether the developed world is accountable – answerable for – these emissions, at least those before major policy actors could reasonably be thought to have known about the ecological damage they did through energy production. The question of projective responsibilities also lies open to political debate. Even if one settled the question of blame, and attributed accountability for cumulative emissions to the developed world, one might think that the essential task going forward is catastrophe prevention, and that the primary consideration ought to be limited emissions, period – thus shutting down the high emissions energy plants typical of the developing world. More directly, whatever theoretical conclusion one draws about the ideal distribution of responsibility, one might conclude, given the stakes, that even an unjust but effective policy response is better than no response.

Second, for practices of responsibility to take hold, the act or harm for which one is being held responsible must be socially located. This is a matter of education and persuasion. We can discuss in the abstract about ideal global policy responses, but until the rancher in Nebraska; the sport utility vehicle (SUV) driver in New Jersey; or the subsistence farmer in the Congo come to see their practices as not only part of a globally significant harm, but as being choices among alternatives and not simply naturally given pathways, the talk of responsibility will be so much angelic hand-waving. Judgments of responsibility must have a target they can hit to be meaningful interventions in our attempts to regulate our common lives. The target is the conscience, by which I mean the field of choice, of individual agents, acting on their own or as the policy representative of others. Put another way, talk of responsibility is premature until the social and epistemological ground is tilled and seeded.

Third, while we can talk about what must be done by various parties to the climate change problem – changes in land use or energy extraction, for example – we cannot ascribe responsibility outside a real network of relations of accountability. This entails two further points. First, the logic of responsibility presupposes a context of exchange, both social and economic. Doubtless we can have duties of beneficence towards those about whom all we know is that they suffer, but responsibility is a subset of justice, and justice requires relationships. A truly global conception of responsibility requires a global conception of justice. Second, the need for a global conception of justice, founded in reciprocity, in turn, presupposes a global culture of common reason and claims. The relevant social and political relations, at the global scale, are still largely interstate relations. We do not have a conception of global responsibility that rests on individual actors, although, under human rights law and rhetoric, individuals can be the objects of these politics. Indeed, one of the chief human rights problems today is that many of the most significant actors are collectives, but not states – they are transnational corporations. I believe it follows from these points that the conception of responsibility we must deal with will be, in the first instance, a responsibility grounded in collectives. I will now say a bit about what that could mean.

4. The ethics of climate change responsibility: individual versus collective perspectives

Current *political* debate on climate change response seem to be based on two types of proposals: historical versus future-oriented.[15] Historical proposals allocate future responsibilities on the basis of past acts – past acts of GHG emission by the developed world, in this case. Those who have done most to generate the problem have the greatest responsibility to pay. Future-based proposals, by contrast, treat history as a sunk cost, and look instead to the marginal impacts of future contributions.

In political debates, especially between the United States and the major developing economies of China, Brazil, Russia, and India (the BRICs), these conceptions lie at loggerheads. From the perspective of the BRICs, had the developed states not emitted so much GHG, the emissions of the developing states would be harmless. Thus put, although China's emissions are rapidly increasing, that fact is only causally and normatively significant because of a baseline set by the incautious development of the West. Ascriptive responsibility for the high marginal cost of BRIC emissions lies with the developed world – and so also accountability (they must incorporate this responsibility into a public understanding), and future responsibilities. While this does not necessarily mean that the BRICs have a free pass for future emissions, it means that their projective

[15] There is an excellent summary of this debate in D. Weijers, D. Eng, and R. Das, 'Sharing the responsibility of dealing with climate change: Interpreting the principle of common but differentiated responsibilities', in J. Boston, A. Bradstock, and D. Eng (eds.), *Public Policy: Why Ethics Matters* (Canberra: ANU E-Press, 2008), ch. 8.

responsibilities should be defined in terms commensurate with a historically limited patrimony of emissions.

By contrast, on the US view (and perhaps *sotto voce* on the European view), these historical emissions are morally blameless, since it is only recently that states realised that GHGs were harmful at all. Moreover, the problem of climate change will require great efforts from all emitters, and it would be simply irresponsible to create an international system without serious efforts and incentives put before all states. Even after technology transfer and the interstate income flows that would follow from international trading, there is no feasible way to limit BRIC responsibility in any way that is more than symbolically reflective of differing historical responsibilities. Given the clash between these views, as well as the short-term self-interest of state leaders, the debate between these moral positions is seen as an explanation, indeed an excuse, for inaction.

Within philosophical debate, however, it is harder to see a clash. Most philosophers and economists are, at root, moral cosmopolitans, in the following sense: they believe that what matters, fundamentally, is the welfare of people taken as individuals, independent of the contingencies of attachment to particular states and territories. No morality that can survive critical reflection can endorse a world that accepts the stark differences in life-chances of children born in Western Europe, say, versus Sub-Saharan Africa. Nor can one think that we must weigh equally the costs to an affluent American of moving from a system of private transport to a socialised one, to the costs of an Indian peasant, asked to forgo the advantages of a truck to bring his produce to market. Any other view is to moralise an international status quo that is itself not even morally neutral, but a product of deliberate immiseration and subordination by the developed world towards the rest.

Once we accept the equal weight of the moral claims of individuals to decent lives and prospects, wherever located, we can see that the historical and future approaches are concurrents, not competitors. Both history and future-directed moral equality dictate approaches to climate mitigation that place nearly all the costs of mitigation and adaptation on the developed world, to be handled through a variety of wealth and income transfer mechanisms. This point about ethical convergence is made from the perspective of utility by Peter Singer, and from the perspective of rights (rights to a decent existence) by Henry Shue.[16] We do not need to

[16] See P. Singer, *One World: The Ethics of Globalization* (New Haven, CT: Yale University Press, 2002), at 14–50 (ch. 2); H. Shue, 'Global Environment and International Inequality'

endorse the further Chinese argument, of a right to unconstrained development, to see that the primary burden of mitigation costs should fall elsewhere.[17]

One might conclude that no more philosophical discussion is needed, except to further underscore the point that current practices will weigh most heavily on the world's most vulnerable, both in this and future generations.[18] What we need, instead, is an account of a political path towards the neighbourhood of what cosmopolitan justice prescribes – a shifting of resources to improve the lives of the least well-off regardless of nationhood.

As a matter of first principle, I believe that the cosmopolitan justice approach is sound, and that ideally, climate change responsibility should take national groupings as, at most, instrumentally significant – administratively convenient ways to organise production and transfer. But the purely cosmopolitan approach still misses something important, namely the political and motivational force of collective conceptions, particularly (in the modern age) conceptions that attach to the nation-state. These conceptions – part of the social embodiment of responsibility – are not mere sociology, but essential to understanding the potential of our responsibility system.

So what would a national and historical perspective mean for climate change costs? I will develop the answer to this question in more depth, but the first point to recognise is that just as the events of our individual histories accumulate to us, as parts of our identities and as part of the fabric of our accountability, so too do the events of our collective histories. I said before that faultless harms may still accrue to our account, demanding repair. Should I, as a farmer, accidentally and unforeseeably drain my region's water table and so deprive my neighbour of his water, I cannot simply accept the new state as the normative baseline – rather,

(1999) 75 IA 531. See also H. Shue, 'SBSTA Technical Briefing: Historical Responsibility', 4 June 2009, at http://unfccc.int/files/meetings/ad_hoc_working_groups/lca/application/pdf/1_shue_rev.pdf.

17 Nor should we endorse China's failure to adopt emissions-limiting policies. The point in the text is that the West should shoulder the principal burden of mitigation independent of China's specific responsibility to sustainable development.

18 There is no economic or philosophical consensus about the correct discount rate, if any, to be applied to the interests of future generations. For a discussion of discount rates in the context of climate change, see M.L. Weitzman, 'Why the Far-Distant Future Should be Discounted at Its Lowest Possible Rate' (1998) 36 JEEM 201; E. Posner and D. Weisbach, *Climate Change Justice* (Princeton University Press, 2010), ch. 7; D.A. Farber, 'From Here to Eternity: Environmental Law and Future Generations' (2003) Ill LR 289.

I must work to restore my neighbour's access to water, at cost to my own baseline. This holds true even if it was my father or grandfather who sank the well that drained my neighbour's access to water. Perhaps we will come to a conclusion that bygones are bygones in this case – but that conclusion will follow from complex considerations of fairness and the impossibility of projecting counterfactual futures.[19] It will not follow simply from the fact that the original act was faultless, nor that it was done by my ancestor, not me. Insofar as I stand in a line of moral succession, identifying with a family line, I am responsible for these claims, independent of the positive law of inherited debt.

The claims of a collective past weigh also, independent of a current generation's fault. This point emerged recently in the statements of French President François Hollande, commemorating the end of France's colonial slave system. While Hollande insisted on the clean hands of the Republic in the matter of slavery, since none of the Republics tolerated its legal existence, he followed Jacques Chirac's lead, in the matter of French complicity in the German genocide, by declining to take that historical fact as an absolution. Whatever the Republic's views of slavery, France had profited greatly from it. And so Hollande apologised. The instability in Hollande's view came from the separate claim of reparations, particularly in relation to Haiti, which Napoleonic France had required to repay the costs of its self-liberation. Here he cynically invoked the words of Aimé Césaire, to declare that the crime of slavery was so great, money could not assuage the guilt.[20]

Whatever one might think about the claims of reparations for slavery as against a broader (and equally deep reaching) obligation by France towards ex-colonies, or more generally towards the world's poorest, it is clearly important to anchor France's moral identity in an account that takes its full history of slavery, colonisation, and exploitation seriously. That history defines modern France, as much as its contemporary social democracy and relatively generous international aid programmes. Its forward-looking responsibilities must be understood in terms of the specific character of its national identity – that is to say, in an identity rooted in both past acts and future ambitions.

[19] I discuss the supersession of historical claims in C.L. Kutz, 'Justice in reparations: The problem of land and the value of cheap talk' (2004) 32 PPA 277.

[20] F. Hollande, 'Discours sur l'esclavage', 10 Mai 2013, at www.elysee.fr/assets/pdf/intervention-du-president-de-la-republique-a-l-occasion-de-la-journee-nationale-des-memoires-de-la-traite-de-l-esclavage-et-leurs-abolitions.pdf.

The case of GHG emissions is simpler in one way, but more complicated in another. We can remove fault from the equation, and so remove questions of blame, guilt, and guilt-based reparations from the discussion. But the historical legacy attaches to the collective transformation of our environment into sources of carbon-based energy for our shared creation of industrial life. Insofar as this history is ours, so are the traces of responsibility. To be a citizen of a state is to come in a family lineage (whenever one's ancestors were adopted into the territory), to be bearer of responsibility for that lineage. We must face the future in the shadow of the collective past.

5. Collective guilt and collective responses

I have asserted more than argued for the relevance of history in thinking through forward-looking reparative responsibilities. I have felt entitled to this assertion because I do not think that the relevance of the past is seriously in debate. I now want to complicate the picture of responsibility in one more direction, however, and more controversially. Talk about responsibilities is itself best seen as anchored in a moral psychology. And talk about national responsibilities is best seen as anchored in a conception of *collective guilt*. This is controversial because collective guilt – or, more accurately, demands that a nation or people act on the basis of collective guilt – is usually thought to be the toxic waste of social psychology. Claims of collective guilt form the basis for genocide and other crimes of race. Even to raise the question, from the outside, of whether collective guilt is appropriate is to stir up a cauldron of trouble, bringing out people's strongest individualistic inclinations and blame-shifting arguments.[21]

I do not want to deny the pitfalls of collective guilt. But I do want to take a chance here and try to show how collective guilt might be thought of as a social *resource* rather than a social curse, and how it might be used to induce the participation of individuals in schemes to solve collective harms. In particular, a guilt-based system can provide the motivation necessary to legitimate the imposition of nation-based carbon taxes.

[21] One recent example that makes the point sharply is the way in which any non-Israeli's use of the word 'apartheid' to characterise the Palestinian occupation meets sharp criticism from within Israel, even as the word is routinely used internally by the Israeli Left. See J. Goldberg, 'Is Israel an Apartheid State?', Bloomberg View, 29 April 2014, at www.bloombergview.com/articles/2014-04-29/is-israel-an-apartheid-state.

Note that I use the term 'induce' rather than 'justify' with respect to participation, since I take myself (and others) to have shown already that participation in a collective act that does wrong can justify imposition of reparative responsibilities on those individuals. I will shortly explain the form I believe this accountability takes, and why its basis must rest on a thicker reed than collective action alone offers. But my principal focus is on collective guilt – or feelings of complicity, if you prefer – as a motivational rather than normative resource.

As I suggested earlier, attempts to justify political programmes out of collective guilt are likelier to breed resentment than support. New Zealand's land reparations to the Maori and the limited case of US reparations to interned Japanese-Americans are two of the rare success stories of reparations programmes self-imposed by a state and accepted by its public. Notably, both programmes were only feasible years after the original injury.

These reparations programmes reflected real policy achievements. What is discouraging is that they might also be thought of as easy cases. In all three cases, public support benefited from the direct legislative or judicial acknowledgement that grave wrongs had been done as a matter of state policy.

The problem is forward-looking: how to coordinate a solution. This problem obviously intersects the historical perspective as well. Whatever the technical solution to climate change, it will be costly – as costly as any technical accomplishment in human history. The cost will probably be more than any nation-state or international organisation can bear.[22] Even if one nation – say, the United States, could bear the costs on its own, it is politically unimaginable. Moreover, a coordinated solution, such as one involving a global system of tradable emissions permits and/or harmonised taxes, will tend to drive down carbon reduction costs for all parties, through the logic of comparative advantage.[23] So funding the technical solution requires finding a way to coordinate among many payers. The problem of coordination is hard enough in the abstract, since there are, by most estimates, more than enough states in a position to shoulder the burden of mitigation – that is, the technical approach

[22] Note that according to Guzman, mitigation efforts could be worthwhile even if only the United States bears the costs, in self-interested terms.

[23] N. Stern et al., *STERN REVIEW: The Economics of Climate Change*, 449 et seq. (part VI, 'International Collective Action') at http://mudancasclimaticas.cptec.inpe.br/~rmclima/pdfs/destaques/sternreview_report_complete.pdf.

could be funded even if one or more contributors decide to ride free. Thus, there are a great number of possible arrays of contributors, rather than a single coordination solution. Still, a principle of equal division might have seemed a fair solution, even if it imposes costs where none need be borne, since any particular state could have escaped contribution. What makes the problem more difficult is the way history hangs over the coordination problem, lending a dimension of moral argument to the problem of division – a moral dimension not exhausted by abstract fairness in division.

What can the dark motivations of guilt supply to the problem of coordinating mitigation costs? We think of 'guilting' people as the worst possible way of motivating them – as likely to spur resistance or resentful compliance as genuine conformity. While fear of guilt may itself be a potent moral emotion, stirring us to act rightly against impulse, when the wrongful acts are in the past, guilt would seem to be entirely paralysing.

But it does seem that guilt can provide a positive motivation, not just a paralysing one, when one thinks about guilt as a way of orienting us around the historical dimension of our act. Here guilting someone may provoke not just resistance but thought – it can make clear another pattern of interpretation of how we act. In the individual case, to point out that one has, in fact, acted shabbily – say, by indulging oneself in what one thought at the time was an important principle of self-realisation, and what one later in life regards as self-dramatisation – can be a spur to understanding how one is caught in a web of obligations. Guilt here does not necessarily move one to try to repair the past, but to understand it. Or so I want to suggest.

If guilt can be a motivating emotion, then it must be one that we can feel – and not just as a passing fancy or an induced cringe, but as a sustainable sense that we *owe something*, that we have a duty of repair in virtue of some wrong to which we are attached. We speak most easily of guilt in cases of direct, personal violation of a norm, usually in relation to an act or omission of our own. Shame is the more vicarious emotion – one easily felt at the disgrace, say, of a member of one's family. So this presents a challenge already, for with the exception of a few industrialists, none of us contributes to global warming in a way that would seem to license talk of guilt, individual and collective. To talk in this abstract way, in the context of climate change, is perhaps already to stretch the semantics of 'guilt' beyond what it can bear. And yet what I am after – what I take to be a genuinely possible emotional state – is one that looks to what we have done as a basis for a duty of repair to those harmed by our acts.

The route to an account of such an emotion, I believe, goes by way of an understanding of collective action. I have developed that account at length in other work.[24] In my view, collective obligations can arise from a common and spontaneous perception of a need for supra-individual action – of a situation that calls for us to orient ourselves and our agency around the projects of an *us*.

Consider, as an example, the Boston Marathon bombing of 2013. People were gathered at the course end to celebrate the winners. There was a loud flash, a bang, screaming, and blood. Some ran away, moving separately, escaping the danger and the chaos. But many ran into the smoke, looking for the worst injured. One of the most moving photos of the scene involved two men rushing a third, badly injured man, to medical help – having already engaged in the difficult business of providing a tourniquet for his leg.[25] They volunteered, as it were, for the collective mission. Assume, as is probably the case, that one person alone could not both tie off the bleeding limbs and bring the victim to medical care. Before the collective action is launched, each witness to the injury has an obligation to the victim, to render what assistance she can. But once they become aware of the other potential rescuer's presence and readiness, the obligation transforms, from one running between individuals, to one that flows from the rescuers as an incipiently cooperating group to the victim. Each individual's planning and deliberation shifts from the question of what she should do – form a group or not – to what *they* should do, for example how to deploy most efficiently their individual and collective capacities.[26]

We can modify the example to suit the context of climate change. Imagine Janice, who has just returned from a conference on climate change, and who is now inspired to do her part of reducing carbon emissions by turning off her car whenever idling more than seven seconds. She realises that this gesture is nothing but narcissism unless many others do the same, or make other individual gestures at individual

[24] See Kutz, *Complicity*, n. 9; and also C.L. Kutz, 'The Collective Work of Citizenship' (2002) 8 LT 471.

[25] T. Rohan, 'In Grisly Image, a Father Sees His Son', *New York Times*, 16 April 2013. The backstory of one of the men, peace activist Carlos Arredondo, is very poignant as well.

[26] See Pierik, 'Shared Responsibility in International Law: A Normative-Philosophical Analysis', n. 10, this volume.

reduction. Fortunately, many of us join her, and we note the growing trend in behaviour at traffic lights, in parking lots, and read about it in the news. At that point we are co-participants in a collective project of carbon reduction. Each of us, like Janice, has shifted in practical orientation towards the problem and the world: each now confronts it, in instrumental stance of deliberating about how we together will act.

In both these cases, there is a collective obligation, to be sure – an obligation of each individual to do his or her part in achieving a goal that can only be achieved together, if it is to be achieved at all. It is essentially collective, insofar as it makes reference to the group formed around the future project of relieving suffering. But it is at the same time individual, grounded in individual claims to help, and individual duties to relieve suffering. The morality of projective responsibility, in other words, is a morality of collaboration.

Getting the place of commitments right matters because it is only through a less confining form of collective action, I believe, that we can get an accurate understanding of the normative situation at stake in climate change. Establishing our responsibility, as citizens of developed states, for carrying a significant burden of carbon reduction costs, means showing how the problem of atmospheric CO_2 is a function of our collective action. But emitting CO_2 together is not plausibly seen as a matter of agreement, much less joint commitment. I suggest, however, that it can nonetheless be seen as a form of collective action. Indeed, many mass phenomena can be seen in such terms, as individuals responding to one another and so jointly constituting a normative system that guides individual choice. This is, basically, an account of a trend or *Zeitgeist*: individual orientation around widespread emergent social norms. In such cases, a collective behaviour moves beyond mere parallelism because of the individual roles in sustaining the social norm.

I now modify the discussion again, from prospective to reparative responsibility. Consider tailpipe emissions, especially in the United States, from large and inefficient automobiles.[27] The taste for such automobiles was a product of many factors, including low fuel prices; but also of socially reinforced trends of admiring (rather than disdaining)

[27] I put aside the carbon emissions generated by industrial production, taking place in one state but consumed in another. One can see such production as a matter of cooperation between producers and the consumers who look to take advantage of the reduced costs of mass production, and so the emissions generated by the production are fairly attributable to the consumers as well.

large SUVs; collective action effects of individuals feeling that they were endangered by others' large cars unless they too bought large cars; and the general dis-inhibiting effect of seeing others in such cars as well. The trend of SUV purchases exploded, helped out by the forces of corporate marketing to be sure. No one individual's choice of what car to drive probably made a difference to anyone else's behaviour, taken on its own – but overall a network of collective choices was built up out of these individual interactions. And so, in such a case, we can say that the global increase of CO_2 emissions is attributable to the collective, and not merely parallel, acts of US consumers. The same phenomenon happened in reverse a couple of years ago, when oil prices first spiked and awareness of global warming began to emerge. In the United States large cars moved from the category of admired to scorned, and the Prius became the new Hummer. The shift in the *Zeitgeist* reflected, again, interdependent patterns of approval, criticism, and reinforcement. None of it occurred by way of agreement or commitment, but the interdependency was sufficient to make this a case of collective action.

The account I have just sketched, of mutual orientation and stabilisation of a norm, can account for the collective aspect of contemporary emissions. It can, therefore, partially ground a reparative duty. But it does so by locating the responsibility of American consumers on the same ground as that of, say, Indian and Chinese consumers. It does not account for the problems of history, and history's inequities. To do that, we need an account that can reach back over time. This may seem a stopping point. How can we connect, say, the carbon emissions of third millennium drivers with the emissions of 1890s industrialists? The story of interdependent adjustment cannot do it.

Instead I offer a tentative suggestion: there can be cases of asymmetric collective action – that is, action that is collective with respect to some participants, and not collective with regard to others (or at least not mutually collective). In particular, we can regard ourselves as collective participants in a shared history with our predecessors, even if they would not have regarded us as co-participants in their shared project. The possibility of such asymmetry should not be doubted. Take, for example, an overly zealous fan at a soccer match. He takes it upon himself to help his team by shining a mirror into the eyes of the goalie on the opposing team. He sees himself as a member of the soccer team writ large, entitled to credit for their win (if they win). The actual team on the field is not only ignorant of his participation, but would demand that he stop immediately if they knew, because of the poor sportsmanship. It is plausible to say that the fan is acting jointly with the team, but the team is not acting jointly with him.

We moderns might fall into the same boat. As Ernest Renan and Benedict Anderson have shown, national identities are projects of active imagination – of new generations seizing aspects of the past and maintaining some while repressing others.[28] To be a national, a member of a nation, is to participate in, and not merely accept, this process – maintaining myths, enmities, and allegiances with the past. The work of maintaining such an identity, at least for those who share it, carries with it responsibilities for bearing the burden of that identity. It is our patrimony, and as such is both burden and inheritance – the family estate that must be kept in repair to be worth keeping at all. As an anchor to a collective identity, it exists apart from who we are and yet it is made through our process of self-definition in relation to that anchor.

6. Guilt and taxes

I will now bring the question of guilt back to bear. I have been invoking a notion of collective responsibility and the importance of the individual emotion of guilt, as anchors for a climate change policy. I now want to suggest that guilt can be the anchor of a tax system in particular. But I want to emphasise first that it is individual feelings of guilt I refer to, not collective guilt. While some writers, notably Margaret Gilbert, believe in the existence of collective emotions, such as guilt, I am skeptical about such claims.[29] I believe, instead, that talk of collective emotions makes sense, if at all, as a way of speaking about a complex of emotions held by individuals, partly in response to an external stimulus in the world, and partly in response to our inherent and powerful interest in coordinating our emotions with one another. To take an obvious example, we speak naturally of the collective pride of Spaniards in their 2010 Soccer World Cup victory. But it would require more metaphysics and philosophical argument than necessary to justify any literal sense to the claim that some entity called 'Spain' felt an emotion called 'pride'. Rather, and most naturally, many Spaniards found themselves in an interlocking and

[28] E. Renan, 'Qu'est-ce qu'une nation?' ['What is a nation?'], Conférence faite en Sorbonne, le 11 mars 1882, at http://fr.wikisource.org/wiki/Qu%E2%80%99est-ce_qu%E2%80%99une_nation_%3F; B. Anderson, *Imagined Communities: Reflections on the Origin and Spread of Nationalism* (London: Verso, 1991).

[29] M. Gilbert, 'Collective Guilt and Collective Guilt Feelings' (2002) 6 JE 115.

intersubjective emotional experience in relation to their team, in which each person's pride mirrored another's. The result is a wave of emotion – a wave made up of individual emoters.

We can make a similar point about guilt. I think it does not make sense to say that the United States, or Goldman Sachs, or any other collective, feels guilt or shame – except as a summary of the attitudes of individual members. Nonetheless, I think an acknowledgement of collective responsibility can be a basis for individual guilt in a way that does reflect the fundamentally collective structure of the situation. On my view, collective responsibility just is individual responsibility for collective acts – but it is a basically non-causal form of responsibility, in which I am answerable in part for what you have done, because what you have done is part of a project you shared with me. I call this 'inclusive responsibility', as opposed to my exclusive responsibility for the acts or harms for which I am directly, personally responsible. In the present case, ascriptions of collective responsibility, including for emissions of prior generations, pose deliberative problems for individuals: how ought they feel, or act, in relation to what the collective has done?

Remorse is one possible response – but given the ignorance of prior generations to the effects on the environment, anything but the most abstract sense of remorse seems peculiar. Nonetheless, a sentiment of reparative guilt is easily derived – perhaps not as a free-standing emotion, but as an element that figures into the further deliberations about what kind of burden individuals from developed states ought to bear in climate change. John Rawls's approach to understanding the import of fairness provides an example. While his decision-theoretic argument for the difference principle is the best known, I believe his more powerful exposition stems from the arbitrariness of fortune, and the responsibility of co-citizens to build institutions that can correct for that arbitrariness. The arbitrariness of fortune is connected to something we might consider instead as *beneficiary* (or survivor's) guilt, and the response to such guilt is to think through what a principle of fair contribution would look like – why a robust conception of democratic equality, in Rawls's terms, requires transfers from the advantaged to the disadvantaged.

The resource of guilt, then, may enable us to continue our discussion of climate corrective institutions with greater control. It may even point a thumb on the scale in relation to the central institutional question in climate change policy: whether a 'cap and trade' or a 'carbon tax' architecture would better promote reduction in carbon emissions. Both function through the internalised discipline of market mechanisms, although both also rely on a significant role for the state in monitoring and enforcing compliance. Roughly, a cap-and-trade model relies on an initial agreement to allocate carbon emissions permits either in the aggregate to different states, or specifically to carbon emitters within states. Firms that can more cheaply reduce their emissions (through their current practice or through accessible improvements) below the permitted level can then sell their excess permitted capacity to those firms facing steep costs for actual reductions. Because of the great international differentials in access to carbon reducing technology, a global trade offers significant efficiency advantages.

At the same time, permit trading presents a number of concerns. The chief one discussed in the literature has to do with the temptations of corruption and the problem of enforcement. Under a global system, presumably states would be responsible for enforcing their own emitters' compliance with permits – but states would have almost no incentive for doing so. Say country A is allocated a small number of permits, and is already using expensive reduction technology. It will seek to buy from poorer country B its unused permit capacity, if doing so is cheaper than making its own reductions. So far so good – global emissions drop at the lowest cost. But note that country B has every incentive to collect the price of the permits it has sold (or to pass that money on to its domestic producer) – and no incentive to actually enforce the reduced net amount of emissions capacity among its producers.[30] Knowing this, country A's citizens have no reason to support the scheme in the first place, which they might regard as merely punitive to their state, without providing any economic benefit. Whether or not they feel specially responsible for climate change policy, such a policy would make them mugs.

A carbon tax scheme, by contrast, sets a price paid by carbon producers at whatever level is sufficient to shift production towards more efficient means, or to enable the collecting state otherwise to offset the carbon emissions. Now there are technical problems estimating or adjusting the level of the carbon tax – though the problems may not be insuperable. But the carbon tax system has a major motivational advantage: motivations line up much more clearly with compliance. Under such a system, the taxes are collected by each state. Each state therefore has an incentive to maximise its tax revenues. Rich country A's citizens can accept a higher tax rate, potentially, because they can see that money

[30] This discussion is indebted to G.E. Metcalfe and D. Weisbach, 'The Design of a Carbon Tax' (2009) 33 Harv ELR 499.

as flowing to cure inequities that would otherwise result from an even-handed assessment of climate change costs – for example, aid to the poor in their own state, who will be more affected by rising heating costs, or technology transfer to poorer nations. And poor country B can see itself as the beneficiary of a global tax scheme that treats its obligations to reduce emissions as commensurate with its own responsibilities. More generally, a carbon tax scheme might be organised in a way that is commensurate with the assessment not just of differential collective responsibility by various states, but also shared responsibility for the global problem. Such a policy response recognises the weight of history while also confronting the future.

I can put the point more generally. We conceive of taxes, domestically, as a way in which the collective burdens of citizenship are shared, by the principles of fairness that are both responsive to local norms and priorities, as well as to universal considerations, such as basic vulnerability, diminishing marginal utility, and proportionality to benefit. The particular tax burden appropriate to an individual is fixed through a combination of theoretical, administrative, and political considerations, and as such is a fully institutional obligation. But its institutional artificiality does not undermine the moral point that one should pay one's share of taxes – that moral point, which is properly anchored in a sense of warranted guilt or shame if one cheats, is prior to the institutional determination. It is a matter of the basic morality of community membership: one has a moral obligation, as an individual, to meet the demands of collective membership. This does not distinguish taxes from the morality of the domestic marketplace: observing constraints of meeting promises and bargaining in good faith are also moral demands that are logically prior to particular bargains and situations. But the morality of taxes points to an understanding of shared responsibility as the morality of the marketplace does not. Taxes anchor themselves in a public morality; markets in a private morality.

7. Concluding remarks

I have argued thus far that the responsibility to mitigate climate change reflects both facts about a shared history and a global responsibility of the fair division of the benefits and burdens of development. These intersecting, vertical and horizontal, collective obligations find their natural expression in the morality of taxation, of individual obligations in relation to our shared identities, as citizens of nations existing over time, and as equal members of an interdependent and mutually vulnerable world. A sense of guilt over historically imprudent development, as well as over undeserved inequalities, can provide the legitimacy such a daunting tax bill demands. By contrast, while the demands of a market-based system are also anchored in a common conception of the problem of global warming, those demands are not easily seen as incidental to the individual obligations of citizenship. This suggests not only that the internal, moral psychological mechanisms of compliance will be weaker for a permit system, but that it will be much harder to construct a narrative to 'sell' the system to separate polities. Put conversely, market-based systems work best where they can legitimate themselves on grounds of efficiency rather than justice. But the demands of climate change are much too strong for efficiency to do the motivational work.

This discussion of the moral foundations of a conception of shared responsibility is not meant to provide a knock-down argument for the superiority of a tax mechanism for distributing burdens. My aim was instead much more modest: to indicate the continuities between an individual conception of moral responsibility and a collective, or shared, conception of legal-political responsibility. The moral emotion of guilt is the matrix in which both are embedded. Guilt and taxes may not be the happiest combination in the quiver of institutional designers, but they are among the most forceful and specific.

13

How to Keep Promises: Making Sense of the Duty Among Multiple States to Fulfil Socio-Economic Rights in the World

MARGOT E. SALOMON*

1. Introduction

This chapter explores bases for assigning positive duties of international assistance and cooperation to fulfil socio-economic rights in the world.[1] A difficulty at present is that states can only be said to have imprecise obligations to fulfil socio-economic rights beyond their borders: they are largely aggregated duties of an undifferentiated international community (to use Philip Alston's term), to cooperate in addressing hunger,

* Dr Margot E. Salomon is Acting Director at the Centre for the Study of Human Rights, London School of Economics and Political Science where she also directs the Laboratory for Advanced Research on the Global Economy, and is Associate Professor in the Law Department. This chapter is adapted from the extended coverage found in the work M.E. Salomon, 'Deprivation, Causation and the Law of International Cooperation', in M. Langford, W. Vandenhole, M. Scheinin, and W. van Genugten (eds.), *Global Justice, State Duties: The Extraterritorial Scope of Economic, Social and Cultural Rights in International Law* (Cambridge University Press, 2013), 259. All websites were last accessed on 5 June 2014.

[1] Although the Committee on Economic, Social and Cultural Rights (CESCR) has not formally elaborated any distinction between obligations of 'international assistance' and of 'cooperation', international assistance tends to be equated with the transfer of resources between states, as well as at times with technical support. International cooperation is understood more broadly, encompassing requirements of separate and joint action towards the realisation of socio-economic rights, including through the creation of an internationally enabling environment conducive to those ends. More recent instruments, such as the Convention on the Rights of Persons with Disabilities, New York, 13 December 2006, in force 3 May 2008, 2515 UNTS 3, but also the Convention on the Rights of the Child, New York, 20 November 1989, in force 2 September 1990, 1577 UNTS 3 (CRC), as well as the Declaration on the Right to Development, UN Doc. A/RES/41/128, Annex, UNGAOR, 41st Sess., Supp. No. 53, at 186, UN Doc. A/RES/41/53 (1986), refer only to international cooperation in the achievement of the relevant rights therein, reflecting the preference of high-income countries to do away with the idea that resource transfer constitutes a legal obligation.

malnutrition, and related deprivations that find expression in human rights treaties.

There are two main benefits that could come from determining the bases for assigning obligations in this area. First, clarity as to the scope of obligations of international assistance and cooperation could compel states to act in order to give them effect. Second, it would facilitate the determination of a breach of an international obligation of a state or states and thus responsibility for an internationally wrongful act. International responsibility could be attributed as a result of an action or omission – things states have and have not done to contribute to securing socio-economic rights elsewhere. Insofar as all states are bound by obligations of international cooperation under the United Nations (UN) Charter,[2] and states party to the relevant treaties addressing economic, social, and cultural rights are bound by obligations of international assistance and/or cooperation,[3] a central task that remains is to identify the basis or bases upon which duties might be disaggregated and thus more clearly assigned.

[2] Charter of the United Nations, San Francisco, 26 June 1945, in force 24 October 1945, 1 UNTS 16 (UN Charter).

[3] The sources of the obligation to cooperate internationally in the realisation of socio-economic rights can be traced back to the UN Charter's emphasis on international cooperation in the achievement of social justice and human rights, which forms a defining element of that foundational treaty (Articles 1(3), 55 and 56). The Universal Declaration of Human Rights, Paris, 10 December 1948, UN Doc. A/RES/217A(III), UNGAOR, 3rd Sess., UN Doc. A/810 (1948), recognises the significance of international cooperation in the realisation of human rights (Articles 22 and 28); and obligations of international assistance and cooperation in the International Covenant on Economic, Social and Cultural Rights, New York, 16 December 1966, in force 3 January 1976, 993 UNTS 3 (ICESCR) and similar formulations in the CRC, n. 1, form part of the general legal obligations in those widely ratified treaties: ICESCR, ibid., Article 2(1) provides that '[e]ach State Party to the present Covenant undertakes to take steps, individually and through international assistance and cooperation, especially economic and technical, to the maximum of its available resources, with a view to achieving progressively the full realization of the rights recognized in the present Covenant by all appropriate means, including particularly the adoption of legislative measures.' The 1986 Declaration on the Right to Development, n. 1, at Article 4(2) asserts the following: 'As a complement to the efforts of developing countries, effective international cooperation is essential in providing these countries with appropriate means and facilities to foster their comprehensive development.' The UN Millennium Declaration, UN Doc. A/RES/55/2 (18 September 2000), UN GAOR, 55th Sess., Supp. No. 49, at 4, UN Doc. A/55/49 (2000), recognises a 'shared responsibility' for managing worldwide economic and social development. International cooperation for human rights has found its most recent reaffirmation in the Convention on the Rights of Persons with Disabilities of 2006, n. 1.

When it comes to positive duties to fulfil socio-economic rights, causation may provide a basis for assigning obligations of international assistance and cooperation, however it hardly exhausts the possible grounds in this regard. States acting singly or jointly need not have caused harm in order to be under a positive duty to address the non-fulfilment of socio-economic rights elsewhere, nor in order to be held responsible for an internationally wrongful act derived from a failure to comply with a human rights obligation to assist and cooperate internationally.

Although it may be difficult to conclude that there exists a legally binding obligation for a given state to provide any particular form of material assistance to any other specific state(s), decades of UN consideration and standard setting in this and related areas have advanced interpretations of the obligation whereby economic, financial, monetary, and other policies should be designed in such a way as to avoid causing injury to the interests of other states and to the rights of their peoples,[4] and, moreover, should actively seek to address existing deprivations.[5] I have elsewhere explored the former issue whereby international policies that impact, for example, on the right to food and on the right to an adequate standard of living, are concerned with possible breaches of obligations to 'respect' socio-economic rights elsewhere (i.e., do no harm).[6] This chapter, for its part, addresses the parameters of a state's obligations to 'fulfil' socio-economic rights beyond its own borders.

When seeking to confront deprivation, obligations to fulfil socio-economic rights beyond borders are not limited to the transfer of financial resources and related aid. Although in this area the strongest argument regarding the role of individual states may be for a general duty amongst developed states to provide 0.7 per cent gross national income (GNI) in official development assistance,[7] states also have duties

[4] P. Alston and G. Quinn, 'The Nature and Scope of States Parties' Obligations under the International Covenant on Economic, Social and Cultural Rights' (1987) 9(2) HRQ 156, at 191; see generally, M. Bulajić, *Principles of International Development Law: Progressive Development of the Principles of International Law Relating to the New International Economic Order*, 2nd edn (Dordrecht: Martinus Nijhoff Publishers, 1993); M.E. Salomon, *Global Responsibility for Human Rights: World Poverty and the Development of International Law* (Oxford University Press, 2007).

[5] Salomon, ibid.

[6] Salomon, 'Deprivation, Causation and the Law of International Cooperation', n. *.

[7] Notwithstanding the various arguments questioning the benefits of aid, see, among others, D. Moyo, *Dead Aid* (London: Allen Lane [Penguin Books], 2009); R.C. Riddell, *Does Foreign Aid Really Work?* (Oxford University Press, 2008).

when acting collectively, and through myriad methods beyond the transfer of resources. These could include addressing trade protectionism by industrialised states,[8] as well as the policies of importing states that fuel resource-cursed countries[9] including international corruption[10] and support for illicit financial flows out of poor countries through tax havens and secrecy jurisdictions.[11] A failure to comply with the obligation of international cooperation for the realisation of human rights can also be found in a global policy of the past four decades that has been marked by gross inequality in wealth and income[12] under a scheme that one commentator pointedly refers to as 'accumulation by

[8] See I. Goldin and K. Reinert, *Globalization for Development: Trade, Finance, Aid, Migration, and Policy* (New York/Washington, DC: World Bank/Palgrave Macmillan, 2006), at 66, 75: 'What are the costs of trade protectionism for the developing world? A number of studies have tried to assess this. To take one example, the World Bank has considered the impact of a "pro poor" trade liberalization scenario. This scenario involves only tariff reductions and agricultural subsidies reform. The welfare gains to developing countries of this liberalization scenario are estimated to be over US$250 billion in 2003 prices. This is four times the value of foreign aid . . . The possibility of exports helping to alleviate poverty is significantly curtailed by trade protectionism in rich countries. This occurs in the form of tariffs, subsidies, quotas, standards, and regulations . . . Rich-country protectionism poses a significant barrier to poverty alleviation, not to mention the overall participation of the developing world in the global economy.'

[9] For an overview and sources on the correlation between the export of high-value extractive resources such as oil, gas, metals, and gems, and curses such as authoritarianism, corruption, conflict, and economic dysfunction, see L. Wenar, 'Clean Trade in Natural Resources: A Policy Framework for Importing States and Multinationals in the Extractive Industries' (2010) at www.cleantrade.org/policy_brief.pdf.

[10] Ibid., at 7: 'The Netherlands allowed tax deductions on bribes to foreign officials until 2006. It was not until 2009 that Britain successfully prosecuted a foreign corruption case. "Facilitation payments" are still permitted by Australia, Canada, New Zealand, South Korea and the US. Export credit agencies in many [resource] importing states fund and insure firms that pay off local officials.' See, further, P. Maass, *Crude World: The Violent Twilight of Oil* (London: Peter Lane [Penguin Books], 2009). As for recent developments, note the illegality of facilitation payments and the extraterritorial reach of the United Kingdom's Bribery Act 2010 c. 23, in force 1 July 2011.

[11] See D. Kar and D. Cartwright-Smith, 'Illicit Financial Flows from Africa: Hidden Resource for Development' (Global Financial Integrity, 2010), www.gfintegrity.org, at 1: 'This massive flow of illicit money out of Africa is facilitated by a global shadow financial system comprising tax havens, secrecy jurisdictions, disguised corporations, anonymous trust accounts, fake foundations, trade mispricing, and money laundering techniques. The impact of this structure and the funds it shifts out of Africa is staggering.' See also N. Shaxson, *Treasure Islands: Tax Havens and the Men Who Stole the World* (London: The Bodley Head, 2011).

[12] See M.E. Salomon, 'Why Should it Matter that Others Have More: Poverty, Inequality and the Potential of International Human Rights Law', Proceedings of the Oxford University Conference on International Law and Global Justice (2011) 37(5) RIS 2137.

dispossession'.[13] Cooperative conduct to fulfil human rights can take the form of domestic regulatory measures and policies with international effect or of international measures and policies.

The obligations of which we speak were not borne of globalisation; the treaties that underpinned the new world order in 1945 underscored 70 years ago that cooperation was essential to the establishment of a peaceful and just world. That said, the harms of globalisation and its attendant institutions reinforce the current significance of obligations of international assistance and cooperation to the ends of socio-economic justice. The forces of globalisation compel the cosmopolitan ethic that animates these obligations today.

2. Bases for assigning obligations of international assistance and cooperation

2.1 The International Covenant on Economic, Social and Cultural Rights and the Committee

In a state-centric system that remains largely circumscribed territorially, international human rights law generally recognises that the primary obligation to fulfil socio-economic rights rests with the state acting domestically. Whereas extraterritorial obligations to 'respect' and 'protect' socio-economic rights exist alongside those of the domestic state, international action to fulfil socio-economic rights by states other than the rights-holders' own, where required, is often said to be based on a secondary or subsidiary duty in those circumstances where the primary duty-bearer is unable or unwilling to fulfil said obligations. However, this latter point should not be overstated: the obligation to cooperate internationally to fulfil socio-economic rights is determined on the basis of the failure of rights-holders to exercise their rights[14] and since

[13] D. Harvey, *A Brief History of Neoliberalism* (Oxford University Press, 2005), 160 et seq. Harvey's accumulation of dispossession comprises four main features: privatisation and commodification; financialisation; the management and manipulation of crisis; and various forms of state redistributions in wealth and income that flow from lower to upper classes.

[14] The significance of distinguishing between whether the domestic state is unable or unwilling to comply with its obligations is important in determining its own responsibility for failure to meet its human rights obligations, inability giving rise to possible defences that might preclude wrongfulness. However the distinction bears no relevance as regards the assignment of secondary duties to external states, which is determined on the basis of the failure of the rights-holders to exercise their rights. See L. Wenar,

socio-economic rights remain so dramatically unmet globally we should best understand these obligations amongst external states to remedy the state of affairs as complementary to those of the right-holder's own state.[15] To ignore the existence of an obligation to take remedial international action would be to hollow out the value of the positive obligation of international cooperation for the realisation of socio-economic rights. It is difficult, however, to determine when an obligation of international assistance and/or cooperation has been breached for the purpose of determining international responsibility, because there is a paucity of judicial elucidation as to what directives would indicate that a given state was required to act in a particular situation, and how, in order to contribute to fulfilling socio-economic rights in the world.

The Committee on Economic, Social and Cultural Rights (CESCR or Committee) has given little detailed direction as to the content of the obligation of international assistance and cooperation under the International Covenant on Economic, Social and Cultural Rights (ICESCR or Covenant),[16] the general human rights treaty on the subject of socio-economic rights. On the terms of the treaty itself, states that might be said to have particular duties are those with economic and technical capacity. This basis is deduced from the 'obligation of all States parties to take steps, individually and through international assistance and cooperation, especially economic and technical', towards the full realisation of the rights.[17] Arguably, it can be further deduced from Article 23 of the Covenant that a particular duty also rests with states that are most influential when it comes to the 'conclusion of conventions and the adoption of recommendations' that would propel 'international action for the achievement of the rights' recognised in the Covenant.[18]

'Responsibility and Severe Poverty', in T.W. Pogge (ed.), *Freedom from Poverty as a Human Right: Who Owes What to the Very Poor?* (Oxford University Press/UNESCO, 2007), 255, at 265. Analogously, the responsibility of the international community to protect people from gross violations of human rights is triggered by the 'manifest failure' of national authorities to afford protection and not whether that failure is due to a government's inability or unwillingness. 2005 World Summit Outcome, UN Doc. A/RES/60/1 (24 October 2005), para. 139. I thank Jennifer Welsh for bringing this aspect of paragraph 139 to my attention.

[15] Salomon, *Global Responsibility for Human Rights*, at 189–195. [16] ICESCR, n. 3.

[17] Article 2(1) ICESCR, n. 3. On technical assistance, see also Articles 22 and 23.

[18] Article 23 ICESCR, n. 3: 'The States Parties to the present Covenant agree that international action for the achievement of the rights recognized in the present Covenant includes such methods as the conclusion of conventions, the adoption of recommendations, the furnishing of technical assistance and the holding of regional meetings and

Only one general basis for assigning obligations has so far been adopted by the Committee: that international cooperation for development and thus for the realisation of economic, social, and cultural rights, while an obligation of all states, 'is particularly incumbent upon those States in a position to assist', a point to which we will return.[19] A second and merely hortatory reference indicates that the inability of people in developing countries to exercise their socio-economic rights is 'of common concern to all countries',[20] the Committee's pronouncement on the existence of a 'common concern' implying an *erga omnes* or indeed an *omnium erga omnes* obligation.[21]

2.2 *Causation as a basis for assigning obligations of international cooperation*

The allocation of injury or loss to a wrongful act requires the existence of a causal link that also meets the criterion of, for example, directness, foreseeability or proximity.[22] A finding of international responsibility may *subsequently* (as part of, or separate from, the reparations owed) indicate a basis for assigning obligations of international assistance and cooperation: a state or states found to have caused harm could reasonably be said thereby to have particular duties of international cooperation when it comes to giving effect to its (treaty) obligations in the area of

technical meetings for the purpose of consultation and study organized in conjunction with the Governments concerned.'

19 CESCR, General Comment No. 3, 'The Nature of States Parties' Obligations' (Article 2(1) of the Covenant) (5th Sess., 1990), UN Doc. E/1991/23 (1991), Annex III, para. 14.

20 CESCR, General Comment No. 14, 'The Right to the Highest Attainable Standard of Health' (Article 12) (22nd Sess., 2000), UN Doc. E/C12/2000/4 (2000), para. 38.

21 '[O]bligations *erga omnes*, according to which there are some obligations with respect to which every State has a right to insist on their observance; and that of *obligations omnium*, according to which some obligations are incumbent upon all States without exception'. On obligations omnium, see, generally, P. Weil, 'Towards Relative Normativity in International Law' (1983) 77(3) AJIL 413. The definition just provided is from J. Tasioulas, 'In Defence of Relative Normativity: Communitarian Values and the Nicaragua Case' (1996) 16(1) OJLS 85, at 86.

22 Commentary to the Articles on Responsibility of States for Internationally Wrongful Acts, ILC *Yearbook* 2001/II(2) (ARSIWA Commentary), Commentary to Article 31, para. 10. The ILC remarks: 'In other words, the requirement of a causal link is not necessarily the same in relation to every breach of an international obligation ... The notion of a sufficient causal link which is not too remote is embodied in the general requirement in article 31 that the injury should be in consequence of the wrongful act, but without the addition of any particular qualifying phrase.' (Ibid.)

socio-economic rights. However, concluding that causation should offer the sole or primary basis for assigning obligations of international assistance and cooperation is unduly restrictive. States acting singly or jointly need not have caused harm in order to be under a positive duty to address the non-fulfilment of socio-economic rights elsewhere, nor in order to be held responsible for an internationally wrongful act derived from a failure to comply with an obligation to assist and cooperate internationally. Notably, as per Article 2(1) of the ICESCR as elsewhere, they are under a prescriptive obligation to act towards the fulfilment socio-economic rights, regardless of causation.[23]

Insofar as causation might shape the scope of subsequent obligations, a broader reading of the causation doctrine could have obligations assigned on the basis of the contribution that a state has made through its conduct to the emergence of the problem (historically or recently) and/or to the persistence of the problem. Obligations of international cooperation could be determined on the basis of the relative power it wields in international affairs manifested as influence over the direction of international trade, investment, taxation, finance, environmental policy, and development cooperation.

When it comes to the obligations of states other than the right-holder's own to respect and protect socio-economic rights, in addition to direct causation, international legal responsibility could be attributed on the grounds that the actions or omissions (whether international or internal decisions with external effect) had reasonably foreseeable international consequences[24] and/or because of the lack of due diligence undertaken to prevent the violation or to respond to it as required.[25] In the case of indivisible harms whereby establishing direct causal links between the actions of a particular state and its impact on the exercise of rights can be difficult, causation determined via a 'but for' test and an assessment as to whether sufficient precaution was taken can be important elements in attributing responsibility. If we take the case of biofuels: global food prices would not have skyrocketed but for the European Union and

[23] M.E. Salomon and I. Seiderman, 'The Maastricht Principles on Extraterritorial Obligations of States in the area of Economic, Social and Cultural Rights', *Special Section on International Law, Human Rights and the Global Economy: Innovations and Expectations for the 21st Century*, Guest Editor M.E. Salomon, (2012) 3(4) GP 458.

[24] See, *Munaf* v. *Romania*, Communication No. 1539/2006, Human Rights Committee, Admissibility and Merits, UN Doc. CCPR/C/96/D/1539/2006 (21 August 2009), para. 14.2.

[25] *Velásquez Rodriguez* v. *Honduras*, IACtHR, (Ser. C) No. 4 (1988), para. 172.

United States (US) policies on production.[26] Similarly if we consider agricultural subsidies, in the *United States–Cotton* case brought by Brazil against the United States, the World Trade Organization (WTO) Panel, as upheld by the Appellate Body, found that the world market price for cotton on which so many developing country farmers rely would have increased significantly had it not been for the US subsidies provided to its cotton producers, users, and/or exporters.[27] In short, the violations of the socio-economic rights abroad would not have occurred but for the actions and omissions of the relevant states, including their *prima facie* failures to exercise due diligence in order to prevent the harms.[28] These indirect causal links could offer a basis for subsequently assigning particular duties of international assistance and cooperation, including as part of reparations where a state is found internationally responsible based on the failure to exercise due diligence.

[26] Salomon, 'Deprivation, Causation and the Law of International Cooperation', n. *, at 263–272.

[27] The price suppression claim by the Panel – upheld by the Appellate Body – was determined via the application of a 'but for' test. In upholding Brazil's claim, the Panel examined whether the world market price for cotton would have increased significantly 'but for these subsidies'. *United States – Subsidies on Upland Cotton*, Appellate Body Report, 3 March 2005, WT/DS267/AB/R, para. 763(c)(i)(B). The subsidies paid by the United States to its 25,000 cotton farmers exceed the entire GNI of virtually every cotton exporting country in West and Central Africa. B. McGivern, *WTO Appellate Body Report: United States-Cotton Case Summary*, 10 June 2008, White and Case LLP, Geneva. In Benin alone, the fall in cotton prices in 2001–2002 was linked to an increase in poverty from 37 per cent to 59 per cent. United Nations Development Programme (UNDP), *Human Development Report 2005: International Cooperation at a Crossroads: Aid, Trade and Security in an Unequal World* (New York: Oxford University Press, 2005), 131.

[28] Due diligence could require *ex ante* impact assessments on cross-border or global impacts. In the *Pulp Mills case* the ICJ concludes that it 'may now be considered a requirement under general international law to undertake an environmental impact assessment where there is a risk that the proposed industrial activity may have a significant adverse impact in a transboundary context'. Moreover, due diligence would not be considered to have been exercised where there was liable to be a negative effect and the relevant party failed to undertake an impact assessment. *Pulp Mills on the River Uruguay (Argentina* v. *Uruguay)*, Judgment, ICJ Reports 2010, 14, para. 204. As for international decision making – human rights treaty bodies regularly call upon states to prepare human rights impact assessments of the trade and investment agreements that they conclude, and call on other actors in urging the use of mechanisms for measuring human rights impact of their international policies: UN Committee on the Rights of the Child, concluding observations on El Salvador, UN Doc. CRC/C/15/Add.232 (2004), para. 48; Committee on the Elimination of Discrimination against Women, concluding observation on Philippines, UN Doc. CEDAW/C/PHI/CO/6 (2006), para. 26, CESCR, 'Statement on Globalization and Economic, Social and Cultural Rights', UN Doc. E/1999/22-E/C.12/1998/26 (1998); ch. VI, sect. A, para. 515, at para 7.

Indirect causation might also be relevant insofar as the very design of existing global arrangements causes and/or fails to remedy widespread deprivation. On this account, the failure is that of the international political economy as a whole, and all states – to greater or lesser degrees – are thereby responsible for 'causing' the harms and are duty-bound to remedy them.[29] (That said, this structural thesis leads us back to having to disaggregate duties.)

2.3 *Historical responsibility as a basis for assigning obligations of international cooperation*

On this account, contemporary obligations would be assigned on the basis of historical responsibility for past exploitation. Although not a precondition, the harmful effects of past actions may be traceable to current deprivations in the form of the non-fulfilment of socio-economic rights and/or can be shown to have benefited the external state over time. It follows that, initially, a form of corrective justice should be forthcoming to the extent that certain countries have been disadvantaged as a result of past injustices,[30] and on the principle that people should not benefit from their wrongdoing and should compensate those who have suffered as a result. The basis of historical responsibility takes a compensatory approach based on some determination of liability for contributing to a problem. Needless to say, it is a claim traditionally advanced by developing countries and is politically contentious.[31] In practice, however, former colonial powers do tend to direct international assistance to their former colonies, in particular based on a moral sense of historical responsibility; recent empirical studies demonstrating the long-term effects of colonialism and slavery on current economic performance could provide a legal grounding.[32] Historical responsibility as a relevant basis for assigning obligations of

[29] See further, Salomon, *Global Responsibility for Human Rights*, n. 4; 1986 Declaration on the Right to Development, n. 1, Article 3(1): 'States have the primary responsibility for the creation of national and international conditions favourable to the realization of the right to development.'

[30] D. Shelton, 'Describing the Elephant in the Room', in J. Ebbesson and P. Okowa (eds.), *Environmental Law and Justice in Context* (Cambridge University Press, 2009), 55, at 61.

[31] It has been given considerable focus in climate change debates as part of 'climate debt' demands. See the submission by the state of Bolivia to the Ad Hoc Working Group on Long-term Cooperative Action: Outcome of the World People's Conference on Climate Change and the Rights of Mother Earth (April 2010).

[32] N. Nunn, 'The Long-Term Effects of Africa's Slave Trades' (2008) 123(1) QJE 139.

international assistance and cooperation should not preclude the adoption of other bases, including notably that of capacity.

2.4 *Capacity as a basis for assigning obligations of international cooperation*

As noted, CESCR has emphasised that particular obligations of international assistance and cooperation are incumbent on those states in 'a position to assist', and as such indicates capacity as a basis for assigning obligations. Capacity offers both a specific and a general requirement: specific in that it is one of the bases that points to the requisite international duty-bearers, and general in that it is a prerequisite to discharging any obligation. Thus, one could argue, for example, that historical responsibility should form a basis for assigning international obligations, but capacity would still be a necessary element in order to see that obligation fulfilled.

A full examination of what constitutes capacity to assist is beyond the scope of this chapter, however the list could include economic, technical, and technological capacities, available resources, and influence, including in international decision-making processes.[33] In the narrower context of providing disaster relief and humanitarian assistance in times of emergency, we see capacity as the basis for assigning obligations to cooperate. CESCR refers to the requirement that 'each State should contribute to this task to the maximum of its capacities'. Furthermore, all states are to fulfil their 'collective responsibility' due to the risk of the spread of disease across borders. In the case of humanitarian assistance, the dilemma of choosing amongst a multiplicity of possible duty-bearers is resolved by the Committee: the degree to which each state should assist depends on its individual (maximum) capacity – with the 'economically developed states parties [having] a special responsibility . . . to assist the poorer developing states'.[34] In the *Genocide* case, the International Court of Justice (ICJ) took the approach of devising allocative principles to identify states with the greatest duty to prevent genocide. Criteria

[33] See 'Maastricht Principles on Extraterritorial Obligations of States in the Area of Economic, Social and Cultural Rights' (2011), at www.maastrichtuniversity.nl, Principle 31; Salomon, *Global Responsibility for Human Rights*, n. 4, ch. 5: 'Attributing Global Legal Responsibility', 180.

[34] CESCR, General Comment No. 14, n. 20, para. 40.

included 'the capacity to influence effectively' (the action of persons likely to commit, or already committing, genocide) and the 'geographical distance of the State concerned from the scene of the events'.[35]

A turn to capacity, and thus differentiated duties, as a basis for assigning obligations in the area of socio-economic rights, is bolstered by what one commentator sums up as the dissolution of the 'traditional egalitarian fiction and the emergence of a new legal polycentricity',[36] which has been brought to the fore by the principle of 'common but differentiated responsibility' (CBDR) in international environmental law. In advancing an ethic that certain countries will take the lead in meeting internationally agreed objectives, the approach based on CBDR serves to influence the interpretation of environmental instruments, as well as affirms the contemporary significance of global partnerships.[37] The principle of CBDR is justified intellectually based on the reality of both historical differences in the contributions made by developed and developing states to global environmental problems, the responsibility of developed countries for present and future pursuit of sustainable development, differences in respective economic and technical capacity to tackle the problems, as well as different needs. Thus, it translates into differentiated environmental standards set on the basis of the range of factors, including special needs and circumstances, future economic

[35] *Application of the Convention on the Prevention and Punishment of the Crime of Genocide (Bosnia and Herzegovina* v. *Serbia and Montenegro)*, Judgment, ICJ Reports 2007, 43, para. 430 (*Genocide* case).

[36] P.H. Sand, 'The Evolution of International Environmental Law', in D. Bodansky, J. Brunnée and E. Hey (eds.), *The Oxford Handbook of International Environmental Law* (Oxford University Press, 2007), 29, at 40.

[37] See Rio Declaration on Environment and Development, UN Doc. A/CONF.151/26 (Vol. I) (1992); (1992) 31 ILM 874, Principle 7: 'States shall cooperate in a spirit of global partnership to conserve, protect and restore the health and integrity of the Earth's ecosystem. In view of the different contributions to global environmental degradation, States have common but differentiated responsibilities. The developed countries acknowledge the responsibility that they bear in the international pursuit of sustainable development in view of the pressures their societies place on the global environment and of the technologies and financial resources they command'; UN Framework Convention on Climate Change, New York, 9 May 1992, in force 21 March 1994, 1771 UNTS 107, Article 3(1): 'The Parties should protect the climate system for the benefit of present and future generations of humankind, on the basis of equity and in accordance with their common but differentiated responsibilities and respective capabilities. Accordingly, the developed country Parties should take the lead in combating climate change and the adverse effects thereof.'

development of countries, and historical contributions to the creation of an environmental problem.[38]

In international environmental law, the principle of CBDR does not in itself offer a basis for assigning obligations of international cooperation, nor for dividing duties amongst those states with the greater responsibilities. These are fleshed out in the provisions of a given instrument that differentiates specific duties by category of states.[39] It is a principle that recognises that states should – for the range of reasons provided earlier – possess different duties, and underpins steps that allow for differential treatment to those ends. Its practical application can take the form of, for example, increased time to implement treaty commitments, exemptions, burden sharing through the allocation of funding, and the transfer of technology. CBDR might be said to offer a general principle of equity, with differential treatment concerned with the realisation of substantive equality over time aimed at enhancing the social and economic development of those worst-off in the world. As such, it seeks to provide remedial measures aimed at achieving what the drafters agree would be a more just society.[40] In sum, although the principle of CBDR may represent merely 'the nucleus of an emerging framework of global burden sharing',[41] it can be seen as part of a broader normative development in international law that requires action on the part of those 'in a position to assist'. It also points to an emerging procedural requirement for states to

[38] The Centre for International Sustainable Development Law, 'The Principle of Common but Differentiated Responsibilities: Origins and Scope', Legal Brief for the World Summit on Sustainable Development 2002 (Johannesburg, 26 August 2002), at http://cisdl.org/public/docs/news/brief_common.pdf.

[39] See for example, Convention on Biological Diversity, Rio de Janeiro, 5 June 1992, in force 29 December 1993, 1760 UNTS 79, Article 20(2): 'The developed country Parties shall provide new and additional financial resources to enable developing country Parties to meet the agreed full incremental costs to them of implementing measures which fulfil the obligations of this Convention and to benefit from its provisions.'

[40] D. Shelton, 'Equity', in D. Bodansky, J. Brunne´e, and E. Hey (eds.), *The Oxford Handbook of International Environmental Law* (Oxford University Press, 2007), 639, at 659.

[41] J. Brunnée, 'Climate Change, Global Environmental Justice and International Environmental Law', in J. Ebbesson and P. Okowa (eds.), *Environmental Law and Justice in Context* (Cambridge University Press, 2009), 316, at 327; and see J. Scott and L. Rajamani, 'EU Climate Change Unilateralism' (2012) 23(2) EJIL 469, at 477: 'Although the CBDRRC [common but differentiated responsibilities and respective capabilities] principle has come to play a pivotal role in international environmental law, the core content of the CBDRRC principle, as well as the nature of the obligation it entails, is deeply contested.'

coordinate with each other in the allocation of particular duties necessary to discharge their respective obligations to cooperate effectively.[42]

2.5 *Capacity and the matter of cost*

When relying on those states with the capacity to assist in fulfilling obligations, the division of duties is determined also according to states that could most easily avert or redress the threat or violation to basic well-being in a given situation. The converse is that should it be too difficult for a state to avert or redress the human rights threat or violation, then there is no obligation to do so.[43] A consideration of capacity as a basis for assigning obligations of international cooperation thus begs the subsequent question as to where the line is to be drawn.

In meeting its positive obligations of international assistance and cooperation to fulfil socio-economic rights beyond territory, the question arises as to what would constitute an unreasonable cost on the part of a state acting internationally. It might be assumed that a state having broadly secured a high level of socio-economic rights for its people is in a position to take steps to fulfil socio-economic rights abroad, perhaps requiring an expenditure of financial or other resources. This approach takes as its starting point that states can act in fulfilling rights elsewhere because socio-economic rights have been realised at home. Ooms and Hammonds recognise the risk that this approach invites when it comes to rights that are progressively realised and indeterminate. They argue with regard to the right to health for example, that in order to avoid a situation whereby high-income countries could endlessly refute their obligations of international assistance by referring to their domestic obligations to achieve the 'moving target of the highest attainable standard of health', any country that has realised the *minimum* essential level of health domestically is duty-bound to contribute to that same standard elsewhere

[42] See 'Maastricht Principles on Extraterritorial Obligations of States', n. 33, Principle 30; O. De Schutter, A. Eide, A. Khalfan, M. Orellana, M.E. Salomon, and I. Seiderman, 'Commentary to the Maastricht Principles on the Extraterritorial Obligations of States in the area of Economic, Social and Cultural Rights' (2012) 34(4) HRQ 1084, at 1149; A. Khalfan, 'Division of Responsibility Between States', in M. Langford, et. al. (eds.), *Global Justice, State Duties: The Extraterritorial Scope of Economic, Social and Cultural Rights in International Law* (Cambridge University Press, 2013), 299.

[43] See Wenar on the 'least-cost principle': Wenar, 'Responsibility and Severe Poverty', n. 14, at 269.

before aiming for the (progressively realisable) highest attainable standard of health.[44]

I would propose a more exacting test: a state that has not ensured the minimum essential level of rights at home could *still* be said to have positive obligations to fulfil the human rights of people outside its borders on the basis of an objective determination as to what constitutes the 'adequate and reasonable' use of its 'available resources' towards the realisation of rights.[45] A state that has not fulfilled the minimum essential levels of socio-economic rights at home might nonetheless be required to comply with its obligations to people elsewhere if, by objective criteria, it can be said to possess adequate resources. In circumstances whereby the state is deemed to possess the resources necessary to meet minimum standards at home and contribute to the fulfilment of rights in the world, it would be for that state to justify any retrogression in the exercise of the rights of its own citizens that occurs alongside the dispensation of foreign assistance.[46] These tests may go some way to addressing the problem of multiplicity just touched on at least in the area of resource transfer: all states that have fulfilled basic socio-economic rights at home, or are determined objectively to possess adequate resources but have shown themselves unwilling to fulfil their minimum obligations at home, are all

[44] G. Ooms and R. Hammonds, 'Taking Up Daniels' Challenge: The Case for Global Health Justice' (2010) 12(1) HHR 29, at 36.

[45] The references to the requirement to use maximum available resources are found in Article 2(1) ICESCR, n. 3, and Article 4 CRC, n. 1. In a 2007 statement, CESCR indicated that under a future communications procedure, it would apply an 'adequate and reasonable' test in determining whether a state party acting at the domestic level has failed to take steps to the maximum of its available resources in meeting its obligations under the Covenant. CESCR, 'Statement on an Evaluation of the Obligations to Take Steps to the "Maximum Available Resources" under an Optional Protocol to the Covenant' (38th Sess., 2007), UN Doc. E/C12/2007/1 (2007), para. 8. CESCR indicates that the requirement is for 'principled policy-making' to be undertaken. Article 8(4) of the new Optional Protocol to the International Covenant on Economic, Social and Cultural Rights directs the Committee in its examination of communications towards a reasonableness standard of review: '[w]hen examining communications under the present Protocol, the Committee shall consider the reasonableness of the steps taken by the State Party in accordance with part II of the Covenant. In doing so, the Committee shall bear in mind that the State Party may adopt a range of possible policy measures for the implementation of the rights set forth in the Covenant.' Optional Protocol to the ICESCR, 10 December 2008, in force 5 May 2013.

[46] CESCR, General Comment No. 3, n. 19, para. 9: 'any deliberately retrogressive measures . . . would require the most careful consideration and would need to be fully justified by reference to the totality of the rights provided for in the Covenant and in the context of the full use of the maximum available resources'.

equally required to contribute to the fulfilment of rights elsewhere. The subsequent determination as to which foreign state(s) should assist which particular recipient state(s), and how, becomes merely a matter of coordination.

At least two issues should be highlighted here: that eliminating deprivation globally is a manageable collective enterprise, and that the perpetuation of need is avoidable under just international institutions. Although mechanisms for financial global redistribution akin to the national welfare state do not exist at present,[47] substantial improvements in the position and living conditions of the world's poor are possible at small opportunity costs to the rich world. Doubling the wealth of all in the bottom two quintiles would take only 1.55 per cent of the wealth of the top 1 per cent of the human population;[48] 0.7 per cent of the global product, or less than 1 per cent of the combined GNIs of the high-income countries, is all that is needed to address the aggregate shortfall from the World Bank's two US dollar-a-day poverty line.[49] A mere 0.1 per cent of the GNI of the sixty-six economies classified as high-income by the World Bank is all that would be required to meet what CESCR considers to constitute the core obligations as regards the right to health.[50] Because taken together funds are easily available, and because meeting global need requires resources beyond that of any one state, obligations of international cooperation (differentiated by capacity) need also include the collective duties of the appropriate members of the international community of states, in this case as regards the transfer of financial resources.

It is immaterial to the finding of a breach of an obligation of conduct for a single state whose responsibility is in issue to claim that it could make little difference on its own in the prevention of a violation, even had it used all means reasonably at its disposal, as the ICJ has noted in a different context: 'the more so since the possibility remains that the combined efforts of several states, each complying with its obligation to prevent, might have achieved the result [of averting the harm] . . . which

[47] R.H. Wade, 'Globalization, Growth, Poverty, Inequality, Resentment, and Imperialism', in J. Ravenhill (ed.), *Global Political Economy*, 2nd edn (Oxford University Press, 2008), 373, at 403.

[48] T.W. Pogge, 'Growth and Inequality: Understanding Recent Trends and Political Choices' (2008) 55(1) *Dissent* 66, at 72.

[49] Ibid., at 73.

[50] Ooms and Hammonds, 'Taking Up Daniels Challenge', n. 44, at 37. In December 2013, there were seventy-five high-income economies: see http://data.worldbank.org/about/country-classifications/country-and-lending-groups#High_income.

the efforts of only one state were insufficient to produce'.[51] In addition, although it is not certain that a given intervention would have prevented the harm, that actuality is irrelevant to establishing responsibility.[52] In circumstances where more than one state is responsible, each state is separately responsible for conduct attributable to it and that responsibility is not diminished by the fact that it is not the only responsible state. This is equally the case in a situation where a single course of conduct is at the same time attributable to several states and is internationally wrongful for each of them.[53] The preliminary conclusions on this matter are twofold: on the one hand, we can recognise the existence of collective legal obligations while relying, so far, on an individualised regime of legal responsibility in the event of a breach of those obligations. On the other hand, the truly collective action required to fulfil this obligation might best invite the application of a standard of joint and several responsibility whereby the victim could claim for the full amount against any wrongdoing state, even if no one state is likely to be able adequately to compensate for the collective failure when it comes to reparations, and other methods will need to be devised. The responsible state will also have the option, in principle, of claiming against the other wrongdoing states for their contribution to the harm.[54] As Nollkaemper and Jacobs rightly point out, when obligations require collective action, it is reasonable for shared responsibility to be implied in the event of a breach.[55] The standard of joint and several responsibility is instructive, as Judge Simma explains in his separate opinion in the *Oil Platforms* case: 'on the one hand it recognizes the difficulty of a finding of responsibility where apportionment is impossible. On the other hand, it excludes as unfair a solution in which no one would be held responsible'.[56]

[51] *Genocide* case, n. 35, para. 430.

[52] Ibid. Although the ICJ concluded in the *Genocide* case that it is not irrelevant to the determination of financial compensation since the actual damage could not be causally linked to the wrongdoing state. Ibid., para. 462.

[53] ARSIWA Commentary, n. 22, Commentary to Article 47.

[54] Nollkaemper and Jacobs highlight, however, that in practice, 'the decentralized nature of the international legal order, combined with the lack of courts with compulsory jurisdiction, suggests that the international legal order is much less conducive to application of joint and several responsibility'. P.A. Nollkaemper and D. Jacobs, 'Shared Responsibility in International Law: A Conceptual Framework' (2013) 34(2) MIJIL 359, at 423.

[55] Ibid., at 394.

[56] *Oil Platforms (Islamic Republic of Iran v. United States of America)*, Judgment, ICJ Reports 2003, 161, Separate Opinion of Judge Simma, para. 68. On joint and several responsibility see Salomon, 'Deprivation, Causation and the Law of International Cooperation', n. *. See also

The second issue warranting note is that poverty and the widespread violation of socio-economic rights are avoidable through the creation of fairer international institutions,[57] the imperative being to elaborate, interpret, and apply international rules in a manner consistent with internationally accepted standards of decency, in many instances as articulated through human rights.[58] International cooperation is not limited to the distribution of resources and goods, but also includes the establishment of just institutional procedural principles[59] and a system of rules that distributes the consequential effects of the law fairly.[60]

3. Accountability

Undoubtedly there currently exist accountability failures in the area of ensuring socio-economic rights globally. There has been little done to

P. d'Argent, 'Reparation, Cessation, Assurances and Guarantees of Non-Repetition', in P.A. Nollkaemper and I. Plakokefalos (eds.), *Principles of Shared Responsibility in International Law: An Appraisal of the State of the Art* (Cambridge University Press, 2014), 208; L.A. Kornhauser, 'Incentives, Compensation, and Irreparable Harm', Chapter 5 of this volume, 120; and A. van Aaken, 'Shared Responsibility in International Law: A Political Economy Analysis', Chapter 6 of this volume, 153.

57 See Pogge, 'Growth and Inequality', n. 48, at 73–74; T.M. Franck, *Fairness in International Law and Institutions* (Oxford: Clarendon Press, 1995).

58 See 'Maastricht Principles on Extraterritorial Obligations of States', n. 33, Principles 17 and 29(a). See also the work of R. Howse that points to the positive impact that would come to bear on poverty through changing the interpretative practices and culture surrounding the existing rules (especially integrating existing positive international human rights law into the interpretation of economic rules), over changes to the formal rules themselves. R. Howse, 'Accountability Issues in International Economic Governance', Conference on the Accountability for Human Rights Violations by International Organizations, International Law Association Belgian Branch, Brussels, March 2007 (on file with author); R. Howse, 'Mainstreaming the Right to Development into International Trade Law and Policy at the World Trade Organization', UN Doc. E/CN.4/Sub 2/2004/17 (9 June 2004); R. Howse and R. Teitel, 'Global Justice, Poverty, and the International Economic Order', in S. Besson and J. Tasioulas (eds.), *The Philosophy of International Law* (Oxford University Press, 2010), 437, at 447.

59 V. Zanetti, 'Egalitarian Global Distributive Justice or Minimal Standard? Pogge's Position', in A. Follesdal and T.W. Pogge (eds.), *Real World Justice: Grounds, Principles, Human Rights, and Social Institutions* (Berlin: Springer, 2005), 199, at 208; and see Franck, *Fairness in International Law and Institutions*, n. 57.

60 Franck, ibid., at 8; Salomon, *Global Responsibility for Human Rights*, n. 4. For two proposals aimed at embedding systems of distributive justice (the consideration or adoption of which might themselves constitute giving effect to aspects of the obligation of international cooperation for the realisation of socio-economic rights), see the work of Thomas Pogge on the Health Impact Fund at www.healthimpactfund.org, and of Leif Wenar on Clean Trade at www.cleantrade.org.

address wide-scale violations of socio-economic rights in a system, in large part, structured around redress for individual territorial victims of human rights violations. So far there is inadequate mobilisation in response to CESCR's view that poverty reflects 'a massive and systemic breach' of international human rights law.[61] The adoption by the General Assembly of an Optional Protocol to the ICESCR in 2008[62] offers some possibilities of redress for the breach of obligations by those states other than the right-holder's own, including when the obligations are shared among several states parties. Through its system of inter-state complaints,[63] and the inquiry procedure triggered by reliable information indicating grave or systematic violations of Covenant rights,[64] the Committee could address issues regarding the failure of a state (or states) to comply with their positive obligations of international cooperation in a manner that it cannot readily consider in the context of individual communications.

Extraterritorial obligations, and notably international cooperation for development and thus for the realisation of economic, social, and cultural rights, are understood both normatively and practically as essential to fulfilling the aspirations of many countries and the human rights of their peoples. Under the Optional Protocol there would seem to be no procedural bar to having, for example, a developing state, acting in its capacity as an injured state to which the obligation is owed (or as non-injured state(s) acting in the wider common interest), from invoking the responsibility of a developed state (or several states) under the inter-state procedure (subject to a declaration recognising the competence of the Committee to receive communications), for non-compliance with its negative and positive international obligations. In the former case, a developing country could submit a communication claiming that other state parties (or another state party) are not meeting their obligations of international assistance by failing to contribute 'the maximum of its available resources' towards the socio-economic rights of its people.[65]

[61] CESCR, 'Statement on Poverty and the International Covenant on Economic, Social and Cultural Rights' (25th Sess., 2001), UN Doc. E/C.12/2001/10 (2001), para. 4.

[62] Optional Protocol to ICESCR, n. 45. [63] Ibid., Article 10.

[64] Ibid., Articles 11 and 12.

[65] As discussed earlier and further see, 'Maastricht Principles on Extraterritorial Obligations of States', n. 33, Principle 33: 'As part of the broader obligation of international cooperation, States, acting separately and jointly, that are in a position to do so, must provide international assistance to contribute to the fulfilment of economic, social and cultural rights in other States.'

Further, a developing country could submit a communication claiming that other state parties (or another state party) are not taking the necessary steps, separately, and jointly through international cooperation, to create an international enabling environment conducive to the universal fulfilment of economic, social, and cultural rights by failing to elaborate or review multilateral and bilateral agreements, so as to render them consistent with international human rights standards.[66] As for concerns pertaining to grave or systematic violations under the inquiry procedure, where the Committee is granted competence it should have no shortage of issues to examine in a world where the realisation of human rights is being brought to its knees by food, financial, and environmental crises.

4. Concluding remarks

As a matter of positive international human rights law obligations of international assistance and cooperation are not discretionary. But unless we begin to see delineated what is required, when, and by which state(s), they may as well be voluntary. While this chapter has only begun to address how we might think about establishing international responsibility in a world of great deprivations where duties to confront need extend beyond the right-holder's own state, it is clear that our doctrines and mechanisms are hardly fit for purpose. A thoughtful commentator remarked recently that the biggest blind spot in global human rights is the political economy,[67] it is high time this changed or justice will continue to evade us.

[66] Ibid., Principle 29.
[67] V.K. Nagaraj, 'Global Human Rights: For Futures unlike the Past', OpenDemocracy, 31 July 2013, at www.opendemocracy.net.

14

Pirate 'Gaolbalisation': Dividing Responsibility Among States, Companies, and Criminals

EUGENE KONTOROVICH*

1. Introduction

Piracy is the prototypical 'universal' offence that injures many nations at once. A pirate attack will directly injure i) the victim vessel's flag state; ii) the victim vessel's owner's state; and iii) the states of the typical multinational crew. Usually, i–iii all involve different countries; and the pirates themselves hail from yet another one. Moreover, pirate attacks result in significant increases in maritime insurance policies for the affected regions, thus spreading the cost of the problem even more broadly. On the high seas, where no nation has sovereignty, responses to piracy require shared responsibility. Alongside shared responsibility among nations, piracy introduces a second axis of distributed responsibility: the division of responsibility between states and private actors. Because pirates act outside of state territory and directly target private interests, the latter have a significant role in the response.

For nearly two centuries, piracy has received little attention in international law. Customary prohibitions were codified and somewhat expanded in the high seas regime of the United Nations Convention on the Law of the Sea (LOSC)[1] and its successors, but the subject was generally seen as an anachronism. A significant rise in piracy in several vital shipping lanes since the start of the twenty-first century has led nations to look for new solutions to the old problem, with relatively little legal guidance or recent precedent.

Especially in response to the surge in Somali piracy, nations have developed a unique model of shared responsibility that deserves further

* Professor, Northwestern University School of Law. All websites were last accessed on 5 June 2014.

[1] United Nations Convention on the Law of the Sea, Montego Bay, 10 December 1982, in force 16 November 1994, 1833 UNTS 3 (LOSC).

study. This complex regime has had the advantage of providing a prompt and relatively effective set of solutions to a pressing international problem. It also raises multidimensional problems of shared responsibility between the actors involved. First, private parties (shippers and security companies) have assumed primary responsibility for piracy suppression nominally allocated to states. Second, nations have divided their suppression role both horizontally and vertically, with apprehension, prosecution, and incarceration of suspects each handled by different groups of nations. Let us call this 'gaolbalisation' – when globalisation, outsourcing, and off-shoring meet gaol, or jail.

These arrangements are quite attractive from an efficiency perspective. At each stage, the most efficient provider of the relevant service assumes responsibility, accompanied with side payments from the transferring nation and other interested parties, who essentially subcontracts parts of the criminal process to other countries. Yet the efficiency of such practices depends in part on mechanisms for assigning responsibility for international law violations, which still remain undeveloped because of the multilayered nature of the phenomenon. This chapter examines such arrangements and the relevant positive law, but also assesses them from an efficiency perspective. Such explicit contractual arrangements to deal with a global public goods problem are an appropriate place to introduce economic logic into public international law.

2. *Ex ante* responsibility – suppression and deterrence

2.1 Role of states

The response to maritime piracy presents one of the most complex scenarios of shared responsibility in international law. Piracy involves stakeholders from multiple different nations – the flag state, the owners' state, the coastal state, the pirates' home state, and the apprehending state may all have some responsibility for responding to the problem. International law classifies pirates as *hostis humani generis* – enemies of all mankind.[2] This is reflected in the principal legal consequence of piracy. Any nation can stop and arrest pirates on the high seas,[3] and any nation may prosecute any pirates that fall in its hands.

[2] See E. Kontorovich, 'The Piracy Analogy: Modern Universal Jurisdiction's Hollow Foundation' (2004) 45 Harv ILJ 183, at 232–234.
[3] Article 105 LOSC, n. 1.

Indeed, the LOSC treats piracy suppression as a general *responsibility* incumbent on all states. In its first provision on piracy, dubbed '*Duty to cooperate in the repression of piracy*', the Convention provides that '[a]ll States shall cooperate to the fullest possible extent in the repression of piracy on the high seas or in any other place outside the jurisdiction of any State.'[4] The drafters' Commentary to the first Law of the Sea Convention stresses that 'any State having an opportunity [to take] measures against piracy, and neglecting to do so, would be failing in a duty laid upon it by international law'.[5] It also favourably cites the Harvard Draft Convention on Piracy, which went so far as to state that legal claims could be brought against any nation that does not take sufficient steps to bring pirates to justice.[6] This is strong and unusual language; international law rarely obligates nations to take particular actions against foreign or extraterritorial conduct. Moreover, the language of Article 100 LOSC speaks only of a duty to 'cooperate', which is much more nebulous than a duty to take particular measures, and Article 105 makes clear that *prosecution* itself is not obligatory.

Despite the 'duty' created by the LOSC and its Commentaries, state practice does not reveal or suggest any practical or concrete obligation upon countries. Failure to repress piracy may be in the abstract a breach of an international responsibility, which may fall on many states, but not an injury in itself. Certainly no legal claims have been brought for insufficient pirate suppression. The narrow interpretation of LOSC's general language may be attributable to the problems inherent with global, general duties.[7] When a duty to do a particular thing is laid upon all nations, it creates predictable collective action and free-rider problems.[8] The failure of the Article 100 'duty' to find reflection in state practice underscores the difficult of widely shared, abstract duties toward unknown third parties.[9]

[4] Article 100 LOSC, n. 1 (emphasis added).

[5] Report of the International Law Commission to the General Assembly, 11 UNGAOR 8th Sess., Supp. No. 9, UN Doc. A/3159 (1956), reprinted in ILC *Yearbook* 1956/II, A/CN.4/SER.A/1956/Add.l, 253, Commentary to Article 38, at 282, para. 2. The piracy provisions in the first Law of the Sea Convention were transferred directly to the 1982 LOSC, n. 1.

[6] Ibid., Commentary to Article 38, at 282, para. 1; see also Harvard Research in International Law, 'Draft Convention on Piracy and Comments' (1932) 26 AJIL (Supp.) 739.

[7] P.A. Nollkaemper and D. Jacobs, 'Shared Responsibility in International Law: A Conceptual Framework' (2013) 34 MIJIL 359.

[8] See E. Kontorovich, 'The Inefficiency of Universal Jurisdiction' (2008) Ill LR 389, at 397–398; n. 42.

[9] The 'duty' to repress piracy may best be understood in the context of maritime law's unusual but longstanding tradition of affirmative duties of assistance on the high seas. The

Instead, there is general agreement, as expressed in numerous United Nations (UN) resolutions, that the primary responsibility for suppressing piracy should fall on the pirate's home state – the place where the pirates are based.[10] The home state is generally speaking the cheapest cost-avoider.[11] Capturing pirates in the vast expanse of the high seas is haphazard and expensive. Even pirates spend most of their time on land, and this is where they are most easily located and captured. Because this occurs within the territory of a sovereign state, which has exclusive authority to police crimes within its borders, it also has the primary responsibility for doing so. Indeed, coastal states typically take the lead role in suppressing piracy – examples include Nigeria today and China a decade ago.

Yet sometimes coastal states have the political will but not necessarily the tactical resources to fully deal with a pirate problem. In such cases, it appears both efficient and expected for such countries to be offered assistance from affected and interested states. Thus the primary responsibility falls on the coastal state because it is the cheapest cost-avoider, yet those who wish the costs to be avoided can be expected to contribute. A well-regarded model of this developed in response to a surge of piracy in the Straits of Malacca at the turn of the millennia. Indonesia and Malaysia lacked the naval sophistication to catch the pirates. They were also very resistant to direct assistance by other nations, which they saw as interfering in their sovereign affairs. The much richer nations of Singapore and Japan provide resources, assets, and organised an effort that quickly suppressed the pirate problem.[12] The efforts were widely seen as a model of international cooperation – made possible by coastal states, and financed by regional states.

LOSC obligates vessels to come to the assistance of distressed mariners, see Article 98 LOSC, n. 1. The pirate suppression duty could be understood in a more limited sense in connection to the assistance duty, as applying to ships reasonably near a national warship, thus significantly reducing the problem of several responsibility (Article 100 LOSC speaks of 'states' and not their flagged vessels, and thus presumably only applies to warships).

[10] This practice follows the analogy to the general duty to render assistance discussed in the prior note. Article 98(2) of the LOSC imposes particular rescue duties on coastal states; pirates typically operate at least in part off the coast of their home state.

[11] See G. Calabresi, *The Cost of Accidents: A Legal and Economic Analysis* (New Haven, CT: Yale University Press, 1970), 135.

[12] P. Lehr (ed.), *Violence at Sea: Piracy in the Age of Global Terrorism* (London: Routledge, 2007); but see, C.Z. Raymond, 'Piracy and Armed Robbery In the Malacca Strait: A Problem Solved?' (2009) 62 NWCR 31.

However, when the coastal state neglects to take appropriate measures to suppress pirates, it can expect to be held accountable by victim-nations. The situation would pose the common problem of nations failing to prevent cross-border attacks from within their territory.[13] However, pirates typically operate from very weak or failed states that *cannot* control their coastlines and for whom any liability imposed by international law would matter relatively little. Historically, pirates have always hidden in bays and harbours of weak states (classically, the weakly-held Caribbean possessions of the crumbling Spanish Empire). The victim states would complain to the coastal state, which would protest its inability to control the problem. Failed states are essentially judgment-proof.[14] Thus the easy answer of holding the coastal state responsible is sometimes not an option.

2.2 *Private vs. public action*

An important second axis of shared responsibility is not cross-national, but public/private. Counter-piracy security and enforcement can be provided by national navies or by private security forces embarked on merchant vessels. Indeed, one reason for the breakout success of Somali pirates in 2008 was that at the time, no vessels transiting the region had armed security forces, making them easy targets. Some shippers responded by equipping their vessels with non-lethal countermeasures, which reduced pirate success rates. The introduction of armed security details has an even more dramatic effect on pirate success rates: no ship with armed guards has been successfully pirated. The private response is much cheaper than naval interdiction: it consists of a few men with rifles on each ship instead of dozens of destroyers. Because the shippers have the best information on the speed of their vessel, the value of their cargoes, and the costs of delay, and fully internalise the benefits of security, they are in the best position to take appropriate preventative measures. Thus the public 'duty' to suppress piracy should be thought of as one that can be shared or fulfilled not just by a nation's warship.

[13] See, e.g., *Military and Paramilitary Activities in and against Nicaragua (Nicaragua* v. *United States of America)*, Merits, ICJ Reports 1986, 14.

[14] This is particularly true if one thinks that a reputation for compliance is the principal (social) currency of international law. See A.T. Guzman, *How International Law Works: A Rational Choice Theory* (Oxford University Press, 2008), 71–100.

Despite the extensive media attention focused on naval counter-piracy efforts, in terms both of economic cost and effectiveness, private deterrence efforts vastly overshadow military ones in actually preventing piracy. Pirates initially prayed on slow-moving vessels; such a leisurely pace saves fuel. In the face of the Somali piracy spike, new industry guidelines recommended proceeding at greater speed through dangerous waters. Such navigational solutions (including rerouting) represented fully one-third of the costs attributable to piracy in 2012 (USD 5.7–6.1 billion in total), with security guards and equipment constituting another 29 per cent.[15] By contrast, military deterrence amounted to only 19 per cent of the cost. In recent years, the military costs have been between USD 1.1 and 1.3 billion, with private avoidance and security costs nearly three times that. Similarly, the cost of prosecution and imprisonment amounted to less than USD 15 million in 2012, and the cost of the various UN and other international agencies and non-governmental organisations that deal with piracy (and pick up some of the prosecutorial tab) have been a mere USD 24 million – these costs are shared across many countries.[16]

The prominent role of private interests stems from the nature of piracy – attacks on largely private economic activity outside of national borders. Principles on the rights and responsibilities of shippers are increasingly being worked out in international fora, through best practices guidelines and other voluntary standard-setting by trade associations like the influential Baltic and International Maritime Council, the International Maritime Bureau, and agencies such as the International Maritime Organization.

Ultimately, governmental piracy suppression represents a public subsidy for maritime shippers: the government pays for their security. In some cases the subsidy is quite explicit: several European nations place their armed forces on their flagged merchant vessels in lieu of private security. The choice between navies and security contractors is on one level the traditional choice between government and private provision of public services. In this context, there is little reason to think there are market failures necessitating such action. Moreover, the publicly provided security creates moral hazard for the masters of vessels, encouraging them to take routes they otherwise might not have if they had to provide security. Moreover, on the high seas, there is no background provision of security by a home state. For example, a distress call by a

[15] J. Bellish, 'The Economic Cost of Somali Piracy, 2012', Oceans Beyond Piracy Working Paper (2013), at http://oceansbeyondpiracy.org/sites/default/files/ecop2012final_2.pdf, at 1.

[16] Ibid, at 4.

Liberian-flagged Russian-owned vessel may be answered by an American warship. Thus substituting public security in the form of naval vessels for private security creates cross-national subsidies. These make it even harder to measure the cost-effectiveness of the subsidy.

Instead, the proper locus for primary responsibility should be with shippers themselves. Firstly, the shippers largely internalise the benefits of the security they provide, leading them to take the proper levels of care. They also have an informational advantage as to the appropriate security measures, given the specifics of the vessel, cargo, and numerous other factors. Only a tiny percentage of vessels fall victim to pirates even in the most dangerous waters, and thus the appropriate *ex ante* precautions can vary considerably. It seems armed security is the dominant solution, with 70 per cent of vessels transiting the Suez Canal now employing such measures, but this will also fluctuate with the fortunes of the local pirates. While the combined cost of private measures considerably exceeds public ones, it is also much more successful. The decline in successful pirate attacks in 2011 and the dramatic and sudden end to effective Somali pirate attacks in the following years are generally attributable to the broad adoption of armed security by shippers.

Moreover, several mechanisms reinforce the primary responsibility of shippers. On one hand, safety improvements result in better insurance terms. Moreover, given maritime insurers' more general interest in piracy suppression, they are well placed to price safety measures in a way that reflects some of their general deterrent effects, not just their specific deterrent effects. On the other hand, a shipper's failure to take adequate precautions – either navigational or security – can be policed *ex post* through the standard domestic tort system,[17] or contractually with the charterers. There are legal limits to private anti-piracy efforts. The LOSC provides that only national warships can *arrest* suspected pirates on the high seas.[18] The purpose of the restriction is to limit the use of force on the high seas, and greatly restrict possible inappropriate interferences with the freedom of navigation. Thus private security can only reduce the returns to piracy, but not incapacitate the pirates.

[17] For example, the famous *Maersk Alabama* capture was dramatically ended by the US Navy SEALS assault on the pirates. Numerous *Alabama* crewmembers that were held hostage have sued the company for failing to take adequate precautions. See R. McCabe, 'Warnings on pirates ignored, Maersk lawsuits say', The Virginian-Pilot, 26 May 2013, at http://hamptonroads.com/2012/05/warnings-pirates-ignored-maersk-lawsuits-say. Indeed, several subsequent attacks on the same vessel were repelled by armed security details hired after the hijacking.

[18] Article 107 LOSC, n. 1.

One major constraint on shippers' use of armed security is national restrictions on such measures. These restrictions can come from the flag state, the vessel owner's state, or port states. Dealing with the multiple inconsistent regulations is itself a problem for shippers. Indeed, there have been several high-profile incidents in which vessels carrying security details have been arrested on weapons charges when coming into a port.[19] One of the major subjects of discussion in anti-piracy efforts is how nations should align their rules on the employment of security personnel and the use of force, but no clear approach has been developed.

To some extent, such questions will be resolved in light of the market response. Flag states compete for vessels. Home-port jurisdictions that restrict private security may find themselves less attractive bases, and may also be expected to provide a higher level of military force. Ports of call that restrict armed vessels will be more expensive to ship to. Indeed, after several years of broad governmental resistance to any use of armed force, the trend has swung significantly in the opposite direction, with nation after nation dropping or relaxing such limitations. Still, nations in pirate-affected areas continue to take strong measures against private security forces; India, in late 2013, invoked weapons charges in arresting a US private vessel, the *Seaman Guard*, that provides armed escort to cargo ships.[20] Still, this raises the interesting issue of the extent to which the Article 100 duty of states to cooperate in suppressing piracy implicates a responsibility to cooperate with private actors – by not restricting them – when such efforts are clearly the cheapest and most effective measures of reducing both the total number of pirate attacks and their success rate. A descriptive understanding of the economics of pirate suppression suggests that the broad shared responsibility of states to suppress piracy should be considered one that is not only shared with other states, but with private actors as well.

3. *Ex post* responsibility: division of labour and specialisation

The international efforts against Somali pirates have developed a fascinating model for distributing *ex ante* responsibility[21] for enforcing

[19] 'Nigerian navy detains Russian crew over arms', BBC News, 12 October 2012.

[20] 'Report of suicide bid underscores desperation of US ship's crew jailed in India', FoxNews.com, 22 October 2013.

[21] *Ex post* responsibility refers to liability for internationally wrongful outcomes, whereas *ex ante* responsibility refers to duties or obligations to take or not take certain measures,

international law against pirates. The model evolved organically and incrementally, without having been planned. Indeed, the model represents a rejection of the more centralised methods of pirate suppression proposed by many experts, such as an international piracy court.[22] The current system reflects an explicitly economic logic – a specialisation of labour and a drive for efficiency. In this arrangement, the traditionally unified enforcement function is disaggregated, and different nations assume responsibility for the arrest, prosecution, and detention of the pirates. The broad diffusion of roles raises complex questions of shared responsibility, which should be resolved with an eye to preserving the explicitly efficiency-minded features of the system.

The surge in Somali piracy in 2008 lead dozens of nations to commit military resources to disrupting the attacks in the Gulf of Aden and Indian Ocean. These forces prevented many hijackings and apprehended hundreds and thousands of suspected pirates. Yet over 90 per cent of them were immediately released because patrolling nations had concerns about taking them back for trial. Some of the concerns focused on the actual costs of the trials. With the elaborate procedural protections and requirements of Western countries in particular, such trials could require disproportionate significant resources. One German trial, for example, took more than one year and more than 100 separate court dates. Apart from the actual costs of trial, such jurisdictions worried about the long-term responsibility they would assume by taking Somalis into their territory. If acquitted, or upon completion of their sentence, they could not necessarily be repatriated to Somalia, and might claim asylum and receive state support benefits.[23]

The answer to this has been for capturing nations to send most suspects for trials in one of several regional states – primarily Kenya and Seychelles, and more recently Tanzania and Mauritius. Thus a division of labour based on specialisation and comparative advantage

regardless of whether liability would attach for breach. See Nollkaemper and Jacobs, 'Shared Responsibility in International Law: A Conceptual Framework', n. 7, at 365–366, 393–394.

[22] See, e.g., E. Andersen, et al., (eds.), *Suppressing Maritime Piracy: Exploring the Options in International Law* (ASIL, One Earth Future Foundation, Academic Council on the United Nations System, Workshop Report, 2009), at http://acuns.org/wp-content/uploads/2012/06/SuppressingMaritimePiracyExploringOptionsIntlLaw.pdf, at 11–14.

[23] Such concerns appear justified. The few Somalis that have been acquitted or released in European countries have not been sent back, and will apparently remain there indefinitely.

has emerged. Western and Asian nations, generally among the most developed, provide the ships to patrol the oceans looking for pirates. Such a commitment requires pre-existing expeditionary naval assets that most nations do not possess. At the same time, there is also likely to be a rough correlation between the size of a nation's navy and its share of international trade.

While the naval component enjoyed broad participation, it is also worth noting that this was achieved not through the promulgation of top-down duties, but through a coincidence of interests. For many Western navies, having vessels in the region was already useful for anti-terror patrol. For Russia and China, the mission offered the opportunity of a rare out-of-region deployment unopposed by the United States. Indeed, for China it was an invaluable training, its first out of region deployment in half a millennia. For several European nations facing budget-cutting austerity, it was an opportunity to prove the relevance of post–Cold War maritime forces.

Yet nations that could most efficiently provide enforcement tools tend to be the most expensive for conducting adjudication because of a highly developed legal system and robust procedural rights. As a result, the apprehending nations entered into a series of agreements with regional states to transfer apprehended pirates to them for trial. The agreements were incremental, bilateral (or with the European Union), and contractual in nature, memorialised through Memoranda of Understanding (MoUs) between sending and receiving nations. The first use of such an arrangement was an ad hoc deal between the United States and Kenya in 2006. After the piracy explosion in 2008, the United States, European Union (EU), individual European nations, and several others began hammering out MoUs with Kenya. Subsequent agreements between the EU as well the United States, individual EU nations, and others on one hand, with most significantly, Seychelles,[24] Mauritius,[25] and Tanzania

[24] 'Exchange of Letters between the European Union and the Republic of Seychelles on the Conditions and Modalities for the Transfer of Suspected Pirates and Armed Robbers from EUNAVFOR to the Republic of Seychelles and for their Treatment after such Transfer', 26 October 2009, (2009) 315 OJEU 37.

[25] 'Agreement between the European Union and the Republic of Mauritius on the conditions of transfer of suspected pirates and associated seized property from the European Union-led naval force to the Republic of Mauritius and on the conditions of suspected pirates after transfer', 14 July 2011, (2011) 245 OJEU 3. 'Announcement: UK signs agreement with Mauritius to transfer suspected pirates for prosecution', Foreign and Commonwealth Office, 8 June 2012.

have followed. Each agreement differs from the others in some particulars.

The agreements provide that the receiving state will receive and try pirate suspects sent to it, while also providing minimum human rights and due process that the defendants must receive.[26] (The Kenyan MoUs give the receiving country less discretion on accepting transferees, while subsequent deals allowed for much greater case-by-case refusal by the receiving nation.) The sending states generally reimburse the receiver for the actual expenses of trial, and often provide additional financial incentives. While the agreements do not specify any quid pro quo consideration on the part of the sending nations, it is clear that the understandings involved side payments to the receiving state to compensate it for the burden on their already strained criminal justice system, and provide an incentive to take such cases.[27] The payments come in the form of foreign aid from sending states, as well as legal assistance from the United Nations Office of Drugs and Crime (UNODC). The support both assured that the sending nation's legal standards would be met while providing rents for the receiver.

The outsourcing model for trial creates significant efficiencies. They take advantage of the lower-cost justice systems in the regional nations. For example, Kenyan and Seychellois trials would often last just a day or so, compared to months-long proceedings in European countries, Japan, and South Korea. Similarly, the daily costs of imprisonment are much lower. While offshoring criminal justice in such ways could be controversial in national legal systems, it seems more easily justifiable as a response to an international legal wrong.[28] Because piracy is an

[26] See E. Kontorovich, 'Introductory Note to Exchange of Letters Between the European Union and the Government of Kenya on the Conditions and Modalities for the Transfer of Persons Suspected of Having Committed Acts of Piracy', (2009) 48 ILM 747.

[27] While the text of the EU's MoU with Kenya and Seychelles have been made public, other agreements with those nations, such as those by the United States and United Kingdom have not been, see ibid. The EU-Mauritius agreement specifically refers to undetermined 'financial assistance', n. 25, see Article 7(3). The EU and individual member states have pledged nearly 4 million euros to the Seychelles for 'capacity building'. See 'The EU-Seychelles Relations-Cooperation beyond Development', at http://eeas.europa.eu/delegations/mauritius/eu_seychelles/index_en.htm.

[28] Perhaps the closest precedent to such an arrangement was the extraterritorial trial of the Lockerbie bombing suspects in the Netherlands. In respect to incarceration, some African war criminals, like Charles Taylor, have been incarcerated in Europe because their home country could not provide adequate security. Finally, the Netherlands and Belgium have worked out an efficiency-based penal outsourcing arrangement for ordinary municipal criminals.

international offense falling under universal jurisdiction, all nations have some responsibility to respond to it. From a global perspective, it makes sense for all aspects of enforcement – naval action, prosecution, and incarceration – to be provided by the lowest-cost effective provider.

Conventional international law does not seem to take this approach. The LOSC seems to place the primary responsibility for all enforcement on the capturing state; indeed, a plain reading of the universal jurisdiction provision seems to authorise trial and punishment solely by the capturing nation.[29] Yet the identity of the capturing nation, from among those that have allocated naval resources, is entirely fortuitous. Indeed, capturing nations may tend to be relatively high-cost trial jurisdictions. Under such circumstances, resting full responsibility on the capturing state would be inefficient, and moreover, result in a lower incidence of capture and trial. State practice entirely resists the narrow reading of the LOSC, a notable episode where customary practice reinterprets a treaty provision to make it consistent with an efficient sharing of *ex ante* responsibility among states.[30]

Another way to understand the tension between practice and Article 105 of the LOSC is that the cheapest justice provider cannot be identified in advance, or described effectively in treaty language. Thus the treaty norm places default responsibility on the capturing nation, but allows it to contract around the rule when and if it can identify the more efficient justice providers.[31] It bears noting that the capturing states still send some pirates for trial back in their own courts. This almost invariably happens when the captured Somalis are suspected of attacking the capturing nation's own vessels. These can be seen as 'high value' defendants from the perspective of the capturing state, where its private benefits of prosecuting are higher than in the typical case.

All this suggests that nations have developed a kind of market model for the enforcement of international law against piracy. This helps shed

[29] Article 105 LOSC, n. 1.

[30] House of Commons Foreign Affairs Committee Report, 'Piracy off the coast of Somalia', Written evidence from Dr Douglas Guilfoyle, legal issues relating to counter-piracy operations off the coast of Somalia, Session 2010–12, PIR 06, at www.publications.parliament.uk/pa/cm201012/cmselect/cmfaff/writev/1318/m06.htm.

[31] This helps reconcile the views of those who read Article 105 as mandatory, with those scholars who see no particular primacy for the capturing state in the universal jurisdiction framework. The LOSC may not be mandatory, but rather a default rule. R. Geiss and A. Petrig, *Piracy and Armed Robbery at Sea: The Legal Framework for Counter-Piracy Operations in Somalia and the Gulf of Aden* (Oxford University Press, 2011), at 189–190.

light on the conduct of Kenya, which less than a year after signing the MoUs and accepting over 100 pirate suspects for prosecution, announced that it was terminating the arrangements. Though Kenyan authorities were not explicit about the reason, there were suggestions the arrangement was not as financially favourable as they had anticipated. Thus Kenya was engaged in contractual hold-up, trying to renegotiate its deal. However, capturing states responded by encouraging new entry into the market, signing deals with Seychelles and other regional states. Broadening the market presumably brings down the implicit price per pirate, and reduced Kenya's hold-up power. Indeed, Kenya again began accepting pirates for prosecution on an ad hoc basis after the deals with Seychelles were worked out.

The outsourcing of prosecution turned out to only be the first stage in disaggregating responsibility for pirate suppression. Perhaps the most expensive and least desirable and prestigious aspect of dealing with pirates is their incarceration. Nations like Seychelles, with a tiny prison system, or Kenya, with an overcrowded one, are reluctant to assume a costly long-term liability in the form of a permanent pirate population. Thus a second tier of agreements emerged between prosecuting nations and Puntland and Somaliland,[32] two semi-independent breakaway regions of Somalia from which many but not all of the pirates hail. These deals contemplate the transfer of the convicted pirates to the Somali regions to serve the remainder of their sentences.[33] Again, UNODC was central in facilitating these agreements, by building prison facilities and training Puntland personnel to bring their penal systems up to minimum standards. Like the prosecuting states, the Somali regions apparently receive some additional foreign aid support for their participation in this arrangement.[34]

Thus the enforcement of anti-piracy law is ultimately divided three ways – capture by one country, prosecution by a second, and detention by a third. UNODC facilitates these arrangements by providing financing and oversight. One important lesson from the solution to the piracy prosecution conundrum is that *ex ante* responsibility can be effectively apportioned contractually: such duties need not be understood as

[32] 'Pirates transfer agreement solves global problem', WorldNews, 4 April 2012, at http://article.wn.com/view/2012/04/04/Pirates_transfer_agreement_solves_global_problem/.

[33] "Mauritius-Somalia: Agreement on the transfer of sentenced pirates signed', Republic of Mauritius News, 28 May 2012, at www.gov.mu/English/News/Pages/Mauritius-Somalia-Agreement-on-the-transfer-of-sentenced-pirates-signed.aspx.

[34] While the particulars of these arrangements have not been made public, at least some transfers apparently require the consent of convicts and the original capturing state.

responsibility to take action, but rather to pay for it. This allows for a more fine-tuned apportionment of duties in international law. The quasi-contractual nature of these arrangements do raise the question of where to turn when one nation acts opportunistically, by, say, releasing pirates that it has already accepted consideration for, or providing inadequate levels of due process at trial or proper conditions in incarceration. One function that UNODC appears to play is monitoring the implementation of these arrangements.

The current distribution of *ex ante* responsibility among states for suppressing piracy developed incrementally and informally, rather than through centralised decisions and top-down mechanisms. Indeed, numerous UN and academic reports favoured a more centralised approach, using international courts and prison facilities to prosecute and detain pirates. Such proposals were criticised as not being cost-efficient, and obscuring the ultimate questions of responsibility, such as where would the courts and prisons be located, and who would administer them. Such centralised solutions proved slower and less flexible than the market-based approach to pirate justice, which nations implemented gradually and incrementally – but immediately. Indeed, the transfer arrangements were originally seen by many as a stop-gap until a fully internationalised solution would emerge, but in practice they have eliminated the impetus for such a solution.

4. Liability for downstream violations

The multiple levels of transfer raise the question of who bears legal responsibility for human rights violations by receiving states. Transfers from Western nations are generally pursuant to MoU that stipulate human rights protection for the transferee. This raises the question of who is ultimately responsible for the treatment of the detainees: the capturing (and first transferring) state, the final transferring state, the unrecognised entity (Somaliland and Puntland) that may be the ultimate destination, or UNODC, the agency proving assistance to the process? The question is not hypothetical: pirates captured by Germany and sent to Kenya successfully sued the former in a Cologne administrative court, arguing that the transfer itself violated their human rights because of inadequate conditions in Kenya.[35]

[35] C. Ahlborn, 'Adjudicating Somali Piracy Cases – German Courts in a Double Bind', 3 January 2013, CJICL Blog, at www.cjicl.org.uk.

Under current understandings of state responsibility reflected in the ILC Articles on State Responsibility,[36] responsibility rests only on the state that actually violates a suspected or convicted pirate's rights. Sending states would not be responsible for downstream violations. Yet this requires some qualifications. *Non-refoulement* is itself a right that is violated by transferring someone to a state where their rights are likely to be violated. The *non-refoulement* right is violated by the sending state at the moment of transfer. Thus the responsibility of sending states for *non-refoulement* is distinct from any responsibility for violations by receiving state. *Non-refoulement* can be violated even if there is ultimately no abuse by the receiving state, if such abuse was objectively likely at the time of transfer, and if it was not likely, actual abuse does not retroactively create responsibility upstream. In anticipation of *non-refoulement* concerns, the MoUs contain assurances of human rights guarantees for transferees. Under European human rights precedents, such diplomatic assurances do not always get the sending state off the hook, and thus the agreements also provide varying degrees of monitoring by the sending states.[37]

The re-transfer to Somali regions raises additional wrinkles. The MoUs typically require the original sending state's permission for subsequent re-transfer. This again brings in the responsibility of the original sender (the capturing state), which becomes a joint participant with the trial state in the decision to transfer to the third state. The liability on the part of the capturing state is not vicarious, but direct, because of its role in the transfer decision. This raises the question of whether the original transferring state can divest itself of responsibility for further transfers by not requiring its agreement to such subsequent action.[38] It would seem that this is fully captured in the original *non-refoulement* responsibility. Where subsequent re-transfer to dubious countries is likely, satisfying the

[36] Articles on Responsibility of States for Internationally Wrongful Acts, ILC *Yearbook* 2001/II(2).

[37] See Geiss and Petrig, *Piracy and Armed Robbery at Sea*, n. 31, at 203–206.

[38] For example, the EU-Mauritius agreement is ambiguous on responsibility for subsequent transfer. Mauritius may transfer convicts 'after consulation with the EU'. Where there are 'serious concerns about the human rights situation in that other State' transfer cannot occur 'before a satisfactory solution will have been found through consultations between the Parties'. See EU Council Decision 9298/2/11 (6 July 2011), 'Agreement between the European Union and the Republic of Mauritius on the conditions of transfer of suspected pirates', n. 25, Article 4(8). This leaves it ambiguous whether the EU state's consent is ultimately required for risky transfers.

original *non-refoulement* obligation may require assuming shared responsibility for subsequent re-transfers.

While these arrangements raise very complex questions about the allocation of responsibility for human rights violations, they also offer a possible solution. The piracy transfer process is fundamentally contractual. The essence of the transfer agreements is that the upstream sending states compensate downstream receiving states for a service (prosecution or incarceration). Because of the nature of the arrangements, the allocation of responsibility can be shifted among the parties by prior agreement.[39]

From a normative economic perspective, in a zero-transaction context, it does not matter which state in the chain has responsibility in international law so long as it is clearly allocated.[40] Thus the parties can reallocate liability among themselves through formal or informal indemnity arrangements. Typically, the last actor in the chain of causation would have responsibility for human rights violations. However, the continued involvement of upstream actors through monitoring and so forth suggest the entire string of transfers may be viewed as a joint enterprise. For the purposes of efficiency, it is more important to have responsibility clearly allocated. Moreover, many standard arguments for joint and several liability do not apply in the public law context, where it is unlikely that either sovereign participant will be insolvent.[41] Thus from an efficiency perspective, it makes sense to clearly assign full responsibility to the most recent custodial country, which exercises the greatest degree of control at the relevant time. Thus Kenya, for example, would be solely responsible for its abuse of pirates in its custody. Given that Kenya receives compensation from the sending states, it can price its potential exposure into the deal. To put it differently, the trial states acts as an independent contractor for the capturing state, and is largely outside its control. In accepting this undertaking, the trial state presumably accepts not just the pirates themselves, but all the relevant responsibility.

[39] See Nollkaemper and Jacobs, 'Shared Responsibility in International Law: A Conceptual Framework', n. 7, at 393–394.

[40] While transaction costs are obviously positive in the real world, the bargaining between sending and receiving nations appears quite flexible, and even open to renegotiation. Unlike many other public law parties, there are multiple participants on both the sending and receiving side, with the possibility of further entry. Thus neither has monopoly power, limiting the possibilities for hold-up and other strategic behaviours.

[41] Ibid.

Indeed, the agreements can build in indemnity claims for the original *non-refoulement* obligation. Presumably, that duty on the part of transferring states is 'personal' to that state and non-transferable. However, since the capturing state is contracting for an acceptable place to send the pirates, if a court were to find transfer barred by *non-refoulement*, one could imagine the sending state demanding a 'refund' from the receiving state. That is, the 'diplomatic assurances' that accompany transfer agreements can also be seen as warranties of fitness for the intended purpose by the receiving state. Making such provisions more explicit would be advisable, and give receiving states clearer incentives to not chisel on the deal.

The re-transfer to Somali regions poses the greatest problem for the allocation of responsibility. The ultimate recipients are not recognised state actors and cannot have international legal responsibility. Moreover, the relevant state, Somalia, is a failed state and is effectively 'judgment proof'. Thus responsibility for violations there should properly rest with the last sending state.

5. Extensions: market-based allocation of responsibility

The emergence of an efficiency-seeking distribution of *ex ante* responsibility for piracy suppression suggests that similar efficiency-based rules should apply to responsibility for international legal breaches in this context. It also illustrates the possibilities of distributing responsibility among nations through agreement, particularly where lower-cost nations are recruited to carry out functions by higher-cost ones.

The 'outsourcing' or 'gaolbalisation' model that has developed in the piracy suppression context has applications to other similarly structured phenomenon. Take migration and refugee issues, for example. Several countries have recently begun outsourcing the purported refugees that come to their shores to third countries. A similar efficiency rationale is at play. The acceptance of refugees can be done by any country where they do not face persecution. However, migrants naturally flock to the affluent countries with generous social services. These may be the most expensive providers of refugee-acceptance services. Thus these nations can contract with lower-cost refuges to create a truly efficient situation. It ultimately allows for the absorption of larger numbers of refugees outside their home countries by not exhausting the tolerance of a small number of most-desired refuges.

These deals have all been made by 'destination' nations that refugees travel through to get to the place of their choice. What makes transfer arrangements legally possible is that the receiving nation's obligation to a refugee is not to take them in, but not to send them back to their country of origin. Refuge is from something, not to something. Naturally, the ultimate receiving state would have to satisfy minimum human rights criteria to avoid *non-refoulement* problems. But as with pirates, that contractual nature of the activity would suggest that all else equal, the receiving state would assume full responsibility for any abuses within its jurisdiction.

6. Conclusion

Piracy is unusual in international criminal law, as the relevant treaties impose an affirmative duty on states to cooperate in suppressing it. In most international piracy contexts – from the Gulf of Guinean to the Straits of Malacca – nations not surprisingly fail to meet this obligation, raising questions about the responsibility of coastal and other states that fail to take reasonable measures to suppress pirates.

However, the international response to Somali piracy in recent years has developed into a complex, multi-sided enterprise in which international law enforcement duties are disaggregated among states. The traditionally unified functions of policing, prosecution, and incarceration have been divided and assigned to different countries, based largely on considerations of economic efficiency and comparative advantage. At the same time, the advantages of this sophisticated arrangement raise particularly complex questions about responsibility for international wrongs that might be committed in the international chain of pirate custody. Given the underlying efficiency logic of arrangements, and their effectively contractual nature, this may be a particular apt context for drawing principles of state responsibility from private law contract principles.

15

The Global Financial Crisis and Collective Moral Responsibility

SEUMAS MILLER*

This chapter is divided in four sections. In section 1 (Introduction: the problem(s)), I outline the nature of the problem to be addressed: collective moral responsibility for the Global Financial Crisis (GFC).[1] In section 2 (Collective moral responsibility), the key theoretical notion to be deployed, namely, collective moral responsibility is defined and defended.[2] In section 3 (Collective action problems), I identify the central role of collective action problems in the GFC and provide an account of the specific type of collective action problems in question. In the final section (Embedding collective responsibility), I explore the ways in which collective moral responsibility can be embedded functionally, structurally, and culturally in relevant global financial institutions and markets. In so doing I rely on a mix of ethico-philosophical analysis and institutional description.

1. Introduction: the problem(s)

It is uniformly agreed that the GFC and its aftershock, the so-called Sovereign Debt Crisis (SDC), constitute the greatest global economic calamity since the Great Depression. The main aspects of the problem

* Seumas Miller is a professorial research fellow at the Centre for Applied Philosophy and Public Ethics (an Australian Research Council Special Research Centre) at Charles Sturt University (Canberra) and the 3TU Centre for Ethics and Technology at Delft University of Technology (The Hague). All websites were last accessed on 5 June 2014.

1 N. Dobos, C. Barry, and T. Pogge (eds.), *Global Financial Crisis: The Ethical Issues* (London: Palgrave Macmillan, 2011). On the specifically economic and financial aspects of the GFC see P. Krugman, *The Return of Depression Economics and the Crisis of 2008* (New York: Norton and Company, 2008); and G. Soros, *The New Paradigm for Financial Markets: The Credit Crisis of 2008 and What it Means* (New York: Perseus Books, 2008).

2 See, for example, vol. 30 (2006) of MSP, dedicated to 'Collective Responsibility', and, in relation to international law and institutions, P.A. Nollkaemper and D. Jacobs, 'Shared Responsibility in International Law: A Conceptual Framework' (2013) 34 MIJIL 359.

have included frozen credit markets; the sub-prime mortgage crisis; slow and inconsistent policy responses; escalating sovereign debt; and an unfolding global (or near global) recession. The crisis has involved major corporate investment and mortgage banking collapses and bailouts in the United States (US) (Lehman Brothers, Freddie Mac, and Fannie Mae); United Kingdom (UK) (Northern Rock); and Europe (Fortis, Hypo). It is also having a devastating effect on home owners who cannot pay their mortgages (foreclosures); retirees whose pension funds have plummeted in value; employees whose jobs have been lost or are at risk in the recession; and taxpayers whose money is being injected into the banking system in vast quantities to rescue it.

Unethical, including imprudent, practices have been identified as being among the principal causes of the crisis. These practices include: first, reckless and predatory lending by banks; second, developing highly leveraged investment banks; third, the selling of toxic financial products, notably non-transparent packaged bundles of mortgages assessed by ratings agencies as high quality because the investment banks that packaged them had good risk assessment processes; fourth, massive frauds (e.g., Bernie Madoff's Ponzi scheme); fifth, allowing the growth of unsustainable debt by governments and, indeed, whole economies; sixth, excessively loose monetary policy by central banks; and seventh, the negligence and/or complicity of legislators and regulators regarding all of the above.

While the crisis has evidently eased at the time of writing, the bad news regarding unethical behaviour, and accompanying financial risk, continues. Perhaps the most prominent recent inflection of the GFC, at least in its moral aspect, is the London Interbank Offered Rate (LIBOR) scandal in the international banking sector. LIBOR is a globally important benchmark calculated for ten major currencies, formerly administered by the British Bankers' Association and published daily; it has been subject to manipulation by many, if not most, of the leading global banks.[3] The unfolding LIBOR scandal itself comes hot on the heels of post-GFC money laundering scandals (e.g., HSBC); facilitating tax evasion through offshore accounts (e.g., UBS); and an ongoing series of rogue traders who have wreaked havoc (e.g., the so-called London Whale at JP Morgan Chase).

[3] H.M. Treasury, 'The Wheatley Review of LIBOR: Final Report' (London, September 2012), at www.gov.uk/government/uploads/system/uploads/attachment_data/file/191762/wheatley_review_libor_finalreport_280912.pdf. LIBOR is now administered by the NYSE Euronext.

In short, evidently banks and other financial service providers have not mended their unethical ways. Moreover, it seems that large-scale corporate collapses and corruption scandals in the global financial sector in general, and the global banking sector in particular, are a recurring phenomenon.

Central among these macro-institutional aspects is surely the phenomenon of global financial institutions that are 'too big to fail'.[4] Thus there were a number of bailouts of major banks and other financial institutions following the decision in 2008 to allow Lehman Brothers to fail; a decision that is thought to have virtually brought the international financial system to its knees. Importantly, for our concerns here, the phenomenon of banks that are 'too big to fail' has morphed into the phenomenon of banks that are 'too big to manage' and, indeed, 'too big to jail' or, less colloquially, 'too big to regulate'.

I take it that a fundamental problem that needs to be addressed in relation to the described ongoing cycle of banking scandals is widespread, unethical, or imprudent behaviour amounting at times to institutional corruption. However, a principal contributing cause to institutional corruption is the existence of *collective action problems*. For example, excessive commercial competition between banks often leads to lax lending practices. As I have also argued elsewhere,[5] a principal remedy for institutional corruption driven or exacerbated by collective action problems consists in *institutionally* embedding (functionally, structurally, and culturally) *collective moral responsibility*. Accordingly, in this chapter my task is threefold: first, establish and defend an appropriate theoretical notion of collective moral responsibility and display its relationship to institutional responsibilities; second, establish and defend an appropriate theoretical notion of the collective action problems in play; and third, explore the ways in which collective moral responsibility can be institutionally embedded functionally, structurally, and culturally in relevant global financial institutions and markets for the purpose of substantially reducing the forms of institutional corruption in question.

[4] See, for example, US Attorney-General Eric Holder's answers to the Senate Judiciary Committee as reported in A.R. Sorkin, 'Realities Behind Prosecuting Big Banks', *The New York Times*, 12 March 2013, at B1.

[5] S. Miller, 'The LIBOR Scandal: Culture, Corruption and Collective Action Problems in the Global Banking Sector', in J. O'Brien and G. Gilligan (eds.), *Integrity, Risk and Accountability in Capital Markets: Regulating Culture* (Oxford: Hart Publishing, 2013), 111.

2. Collective moral responsibility

Collective moral responsibility is a species of moral responsibility. Here we need to distinguish *moral* responsibility (including collective moral responsibility) from *causal* responsibility.[6] A person or persons can inadvertently cause a bad outcome without necessarily being morally responsible for so doing. Moral responsibility typically requires not only causal responsibility, but also an intention to cause harm or the knowledge that one's action will or may well cause harm, whether harm to persons or institutions or (more likely in the kinds of cases under consideration here) to both. We also need to distinguish moral responsibility for actions and moral responsibility for omissions, and retrospective from prospective moral responsibility.

All these distinctions in respect of individual moral responsibility are mirrored in the case of collective moral responsibility. Hence the various different but related questions that arise are, first, who are collectively morally responsible for the GFC by their acts or omissions? And, second, who are collectively morally responsible for ensuring it does not recur? In this chapter my primary concern is with the latter question, and this is the focus of the final section on institutionally embedding collective moral responsibility.

In this section I will argue that collective moral responsibility is to be understood as joint moral responsibility: the joint moral responsibility of individual human actors engaged in morally significant joint actions. I will further argue that the notion of joint action can be enriched so as to encompass action in accordance with joint procedures (e.g., conventions), joint institutional mechanisms (e.g., benchmarks such as LIBOR) and, finally and importantly, organisational action (i.e., multi-layered structures of joint action). The upshot of this analysis is that individual human actors are, at least in principle, collectively (jointly) morally responsible for morally significant organisational action.

2.1 Collective responsibility as joint responsibility

Elsewhere I have elaborated and defended a relational account of collective moral responsibility; specifically, that of collective responsibility as

[6] And also from notions of accountability and liability. See Nollkaemper and Jacobs, 'Shared Responsibility in International Law: A Conceptual Framework', n. 2, at 365 et seq. for discussions of these notions in the international legal context. See also Chapter 2 of this volume, R. Pierik, 'Shared Responsibility in International Law: A Normative-Philosophical Analysis', 36; and Chapter 5 of this volume, L.A. Kornhauser, 'Incentives, Compensation, and Irreparable Harm', 120.

joint responsibility.[7] On this view, collective responsibility is responsibility arising from joint actions and omissions. Roughly speaking, a joint action[8] can be understood thus: two or more individuals perform a joint action if each of them intentionally performs an individual action (or omission), but does so with the (true) belief that in so doing they will jointly realise an end which each of them has. On this view of collective responsibility as joint responsibility, collective responsibility is ascribed to individual human beings only, albeit jointly. Each member of the group is individually morally responsible for their contributory action, and also for the outcome of the set of actions. However, each is individually responsible for that outcome, *jointly with the others*; hence the conception is relational in character. Thus in a million-dollar bank heist each member of the gang is responsible jointly with the others for the theft of the million dollars because each performed his contributory action in the service of that collective end (the theft of the million dollars).

Naturally, the contributory actions may differ greatly in respect of their importance in relation to the realisation of the collective. For example, in our bank heist scenario the contributory action of one of the look-outs might be far less important than that of the safe-blower; the action of one of the look-outs might be neither necessary nor sufficient for the success of the bank heist, whereas the action of the safe-blower is undoubtedly necessary for this outcome. This difference might be reflected in the share of the 'loot' each receives (supposing the heist is successful); the safe-blower's share would be much greater than that of the look-out.

A further point to be noted here is the distinction between an individual action that is constitutive of the joint action, and an action that is not constitutive but which, nevertheless, assists or otherwise facilitates the performance of the joint action. An example of the latter is the person who illegally sells the explosives to the safe-blower and assists the bank heist, but who might not have any interest in, or even specific knowledge of, the bank heist.

2.2 *Joint action*

The key notion of joint action underpinning collective responsibility can be construed very narrowly or more broadly. On the narrowest construal we have what I will call *basic* joint action. Basic joint action involves two

[7] S. Miller, 'Collective Moral Responsibility: An Individualist Account' (2006) 30 MSP 176.

[8] S. Miller, 'Joint Action' (1992) 21(3) PP 275; and S. Miller, 'Intentions, Ends and Joint Action' (1995) 24(1) PP 51.

co-present agents each of whom performs one basic individual action, and does so simultaneously with the other agent, and in relation to a collective end that is to be realised within the temporal and spatial horizons of the immediate face-to-face experience of the agents. A basic individual action is an action an agent can do at will without recourse to instruments other than his or her own body. An example of a basic individual action is putting one's hand in the till and seizing a wad of banknotes; an example of a basic joint action is two people lifting a safe onto the back of a truck.

If we construe joint action more broadly we can identify a myriad of other examples of joint action. Many of these involve the intentions and ends of multiple institutional actors directed to outcomes outside the temporal and/or spatial horizon of the immediate experience of those actors (e.g., the members of a management team setting revenue targets and developing strategies in the context of a plan to grow their business over a five-year period).[9]

Basic joint actions can also be distinguished from, what I will call, *joint procedures*. An agent has a joint procedure to x, if he x's in a recurring situation, and does so on condition that other agents x. (Procedures are different from repetitions of the same action in a single situation; for example, rowing or skipping.) Languages consist in large part in joint procedures governing the use of utterance types; English language users utter the term, 'The City', when they intend to refer, and to be taken by hearers to be referring, to London's financial district. Moreover, joint procedures are followed in order to achieve collective goals (e.g., communication). Joint procedures are in fact conventions.[10]

As will become evident later in this chapter, it is important to make some further distinctions beginning with the distinction between conventions and social norms. Social norms are regularities in action involving interdependence of action among members of a group, but regularities in action that are governed by a moral purpose or principle.[11] For example, avoiding telling lies is a social norm.

[9] S. Miller, *The Moral Foundations of Social Institutions: A Philosophical Study* (New York: Cambridge University Press, 2009), chapter 1: 'A Teleological Account of Institutions', 37; and chapter 2: 'The Moral Foundations of Institutions', 56.

[10] S. Miller, *Social Action: A Teleological Account* (New York: Cambridge University Press, 2001), chapter 3: 'Conventions', 91.

[11] Ibid., chapter 4: 'Social Norms', 123.

We can also distinguish between joint procedures (in the aforementioned sense) and, what I will call, *joint mechanisms.*[12] Examples of joint mechanisms are the device of tossing a coin to resolve a dispute and voting to elect a candidate to office. Joint mechanisms are typically – but not necessarily – constitutive elements of social institutions[13] and when they are, they are joint institutional mechanisms.

Joint mechanisms consist of: (a) a complex of differentiated but interlocking actions (the input to the mechanism); (b) the result of the performance of those actions (the output of the mechanism), and; (c) the mechanism itself. Thus a given agent might vote for a candidate. He or she will do so only if others also vote. But further to this, there is the action of the candidates, namely, that they present themselves as candidates. That they present themselves as candidates is (in part) constitutive of the input to the voting mechanism. Voters vote *for candidates*. So there is interlocking and differentiated action (the input). Further, there is some result (as opposed to consequence) of the joint action; the joint action consisting of the action(s) of putting oneself forward as a candidate and of the actions of voting. The result is that some candidate, say, Jones, is voted in (the output). That there is a result is (in part) constitutive of the mechanism. That to receive the most number of votes is to be voted in, is (in part) constitutive of the voting mechanism. Moreover, that Jones is voted in is not a collective end of all the voters (although it is a collective end of those who voted for Jones). However, that the one who gets the most votes – whoever that happens to be – is voted in, is a collective end of all (or nearly all) of the voters.

Joint mechanisms play a central role in institutional action and, as is the case with conventions and social norms, it is important for my purposes in this chapter that they can be understood in purely individualist terms by recourse to my core notion of joint action. For in that case the participants in morally significant joint mechanisms are, at least in principle, collectively (jointly) morally responsible for the input and output of these mechanisms.

On this account of joint institutional mechanisms, to take LIBOR manipulation as an example, the various relevant bank submitters, traders, and/or managers involved in some particular episode of LIBOR interest-rigging can be ascribed collective moral responsibility for this

[12] Ibid., chapter 5: 'Organisations, Agency, and Action', 160; and Miller, *The Moral Foundations of Social Institutions*, n. 9, chapter 1: 'A Teleological Account of Institutions', 37.
[13] Miller, *The Moral Foundations of Social Institutions*, n. 9.

particular corrupt (joint) action, and for any (personal and/or institutional) harm that might result from it. Each is also individually responsible for his or her contributory individual action or omission (e.g., a manager who signed off on a particular submission).

Note that in most of the scandals in question, the network of joint actions and omissions can be quite wide and complex without necessarily involving all, or even most, personnel in a given institution.

Further, responsibility for the cumulative damage done by an ongoing series of such episodes of corrupt action by numerous bank personnel from different institutions and on multiple occasions, might conceivably also be ascribed to the entire large group, albeit there are various barriers to fixing collective moral responsibility on large groups in which each member only makes a small causal contribution. In this connection let us consider organisational action and, specifically, layered structures of joint institutional action.

2.3 Organisational action as joint action

Organisations consist of an (embodied) formal structure of interlocking roles.[14] An organisational role can be defined in terms of the agent who performs certain tasks; the tasks themselves; procedures (in the aforementioned sense); and conventions. Moreover, unlike social groups, organisations are individuated by the kind of activity that they undertake, and also by their characteristic ends. Many organisations are also social institutions. Social institutions are organisations with a moral dimension by virtue of, for example, the authority relations they involve and the fact that their collective ends are also collective goods.[15] Thus governments have as a collective end the regulation of other institutions (a collective good), universities the end of discovering knowledge (a collective good), and so on.

A further defining feature of organisations is that organisational action typically consists in, what I have elsewhere termed, a *multi-layered structure of joint actions.*[16] One illustration of the notion of a layered

[14] Miller, *Social Action*, n. 10, chapter 5: 'Organisations, Agency, and Action', 160; and Miller, *The Moral Foundations of Social Institutions*, n. 9, chapter 1: 'A Teleological Account of Institutions', 37; and chapter 2: 'The Moral Foundations of Institutions', 56.

[15] Ibid., Miller, *The Moral Foundations of Social Institutions*, chapter 2.

[16] Miller, *Social Action*, n. 10, chapter 5: 'Organisations, Agency, and Action', 160; and Miller, *The Moral Foundations of Social Institutions*, n. 9, chapter 1: 'A Teleological Account of Institutions', 37; and chapter 2: 'The Moral Foundations of Institutions', 56.

structure of joint actions is a firm competing in a market place. Suppose at an organisational level a number of joint actions ('actions') are severally necessary,[17] and jointly sufficient to achieve some collective end. Thus the 'management action' of the home loans management team in a bank in setting the interest rates of the bank's home loans; the 'compliance action' of the bank's legal team in ensuring the loans and their associated lending processes are compliant with the relevant laws and regulations; and the 'sales action' of the home loans sales team in the provision of home loans in accordance with sales targets might be severally necessary, and jointly sufficient to achieve the collective end of maximising the bank's profits from home loans. These 'actions' taken together constitute a joint action.

At the first level there are individual actions directed to three distinct collective ends: the collective ends of (respectively) setting the interest rates; ensuring compliance; and meeting home loan targets. So at this level there are three joint actions, namely, the members of the management team setting interest rates; the members of the legal team ensuring compliance; and the members of the sales team meeting sales targets. However, taken together these three joint actions constitute a single joint action. The collective end of this second level joint action is to maximise revenue from home loans; and from the perspective of this second level joint action, and its collective end, these (first level joint) constitutive actions are (second level) individual actions. I note that typically in organisations not just the nature, but the quantum of the individual contributions made to the collective end will differ from one agent to another.

Accordingly, given that 'the action' of (say) a bank in maximising its revenue from home loans in a given period is to be understood as a multi-layered structure of joint actions, and given this joint action is morally significant, then the various participants in it are collectively (jointly) morally responsible for its outcome. Here it is important to note that within the set of individuals who are collectively morally responsible for some outcome, the degree of individual responsibility that some have (jointly with others) might be greater than the degree of individual responsibility that others have (e.g., managers will typically have a higher

[17] Here there is simplification for the sake of clarity. For what is said here is not strictly correct, at least in the case of many actions performed by members of organisations. Rather, typically some threshold set of actions is necessary to achieve the end; moreover the boundaries of this set are vague.

degree of individual responsibility than their subordinates). Indeed, if the contribution of some individuals is minute and they are only very indirectly connected to some morally significant outcome, then their degree of moral responsibility may well diminish to the point of non-existence.

Moreover, in the case of collusion between members of different organisations, some of the constitutive joint actions involved in the multi-layered structure of joint action may well be far less important than others. Additionally, in such cases, as elsewhere, we have to distinguish between lower level joint actions which are *constitutive* of some higher level joint action and lower level joint or individual actions which assist, fail to prevent, or otherwise facilitate the higher level joint action in question, but which are not constitutive of it. For example, persons who are well aware that their colleagues are engaged in fraudulent activity but, nevertheless, fail to do their duty and report this activity may well be culpable in that they failed to contribute to the prevention of unlawful activity.

Further, in some cases of collective moral responsibility no one is *fully* morally responsible for the adverse outcome; rather each has a share, so to speak, of the collective moral responsibility in question. The GFC is a case in point. No single individual (or, for that matter, organisation) is *fully* morally responsible for the credit crisis, housing bubbles, near global recession, and other constitutive elements of the GFC. This is, of course, not to say that no one has *any* moral responsibility. On the conception of collective moral responsibility as joint moral responsibility, each member of the salient group in question must have *some* degree of moral responsibility (jointly with others).[18]

Naturally, multiple individuals could be collectively *causally* responsible for some adverse outcome without any individual having any *moral* responsibility. Nineteenth-century – as opposed to, say, twenty-first-century – contributors to human induced harmful global climate change are a case in point; nineteenth-century contributors did not know, and could not have known, the harm they were causing.[19] Moreover, even if a set of individuals do know that they are collectively causing harm, they

[18] For arguments against collectivist theories of collective moral responsibility which allow the possibility of collective moral responsibility without any individual moral responsibility, or with collective moral responsibility above and beyond aggregate (and/or joint) moral responsibility, see S. Miller, 'Against the Moral Autonomy Thesis' (2007) 38(3) JSP 389; and S. Miller and P. Makela, 'The Collectivist Approach to Collective Moral Responsibility' (2005) 36(5) *Metaphilosophy* 634.

[19] See on historical contributions also Chapter 11 of this volume, H. Shue, 'Transboundary Damage in Climate Change: Criteria for Allocating Responsibility', 321; and Chapter 12

may not be collectively morally responsible for that harm by virtue of not being able to organise themselves sufficiently to avert that harm, or at least being unable to do so within the relevant time frame. This was arguably true in the late 1990s of government officials in relation to harmful human-induced climate change, even if it is no longer true.[20]

Let us now turn to our second task, namely, that of identifying and analysing the type of collective action problem and associated perverse incentive structures implicated in the GFC.

3. Collective action problems

A paradigmatic collective action problem is the 'tragedy of the commons' scenario in which it is in the individual interest of each to continue to use some common resource, but it is not in the collective interest, at least in the long term; so the collective action problem is such that it has a perverse incentive structure leading to an outcome harmful to everyone.[21] Thus it is in the interest of each fishing boat to continue to catch fish, irrespective of whether others do so since it provides a livelihood. Indeed, the fisherman are in *de facto* competition with one another in that each is seeking over time to get a larger share of the total fish stock than his competitors. Unfortunately this behaviour, whether explicitly competitive or not, is not in the collective interest, at least in the long term, since eventually the stock of fish will be depleted to the point where no one can make a living from fishing in the area in question.

As a response to this kind of problem, the fishermen might agree to a quota system whereby each restricts his catch to a certain amount, thereby ensuring the long-term sustainability of fishing in the area.

3.1 Free-riding

However, such cooperative schemes give rise to the so-called free-rider problem. It is in the individual interest of each to ignore his quota, if he can

of this volume, C.L. Kutz, 'Shared Responsibility for Climate Change: From Guilt to Taxes', 341.

20 S. Miller, 'Collective Responsibility, Epistemic Action and Climate Change', in N.A. Vincent, I. van de Poel and J. van den Hoven (eds.), *Moral Responsibility: Beyond Free Will and Determinism* (Heidelberg: Springer, 2011), 219.

21 An earlier version of some of the material in this section appeared in Miller, 'The LIBOR Scandal: Culture, Corruption and Collective Action Problems in the Global Banking Sector', n. 5.

get away with it. Moreover, if compliance is not enforced, then each may well free-ride. Unfortunately, the consequence of large numbers of individuals free-riding is that the system collapses. The solution to the problem is, of course, to enforce compliance with the cooperative scheme. Indeed, over time if the scheme becomes entrenched, is subject to regulatory authorities, and so on, then it becomes an institutional arrangement.

Unfortunately, enforcement is probably not a sufficient condition for compliance, although it is a necessary one. Notoriously, a population that does not for the most part want to comply cannot in the long term be forced to do so; there are simply too many opportunities for non-compliance and too few enforcers for this to be practicable. This is the Achilles heel of one-dimensional regulatory-enforcement models. Let us refer to this as the 'insufficiency of enforcement mechanisms' problem.

Moreover, the enforcement 'solution' simply elevates the initial problem to a different level. Specifically, why should the enforcer adequately enforce the quota system when it is not in his individual rational self-interest to do so; for example, when he is bribed to look the other way, when he has a financial interest in specific fishing boats, or when he simply does not feel like making the effort? Why does the enforcer necessarily pursue the collective self-interest embodied in the quota system when it is not in his individual rational self-interest to do so? Within the rational self-interest model, the answer can only be that the enforcer's compliance with the requirements of his role is itself enforced; that is, a *meta*-enforcer is invoked. But irrespective of whether this meta-enforcer is an individual or a collective, the same problem will recur: who enforces the compliance of the meta-enforcer?

Moreover, the problem persists irrespective of whether the enforcer, the meta-enforcer and so on exist in a single, layered, hierarchical structure (e.g., a hierarchical bureaucracy), or under some non-unitary and relatively non-hierarchical arrangement (e.g., a cooperative scheme), whose enforcers are themselves subject to enforced democratic control. In the former case, the individual or group at the apex of the hierarchical structure is not itself subject to enforcement; this guard has no guard. In the latter case, the 'enforcement buck' stops with multiple enforcers ('the people'), notwithstanding that their own compliance with the cooperative scheme is enforced by the first level enforcers. There is, as it were, a circle of enforcement.[22] Unfortunately, the links in this and other

[22] J.B. Braithwaite, 'Cultures of Redemptive Finance', in J. O'Brien and G. Gilligan (eds.), *Integrity, Risk and Accountability in Capital Markets: Regulating Culture* (Oxford: Hart

'circular' enforcement chains of rationally self-interested actors are weak and, therefore, not secure. For if the large and diffuse set of individuals ('the people') are to be rationally self-interested meta-enforcers, then they must themselves be appropriately organised and possessed of an effective enforcement capacity. But in that case there are competing enforcement regimes and hence no guarantee that the enforcement capacity of the first level enforcers who enforce the compliance of 'the people' will be effective. Let us refer to this regress problem of enforcement as the 'who guards the guards?' problem.

3.2 Collective action problems in the global banking sector

Collective action problems are, I suggest, endemic in the global banking sector. At the micro-level there is the problem of excessive remuneration. Executives receive huge remuneration packages consisting in large part of bonuses. Yet empirical studies have consistently demonstrated that there is no significant correlation between large executive remuneration packages and executive performance as measured in terms of medium to long-term profitability and/or share price (the favoured, if flawed, measure of performance).[23] In the absence of external regulatory or other intervention, competition among corporations for senior executives has driven up executive remuneration packages to extraordinarily high, and completely unjustified, levels. However, the competitive arrangement in question does not remotely approach the pure competition market model beloved by economists, in which neither buyers nor sellers can individually or collectively unduly influence the price at which goods are exchanged. Rather, it takes place in the context of increased management power relative to shareholder – and board – control due in large part to a shift in share ownership from direct individual ownership to indirect share ownership, and to share ownership in the hands of institutional share funds and (relatedly) in corporate power structures (dominated by managers). Accordingly, the sellers (the managers) can collectively and over time unduly influence (upwardly) the price at which their labour is sold to the buyers (the shareholders via their boards). Specifically, executive managers compete with one another for financial rewards within a

Publishing, 2013), 284 assumes that the problem of guarding the guards can be overcome with this notion of a non-hierarchical circle of enforcement.

[23] S. Elaurant, 'Corporate Executive Salaries – The Argument from Economic Efficiency' (2008) 13(2) EJBEOS 35.

competitive framework in which there is insufficient downward pressure on the overall level of those rewards from those who ultimately have to provide them (the shareholders). This is a collective action problem in which increased competition produces the perverse outcome of grossly inflated executive remuneration. And there is an additional perverse outcome. To the extent that there is a relationship between high executive remuneration and corporate performance, it is purely a relationship between remuneration and short-term profits and share price and, to that extent, part of the problem rather than the solution.

At the mezzo- and macro-institutional levels there are various collective action problems. For example, in the 'good' times, the banks engage in fierce competition for depositors' funds and as lenders to homebuyers, investors, and so on. This contributes to housing bubbles, speculative investor bubbles, over-leveraged banks, and so on. Eventually, indeed predictably, the bubble bursts. Investors 'sensing' the bubble is about to burst begin to sell en masse to a diminishing pool of buyers; stock prices collapse. Over-leveraged investment banks, in particular, are at great risk from those who have borrowed heavily from them but are now unable to pay them back. In addition, depositors become increasingly nervous and banks fear a run on their deposits. Accordingly, in these 'bad times' it now becomes of critical importance to each bank that it is regarded as being safe and secure, especially relative to other banks.

The general form of the collective action problem is that each bank in pursuing its own rational self-interest threatens the collective self-interest of the banking sector (not to speak of the economic system, more generally). How is this so? Why does the market mechanism not simply come into play? Why do not the weaker banks fail and the stronger banks pick up their residual business, as outlined in Economics 1? Part of the problem is that a run on one bank can lead to contagion, even if the damage arising from the failure of any one bank on its own would be containable. But the problem is far greater than this in the global banking sector. For it turns out that pretty much all of the leading banks in the global banking sector are 'too big to fail'. For example, according to the respected international body, the Financial Stability Board, there are no less than 29 banks that are 'systemically important financial institutions'.[24] It follows that while the banks are in competition with one another at one level, at another level

[24] Financial Stability Board, 'Financial Stability Board reports to G20 Leaders on progress in implementing financial regulatory reforms', Press Release ref. no: 61/2011, 4 November 2011, at www.financialstabilityboard.org.

each requires every other *not* to fail on pain of systemic collapse. Hence, there is a collective action problem: the pursuit of individual self-interest is ultimately at odds with collective self-interest.

The problem of guarding the guards has a specific form in the global banking sector and there is a problem not only with the regulators (the guards) *per se* (e.g., in respect of the intensity and effectiveness of their enforcement activities), but also with the governments who frame the regulations (the legislatures).

National governments and (relatedly) regulators have an ambiguous role when it comes to global markets, including global financial markets. For national governments and their regulators are to some extent partisan, and (understandably) seek to look after the economic interests of their own industries and businesses, including their own financial and banking sector (e.g., the 'City' in the case of UK regulators). Moreover, in the absence of a uniform set of global regulations and a single global regulator with real authority, regulators operating at a national level can be played off against one another by multinational corporations.

In the case of the global banking sector, regulation and integrity assurance are ultimately in the hands of national governments. However, national governments and their regulatory authorities are not simply umpires, they are also players in the financial – and, more generally, corporate – 'game'. For example, the UK government and its financial regulator (formerly the FSA) cannot be expected to regulate entirely impartially in the interests of ethical ends and principles, given the substantial interest the UK government has in ensuring that the London-based UK corporate and financial sector retains, and increases the benefits accruing to it from global financial markets.

In short, the 'guards' in the global financial sector, *viz.* national governments and their regulators, confront a collective action problem that compromises their independence and, as a consequence, partially undermines their capacity to function as guards.

Another kind of collective action problem in the global financial sector arising at the macro-level arises from the capacity for powerful nation-states to distort the normal workings of markets – themselves a social institution of sorts[25] – and thereby creating collective action problems and associated perverse incentive structures.[26] For instance, Martin Wolf

25 Miller, *The Moral Foundations of Social Institutions*, n. 9, chapter 1: 'A Teleological Account of Institutions', 37; and chapter 10: 'The Business Corporation', 277.

26 M. Wolf, *Fixing Global Finance* (Baltimore: John Hopkins University Press, 2008).

argues that China, other Asian exporting countries, and the oil exporting economies have pegged their exchange rates to the US dollar and, as a consequence, their currencies have not been re-valued upwardly, leading to a reduction in their exports and an increase in their imports. Rather, these economies have accumulated vast surpluses which they have in turn invested in the United States, in particular. The US economy has responded to the availability of large amounts of cheap cash by going on a borrowing binge. However, in the absence of sufficient opportunities for investment in US infrastructure and other projects in, so to speak, Main Street, the US banking system artificially created opportunities for investment in sub-prime mortgages, securitisation and the like. Successive US governments encouraged this process, since it seemed to provide an almost limitless supply of cheap housing, cheap consumer goods, and a booming stock market. In short, the glut in savings was used to fuel speculative booms in housing and other sectors of the US economy. Inevitably, of course, the boom was followed by a bust: the Global Financial Crisis.

Whether or not Wolf's account is correct, it does draw attention to an important category of collective action problems in the global financial sector, namely, those largely created by national governments (as opposed to ones that governments and their regulators have failed to prevent or curtail).

International public institutions such as the International Monetary Fund (IMF) and the European Union (EU) are implicated in some of these collective action problems in respect of their roles as supervisors and/or regulators. Perhaps the IMF has been overly influenced by free market doctrines, such as the efficient markets hypothesis and, as a consequence, was less helpful before, during, and after the GFC than otherwise might have been the case. Moreover, notwithstanding its supra-national status, the EU, in particular, has arguably been a source of *additional* collective action problems, as opposed to a solution to pre-existing ones. For example, it has provided a straightjacket for debtor nations such as Greece who as a result of using a common currency with their trading partners, such as Germany, cannot devalue their currency and, thereby, reduce their imports and increase their exports. Indeed, it is claimed that the creation of a currency union (the Eurozone) without simultaneously creating a fiscal union and various other centralising features was a collective action disaster waiting to happen. According to Paul Krugman: 'Members of a currency area, it turns out, should have high integration of bank guarantees, and a system of lender of last resort provisions for governments as well as ... high labour mobility ... and fiscal integration. The euro area has none of these.'[27]

3.3 *Collective action problems and collective moral responsibility*

Let me now turn to the analysis of these various collective action problems and the role that collective moral responsibility might play in their amelioration.

As a preliminary to my own analysis we must first identify the deficiencies in the rational choice model standardly used to explicate such problems. The rational choice model assumes rational self-interested individuals in competition with one another. This is fine as far as it goes. However, it does not leave room for rational individual action performed in the collective self-interest and/or in accordance with socially engendered moral principles and purposes; yet the latter are ubiquitous features of human collective life, including in the economic sphere.

Importantly, this one-sided fixation with individually rational self-interested action eliminates the possibility, in effect, of finding a solution to collective action problems of the kind in question. This can be seen in the failure to find solutions to the problems described previously of the 'insufficiency of enforcements mechanisms' and of 'who guards the guards'.

What is needed at this point is the acceptance that individual human agents can, and often do, engage in action-determining reasoning from collective goals and interests to individual actions: collective goals and interests to which members of social groups and organisations are strongly committed. Importantly, such acceptance does not imply any commitment to an irreducibly collective agent (or irreducibly collective reasoner). Indeed, any such commitment would simply be the application of the rational choice model at the collective rather than the individual level and, as such, would not provide a solution to the problem at hand but simply elevate it to the higher level. Nor does it necessarily imply some ultimate individually rational, self-interested reason that motivates the possession of the collective goals and interests in question; rather, collective goals and interests may well in many cases function as ground-level explanations of behaviour.

[27] P. Krugman, 'Revenge of the Optimum Currency Area', *The New York Times*, 24 June 2012.

On this view of individual reasoning from common goals and collective interests to their own individual action, what is called for is a conception of an individual human agent *qua member of a social group or organisation* (e.g., qua banker). In short, the individual internalises the collective goals and interests of the social group or organisation to which he or she belongs. Crucially, these collective goals and interests can, and often do, transcend the role occupant's prior and limited, individually rational self-interested, goals and interests. Moreover, the collective goals and interests in question can, and often are, embraced by the individuals involved on the grounds that they are desirable from an impartial or, at least, collective standpoint. This capacity of individuals to reason from, and act in accordance with, collective goals and interests is not without its problems. For example, the collective goals in question might be inherently morally problematic (e.g., those of the Third Reich), or the collective interest of the members of an organisation in question might be at variance with the interests of the wider society (e.g., the members of an investment bank with a business model based on constructing and on selling toxic financial products).

In order to get an understanding of reasoning of individual agents acting qua members of a social group or organisation engaging in joint action to realise a collective end which is also a collective good, it might be helpful to remind ourselves of the basic structure of means/end reasoning. Roughly speaking, individual means/end reasoning proceeds in the following manner.

First, identify the end that one has. Second, identify the means to that end. Third, perform the action that is the means to the end.[28] Notice that here ends are not necessarily goods or benefits; they are simply ends.

In the case of cooperative schemes – involving as they do, joint actions directed to collective ends – matters are more complicated. But here is a rough summary of such reasoning.

First, agent A has end e, and agent B also has end e, and so does C, etc. Moreover, A has end e only on condition that B has end e, and so on. Second, A and B and C, etc. believe that e cannot be achieved other than by A, B, C, etc. each performing some action x.[29] Third, A, B, C, etc. each has the true belief that each other has performed, is performing, or will

[28] Or at least conclude that one ought to perform the action x. See Miller, *Social Action*, n. 10, chapter 4: 'Social Norms', 123.

[29] Or at least that each x-ing is the best means to realising e. Here the notion of a best means is fully determined by the end e (e.g., that x is better than (say) y, because x more fully realises e).

perform x, and these beliefs are a matter of common knowledge. Four, A, B, C, etc. each performs. Notice once again that here ends are not necessarily goods or benefits; they are simply ends.

Now let us consider means/end reasoning in relation to ends that are also regarded as goods or benefits.

First, agent A comes to have e as an end for the reason that he regards e as a good or benefit, G. Second, agent B has end e, and agent C also has end e, and so does D, etc. A, B, C, etc. have e as an end for the reason that they regard e as a good, or benefit, or as a means to some other good or benefit. Note that here A has end e only on condition that B has end e, and so on. So e is a collective end.

Second, if A and/or B, etc. have competing ends, e overrides the other ends, and does so by virtue of the greater importance that A and B attach to the goods or benefits that the realisation of e will bring.

Third, A and B and C, etc. believe that e cannot be achieved other than by A, B, C, etc. each performing some action x.

Fourth, A, B, C, etc. each has the true belief that each of the others has performed, is performing, or will perform x, and these beliefs are a matter of common knowledge.

Fifth, A, B, C, etc. each performs x.

I suggest that this is the basic structure of practical means/end reasoning in joint actions performed to produce what are mutually believed to be benefits or goods. Moreover, this basic structure does not change in the case of complex joint actions, such as those constitutive of joint institutional mechanism (e.g., the LIBOR mechanism), and crucially for our purposes here, those constitutive of organisational action (e.g., actions of officers, managers, employees in a corporation in a market).

Viewed from this perspective, the solution to collective action problems is joint action, typically an enforceable cooperative scheme, in which there is a collective end, the realisation of which removes or at least curtails the collective action problem. Notice that for the kinds of collective problems under discussion here, namely, collective action problems in the global finance sector, the enforceable cooperative schemes in question are *institutional* arrangements (of which more in the final section). Moreover, this collective end is a collective good and, as such, has motivational force for the participants in the joint action. Naturally, individualist self-interest remains a problem and, as stated, enforcement is an additional requirement. However, framing the issue in this manner enables us to see: first, collective self-interest and/or a collective good may in fact be constitutive of individual self-interest (e.g., a banker's individual self-interest is constituted in part by his participation in and contribution to the realisation of the collective ends of the bank which employs him); second, collective self-interest and/or collective goods may in fact override individual self-interest; third, individual self-interest does not necessarily dominate collective self-interest and/or collective goods (e.g., the success of his bank might be more important to a bank manager than his own pay packet); and fourth, in cases where collective self-interest and/or collective goods have motivational force which is overridden by individual self-interest, enforcement is *necessary*; however, enforcement is *not sufficient* for compliance given the previously elaborated problem of the insufficiency of enforcement mechanisms. In relation to the fourth point, I note that given the motivational role of collective self-interest and/or collective goods, enforcement does not have to be sufficient for compliance.

Finally, I note that framing collective action problems in this manner allows us to offer at least a partial solution to the problem of guarding the guards. Here there are three relevant points to be made. First, the individual enforcers are themselves engaged in joint action to realise a collective end, which is a collective good to which they are, at least *pro tanto*, committed, namely, that of ensuring the compliance of participants with the requirements of the cooperative scheme(s). Accordingly, qua *bona fide* enforcers are motivated by collective self-interest and/or this proximate collective good, as well as by individual self-interest. Second, the enforcement team is itself a participant in, and contributor to, the larger collective end of the cooperative scheme(s), be it an organisation or industry, in which they enforce compliance; so they have this further collective self-interest and/or collective good as motivating factors. Third, enforcers are in fact dependent on the cooperation of the majority of those whose compliance they enforce. Indeed, enforcement is itself a joint action of sorts between the enforcers, on the one hand, and the broad mass of those whose compliance with the larger cooperative scheme is required, on the other. Consider in this connection that combating fraud is dependent on the co-workers of fraudsters reporting the latter's fraudulent activities.

4. Institutionally embedding collective moral responsibility in the global banking sector

Having provided accounts of collective moral responsibility and collective action problems it is now time to turn to the matter of institutionally embedding collective responsibility in relevant global financial institutions and markets.[30] As already mentioned, this is primarily an exercise in respect of prospective, as opposed to retrospective, moral responsibility. As such, it requires that matters of institutional redesign, implementation, and ongoing compliance be attended to. Notice also that for this purpose I understand social institutions to have three fundamental dimensions, namely: function (collective ends, normatively understood), structure, and culture.[31]

The generic solution to this kind of collective action problem in question is at least in part, as we saw with the tragedy of the commons over-fishing example, an enforced cooperative scheme: enforced cooperative schemes are one important way to embed collective moral responsibility in institutional settings suffering from harm-inducing collective action problems.

Thus in relation to the micro-institutional problem of excessive executive salaries, presumably the relevant cooperative scheme to be designed and implemented could be the enforced removal of bonuses, or at least an enforced cap on bonuses. As far as the mezzo- and macro-institutional problems are concerned, the cooperative schemes in question would consist in more stringent enforceable measures such as capital-to-lending ratios, disclosure requirements, and new institutional devices (e.g., in relation to global benchmarks such as LIBOR), but also a return to past institutional arrangements (e.g., the segregation of retail from investment functions).

However, enforced cooperative schemes cannot be the whole of the solution because of the aforementioned problem of the insufficiency of enforcement mechanisms, and that of guarding the guards. In relation to the former problem, developing and maintaining an ethical culture – one that takes its collective moral responsibilities seriously – is an important part of the solution. In relation to the latter, matters are more difficult. However, removing lopsided power structures (e.g., banks that are too big to regulate), creating or redesigning independent agencies, such as the IMF and World Bank, and credit rating agencies,[32] and mobilising

[30] Earlier versions of some of the material in this section appeared in S. Miller, 'Global Financial Institutions, Ethics and Market Fundamentalism', in N. Dobos, C. Barry, and T. Pogge (eds.), *The Global Financial Crisis: Ethical Issues* (London: Palgrave Macmillan, 2011), 24; and Miller, 'The LIBOR Scandal: Culture, Corruption and Collective Action Problems in the Global Banking Sector', n. 5.

[31] Miller, *The Moral Foundations of Social Institutions*, n. 9.

[32] Credit rating agencies were found to be conflicted in relation to toxic financial products since they were funded by the very investment banks whose product they were assessing.

consumers and clients (e.g., by way of class actions) are surely part of the answer. In each case they are part of the answer because they have the potential to both strengthen the hand of the enforcers and also hold them to greater account. On the other hand, certain collective action problems created by powerful nation-states, such as the United States and China, cannot be solved merely by strengthening the hand of enforcers.

4.1 *Institutionally embedding collective moral responsibility*

Before proceeding further it is important to clarify the notion of institutionally embedding collective moral responsibility in relation to collective action problems. It is also important to further clarify the relationship between individual and collective *moral* responsibility, on the one hand, and individual and collective *institutional* responsibility on the other. In doing so the relevant notion of the *distribution of individual moral responsibilities* in the context of the forms of collective moral responsibility in question will come into view.[33] As noted earlier, our concern here is principally with prospective rather than retrospective moral responsibility.

Prior to the establishment of an institutional arrangement of the kind in question (an enforceable cooperative scheme) there is typically a collective moral responsibility to deal with some collective action problem, be it over-fishing or reckless and predatory lending in the retail banking sector. Moreover, those who have this collective (i.e., joint, moral responsibility) are quite often multiple and diverse (e.g., bankers; regulators; members of the legislature; and borrowers). However, since the design and implementation of the institutional 'solution' to the problem has not yet taken place, the collective moral responsibility of these agents is relatively inchoate and, as a consequence, the accompanying individual moral responsibilities unspecified.

But once the specific institutional arrangement – the enforceable cooperative scheme – has been designed and implemented matters are different. There is now not only a collective end which is a collective good (e.g., the cessation of reckless and predatory lending) but a specific institutional means to achieve this end, such as strictly applied lending

[33] For more detail in relation to the following discussion see Miller, *The Moral Foundations of Social Institutions*, n. 9, chapter 2: 'The Moral Foundations of Institutions', 56; chapter 4: 'Collective Moral Responsibility', 120; and Miller, 'Collective Moral Responsibility: An Individualist Account', n. 7.

criteria for home loans, and an enforcement mechanism, for instance a banking regulator with stringent oversight and disciplinary powers. Importantly, the institutional rights and duties of the role occupants in this enforceable cooperative scheme (e.g., those of a bank loans officer) have been specified in a manner that (presumably) ensures the scheme achieves its collective end. In short, the original somewhat inchoate collective moral responsibility to solve the collective action problem has been discharged by means of an institutional arrangement, namely, an enforceable cooperative scheme.

Notice that whereas each institutional role occupant has an *individual* institutional responsibility for example, (to revert to the fishing scenario) that of each fisherman to meet his quota, it is the combination of all the contributing institutional actors, for instance the individual fishermen and regulators of the fishing industry, that realises the collective end of the enforceable cooperative scheme. Accordingly, each institutional actor is not only discharging his individual institutional responsibility (e.g., by meeting his quota), each is also (simultaneously) doing his or her part to jointly discharge the *collective* institutional responsibility of the cooperative scheme (e.g., to act jointly to reduce the quantum of fish caught so as to enable sustainable fishing).

Moreover, these individual and collective *institutional* responsibilities are *also* individual and collective *moral* responsibilities; or, at least, they are if we assume the cooperative scheme in question realises a collective good; does not involve any rights violations; is fair and reasonable; and so on. Thus, in the banking scenario the individual institutional responsibility of the loans officer to strictly apply the home lending criteria is also an individual moral (epistemic) responsibility. Moreover, the development of an appropriate set of such criteria, neither overly permissive nor overly restrictive, is a joint moral (epistemic) responsibility of the relevant bank personnel. Again, the collective institutional responsibility on the part of supervisory banking staff in multiple banks and on the part of bank regulators and other enforcers – discharged by way of each discharging their individual institutional supervisory and enforcement responsibilities jointly with others – is also a collective (i.e., joint) moral (behavioural) responsibility.

It should now be evident what is meant by institutionally embedding collective moral responsibility. For the original somewhat inchoate collective moral responsibility, and its accompanying unspecified individual moral responsibilities, have now been transformed by way of an institutional arrangement into a collective moral responsibility with specific content, and an accompanying set of well specified individual moral responsibilities (the moral rights and duties definitive of the constitutive institutional roles).

The notion of collective moral responsibility in play here (i.e., joint moral responsibility), applies vertically as well as horizontally. It applies horizontally in so far as there are multiple coordinated morally significant joint actions of individuals at the same organisational level or in an unstructured group. It applies vertically in so far as the collective moral responsibility in question involves the joint actions of individuals at different levels in hierarchical organisations (e.g., loan officers and their supervisors). Here there is a need to recall the conception outlined in section 2 of organisational action as multi-layered structures of joint action. This conception makes possible the ascription of collective (joint) moral responsibility to members of an organisation engaged in organisational action. Likewise, the related conception of a joint procedural mechanism outlined in section 2 makes possible the ascription of collective (joint) moral responsibility to participants in various sub-institutional mechanisms, such as the LIBOR benchmark-setting process.

Further, that the distribution of individual *moral* responsibilities in an institutional arrangement which is an enforceable cooperative scheme mirrors the distribution of individual *institutional* responsibilities in that scheme. Roughly speaking, each discharges his or her individual moral responsibility in so far as he or she discharges his or her individual institutional responsibility. Moreover, in doing so each contributes to discharging – jointly with others – the collective moral responsibility (which mirrors the collective institutional responsibility of the scheme).

In general, whereas any given participant in such an institutional cooperative scheme is only partially morally responsible for the realisation of the collective good realised by the scheme, each is, nevertheless, fully morally responsible for their own individual contribution. However, this is not necessarily the case. For example, a subordinate may have diminished individual moral responsibility for his or her institutional action which has untoward moral consequences, if he or she carried it out under a (lawful) instruction from a superior

Let us now proceed to a discussion of how collective moral responsibility might be institutionally embedded in the global banking sector.

4.2 Function

The problem of guarding the guards has a specific form in the global banking sector, and there is a problem not only with the regulators (the guards) *per se* (e.g., in respect of the intensity and effectiveness of their enforcement activities), but also with the regulations themselves, and hence with the governments who frame the regulations (the legislatures).

It is one of the principal tasks of those who design and oversee the market system, including governments and – under the direction of governments – regulators, to ensure that the ultimate purposes (function) of banks are in fact achieved. However, if one looks for example at the objectives of many regulators, one typically finds only limited aims (e.g., to reduce crime and protect consumers), and procedural concerns (e.g., to promote competition and efficiency). There is little or no reference to the ultimate ends of markets in general (i.e., the outcome the invisible hand is supposed to bring about) and of the banking sector in particular.

On the teleological account of organisations and markets elaborated in detail elsewhere,[34] the latter are essentially complex structures of joint action and, as such, have collective ends; normatively speaking, these ends are collective goods.[35] Presumably, financial institutions are no different from any other social institution in this respect. That is, there is a need to identify collective ends that are collective goods and, as such, provide the *raison d'etre* for their existence. However, evidently in the case of the financial services sector in particular, the prior fundamental ethical question as to the ultimate institutional ends of this sector remains unanswered or is, at least, contested. Yet without an answer to this question governments, regulators and policy makers cannot give rational direction to the financial services sector. They cannot, for example, determine whether or not the financial services sector is doing its job or whether it has become bloated and economically dysfunctional (as many commentators now claim) by virtue of, for example, ceasing to serve the interests of the 'real' economy (so-called Main Street).

Importantly, the regulatory 'system' (i.e., the national and international network of enforceable cooperative schemes for the financial services sector) is also without direction; it does not know what ends other than harm reduction and the promotion of efficient markets it is seeking to embed in its target institution – the financial services sector. The implication of this for our conception of enforceable cooperative schemes solving collective action problems is that the specific collective ends of those schemes remains underspecified and, therefore, so to an

[34] Miller, *The Moral Foundations of Social Institutions*, n. 9, chapter 1: 'A Teleological Account of Institutions', 37.

[35] Ibid., chapter 2: 'The Moral Foundations of Institutions', 56.

extent does the content and scope of the rules to be enforced; after all, these rules must in part be determined by the purposes of the cooperative scheme.

Consider in this connection, for example, the purposes of corporate financial service providers in capital markets. Let us accept what is agreed on all hands to be the case, namely, that they have as *a* purpose to maximise shareholder value. But suppose, as argued earlier, that this is merely a proximate end or purpose and that these financial service providers have some further, indeed ultimate, purpose to which this proximate purpose is merely a means. Let us posit that this ultimate end is to make an adequate quantum of capital available at reasonable costs to productive firms.[36] Qua ultimate institutional purpose, the provision of capital to productive firms at reasonable costs gives direction to governments, regulators, and policy makers in their various roles, albeit it can only usefully do so if it is further elaborated.

4.3 Structure

As we have seen, the collective responsibilities of industries to realise their institutional purposes, including the collective responsibilities of banks and other financial service providers, typically consist of highly dispersed individual responsibilities that attach to individual persons within firms; individual firms within the industry; institutions outside the industry; and so on and so forth. The collective responsibility, for example, to lower the cost of capital is not one that can be discharged by any one, or even a small group, of market actors within a given capital market. Given the diffuse character of such collective responsibilities – and its attendant incentive structure – many industries, financial service providers included, will not discharge these collective responsibilities and, as a consequence, these industries will not adequately realise their institutional purposes. Hence the need (and resultant responsibility) on the part of governments, in particular, to intervene to adjust these incentive structures and, if necessary, to design appropriate institutions or sub-elements thereof.

[36] J. Coffee suggests as much in a paper entitled 'Law and the Market: The Role of Enforcement', presented at 'The Dynamics of Capital Market Governance: Evaluating the Conflicting and Conflating Roles of Compliance, Regulation, Ethics and Accountability' Workshop held at the Australian National University on 14–15 March 2006 (on file with the author).

Micro-, mezzo-, and macro-institutional structural problems also need to be addressed if the collective moral responsibility for combating institutional corruption and other harms is to be adequately discharged. These problems include specific institutional conflicts of interest (e.g., in relation to LIBOR), but also macro-structural aspects of the various collective action problems that are in play. Evidently, the corruption-inducing collective-action problems arising from commercial competition between the investment arms of banks in a market context in which there is an overriding imperative to maximise profit, and in which many of these banks are 'too big to fail', looks to be too great to be overcome other than by substantial institutional redesign. The redesign in question would involve splitting the investment from the retail arm of banks to form two separate institutions[37] – or, at the very least, iron-clad segregation within one institution, if that is possible – and 'down-sizing' banks 'too big to fail' and, therefore, 'too big to regulate'.

This is not to deny that there are the standard market incentives and disincentives in place which (respectively) encourage ethical behaviour and discourage unethical behaviour especially, but not exclusively, among independent financial advice providers. These incentives do exist and they are strengthened by greater emphasis on appropriately communicated disclosure, enhanced financial literacy of consumers/clients, and the like.

Nevertheless, market incentives and disincentives are heavily influenced by the particular (as it were) macro-institutional structure of the market in question and, in the case of the financial service industry in many countries, that structure is characterised by a small number of large, vertically integrated organisations. Moreover, functionally, these organisations are market actors driven by the profit motive. It follows that the pervasive culture in these organisations will be reflective of this function and structure, and will not be sufficiently responsive to the relevant normative purposes and ethical principles.

Naturally, these national macro-institutional frameworks and their constitutive function(s), structure, and culture(s) are not immutable. National governments and regulators can introduce reform across the whole spectrum of their national financial products and services sector. Here there is a need for a focus on specific 'fit for purpose' regulation and integrity regimes for product manufacturers, bankers, and financial advisors alike.

[37] Perhaps in accordance with the so-called Volcker Rule originally within the Dodd-Frank Wall Street Reform and Consumer Protection Act, 111th Congress (2009–2010), H.R.4173, but subsequently watered down.

At the global level, as we have seen, matters are somewhat more problematic and, of course, in some cases the global and the national are not easily separated. Nevertheless, perverse incentive structures arising from collective action problems at the global level can be addressed by recourse to interventions that reconfigure the incentive structures.[38] Such interventions can take the form of solving jurisdictional problems in global settings, and increasing enforcement options, and/or the intensity of enforcement.

Global widening of the possibility of class action in relation to corporate price-fixing has been suggested. While obviously of great importance, these jurisdictional and enforcement methods are not always sufficient. Other options are themselves market-based; for example, reduce supply of a product or service by factoring in real costs (and requiring that they be paid); reduce demand for a product by high sales tax; or limiting availability. Some of these options may need to involve ambitious innovations to the market system itself, including the global financial system.

4.4 Culture

Whether or not the members of some organisation internalise the *desirable* ends and principles of an organisation – as opposed to undesirable ones – is in part a matter of institutional culture. Institutional culture is in turn dependent on the extent to which the collective moral responsibility to achieve desirable ends, and eschew corrupt practices, is embedded in the organisation by way of explicit institutional mechanisms (e.g., formal continuing education programmes in professional ethics; whistle-blower protection schemes; and remuneration systems that do not encourage excessive risk-taking), and implicit practices (e.g., managers who acknowledge their mistakes; and employees who are unafraid to voice their concerns).

If, on the other hand, the prevailing ethos or culture of an organisation, and perhaps even ideology or central elements of a sector, downplays desirable institutional goals and other ethical considerations in favour of the pursuit of individual self-interest, then it should hardly surprise when individual self-interest overrides compliance with ethical principles, even ones enshrined in the law. This is no doubt especially the

[38] See S. Rose-Ackerman, *Corruption and Government: Causes, Consequences and Reform* (Cambridge University Press, 1999) for a variety of types of prescription, including adjusting incentive structures, in relation to corruption.

case in a context of high temptation and opportunity, on the one hand, and low risk of detection and conviction, on the other (e.g., LIBOR manipulation by bank traders motivated by large bonuses in a context of an oversight body with a structural conflict of interest).

The point here is not necessarily that the majority of individuals themselves engage in corrupt or unethical practices, but rather that in certain cultural or ideological contexts they may well refrain from reporting or otherwise preventing a minority from doing so. Many key elements of integrity systems such as ethics codes, codes of practice, education programs, and the like, do not exist for the most part directly to prevent or deter the few people who are wrongdoers from doing wrong, but rather to ensure that the many are intolerant of the wrongdoing of the few. In this context it is perhaps worth pointing out that most fraudsters are detected and convicted as a consequence of the disclosures of their colleagues.

An important potential engine of ethico-cultural education in the context of large, hierarchical organisations driven by commercial interest is the 'professionalisation' process at the occupational level.[39] Here we need to bear in mind that many occupations are not, and ought not to become, professions in the traditional sense of that term. In such cases the analogue of full-blown professionalisation is, what might be termed, occupational ethical acculturation: a process involving many, but not all, of the elements of professionalisation.

The process of occupational ethical acculturation in large banking organisations would consist in such things as the establishment for the occupational group in question of an independent occupational association; the creation and utilisation of codes of ethics; ongoing professional ethics education; reward and remuneration systems designed to realise the ultimate institutional purposes of the organisation, rather than to maximise short-term profits and share prices (or line the pockets of executive managers); establishment of complaints processes conducted by the association; independent (of management) and well-resourced anti-corruption units within the banking organisation itself; appropriate whistle-blowing legislation (including legal protections), and the like. Such measures can assist in the generation and maintenance of a culture of collective moral responsibility and, not the least, one that is intolerant of corruption.

[39] See A. Alexandra and S. Miller, *Integrity Systems for Occupations* (Aldershot: Ashgate, 2010). This is, of course, not to exclude other relevant measures, such as flatter, more democratic, management structures.

A marked feature of the GFC is the extent to which traditional 'gatekeeper' professions, such as lawyers and auditors, have been implicated in corruption scandals. Evidently, there is a need to reinvigorate these professions and strengthen their independence of management and commitment to their core professional values. Elsewhere,[40] I have set forth a range of measures in this regard.

Another area that might be looked at is the full professionalisation of occupations that have not traditionally been professions. Given the nature of some of the problems identified in the banking sector (e.g., conflation of lending and *de facto* selling roles), perhaps there is a need to establish the profession of banker (or at least extend the range of ethical and legal duties). Such a process of professionalisation might include, crucially, attaching to (relevant categories of) bankers a fiduciary duty grounded in the vulnerability of the needy (e.g., home buyers) and so on.

Still other options are based on the importance of reputation to the self-interest of market actors. For example, a reputational index (comprised of objective indicators of ethical 'health') could be constructed, an ethics audit conducted (by an independent body) – the results of which would give a comparative picture of the various firms in the industry – and these results promulgated.[41]

5. Conclusion

In this chapter I have done the following: first, established and defended the theoretical notion of collective moral responsibility as joint moral responsibility, and displayed its relationship to institutional responsibilities; second, offered and defended a normative theoretical account of the collective action problems in play in the GFC and their possible solutions which is wider than that provided by rational self-interested actor models; and third, explored the ways in which collective moral responsibility can be institutionally embedded functionally, structurally, and culturally in relevant global financial institutions and markets for the purpose of substantially reducing the forms of widespread imprudent, unethical, and corrupt behaviour in question by way of addressing various identified collective action problems.

[40] Ibid.

[41] For further details on this and other reputational devices see ibid., chapter 5: 'Ethical Reputation Indexes and Ethics Audits', 99.

INDEX

Lightning Source UK Ltd.
Milton Keynes UK
UKHW020121170619
344535UK00018B/405/P

9 781107 514621